THE ULTIMATE BOOK OF FISH & SHELLFISH

THE ULTIMATE BOOK OF FISH & SHELLFISH

A comprehensive cooking encyclopedia and guide, including 300 fantastic step-by-step recipes and over 1500 fabulous photographs

Contributing Editor KATE WHITEMAN

This edition is published by Hermes House, an imprint of Anness Publishing Ltd
Hermes House, 88–89 Blackfriars Road, London SE1 8HA
tel. 020 7401 2077; fax 020 7633 9499;
www.hermeshouse.com; www.annesspublishing.com

If you like the images in this book and would like to investigate using them for publishing, promotions or advertising, please visit our website www.practicalpictures.com for more information.

Publisher: Joanna Lorenz
Editorial Director: Helen Sudell
Editor: Joy Wotton
Designer: Nigel Partridge
Authors: Pepita Aris, Marlena Spieler, Kate Whiteman
Photography: William Lingwood, assisted by Vanessa Davies
Food for Photography: Sunil Vijayakar, Tonia Hedley (recipes) and Annabel Ford (reference)
Illustrator: Madeleine David

ETHICAL TRADING POLICY
Because of our ongoing ecological investment programme, you, as our customer, can have the pleasure and reassurance of knowing that a tree is being cultivated on your behalf to naturally replace the materials used to make the book you are holding. For further information about this scheme, go to www.annesspublishing.com/trees

A CIP catalogue record for this book is available from the British Library.

NOTES
Bracketed terms are intended for American readers.

For all recipes, quantities are given in both metric and imperial measures and, where appropriate, in standard cups and spoons. Follow one set, but not a mixture, because they are not interchangeable.

Standard spoon and cup measures are level. 1 tsp = 5ml, 1 tbsp = 15ml, 1 cup = 250ml/8fl oz.

Australian standard tablespoons are 20ml. Australian readers should use 3 tsp in place of 1 tbsp for measuring small quantities of gelatine, flour, salt, etc.

American pints are 16fl oz/2 cups. American readers should use 20fl oz/2.5 cups in place of 1 pint when measuring liquids.

Electric oven temperatures in this book are for conventional ovens. When using a fan oven, the temperature will probably need to be reduced by about 10–20°C/20–40°F. Since ovens vary, you should check with your manufacturer's instruction book for guidance.

Medium (US large) eggs are used unless otherwise stated.

CONTENTS

Cooking with Fish

Since humans evolved as hunter-gatherers, the world's rivers, lakes and seas have served as a limitless pantry, providing a bountiful supply of fish and shellfish almost infinite in its variety. From tiny streams and brackish ponds to great oceans, all waters yield some kind of fish or shellfish, almost all of them edible, although in many cases you might not guess this from their outward appearance.

Although for many years fish was undervalued in the Western world, particularly in areas far from a coast, its importance as a highly nutritious and delicious food is now universally recognized. As controversial farming methods make many important foods such as meat, dairy produce and cereals less attractive than they once were, fish has really come into its own as a healthy alternative.

Cooking with Fish

There is no doubt that fish is good for you. All fish and shellfish is low in fat and high in proteins, minerals and vitamins; oily fish can actually improve your health by lowering cholesterol levels and unclogging arteries. The Japanese, whose diet consists largely of fresh raw fish, have the lowest incidence of heart disease in the world.

Good health is only one of many reasons to eat fish, however. When properly prepared and cooked, it can be among the most delicious foods imaginable. Unfortunately, too many of us were brought up on institutional offerings of heavily-breaded deep-fried scampi (shrimp), or unpalatable, overcooked or watery fish, whose delicate flavour was often rendered tasteless, or masked with floury sauces. Well-cooked fish is quite another matter. Really fresh fish needs little cooking or embellishment, and most takes very little time to prepare, a huge bonus for the modern cook. It is easy to rustle up an elegant fish dish in under half an hour.

Every fish and shellfish has its own unique flavour, offering something for all tastes. It is unlikely that there is a recipe for a piscatorial dessert, but fish and shellfish can feature in every other part of a meal, including appetizers, main courses, salads and savouries.

It is hard to understand why fish has been undervalued for so long. Perhaps it has something to do with the fact that it was traditionally eaten on fast days, as a substitute for meat, so is associated with self-denial and penance. In times of plenty, easily-obtainable seafoods, such as salmon and oysters, were regarded as foods fit only for the poor. Medieval apprentices complained bitterly and refused to eat oysters more than three times a week. Bland, easily-digested white fish was perceived as invalid food and rejected by those with more robust constitutions.

Probably the reason for eschewing fish was lack of understanding of how to prepare it. Skinning, filleting, scaling and shelling all seemed like rather hard work. Nowadays, despite the demise of many fishmongers, there is no need to do all the hard work yourself. Just visit your local supermarket and choose ready-prepared fish or, better still, follow the instructions given in this book, which will guide you through the complexities of handling and preparing all kinds of fish and shellfish.

Fish and shellfish are rewarding to cook and extremely versatile. Although some types have become scarce through over-fishing, and therefore very expensive, the price of others has plummeted, thanks to advances in fish farming. Salmon, for example, has come full circle. Once despised as

Above: Octopus and baby squid on sale at Tsukiji fish market in Tokyo.

Below: In many areas good fish stalls, like this one in Venice, Italy, are becoming increasingly hard to find.

being too common, its subsequent rarity made it one of the most expensive and sought-after fish. Now, once again, it has become one of the cheapest types of fish available. Be wary, however, of buying very cheap farmed fish. Careless farming results in poor quality specimens. Poor fish farming can also promote diseases, which may spread to other sea creatures in their natural habitat. Consumers must not repeat the mistakes of the past, when demand for ever-cheaper meat and other foods had disastrous consequences in terms of health and ecology. Fish and shellfish are superb natural foods and should remain so. That said, well-managed fish and shellfish farms produce healthy specimens and help counteract the effects of over-fishing of wild stocks.

The variety of edible underwater creatures is staggering. I often wonder which intrepid (or desperately hungry) soul was the first to imagine that a hideous lumpfish, snake-like eel or multi-limbed octopus might serve as a snack, or spot the potential in a spider crab, sea urchin or slimy sea cucumber for providing a palatable meal. Imagine what pleasures we might have missed had our ancestors been repelled by the appearance of such strange creatures. With a few poisonous exceptions, almost everything that swims, crawls, scuttles or merely lurks in the water can supply us with food.

One of the greatest pleasures when travelling is to visit the local fish market and see the dazzling array of brightly coloured fresh fish and shellfish set out on the stalls. However strange their shapes and forms, all have a unique beauty and character. Modern methods of fishing and transportation have made sea creatures from all over the world accessible to adventurous cooks, so allow yourself the pleasure of experimenting and enjoy the infinite variety of textures, flavours and colours of the fruits of the sea.

Right: There are fish and shellfish from all over the world on sale on this stall at an indoor market in the Champagne region of France.

EQUIPMENT

Although it is perfectly possible to prepare and cook fish without special equipment, there are a few items which make the process much easier. Some, such as the fish kettle, take up quite a lot of storage space; other gadgets, such as the fish scaler, are quite tiny, but all will prove invaluable for fish and shellfish cooking.

KNIVES, SCISSORS AND SCALERS

Chef's knife

A large heavy knife with a 20–25cm/ 8–10in blade is essential for cutting fish steaks and splitting open crustaceans, such as crayfish and lobster.

Filleting knife

For filleting and skinning fish, you will need a sharp knife with a flexible blade, which is at least 15cm/ 6in long. This type of knife can also be used for opening some kinds of shellfish. It is essential to keep a filleting knife razor sharp.

Oyster knife

This short, stubby knife – sometimes called a shucker – has a wide, two-edged blade to help prise open the shells of oysters and other bivalves. Make sure that it has a safety guard above the handle to protect your hands.

Kitchen scissors

A sturdy, sharp pair of scissors that have a serrated edge are needed for cutting off fins and trimming tails.

Fish scaler

Resembling a small, rough grater, a fish scaler makes short work of a task that few relish.

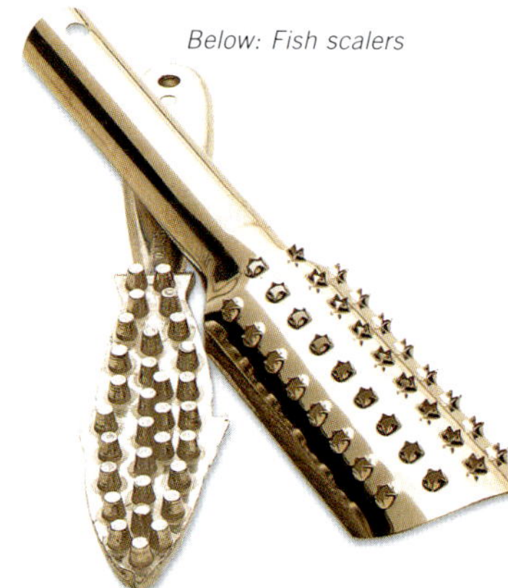

Below: Fish scalers

Below: Chef's knife

Below: Filleting knife

Below: Scissors

Left: Oyster knives

PANS

Fish kettle

Long and deep, with rounded edges, this attractive utensil has a handle at either end, and a tightly-fitting lid. Inside is a perforated rack or grid on which to lay the fish. This, too, has handles, and enables the cook to lift out the fish without breaking it. Most modern fish kettles are made of stainless steel, but they also come in enamelled steel and copper with a tin-plated interior. Fish kettles are used on the hob (stovetop) and are invaluable for cooking whole large fish, such as salmon and sea trout. They can also be used for steaming other foods.

Above: A fish kettle takes up a lot of storage space in the kitchen, but if you want to cook whole fish, such as salmon, it is well worth buying.

Right: Oval frying pan

Right: Griddle pan

Right: Chinese bamboo steamers

Above: Stainless steel steamers

Oval frying pan

Such a simple idea, but intensely practical, this large pan enables you to cook whole fish flat instead of bending them to fit a round pan and spoiling their shape.

Griddle pan

A ribbed cast-iron griddle pan is ideal for searing and cooking fish. They can be round, oval or rectangular. Some of the large griddles need to be used over two electric rings or gas burners on top of a stove.

Steamer

If you steam food frequently, a stainless steel steamer set is a good investment. They have a lidded, deep outer pan and a perforated inner basket. Choose the widest type that you can find. Chinese bamboo steaming baskets are an economical alternative. They come in a variety of sizes, from very small dim sum baskets to very wide baskets that are about 35cm/14in across. Chinese steaming baskets can be stacked one on top of the other so that several layers of food can be cooked at one time. Cheapest of all is a small, collapsible, perforated steamer, which unfolds like a flower to fit any pan.

Above: A single-handled wok can be used for steaming and deep-frying as well as stir-frying.

Below: Double-sided hinged rack

Above: Barbecue grilling rack for whole large fish

Below: Sardine rack

Wok

A 35cm/14in wok with a lid will be large enough to cope with most types of fish and will prove invaluable in the kitchen. There's no need to reserve this piece of equipment for stir-frying; a wok also makes an effective steamer and can be used for deep-frying.

SPECIALIST ITEMS

Barbecue grilling rack

A hinged rack in the shape of a fish makes cooking – and turning – a single large fish relatively easy. Also available are shaped racks designed to hold 6–12 sardines. These can be rectangular or round. More useful for general purposes is a double-sided hinged grill rack. These can be square or rectangular and have long handles so that several steaks or fish can be cooked on a barbecue and turned over simultaneously. However, the flat sides do tend to squash the delicate flesh of some fish. Always oil grilling racks before use to prevent the fish from sticking to them.

Smoker

The cheapest home-smoker is a lidded metal box with a rack to hold the fish. Smoke produced by placing dampened aromatic wood chippings or herbs on the coals gives extra flavour. More convenient (and much more expensive) are electric smokers. Stovetop models can be used indoors.

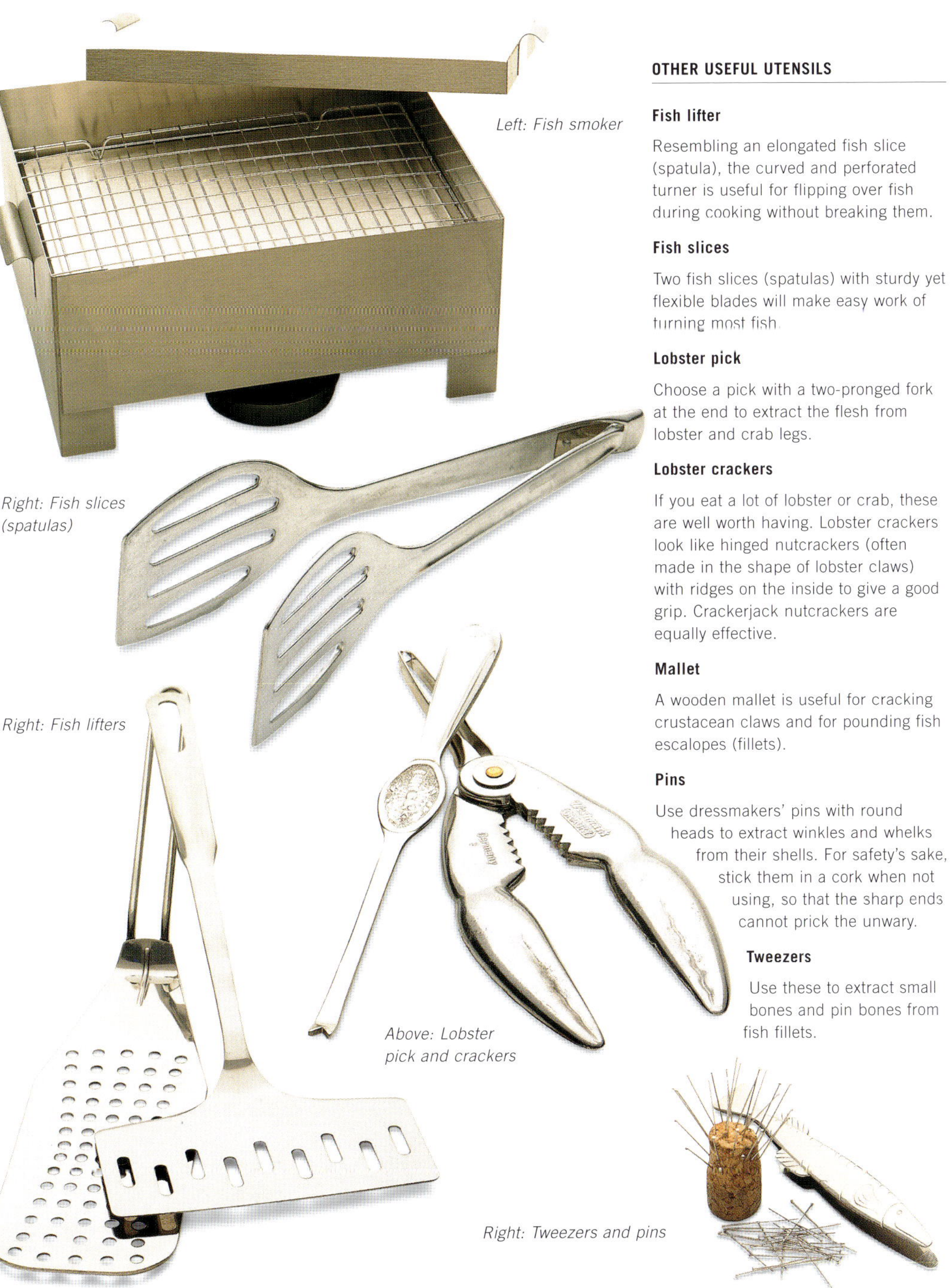

Left: Fish smoker

Right: Fish slices (spatulas)

Right: Fish lifters

Above: Lobster pick and crackers

Right: Tweezers and pins

OTHER USEFUL UTENSILS

Fish lifter

Resembling an elongated fish slice (spatula), the curved and perforated turner is useful for flipping over fish during cooking without breaking them.

Fish slices

Two fish slices (spatulas) with sturdy yet flexible blades will make easy work of turning most fish.

Lobster pick

Choose a pick with a two-pronged fork at the end to extract the flesh from lobster and crab legs.

Lobster crackers

If you eat a lot of lobster or crab, these are well worth having. Lobster crackers look like hinged nutcrackers (often made in the shape of lobster claws) with ridges on the inside to give a good grip. Crackerjack nutcrackers are equally effective.

Mallet

A wooden mallet is useful for cracking crustacean claws and for pounding fish escalopes (fillets).

Pins

Use dressmakers' pins with round heads to extract winkles and whelks from their shells. For safety's sake, stick them in a cork when not using, so that the sharp ends cannot prick the unwary.

Tweezers

Use these to extract small bones and pin bones from fish fillets.

Buying and Preparing Fish

Fish is only worth buying if it is absolutely fresh, and it is best if you eat it on the day you buy it. Fresh fish have shiny skin with a metallic glint and they are covered with a transparent mucus that becomes opaque when the fish is old and stale. The eyes should be clear, bright and slightly bulging. The flesh should feel firm and springy when you press it lightly with your finger; if it feels limp and your finger leaves an indentation, the fish is past its best. Stale fish has an unpleasant "fishy" smell, the skin looks dull, dryish and unattractive and the eyes are sunken.

The best test of freshness for whole fish is to open up the gills; they should be a clear red or rosy colour, not a dull brown. Look for a firm tail and plentiful, shiny close-fitting scales. A fish which has been dead for an unacceptable length of time, or which has not been properly kept, will shed its scales all over the counter. Seafish should have a pleasant odour, redolent of seaweed; freshwater fish should smell of waterweeds. There should never be more than a hint of a "fishy" smell.

Ready-prepared white fish fillets, steaks and cutlets should be neatly trimmed, with moist, firm, translucent flesh. If you must buy frozen fish, make sure that it is frozen solid, with no sign of thawing, and that the packaging is not damaged.

When buying fish, shop with an open mind and be prepared to purchase whatever looks freshest and best on the day. If you want a specific type of fish, it is best to ask the fishmonger in advance so that it can be bought fresh from the market for you. It pays to develop a relationship with one particular fishmonger – if you show that you are really interested in what you are buying, you are sure to get a much better standard of service.

An accommodating fishmonger will gut and clean your fish for you and even scale, skin and fillet it. It is not unreasonable to expect this service, but it does take time. At busy periods, therefore, be prepared to place an order and come back later to collect it. However, if you do have to prepare fish yourself, don't despair; it is really not difficult, given a sharp, flexible knife and a little dexterity.

Quantities

Allow about 175g/6oz fish fillet, cutlets or steaks per serving for a main course. There is a lot of wastage in whole fish, so allow at least 300g/11oz per person if buying fish this way.

Storing fish

Fresh fish should be eaten as soon as possible after purchase, but most types can be kept in the refrigerator for a day or overnight if necessary. Remove any wrapping or packaging and rinse the fish in very cold water. Pat dry with kitchen paper and place on a plate. Cover with clear film (plastic wrap) and store at the bottom of the refrigerator.

Frozen fish

Although fresh fish is much nicer than frozen, for practical reasons it is not always possible to buy it, and on some occasions frozen fish may be your only option. Of course, you cannot apply the usual tests for freshness – prodding, smelling and judging the colour – so it is important to buy frozen fish from a reputable store with a quick turnover. Transport it in a freezer bag if possible and get it home and into your own freezer without delay. White fish can be kept in the freezer for three months and oily fish for two months.

Commercially frozen fish is frozen extremely rapidly and at a lower temperature than can be attained by the average domestic freezer. This preserves the delicate texture of the flesh. It is not advisable to freeze fish at home, but if you must, it should be kept at –18°C/0°F or below.

Thawing fish

If possible, thaw frozen fish overnight in the refrigerator. If you need it in a hurry, microwave the fish on the defrost setting. Separate the pieces as soon as they are thawed enough and spread out in an even layer. Remove from the microwave while still slightly icy; if fish is over-thawed it will become dry.

ROUND FISH

Scaling

Smooth-skinned round fish, such as trout and mackerel, do not need scaling. For others, such as sea bass, mullet and snapper, it is essential.

First, trim off all the fins with a strong pair of scissors. Take care with the dorsal fins on the back, as they can have sharp spines. Work in the sink, preferably under running water, or the scales will fly all over your kitchen. Otherwise you can cover the fish with a damp cloth to catch the scales. Ideally, you should use a proper fish scaler to do the job, but the back of a round-bladed knife will do almost as well. Always scale fish before filleting if you are going to cook it with the skin on.

1 Wash the fish under cold water. Cut off the three fins that run along the stomach, and the dorsal fins on the back, using strong, sharp scissors.

2 Hold the fish firmly by the tail (a cloth will give a better grip). Using a fish scaler or the back of a knife, and working from tail to head, scrape against the lie of the scales to remove them. Wash the fish again to detach any clinging scales.

Gutting/cleaning

This is a messy job, so always work on several layers of newspaper topped with greaseproof (waxed) paper. There are two ways of gutting a whole round fish: through the belly or through the gills. The former is the more usual method for round fish, but gutting through the gills is preferred if splitting the fish open would spoil its appearance. In either case, the gills should be removed before the fish is cooked, because they taste bitter. Do this by holding the fish on its back and opening the gill flaps. Push out the frilly gills and cut them off at the back of the head and under the jawbone with a sharp knife.

Cleaning through the belly

1 Starting at the site of the anal fin, slit open the belly from tail to head, using a short sharp knife.

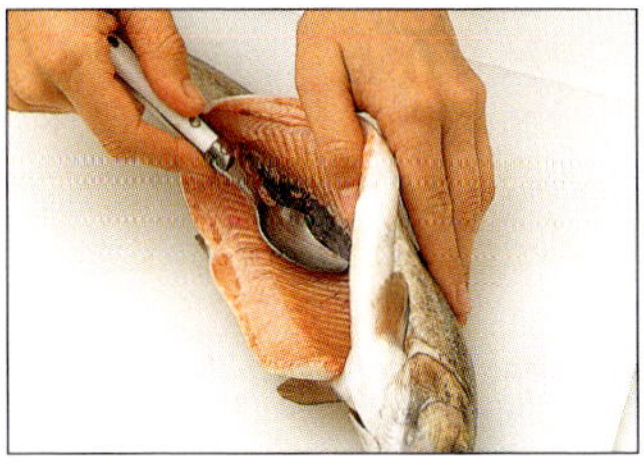

2 Gently pull out the innards, severing them at the throat and tail if necessary. Keep any roes and red mullet livers, which are a great delicacy, but discard everything else, having first wrapped the innards thoroughly. Use a tablespoon to make sure the cavity is empty, removing any blood vessels adjacent to the backbone. Wash the cavity thoroughly, then pat the fish dry with kitchen paper.

Cleaning through the gills

1 Lay the fish on its back. Make an incision in the bottom of the belly, near the tail. Locate the end of the innards, and snip through it.

2 Cut through the bone under the lower jaw. Open the gill flaps, insert your fingers into the cavity and gently pull out the innards; these will come away through the flaps, leaving the belly intact. Wash the fish thoroughly and then pat it dry.

Boning bony fish such as mackerel and herring

1 Having removed the fins and cleaned the fish through the belly, open the fish out like a book and lay it on a board, with the skin side uppermost. Press down firmly with your fingers right along the length of the backbone.

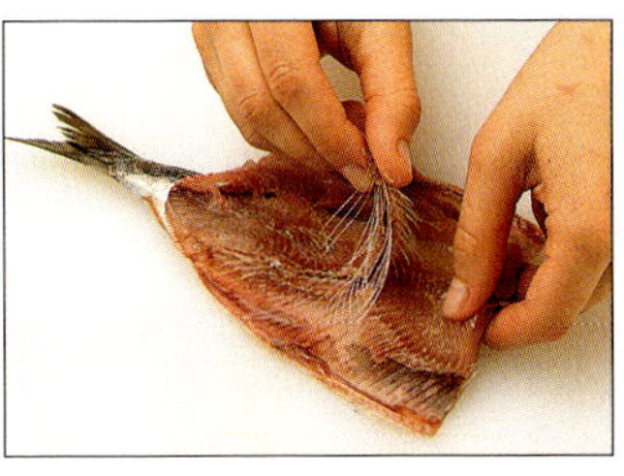

2 Turn the fish over and gently pull the backbone away from the flesh. Cut off at the tail and pick out any small loose bones. Rinse the fish and pat dry.

Filleting round fish

1 Lay the fish on a board with the back away from you and the tail towards you. Lift the gill fin and make a diagonal cut behind the fin to the top of the head.

2 Insert the knife about halfway down the fish as close to the backbone as possible. Cut towards the tail, keeping the knife flat to the bone. Lift up the released fillet, turn the knife towards the tail and carefully slide it along the bone to free the fillet completely.

3 Turn the fish over and repeat on the other side. Remove any small pin bones from the fillets with tweezers.

Removing pin bones from fillets

1 There are always some small bones left in a fillet. Run your finger down the fillet to locate them and lift them out with tweezers.

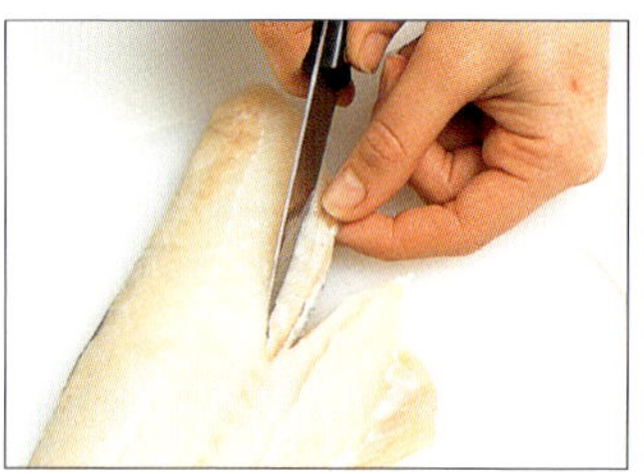

2 Round fish also have tiny pin bones just behind the gill fins. To remove these, make a diagonal cut on either side of the line of bones with a sharp knife. Remove the V-shaped piece of flesh together with the bones.

Flat fish roes

During the breeding season, flat fish contain large roes. In the female fish, these consist of thousands of tiny eggs, which add very little to the flavour of the fish, but weigh quite a lot. So in effect, you are paying for a useless part of the fish.

The soft roes in the male fish, however, are delicious, so do not throw them away. Shallow fry them *à la meunière* in a little butter and serve as a savoury or as a garnish for the cooked fish. They are also excellent dipped in egg and breadcrumbs and then deep-fried in hot oil.

Gutting/cleaning flat fish

Flat fish are generally sold already cleaned, but it is easy to gut them yourself if necessary. Trim off the fins with sharp kitchen scissors. Make an incision just below the gills, then insert your fingers and pull out the innards, including the roe. Wrap the innards in several layers of newspaper before disposing of them. Retain the roe if you like to eat it.

Filleting flat fish

Four fillets can be obtained from flat fish, two from each side. However, the fillets won't be equal in size because the structure of the fish is not regular.

1 Lay the fish on a board with the dark skin facing up and the head pointing away from you. Using a large sharp knife, cut around the head and right down the centre line of the fish, taking the blade of the knife all the way through to the backbone.

2 Working from the head of the fish to the tail, insert the point of the knife under the flesh at the head end. Starting with the left-hand fillet, hold the knife almost parallel to the bones and carefully free the fillet with long stroking movements of the knife.

3 Turn the fish so that the head is towards you and remove the second fillet in the same way.

4 Turn the fish over and repeat the process on the other side.

Skinning whole flat fish

Traditionally, Dover sole are skinned only on the dark side, but other flat fish, such as plaice, flounder or halibut, are skinned on both sides.

1 Lay the fish on a board with the dark skin facing up and the tail towards you. Slit through the skin just below the tail and loosen the skin on both sides.

2 Using a cloth, hold the tail down firmly with one hand. Use the other hand to pull away the skin quickly and firmly towards the head.

Skinning fish fillets

Round and flat fish fillets are skinned in the same way. A really sharp knife is essential for a clean cut.

1 Lay the fillet on a board with the skin side down and the tail towards you. Dip your fingers in a little salt to stop them slipping and grip the tail firmly. Angle the knife blade down at 45° towards the skin and cut with a slight sawing action.

2 Working from the tail to the head, cut along the length of the fillet, folding the flesh forwards as you go and making sure you keep the skin taut.

Filleting fish
Fish fillets are always a popular choice, because there is no wastage, very few bones and, perhaps most importantly, someone else has done all the hard work. But it is often more practical and cheaper to fillet and skin the fish yourself, with the added bonus that you are left with the head and bones for making stock. Remember to wash the fish heads thoroughly first and then remove the gills before using them for stock.

Preparing fish fillets for cooking

Fish fillets can be cooked whole and flat, rolled and secured with a cocktail stick (toothpick), or cut into cubes.

If you are cooking the fillets whole, trim them neatly with a sharp knife, cutting off any very thin flaps of flesh along the edges.

To roll a fillet, lay it on a board skinned-side upwards. Roll the head end (the wider part) towards the tail and tuck the tail underneath. Secure the rolled fillet with a cocktail stick.

To cube a skinned fillet, use a sharp knife to cut along the length of the fillet, making strips of the desired width. This is easier if you follow the natural long lines of the flesh. Then cut each strip across into cubes.

Boning cod steaks

Cod steaks are often cooked with the bone in, or you may wish to remove it for a special meal.

1 Stand the cod steak upright on a chopping board, then insert a sharp knife at the right hand side at the top of the bone.

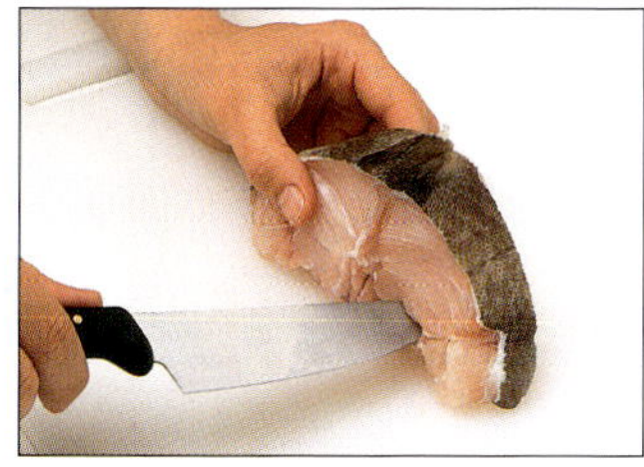

2 Cut firmly downwards, following the curve of the bone and keeping the knife blade as flat to the bone as possible. Repeat the process on the other side.

3 Lay the steak flat on the chopping board. Carefully lift the flesh away from the bone. Make a small cut across the top to release the bone. Fold the flesh into the middle to make a neat, boneless steak.

COOKING FISH

Fish is an extremely versatile food and there are any number of quick and delicious ways to cook it, "quick" being the operative word, since it is all too easy to overcook the delicate flesh. Almost any cooking method suits fish, except boiling, although simmering is fine for hearty soups. Because fish is so delicate, it is always better to undercook rather than overcook it; you can always give it a little extra cooking, but there is no redressing the dry texture and lack of flavour once it is overdone.

It is impossible to give precise cooking times for fish, because so many factors come into play: the thickness of fillets, for example; whether they are much thinner at one end than the other; the type of fish and so on. Fish is cooked when the internal temperature reaches about 63°C/145°F. You can use a meat thermometer to test this, but with experience you will soon be able to judge by eye.

To test whether fish fillets are cooked, insert a small knife into the centre and part the flesh; it should look opaque rather than translucent. Ease the flesh away from the bone; it should just come away, not fall off easily. Alternatively, press a fork into the thickest part of the fillet. If the prongs go in only halfway, cook the fish for a little longer. If the prongs sink in, meeting a slight resistance near the bone, then the fish is done.

Always take the fish out of the refrigerator at least 30 minutes before cooking to be sure that it cooks evenly.

Cooking without heat

Very fresh fish can be "cooked" without heat by being marinated or soused with lemon juice or white wine vinegar. The acids soften the flesh and turn it opaque. The classic dish of this type is ceviche, where cubes or strips of firm white fish (turbot, cod, halibut, snapper, etc.) are marinated in lemon juice, salt and finely chopped chilli for at least 2 hours, until the flesh turns pearly white.

Cooking "au bleu"

This old-fashioned method of cooking is mainly used for freshwater fish, such as trout, carp, tench or pike, which are still alive or exceedingly fresh. The fish is killed, cleaned through the gills, then sprinkled with boiling vinegar, which turns the slime on its skin a steely blue colour (hence "au bleu").

Enough court-bouillon to cover the fish is heated. The fish is placed in a flameproof dish or fish kettle and the court-bouillon is poured over the fish. The dish or kettle is covered and the fish is simmered gently until it is just cooked. The cooked fish can be served hot or cold. If necessary, the fish should be scaled before being served.

Baking

Whole fish and some chunky fish steaks and fillets, such as cod or halibut, are perfect for baking. Because the flesh is delicate, it is best to bake fish at a lower temperature than would be used for meat, and certainly no higher than 200°C/400°F/Gas 6.

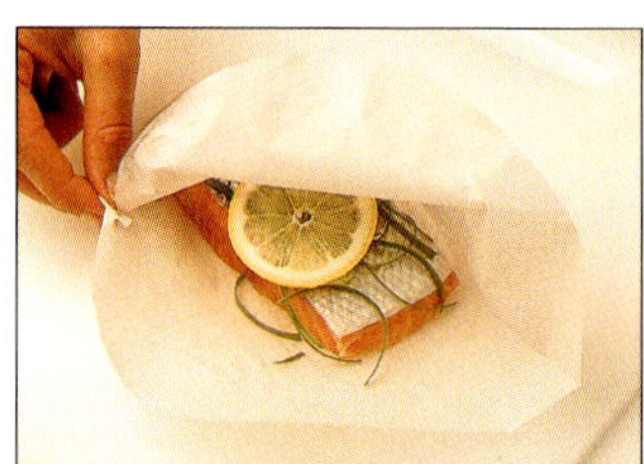

Baking *en papillote* (in a parcel) is an extremely healthy way of cooking, because it uses no fat and retains all the flavour of the fish.

Court-bouillon

This flavoured stock is invaluable for poaching fish or shellfish. The recipe makes about 1 litre/1¾ pints/4 cups.

1 Slice 1 small onion, 2 carrots and the white part of 1 leek.

2 Place the vegetables in a pan and add 2 parsley stalks, 2 bay leaves, 2 lemon slices, 300ml/½ pint/1¼ cups dry white wine and 90ml/6 tbsp white wine vinegar. Add 30ml/2 tbsp salt, a few white peppercorns and 1 litre/1¾ pints/4 cups water.

3 Bring to the boil, lower the heat and simmer for 20 minutes. Strain and leave to cool before using.

Braising

This is another excellent cooking method for whole fish or large fillets.

1 Butter a flameproof dish and make a thick bed of thinly sliced or shredded vegetables, such as a mixture of carrots, onions, fennel and celery.

2 Place the fish on top and pour on enough white or red wine and/or fish or chicken stock to come nearly halfway up the fish.

3 Sprinkle over 15ml/1 tbsp chopped fresh herbs, cover with buttered greaseproof (waxed) paper and bring to the boil. Braise at a low temperature on top of the stove or in a preheated oven at 180°C/350°F/Gas 4, allowing about 20 minutes for a 1kg/2¼lb fish; 10–15 minutes for large fillets.

Fish stock

For many recipes, a good fish stock is essential. It is very simple to make. White fish bones and trimmings make the best stock. Ask the fishmonger for these whenever you buy fish; even if you cannot make stock that day, you can freeze them for later use. To make about 1 litre/1¾ pints/4 cups stock, you will need 1kg/2¼lb white fish bones, heads and trimmings.

1 Wash the fish heads thoroughly then remove the gills. Chop the heads and bones if necessary. Put them in a large pan.

2 Coarsely chop the white part of 1 leek (or ½ fennel bulb), 1 onion and 1 celery stick. Add these to the fish heads and bones in the pan.

3 Add 150ml/¼ pint/⅔ cup dry white wine. Toss in 6 white peppercorns and a bouquet garni, add 1 litre/1¾ pints/4 cups water.

4 Bring to the boil, lower the heat and simmer for only 20 minutes (no longer). Strain through a sieve lined with muslin (cheesecloth).

Frying

Shallow frying or pan-frying

For this popular method, pieces of fish (fillets, steaks or cutlets) or small whole fish are cooked in a little fat in a shallow pan to caramelize and colour the outside. This can either be a prelude to another cooking method or the fish can be fully cooked in the pan. Before frying, the fish can be coated with flour, breadcrumbs or oatmeal. Plain fish can be fried without fat using a non stick pan, but it will have to be cooked carefully to prevent drying out.

Frying in butter gives the best flavour, but it burns easily, so should be combined with a small amount of oil. Alternatively, use clarified butter or just oil. Heat the fat in the pan until very hot, put in the fish and seal briefly on both sides. Lower the heat and cook the fish gently until done. If the pieces of fish are large or the recipe is more complex, it may be necessary to finish cooking in a moderate oven.

Deep-frying

Because fish is delicate, it must be coated in flour or some kind of batter before being deep-fried. This seals in the flavoursome juices, so that the fish is deliciously crisp on the outside and moist inside. Most fish is suitable for deep-frying, from tiny whitebait to large chunky fillets.

Use plenty of oil and make sure that it is really hot (180–190°C/350–375°F) before putting in the fish. Use an electric deep-fryer, or test by carefully dropping a cube of bread into the hot oil; if it browns within 30 seconds, then the oil is hot enough. Larger pieces of fish should be cooked at a slightly lower temperature than small pieces like goujons. This allows the heat to penetrate to the centre before the outside burns. Do not cook too many pieces of fish at the same time, or the temperature of the oil will drop. Oil used for frying fish should never be used for any other purpose, as it will inevitably impart a fishy flavour.

1 Heat the oil in a deep-fryer to 180°C/350°F. Dip the fish in seasoned flour, add to the oil and cook until golden.

2 Drain the fish on a double thickness of kitchen paper before serving.

Goujons of sole or plaice

The name goujon comes from the French for gudgeon, which are small freshwater fish often served crisply fried. Goujons are strips of fish, such as sole, plaice or flounder; which are deep-fried and served with tartare sauce. They are ideal for persuading children to eat fish, especially if they can eat them with their fingers.

SERVES FOUR

INGREDIENTS

- 8 sole, plaice or flounder fillets
- 120ml/4fl oz/½ cup milk
- 50g/2oz/1 cup plain (all-purpose) flour
- vegetable oil, for deep-frying
- salt and ground black pepper

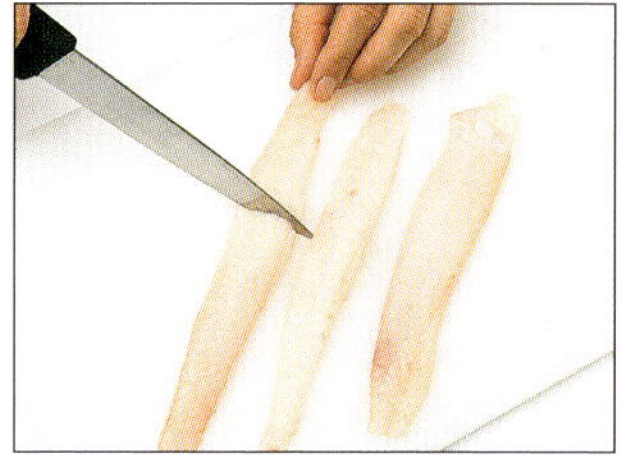

1 Skin the fish fillets and cut them into 7.5 x 2.5cm/3 x 1in strips. Season the milk with a little salt and pepper. Pour it into a shallow bowl, and place the flour in another bowl or spread it out on a plate.

2 Dip the fish strips first into the milk, then into the flour. Shake off the excess flour.

3 Fill a large pan one-third full with vegetable oil. Heat to about 185°C/360°F or until a small cube of bread dropped into the oil turns brown in 30 seconds.

4 Carefully lower the fish strips into the hot oil, adding 4 or 5 at a time. Fry for about 3 minutes, turning them occasionally using a slotted spoon, until the strips rise to the surface and turn golden brown in colour.

5 Lift out each piece of cooked fish with a slotted spoon and drain them on a double thickness of kitchen paper. Keep the cooked goujons hot in the oven while you cook successive batches.

Stir-frying

This quick-cooking method is perfect for fish, prawns (shrimp) and squid.

1 Cut the fish or squid into bite-size strips; leave prawn tails whole, with the tail shells intact. Toss them in a little cornflour (cornstarch).

2 Heat a little oil in a wok over a very high heat, add a few pieces of fish or shellfish and stir-fry for a few moments.

Searing

This method is best for thickish fillets that have not been skinned or small whole fish, such as sardines and red mullet.

1 Smear the base of a heavy frying pan or griddle with a little oil and heat until smoking. Lightly brush both sides of the fish with oil and put it into the hot pan.

2 Sear for a couple of minutes, until the skin is golden brown, then turn the fish over and cook on the other side.

Grilling and Cooking on the Barbecue

Fish steaks, thick fillets and relatively small whole fish, such as sardines, red mullet or trout, can be grilled (broiled) or cooked on a barbecue, as can crustaceans. The grill (broiler) should be preheated to a very high heat so that the fish juices are sealed in quickly. Griddle pans are better than overhead grills, but either will do. Grilling on a barbecue can be a little more tricky, as bastes or marinades used to keep the fish moist can drip and cause flare-ups.

All grilled fish will benefit from being marinated for 1 hour in a mixture of oil and lemon juice before being cooked. If the fish is to be cooked whole, make several slashes down to the bone on either side to make sure that the fish cooks quickly and evenly. Brush the grill rack and fish with oil to prevent sticking. Thin fillets need only be grilled on one side, without a grill rack. Brush the grill pan with oil. Place it under the grill until hot, then pass both sides of the fish through the oil before grilling on one side only; the underside will cook at the same time.

Microwaving

Fish can be cooked successfully in a microwave oven. As long as it is not overcooked, it will be moist and full of flavour. Always cover the fish with clear film (plastic wrap). Cook it on full power (100 per cent) for the shortest possible time recommended in your handbook, then give it a resting period to allow it to finish cooking by residual heat. Cooking time depends on the thickness and density of the fish. The following are general guidelines for 500g/1¼lb fish, but test before the end of the given time to check that the flesh is still succulent.

Whole round fish, thick fillets, steaks and cutlets: cook for 4–5 minutes, then leave to stand for 5 minutes.

Flat fish, thin fillets: cook for 3–4 minutes, then rest for 3–4 minutes.

Fish with denser flesh (monkfish, tuna, skate, etc): cook for 6–7 minutes, then leave to stand for 5 minutes.

Cook fillets in a single layer, thinner parts towards the centre, or tuck a thin tail end underneath a thicker portion.

Fish can also be microwaved whole, provided that they will fit in the oven. Slash the skin in several places to prevent it from splitting. Turn the fish over halfway through cooking.

Poaching

Cooking in a stock or court-bouillon brings out the flavour of fresh fish.

1 A whole fish can be poached in a fish kettle, provided it is not too large, while portions are best placed in a single layer in a shallow heatproof dish.

2 Cover with cold court-bouillon or stock, add a few herbs and flavourings.

3 Lay some buttered or greaseproof (waxed) paper on top and heat until the liquid just starts to tremble. At this point, thin pieces of fish may be done. Continue to cook thicker pieces at a bare simmer either on top of the stove or in the oven, until the flesh is just opaque. For 1kg/2¼lb fish allow 7–8 minutes. To serve the fish cold, leave it to cool in the poaching liquid.

Butter sauce for poached fish

Poached fish needs very little enhancement other than a simple sauce that has been made from the poaching liquid.

1 Remove the cooked fish from the poaching liquid and keep it hot while you make the sauce.

2 Strain the liquid into a pan and place it over a medium heat. Simmer gently until the liquid has reduced by half.

3 Whisk in some cold diced butter or a little double (heavy) cream to make a smooth, velvety sauce. Season to taste. Pour the sauce over the fish and serve.

Roasting

This is more usually associated with meat, but it is an excellent method of cooking whole fish and "meaty" cuts, such as monkfish tails or swordfish steaks. The oven should be preheated to very hot – 230°C/450°F/Gas 8 – with the roasting pan inside. The fish will then be seared by the heat of the pan, and the juices will not escape.

Drizzle a little olive oil over the fish before roasting. For extra flavour, roast it on a bed of rosemary, fennel or Mediterranean vegetables.

Smoking

Although most of the smoked fish we buy has been commercially smoked, it is easy to smoke your own, adding a new dimension to bland tastes.

Hot smoking

This method cooks and smokes the food at the same time, using a special smoker filled with fragrant hardwood chips (hickory and oak are popular), which give the fish a delicious flavour. Domestic smokers are quite small and very easy to use. Some can be used indoors, but on the whole they are best suited to outdoor use, where the smoke can dissipate easily. For large quantities you can use a kettle barbecue. Heat the wood chips to 80–85°C/176–185°F, place the fish on the rack, put on the lid and smoke until the fish looks like pale burnished wood.

Cold smoking

This method cures but does not cook the fish. It must first be salted in dry salt or brine, then hung up to drip dry before smoking at 30–35°C/86–95°F.

Tea smoking

This Chinese method of smoking is usually used for duck, but imparts a wonderful flavour to oily fish, such as mackerel and tuna, and shellfish such as scallops and mussels.

1 Line a wok with foil and sprinkle in 30ml/2 tbsp each of raw long grain rice, sugar and aromatic tea leaves.

2 Place a wire rack on top of the wok and then arrange the fish in a single layer on the rack. Cover the wok with a lid or more foil and cook over a very high heat until you see smoke.

3 Lower the heat slightly (some smoke should still escape from the wok) and cook until the fish is done. A mackerel fillet takes 8–10 minutes, large prawns (shrimp) 5–7 minutes.

Steaming

Many people assume that steaming will result in bland, flavourless fish. Far from it; this method of cooking enhances the natural flavour and the fish remains moist and retains its shape, even if you overcook it.

Steaming is the healthiest way of cooking fish. It uses no fat and because the fish is not in contact with the cooking liquid, fewer valuable nutrients are lost in the process.

1 Half-fill the base pan of a steamer with water and bring it to the boil. Place the fish in a single layer in the steamer basket, leaving room to enable the steam to circulate freely.

2 Lower the fish into the steamer, making sure that the insert stands well clear of the boiling water.

3 Lay a sheet of greaseproof (waxed) paper over the surface of the fish, then cover the pan tightly with a lid or foil and steam until the fish is just cooked.

4 Fish cooks very quickly in a steamer, but take care that the level of the water does not fall too low. Check once or twice during cooking and keep a supply of boiling water on hand to add more.

Alternative steamers

There are plenty of purpose-made steamers on the market, which range from the hugely expensive stainless steel models to modest Chinese bamboo baskets. However, you can easily improvise with a pan, any perforated container (a colander or sieve, for example) and some foil. Make sure that the pan is large enough to hold a good depth of water.

Whatever the type of steamer, remember that the golden rule of steaming is not to allow the boiling liquid to touch the steamer basket or the fish or shellfish.

A Chinese bamboo steamer, which can be used in a wok or on top of a large pan, is ideal for steaming fish or shellfish. If you like, arrange the fish on a bed of aromatic flavourings, such as lemon or lime slices and sprigs of fresh herbs. Alternatively, before adding the fish or shellfish, you can place finely shredded vegetables, seaweed or samphire in the base of the steamer to give extra flavour.

SAUCES FOR FISH AND SHELLFISH

MANY TYPES OF FISH ARE SO DELICIOUS THAT THEY DO NOT NEED TO BE COOKED IN A SAUCE, BUT A GOOD ACCOMPANYING SAUCE WILL CERTAINLY ENHANCE PLAINLY COOKED FISH.

NEVER-FAIL MAYONNAISE

Some people find classic mayonnaise difficult to make, but this simple version takes away the mystique. The essential thing is to have all the ingredients at room temperature before you start. Be aware that this recipe contains raw eggs. If this is a concern, use bought mayonnaise instead.

SERVES FOUR TO SIX

INGREDIENTS

- 1 egg, plus 1 egg yolk
- 5ml/1 tsp Dijon mustard
- juice of 1 large lemon
- 175ml/6fl oz/¾ cup olive oil
- 175ml/6fl oz/¾ cup grapeseed, sunflower or corn oil
- salt and ground white pepper

1 Put the whole egg and yolk in a food processor and process for 20 seconds. Add the mustard, half the lemon juice and a generous pinch of salt and pepper. Process for about 30 seconds, until thoroughly mixed.

2 With the motor running, pour in the oils through the feeder tube in a thin, steady stream. Process until the oils are incorporated and the mayonnaise is pale and thick. Taste and add more lemon juice and seasoning, if necessary.

VARIATIONS

Vary the oil according to the fish the mayonnaise is to accompany. Use all olive oil for robust fish such as salmon or tuna, a mixture of olive and light vegetable oil for more delicate fish.

BEURRE BLANC

Legend has it that this exquisite sauce was invented by a cook who forgot to put egg yolks into a béarnaise sauce. Whether or not this is true doesn't matter: this light sauce goes perfectly with poached or grilled (broiled) fish.

SERVES FOUR

INGREDIENTS

- 3 shallots, very finely chopped
- 45ml/3 tbsp dry white wine or court-bouillon
- 45ml/3 tbsp white wine or tarragon vinegar
- 115g/4oz/½ cup chilled unsalted (sweet) butter, diced
- lemon juice (optional)
- salt and ground white pepper

1 Put the shallots in a small pan with the wine or court bouillon and vinegar. Bring to the boil and cook over a high heat until only about 30ml/2 tbsp liquid remains. Remove the pan from the heat and then leave to cool until the liquid is just lukewarm.

2 Whisk in the chilled butter, one piece at a time, to make a pale, creamy sauce. (Make sure each piece is fully incorporated before adding the next.) Taste the sauce, then season with salt and pepper and add a little lemon juice to taste, if you like.

3 If you are not serving the sauce immediately, keep it warm in the top of a double boiler set over barely simmering water.

HOLLANDAISE SAUCE

This rich sauce goes well with any poached fish. Serve it warm. As the egg yolks are barely cooked, do not serve to children, the elderly or invalids.

SERVES FOUR

INGREDIENTS

- 115g/4oz/½ cup unsalted (sweet) butter
- 2 egg yolks
- 15–30ml/1–2 tbsp lemon juice or white wine or tarragon vinegar
- salt and ground white pepper

1 Melt the butter in a small pan Put the egg yolks and lemon juice or vinegar in a bowl. Add salt and pepper and whisk until completely smooth.

2 Pour the melted butter in a steady stream on to the egg yolk mixture, beating vigorously with a wooden spoon to make a smooth, creamy sauce. Alternatively, put the mixture in a food processor and add the butter through the feeder tube, with the motor running. Taste the sauce and add more lemon juice or vinegar, if necessary.

PARSLEY SAUCE

Forget the pallid, lumpy parsley sauce of your youth; when this classic sauce is well made it is delicious. Serve it with poached cod, haddock or any white fish. If possible, use the poaching liquid to enhance the flavour of the sauce.

SERVES FOUR

INGREDIENTS

- 50g/2oz/¼ cup butter
- 45ml/3 tbsp plain (all-purpose) flour
- 300ml/½ pint/1¼ cups milk
- 300ml/½ pint/1¼ cups poaching liquid from the fish (or an extra 300ml/½ pint/1¼ cups milk)
- 60ml/4 tbsp double (heavy) cream
- lemon juice (see method)
- 90ml/6 tbsp chopped fresh parsley
- salt and ground black pepper

1 Melt half the butter in a small pan, add the flour and stir for 2–3 minutes to make a smooth roux. Take the pan off the heat, add a couple of spoonfuls of milk and stir in until completely absorbed. Continue to add small quantities of milk and poaching liquid, if available, stirring until the sauce has the consistency of double cream. Add the rest of the milk and poaching liquid and whisk thoroughly to break down any lumps.

2 Return the pan to the heat and bring the sauce to the boil. Lower the heat and simmer gently for about 5 minutes, stirring frequently. Stir in the cream and lemon juice to taste, and season with salt and pepper. If the sauce is at all lumpy at this stage, whisk it thoroughly with a hand-held blender or a balloon whisk.

3 Stir in the parsley, then whisk in the remaining butter and serve hot.

MUSTARD AND DILL SAUCE

Serve this fresh-tasting sauce with any cold, smoked or raw marinated fish. Note that it contains raw egg yolk.

SERVES FOUR

INGREDIENTS

- 1 egg yolk
- 30ml/2 tbsp brown French mustard
- 2.5–5ml/½–1 tsp soft dark brown sugar
- 15ml/1 tbsp white wine vinegar
- 90ml/6 tbsp sunflower or vegetable oil
- 30ml/2 tbsp finely chopped fresh dill
- salt and ground black pepper

1 Put the egg yolk in a small bowl and add the mustard with a little soft brown sugar to taste. Beat with a wooden spoon until smooth. Stir in the white wine vinegar, then gradually whisk in the oil, a little at a time, mixing well after each addition.

2 When the oil has been completely amalgamated, season the sauce with salt and pepper, then stir in the finely chopped dill. Chill for an hour or more before serving.

CRAWFISH SAUCE

This sauce, also known as Nantua sauce, is perfect for using up the shells left over from seafood recipes. It can be made with other crustaceans, such as lobster or large prawns (shrimp). Use it to enhance any white fish or shellfish.

SERVES FOUR

INGREDIENTS

- 1 cooked crawfish (rock lobster), about 450g/1lb
- 40g/1½oz/3 tbsp butter
- 15ml/1 tbsp olive oil
- 45ml/3 tbsp brandy
- 500ml/17fl oz/generous 2 cups fish or shellfish stock
- 15ml/1 tbsp plain (all-purpose) flour
- 45ml/3 tbsp double (heavy) cream
- 2 egg yolks
- salt and ground white pepper

1 Remove the tail meat from the crawfish and keep for another recipe. Break up the shells and legs and crush them coarsely in a food processor.

2 Melt 25g/1oz/2 tbsp of the butter in the oil in a pan, add the shells and cook for about 3 minutes, stirring frequently. Add the brandy and stock, bring to the boil, then simmer for 10 minutes.

3 Mash the remaining butter with the flour to make *beurre manié*. Whisk this into the sauce, a small piece at a time, and cook gently until thickened. Season the sauce and strain it through a fine sieve. Stir in the cream and bring back to just below boiling point.

4 Beat the egg yolks lightly in a bowl and mix in a couple of spoonfuls of the hot sauce. Return the mixture to the pan and cook gently until smooth. Adjust the seasoning and serve.

Buying, Preparing and Cooking Shellfish

The term "shellfish" is loosely applied to seafood other than fish. Strictly speaking, it means aquatic invertebrates with shells or shell-like carapaces. This includes the crustaceans – lobsters, crabs, prawns (shrimp) and similar creatures – as well as some molluscs, such as clams, mussels and oysters. For convenience, however, the category extends to other molluscs too, such as the cephalopods (octopus, squid and cuttlefish) and lesser known sea creatures, such as sea urchins.

When discussing shellfish, it is impossible to divorce preparation and cooking techniques, since one is bound up so closely with the other. Lobsters and crabs, for instance, are cooked live; mussels are opened and cooked in one simple process.

Crustaceans and molluscs need very little cooking to enhance their already superb flavour. Indeed, many molluscs can be eaten raw, provided they are extremely fresh and come from unpolluted waters. Crustaceans of all types must be cooked; unlike fish, the larger specimens can be boiled. Many of the methods used for cooking fish are suitable for shellfish – poaching, frying, grilling (broiling) and steaming.

CRUSTACEANS

Lobsters and crabs

Buying

Live lobsters or crabs should smell very fresh and still be lively and aggressive when picked up. The tails of lobsters should spring back sharply when they are opened out. Crabs should feel heavy for their size, but you should make sure this is not because there is water inside the shell. Shake them – any sloshing sounds are a bad sign. The shell should neither be soft nor should it contain any cracks or holes.

Lobsters in particular command a high price, which reflects the effort involved in catching them. It is a good idea to check that lobsters and crabs have both claws, as one may often be lost in a fight. If a claw is missing, make sure the price is reduced accordingly.

Preparing and cooking a live lobster

1 The most humane way to kill a live lobster is to render it unconscious by placing it in a freezerproof dish or tray and covering it with crushed ice. Alternatively, put the lobster in the freezer for 2 hours.

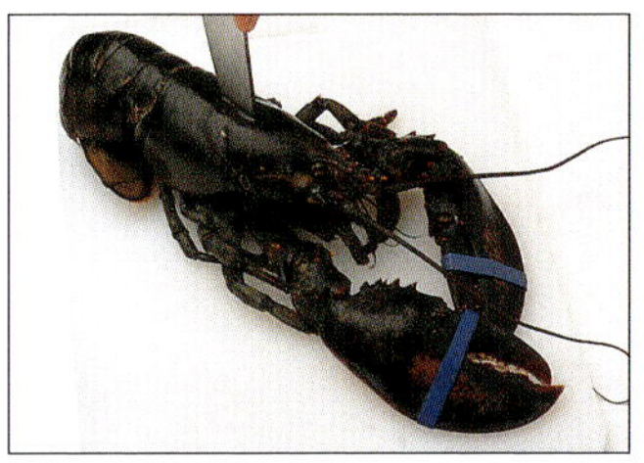

2 When the lobster is very cold and no longer moving, place it on a chopping board and drive the tip of a large, sharp heavy knife or a very strong skewer through the centre of the cross on its head. According to the experts, death is instantaneous.

3 If you can't face stabbing the lobster, put it in a large pan of cold, heavily salted water and bring slowly to the boil. The lobster will expire before the water boils.

4 Alternatively, you can add the comatose lobster to a large pan of boiling water. Plunge it in head first and immediately clamp on the lid. Bring the water back to the boil.

5 Lower the heat and simmer the lobster gently for about 15 minutes for the first 450g/1lb and then allow 10 minutes more for each subsequent 450g/1lb, up to a maximum of 40 minutes.

6 When cooked, the lobster will turn a deep brick red. Drain off the water and leave to cool, if not eating hot.

If cooking two or more lobsters in the same pan, wait until the water comes back to the boil before adding the second one. More than two lobsters should be cooked separately.

Always buy cooked lobsters or crabs from a reputable supplier who cooks them fresh every day. The colour should be vibrant and the crustaceans ought to feel heavy for their size. Cooked lobsters should have their tails tightly curled under their bodies; avoid specimens with floppy tails, which may have been dead when they were cooked.

Quantities

When calculating how much you should buy, allow about 450g/1lb per person.

Storing

For practical reasons you will wish to cook live lobsters or crabs on the day you buy them, unless you want them live in your bathtub.

If you cannot pop them straight into the pot, live crustaceans can be wrapped in wet newspaper or covered in a very damp dishtowel and kept in the coldest part of the refrigerator. If you intend the crustaceans to be unconscious when you kill them, you may want to put them in the freezer for a couple of hours or submerge them in crushed ice.

Removing the meat from a boiled lobster

1 Lay the lobster on its back and twist off the large legs and claws.

2 Carefully crack open the claws with a wooden mallet or the back of a heavy knife and remove the meat, keeping the pieces as large as possible. Scoop out the meat from the legs with a lobster pick or the handle of a small teaspoon.

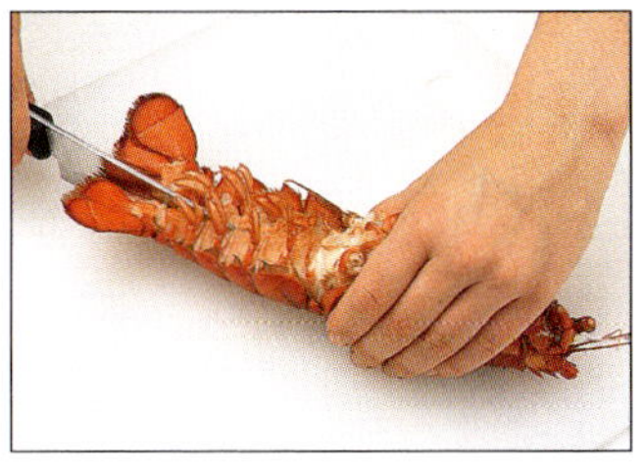

3 On a chopping board, stretch out the body of the lobster so that its tail is extended. Turn it on to its back and, holding it firmly with one hand, use a sharp, heavy knife to cut the lobster neatly in half along its entire length.

4 Discard the whitish sac and the feathery gills from the head and the grey-black intestinal thread that runs down the tail.

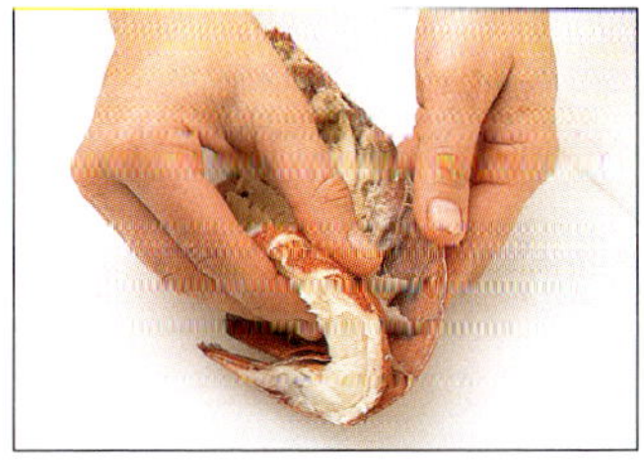

5 Carefully remove all the meat from each half of the tail – it should come out in one piece.

6 Keep the greenish tomalley (liver) and the coral (roe), which are delicious. This roe is only to be found in the female or "hen" lobsters. Like the tomalley, it is usually added to a sauce. The creamy flesh close to the shell can also be scraped out and used in a sauce.

Grilling lobster

Preheat the grill (broiler) to high. Boil the lobster for 3 minutes only, then drain, split in half and clean.

Lay the halves of the lobster cut side up in a grill pan, brush generously with melted butter and cook for about 10 minutes, spooning on more melted butter halfway through.

If the lobster has already been killed by stabbing, it can just be split and cooked for about 12 minutes.

Cooking lobster on the barbecue

Prepare the lobster as for grilling (broiling). Brush the cut sides with butter seasoned with garlic or cayenne. Grill cut side down over moderately hot coals for about 5 minutes, then turn the halves over and grill them on the shell for 5 minutes more. Turn the lobster halves over once more, brush the flesh with more melted butter and grill it flesh side down for 3–4 minutes more.

Preparing a live crab

To kill a crab humanely, chill it by submerging it in ice, or leave it in the freezer for a couple of hours until it is comatose (see Preparing and cooking a live lobster, page 26). When the crab is no longer moving, lay it on its back on a chopping board, lift up the tail flap and look for a small hole at the base of a distinct groove. Drive an awl or sturdy skewer into this hole, then carefully push the skewer between the mouth plates between the eyes. The crab is now ready for cooking.

Alternatively, if stabbing a crab does not appeal to you, the live crab can be killed and cooked simultaneously. There are two ways of doing this. Either plunge the crustacean into a large pan of salted, boiling water, bring back to the boil and cook for 10–12 minutes; or place it in a pan of cold salted water and bring it slowly to the boil. The latter method is reckoned to be the more humane, because the crab becomes sleepy as the temperature rises and succumbs well before the water reaches boiling point. Whichever way you choose, calculate the cooking time from the moment that the water boils, and do not boil the crab for more than 12 minutes, whatever its size.

Removing the meat from a cooked crab

1 Lay the cooked crab on its back on a large chopping board. Hold the crab firmly with one hand and break off the tail flap. Twist off both the claws and the legs.

2 Stand the crab on its head and insert a heavy knife between the body and shell. Twist the knife firmly to separate them so that you can lift the honeycomb body out.

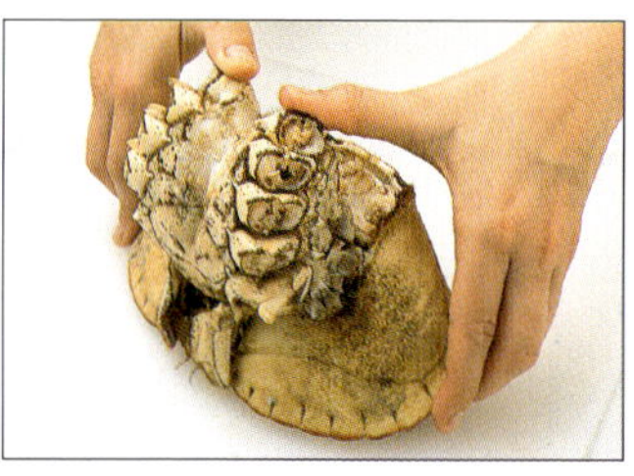

3 Alternatively, hold the crab firmly and use your thumbs to ease the body out of the shell.

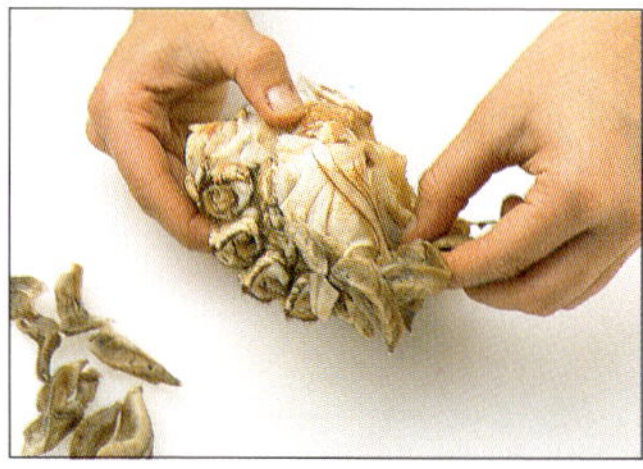

4 Remove and discard the feathery, grey gills (these are unattractively but descriptively known as "dead men's fingers"), which are attached to either side of the body.

5 Press down on the top shell to detach the spongy stomach sac – this is found directly behind the mouth. Cut the honeycomb body into quarters with a large, heavy knife.

6 Carefully pick out the white meat, using a skewer.

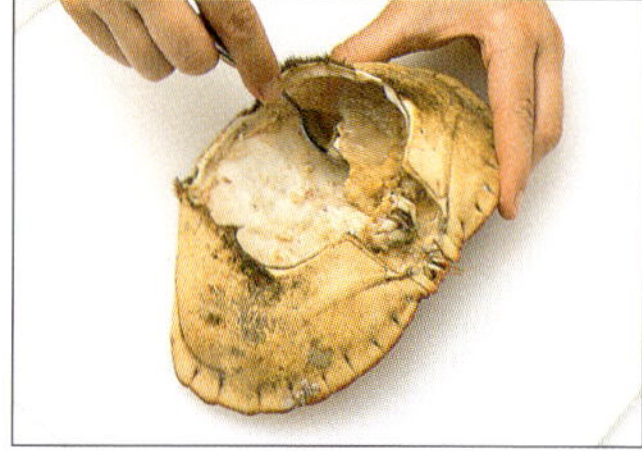

7 Use a teaspoon to scoop out all the creamy brown meat from the back shell, then scoop out the thin solid brown meat from inside the flaps.

8 Crack open the claws and legs with a mallet (or use the back of a heavy knife), then remove the claw meat in the largest possible pieces. Pick or scrape out the leg meat with a lobster pick or a skewer. The smallest legs can be kept whole and used to make a delicious shellfish stock.

Prawns, Shrimps, Langoustines and Crayfish

Buying

There is some confusion over the terms prawn and shrimp. In America, the word shrimp refers to all sizes and types of prawns, but in most countries shrimps are a tiny separate species.

Prawns and shrimp are not sold alive, but crayfish must be as their flesh deteriorates quickly after death and can become poisonous. All fresh raw prawns and shrimp should have crisp, firm shells and a fresh smell. Do not buy any that smell of ammonia. If you cannot buy fresh prawns or shrimp, buy frozen. Transport them in a freezer bag and get them into your freezer as quickly as possible. Do not buy frozen prawns or shrimp that have been thawed.

Quantities

If you buy them with the shells on, allow about 300g/11oz prawns or shrimp per serving. Some crustaceans – Dublin Bay prawns, for example – tend to be sold shelled, without the heads. If you buy these in the shell, remember that there will be a lot of wastage (up to 80 per cent) so buy a generous amount. Keep the shells to flavour sauces and stocks.

Storing

Fresh prawns and shrimp should be eaten as soon as possible after purchase. Crayfish – including the yabby – are the exception. They are none too fussy about what they eat, so it is best to purge them after purchase. Place them in a bowl, cover with a damp dishtowel and leave in the coldest part of the refrigerator for 24 hours.

Poaching langoustines or prawns

Raw langoustines or prawns are best poached in sea water. Failing that, use a well-flavoured *nage* (fish stock) or heavily salted water. Bring the poaching liquid to the boil in a large deep pan, drop in the crustaceans and simmer for only a minute or two, depending on their size. Be careful not overcook the shellfish, or the delicate flesh will become tough.

Peeling and deveining raw prawns

Raw prawns and large shrimp are often peeled before cooking. Raw prawns must have their intestinal tracts removed before cooking, a process that is known as "deveining". It is not necessary to devein very small shrimp.

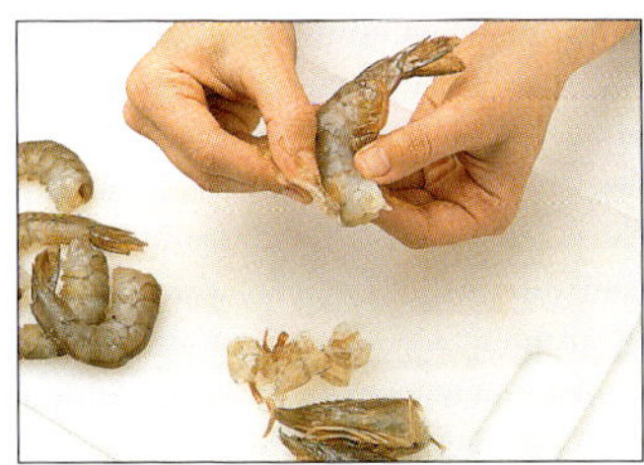

1 Pull off the head and legs from each prawn or shrimp, then carefully peel off the body shell with your fingers. Leave on the tail "fan" if you like.

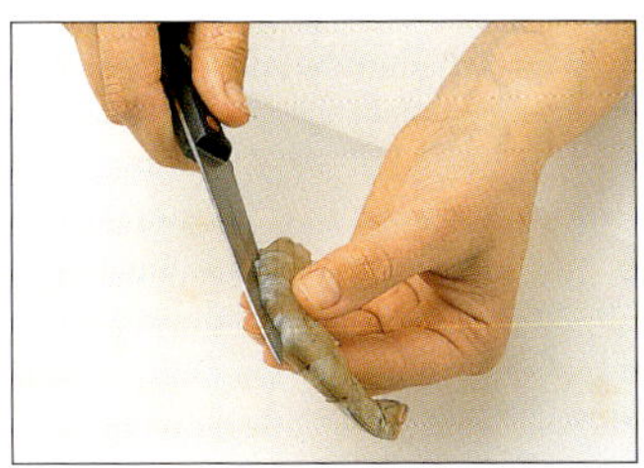

2 To remove the intestinal vein from prawns, make a shallow incision down the centre of the curved back of the prawn using a small sharp knife, cutting all the way from the tail to the head.

3 Carefully pick out the thin black vein that runs the length of the prawn with the tip of the knife and discard.

Grilling or cooking langoustines or large prawns on the barbecue

This method is also suitable for crayfish. The shellfish can be raw or cooked.

1 Preheat the grill (broiler) or barbecue to hot. Butterfly the shellfish by laying them on their backs and splitting them in half lengthways, without cutting right through to the back shell.

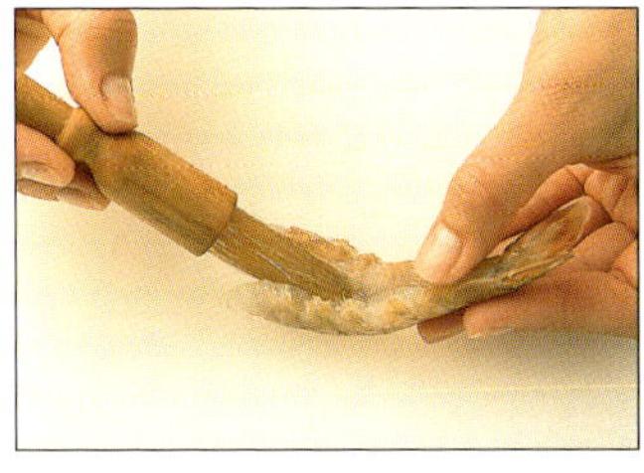

2 Open the shellfish out like a book and brush the cut sides all over with a mixture of olive oil and lemon juice.

3 Lay the shellfish in a grill (broiler) pan or on a barbecue rack. Cook for 2–3 minutes on each side; cooked shellfish for about half this time. To make sure they keep their shape, you could thread the butterflied shellfish on to skewers before cooking.

Peeling cooked prawns, langoustines and crayfish

1 Twist off the heads and, in the case of langoustines, the claws.

2 Squeeze the shellfish along their length and pull off the shell and the legs with your fingers.

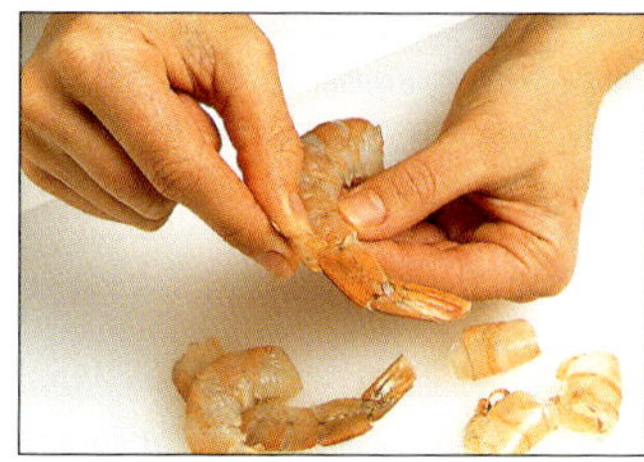

3 To keep the tail fan, carefully peel off the last piece of body shell, otherwise, squeeze the end of the tail and remove.

Fantail or phoenix prawns

This way of serving large prawns (shrimp) comes from China. The cooked prawns, with their bright red tails, are supposed to resemble the legendary phoenix, which in China is a symbol of dignity and good luck.

1 Remove the heads from the prawns and peel away most of the body shell with your fingers. Leave a little of the shell to keep the tail "fan" intact.

2 Make a long shallow incision in the back of each prawn and remove the black intestinal vein with the point of the knife.

3 Hold the prepared prawns by the tails and dip them lightly in a little seasoned cornflour (cornstarch), and then in a frothy batter before deep-frying them in hot oil until the tails, which are free from batter, turn red.

Potted Shrimp

These are very simple to make and will keep for several days. If possible, use fresh, not frozen, brown shrimp. They are tedious to peel, but worth the effort. Serve with buttered brown bread or toast and lemon wedges.

SERVES FOUR

INGREDIENTS

- 350g/12oz/1 1/2 cups butter
- 225g/8oz cooked peeled shrimp, thawed if frozen
- 1 bay leaf
- 1 large blade of mace or 2.5ml/ 1/2 tsp ground mace
- ground black pepper and cayenne pepper

1 Melt 250g/9oz/generous 1 cup of the butter in a pan. Add the shrimp, bay leaf, mace and seasoning. Heat gently, then discard the bay leaf and mace. Divide the shrimp between four ramekins and leave to set.

2 Clarify the remaining butter, by placing it in a small pan and heating very gently over a low heat until melted and foaming. Strain through a sieve lined with muslin (cheesecloth) into a small bowl, leaving the milky solids at the base of the pan.

3 Spoon the clarified butter over the potted shrimp, making sure they are completely covered. When cool, transfer the ramekins to the refrigerator and chill for up to 2–3 days, until ready to serve.

MOLLUSCS

Bivalves (mussels, clams, oysters and scallops)

Buying

Like other types of shellfish, molluscs deteriorate rapidly, so you must make sure that they are alive when you cook them. Scallops are an exception, as they are often sold already opened and cleaned. Bivalves such as mussels, clams and oysters should contain plenty of sea water and feel heavy for their size. Do not buy any that have broken shells. If the shells gape, give them a sharp tap on a hard surface. They should snap shut immediately; if they don't, do not buy them as they will either be dead or moribund.

Quantities

When buying mussels, clams or similar shellfish, allow about 450g/1lb per person, as the shells make up much of the weight. Four or five scallops will serve one person as a main course.

Storing

Mussels, clams and other bivalves must be eaten within one day of purchase, but will keep briefly stored in the refrigerator. Tip them into a large bowl, cover with a damp cloth and keep them in the coldest part of the refrigerator (at 2°C/36°F) until ready to use. Some people advocate sprinkling them with oatmeal and leaving them overnight to fatten up. Oysters can be kept for a couple of days, thanks to the sea water contained in their shells. Store them cupped side down. Never store shellfish in fresh water, or they will die. Ready-frozen bivalves should not be kept in the freezer for more than 2 months.

Preparing

Scrub bivalves under cold running water, using a stiff brush to remove any sand or dirt. Open the shellfish over a bowl to catch the delicious juice. This will be gritty, so must be strained before being used. Cockles (small clams) usually contain a lot of sand. They will expel this if left overnight in a bucket of clean sea water or salted water.

Cleaning mussels

1 Wash the mussels in plenty of cold water, scrubbing them well. Scrape off any barnacles with a knife.

2 Give any open mussels a sharp tap; discard any that fail to close.

3 Pull out and discard the fibrous "beard" that sprouts between the two halves of the shell.

Moules Marinière

1 Chop 1 onion and 2 shallots. Put in a large pan with 25g/1oz/2 tbsp butter and cook over a low heat until translucent.

2 Add 300ml/½ pint/1¼ cups white wine, a bay leaf and a sprig of fresh thyme. Bring to the boil. Add 2kg/4½lb cleaned mussels, cover the pan tightly and steam over a high heat for 2 minutes. Shake the pan vigorously and steam for 2 minutes more. Shake again and steam until all the mussels have opened. Discard any closed ones.

3 Stir in 30ml/2 tbsp chopped fresh parsley and serve immediately.

Steaming mussels

This method opens and cooks the shellfish all at once. It is also suitable for clams, cockles and razor-shells.

1 Put a few splashes of white wine into a wide pan. Add some finely chopped onion and chopped fresh herbs, if you like, and bring to the boil.

2 Add the mussels, cover the pan and shake over a high heat for 2–3 minutes. Remove the mussels that have opened.

3 Replace the lid and shake the pan over a high heat for another minute or so. By this time all the mussels that are going to open should have done so; discard any that remain closed.

4 Strain the cooking liquid through a sieve lined with muslin (cheesecloth).

5 The cooking liquid can be reheated and used as a thin sauce, or heated until it has reduced by about half. For a richer sauce, stir in a little cream.

6 The mussels can be eaten as they are, or the top shell can be removed and the mussel served on the half shell. Alternatively, they can be grilled (broiled), but take care not to overcook.

Grilling mussels and clams

Steam open the molluscs and remove the top shell. Arrange in their half shells in a single layer on a baking sheet. Spoon over a little melted butter flavoured with chopped garlic and parsley. Top with fresh breadcrumbs, sprinkle with a little more melted butter and cook under a hot grill (broiler) until golden brown and bubbling.

Opening clams and razor-shells

The easiest way to open clams or razor-shells is by steaming them, in the same way as you do for mussels. However, this method is not suitable if the clams are going to be eaten raw like oysters.

1 Protect your hand with a clean dishtowel, then cup the clam in your palm, holding it firmly. Work over a bowl to catch the juices.

2 Insert a sharp pointed knife between the shells. Run the knife away from you to open the clam, twisting it to force the shells apart.

3 Cut through the hinge muscle, then use a spoon to scoop out the muscle on the bottom shell. This part of the mollusc should be discarded.

Opening small clams in the microwave

1 Thin-shelled molluscs like small clams can be opened in the microwave. Place them in a bowl and cook on full power (100 per cent) for about 2 minutes.

2 Remove the open molluscs and repeat the process until all have opened. Do not try to open large clams, oysters or scallops this way, as the thick shells will absorb the microwaves and cook the molluscs before they open.

Opening scallops in the oven

The easiest way to open scallops is to place them, rounded side down, on a baking sheet and place them in an oven preheated to 160°C/325°F/Gas 3 for a few moments until they gape sufficiently for you to complete the job by hand.

1 Spread the scallops in a single layer on a baking sheet. Heat them until they gape, then remove them from the oven.

2 Grasp a scallop in a clean dishtowel, flat side up. Using a long, flexible knife, run the blade along the inner surface of the flat shell to cut through the muscle that holds the shells together. This done, ease the shells apart completely.

3 Lift off the top shell. Pull out and discard the black intestinal sac and the yellowish frilly membrane.

4 Cut the white scallop and orange coral from the bottom shell and wash briefly under cold running water. Remove and discard the white ligament attached to the scallop flesh.

Cooking scallops

Scallop flesh is very delicate and needs barely any cooking; an overcooked scallop loses its flavour and becomes extremely rubbery. Small scallops need to be cooked for only a few seconds; larger ones take a minute or two.

Scallops can be pan-fried, steamed, poached and baked au gratin. They are also delicious grilled (broiled).

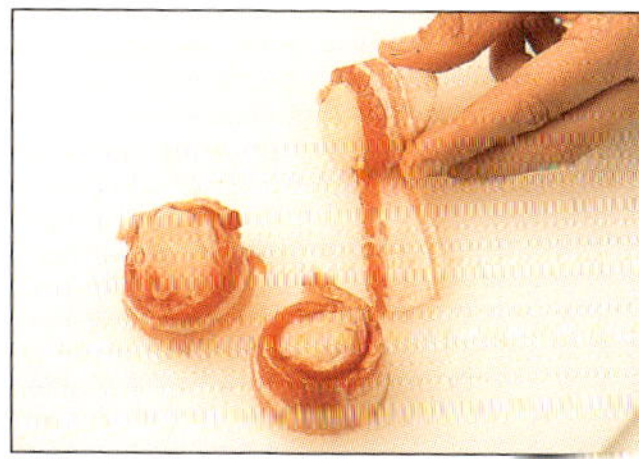

Wrap scallops in thin strips of bacon or pancetta before grilling (broiling) them to protect the delicate texture and add extra flavour.

Opening oysters

You really do need a special oyster knife if you are to open – or shuck – oysters successfully. If you haven't got one, use a strong knife with a short, blunt blade.

1 Scrub the shells under cold running water. Wrap one hand in a clean dishtowel and hold the oyster with the cupped shell down and the narrow hinged end towards you.

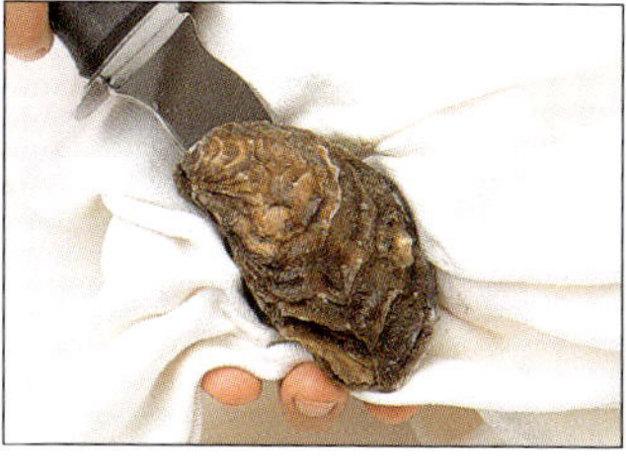

2 Push the point of the knife into the small gap in the hinge and twist it to and fro between the shells until the hinge breaks. Lever open the top shell.

3 Slide the knife along the inner edges of the top shell and sever the muscle that joins the oyster to the shell. Lift off the top shell, leaving the oyster in its juices in the bottom shell.

Cooking oysters

Oysters are best eaten raw with just a squeeze of lemon or a dash of Tabasco sauce. If you prefer to cook them, do so very briefly. They can be poached or steamed for a minute or two and served with a white wine sauce; grilled (broiled) like mussels or clams; deep-fried in cornmeal batter; or added to meat, fish or shellfish pies or casseroles.

Gastropods (winkles, whelks and abalone)

Small gastropods such as winkles (also known as periwinkles), whelks and limpets need little preparation other than a quick rinse under cold running water. They are removed from the shell after cooking, either with a small fork or, in the case of winkles, with a dressmakers' pin. Larger gastropods, such as abalone (or their cousins, the ormers) and conch, must be removed from the shell and beaten vigorously to tenderize them before cooking. In some fishmarkets, especially those in California, tenderized abalone is sold in slices.

Cooking abalone or ormers

There are two schools of thought when it comes to cooking abalone. One claims the best way is to marinate the flesh, then cook it briefly in butter; the other claims that if abalone is to be truly tender, it needs long, slow cooking. Both methods work equally well, but only if the abalone has been thoroughly beaten first.

Boiling winkles or whelks

Ideally, these shellfish should be boiled in sea water, so if you gather them yourself, take home a bucket (pail) of water in which to cook them. Otherwise, use heavily salted water. Bring this to the boil in a pan, add the winkles or whelks and simmer for about 5 minutes for winkles; 10 minutes for whelks.

To test whether winkles or whelks are ready, use a fork or dressmakers' pin to remove the body from the shell. It should come out easily. If not, cook for a little longer, but do not overcook, or the winkles will become brittle and the whelks tough.

Cephalopods (octopus, squid, cuttlefish)

Buying

You may have seen Mediterranean fishermen flailing freshly caught octopus against the rocks to tenderize them. It is said that they need to be beaten at least a hundred times before they become palatable. Fortunately for the consumer large octopus are usually sold already prepared, so we are spared this unpleasant task. Small octopuses can be dealt with in much the same way as squid, but even they have tough flesh which needs to be beaten with a wooden mallet before being cooked.

Most fishmongers and supermarkets now sell ready-cleaned squid, but cuttlefish are more usually sold whole. Both are easy to clean, and are prepared in similar ways. When buying fresh squid, look for specimens that smell fresh and salty, have good colour and are slippery. Avoid squid with broken outer skins, or from which the ink has leaked.

Quantities

The amount of octopus or squid that will be required will depend on how substantial a sauce you are going to serve. As a general guide, 1kg/2¼lb octopus, squid or cuttlefish will be more than ample for six people.

Storing

As for fish.

Cleaning and preparing octopus

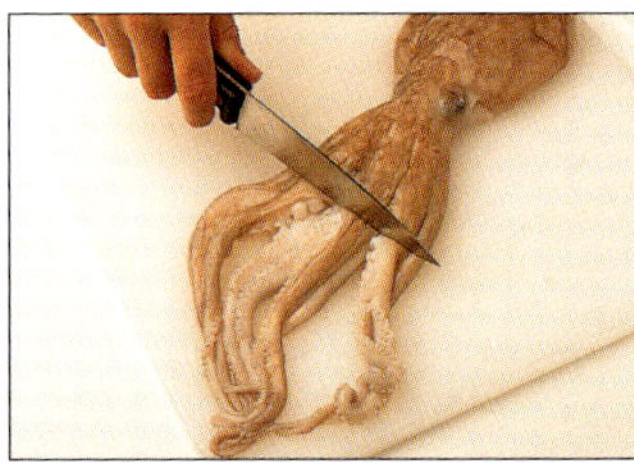

1 Cut the tentacles off the octopus and remove the beak and eyes. Cut off the head where it joins the body and discard it. Turn the body inside out and discard the entrails.

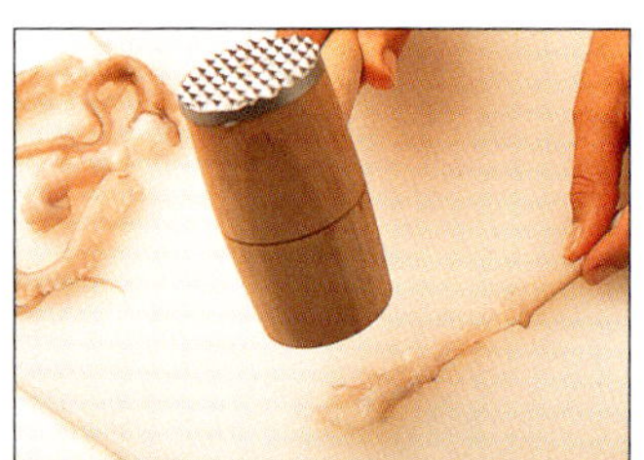

2 Pound the body and tentacles with a mallet until tender, then place in boiling water and simmer very gently for at least 1 hour, or until tender. Serve with a flavoursome sauce.

Baby Octopus and Red Wine Stew

Baby octopuses are tender and delicious, particularly cooked in a stew with the robust flavours of red wine and oregano. Unlike large octopuses, they need no tenderizing before cooking.

SERVES FOUR

INGREDIENTS

- 900g/2lb baby octopuses
- 450g/1lb onions, sliced
- 2 bay leaves
- 60ml/4 tbsp olive oil
- 4 garlic cloves, crushed
- 450g/1lb tomatoes, peeled and sliced
- 15ml/1 tbsp each chopped fresh oregano and parsley
- salt and ground black pepper

Put the octopuses in a pan of simmering water with a quarter of the sliced onion and the bay leaves. Cook gently for 1 hour. Drain the octopuses and cut into bitesize pieces. Discard the heads. Heat the olive oil in a pan, add the remaining onions and the garlic cloves and cook for 3 minutes. Add the tomatoes and herbs, season with salt and pepper and cook, stirring, for about 5 minutes until pulpy, then cover the pan with a lid and cook very gently for 1½ hours.

Cleaning and preparing squid

1 Rinse the squid thoroughly under cold running water. Holding the body firmly in one hand, grasp the tentacles at the base with the other, and gently but firmly pull the head away from the body. As you do this the soft, yellowish entrails will come away.

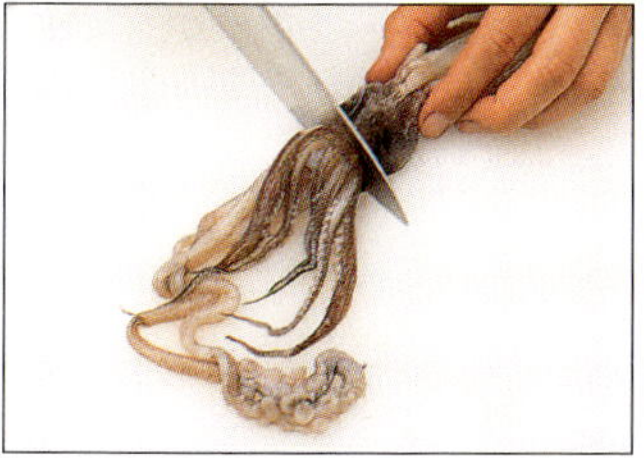

2 Use a sharp knife to cut off the tentacles from the head of the squid. Reserve the tentacles but discard the hard beak in the middle.

> **Squid ink**
> This can be used as a wonderful flavouring and colouring for home-made pasta and risotto, or to make a sauce. Having removed the ink sac, put it in a small bowl. Pierce it with the tip of a knife to release the thick, granular ink. Dilute this with a little water and stir until smooth. Use the ink right away, or freeze it for later use.
>
> There is ink in an octopus too. It is found in the liver and is very strongly flavoured. Like squid ink, it should be diluted in water before being used.

3 Remove and reserve the ink sac, then discard the head.

4 Peel the purplish-grey membrane away from the body.

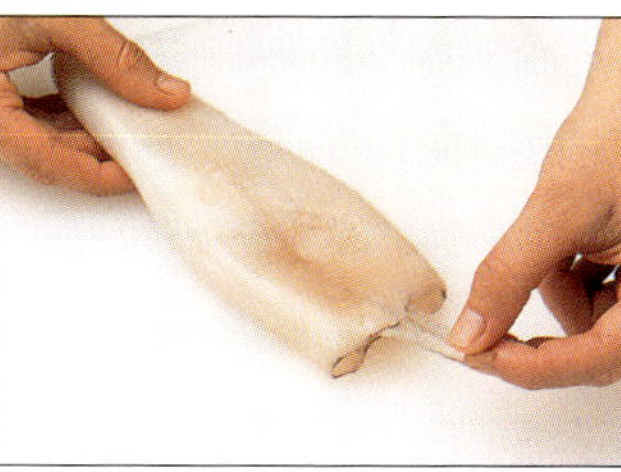

5 Pull out the "quill". Wash the body under cold running water.

6 Cut the body, flaps and tentacles to the required size.

Cooking squid

Squid is often cut into rings and deep-fried. It can also be stewed, stuffed and baked, or sliced and stir-fried.

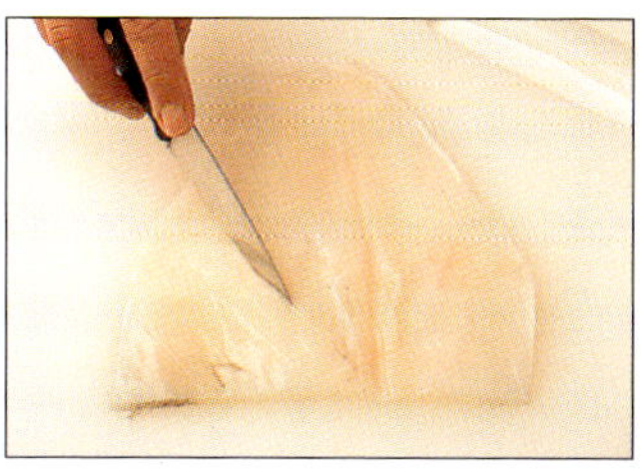

1 For stir-frying, slit the body from top to bottom and turn it inside out. Flatten it and score the inside lightly with a knife to make a criss-cross pattern.

2 Cut each piece lengthways into ribbons. These will curl when stir-fried.

Cleaning and preparing cuttlefish

Cut off the tentacles and remove the beak from the cuttlefish. Along the length of the body you will see the dark line of the cuttle bone. Cut along this line and remove the cuttle bone. Prepare in the same way as squid. The body is usually left whole.

> **Sea urchins**
> There are several edible varieties of sea urchin. They are particularly popular in France, where they are served raw, or lightly cooked in salted water and eaten like boiled eggs. The tops are sliced off and fingers of bread are then dipped into the coral flesh.

A Catalogue of Fish and Shellfish

The almost infinite variety of edible sea and freshwater fish has always been an inspiration to cooks, who love them for their fresh flavour, versatility and nutritious qualities. There is a host of delicious shellfish, each with its own unique flavour and all evoking the unmistakable tang of the sea. Once, we were limited to eating only fish and shellfish from local waters, but now, thanks to modern transportation methods, a whole new world of exciting species is available to cooks. This chapter is designed to help you to identify the fish and shellfish you may find on the fishmonger's slab and to give you an indication of how it can be cooked.

SEAFISH

There are two main categories of seafish: round and flat. Those that live on or near the sea bed are known as demersal fish. Flat fish are demersal fish, spending most of their time on the sea bed and doing very little swimming. Consequently they have delicate white flesh with little muscle tone. The nutritious oil of "white" fish is concentrated in the liver.

In "oily" fish, this oil is dispersed throughout the flesh. Oily fish tend to swim in shoals near the surface of the sea; they are known as pelagic fish.

ROUND WHITE FISH

THE SEA BASS AND GROUPER FAMILY

This large and important family of fish is known as *perciformes* because they all share some of the characteristics of perch. They have at least some spiny fins, a V-shaped tail and pectoral fins set high on the body. The pelvic fins have one spiny ray each.

Various species of perciformes are found in the Indian and Pacific oceans and the Caribbean, and also in Mediterranean and Atlantic waters.

Sea bass *(Dicentrarchus labrax)*

Among the finest of all fish, sea bass are as good to look at as they are to eat. They have an elegant, sleek shape rather like salmon, and a beautiful silvery body with a darker back and a white belly. They can grow to a length of 90cm/36in and weigh up to 7kg/15½lb, although the average weight is 1–3kg/2¼–6½lb.

Habitat Sea bass are voracious predators that live in small shoals close to rocky coasts in Great Britain and the Mediterranean. They can also be found in salt water lakes and large river estuaries. They can be caught in traps or trawled, but the best are line-caught. Because sea bass are in such demand, wild fish have become prohibitively expensive. They can, however, be farmed successfully, and there are sea bass farms all over the Mediterranean.

Other names The French for sea bass is *bar*; owing to their ferocity, they are also known as *loup de mer* (sea wolf). In Italian, they are *spigola* or *branzino*; their Spanish name is *lubina*.

Buying Sea bass are available all year round, as whole fish or as fillets. They are best in spring and early summer, before they spawn. Line-caught, wild sea bass have the finest texture and flavour, but farmed fish are an acceptable and much cheaper alternative. Look for bright, silvery skin and clear eyes. Allow about 200g/7oz per serving.

Cooking Sea bass have very few small bones and fine, firm flesh that holds its shape well during cooking. They are versatile fish with a delicate flavour and can be cooked by almost any method – grilled (broiled), baked, braised, poached, shallow or stir-fried, or steamed over seaweed or samphire. A whole poached sea bass, skinned and served cold with mayonnaise, makes a wonderful party dish. Plainly cooked sea bass can be served with any number of sauces, from *beurre blanc* to fresh tomato coulis and Asian sesame dressing. A classic French dish is *bar au fenouil*; grilled sea bass served on a bed of fennel twigs flamed with Pernod. Sea bass are highly prized in China, where they are braised with ginger and spring onions (scallions), while the Japanese slice the flesh wafer-thin and use it raw.

Alternatives Few fish can equal sea bass for flavour, but good substitutes in most recipes are grey mullet, sea bream (porgy), grouper and John Dory.

Right: Sea bass

Scaling sea bass

The skin of sea bass is excellent to eat, and it becomes deliciously crisp when grilled (broiled) or pan-fried. It does, however, have very hard scales, so it is essential to scale sea bass before cooking. Ask your fishmonger to do this, or follow the instructions in the section on Buying and Preparing Fish.

Other varieties *Dicentrus punctatus* (speckled bass) takes its Latin name from the small black spots on its back and sides. It is found mainly in the southern Mediterranean and is very similar to sea bass. Two other varieties come from North America and southern seas; striped bass and black bass. Both are excellent fish, but neither tastes quite so fine as sea bass.

Stone bass/Wreckfish *(Polyprion americanum)*

This ugly cousin of the sea bass lives in deep Atlantic waters, often amid wrecked ships at the bottom of the sea, which is how it came by its alternative name. This makes it difficult to catch; it can only be line-fished at a depth of more than 150m/500ft, so it is seldom found in stores and markets. Its Italian name is *cernia di fondale* (bass from the deep). It has dark skin and large, bony fins, and the end of its tail is straight, not V-shaped like the tails of other types of bass.

Cooking If you do find stone bass for sale, it is likely to be as fillets or steaks, which can be cooked in the same way as any other white fish.

Comber *(Serranus)*

These smaller members of the grouper family have reddish or brownish skin with wide vertical markings. *Serranus scriba* is so called because its markings are said to resemble scribbles.

Cooking Comber have delicious firm white flesh. The whole fish can be poached, steamed, braised or baked. Fillets and steaks can be grilled (broiled), pan-fried or steamed.

THE SEA BREAM FAMILY

There are approximately two hundred species of sea bream, some of which, unusually for seafish, are vegetarian. They have tall, compact bodies and slightly snub noses.

Habitat Sea bream are found in all warm and temperate coastal waters, including the Atlantic, up to the Bay of Biscay.

Above: Sea bass fillets

Gilt-head bream *(Sparus aurata)*

This beautiful fish is considered the finest of all sea bream. It has silver scales, a gold spot on each cheek and a golden crescent in the middle of its head from which it takes its name. Its dense, juicy white flesh has been highly prized for thousands of years; the ancient Greeks and Romans considered it a fish fit for feasting, and it was sacred to Aphrodite, the goddess of love. One wonders what she would have made of the fact that gilt-head breams are hermaphrodite, starting as male and becoming female as they mature.

Other names Gilt-heads are also known as royal bream. Sometimes in English they are called *daurade* (also spelt *dorade*), as in French. The Italian name is *orata*, the Spanish is *dorada*.

Buying Gilt-heads grow to a length of 60cm/24in and can weigh up to 3kg/ 6½lb. They are sold whole or as fillets. There is a high percentage of wastage, which makes this quite an expensive fish. Nowadays, gilt-heads are farmed successfully in the Mediterranean, which makes them a little less costly. Fresh gilt-head bream should have bright, shiny scales.

Cooking All bream have numerous wide scales that must be removed before cooking, or the diner will experience a most unpleasant mouthful. Whole gilt-head bream can be treated like sea bass or sole – baked, grilled (broiled), poached, steamed in seaweed or braised. Score the flesh in several places on both sides before the fish is grilled or baked whole, to make sure of even cooking. The dense flesh is robust enough to withstand spicy or aromatic flavours. A classic French dish is *daurade rôtie*, where the fish is covered with alternate strips of pork fat or bacon and anchovy fillets, then wrapped in greaseproof (waxed) paper and baked.

Gilt-head fillets can be pan-fried, grilled or baked. Very fresh fish can be used raw to make *sashimi*.

Red bream *(Pagellus bogaraveo)*

This tall rosy-red fish has a pronounced black spot above the pectoral fin on each shoulder. It grows to about 50cm/ 20in and is usually sold already filleted. Red bream lives deep in the sea and feeds on crustaceans and molluscs, which make it particularly tasty. It is found in northern European waters, but swims southwards in winter to spawn, and is a much sought after fish in Spain and Portugal.

Other names Young red bream have small blue spots on their backs and are sometimes known as blue-spotted bream. In French, red bream is rather rudely called *dorade commune* (common bream); the Italians call it *pagro*, *pagello* or *occhialone*, meaning "big eye". The Spaniards call it *besugo*.

Cooking Extremely fresh red bream can be eaten raw as *sashimi*. Whole fish and fillets should be cooked in the same way as snapper, bass or red mullet.

Black bream *(Spondyliosoma cantharus)*

This large bream is sometimes found in the North Sea. It is actually dark grey, with beautiful golden stripes running from head to tail. Unlike the gilt-head, it is unisexual and monogamous. Like gilt-head bream, it can be baked, grilled (broiled), poached, steamed in seaweed or braised. The flavour and texture are similar but not so fine.

Above, from front: gilt-head bream, red bream and black bream

Ray's bream *(Brama brama)*

These large shoaling fish live in depths of 100m/328ft and below, but come up to the surface in summer, sometimes with tragic consequences, as the eponymous John Ray found when he discovered huge quantities of the fish stranded on the coast of Britain in the 17th century. Ray's bream are brownish-grey, with firm flesh and a good flavour. They should be cooked in the same way as other bream.

Dentex *(Dentex dentex)*

These relatives of the sea bream are particularly popular in Mediterranean countries, in whose waters they are found. They are also found to a lesser extent in the East Atlantic. Their colour varies with their age; young dentex are grey, changing first to reddish pink, then to a beautiful steel blue with a sprinkling of dark spots.

Other names *Denté* in French, *dentice* in Italian and *dentón* in Spanish.
Cooking Dentex can grow up to 1m/39in in length, but they are best eaten when 30cm/12in long. Fish this size can be grilled (broiled) whole or baked with herbs. Larger specimens should be cut into steaks and grilled or fried.

Porgy *(Pagrus pagrus)*

The eponymous hero of *Porgy and Bess* took his name from these rosy-tinted North American relatives of the bass, variations of which are also found in the Atlantic coastal waters around Africa. Porgies grow to a length of up to 75cm/30in and can be cooked whole or as steaks – baked, grilled (broiled), poached, steamed or braised, using any of the recipes for bream.

Unusual species of bream
Among the many varieties of bream, there are a number whose names describe their appearance.

The **two-banded bream**, a fish which makes very good eating, has two distinct vertical black bands fore and aft.

Annular bream, which is the smallest of its group, has a dark ring round its tail, as does **saddled bream**, while **sheepshead bream** has an upturned snout.

The small varieties, such as annular bream and saddled bream, are used for making soup.

A classic Tuscan dish, *sarago e parago*, uses two different kinds of small bream, boned and stuffed with raw ham and rosemary, then grilled (broiled) over a wood fire.

THE COD FAMILY

This large family of fish includes haddock, hake, ling, whiting and many other related species of white-fleshed fish. Most of them come from the Atlantic and other cold northerly waters, although hake is found in the warmer Mediterranean and is very popular with the Spaniards and Portuguese.

Cod *(Gadus morruha)*

Long, torpedo-shaped fish with vibrant yellowish-brown mottled skin and a whitish belly, cod have a large head with a snub nose, a protruding upper jaw and a whiskery barbel on the chin which acts as a sensor as they search for food on the sea bed. They can live for over 20 years and grow to a length of 6m/20ft (weighing up to 50kg/110lb), although such specimens are sadly rare and most commercially fished cod weigh between 3 and 8kg/6½ and 17½lb.

Habitat Cod prefer to live in cold water with a high salt content. They hatch in huge numbers (a single female can lay up to five million eggs) close to the surface of the water, but gravitate down to the sea bed where they feed on crustaceans, molluscs and worms. Large cod also feed on smaller fish. Cod can be caught in trawler nets or line-caught. Trawled fish are often damaged in the nets.

For years, cod was so plentiful that it was regarded as an inferior fish, fit only to be deep-fried or masked with an unpleasant floury white sauce. All too often, its succulent, flaky white flesh was overcooked, making it watery or dry. Today, overfishing has depleted stocks so much that now it has become relatively scarce and therefore more highly appreciated. As the great French chef Auguste Escoffier predicted in the 19th century: "If cod were less common, it would be held in as high esteem as salmon;" (at that time, regarded as the king of fish) "for, when it is really fresh and of good quality, the delicacy and delicious flavour of its flesh admit of its ranking among the finest of fish".

Other names In France, fresh cod is called *cabillaud*. In Italy, it is *merluzzo* and in Spain, *bacalao* (which can also mean salt cod).

Buying Cod is most commonly trawled or netted, but it can also be line-caught. The first two methods can damage the delicate flesh, so try to buy the superior line-caught fish if possible.

When you buy a whole small cod or codling, the skin should be shiny and clear. There is a lot of wastage in whole cod, which makes these fish very expensive, so they are more usually sold as steaks and fillets. Shoulder steaks have the finest flavour. Try to buy thick cuts from the shoulder or middle of the fish and always check that the flesh is very white. Never buy cod with discoloured patches on the flesh. The fresher the fish, the firmer and flakier the flesh will be.

Cooking Cod holds its texture well and can be cooked in many different ways, but it is vitally important not to overcook it. The flavour is robust enough to take quite strong and spicy flavours. Whole fish can be poached in a court-bouillon and served cold with mayonnaise, green sauce or tartare sauce. Cod can also be baked or roasted in the oven or braised in white wine.

Above: Cod fillet and steaks

Most cooking methods are suitable for cod fillets and steaks, except for grilling (broiling), which can destroy the flaky texture. They can be poached, steamed, braised in tomato sauce or topped with a crust of breadcrumbs and herbs and baked. They are also delicious floured and sautéed, or coated with batter and deep-fried. Cod makes an excellent substitute for more exotic fish in curries. A classic English dish is poached cod with parsley sauce. Fresh and smoked cod fillets can be used to make fish cakes, croquettes, fish pies, salads and mousses.

Cod can be salted or dried (see Dried and Salted Fish). The roe is often smoked and used to make *taramasalata*. Frozen cod is usually frozen at sea to retain freshness and flavour, but is never so good as fresh fish. It is available as steaks, fillets, breaded cuts and fish fingers (sticks). The liver produces cod liver oil, which tastes disgusting but is good for you.

Alternatives Any firm-fleshed white fish can be substituted for cod, including flat fish such as brill, halibut and turbot.

Above: Cod

Above: Haddock

Coley *(Pollachius virens)*

Traditionally regarded as cod's poor relation, fit only for feeding to the cat, coley has unappealing greyish flesh, which is responsible for its low price. Long and slim, the fish has a protruding lower jaw and no barbel. The skin on the back is dark grey, lightening to mottled yellow on the sides and almost white on the belly. Coley generally weigh 5–10kg/11–22lb, but smaller fish do appear on the fishmonger's slab.

Habitat Coley live in huge shoals in both deep waters and near the surface. They prefer cold, very salty water. They are voracious predators who prey on herring and have cannibalistic tendencies.

Other names Coley are also known as saithe, coalfish and pollock (not to be confused with pollack). In French, they are *lieu noir*, in Italian *merluzzo nero* and in Spanish *abadejo*.

Buying Coley are sometimes sold whole, weighing 1–4kg/2¼–8¾lb, but are more usually sold as steaks, cutlets and fillets. The unattractive grey flesh looks off-putting, but whitens during cooking. It should feel firm to the touch. Coley must be extremely fresh, or the flesh will become woolly and unpleasant.

Cooking Coley is less fine than cod in texture and flavour. Rubbing the greyish flesh with lemon juice helps to whiten it, but the colour can also be masked by coating the fish in batter or using it in a fish pie, casserole or fish cakes. It will withstand robust flavours and can be baked, braised, grilled (broiled) or fried. Smoked coley has an excellent flavour, but is seldom available commercially. It is worth smoking at home.

Alternatives Haddock, cod or any firm-fleshed white fish can be used instead of coley.

Haddock *(Melanogrammus aeglefinus)*

These are generally smaller than cod, growing up to 1m/39in long and weighing 1–2kg/2¼–4½lb. They have dark brownish-grey skin with a black lateral line and a black spot above the pectoral fin (purportedly the thumb print of St. Peter). Their eyes are large and prominent. They live close to the sea bed and prefer water with a high salt content.

Haddock is often considered to be interchangeable with cod, but its white flesh has a more delicate flavour and a softer, less flaky texture.

Habitat Haddock are shoaling fish which live at the bottom of cold northern seas in Europe and North America. They feed on molluscs, worms and other small fish and spawn in the coldest, saltiest water they can find, off the coast of Norway and the Faroes, for example.

Other names In North America, young haddock are known as scrod. In French, the fish is called *aiglefin* (from the Latin name). Confusingly, the French for smoked haddock is *haddock*. In Italian, haddock is *asinello*; in Spanish it is *eglefino*.

Buying Fresh haddock is at its best in winter and early spring, when the cold has firmed up the flesh. You may find whole small haddock (weighing 450g–2kg/1–4½lb) at the fishmonger's, but the fish is usually sold as fillets. Before you buy, prod the flesh to make sure that it is firm.

Cooking Fresh haddock is a versatile fish, which can be cooked in the same way as cod. When cooking whole haddock, leave the skin on to hold the delicate flesh together.

Haddock is the perfect fish for deep-frying and it makes wonderful fish and chips (French fries). It also makes excellent lasagne and pie, especially when the fresh fish is mixed with an equal quantity of smoked haddock.

Below: Haddock fillets

Hake *(Merluccius merluccius)*

This most elegant member of the cod family is a long, slim fish with two spiny dorsal fins, bulging eyes and a protruding lower jaw without a barbel. The head and back are dark steely grey and the belly is silvery white. The inside of the mouth and gills is black. A mature fish can grow up to 1m/39in, but the average length is 30–50cm/12–20in.

Habitat Hake are found in most temperate and cold waters. By day, they live near the sea bed, but at night they move to the surface to hunt oily fish such as herring, mackerel and sprats.

Other names The French have several names for hake: *merlu*, *colin* and *merluchon* (small immature fish). The Spanish call it *merluza*. In Italian, it is *nasello*. In North America, hake is often known as ling or whiting, although it is far superior to the European whiting.

Buying Owing to overfishing, hake are becoming quite scarce and expensive. Hake can be trawled or caught on long lines. Try to buy line-caught fish, which have a better texture. Hake must be very fresh, or it becomes flabby. The flesh has a pinkish tinge; it will always feel quite soft to the touch, but should never feel limp. Whole fish should have bright eyes and smell of the sea.

When calculating how much hake to buy, allow for 40 per cent wastage for whole fish. Keep the head, as it makes particularly delicious soup or fish stock.

Hake is usually sold as cutlets or steaks. Those cut from near the head have the best flavour. The fish has few bones and these are easy to remove. Avoid buying fillets, as they tend to disintegrate during cooking.

Cooking Whole hake can be poached, baked or braised in wine, lemon juice and fresh herbs or tomato sauce. Like all fish, it should never be overcooked. Steaks can be grilled (broiled), coated in egg and breadcrumbs and deep-fried, or sautéed in olive oil and garlic. They can also be layered with potatoes and onions, or with tomatoes and cheese and baked *au gratin*. Light buttery sauces go well with hake, as does caper sauce. Shellfish such as mussels and clams are perfect partners. A popular Spanish hors d'oeuvre is *escabeche* – marinated hake served cold.

Alternatives Both haddock and cod can be substituted for hake in any recipe.

Other varieties North American silver hake is a small, streamlined fish with an excellent flavour. Varieties of hake are also found in the warmer waters of South America and southern Africa, but don't taste as good as northern hake.

Above: Ling

Ling *(Molva molva)*

This fish has a long, slender greenish-brown body with a silver lateral stripe, no scales and a barbel on the lower jaw. It is the largest relative of the cod, growing to a length of 1.8m/6ft.

Habitat Common ling live in the Atlantic, often in proximity to rocks, where they feed on round and flat fish, small octopuses and crustaceans. A smaller relative is found in the Mediterranean.

Other names Mediterranean ling are sometimes known as blue ling. They have larger eyes and a shorter barbel than common ling, and are esteemed for their superior flavour. Both varieties are known as *lingue* in French, *molva occhiona* in Italian and *maruca* in Spanish. Rock ling are available in Australia. In Scandinavian countries ling is salted, dried and sold as *lutfisk* or *klipfisk* (see Dried and Salted Fish).

Buying As with all fish, the best ling are line-caught. You may find small whole ling on the fishmonger's slab, but the fish is more commonly sold as fillets or middle-cut cutlets. Ling is available most of the year, except in high summer.

Cooking Ling has firm flesh with a fairly good flavour and is sometimes substituted for monkfish. Whole fish can be baked or braised, or made into casseroles, soups and curries. Fillets and cutlets can be grilled (broiled) or pan-fried, and served with a sauce.

Alternatives Any member of the cod family can be substituted. For a more extravagant substitute, use monkfish or conger eel.

Pollack *(Pollachius pollachius)*

These attractive fish have steely grey backs and greenish-yellow bodies with a curved lateral line. They have a protruding lower jaw and no barbel. Pollack are smaller than cod, growing to a length of less than 1m/39in.

Habitat Pollack can live in shoals near the surface of the sea, where they feed on sprats and herrings, or close to the bottom where they eat deep-sea prawns (shrimp) and sand-eels.

Other names Its yellow colour gives pollack the name of *lieu jaune* in French. It is also known as *merluzzo giallo* in Italian and *abadejo* in Spanish.

Buying Pollack are at their best in autumn (fall) and winter. They are usually sold as fillets, cutlets or steaks. If you need a whole fish, look for a superior line-caught specimen.

Above: Hake

Above: Pouting

Cooking Pollack has a drier texture and less pronounced flavour than cod, so it benefits from a creamy, highly flavoured sauce. It is good for fish pies and soups and can be baked, braised, deep-fried or sautéed. It is suitable for any recipe for cod, haddock, hake or ling.

Pouting *(Trisopterus luscus)*

This sulky-sounding fish is a poor (and cheap) relation of the whiting and often caught in the same nets. It is comparatively small (about 25cm/10in long), with light brown papery skin.
Other names It is also known as pout. In French it is *tacaud*, in Italian *merluzzo francese* and in Spanish *faneca*.
Buying Pouting goes off extremely quickly and must be eaten very fresh. Your nose will soon tell you if the fish is past its best. If possible, buy a whole fish and ask the fishmonger to fillet it. Then cook it as soon as you can, as the fillets will rapidly deteriorate.
Cooking As for whiting.

Whiting *(Merlangus merlangus)*

Similar in appearance to haddock, whiting are small fish (generally about 30–40cm/12–16in long). They have greenish-grey skin, a silvery belly and a black spot at the base of the pectoral fin. The head is pointed, with a protruding upper jaw and no barbel.
Habitat Whiting are found all over the Atlantic, from Iceland to northern Spain. They feed on crustaceans and small fish such as sand-eels and herrings and are often found near rocky shores.
Other names Its old name was merling. The French call it *merlan*, the Italians *merlano* and the Spanish *merlán*.
Buying The fact that it is abundant all year and has soft, rather unexciting flesh means that whiting is cheap and tends to be undervalued. However, really fresh whiting is well worth buying. Whole fish should be scintillatingly shiny. Fillets should be pearly white and feel soft but definitely not flabby.

Below: Whiting

Stale whiting may have a woolly texture and taste unpleasant, so make sure that you buy only absolutely fresh fish. Whiting are small, so allow two fillets per serving. You may find whiting boned through the back, leaving the two fillets attached.
Cooking The whiting's meltingly tender flesh makes it an ideal basis for a soup, as it contributes a velvety texture. It is also excellent for quenelles and fish mousses. Whiting is a versatile fish that can be coated in breadcrumbs or batter and fried. It can also be pan-fried, grilled (broiled) or gently poached in wine or court-bouillon and served with a lemony sauce or flavoured butter. Whatever cooking method you use, make sure the whiting is well seasoned.
Alternatives Plaice, flounder or sole can be used, and all of the cod family.

Whiting en colère

A once immensely popular dish was *merlan en colère* ("angry whiting"). Whole fish were baked with the skin on, then curled around so that their tails could be stuck through their eye sockets or into their mouths. Presumably the name came from the assumption that the fish was chasing its own tail in anger. Mercifully, this method of serving whiting has fallen out of favour.

THE GURNARD FAMILY

Gurnard are curious, almost prehistoric looking fish with cylindrical bodies, high, armour-plated heads with wide mouths, and strange pectoral fins with the three lowest rays divided into "fingers". They use these to explore the sea bed. Another curiosity is the grunting noise they emit, caused by vibrating the swim bladder – for what purpose, no one has yet discovered.

Below: Gurnard

Gurnard weigh between 100g/3¾oz and 2kg/4½lb. There are several types, which are distinguished by their colour; all have lean white flesh with a firm texture but rather insipid taste. They are rich in iodine, phosphorus and protein.

Habitat Gurnard are found in the Atlantic and Mediterranean. They live on or near the sea bed, using their "fingers" to seek out crabs, prawns (shrimp) and small fish in the sediment.

Other names Also known as sea robin and gurnet. The French name, *grondin*, echoes the grunting sound they make. In Italian, they are *capone* (meaning large head); in Spanish, [illegible]

Grey gurnard *(Eutrigla gurnardus)*

These fish have brownish-grey backs and silvery bellies. They grow to a maximum length of 45cm/18in. The lateral line is scaly and should be [illegible] before cooking.

Red gurnard *(Aspitrigla cuculus)*

The most attractive member of the gurnard family, this pinkish-red fish has bony extensions to the lateral line, which give it the appearance of vertical stripes on its back. It has the finest flavour of all the gurnards and is sometimes substituted for red mullet.

Above: Tub gurnard

Tub gurnard *(Trigla lucerna)*

This larger gurnard is orangey-brown with bright orange pectoral fins. It is an excellent swimmer and sometimes leaps right out of the water, high above the surface, which explains its alternative name of flying gurnard.

Buying Gurnard are bony fish with an unexceptional flavour, so they tend to be cheap. They are usually sold whole – ask the fishmonger to remove the spiny fins and the skin. Beware, especially in France, of buying red gurnard masquerading as red mullet (*rouget*). The latter is vastly superior.

Cooking Small gurnard are best used in soups and stocks. Larger fish can be braised or baked on a bed of vegetables with a little white wine. Take care when eating whole gurnard, as they are very bony. Fillets can be coated in breadcrumbs and fried, or steamed and served with a Mediterranean sauce.

Alternatives Red or grey mullet can be used in any gurnard recipe, and will generally give a better result.

Scorpion fish *(Scorpaena scrofa, Scorpaena porcus)*

Like gurnard, scorpion fish have huge heads and armour-plated cheeks. Their enormous scaly heads have loose folds of skin above and between the eyes. The dorsal fin is made up of large poisonous spines. The smaller brown scorpion fish has a finer flavour than its larger cousin.

Habitat Scorpion fish are found throughout the Mediterranean and off the coast of North Africa. They also live in Atlantic waters, ranging from the English Channel to Senegal.

Other names The French for scorpion fish is *rascasse* (*chapon* in the south of France). Italians call it *scorfano*; in Spanish it is *cabracho* or *rascacio*.

Buying Scorpion fish are usually sold whole. You should allow for a huge amount of wastage; a 2kg/4½lb fish will serve only four people.

Cooking Scorpion fish is best known as an essential ingredient in bouillabaisse. Whole fish can be baked or braised with fennel; scorpion fillets can be cooked *à l'antillaise*, braised with tomatoes, potatoes and red (bell) peppers.

Alternatives Monkfish, snapper, John Dory or gurnard can be used in a pinch.

Above: Scorpion fish

THE MULLET FAMILY

Over a hundred species of mullet are found in temperate and tropical seas. These belong to two main groups, grey and red, which are unrelated and very different in appearance and flavour.

Grey mullet *(family Mugilidae)*

Varieties of grey mullet are found all over the world. These beautiful silvery fish resemble sea bass, but have larger scales and small mouths, suited to their diet of seaweed and plankton. They are shoaling fish that live in the vicinity of the muddy sea bed, so they sometimes smell and taste rather muddy. A good grey mullet has lean, slightly soft, creamy white flesh with quite a pleasant flavour.

Habitat Grey mullet are found in coastal waters and estuaries all over the world.

Varieties The finest is the golden mullet (*Liza aurata*), which has a thin upper lip and gold spots on its head and the front of the body. It is one of the smallest mullets, growing only to about 45cm/18in. In French, it is known as *mulet doré*. Thick-lipped mullet (*Crenimugil* or *Chelon labrosus*) has, as its name suggests, thick lips and a rounded body. This mullet is sometimes farmed. The thin-lipped mullet (*Liza ramada*) has a golden sheen, a thin upper lip and a pointed snout, which gives it its French name of *mulet porc*. The largest mullet is the common or striped grey mullet (*Mugil cephalus*), which can grow up to 70cm/28in. This fish has a brown body, silvery back and a large head. Its eyes are covered by a transparent membrane. In French it is called *mulet cabot*. There is also a small Mediterranean mullet whose main claim to fame is its ability to leap out of the water to escape predators. This is the leaping grey mullet (*Liza saliens*).

Above: Silver-skinned grey mullet are found all over the world.

Buying Except in France, you are unlikely to find any differentiation between the varieties of grey mullet at the fishmonger. If possible, choose fish that come from the high seas rather than estuaries, as the latter often have a muddy taste and can be flabby. Grey mullet are usually sold whole – ask the fishmonger to scale and skin them for you. Keep the roes, which are delicious. Larger fish may be sold filleted.

Cooking Grey mullet must be scaled before being cooked. Any muddiness can be eliminated by soaking the fish in several changes of acidulated water. Whole fish are very good stuffed with fennel and grilled (broiled). Slash the sides and add a splash of aniseed apéritif before cooking the fish, and serve with a buttery sauce. Mullet roe is a delicacy and can be eaten fresh, fried in butter or used in a stuffing for a baked fish. When salted and dried, mullet roe is the authentic basis of taramasalata and *bottarga* or *boutargue*.

Below: Red mullet are considered one of the finest seafish.

Red mullet *(Mullus surmuletus and Mullus barbatus)*

These are among the finest of all seafish. They are small (up to 40cm/16in long), with pinkish-red skins streaked with gold. Their Roman-nosed heads have two long barbels on the chin. They have lean, firm flesh. The flavour is robust and distinctive.

Other varieties *Mullus surmeletus* is more correctly known as *surmullet*; it has rosy red skin and is larger than *Mullus barbatus*, which has three yellowish stripes along each side and grows to a length of 30cm/12in.
Goatfish Types of red mullet known as goatfish because of their long, beard-like barbels are found in the warm Pacific and Indian Oceans. They are smaller (up to 20cm/8in) and less colourful than cold-water mullet, and they have drier, less tasty flesh.
Habitat Red mullet are found in Atlantic and Mediterranean waters. They live on sandy or rocky areas of the sea bed, feeding on small sea creatures.
Other names Red mullet are usually cooked complete with their livers and sometimes all their guts. These impart a gamey flavour, giving the fish the nickname "woodcock of the sea". In America, all red mullet are known as "goatfish", regardless of size or place of origin. The French for mullet is *rouget*; depending on the variety, it is *rouget barbet*, *rouget de roche* or *rouget de vase* (*Mullus barbatus*). In Italian, red mullet is *triglia*; in Spanish, *salmonete de roca* (*Mullus surmuletus*) or *salmonete de fango* (*Mullus barbatus*).
Buying Red mullet have delicate flesh that is highly perishable, so it is essential to buy extremely fresh fish. They should have bright skin and eyes and feel very firm. The scales should be firmly attached, not flaking off the skin. Because they are small, red mullet are usually sold whole, but large fish are sometimes filleted. The flesh is quite rich, so a 200g/7oz fish will be ample for one person. Ask the fishmonger to scale and gut it for you, and keep the liver, which is a great delicacy.
Cooking The best ways to cook red mullet are grilling (broiling) and pan-frying. Slash the sides before grilling a whole fish to be sure of even cooking. Red mullet marry superbly with many Mediterranean flavours, such as olive oil, saffron, tomatoes, olives, anchovies and orange. They can be cooked *en papillote* with flavourings or made into mousses and soufflés. Very small, bony red mullet are used in bouillabaisse.

THE WRASSE FAMILY

This large family of fish is notable for its varied and dazzling colours. Wrasse range from steely blue to green, orange and golden; in some species, the sexes have different colours. All wrasse have thick lips and an array of sharp teeth. They are small fish, seldom growing larger than 40cm/16in in length.
Habitat Wrasse are found in both Atlantic and Mediterranean waters. They live near rocky coasts, feeding on barnacles and small crustaceans.
Varieties The most common is the ballan wrasse (*Labrus berggylta*), which has greenish or brownish skin, with large scales tipped with gold. Male and female cuckoo wrasse (*Labrus mixtus*) have strikingly different coloration; the males are steely blue with almost black stripes, while the females are orangey-pink with three black spots under the dorsal fin. The name of the five-spotted wrasse (*Symphonus quinquemaculatus*) is self-explanatory, while the brown spotted wrasse is completely covered with spots. Rainbow wrasse (*Coris julis*) have spiny dorsal fins and a red or orange band along the body.

Right: Common wrasse

Below: Brown spotted wrasse

Other names In French, wrasse is variously known as *vielle*, *coquette* and *labre*. In Italian, it is *labridi*; in Spanish *merlo*, *tordo* or *gallano*.
Buying Wrasse are available in spring and summer. Look for scintillating skin and bright eyes. Ask the fishmonger to scale and clean the fish. Allow at least 400g/14oz per serving.
Cooking Most wrasse are fit only for making soup, but some larger varieties, such as ballan wrasse, can be baked whole. Make a bed of sliced onions, garlic, smoked bacon and potatoes, bake at 200°C/400°F/Gas 6 until soft, then add the wrasse, moisten with white wine and bake for 10–15 minutes.

Oily Fish

Fish such as herrings, mackerel and sardines have always been popular because they are cheap and nutritious, but now they are considered the ultimate "good for you" food. In recent years they have received an excellent press, owing to their healthy properties. Not only do they contain protein and vitamins A, B and D, but the Omega-3 fatty acids in their flesh are known to reduce the risk of clogged arteries, blood clots, strokes and even cancer. People who eat fish regularly tend to live longer – the Japanese, among the world's greatest fish eaters, have one of the lowest rates of heart disease.

Oily fish are pelagic fish, which swim near the surface of the sea and live in shoals that can be quite enormous. The largest family of oil-rich fish are the *clupeiformes*: herrings and their relatives – sardines, anchovies, sprats and pilchards. Other oily fish are smooth-skinned mackerel and tuna.

Below: Herring

THE HERRING FAMILY

Herring *(Clupea harengus)*

There are numerous different varieties of herring, each confined to its own area – the North Sea, Baltic, White Sea (an inlet of the Barents Sea), the coast of Norway and many colder coastal areas. Herring are prodigiously fertile fish, which is just as well, since they have been overfished for centuries and are becoming more scarce.

Herring are slender silver fish with a central dorsal fin and large scales. They seldom grow to a length of more than 35cm/14in. Their oily flesh can be cured in many ways, including smoking, salting, drying and marinating in vinegar and spices.

Habitat Herring live in huge shoals in cold northerly waters, where they feed on plankton. They are migratory fish which come inshore to spawn. They sometimes change their habitual route for no apparent reason, so that there may be a glut in a particular area for several years, but no herring at all the next year.

Boning a whole herring

Herring must be scaled before cooking; the scales virtually fall off by themselves, so this is easy to do. Whether or not you leave the head on is a matter of choice.

1 First scale the herring, then slit the belly with a sharp knife and remove the innards.

2 Lay the fish on a chopping board, belly-side down. With the heel of your hand, press down firmly all along the backbone.

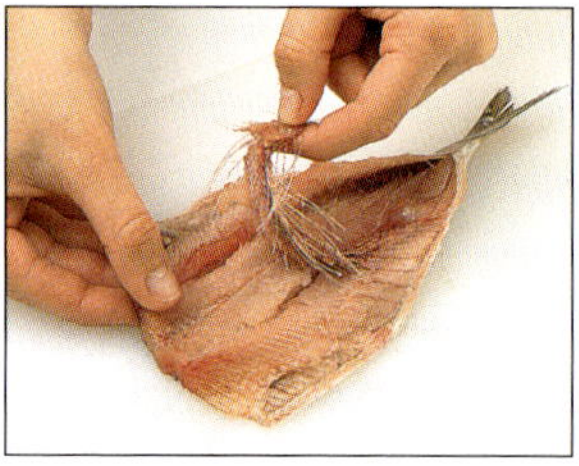

3 Turn the herring over and lift off the backbone. You will find that most of the small side bones will come away with it.

Varieties Herring are mostly known by the name of the region where they are located – North Sea, Norwegian, Baltic, for instance. Each variety has its own spawning season, which influences the eating qualities of the fish.

Buying Like all oily fish, herring must be absolutely fresh, or they will taste rancid. They are at their best before they spawn. Look for large, firm fish with slippery skins and rounded bellies containing hard or soft roes; hard roes are the female eggs, soft roes the male milt. Soft herring roes are considered a particular delicacy. By running your hands along the belly of the fish, you will be able to tell whether the roes are hard or soft.

Once they have spawned, herrings lose condition and weight and their flesh becomes rather dry. If the fishmonger cleans them for you, be sure to keep the roe. As herrings contain numerous soft bones, you might ask him to bone or fillet them for you. They can be gutted either through the belly or through the gills, leaving the roe inside.

Above: Herring fillets

Herring roes

Soft roes have a creamy, melting texture. They can be tossed in seasoned flour, gently fried in butter and served as they are, or they can be devilled with cayenne pepper and Worcestershire sauce and served on hot toast. They also make a delicious omelette filling. Poached in stock and mashed, they can be used as a spread, in a stuffing for whole baked herrings or added to a sauce or savoury tart filling. Hard roes have a grainy texture, which people tend either to love or loathe. They can be baked or braised under the fish to add extra flavour.

Above: Soft herring roes

Cooking The oiliness of the flesh makes herrings particularly suitable for grilling (broiling) and cooking on a barbecue. Score whole fish in several places on both sides for even cooking. Herring benefit from being served with an acidic sauce, such as gooseberry or mustard, to counteract the richness.

Whole herrings are excellent baked with a stuffing of breadcrumbs, chopped onions and apples. They are also good wrapped in bacon and grilled (broiled), or grilled with a mustard sauce. Both whole herrings and fillets are delicious rolled in oatmeal and then pan-fried in bacon fat. Serve them with a little lemon juice.

Herring fillets can be made into fish balls, or cooked in a sweet-and-sour sauce made with tomato ketchup, wine vinegar, honey and Worcestershire sauce. They are also delicious soused in a vinegary marinade flavoured with herbs and spices.

Fillets are also traditionally made into rollmops or smoked to make kippers – these processes are explored fully in the chapters on Pickled and Smoked Fish.

Alternatives Sardines, sprats and mackerel can be cooked in the same way as herrings.

Above: Anchovies

Anchovies *(Engraulis encrasicolus)*

These small slender fish seldom grow to more than 16cm/6¼in; the average length is only 8–10cm/3¼–4in. They have steely blue backs and shimmering silver sides, and the upper jaw protrudes markedly. Most anchovies are sold filleted and preserved in salt or oil, but if you are lucky enough to find fresh fish, you are in for a treat.

Habitat Anchovies are pelagic fish and are found in tightly packed shoals throughout the Mediterranean, in the Black Sea (where, sadly, pollution has depleted stocks) and the Atlantic and Pacific Oceans.

Other names In French, anchovy is *anchois*, in Italian *acciuga* or *alice*, in Spanish *boquerón*.

Buying Ideally, fresh anchovies should be cooked and eaten straight from the sea. The best anchovies come from the Mediterranean and are at their peak in early summer. By the time they have been exported, however, they will have lost much of their delicate flavour. When buying fresh anchovies, look for scintillating skins and bright, slightly bulging eyes.

Preparing You are unlikely to find a fishmonger willing to clean anchovies for you, but they are easy to prepare at home. To gut, cut off the head and press gently along the body with your thumb to squeeze out the innards. To fillet, run your thumbnail or a stubby blunt knife along the length of the spine from head to tail on both sides and lift off the fillets.

Freezing Since fresh anchovies are hard to come by, it is worth freezing them when there are plentiful supplies. Remove the heads and clean the fish, then pack them head-to-tail in a shallow freezer box, separating the layers with sheets of clear film (plastic wrap) or plastic. Cover the box with a lid and freeze. Thaw before using.

Cooking Whole anchovies can be grilled (broiled) or fried like sardines, or coated lightly in egg and flour and deep-fried. They make an excellent *gratin* when seasoned with olive oil and garlic, then topped with breadcrumbs and baked. Fillets can be fried with garlic and parsley, or marinated for 24 hours in a mixture of olive oil, onion, garlic, bay leaves and crushed peppercorns. Anchovy essence (extract) and anchovy paste are useful ingredients.

Sardines and Pilchards *(Sardinia pilchardus)*

It is a common misconception that sardines and pilchards are different fish; in fact, a pilchard is merely a larger, more mature sardine. Even the largest pilchards grow to only 20cm/8in, while sardines may be only 13–15cm/5–6in long. They are slim fish, with blue-green backs and silvery bellies. They have thirty scales along the mid-line on either side. Their flesh is compact and has a delicious, oily flavour. Canned sardines and pilchards are very popular as store-cupboard (pantry) items because they are convenient and easy to prepare.

Left: Sardines

Habitat Sardines take their name from Sardinia, where they were once abundant. They are pelagic shoaling fish, and are found throughout the Mediterranean and Atlantic. Various related species are also found in other parts of the world.

Other names Sardines are easy to recognize on foreign menus: they are *sardine* in French, *sardina* in Italian and Spanish, and *pilchard* or *sardine* in German. Confusingly, the French use the word *pilchard* when speaking of canned herring.

Buying Sardines are at their best in spring and early summer. They do not travel well, so try to buy fish from local waters and avoid any damaged or stale-looking specimens. Small sardines have the best flavour, but larger fish are better for stuffing. Depending on the size, allow 3–5 sardines per serving.

Cooking Sardines should be scaled and gutted before being cooked. This is easy to do; just cut the head almost through from the backbone and twist, pulling it towards you. The innards will come away with the head. Whole sardines are superb simply grilled (broiled) plain or cooked on a barbecue, which crisps the skin. They can be coated in breadcrumbs, fried and served with tomato sauce, made into fritters or stuffed with capers, salted anchovies or Parmesan and baked. They make an excellent sauce for pasta and are also delicious marinated and served raw.

Alternatives Large anchovies or sprats can be used instead of small sardines.

Above: Sprats

Below: Pilchards

Sprats *(Sprattus sprattus)*

These small silvery fish look very similar to sardines or immature herrings, but are slightly squatter. Once the sprat was an important fish, but they are seldom sold fresh these days, being mostly smoked or cured, or sold as fishmeal.

Habitat They are abundant in the Baltic, North Sea and the Atlantic, and, since they can tolerate low salinity, are also found in fjords and estuaries. In addition to being sold fresh, sprats are available smoked or canned in oil.

Other names Sprats are sprat in French, *papalina* in Italian and *espadin* in Spanish. Smoked sprats are called *brisling* in Norway.

Cooking Sprats can be cooked in the same way as anchovies and small sardines. They have very oily flesh and are delicious when fried in oatmeal or deep-fried in batter.

Raw sprats can be marinated in vinaigrette; they are often served as part of a Scandinavian smorgasbørd.

Above: Whitebait

Whitebait

This name is given to tiny silver fish – only about 5cm/2in in length – that are caught in summer as they swim up estuaries. The name can refer to immature sprats or herrings, or to a mixture of both fish.

Other names Whitebait are *blanchaille* in French; this name is also used to describe tiny freshwater fish. The Italian name for them is *bianchetti*; the Spanish *aladroch*.

Buying Whitebait do not need to be cleaned. They are available fresh in spring and summer, and frozen all year round. Allow about 115g/4oz per person when serving them as an appetizer.

Cooking Whitebait are cooked whole, complete with heads. They are delicious deep-fried and served with brown bread and butter. Prepare them for cooking by dunking them in a bowl of milk, then shake them in a plastic bag containing flour seasoned with salt and cayenne pepper. Deep-fry until very crisp.

"Blue" fish

Although they are not related to each other, several species of particularly oily fish are known collectively as "blue" fish. All have very smooth, taut skin with virtually undetectable scales and firm, meaty flesh. Varieties of blue fish are found in almost all temperate and tropical seas.

Mackerel *(Scomber scombrus)*

These streamlined fish are easily identified, thanks to their beautiful greenish-blue skin. They have wavy bands of black and green on their backs, while the bellies are silvery. The smooth, pale beigey-pink flesh is meaty, with a distinctive full flavour.

Habitat Mackerel are pelagic shoaling fish, often found in huge numbers in the North Atlantic, North Sea and Mediterranean. They spend the winter near the bottom of the cold North Sea, not feeding at all.

Below: Mackerel

Below: Jack mackerel, which are not true mackerel, are common in New Zealand.

Other names Larger mackerel are known as *maquereau* in French; small specimens are called *lisette*. In Italian, mackerel is called *sgombro* and in Spanish it is known as *caballa*.

Buying Mackerel are delicious when extremely fresh, but not worth eating when they are past their best. They are in their prime in late spring and early summer, just before spawning. Look for firm fish with iridescent skin and clear, bright eyes. Small mackerel are better than large fish. Larger specimens are sometimes sold filleted, and either sold fresh or smoked. Mackerel is a popular canned fish, and may be canned in either oil or tomato sauce.

Cooking Whole mackerel can be grilled (broiled), cooked on a barbecue, braised or poached in court-bouillon, white wine or cider. Slash both sides of each fish before cooking them over direct heat. Like herrings, they need a sharp sauce to counteract the richness of the flesh; classic accompaniments are gooseberry, sorrel, horseradish or mustard sauce. Fillets can be cooked in the same way as herring – coated in oatmeal and fried, or braised with onions and white wine. Raw mackerel fillets can be marinated in sweet-and-sour vinaigrette to make an appetizer.

Below: Mackerel fillets can be cooked in the same way as herring – they are especially good lightly coated in oatmeal and pan-fried.

Bluefish *(Pomatomus saltatrix)* Found in the Mediterranean and American Atlantic waters, bluefish are highly aggressive and are often fished for sport. They have shiny blue-green backs and masses of very sharp teeth. Bluefish are hugely popular in Turkey, where they are displayed in fish markets with their bright red gills turned inside out like elaborate rosettes to indicate their freshness. The flesh of bluefish is softer and more delicate than that of mackerel, but they can be cooked in the same way.

Right: Bluefish in a Turkish market with their bright red gills displayed.

Other varieties of mackerel

Chub mackerel *(Scomber japonicus colias)* are similar to Atlantic mackerel, but are also found in the Mediterranean and Black Sea. They have larger eyes and less bold markings on their backs. **Spanish mackerel** *(Scomber colias)* have spots below the lateral line. The rarer *Orcynopsis unicolor* is found near the coast of North Africa. It has silvery skin with spots of gold.

Horse mackerel *(Trachurus trachurus)* or **scad** and similar fish such as **jack mackerel** and **round robin** vaguely resemble herrings and are not, despite their name, true relatives of mackerel. They are perfectly edible, but their flesh is rather insipid and they tend to be bony. They can all be cooked in the same way as mackerel.

THE TUNA FAMILY

Tuna has been a popular food for centuries. The fish were highly prized by the Ancient Greeks, who mapped their migratory patterns in order to fish for them. The Phoenicians preserved tuna by salting and smoking it, and in the Middle Ages it was pickled. A shoal of immense tuna fish travelling through the high seas is a magnificent sight, although satellite tracking has robbed the experience of some of its excitement. These beautiful, torpedo-shaped fish can grow to an enormous size (up to 700kg/1540lb). They have immensely powerful muscles and firm, dark, meaty flesh. There are many varieties of tuna, but due to centuries of overfishing, only about half a dozen varieties are available commercially.

Habitat Tuna are related to mackerel and are found in warmer seas throughout the world, as far north as the Bay of Biscay.

Other names Tuna is also known as tunny fish. In French, it is *thon*, in Italian *tonno*, in Spanish *atún*. In Japan, where raw tuna is eaten as *sashimi*, it is called *maguro*.

Buying Tuna is usually sold as steaks. It is a very substantial fish, so allow only about 175g/6oz per serving. Depending on the variety, the flesh may range from pale beigey-pink to deep dark red. Do not buy steaks with heavy discolorations around the bone, or which are dull-looking and brownish all over. The flesh should be very firm and compact.

Below: Tuna steaks

Cooking Tuna becomes greyish and dry when overcooked, so it is essential to cook it only briefly over high heat, or to stew it gently with moist ingredients like tomatoes and (bell) peppers. It has become fashionable to sear it fleetingly, leaving it almost raw in the middle; if this is not to your taste, cook the tuna for about 2 minutes on each side – no more.

The following cooking methods are suitable for most types of tuna. Steaks can be seared, grilled (broiled), baked or braised. They benefit from being marinated for about 30 minutes before cooking. Tuna marries well with Mediterranean vegetables, such as tomatoes, (bell) peppers and onions, as well as olives. Most varieties can be eaten raw as *sashimi*, *sushi* or *tartare*, but they must be absolutely fresh. Thinly sliced raw tuna can be marinated in vinaigrette or Asian marinades. Tuna fillets are delicious cut very thin, dusted with flour and cooked like veal *scaloppine* in butter. Grilled (broiled) fresh tuna makes a superb alternative to canned in a classic Salade Niçoise.

Albacore *(Thunnus alalunga)*

Also known as longfin, because of its long pectoral fins, this tuna is found in temperate and tropical seas, although only the smaller specimens venture into the North Sea. Albacore has pale, rosy flesh whose colour and texture resemble veal. Once known as "Carthusian veal", it could be eaten by monks when eating meat was not permitted. It is frequently used for canning.

Other names Albacore is also known as "white" tuna. In French it is *thon blanc* or *germon*; in Italian *alalunga* and in Spanish *atún blanco* or *albacora*.

Cooking Because its rosy-white flesh is so akin to veal, albacore is often cooked in similar ways – as escalopes (scallops) or larded with anchovy fillets and pork back fat, and braised.

Above: Bigeye or blackfin tuna steaks

False albacore *(Euthynnus alletteratus)*

This comparatively small tuna (weighing about 15kg/33lb) is found only in warmer waters, generally off the coast of Africa. It is highly sought-after in Japan, where it is used for *sashimi*.

Bigeye *(Thunnus obesus)*

This fat relative of the bluefin is found in tropical waters. It has rosy flesh and is substituted for bluefin when that superior tuna is unavailable. It is sometimes known as blackfin tuna. Other languages continue the rather rude reference to its obesity; In French, it is *thon obèse*, in Italian, *tonno obeso* and in Spanish *patudo*.

Bluefin *(Thunnus thynnus)*

Considered by many to be the finest of all tuna, bluefin are also the largest, and can grow to an enormous size (up to 700kg/1,540lb), although the average weight is about 120kg/264lb. Bluefin have dark blue backs and silvery bellies. Their oily flesh is deep red and has a more robust flavour than albacore. Bluefin is the classic tuna for *sushi* and *sashimi*.

Habitat Bluefin are found in the Bay of Biscay, the Mediterranean and tropical seas. They are very strong swimmers and a dense shoal of bluefin powering its way through the sea is an awesome sight.

Left: Bluefin tuna

Other names In Australia, the fish is known as Southern bluefin. Owing to its bright red flesh, bluefin is *thon rouge* in French. In Italian it is merely *tonno*; in Spanish it is known as *atún*.
Buying Bluefin tuna is extremely expensive, largely because the Japanese will pay almost any price for it. It has an almost gamey flavour and is best when it has been kept for a week. Once the flesh has turned from bright red to light brown, however, it should be avoided at all costs – the tuna is past its prime.

Bonito *(Sarda sarda)* and Skipjack *(Katsuwonus pelamis)*

These fish fall somewhere between mackerel and tuna. There are two main types of bonito: Atlantic *(Sarda sarda)* and skipjack or oceanic. The Atlantic bonito is also found in the Mediterranean and Black Sea; skipjack is most commonly found in the Atlantic and Pacific Oceans.

Bonito are inferior to true tuna in quality and taste, with pale flesh which can sometimes be rather dry. Skipjack are usually used for canning. They are popular in Japan, where they are known as *katsuo* and are often made into dried flakes (*katsuobushi*), which is a main ingredient of *dashi* (stock).

Other names
Skipjack have dark blue parallel lines along their bellies and are sometimes known as "striped tuna". This gives them the French name *bonite à ventre rayé* (striped belly). In Italian they are *bonita*; in Spanish, *listado*.

Frigate mackerel *(Auxis rochei)*

Despite its name, this fish is actually a tuna that is found in the Pacific and Indian Oceans. It grows to only about 50cm/20in and has red, coarse flesh. Some are small enough to cook whole.

Yellowfin *(Thunnus albacores)*

These large tuna are fished in tropical and equatorial waters. Weighing up to 250kg/550lb, they resemble albacore, but their fins are yellow. They have pale pinkish flesh and a good flavour.
Other names Confusingly, the French and Italians call yellowfin *albacore* and *tonno albacora* respectively. In Spanish, it is *rabil*.

Above: Bluefin tuna steaks

Buying Since yellowfin tuna come from warm oceans, in Europe they are generally sold frozen as steaks. Make sure that they have not begun to thaw before you buy. Frozen yellowfin is available all year round.
Cooking Very fresh yellowfin can be eaten raw as *sashimi* or *sushi*, but is better cooked in any recipe that is suitable for tuna.

Salade Niçoise
Tuna is the essential ingredient of this substantial Provençal salad, whose other components consist of whatever is fresh and available. Although the salad can be (and often is) made with drained canned tuna, it is infinitely nicer to use freshly seared or grilled (broiled) fish. Arrange some shredded cos or romaine lettuce in a salad bowl and add the tuna, some quartered hard-boiled eggs, thickly-sliced cooked new potatoes, tomato wedges, crisply cooked green beans, some black olives and a few anchovy fillets. Just before serving, toss the salad in a little garlic-flavoured vinaigrette dressing.

Flat Fish

All flat fish start life as pelagic larvae, with an eye on each side of their head like a round fish. At this stage, they swim upright near the surface of the sea. As they mature, the fish start to swim on one side only and one eye moves over the head on to the dark-skinned side of the body. Later, they gravitate to the sea bed and feed on whatever edible creatures pass by. Because they do not have to chase their food, their flesh is always delicate and white, without too much muscle fibre. They have a simple bone structure, so even people who are nervous about bones can cope with them. With the exception of flounder, flat fish are seldom found outside European waters. Dover sole, turbot and halibut possibly rank as the finest fish of all.

Above: Brill

Brill *(Scophthalmus rhombus)*

Similar to turbot in appearance and taste, brill is regarded as the poor relation, although it has fine softish white flesh with a delicate flavour. Brill can grow to about 75cm/30in and can weigh up to 3kg/6½lb, but are often smaller. The fish have slender bodies, and there are small, smooth scales on the dark grey skin on the top. The underside is creamy or pinkish white.

Habitat Brill live on the bottom of the Atlantic, Baltic Sea and Mediterranean.

Buying Many people prefer turbot to brill; others think that brill is every bit as good as its plumper friend. Brill is considerably cheaper than turbot and available almost all year round, as whole fish or fillets. Brill lose condition after spawning and can contain a great deal of roe just before, so avoid buying them at that time. There is a high percentage of wastage in all flat fish, so you will need a 1.5kg/3–3½lb fish for four.

Cooking Brill can hold its own against robust red wine and is often cooked in a *matelote* (fish stew) or red wine sauce. Small fish (up to 2kg/4½lb) are best cooked whole; they can be baked, braised, poached, steamed, pan-fried or grilled (broiled). Whole poached brill is excellent garnished with prawns (shrimp) or other shellfish. Fillets of brill *à l'anglaise* are coated in egg and breadcrumbs and pan-fried in butter.

Other names In French, brill is *barbue*, in Italian *rombo liscio*, "smooth turbot"; its Spanish name is *rémol*.

Alternatives Any halibut, sole or turbot recipe is suitable for brill.

Left: Dab

Dab *(Limanda limanda)*

There are several related species of dab, none of which has much flavour. European and American dabs are small lozenge-shaped fish, which seldom grow to more than 35cm/14in. They have brownish, rough skin and a lateral line.

Habitat Dabs are found in shallow water on the sandy bottom of the Atlantic and off the coast of New Zealand.

Other names The so-called false dabs are more elongated than their European counterparts. In America, dabs are known as sand dabs. In French, they are *limande*, in Italian *limanda* and in Spanish *limanda nordica*.

Buying Dabs are only worth eating when they are very fresh. Near the coast, you may find them still alive and flapping on the fishmonger's slab; if not, make sure they have glossy skins and a fresh smell. Dabs are usually sold whole, but larger fish may be filleted.

Cooking Dabs have rather soft, insipid flesh. Pan-fry them in butter or grill (broil) them. Fillets can be coated in egg and breadcrumbs and fried.

Above: Halibut

Below: Halibut Steaks

Halibut *(Hippoglossus hippoglossus)*

Halibut are the largest of the flat fish, sometimes growing up to 2m/6½ft and weighing well over 200kg/440lb, although they normally weigh between 3kg/6½lb and 15kg/33lb. Halibut have elegant, elongated greenish-brown bodies, a pointed head with the eyes on the right-hand side, and pearly white undersides. The flesh is delicious with a fine, meaty texture.

Habitat Halibut live in very cold, deep waters off the coasts of Scotland, Norway, Iceland and Newfoundland. They migrate to shallower waters to spawn. A warm water variety is found in the Pacific. These fish are voracious predators, which will eat almost any type of fish or crustacean, and will even devour birds' eggs that roll off cliffs.

Other names Beware of Greenland halibut *(Reinhardtius hippoglossoides)*, which is a vastly inferior fish. True halibut is called *flétan* in French and *halibut* in Italian and Spanish.

Buying Whole young halibut, called chicken halibut, weigh 1.5–2kg/3½–4½lb, and one will amply serve four. Larger fish are almost always sold as steaks or fillets. Go for steaks cut from the middle rather than from the thin tail end, and allow 175–200g/6–7oz per serving. Fresh raw halibut can be used for *ceviche*, *sashimi* and *sushi*.

Cooking Chicken halibut can be baked, braised, poached or cooked *à la bonne femme*, with shallots, mushrooms and white wine. The flesh of large halibut can be dry, so should be braised or baked with wine or stock.

Alternatives Brill can be substituted for halibut in any recipe. Turbot or John Dory can also be used.

Flounder *(Platichthys flesus)*

Another large family of fish, species of flounder are found in many parts of the world, from Europe to New Zealand. The mottled greyish-brown skin has orange spots and is rough. Flounders can grow to 50cm/20in, but they usually measure only 25–30cm/10–12in. They sometimes hybridize with plaice, which they resemble, having a similar soft texture and undistinguished flavour.

Habitat Flounders live close to the shore and are sometimes found in estuaries. They spend their days on the sea bed, not feeding, but become active at night.

Other names Many types of flounder are found in America, where they are variously known as summer, winter and sand flounders. Other varieties have such descriptive names as arrowtooth, black, greenback and yellowbelly. In France, they are called *flet*, in Italy, *passera pianuzza*; in Spain, *platija*.

Buying Like dabs, flounders must be extremely fresh. Apply the same criteria.

Cooking As for dabs, brill or plaice.

Below: Flounder

Megrim *(Lepidorhombus whiffiagonis)*

Small yellowish-grey translucent fish with large eyes and mouths, megrim seldom grow to more than 50cm/20in in length. They have dryish, rather bland flesh and are not considered much worth eating.

Habitat Found mostly to the south of the English Channel.

Other names Megrim is also known by the alternative names of whiff or sail-fluke. In France it is called *cardine franche*; in Italy *rombo giallo* (although you are unlikely to find it on a restaurant menu in either country). In Spain, where it is quite popular, it is called *gallo*.

Buying Megrim are either sold whole or as fillets. The flesh can be a little dry. They need to be extremely fresh, so make sure you smell them before you buy. Allow a 350g/12oz fish or at least two fillets per serving.

Cooking Whole fish can be coated in batter or breadcrumbs and deep-fried, or poached or baked. Their flesh can sometimes be rather dry, so use plenty of liquid. Fillets are best crumbed and deep-fried. Remove the coarse skin before frying or grilling (broiling).

Alternatives Lemon sole, plaice, dab or witch (Torbay sole).

Above: Megrim

Above: Plaice

Plaice *(Pleuronectes platessa)*

These distinctive-looking fish have smooth, dark greyish-brown skin with orange spots. The underside is pearly white. The eyes are on the right-hand side; a ridge of bony knobs runs from behind them to the dorsal fin. Plaice can live for up to 50 years and weigh up to 7kg/15½lb, but the average weight is 400g–1kg/14oz–2¼lb. They have soft, rather bland white flesh, which can sometimes lack flavour.

Habitat Plaice are found in the Atlantic and other northerly waters, and in the Mediterranean. They are bottom-feeding fish which, like flounder, are most active at night.

Other names In France, plaice are *plie* or *carrelet*; in Italy, *passera* or *pianuzza*; in Spain, *solla*.

Buying Plaice must be very fresh, or the flesh tends to take on a woolly texture. These fish are available all year, whole or as fillets, but are best

Left: Plaice fillets

avoided in the summer months, when the flesh is flaccid and tasteless. In fresh plaice, the orange spots on the dark skin will be bright and distinctive. Dark-skinned plaice fillets are cheaper than white-skinned, but there is no difference in flavour. There is a lot of wastage on plaice, so you should allow a whole 350–450g/12–16oz fish per serving, or 175g/6oz fillet.

Cooking Any sole or brill recipe is suitable for plaice. Deep-fried in batter, plaice is a classic "fish and chip shop" favourite. Whole fish or fillets can be coated in egg and breadcrumbs and pan-fried. Steamed or poached plaice is highly digestible and makes good food during illness. For plaice *à la florentine*, bake a whole fish or white-skinned fillets in stock and white wine, lay it on a bed of lightly-cooked spinach, cover with a cheese sauce and grill (broil) until bubbling and browned.

Alternatives Flounder, dab, sole and brill can all be substituted for plaice.

Sole/Dover sole *(Solea solea)*

Arguably the finest fish of all, Dover sole have a firm, delicate flesh with a superb flavour. Their oval bodies are well proportioned, with greyish or lightish brown skin, sometimes spotted with black. The eyes are on the right-hand side. The nasal openings on the underside are small and widely separated, which distinguishes these sole from lesser varieties. Dover sole can weigh up to 3kg/6½lb, but the average weight is 200–600g/7oz–1lb 6oz.

The Ancient Romans adored sole and called them *solea Jovi* ("Jupiter's sandal"). The firm flesh was often preserved. During the reign of Louis XIV of France, sole was regarded as truly fit for a king, and the great chefs of the time created extravagant sole dishes. In the earlier part of the 20th century, it was the mainstay of English fish cooking.

Habitat Dover sole are found in the English Channel and the Atlantic Ocean and also in the Baltic, Mediterranean and North Seas. They come inshore to spawn in spring and summer. For the most part, they spend their days buried in the sand on the sea bed and hunt for food at night.

Other names Sand or partridge sole *(Pegusa lascaris)* are very similar in appearance to Dover sole and are sometimes sold as "Dovers", although they are smaller and inferior fish. Their distinguishing feature is a much larger nasal opening on the underside. Another species, known as "tongues", *(Dicologlossa cuneata)* are smaller still (only 7.5–10cm/3–4in in length). In France, these fish are sometimes sold as baby Dover sole, when they are known as *séteaux* (or *cétaux*) or *langues d'avocat* ("lawyers' tongues"). In French Dover sole is *sole*; in Italian, *sogliola*; in Spanish, *lenguado*.

Buying Sole are at their best three days after being caught, so if you are sure that you are buying fish straight from the sea, keep them for a couple of days before cooking. The skin should be sticky and the underside very white. Nowadays, whole sole are graded by weight;

Above: Dover sole (top) and lemon sole

Below: Turbot

a 225g/8oz fish will serve one person. If you want to serve two, buy a fish weighing at least 675–800g/1½–1¾lb (which will yield four decent-size fillets, but could prove costly). It is best to buy a whole fish; if you ask the fishmonger to fillet it for you, keep the bones and trimmings to make fish stock (and help to justify the cost).

Cooking There are many recipes for sole, but a plain lightly grilled (broiled) fish served with a drizzle of melted butter and lemon juice is hard to beat. Skin both sides before cooking. Small sole can be coated in egg and breadcrumbs and pan-fried or deep-fried; larger specimens can be poached, steamed or cooked in butter *à la meunière*. Fillets can be fried, poached in wine or served with an elaborate sauce, or given an Asian twist with soy sauce, lemon grass and ginger. They can be steamed and rolled up around a stuffing or used to line a mould which is then filled with shellfish mousse.

Alternatives

Nothing tastes quite like Dover sole, but lemon sole, plaice and other flat fish can be cooked in the same way.

Lemon sole *(Microstomus kitt)*

Despite the name, lemon sole is related to dab, plaice and flounder. These fish are oval in shape, with the widest part well towards the head. They have smooth reddish brown skin with irregular marbling and a straight lateral line, very small heads and bulging eyes. The flesh is soft and white, similar to that of plaice but slightly superior. It is a good alternative to the more expensive Dover sole.

Habitat Lemon sole are found in the North Sea and Atlantic Ocean and around the coast of New Zealand. They lead largely stationary lives on the stony or rocky sea bed and vary enormously in size depending on local conditions.

Other names In America, lemon sole are known as yellowtail flounder. In France, they are *limande-sole*, in Italy *sogliola limanda*; in Spain, *mendo limón*.

Buying Lemon sole are available all year round and are sold whole or as fillets. They must be very fresh and should have a tang of the sea.

Cooking Lemon sole are best cooked simply; use them in any dab, plaice or Dover sole recipe.

Turbot *(Psetta maxima)*

What turbot lacks in looks, it makes up for in texture and taste, and it is a clear contender for the fishy crown. Highly prized since ancient times, it was called *le roi de carême* ("the king of Lent") in the Middle Ages. All the great chefs of the time created sumptuous recipes for turbot, marrying the fish with langoustines, truffles, lobster sauce and beef marrow.

Turbot have tiny heads and large, almost circular bodies with tough warty brown skin like a toad. Unusually, the white underside is sometimes pigmented with grey. They can grow to 1m/40in in length and can weigh as much as 12kg/26½lb. The flesh is creamy white, with a firm, dense texture and a superb sweet flavour.

Turbot kettle

In the days of affordable luxury, a whole huge turbot might be steamed in a magnificent diamond-shaped copper turbot kettle with handles on the points and a grid for lifting out the cooked fish.

Nowadays you will find only one of these kettles in the kitchen of a stately home or a fine restaurant. Modern turbot kettles are made of stainless steel or aluminium.

Above: Chicken turbot

Habitat Turbot live on the sea bottom in the Atlantic, Mediterranean and Black Seas, and have been introduced to New Zealand coastal waters. They can be farmed successfully, and this has improved both the quality and the size of the fish.

Other names The name is the same – *turbot* – in French, *rombo chiodato* (studded with nails) in Italian; *rodaballo* in Spanish. Small young turbot, weighing up to 2kg/4½lb, are called chicken turbot.

Buying Turbot is extremely expensive; a really large wild fish can cost several hundred pounds (dollars). Farmed fish are cheaper, but can be fatty. Turbot should have creamy white flesh; do not buy fish with a blue tinge. It is available all year round, sold whole, as steaks and fillets. A chicken turbot weighing about 1.5kg/3–3½lb will feed four people. There is a high percentage of wastage, so if your fishmonger fillets a whole turbot for you, ask for the bones and trimmings to make a superb stock.

Cooking It is neither practical nor economical to cook a whole turbot that weighs more than about 1.5kg/3–3½lb in a domestic kitchen. To cook a chicken turbot, grill (broil) it or poach in white wine and fish stock, using a large frying pan or roasting pan. Traditionally, turbot was poached in milk to keep the flesh pure white, then served with hollandaise sauce. Almost any cooking method is suitable for turbot, except perhaps deep-frying, which would be a waste; it is essential not to overcook it. Creamy sauces such as lobster, parsley and mushroom go well with plainly-cooked turbot. Chunks of poached turbot dressed with a piquant vinaigrette, make a superb salad.

Alternatives Nothing quite equals turbot, but brill, halibut, John Dory and fillets of sole make good substitutes.

Below: Witch

Witch *(Glyptocephalus cynoglossus)*

This member of the sole family has an elongated body like a sole, with a straight lateral line on the rough, grey-brown skin. The flesh tastes rather insipid, and resembles megrim.

Other names Also known as Torbay sole, witch flounder and pole flounder. In French, it is *plie grise*, in Italian *passera cinoglossa*; in Spanish *mendo*.

Buying Witch are available all year round, usually only near the coast where they are caught – mostly off the south-west coast of England. They are only worth eating when very fresh.

Cooking Because these fish taste rather dull, it is important to season them well before cooking. Witch are best grilled (broiled), but any sole recipe is suitable.

Migratory Fish

Certain species of fish undertake an astonishing annual mass migration from one area to another to spawn or feed. They follow a specific route, although how they know which route to take remains a mystery. Each year salmon and sea trout migrate from the sea to spawn in the fresh water of the river; having spawned, they return to the sea, and so the pattern continues. Eels, on the other hand, travel from rivers and lakes to spawn in salt sea water, entailing a journey of thousands of miles. The whole process is truly one of nature's miracles.

EELS *(Anguillidae)*

There are more than twenty members of the eel family. All are slim snake-like fish with smooth slippery skin and spineless fins. Most have microscopic scales, but these are not visible to the naked eye. The *Anguillidae* family are freshwater fish, but other species, such as conger, moray and snake eels, are marine fish. Eels have fatty white flesh with a rich flavour and firm texture.

Eels have been a popular food since Roman times, and were highly prized in the Middle Ages. Their mysterious life cycle gave rise to all sorts of improbable myths; one popular belief was that they were loose horsehairs which came to life when they touched the water. The less fanciful but equally amazing truth was only discovered by a Danish scientist at the end of the 19th century.

Habitat Freshwater eels are born in the Sargasso Sea. Each female lays up to 20 million eggs and both she and her male partner die immediately after the eggs have been laid and fertilized. The eggs hatch into minuscule larvae, which are carried on the ocean currents to the coasts of Europe and America, then back to the rivers where their ancestors matured. This journey takes a year for American eels and between two and three years for European eels. No one has yet fathomed how the babies know which direction to take, since they have never seen "home". When the baby elvers enter the estuaries in huge flotillas, they are tiny transparent creatures not more than 8cm/3¼in long. As they mature, their skin colour changes to yellow, then to green and finally to silver. At this stage, the eels begin the long journey back to the Sargasso Sea, where they spawn and immediately die.

Above: Young eels

Varieties Tiny elvers are known as glass eels (*civelles* or *piballes* in French). Adult European eels (*Anguilla anguilla*) and American eels (*Anguilla rostrata*) are *anguille* in French, *anguilla* in Italian and *anguila* in Spanish. The Japanese eel (*Anguilla japonica*) and Australian eel (*Anguilla australis*) are both known as the shortfinned eel, while *Anguilla dieffenbachii* is the longfinned eel.

Buying You may find tiny elvers for sale in the spring – these are a great delicacy and are extremely expensive. One kilo/two pounds consists of up to two thousand tiny elvers.

Adult eels are at their plumpest and best in autumn (fall) when they have turned silver with almost black backs. Females weigh three times as much as males, so a female silver eel is highly prized. Farmed eels are available all year round. Eels should be bought alive, as they go off very quickly once dead. Ask the fishmonger to kill and skin them and to chop them into 5cm/2in lengths.

Skinning an eel

You will probably prefer to ask your fishmonger to kill and skin your eel, but if this is not possible, this is how to do it yourself. Grip the eel in a cloth and bang its head sharply on a hard surface to kill it. Put a string noose around the base of the head and hang it firmly on a sturdy hook or door handle. Slit the skin all round the head just below the noose. Pull away the top of the skin, turn it back to make a "cuff", then grip with a cloth or two pairs of pliers and pull the skin down firmly towards the tail. Cut off the head and tail. Alternatively, kill the eel and chop it into sections, leaving the skin on. Grill (broil) the pieces, skin up, turning frequently until the skin has puffed up on all sides. When cool enough to handle, peel off the skin.

Cooking Tiny elvers can be tossed in seasoned flour and deep-fried; soak them first in acidulated water to remove the mud. Eel is a versatile fish that can be fried and served with parsley sauce. It is good poached or braised in red wine. If you grill (broil) it, marinate it first, then wrap it in bacon to keep the fish moist. Eel is excellent in soups and casseroles, such as *matelote*, and the rich flesh marries well with robust Asian flavours. Two classic English eel recipes are jellied eels and eel pie with mashed potatoes and green "liquor". Eels are also delicious smoked.

Above: Fierce-looking conger eel, which is a ferocious carnivore.

Conger eel *(Conger conger)*

These marine eels can grow to an enormous size – sometimes up to 3m/9ft 9in, although the average length is 60–150cm/2–5ft. They are ferocious carnivores with long, thick scaleless bodies and very bony firm white flesh, which is quite good to eat.

Habitat Conger eels are found in temperate and tropical seas, living in rocky crevices and wrecks. Many live in deep water, but some prefer to lurk in shallow inshore waters, causing panic among unfortunate swimmers who inadvertently disturb a large specimen.

Other names In French, conger eel is *congre*, in Italian *grongo*, and in Spanish *congrio*.

Buying Conger has the merit of being cheap. It is available from early spring to autumn (fall) and is usually sold cut into chunks or steaks. Ask for a middle cut from near the head end; the tail end is extremely bony. If you are offered a whole conger, ask the fishmonger to fillet it and keep the head and bones for soup or stock.

Cooking Conger is best used for soups or hearty casseroles. Its dense flesh makes it good for terrines. Thick middle cuts can be roasted, poached or braised and served with a *salsa verde*.

Below: Conger eel steaks

Moray eel *(Muraena helena)*

These eels are even more fearsome than the conger eel. They grow to only about 2m/6ft 6in, but are extremely vicious and will not hesitate to bite. Moray eels have long, flattened bodies and thick, greenish leathery skin with a pattern of light spots and no scales. The white flesh is rather tasteless and very bony.

Habitat Most species of moray eel are found in tropical and sub-tropical waters, but some occur in the Atlantic and Mediterranean. These eels typically anchor the tail end of their bodies in rock crevices and corals and wait with their mouths agape for catching prey that comes too close.

Buying Morays are mostly fished for sport and are seldom found in fishmongers. When they are available, they are sold in chunks.

Cooking Morays are really fit only for soup, and are often used in the traditional *bouillabaisse*. They can be cooked gently in (hard) cider, then the flesh removed from the bone and used in fish pies or fish cakes. The tail end is full of sharp bones. Avoid it, unless you are making stock.

Right: Atlantic salmon

THE SALMON FAMILY

Known as the "king of fish", salmon is probably the most important of all fish, prized by sportsmen and gastronomes alike. Various species are found throughout the world, but the finest by far is the Atlantic salmon. All salmon spawn in fresh water. Some species spend their lives in landlocked waters, but after two years, most salmon migrate upstream to the sea to feed before returning to spawn in the rivers where they were born. This arduous trek makes them sleek and muscular. Once they return to fresh water, they stop feeding, only starting again when they go back to the sea.

Salmon have suffered from over-fishing and environmental disturbance, and wild fish have become rare and expensive. Once, it was possible to land salmon weighing 20kg/44lb or more, but such magnificent fish have now disappeared. Fortunately, salmon can be farmed successfully, although early salmon farms produced fish with flabby, bland flesh, often riddled with sea lice, which attacked and further decimated the wild stocks. Lessons have been learned, and it is now possible to buy healthy, well-flavoured farmed salmon.

Atlantic salmon *(Salmo salar)*

These magnificent fish have silvery-blue backs, silver sides and white bellies. In comparison to their large, powerful bodies, their heads are quite small. The heads and backs are marked with tiny black crosses. Salmon's fine fatty flesh is deep pink and firm with a superb, rich flavour.

Habitat Atlantic salmon are found in all the cold northern waters of Europe and America. They are spawned in rivers, then undertake the exhausting journey back to the sea, returning to the river to spawn in their turn. When young salmon, which are 10–20cm/4–8in long, first migrate to the sea, they are called smolts. After a year or two of voracious feeding, they reach a weight of 1–2kg/2¼–4½lb and make their first spawning run; these young fish are called grilse.

Below: Salmon steaks

The males develop elongated hooked jaws; this is just to help them fight the strong currents, since they do not feed during the spawning run. Some fish may spawn only once or twice in their lifetimes; others up to four times.

Salmon were a popular food in the Middle Ages, when they were braised with spices, potted or salted, or made into pies and pâtés. Once they became rarer, they were regarded as a luxury and chefs vied to marry them with extravagant ingredients such as lobster, crayfish and cream. Only recently has salmon once again become affordable.

Other names The deep, cold lakes of Canada and North America are home to landlocked salmon; these are variously known as ouananiche, lake salmon and sebago. In French, salmon are *saumon*, in Italian *salmone*; in Spanish *salmón*.

Buying Salmon are sold whole, as steaks, cutlets, fillets and large middle and tail cuts. The best (and most expensive) salmon are wild fish. Ethical fishmongers will tell you which are wild and which farmed and charge accordingly. Wild salmon are sleeker, with firmer, lustrous skin and deep pink flesh. They are available from spring to late summer. Late-spawning fish which return to the sea in autumn (fall) are known as kelts; because they have not eaten for many months, kelts are thin and in poor condition and are not worth buying. Grilse – young salmon with an average weight of 1.4kg/3lb – are cheaper than large wild fish and will provide a generous meal for two. Scottish and Irish wild salmon are the finest of all; Atlantic salmon from Greenland and Scandinavia is less highly regarded.

The quality of farmed salmon can be variable. The flesh should be firm and dark pink with creamy marbling and not too much fat, not flabby and pale or greyish. Salmon heads are surprisingly heavy, so if you buy whole salmon allow about 350–400g/12–14oz per serving. If buying steaks or cutlets, you will need only about 200g/7oz per person.

Cooking There is almost no limit to the ways in which you can prepare and cook salmon. It can be eaten raw as a salmon *tartare*, *sashimi* or in *sushi*. It can be marinated in oil, lemon juice and herbs or salted and marinated to make *gravad lax*. It can be poached, pan-fried, seared, grilled (broiled), baked or braised, or enveloped in pastry as *saumon en croûte* or *coulibiac*. Poached salmon is delicious hot or cold; a whole fish poached in *court-bouillon* makes a superb festive dish served with plain or green mayonnaise and dressed with cucumber. It is a classic choice for wedding celebrations, for example. It is also excellent with a spicy salsa.
Hot poached salmon cries out for hollandaise or rich seafood sauce or *beurre blanc*. If you do not have a fish kettle large enough for a whole salmon, wrap the fish in foil, moisten with white wine, then bake.

Salmon fillets can be thinly sliced and flash-fried, or sandwiched together with fish or shellfish mousse or vegetable purée and baked or braised. They are delicious made into fish cakes, kedgeree, pâté and mousse. Try them potted in butter flavoured with mace, or as *rillettes*. Steaks can be cooked in red wine, poached, baked *en papillote* with white wine and herbs or Asian flavourings, grilled (broiled), pan-fried or cooked on a barbecue. Salmon is also delicious cold- or hot-smoked. It can be cured in salt and is one of the world's most popular canned fish.

Alternatives Sea trout and good-quality brown or rainbow trout can be used instead of salmon.

Pacific salmon *(Onorhynchus)*

Five species of Pacific salmon are found around the Pacific coast from California to Alaska and another is found in northern Japan. Even the largest, the Chinook or king salmon, is smaller and slimmer than its Atlantic counterpart. Other Pacific salmon include the sockeye or red salmon, chum or dog salmon and pink salmon. None is as fine as Atlantic salmon and all types are frequently sold canned.

Sea trout *(Salmo trutta)*

Although they are closely related to the brown trout, sea trout differ from other species in that they migrate to the sea like salmon. They closely resemble salmon, but have smaller, less pointed heads and squarer tails. Sea trout seldom grow to more than 3kg/6½lb, which makes them more manageable for cooking. They have fine, dark pink flesh, which is beautifully succulent and has a delicate, mellow flavour.

Other names Sea trout are also known as salmon trout or sewin. In French, they are *truite de mer*, in Italian *trota di mare*, and in Spanish *trucha marina*.

Buying Sea trout are always wild, but they do not cost so much as wild salmon. They are sold whole; a 2kg/4½lb fish will serve 4–6 people. They should be bright and silvery with an almost golden sheen.

Cooking As for salmon.

Above: Sea trout

Exotic Fish

Thanks to modern transportation, unusual exotic fish from tropical seas all over the world are now available in European and North American markets. Warm water fish never have quite as good a flavour as those from colder climes, but they add variety to a fish diet and are often very colourful. Do not be alarmed at the prospect of cooking unfamiliar fish; they can be cooked in the same way as other species, and lend themselves to exotic flavourings, so you can experiment with new taste sensations.

Barracouta/Snoek *(Thyrsites atun)*

This long thin fish has smooth blue-grey skin with silver sides and belly, a flat dorsal fin running almost the length of the body and a series of spines near the tail. Barracouta can grow to 2m/6½ft long, but are generally 60–90cm/24–36in in length. The lower jaw protrudes, and there is a single lateral line. The dryish flesh is dark, but whitens on cooking. Barracouta have long, irregular bones. The fish are often canned, which softens the bones and makes them more palatable.

Habitat Barracouta are widely distributed in temperate regions of the southern hemisphere.

Other names In Australia and New Zealand, the name barracouta is often shortened to "couta". In South Africa, these fish are always known as snoek.

Buying Barracouta are not sold fresh in the northern hemisphere, but you may find them canned or smoked.

Cooking Barracouta can be grilled (broiled), fried or baked. They are often pickled in vinegar and spices, and marry well with Asian flavours. Smoked barracouta is absolutely delicious.

Barracuda *(Sphyraena barracuda)*

These fearsome-looking game fish have long slender bodies, forked tails and sharp teeth capable of delivering a vicious bite. They are frequently spotted by divers, who encounter them on coral reefs. There are about twenty

Above: Barracuda

species of barracuda. The largest is the great barracuda, which has dark bars and scattered black blotches on its greenish skin. This fish can grow to over 1m/3¼ft in length. Other species include the yellowtail and the small Pacific and Mexican barracudas. All have meaty, rich, oily flesh, which has the reputation of being toxic. Play safe by not eating raw fish; properly cooked, it is perfectly acceptable.

Habitat Barracuda are found in warm waters, mainly in the Pacific and Caribbean, but sometimes in warmer Atlantic seas. Young fish travel in schools, but older specimens are solitary. They are full of curiosity and will follow divers around the reefs, or even walkers along the shore, which gives them the probably undeserved reputation of being predatory.

Below: Barramundi

Other names In French, barracuda is known as *brochet de mer* because it resembles pike. Italians call it *luccio marina* and in Spain it is *espeton*.

Buying Small barracuda up to 3kg/6½lb are best. Ask the fishmonger to scale and fillet them. Larger fish are often sold already filleted. Barracuda is available all year round.

Cooking The rich flesh of barracuda lends itself well to Asian flavourings. It is oily, so avoid cooking with butter, cream or too much oil. Small whole barracuda can be grilled (broiled), cooked on a barbecue or baked. Fillets and steaks can be curried or marinated in spices and grilled or baked.

Alternatives Any firm-fleshed oily fish, such as tuna or bonito.

Barramundi *(Lates calcifer)*

This beautiful giant perch has an elongated silver body with a dark grey back, a curved lateral line and a protruding lower jaw. Barramundi can grow to an enormous size, often

weighing more than 20kg/44lb; the record catch so far weighed 250kg/ 550lb. The best size for eating is about 10kg/22lb, although whole baby barramundi (or "barra") are popular in Australia. The chunky white flesh has a delicious, quite delicate flavour.
Habitat Barramundi are found in Indo-Pacific waters, from Japan to the East Indies. They often swim close to the shore and are sometimes found in estuaries and brackish water.
Other names Barramundi are sometimes known as giant perch.
Buying You are unlikely to find barramundi outside the Antipodes and Asia. Small fish are sold whole and larger specimens are sold as steaks or fillets. Look for bright skin and white flesh.

Below: Flying fish

Cooking Whole fish can be baked, fried, braised, grilled (broiled) or cooked on a barbecue. Cook fillets and steaks in the same way as bream, porgy and snapper.

Flying fish *(Exocoetidae)*

These are the fish that gave their name to the exocet missile, due to their habit of gliding (not flying) amazing distances through the air at about 60kph/40mph. They are supported by a disproportionately large, highly-developed, wing-like, spineless pectoral fin. Flying fish begin their "flight" below the water, at high speed, bursting through the surface into the air. Only then do they expand their pectoral fins, which allow them to glide for about 30 seconds before dropping tail-first back into the water. Flying fish may look spectacular, but their flavour is less exciting than their appearance.
Habitat Various species of flying fish are found in the Caribbean, Pacific and warm Atlantic waters. They are attracted by bright lights and are sometimes lured by fishermen who hang a lamp over the side of the boat to encourage the fish to "fly" into their nets.
Other names The French call flying fish *exocet*, the Italians *pesce volante*, the Spanish *pez voador.*
Buying Flying fish are usually displayed whole so that customers can admire their exotic shape. Large fish are sometimes filleted. They do not travel well, so are best eaten near the shores where they are caught.
Cooking Whole fish or fillets can be dusted in seasoned flour and deep-fried, baked au gratin or braised with tomatoes and onions.

Fugu fish – delicious or deadly
Ranking high amongst the ugliest fish in the world is the puffer or fugu fish, the eating of which constitutes a kind of Japanese roulette, since the internal organs (roe, liver, kidneys etc, depending on the species) contain a toxin five hundred times more deadly than cyanide. Nonetheless, fugu are regarded as a great gastronomic treat in Japan, where chefs train for many years to learn how to prepare this potentially deadly luxury. One slip of the knife and the lethal poison may be released into the flesh, resulting in instant death to the poor unfortunate who eats it.

Happily, it is now possible to farm fugu fish that are free from toxins, so the health of the gourmet population of Japan should be more secure in future.

Left: Strawberry Grouper

Grouper *(Epinephelus)*

Groupers are members of the extensive sea bass family. Dozens of species of these non-shoaling carnivorous fish are found in all the warm seas of the world; all have firm white flesh and make good eating. They look extremely gloomy, with upturned protruding lower lips, giving them the appearance of permanently sulky teenagers. They have beautiful colouring, often with mottled skin. One of the largest is the spotted jewfish or giant grouper, which can weigh more than 300kg/660lb; even larger is the Queensland grouper, which can weigh over half a ton, and has been known to attack and terrorize divers. Smaller species include the red, black, yellowmouth and Malabar groupers.

Below: Mahi mahi steaks

Habitat Warm water groupers inhabit all warm seas, from Africa to the Caribbean. Most inhabit rocky shores, but many live on deepwater reefs.
Other names In Australia, grouper is called rock or reef cod. In France, *merou*; in Italy, *cernia*; in Spain, *mero*.
Varieties There are two basic types of grouper; red and black. Red groupers have reddish-brown skin with attractive yellowish markings. Black groupers range from pale grey to very dark.
Buying Groupers are available all year round. Fish weighing up to 5kg/11lb are sold whole, or may be filleted or cut into steaks. You are unlikely to find any distinction made between the different varieties of grouper. All taste very similar and are interchangeable.
Cooking Grouper can be cooked in all the same ways as sea bass. It goes well with spices and Caribbean flavourings.
Alternatives Sea bass and bream can be substituted for grouper.

Mahi mahi/Dolphinfish *(Coryphaena hippurus)*

These strange and beautiful fish have long, tapering streamlined bodies, with a high ridge of fin running down the body from the head to the forked, swallow-like tail. They are among the fastest swimmers, with a top speed of 80kph/50mph. Their skin changes colour as they swim, from green and gold to silver and grey, with gold and blue spots. The average weight is about 2.5kg/5½lb, but fish have been known to grow to ten times that weight. The flesh is firm and white, with an excellent sweet flavour.
Habitat Mahi mahi are found in almost all the warm seas of the world. They are very inquisitive fish, which are easy to catch, since they are drawn to objects floating on the water.
Other names Mahi mahi is the Hawaiian name for these fish, which are also known as dorade or dolphinfish, though they are not related to dolphins. In French, they are *coryphene*, in Italian *lampuga* and in Spanish *llampuga*.
Buying Available from spring through to autumn (fall), mahi mahi is sold as steaks or fillets. Do not buy frozen fish, as it is completely lacking in flavour.
Cooking The Hawaiians eat mahi mahi raw, but it is best grilled (broiled) or fried. It marries well with spicy flavours and is delicious with a piquant salsa.
Alternatives Monkfish, John Dory, cod or any firm-fleshed fish can be substituted.

Above: Mahi mahi

Above and left: Parrot fish come in a huge variety of colours.

Parrot fish *(Scarus* spp*)*

Perfectly adapted to living in proximity to coral reefs, parrot fish have hard, parrot-like beaks (evolved from fused teeth) with which they nibble the coral. There are almost a hundred species of parrot fish. All have compact, brightly coloured bodies and large scales. They come in an incredible variety of vibrant hues – green, blue, red and multi-coloured. The largest is the rainbow parrot fish, which can grow up to 1m/3½ft, but most are only 30cm/12in long. Like many types of exotic fish, parrot fish look much better than they taste.

Habitat Parrot fish are found in tropical and sub-tropical seas. They live in large numbers around coral reefs, crushing the coral to reach the soft sea creatures inside, or scraping algae from surrounding rocks.

Other names In French, they are *perroquet*; in Italian *pesce pappagallo;* in Spanish *vieja*.

Buying Many supermarkets now stock parrot fish. Make sure that the colours are clear and bright; avoid fish that look faded. The average fish from the fish market or fishmonger's slab will feed one person; a larger 800g–1kg/1¾–2¼lb fish will serve two. Larger fish are sometimes sold filleted, or can be filleted on request.

Cooking Parrot fish can be rather bland, so spice them up with tropical flavours, such as coconut milk, garlic, chilli and lemon grass. Whole fish can be baked or braised; they look pretty and taste good served with a spicy salsa.

Alternatives Red snapper, bream and John Dory can all be used instead of parrot fish.

Pomfret *(Stromateus* spp*)*

These small silvery fish look rather like coins if seen as though through the eyes of Salvador Dali. Their almost circular bodies have very pointed dorsal and anal fins and curved forked tails, not unlike those of flat fish. Scales are almost absent and the white flesh is fairly soft, with a mild flavour. Together with their close relation, the American butterfish, pomfret make good eating.

Above: Pomfret

Habitat A variety of pomfret is found in the Mediterranean, but the best-flavoured fish come from the Indian and Pacific oceans. Butterfish are found off the north-west coast of America.
Buying Pomfret are available most of the year, either fresh or frozen. Small fish weighing about 400g/14oz are sold whole and will feed one person. Fillets from small fish are rather thin, so it is best to choose a larger fish if possible and ask the fishmonger to fillet it.
Other names Pomfret from the north-west Atlantic are known as butterfish, and in America also go by the names of dollar fish, and pumpkinseed fish, owing to their shape, which in Europe is likened to that of the chestnut. In France, they are called *castagnole du Pacifique*; in Italy *pesce castagna* and in Spain *castagneta*.
Buying Pomfret are available most of the year. A small whole fish weighing about 400g/14oz will feed one person. Fillets from small pomfret are rather thin, so if possible, buy a larger fish and ask the fishmonger to fillet it for you.
Cooking Whole pomfret can be grilled (broiled), fried, baked, poached or steamed. This fish goes well with spices and Asian flavours such as coconut, lemon grass and tamarind. Beloved of Indian chefs, pomfret makes excellent curries and is often cooked in a tandoor as tikka masala. Because the fillets are thin and the flesh is soft, pomfret fillets should be cooked only briefly.
Alternatives Trout can be used instead of pomfret, as can any flat fish.

Pompano *(Alectis ciliaris)* and Jack *(Seriola)*

This large family of fish comprises more than two hundred species. All are oily fish, similar to mackerel, but with a stronger flavour. The dark flesh becomes lighter on cooking. Jacks vary enormously in size and shape, but all have forked tails and virtually scaleless iridescent skin. Among the most common jacks and pompanos are the small leatherjacket, the larger yellowtail, the amberjack and crevalle jack. The best of all for culinary purposes is the Florida pompano, which has white, meaty flesh, while the oddest-looking is the lookdown, a small glum-looking fish with a flat, thin body and a high domed forehead.
Habitat Pompano and jacks are found in warm seas all over the world. They travel in schools, either around coral reefs or, like the Florida pompano, close to the shore.
Other names In Australia and New Zealand, yellowtail jack is known as kingfish. In French, jack is *carangue*; in Italian *carango*; in Spanish *caballa*. Pompano is *palomine* in French; *leccia stella* in Italian and *palometa blanca* in Spanish.
Buying Pompano and jack are available all year round. They are usually sold whole, but may be filleted. Outside Florida, you are likely to find only farmed pompano, but this is of excellent quality.
Cooking Jack can be cooked in the same way as mackerel. The robust flesh lends itself to spicy Asian flavours such as chilli, ginger and coriander. Pompano and jack can be stuffed with breadcrumbs or crab meat and baked, grilled (broiled) or cooked on a barbecue. They can also be cooked *en papillote*, steamed or poached in court-bouillon flavoured with Asian ingredients such as soy sauce or Thai fish sauce and fresh ginger. The Japanese use the fillets raw as *sashimi*.

Below: Yellowtail jack or kingfish

Below: Yellowtail jack steaks

Above: Red and emperor snappers

Snapper *(Lutjanidae)*

More than 250 species of snapper are found in warm seas throughout the world. The best-known and finest to eat is the American red snapper (*Lutjanus campechanus*), which is bright red all over, including the eyes and fins. The silk snapper is similar, but has a yellow tail. Other species include the pink snapper, or *opakapaka*, mutton snapper, which is usually olive green with vertical bars (but can change colour), the yellowtail snapper and the African and Indo-Pacific. All have domed heads with large mouths and big eyes set high on the head. Most snappers weigh between 1.5 and 2.5kg/3¼ and 5½lb, although mutton snappers can weigh up to 10kg/22lb, while yellowtails average only 250g/9oz. Snappers have firm, slightly flaky well-flavoured white flesh.

Habitat Red snapper come from deep waters around Florida and Central and South America. Other varieties are found in warm waters from the Atlantic to the Caribbean and Indo-Pacific.

Other names Snapper from the Indian Ocean and Arabian Sea are known as job or jobfish. In French, *vivaneau*; in Italian, *lutianido*; in Spanish, *pargo*.

Buying Snapper are available all year round. Many fish sold as red snapper are a different, inferior species; true American red snapper have red eyes. A whole fish weighing about 1kg/2¼lb will feed two people, while a 2kg/4½lb fish makes a good meal for four people.

Cooking Snapper is a versatile fish that can be baked, poached, pan-fried, grilled (broiled) and steamed. It lends itself to exotic and Caribbean flavours, such as chilli, mango and coconut.

Alternatives Grey mullet, bream, John Dory and sea bass can be substituted.

Tilapia *(Tilapia)*

Members of the enormous *Cichlids* family, tilapia have only one nostril on either side of their heads. The female is considerably smaller than the male, and scientists have now successfully bred tilapia that produce offspring that are almost exclusively male. Tilapia are freshwater fish, but can also live in salt water and are found in tropical seas. There are many varieties, with colours ranging from grey to bright red. Their flesh is white and moist, with a pleasant, sweet flavour.

Habitat Tilapia are found in warm tropical waters, both fresh and salt. They are farmed all over the world.

Other names In Egypt and Israel, tilapia are sometimes marketed as St. Peter's fish (not to be confused with John Dory).

Buying Tilapia are available all year round. Small fish are sold whole, but larger fish are filleted. A small whole fish (about 350g/12oz) will serve one person; a 675g/1½lb fish serves two.

Cooking Whole tilapia can be stuffed and baked, grilled (broiled) or cooked on a barbecue. The bland flesh benefits from Chinese flavourings and spices. Fillets can be coated in egg and breadcrumbs or batter and deep fried.

Alternatives Carp, bream and zander can be used instead of tilapia.

Above: Tilapia

Cartilaginous Fish

This curious group of fish, called *chondrichthyes*, have no bones. Their skeletons are made entirely of cartilage. Many of these very ancient fish exist only as fossils, but about 500 species are still living, including edible fish such as shark, dogfish, ray and skate. Cartilaginous fish are thought to have evolved from freshwater fish which adapted to life in the sea. Unlike other fish, they have no swim bladders to control buoyancy, but in compensation have developed very large livers, whose high oil content helps the fish to float. This oil is often extracted and used for medicinal purposes.

Almost all cartilaginous fish have long snouts and mouths set well back on the underside of the head. They have several rows of teeth, arranged one behind the other. As one row wears away, they start to use the next. They have stiff fleshy fins and no scales, but their bodies are covered with backward-facing denticles, which give them a rough texture. Once these fish die, the urea they contain turns into ammonia, imparting an unpleasant smell and taste, so it is essential that they are eaten very fresh.

THE SHARK FAMILY

The shark family is a large one, ranging in size from the small dogfish to the huge basking shark, which can weigh up to 4000kg/8800lb, and whose liver alone weighs 500–700kg/1100–1540lb. Edible sharks include porbeagle, blue shark, mako, tope and dogfish. They are an unattractive bunch, with a bad reputation, but some of them make excellent eating. Shark flesh is firm and slightly sweet, with a meaty texture.
Buying Shark is sold as steaks, loin or fillets. The flesh has a faint smell of ammonia, which disappears during cooking if the shark is fresh. However, after a week or so, it becomes very pungent and nothing will get rid of it.
Cooking Shark meat is a match for robust flavours and is excellent in curries. Steaks can be grilled (broiled), pan-fried or cooked on a barbecue. They can be dry, so marinate them in olive oil and lemon juice, or lard them with pork back fat before cooking.

Steaks can also be braised or baked au gratin in a mornay sauce and glazed under the grill (broiler). It makes a good addition to a fish soup or casserole and can be served cold in salads, dressed with a lemony mayonnaise. It is also ideal for home-smoking.
Alternatives Any meaty fish can be used instead of shark in recipes; try monkfish, swordfish and tuna.

Above: Shark loin can be bought as a piece or cut into steaks. The meat can be dry, so is best marinated.

Blue shark *(Prionace glauca)*

This migratory shark has exceedingly sharp teeth and is regarded as a man-eater. It has a sleek indigo-blue back, shading to bright blue on the sides and a snow white belly. It seldom grows to more than 4m/13ft in length. The very white flesh is not especially good, but the fins are used to make the Chinese favourite, shark's fin soup.
Other names In French, blue shark is *peau bleu*, in Italian *verdesca*; in Spanish *tintorera*.

Dogfish *(Scyliorhinus caniculus)*

Three species of these small members of the shark family are commonly eaten; the lesser spotted dogfish, the spur-dog or spiny dogfish *(Squalus acanthius)* and the larger, more portly nursehound *(Scylorhinus stellaris)*. The first has grey-brown skin with numerous brown spots, the second has grey skin, while the nursehound's skin is reddish. The thick rough skin is almost always removed before sale to disguise the shark-like appearance of these fish. Lesser spotted dogfish grow to about 80cm/32in, spur-dogs to 1.2m/4ft and nursehounds to 1.5m/4ft 9in; the fish you find in the market are usually half that size. The flesh is white or pinkish with a firm texture and a good flavour. It is, of course, boneless.
Habitat Different varieties of dogfish are found in cool temperate waters all around the world.

Above: The lesser spotted dogfish, which is generally sold skinned but not filleted, is more commonly known as huss or even rock salmon.

Shark à la Créole

Shark is a very popular fish in the Caribbean and the southern states of North America. This recipe reflects the mixture of the two cultures.

For 4 people you will need 4 shark steaks. First, make a marinade with the juice of 2 limes, 2 crushed garlic cloves, 2 seeded and chopped red chillies, salt and ground black pepper. Dilute the marinade with 15ml/1 tbsp water and pour into a non-metallic dish. Add the shark steaks, turn them over in the marinade so that they are coated, then cover and leave to marinate for several hours in a cool place or in the refrigerator.

When ready to cook, slice 2 red onions, 4 shallots and 4 tomatoes. Seed 2 red or green fresh chillies and chop the chillies finely. Heat 30ml/2 tbsp oil in a shallow pan, add the vegetables and chillies and cook until brown. Drain the shark steaks and lay them on top of the vegetables. Cover and cook gently for about 20 minutes, until tender. Squeeze over the juice of a lime and garnish with chopped parsley. Serve with creole rice and black-eyed beans (peas).

Filleting dogfish

The central cartilage in dogfish is very easy to remove, and there are no small bones. It is usually sold as a whole skinned fish. To fillet, use a sharp knife with a long blade to cut down through the flesh on either side of the cartilage, using the full length of the blade and keeping it as close to the cartilage as possible. The fillets will fall away.

Other names Dogfish are variously known as huss, flake, rigg and even rock salmon, although this last is a complete misnomer. Spur dogs are also known as spinebacks or spiky dogs. In French, they are *petite* or *grande roussette*, depending on their size, or, misleadingly, *saumonette* (little salmon). In Italian they are called *gattopardo* (leopard), in Spanish *pata-roxa*.

Buying Dogfish are sold skinned, often as fillets. They are cheap and available all year round. They must be very fresh, so sniff before you buy to make sure they do not smell of ammonia.

Cooking Dogfish has good firm flesh and can be cooked in the same ways as monkfish and skate. It is excellent in casseroles and chunky soups and is the perfect fish for fish and chips (french fries). It can be grilled (broiled) or cooked on a barbecue with a coating of olive oil, or cooked and flaked and used in salads. It is delicious smoked.

Mako shark *(Isurus oxyrinchus)*

Part of the family of mackerel sharks, mako are swift surface swimmers with streamlined blue-grey bodies and bright white bellies, which grow to 2–3m/6½–9¾ft. They are found in sub tropical and temperate-warm seas. Prized by game fishermen, they have a habit of raiding and damaging fishing nets and lines. Mako sharks have firm white flesh and are usually sold as loins or fillets. The flesh can be rather bland, so it will benefit from a robust marinade.

Other names In French, *taupe bleu*, in Italian *squallo mako* or *ossirina*; in Spanish *marrajo*.

Porbeagle *(Lamna nasus)*

These stocky, dark mole-grey sharks are closely related to the great white shark. They are surface swimmers, found in cold and temperate seas, but little is known about their growth or longevity. Porbeagles are widely regarded as the finest of all the sharks for eating, with firm, meaty pink flesh which is sometimes likened to veal. It is usually sold as loin or fillets.
Other names In French, porbeagle is known as *taupe* or *veau de mer*; in Italian it is *smeriglio*; in Spanish *cailón*.

Cooking Porbeagle so closely resembles veal that it can be sliced into thin escalopes (scallops), dipped in egg and breadcrumbs and then pan-fried like *scallopine alla milanese*. It can also be used in any other shark recipe.

Tope *(Galeorhinus galeus)*

These small grey sharks have pointed upward-tilting noses and serrated triangular teeth. Although edible, they do not taste particularly good and are best cut into chunks and used in mixed fish soups and casseroles.
Other names In French it is *milandre*, in Italian *cagnesca*; in Spanish *cazón*.

Above: Porbeagle, which is sometimes sold in fishmongers and markets by its French name, taupe.

Below: Tope

Ray and Skate *(Raja)*

Although they are different members of the same family, it is virtually impossible to distinguish between ray and skate on the fishmonger's slab, since only the "wings" are sold, never the whole fish. These fish have large, kite shaped bodies with long thin tails and enlarged flattened pectoral fins (the wings). The skin is greyish-brown and smooth, knobbly or even thorny, depending on the species. Ray and skate have short snouts and large mouths on the underside with sharp slashing teeth. They can be differentiated by the shape of the snout; in skate, this is pointed. The largest rays can grow to 2.5m/8ft and weigh up to 100kg/220lb.

The thornback ray (*Raja clavata*) is considered to have the best flavour, but gastronomically speaking, there is little to distinguish between the edible skates and rays. They have moist, meaty pinkish flesh with a fine texture and good flavour. Normally, only the wings are eaten, but the cheeks are regarded as a delicacy, as are the small medallions from the tail known as "skate knobs". The liver also makes good eating.

Habitat Rays and skates are found in cold and temperate waters. They are lazy bottom living fish that hide on the sea bed waiting for their prey to pass by. They have evolved a way of breathing without opening their mouths. Most rays lay eggs, each enclosed in a four-horned black sac known as a "mermaid's purse".

Other names Among the edible rays and skates are the common skate (*raie* in French, *razza* in Italian; *raya* in Spanish), thornback ray or roker, rough skate and butterfly skate.

Below: Skate wing

Buying Skate is available most of the year, but is best in autumn (fall) and winter. Smaller wings are sold whole; if you want a larger piece, then ask for a middle cut. The wings are covered with a clear slime, which regenerates itself even after death. To test for freshness, gently rub off the slime and make sure that it reappears. Even fresh skate smells faintly of ammonia. This is normal, and the smell will disappear during cooking.

Cooking Before cooking skate, wash it well in cold water to eliminate the ammoniac smell. If the skin is still on, leave it and scrape it off after cooking. The classic skate dish is *raie au beurre noir* (with black butter). Poach the wings in water acidulated with a little vinegar or *court-bouillon* for about 10 minutes, then drain and sprinkle with capers. Brown some butter (do not let it burn and blacken) and pour it over the fish. Skate can also be grilled (broiled), deep-fried in batter or curried, and makes a delicious salad. Its gelatinous quality makes it good for soups and fish terrines and mousses.

Alternatives Fillets of brill, sole, John Dory or turbot can be used instead.

Skinning cooked skate

1 Lay the fish on a board. With a blunt knife, scrape off the skin from the thicker part towards the edge.

2 Discard the skin. Scrape the flesh off the cartilage in the same way.

Deep Sea and Game Fish

Deep in the world's oceans live several varieties of fish that never come close to the shore. Many have odd shapes and vibrant colours, which consumers seldom see, since the fish are filleted on board the boats that travel far out to sea to trawl the fish. Most edible deep-sea fish are found around the coasts of New Zealand, South Africa and South America. The Caribbean is home to huge game fish, such as marlin, and keen fishermen will pay vast sums for a day's sport. Little is known about the life cycles of these creatures of the deep, but it is certain that, as stocks of the more common inshore fish decline, we shall see more and more deep-sea fish appearing in the supermarkets.

Antarctic sea bass *(Dissostichus eleginoides)*

Not a true sea bass, this fish is also known as toothfish, icefish and Chilean sea bass. It has only recently been fished commercially, and little is known about it. The white flesh has a good texture and a pleasant flavour, but it does not compare to true sea bass.
Habitat Antarctic sea bass inhabits the southern oceans from Antarctica to the Falklands and Chile.
Buying Available all year round as fillets. Prod the flesh to make sure that it is firm. When buying Antarctic sea bass, make sure that you are not paying for real sea bass, which is a much more expensive fish.
Cooking Cook Antarctic sea bass in the same way as cod or any round white fish. A well-flavoured sauce will enhance the rather bland flavour.

Below: Hoki fillets are very long and thin. The flesh is pinkish white, and has a flaky texture that is similar to hake when cooked.

Grenadier/Rattail *(family Macrouridae)*

There are about fifty species of these curious-looking shoaling fish. They may be the most abundant of all fish, although since they live at depths of between 200m/656ft and 6000m/19,700ft, it is hard to be sure. Grenadiers have large pointed heads that contain sensors to help them navigate in the dark ocean depths, and bodies that taper into filament-like tails (hence their alias). Their swim bladders vibrate to produce a grunting sound. Despite their odd appearance, grenadiers are good to eat. The white flesh has a delicate, fairly moist texture.
Habitat Grenadiers are distributed throughout the world. They live at great depths, feeding on luminous creatures that they can detect even in the dark.
Buying Grenadier fillets are available all year round. You may find fresh fish, but in the northern hemisphere it is more usual to find the fish frozen.
Cooking Fillets can be deep- or pan-fried or brushed with oil and grilled (broiled). They benefit from a creamy sauce and are good baked *au gratin*.
Alternatives Cod, hake, hoki or any other fairly firm white fish can be used instead of grenadiers.

Hoki *(Macruronus novaezelandiae)*

Although hoki resemble grenadiers in appearance, they are actually related to hake and have the same white flesh and flaky texture. They have blue-green backs with silvery sides and bellies, and their tadpole-like bodies taper to a point. The average length of a hoki is 60cm–1m/24–39in.
Habitat Hoki occur in large numbers around the coasts of Southern Australia and New Zealand; a similar species is found around South America. They live at depths of 500–800m/1640–2626ft.
Other names In Australia, hoki are inaccurately called blue grenadier. In New Zealand, they are sometimes called whiptail or blue hake.
Buying Hoki is available all year round, as fillets, loins and other cuts. It is frequently used to make fish fingers (breaded fish sticks).
Cooking The delicate white flesh is suitable for most cooking methods, particularly frying. It can sometimes taste insipid, so is best served with a robust tomato-based sauce or a creamy sauce. Hoki can be cubed for kebabs and is an excellent fish for smoking.
Alternatives Hake, monkfish and huss can be substituted for hoki.

Marlin *(family Istiophoridae)*

More usually fished for sport than for commerce, marlin are magnificent-looking billfish, renowned for their speed and endurance. The name billfish comes from their greatly elongated upper jaw, which forms a bill or spear. They have beautiful slender bodies with smooth iridescent skin and a high dorsal fin, which they fold down when speeding through the water.

There are several species of marlin, the best-known being blue, black (the largest marlin), white (the smallest) and striped. All can attain enormous weights of up to 300kg/660lb but the average size is 160–200kg/352–440lb. The deep pink flesh is high in fat and has a fairly firm texture with a disappointingly undistinguished flavour.
Habitat Marlin are found in warm seas throughout the world. Unusually for predators, they have no teeth, but use

their bill to stun schooling fish, and then to spear them.

Other names In French, marlin are *makaire*, in Italian *pesce lancia*, in Spanish *aguja*.

Buying Marlin are available in summer usually as loins and steaks. Try to buy cuts from smaller fish if possible. In the United States, marlin is almost always sold smoked rather than fresh.

Cooking Cook as swordfish, or cut into cubes and marinate to make ceviche.

Alternatives Swordfish, shark, and tuna can be used instead of marlin.

Sailfish *(Istiophorus spp)*

The sailfish resembles marlin, but looks even more spectacular. It has a beautiful streamlined body with a golden back spotted with blue, and a high, wavy blue dorsal fin which it unfurls like a sail to travel through the water at up to 96kph/60mph. Sailfish are tremendous fighters and will perform amazing aerial acrobatics when hooked.

Habitat As for marlin.

Other names Sailfish are *voilier* in French, *pesce vela* in Italian and *pez vela* in Spanish.

Buying Available in summer as loins and steaks. Buy cuts from smaller fish.

Cooking As for marlin.

Below: Marlin steaks

Orange roughy *(Hoplosthetus atlanticus)*

These ugly, but very delicious fish have orange bodies and fins and massive heads with conspicuous bony ridges and cavities. Although they are not large (the average weight is about 1.5kg/3–3½lb), they are always cleaned and filleted at sea. The pearly white flesh is similar in texture to that of cod, but has a sweet shellfish flavour.

Habitat For many years, orange roughy were believed to inhabit only Icelandic waters. In the 1970s, however, large numbers were found on the opposite side of the world in the deep waters around New Zealand and most of the world's stocks now come from there.

Other names In Australia roughy is sometimes known as sea perch. In French it is *hopostète orange*, in Italian *pesce specchio* (mirror fish); and in Spanish *reloj*.

Buying Orange roughy is available all year round, usually as fillets. If you are

Above: Orange roughy fillets

Above: Redfish

lucky enough to find fresh fish, you are in for a treat; most is frozen at sea.
Cooking Orange roughy holds together well when cooked, and its crab-like flavour marries well with other seafood. It can be used for soups and stews, and is good poached, pan-fried, roasted or steamed. It can also be dipped in batter or egg and breadcrumbs and fried.
Alternatives Cod, haddock or any firm white fish can be substituted.

Redfish/Ocean perch *(Sebastes marinus)*

These beautifully-coloured red fish were once the most important deep-sea fish, with vast catches being landed every year in northern fishing ports. As new varieties of fish have become widely available, however, their popularity has declined. Redfish can grow to about 5kg/11lb. The flesh is white and moist, with a sweet flavour.
Habitat Redfish inhabit the cold, deep waters of the Atlantic and Arctic Oceans. Related species *(Helicolenus* spp*)* are found in the Pacific.
Other names Redfish are known as ocean perch or Norway haddock. In French, they are *rascasse* (not to be confused with their relative, the scorpion fish); in Italian, *scorfano* (ditto); in Spanish, *gallineta nórdica*.
Buying Redfish are available all year round, sold whole or as steaks and fillets. A whole fish weighing 400–600g/14oz–1lb 6oz will feed one person; a 1–1.5kg/2¼–3½lb fish will feed two.
Cooking Redfish is suited to all cooking methods. It marries well with Mediterranean flavours and spices, and is very good baked in a creamy sauce.
Alternatives Hake or cod can be used instead of redfish.

Blackened Redfish

A favourite recipe from New Orleans is blackened redfish, a spicy Creole dish. Fillets of redfish are thickly coated on both sides with a mixture of dried herbs and spices – crushed peppercorns and coriander seeds, cayenne pepper, paprika, dried thyme and oregano – then seared on both sides in a very hot frying pan or griddle until the spice crust is blackened and charred and the fish is cooked. The contrast between the aromatic, crunchy crust and the tender white fish is delicious.
However, this fierce cooking method produces plenty of smoke, so remember to open the kitchen window.

Above: Swordfish

Stuffed Swordfish Rolls

Swordfish steaks can be pounded lightly between two sheets of clear film (plastic wrap) and used to roll around a stuffing. Choose 1cm/½in thick steaks and pound lightly using a meat mallet or rolling pin until they are only 5mm/¼in thick.

Make a stuffing using finely grated Parmesan cheese, breadcrumbs and chopped fresh herbs bound together with an egg. Roll the swordfish steaks around the stuffing and secure with wooden cocktail sticks (toothpicks).

Place the swordfish rolls in a shallow, heavy pan and pour over about 300ml/½ pint/1¼ cups well-flavoured tomato sauce. Bring to the boil, then reduce the heat and simmer for 30 minutes, turning once. Remove the swordfish rolls from the sauce and discard the cocktail sticks. Return to the sauce and serve hot.

Below: Swordfish steaks

Swordfish *(family Xiphiidae)*

Famous as both a culinary and game fish, swordfish differs from other billfish in having neither scales nor teeth. In all other respects, it is as dramatic and graceful to look at as it powers through the water with only the curve of its dorsal fin visible above the surface. Its long "sword" represents up to one-third of its total length and appears to be a powerful weapon, but no one is certain whether it is actually used to kill its prey, or merely to stun small fish. Swordfish can grow to an enormous size, sometimes weighing up to 600kg/1320lb. Their excellent white, meaty flesh is very low in fat and tends to dryness, so it needs careful cooking.

Habitat Swordfish are migratory fish which are widely distributed in warm, deep waters around the world. They occasionally migrate into northern European seas, but are more commonly found in the Mediterranean.

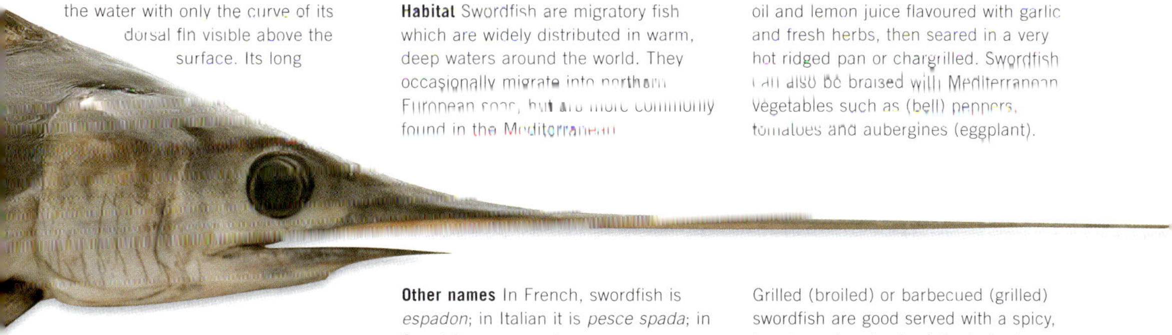

Other names In French, swordfish is *espadon*; in Italian it is *pesce spada*; in Spanish, *pez espada*.

Buying Fresh swordfish is available all year round, usually sold as steaks. Frozen fish is also available, but is best avoided.

Because swordfish is so meaty and substantial, 150–165g/5–5½oz will provide an ample portion for one person. Try to buy fairly thick steaks, as thinner ones are more apt to dry out during cooking.

Cooking It is essential not to let swordfish dry out during cooking, so baste it frequently with olive oil when grilling (broiling) or cooking on a barbecue and serve with a drizzle of olive oil or some herb butter. Swordfish makes excellent kebabs and can withstand a robust or spicy sauce. It is delicious marinated in a mixture of olive oil and lemon juice flavoured with garlic and fresh herbs, then seared in a very hot ridged pan or chargrilled. Swordfish can also be braised with Mediterranean vegetables such as (bell) peppers, tomatoes and aubergines (eggplant). Grilled (broiled) or barbecued (grilled) swordfish are good served with a spicy, tomato and coriander (cilantro) salsa.

Alternatives Shark and tuna can be used instead of swordfish.

Right: Garfish

Miscellaneous Fish

A few fish do not slot neatly into any obvious category. The only connection between the fish described in this chapter is that they are all exceptionally good to eat. They are a strange-looking collection, from the hideously ugly monkfish to the slimline but no more beauteous John Dory and the needle-like garfish with its unappealing phosphorescent green bones. Monkfish and John Dory are seldom sold whole, so there is an enormous amount of wastage, which sadly makes these gastronomically excellent fish extremely expensive to buy.

Garfish/Needlefish *(family Belonidae)*

There are more than fifty species of needlefish. Most inhabit tropical seas, but some, like the garfish, are found in cooler waters, and one species is found only in fresh water. Many people find the needle-like appearance of the garfish off-putting, despite (or perhaps because of) their vibrant silver and blue-green colouring and their long spear-like beaks.

Needlefish can grow to 2m/6½ft, but are more commonly up to 80cm/32in in length. Their bones are a phosphorescent green even when cooked (this coloration is completely harmless), and even their flesh has a greenish tinge, although this whitens on cooking. Despite these physical disadvantages, garfish are good to eat, with firm flesh from which the backbone can easily be removed, since you can hardly miss it.

Habitat Garfish inhabit the Atlantic Ocean and Mediterranean Sea, sometimes straying into fresh water. Other needlefish are found in the tropics, the Black Sea and the Pacific Ocean, while the Atlantic is also home to the saury, another sub-species. When they are frightened or being chased by predators, needlefish sometimes leap out of the water and launch themselves through the air like dangerous missiles. Unfortunate fishermen have been severely injured by their needle-sharp beaks.

Other names The French for garfish is *aiguille* or *orphie*, the Italian is *aguglia*, and the Spanish is *aguja*. Saury is also known as skipper, because of its habit of skipping over the water to escape from predators. Saury and needlefish are *balaou* in French; *costardello* in Italian and *paparda* in Spanish.

Buying Garfish are sold whole. If you do not want to serve the fish that way, ask the fishmonger to clean it and cut it into 5cm/2in chunks.

Cooking To cook a whole garfish, wash it thoroughly inside and out, rub the cavity with lemon juice, then curl the fish around and stick the pointed beak into the tail end so that it forms a ring. Brush with a marinade of olive oil, lemon juice, garlic and chopped parsley and grill (broil) or barbecue for about 15 minutes, basting frequently.

Chunks of garfish or saury can be coated in seasoned flour and pan-fried in butter and oil, or stewed with onions and tomatoes. They are gelatinous fish, so make excellent soups and stews or fish couscous.

John Dory *(family Zeidae)*

These fish were said to be sacred to Zeus, hence the Latin name of *Zeus faber*. The olive-brown bodies of these fish are so slim that they look almost like upright flat fish. Dories have extremely ugly faces and spiny dorsal fins from which long filaments trail. Their most distinguishing feature is a large black spot ringed with yellow right in the middle of their bodies; this is said to be the thumb print of St Peter. The story goes that the saint lifted a John Dory in the Sea of Galilee, leaving his thumb and finger prints on either side, and found in its mouth a gold coin, which he used to pay the unpopular tax collectors. This delightful fable is highly unlikely, since John Dory are not found in the Sea of Galilee, which is a freshwater lake. John Dory is also known as "St Peter's fish". Despite its unattractive appearance, John Dory is one of the most delicious of all fish, with firm, succulent white flesh which is on a par with turbot and Dover sole.

Habitat Dories are found in the Atlantic; those from American coastal waters are known as American dories *(Zenopsis ocellata)*, while fish from the eastern Atlantic, from Britain and Norway to Africa, and from the Mediterranean are European dories *(Zeus faber)*. Another species, from the southern hemisphere *(Zeus japonica)*, inhabits the Indo-Pacific oceans.

Other names The name John Dory is said to come from the French *jaune doré* (golden yellow), which describes

the golden sheen of very fresh dories. Another theory is that it comes from the Italian *janitore* (janitor). However, most countries celebrate the St Peter legend in describing the fish. The French call it *St Pierre*; the Italians *San Pietro*; the Spanish *pez de San Pedro*.

Buying Thanks to its large head, almost two-thirds of a dory's weight is wastage, which makes it a very expensive fish. Small dories weighing 1–2kg/2¼–4½lb are sold whole; a 1kg/2¼lb fish will feed two people. For fillets, buy the largest fish you can afford, otherwise the fillets will be too thin. Allow 150–200g/5–7oz per serving.

Cooking Whole fish can be grilled (broiled), braised, baked, steamed or poached; boiled dory served with mayonnaise is a popular Venetian and Catalan dish. Its succulent flesh goes well with Mediterranean flavours such as tomatoes, fennel, (bell) peppers, olives and saffron. Fillets can be cooked in the same way as sole, brill and turbot. They are superb served with a red wine, white wine or creamy sauce. Small fillets can be used in substantial fish soups such as bouillabaisse and *cacciucco*, or used in combination with other fish in a mixed grill.

Alternatives Brill, sole, halibut and turbot can be used instead of John Dory.

Bouillabaisse

One of the world's great classic dishes is the Provençal fish soup, bouillabaisse. More of a stew than a soup, this dish was originally cooked on the beach by fishermen, using those fish that had little market value, such as spiny scorpion fish. This fish is regarded as the most important ingredient in bouillabaisse. The soup can also contain monkfish, weaver fish, John Dory and other Mediterranean fish, plus small crabs and other shellfish, all cooked with tomatoes, potatoes and onions and flavoured with garlic, olive oil and saffron. Sometimes, the cooking liquid is served on its own as soup, accompanied by garlicky croûtons, with the fish served as a separate course. Nowadays, bouillabaisse is no longer an ad hoc fishermen's stew, but a hugely expensive treat served in the smartest restaurants.

Left: John Dory

Monkfish/Anglerfish *(Lophius piscatorius)*

This extraordinarily ugly fish has an enormous head equipped with a "rod and lure" to catch its food; hence its alternative name of anglerfish. It has a huge mouth fringed with lethally sharp teeth and a dangling "rod" (actually the first spine of the dorsal fin) on its nose. Its comparatively small body has brown, scaleless skin. On the fishmonger's slab, the only part of a monkfish you are likely to see is the tail, since the head is almost always removed because of its extreme ugliness, disproportionate weight and the fact that only the cheeks are worth eating. The tail is quite another matter; it is one of the finest of all fish, with a superb firm texture and a delicious sweetness, rather like lobster meat. In fact, some unscrupulous caterers have been known to pass off monkfish as fresh lobster. The only bone the tail contains is the backbone, which makes it especially easy to prepare and pleasant to eat. Monkfish liver, if you can find it, is considered to be a great delicacy.

Habitat Monkfish are found in the Atlantic and Mediterranean. They lurk on the sea bottom dangling their "fishing rods" to lure passing fish. They are extremely predacious and will sometimes swim up to the surface to prey on small birds.

Varieties The best monkfish are *Lophius piscatorius* and the similar *L. budegassa*, which is highly prized in Spain. American monkfish or goosefish *(L. americanus)* is considered inferior, while New Zealand monkfish *(Kathetostoma giganteum)* is truly a poor relation.

Other names Monkfish is also known as monk or angler. In French, it is *lotte* or *baudroie*, *crapaud* or *diable de mer* ("sea toad" or "sea devil"). In Italian, it is *coda di rospo* or *rana pescatrice* ("fishing frog"); in Spanish, *rape*.

Buying Monkfish is available all year, but is best in spring and summer before spawning. It is sold as whole tails, fillets or medallions. Generally speaking, the larger the tail, the better the quality; avoid thin, scraggy tails. For tails with the bone in, allow about 200g/7oz per person. A 1.5kg/3¼lb tail will serve four to six people. Ask the fishmonger to skin the tail and remove the membrane.

Below: Monkfish

Cooking One of the best ways to cook a whole monkfish tail is to treat it like a leg of lamb; tie it up with string, stud with slivers of garlic and thyme or rosemary leaves, anoint with olive oil and roast in a hot oven. This dish is known as *gigot de mer*. Monkfish can also be grilled (broiled), made into kebabs, pan-fried, poached and served cold with garlicky mayonnaise, or braised with Mediterranean vegetables or white wine, saffron and cream. It goes well with other seafood such as salmon, red mullet and shellfish, and is classically used in bouillabaisse and other fish soups. Thin fillets are delicious marinated in olive oil and lemon juice, then coated with flour and sautéed in butter.

Alternatives Nothing has quite the same nice firm texture as monkfish, but conger eel, John Dory, shark or cod can all be used instead.

Below: Monkfish cheeks, round nuggets of monkfish flesh, are sometimes available from specialist fishmongers.

Preparing monkfish tails

The tails are the best part of the monkfish. Because of their high water content, fillets should be cooked with very little liquid. They are easy to prepare.

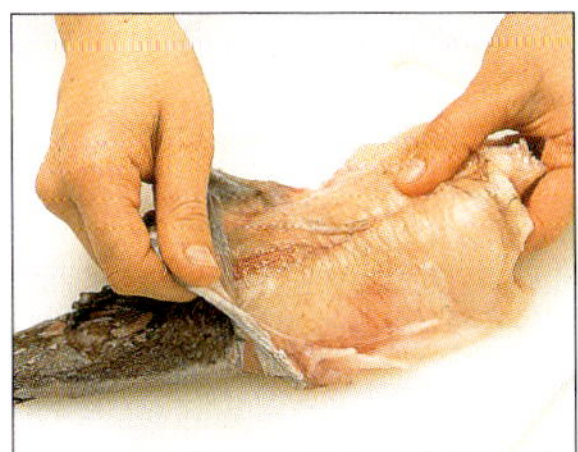

1 Grasp the thick end of the tail firmly with one hand and peel off the skin with the other, working from the thick to the thin end.

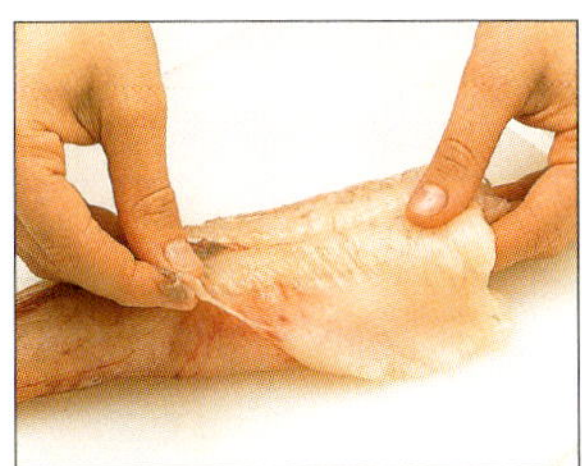

2 Carefully pull off the thin, dark or pinkish membrane.

3 Fillet the tail by cutting through the flesh on either side of the backbone with a sharp knife (there are no small bones). The bone can be used to make stock.

Above: Monkfish tail can be filleted and then roasted like a leg of lamb in a hot oven with olive oil, herbs and garlic.

Opah *(Lampris regius)*

Variously called moonfish, sunfish or mariposa, this beautiful, slim, oval fish has a steel blue back shading into a rose pink belly, with silver spots all over its body. It has glorious red fins, jaws and tail, and, unusually, is the only member of its family. It is toothless and scaleless, and can grow to an enormous size. Some specimens weigh over 200kg/440lb and measure more than 2m/6½ft, although the average weight of those caught is about 20kg/44lb. The flesh is salmon pink, with a flavour similar to tuna.

Habitat Opah are found in warm waters throughout the world, but so far only solitary specimens have been caught, and little is known about them.

Other names In French, opah is *poisson lune*, in Italian, *lampride* or *pesce rè*; in Spanish, *luna real*.

Buying Should you be lucky enough to find opah on the fishmonger's slab, ask for it to be cut into steaks or fillets.

Cooking Treat opah in the same way as salmon or tuna, taking great care not to overcook, and serve with a creamy sauce or mayonnaise.

Alternatives Tuna, shark or salmon.

Freshwater Fish

Nothing can beat the taste of a freshwater fish, caught, cleaned and cooked within a couple of hours of being pulled from the lake or river, especially if you have caught it yourself. The flesh of freshwater fish is fragile, so generally speaking, they are only really good to eat when they are absolutely fresh. Sadly, many of the world's rivers and lakes are so polluted that supplies of good, untainted fish are low, so many of the freshwater fish we buy are farmed. A major problem with all freshwater fish is that they often contain numerous small, very fine bones, which many people find off-putting. Apart from trout and zander, you will find few of the fish in this chapter on the fishmonger's slab; most are eaten by the anglers who catch them for sport. If you are lucky enough to be given a freshly caught fish, you will relish the experience.

Above: Red carp

Barbel *(Barbus)*

These "bearded" fish (the Latin name means "beard") live in fast-flowing rivers. They have brown backs, yellowish sides and white bellies. Barbel have rather tasteless flesh and are extremely bony, so they are not regarded as prime river fish. They are popular in the Loire and Burgundy regions of France, where they are typically poached or braised with a red wine sauce.

Cooking Barbel need strong flavours to enhance their intrinsic blandness. Small young fish can be grilled (broiled) and served with a well-seasoned butter; larger fish (up to 1.75kg/4–4½lb) are best used in a stew, such as *matelote*.

Bream *(Abramis brama)*

The appearance of bream, with their flat oval greenish-brown bodies covered with gold scales, is more attractive than their taste. The bony flesh is soft and bland, and can sometimes taste muddy, since bream live in the silt near the bottom of pools and slow-flowing rivers. Despite this, bream was an extremely popular fish in the Middle Ages. It was caught in fishponds around the country and used in numerous recipes.

Cooking Bream is best used in braised dishes and stews. It should be soaked in acidulated water for several hours before being cooked to eliminate the taste of silt.

Carp *(Cyprinus carpio)*

Carp are members of the minnow family, which contains more than 1500 different species. They are among the hardiest of all fish and can live for hundreds of years. Although they can grow to over 35kg/77lb, most of the carp caught weigh only about 2kg/4½lb; anything larger than this and the keen angler is in seventh heaven. There are three main varieties of carp; the very scaly common carp; the scaleless leather carp and the mirror carp,

Above: Bream

Right: Carp

> **Carp roe**
> This roe has a delicate texture and flavour and is much sought after in France, where it is poached and served in pastry cases or ramekins, or made into fritters, omelettes and soufflés. A classic dish is *tourte de laitances* (soft roe or milt), which combines puréed carp and pike with soft carp roes; the mixture is then baked in a puff pastry tart.

which has only a few large irregularly spaced scales that can easily be removed with a fingernail. All carp are handsome fish with compact, meaty flesh that varies in taste according to how the fish is cooked.

Originally natives of Asia, carp were highly prized by Chinese emperors as ornamental pets and as food; they frequently featured on festive banquets. Travellers along the Silk Routes brought them to Europe, where they proliferated in unpolluted fresh water and became a staple food of Eastern European Jews who lived far from the sea, but could cultivate carp in ponds. The tongues were regarded as a delicacy. Carp are still immensely popular in Chinese cuisine; the lips are considered the finest part, and they command high prices in restaurants.

Habitat In their natural state, carp like living in muddy and polluted waters, which they seem to prefer to clean streams and lakes. Nowadays, they are extensively farmed in clean ponds. In the wild, they are considered the most difficult of all freshwater fish to catch; despite being toothless, they are powerful fighters, and can demolish fishing tackle.

Other names In French, carp is *carpe*, in Italian and Spanish, *carpa*.

Buying Most commercially available carp are farmed and weigh 1–2kg/ 2¼–4½lb. A 2kg/4½lb fish will amply serve four. Look for a plump fish, preferably containing roe or milt, which is considered a delicacy. You may find live carp for sale; if so, ask the fishmonger to prepare the fish, gutting it and removing the bitter gall bladder from the base of the throat. If you buy a common carp, ask the supplier to scale it for you.

Preparing If you have to scale carp yourself, pour boiling water over the fish to loosen the scales before scraping them off.

Cooking Carp is a very versatile fish, which can be delicious if prepared with interesting flavourings. It can be filled with fish mousse or stuffing and baked, and is also excellent braised, opened out and grilled (broiled) or deep-fried, or poached in a sweet-and-sour sauce. A traditional German or Polish Christmas Eve dish is carp cooked in beer or white wine. Carp marries well with Asian flavours such as ginger, soy sauce and rice wine, and makes a good addition to fish stews and soups that have been well flavoured with plenty of tomatoes and garlic.

Carp can be cooked *au bleu*, as described in the chapter on Buying and Preparing Fish, or stewed with red wine and mushrooms to make a *meurette*. A classic dish is *carpe à la Juive*, a sweet-and-sour cold dish made with whole or thickly-sliced carp braised with onions, garlic, vinegar, raisins and almonds. When cooked, the whole fish (or a fish sliced and reformed into the original shape), is left to go cold in the sauce, which solidifies into a flavoursome jelly.

Alternatives Catfish, perch and zander can be substituted for carp.

Above: Catfish

Catfish *(Ictalurus spp)*

These fish take their name from the long whiskery barbels which help them to locate their prey in the muddy waters where they live. There are dozens of species, ranging from tiny fish to gigantic specimens weighing several hundredweight. Catfish are extremely hardy and can live out of

water for a considerable time. These fish are found all over the world, but the best fish for eating are the American species known as bullheads, which have firm, meaty, rather fatty white flesh and very few bones.
Habitat Catfish are bottom-living fish that feed on live and dead prey. They inhabit muddy waters throughout the world and are successfully farmed in the United States and Canada.
Other names In French, catfish is *silure*; in Italian *pesce gatto*; in Spanish *siluro*.
Buying Catfish is sold skinned and usually filleted. Its chunky flesh is filling, so 175g/6oz is ample for one person. Sniff the fish before you buy to make sure that it smells fresh and sweet. Avoid fillets from very large fish, which can be rather coarse.
Cooking The classic southern American cooking method for catfish is to coat it in cornmeal, deep-fry it and serve with tartare sauce. It can also be grilled (broiled) or pan-fried in butter, baked, or cooked like eel, whose flesh it resembles. The tough skin must be removed before cooking. Catfish makes a good addition to fish soups and stews with hearty flavourings such as garlic and tomatoes, or Caribbean spices.
Alternatives Any trout or perch recipe is also suitable for catfish.

Potted Char

When char proliferated in the Lake District in England in the 18th and 19th centuries, potted char became a popular delicacy. It was often sold in white china pots that were decorated with painted fish.

1 To make potted char, flake some leftover cooked fish, removing all skin and bones.

2 Weigh the boned fish. Melt an equal quantity of butter in a pan. Flavour the butter with nutmeg or mace and salt and pepper. Pour the butter over the flaked fish.

3 Put the prepared fish into ramekins. Cover with clear film (plastic wrap) and chill until the mixture is firm.

4 Seal with a thin layer of clarified butter and cover again; it will keep in the refrigerator for a week. Salmon, trout, whitefish and grayling can be prepared in the same way.

Char *(Salvelinus alpinus)*

These trout-like fish are members of the salmon family. They have attractive silvery-green sides dotted with pale spots, and rose-pink bellies.The white flesh is firm and succulent, with a delicate flavour. Sadly, these fish, which once inhabited cold lake waters in large numbers, are becoming increasingly rare in the wild. They can, however, be farmed successfully. The most common varieties are Arctic char, char, brook trout and lake trout. All can be distinguished from trout by their smaller scales and rounder bodies.
Habitat Arctic char are found in cold-water lakes in the United States, Canada, Britain and Iceland. Other species inhabit the lakes of northern France and the Swiss Alps. Brook and lake trout (which are actually char) live in the lakes of North America; Dolly Varden is found from western North America to the Asian coast.
Other names Char is *omble chevalier* in French, *salmerino* in Italian, and *salvelino* in Spanish.
Buying You may be lucky enough to find wild char in summer and early autumn (fall). Farmed Arctic char from Iceland and America are available all year round. Small fish are sold whole; larger char may be cut into steaks.
Cooking Char can be cooked in the same ways as trout. It can be poached, baked, braised, fried, grilled (broiled) or cooked on a barbecue.

Grayling *(Thymallus arcticus)*

A relative of trout, grayling is an attractive silvery fish with a small mouth and a long, high dorsal fin spotted with gold. These small fish (rarely weighing more than 1.2kg/2½lb) have firm white flesh with a delicate trout-like flavour; they are said to smell of thyme when first caught, but their scent and flavour is fleeting, so they should be eaten within hours of being caught.
Habitat Grayling are found in lakes from Europe to North America and the northern coasts of Asia, but as these become more polluted, their numbers are declining.

Other names In France, grayling is called *ombre*; in Italy *temolo*; in Spain *salvelino* or *timalo*.

Cooking Grayling must be scaled before cooking. Pour boiling water over the fish and scrape off the scales with a blunt knife. These fish are excellent brushed with melted butter and grilled (broiled) or pan-fried, preferably on the shore where they were caught. To enhance the faint aroma of thyme, put a few fresh thyme leaves inside the fish. They can also be baked and potted like char.

Gudgeon *(Gobio gobio)*

Small fish with large heads and thick lips, gudgeon have delicious, delicate flesh. They live at the bottom of lakes and rivers all over Europe and, freshly caught and crisply fried, gudgeon were once a common sight in cafés on riverbanks in France.

Other names Gudgeon are *goujon* in French, a name that has come to have a much wider application. Nowadays, deep-fried strips of any white fish are known as *goujons*.

Cooking Gudgeon must be gutted and wiped clean before cooking. Coat them in flour or very light batter and deep-fry until very crisp and golden. Sprinkle with salt and serve with lemon wedges.

Roach *(Rutilis rutilis)*

These members of the minnow family have greenish-grey skin and golden eyes. They can weigh as much as 1.75kg/4–4½lb. Their white flesh is firm and has quite a good delicate flavour. Their greenish roe (which turns red on cooking) is excellent to eat. Roach are not the easiest fish to eat, because they contain so many bones. Use tweezers to remove as many bones as possible before cooking.

Above: Roach

Habitat Roach inhabit sluggish waters in Europe and North America. Unusually for members of the minnow family, they are also sometimes found in brackish coastal waters.

Other names In French, roach is *gardon*, in Italian *triotto*, in Spanish *bermejuela*.

Cooking Small roach can be fried with other tiny fish to make a *friture*. If you can cope with the bones, larger fish can be grilled (broiled) or pan-fried, or baked in white wine.

Pike-Perch/Zander *(Stizostedion lucioperca)*

Zander (sometimes spelt sander) look like a cross between perch and pike, but have a much more delicate and appealing flavour than the latter. They have greenish-grey backs with dark bands, and hard, spiny dorsal fins and gills. Zander can grow quite large, sometimes weighing up to about 5kg/11lb, and fillets from fish this size are delicious and meaty. American pike-perch are known as walleye. Zander can be farmed successfully, and are cooked in the same way as perch.

Perch *(Perca fluviatilis)*

These beautiful fish have greenish-gold skins and coral fins. Their humped backs have a spiky dorsal fin, which makes them difficult to handle. Perch are highly prized for their firm, delicate white flesh and are considered to be one of the finest freshwater fish. They grow slowly and can reach a weight of 3kg/6½lb, but the average weight is only about 500g/1¼lb.

Above: Zander

Habitat Perch are found in sluggish streams, ponds and lakes throughout Europe and North America, and as far north as Siberia.
Other names The American yellow perch is very similar to the common variety and is often simply called "perch". In French, perch is *perche*; in Italian *pesce persico* ("Persian fish"); in Spanish, *perca*.
Cooking Unless perch are scaled the moment they are caught, this is a near impossible task. The only solution is to plunge the fish into boiling acidulated water for a few moments, then peel off the entire skin. Small perch can be pan-fried or deep-fried in oil. Fillets can be pan-fried and served with a buttery sauce such as hollandaise, a herbed béarnaise or *beurre blanc*. Larger fish can be baked, poached or grilled (broiled), or stuffed with seasoned breadcrumbs and braised in wine.

Pike *(Esox lucius)*

Described by Izaac Walton in *The Compleat Angler* as the tyrants of fresh water, pike are indeed fearsome creatures, with their elongated upturned noses and jaws equipped with hundreds of sharp teeth. Pike can grow to an enormous size, sometimes up to 1.5m/5ft. The larger the fish, the better the sport for anglers, but fish this size are not good to eat, as the flesh is dry and tough; the best size for eating is 1–2kg/2¼–4½lb. Pike have soft white flesh that is full of lethally sharp bones. Despite this, they are highly regarded in France. During the spawning season, pike roes can become toxic, so they should never be eaten.

In the Middle Ages, pike were highly prized in France and were cultivated in the fish ponds of the Louvre for the delectation of the king. Monks also farmed the fish to enjoy on meatless days. The voracious appetites of these fish earned them the nickname *grands loups d'eau* ("great water wolves").
Habitat Pike lurk in the streams and ponds of Eastern Europe, Britain and France. They are solitary, aggressive predators who like nothing better than to eat a duckling or water rat. Their close relations, muskellunge and pickerel, are found in the United States and Canada. Fish from fast-flowing streams taste better than those that are fished from ponds.
Other names The large American pike, muskellunge (a corruption of the French for "long mask", *masque allongé*) is also known as musky. In France, pike is called *brochet* (pickerel is *brocheton*); in Italy, *luccio (luccio giovane)*; in Spanish *lucio (lucio joven)*.

Above: Pike are large, fearsome-looking freshwater fish.

Pike Quenelles

The most famous recipe involving pike is *quenelles de brochet,* featherlight oval fish dumplings poached in water or fish stock. To make enough for four people, you need 450g/1lb skinned pike fillets, 4 egg whites, 475ml/16fl oz/2 cups chilled double (heavy) cream, salt, white pepper and nutmeg.

1 Purée the fish until smooth, adding the egg whites one at a time until completely amalgamated. Chill.

2 Whip the cream until stiff, then fold it into the fish mousse. Season and chill for at least an hour.

3 To cook, bring a pan of water or fish stock to a bare simmer. Shape the fish mousse into ovals using two tablespoons dipped in hot water and drop them into the trembling (not boiling) liquid, a few at a time.

4 Poach for about 10 minutes, until the quenelles are cooked through, but still creamy in the centre. Lift the cooked quenelles out of the water with a slotted spoon and drain on kitchen paper.

5 The quenelles are delicious served with a creamy sauce. Alternatively, cover them with a rich béchamel and bake *au gratin.*

Buying Pike are at their best in autumn (fall) and early winter. The best fish to buy are small whole fish weighing 1.2–1.7kg/2½–4½lb, which will feed four to six people. Large pike are sold cut into steaks; these can be tough.
Cooking Scale pike before cooking. Pour over a little boiling water – not too much, as the natural slime on the fish keeps it tender. Whole fish can be stuffed and baked or braised. Small pike are good cooked *au bleu*, or poached in a *court-bouillon* and served with *beurre blanc.* Pike is also traditionally cooked *à la Juive*, like carp. Sorrel, horseradish and similar sharp flavoured ingredients make excellent accompaniments. Fillets and steaks are best marinated for several hours before cooking to offset any dryness. They can then be pan-fried, braised or baked with white wine and served with a creamy shellfish sauce. They can be made into mousses, terrines and fish cakes.

Shad *(Alosa)*

The largest member of the herring family, shad is a migratory fish which spawns in fresh water. It resembles a fat silvery-green herring and can weigh up to 5kg/11lb. The three main species of shad are the allis, thwaite and American. They resemble fat silvery-green herrings. Although the white flesh has a fine, rich flavour, it is full of fine bones, which make eating the fish rather difficult. The best part of the shad is the large-grained roe, which has the wonderfully crunchy texture of caviar and is said by some to have aphrodisiac qualities.
Habitat Allis and thwaite shad are caught in the Loire and Garonne rivers in France during the spawning season. American shad is found all along the coast from Canada to Florida. During the 19th century, American shad were introduced to the Pacific and are now fished from Alaska to southern California. Pollution and overfishing for its highly-prized roe have decimated the numbers of shad in this region.
Other names In French, shad is *alose*, in Italian *alosa*, in Spanish *sábalo.*
Buying Shad are at their best in spring when they are full of roe. They are usually sold whole. A 1.5kg/3–3½lb fish will amply serve four. Ask the fishmonger to clean and scale the fish and persuade him, if you can, to bone it for you. Make sure you keep the roe, which is also good to eat.
Cooking Once the fish is cooked, make a series of incisions about 10cm/4in apart along its length and pull out as many bones as possible with your fingers. Whole shad can be stuffed with fish mousse (whiting is traditionally used), spinach or sorrel and baked, or poached and served on a bed of sorrel with *beurre blanc.* Fillets and steaks are good grilled (broiled), deep-fried or pan-fried and served with tomato sauce; check for small bones before serving. Shad roes are delicious briefly poached, then creamed with butter, cooked finely chopped shallots, cream, egg yolks and lemon juice. Serve them on toast as a rich appetizer or savoury, or use them to garnish a cooked shad.

Sturgeon *(family Acipenseridae)*

You have only to see a sturgeon to know that it is a "living fossil", part of a family of fish which were abundant in prehistoric times. The bodies of these long thin fish are armour-plated with several rows of bony scales that extend along their length. They have long, shovel-shaped snouts, with four whiskery barbels that are used for detecting food. Sturgeons are noted for their longevity, sometimes living more than 150 years, growing to a length of 9m/29½ft and weighing up to 1400kg/3080lb. There are about two dozen species of sturgeon, among them European, Beluga, Sevruga, Oscietra and the sterlet, which is found in Russian rivers. They have firm white flesh with a rich texture. Sturgeon can, however, be dry and somewhat indigestible. The fish is often sold smoked, but its real glory is its roe (caviar), the ultimate luxury food (see Dried and Salted Fish). In Russia, the bone marrow (*vésiga*) of the fish is dried and used in the classic recipe, *coulibiac.*

Habitat Sturgeon are migratory fish that live in the sea but swim into rivers to spawn. Once plentiful in European and American rivers, they are now found mainly in the rivers that feed the Black and Caspian Seas. Recently, they have been successfully farmed in France and California.

Other names In French, sturgeon is called *esturgeon*, in Italian it is *storione*, and in Spanish, *esturión*.

Buying Wild sturgeon is at its best in spring and early summer. Farmed fish is available all year round. It is sold as steaks or large cuts.

Cooking Sturgeon needs careful cooking to make it palatable, and should be marinated or barded with canned anchovy fillets to keep it moist. Its texture is similar to veal, and it is often cooked in the same ways, as breaded fillets or braised steaks. It can be poached in white wine (or, for a touch of luxury, champagne), or baked in a creamy sauce with onions. In Russia, sturgeon is traditionally poached with vegetables and served hot with tomato sauce, or cold with a piquant garnish of mushrooms, langoustines, horseradish, lemon, gherkins and olives. It can also be home-smoked very successfully.

Below: Sturgeon steaks

Above: Brown and rainbow trout

Tench *(Tinca tinca)*

This fat-bodied relative of the minnow has a coppery-green body covered with small scales and a thick coating of slime. Tench are hardy, fighting fish, which make great sport for anglers. They live in sluggish streams and have a tendency to taste muddy, but they make a good addition to a fish stew. They can also be baked or fried, and should be served with a robustly flavoured sauce to enliven the rather bland flesh. They must be scaled and thoroughly cleaned before cooking; scalding them with boiling water helps to remove the scales.

Trout *(family Salmonidae)*

The best-known of all freshwater fish, trout are popular with gourmets and fishermen alike. The two main species are brown trout *(Salmo trutta)* and rainbow trout *(Salmo gairdneri)*. Rainbow trout are probably the more familiar since they are extensively farmed and are available everywhere. They have silvery-green bodies with dark spots and a pinkish band along the sides. Wild fish have moist white flesh with a sweet flavour; farmed rainbow trout are often fed on a special diet to give the flesh a pink tinge, which is considered to be more appealing.

Brown trout come from cold mountain streams and lakes. They have coppery-brown skin dotted with red or orange and brown spots. Their flesh is a delicate pink and their flavour exquisite, but sadly they are seldom found in stores; to enjoy a fresh brown trout, you should befriend an angler.

Golden trout and coral trout are both farmed hybrid trout, with beautiful, vibrantly coloured skin. Their pinkish flesh is more like that of rainbow trout and tastes very similar.

Habitat Rainbow trout are native to America, but have been introduced to many other parts of the world. Brown trout are natives of Europe and have been introduced to America. Golden trout are not found naturally in the wild, but are increasingly farmed for their attractive coloration.

Other names In French, trout is *truite*, in Italian *trota*; in Spanish *trucha*.

Buying Trout are available all year round, usually farmed. Unlike many other fish, they are quite robust and freeze well, so frozen trout are perfectly acceptable. For fresh trout, look for a good coating of slime, bright clear eyes and red gills. Trout are almost always sold whole with the head on. They are very inexpensive, and you should allow one fish per person, unless they are very large.

Cooking Trout are arguably the most versatile of all fish and can be cooked in myriad ways. They are easy to eat, as the flesh falls away from the bone once cooked. The best way to cook a freshly-caught trout is *à la meunière*; dust it with flour, fry in clarified butter until golden brown, and season with lemon juice and parsley. Live trout can be cooked *au bleu*. Other cooking methods include poaching in *court-bouillon*, baking, braising, frying, grilling (broiling) and cooking on a barbecue. Trout marry well with many flavours, such as bacon, onions, garlic and mushrooms.

Left: Coral trout

In Normandy, they are often baked *en papillote* with apples, cider and cream. They are also excellent for home-smoking and make delicious mousses and terrines. A classic, if clichéd, recipe is trout with almonds (hazelnuts make good alternatives). If you find roes in your trout, these can be puréed, mixed with seasoned breadcrumbs and used as a stuffing for the fish.

Alternatives Almost any freshwater fish can be used instead of trout.

Whitefish *(family Salmonidae)*

Members of the salmon family, whitefish are silvery white in colour. They resemble trout, but have larger scales and smaller mouths. They live in cold, clear lochs and lakes in northern Europe and America. In Britain they are sometimes called vendace or powan. They have a pleasant texture and flavour, somewhere between trout and grayling, but not so fine as either.

Left: Golden trout are spectacular in appearance.

DRIED AND SALTED FISH

Since prehistoric times, the dehydrating effects of sun and wind have been used as a means of preserving fish almost indefinitely. Even today, in remote communities, long ropes strung with split and salted fish hung out to dry like washing are a common sight. Any fish can be dried in this way; before the days of frozen fish, fishermen would salt and dry whatever they had caught in their nets – cod, haddock, herring, mackerel and even freshwater fish such as eel, pike, salmon and sturgeon.

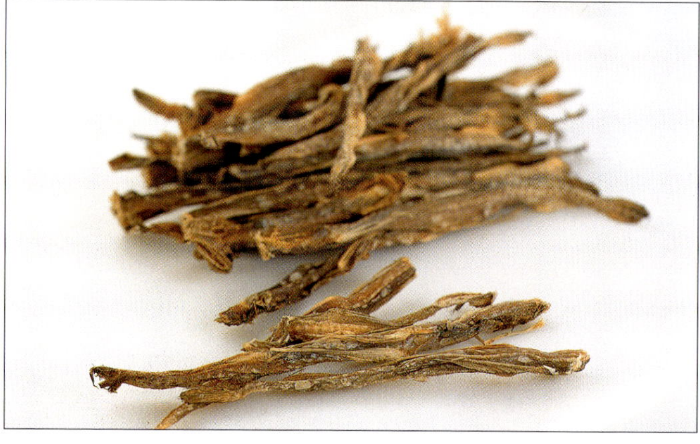

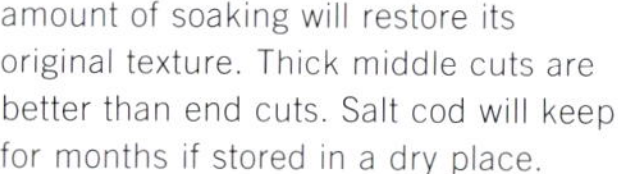

Above: Bombay duck

Dried/Salt cod and Stockfish

The most common commercially available dried fish is cod and its relatives (haddock, ling and pollack). When dried, these look – and feel – like old shoe leather, but once reconstituted in water, the flesh softens and tastes delicious when cooked. Depending on its country of origin, dried cod is known as *baccalà* (Italy), *bacalhau* (Portugal) and stockfish (Scandinavia, northern Europe, the Caribbean and Africa). Stockfish differs from other types of dried cod in that it is not salted before being dried. Whatever the type, dried cod must be soaked for many hours in fresh, cold water – sometimes for up to a couple of weeks – before it becomes palatable. Stockfish needs to be beaten with a rolling pin to tenderize it, and you may find you need a saw to cut it.

The world is divided between those who believe that the result is worth all this effort and those who detest salt cod in all its forms. The Portuguese boast that they have a different recipe for every day of the year. The Scandinavians and the northern Italians love salt cod, too, while the French pound it into a rich creamy mousse, *brandade de morue*, with lashings of olive oil and garlic.

Buying Depending on where you buy it, dried and salt cod may be split down the backbone or sold whole. Make sure you buy the best quality fish, or no amount of soaking will restore its original texture. Thick middle cuts are better than end cuts. Salt cod will keep for months if stored in a dry place.

Below: Salt cod

Preparing Salt cod needs less soaking than stockfish, but it still needs to be left to soften in a bowl of cold water for at least 24 hours. The best way to reconstitute it is to leave the bowl under a running tap (faucet); if this is not practical, change the water every 8–12 hours. Taste the fish before cooking to check that it is not too salty; if it is, continue to soak it.

Cooking Dried and salt cod can be poached or baked. Never cook it in boiling water, as it tends to toughen. It is a classic ingredient of Provençal *allioli*, a salad consisting of vegetables and hard-boiled eggs served with garlic mayonnaise. Olive oil complements it well. In Spain and Portugal, salt cod is often cooked with tomatoes, (bell) peppers, olives, onions and garlic. It marries well with potatoes and split peas in a stew, or on top of a mound of creamy mashed potatoes. Salt cod makes wonderful fish cakes, fritters and mousses.

Bombay duck

Quite why this dried form of a small transparent fish from the Indian sub-continent should be called Bombay

Above: Mojama

Above: Shark's fin

duck, no one knows for sure; it is possibly a corruption of the Bombay name for the fish, *bommaloe macchli*. As soon as the fish is caught, it is filleted and hung on cane frames to dry. Bombay duck is often served as an appetizer or used as a garnish for curries and rice dishes. Uncooked Bombay duck has an unpleasantly pungent smell which fades a little when it is grilled (broiled), but is intensified when it is deep-fried. When grilling (broiling), keep the heat low. It is ready when it is crisp and it curls at the edges. When cold, serve with drinks or crumble over curries or rice.

Mojama

Popular in Spain, Sicily and other countries with an Arabic influence, *mojama*, *mosciame* or *missama* is made from fillets of tuna that are salted, then dried in the sun for about three weeks. It is eaten as a snack with a glass of chilled fino sherry, or served on slices of baguette that have been rubbed generously with garlic and drizzled with olive oil.

Shark's fin

Dried shark's fin is highly prized in China, where it is served at banquets, either braised or as the central ingredient in an extremely expensive soup. The fins from the many species of sharks that inhabit the Indo-Pacific oceans are sun-dried and preserved in lime. In its dried state, shark's fin looks like a very bushy beard, but after long soaking it reconstitutes into a gelatinous, viscous mass with a texture resembling calf's foot jelly. It is highly nutritious and is eaten as a tonic.

SALTED FISH ROE

The best-known and most expensive salted fish roe is caviar, the eggs of the sturgeon. Other salted roes include grey mullet, cod, lumpfish and salmon. In Sweden, bleak roe is compressed into a form of caviar paste called *løjrom* or *kaviar*, which has a pretty orangey-pink colour. It tastes rather sweet, and is definitely an acquired taste.

Caviar

Made from sturgeon roe lightly cured with salt and borax, caviar is the most expensive luxury food in the world. It has a unique texture, and the tiny eggs burst on the roof of the mouth to release a salty liquid with an elusive, incomparable flavour. The three main types of caviar take their names from the species of sturgeon from which the eggs come. The rarest and most expensive is beluga, which comes from the largest fish; one beluga can contain over 50kg/110lb of roe. The dark grey eggs are quite large

Below, clockwise from bottom left: sevruga, oscietra and beluga caviar

and well separated. Oscietra is golden brown, with smaller grains and an oily texture, which many prefer to beluga. Sevruga is the cheapest caviar. It comes from the smallest and most prolific fish and has small pale greenish-grey grains with a markedly salty flavour. Arguably the best caviar of all comes from Iran; the finest is marketed as "Imperial caviar" and each can contains only the eggs from a single fish. The best caviar is "harvested" from fish that are just about to spawn; the eggs are very pale and full of flavour.

Each type of caviar is graded. The finest, malassol, is slightly salted. Second grade caviar is saltier and may be made from a mixture of roes. Inferior quality sevruga roe is pressed into a solid mass (pressed caviar), which squashes the eggs. It has a strong, salty taste and can be oily. It is fine for cooking, however, and has the advantage of being cheaper. The best caviar is always fresh; pasteurization will ensure that it keeps longer, but the quality will be compromised.

Despite its high price, caviar is so sought-after that the world's population of sturgeon is endangered almost to the point of extinction, due to overfishing, poaching and pollution. Sturgeon were once common in European rivers, but are now found almost exclusively in the Caspian Sea. Recently, however, the fish have been farmed successfully in France, so there may be some hope for the future of caviar.

Buying Never buy caviar that seems suspiciously cheap; it may not have been cured properly, or may have been made with damaged eggs. There is a huge illicit trade in second-rate caviar, which can taste unacceptably oily or salty. At worst, it might even poison you. You get what you pay for, so buy the best you can afford from a reputable dealer. Caviar should be kept in the refrigerator at 0–3°C/32–37°F; any warmer and it will become too oily. Once you have opened a can or jar of caviar, eat the contents within a week.

Above: Black and red lumpfish roe

Serving Caviar should be served chilled, preferably on a bed of crushed ice. Never serve or eat it with a silver spoon, as this will react with the caviar and give it a metallic taste. A proper caviar spoon is made of bone, but a plastic one would do at a pinch. Traditionally, caviar is served with *blinis* and sour cream. Chopped hard-boiled (hard-cooked) egg and onions make it go further. It is also delicious with toast and unsalted (sweet) butter. Some people believe that a squeeze of lemon enhances the flavour; others that it spoils the taste. Allow about 25g/1oz caviar per person as a first course. Or use a few grains as a garnish.

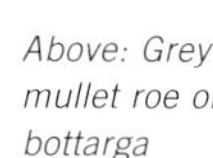

Above: Grey mullet roe or bottarga

Right: Trout caviar

Far right: Salmon caviar, which is also known as keta.

Lumpfish roe

Sometimes known as "mock" or Danish caviar, this is the roe of the arctic lumpfish, which is as unpleasant as its name. The tiny eggs are dyed black or orange-red and look pretty as a garnish for canapés. They can be eaten with sour cream and blinis, but bear no resemblance to real caviar. Lumpfish roe is sold in glass jars.

Grey mullet roe/Bottarga/Tarama

Dried grey mullet roe is a great delicacy and is very nutritious. The orange roe is salted, then dried and pressed. It is usually packed in a sausage shape inside a thin skin, which should be removed before the roe is used. Wrapped in clear film (plastic wrap), it will keep for several months. Grey mullet roe is the traditional ingredient of taramasalata, although smoked cod's roe is often used instead. In Mediterranean countries it is also known as bottarga or *poutargue*.

Salmon caviar/Keta

This is made from vibrant orange-pink salmon roe. The eggs are much larger than sturgeon caviar and have a pleasant, mild flavour and an excellent texture. They make an attractive garnish for fish pâtés and mousses, or can be eaten like caviar with sour cream and blinis. A squeeze of lemon enhances the flavour. The name *keta* comes from the Russian for chum salmon. Salmon caviar is sold in jars. Trout caviar is also available.

Pickled Fish

Pickling in vinegar or brine is another effective way of preserving fish. It is particularly well suited to oily fish such as herrings and eels.

Baltic/Bismarck herring

The herrings are split like kippers (smoked herrings) and marinated in white wine vinegar and spices. The fillets are layered with onion rings and carrot rounds for 24 hours. These are delicious with sour cream.

Maatjes herring

Fat young female herrings (the name means "maiden" or "virgin" in Dutch) are lightly cured in salt, sugar, spices

Below: Maatjes herring

Above: Baltic or bismarck herring

and saltpetre, which turns the flesh brownish-pink. In Holland and Belgium they are eaten with chopped raw onion. The Scandinavian equivalent is *matjes*. These have a stronger flavour and are generally eaten with sour cream and chopped hard-boiled egg.

Pickled herring

Herring fillets are marinated in vinegar and spices, then coated in a sour cream sauce.

Soused herring and Bratheringe

These marinated herrings are simple to prepare at home. In the German version, *bratheringe*, herring fillets are lightly floured and fried until golden, then steeped in a boiled marinade of vinegar, pickling spice and herbs. Soused herring are not fried first.

Below: Pickled herring

Rollmop Herrings

Like *ceviche*, rollmops are not cooked by heat, but by the action of vinegar. For four servings, halve 8 herring fillets lengthways and soak them for several hours in heavily salted water. Make a marinade by mixing about 600ml/1 pint/2½ cups vinegar with 2 bay leaves, 2.5ml/½ tsp coarsely crushed white peppercorns, 15ml/1 tbsp pickling spice and 1 sliced sweet onion in a pan. Bring to the boil, then leave until cold. Drain and dry the herring fillets. Slice a second sweet onion finely. Roll each herring fillet around a little sliced onion and some of the peppercorns and spices. Secure with a cocktail stick (toothpick) and pack tightly into a preserving jar. Pour over the marinade and leave for at least five days before eating.

Below: Rollmop herrings

Rollmops

These consist of herring fillets rolled up, skin side out, around whole peppercorns and pickling spice, and secured with wooden cocktail sticks (toothpicks). The rolls are marinated in white wine vinegar with onion slices and, sometimes, gherkins. Serve rollmops with rye bread and butter, or a cucumber salad with a sour cream and dill dressing.

Gravad lax/Gravlax

A wonderfully succulent Swedish speciality, *gravad lax* has achieved great popularity. It is fresh raw salmon fillet cured with dill, sugar, salt and coarse peppercorns. *Gravad lax* is widely available, often packed with a sachet of dill-flavoured mustard sauce, which makes the perfect accompaniment.

Jellied eels

Market stalls in Britain selling this traditional Cockney dish are becoming increasingly rare, but jellied eels are available frozen and in cans. Jellied eels are made by boiling pieces of eel in a marinade of white wine vinegar and herbs, then leaving them in the liquid with masses of chopped parsley until the mixture sets to a light jelly. Serve with thick slices of bread and butter.

Below: Jellied eels

Below: Gravad lax

Home-cured Gravad Lax

Although almost every supermarket sells ready-cured *gravad lax*, it is very easy to prepare at home. For eight people, you will need 1–1.2kg/2¼–2½lb absolutely fresh middle-cut salmon, boned and cut lengthways into two fillets. For the curing mix, mix together 30ml/2 tbsp coarse sea salt, 30ml/2 tbsp caster (superfine) sugar, 15–30ml/1–2 tbsp coarsely crushed peppercorns (black or white) and a good handful of fresh dill, chopped. Lay one salmon fillet skin side down in a non-metallic dish. Cover with a generous layer of the curing mix. Lay the second fillet on top, skin side up, and sprinkle on the remaining curing mix. Cover with clear film (plastic wrap). Place a wooden board slightly larger than the fish on top and weight down with heavy cans or weights. Leave in the refrigerator for at least 72 hours, turning the salmon every 12 hours and basting it with the juices that have oozed out. To serve, slice the *gravad lax* on the diagonal, a little thicker than you would for smoked salmon. Serve with a mustard and dill sauce.

Canned Fish

This is a very useful staple ingredient. While it never has the subtle texture and flavour of fresh fish, canned fish can be excellent in its own right and is invaluable for salads and sandwiches.

Anchovies

Fillets of this fish are canned in oil (olive oil is best) in small oblong cans or bottled in jars. The salty fillets are a staple ingredient of *salade niçoise* and *tapenade* (olive and anchovy paste), and are used as a topping for pizzas and *crostini*. They can be mashed into butter as a topping for grilled (broiled) fish, or chopped and mixed into tomato sauces. Anchovies enhance the flavour of many non-fish dishes (roast lamb, for example) without making them taste fishy. Once opened, anchovies perish quickly, so try to use the whole can or jar at once. Any leftovers should be submerged in oil and kept for only a day or two. As an alternative to canned anchovies, try salted anchovies, which are packed in barrels with masses of salt and cured for several months. Rinse well before using.

Pilchards

These fish are large, older sardines. They lack the subtle flavour of their younger siblings, so are usually canned in tomato sauce.

Salmon

Canned salmon is quite different in flavour and texture from fresh fish, but is useful to have in the pantry. It is richer in calcium than fresh salmon, because the bones are softened during the canning process and can easily be eaten. Canned salmon was once the mainstay of sandwiches, salads, fish cakes and fish pies, but it has been overshadowed by inexpensive farmed fresh salmon. Canned salmon is available in several grades, from the cheapest pink chum salmon to the best-quality wild red Alaskan fish, which has a better flavour and texture. Canned salmon is good for making mousses, soufflés and fish cakes.

Above: Canned anchovies

Left: Sardines in olive oil, which were the first fish to be canned.

Sardines

These were the first fish to be canned; in 1834, a canning factory opened in Brittany to process the sardines that abounded on the Breton coast. For years, tiny Breton sardines were the best, but these fish have all but disappeared, and most sardines canned in France now come from North Africa. Large numbers of sardines are also canned in Spain and Portugal. The finest sardines are fried in olive oil before canning, a time-consuming process that makes them expensive. Most sardines are beheaded and gutted before being packed raw, complete with backbones, in groundnut (peanut) or olive oil. Inferior or damaged fish are packed in tomato or mustard sauce. Sardines in olive oil are the best; the more expensive varieties are left to mature for at least a year before being sold to soften the bones and mature the flavour. The best way to enjoy them is to serve them whole on hot toast. They can also be mashed with lemon juice and cayenne pepper to make a pâté, stuffed into hard-boiled eggs or made into fresh or toasted sandwiches.

Tuna

In recent years, canned tuna has received a bad press because dolphins were often caught in the tuna nets and slaughtered unnecessarily. Nowadays, tuna canners have become more ecologically aware and most tuna is line-caught. The best canned tuna is the pale albacore, which is usually canned in one solid piece. Cheaper varieties such as skipjack and yellowfin are often sold as chunks or flaky broken pieces. Tuna comes packed in olive oil (the best), vegetable oil or brine, which is healthier and lighter.

Canned tuna is versatile and can be served with pasta, used in sandwiches and salads, or made into a pâté or fish loaf. It is used in the classic Italian dish *vitello tonnato* – loin of veal coated in a thick tuna-flavoured mayonnaise.

Above: Canned tuna

SMOKED FISH

Another ancient and traditional way of preserving fish is smoking. Today it is used less for preserving and more for imparting a unique flavour. There are two methods of smoking fish, cold and hot smoking, which give very different results. For both methods, the fish must first be salted in dry salt or brine. They are then smoked over different types of wood, which impart their distinctive flavour to the fish. Every smokery produces fish with a different texture and taste; it is a matter of individual choice which appeals to you.

COLD-SMOKED FISH

A high degree of skill is required when cold smoking to get the flavour and texture right. It is done at a temperature of 30–35°C/86–95°F, which cures but does not cook the fish. Some cold-smoked fish such as salmon, halibut and trout are eaten raw; others such as kippers (smoked herrings) and haddock are usually cooked, although they can be marinated and eaten as they are.

Smoked salmon

The best-loved of all smoked fish, smoked salmon is made by brining the fish, then dry curing it in sugar with flavourings such as molasses or whisky, and smoking it over wood chips (usually oak). Different wood chips give different flavours; some Scottish and Irish salmon is smoked over a fire made from old whisky barrels, which impart the flavour of the spirit. Depending on the strength of the cure, the type of wood used and the smoking time, smoked salmon can vary in colour from very pale pink to deep brownish-red. The best smoked salmon has a fairly mild flavour and a moist, succulent texture.

Below: Smoked halibut

Above: Smoked salmon

Buying Smoked salmon is usually sold ready-sliced, with the slices separated by sheets of transparent paper. Whole sides are sliced, and the slices are reassembled to restore the original shape of the fillet. Avoid buying sliced fish that is not layered with paper, as the slices stick together. The thinner the salmon is sliced the better; thickly-sliced fish can be coarse. Whole sides are sometimes sold unsliced; these are cheaper, but you need an extremely sharp flexible knife and a degree of skill to slice the fish yourself. The most expensive smoked salmon is made from wild fish, but good-quality farmed fish give excellent results, and it can be difficult to distinguish between the two.

Freshly sliced smoked salmon is best, but vacuum packs are better value and perfectly acceptable when purchased from a reliable supplier. Frozen smoked salmon is also available and can be used at a pinch. Smoked salmon trimmings are much cheaper than slices and are perfect for mousses, pâtés and omelettes. In Jewish delicatessens, you will find *lox*, a heavily-cured salmon with a deep reddish-gold colour.

Serving Top-quality smoked salmon should be eaten just as it is, served with thinly sliced brown bread and butter. Cheaper salmon can be served in traditional Jewish style, with cream cheese as a topping for bagels (add some thin rings of raw onion, if you like), or in sandwiches. Smoked salmon makes a delicious salad. Scraps can be stirred into omelettes, quiches or flans, mixed into pasta, puréed to make mousses, or mashed into hard-boiled egg yolks and piled back into the whites. If you are slicing smoked salmon yourself, slice thinly across the grain, working from head to tail. You will need a very sharp, flexible knife with a long blade.

Cold-smoked trout

A cheaper alternative to smoked salmon is cold-smoked trout, which looks like salmon, but has a more delicate flavour. It can be eaten in the same way as smoked salmon, with thinly sliced brown bread and butter.

Smoked halibut

Sold thinly sliced like smoked salmon, smoked halibut has translucent white flesh and a very delicate flavour. It makes an excellent addition to a plate of assorted smoked fish, or can be used like smoked haddock. The flavour can be enhanced with a mild, creamy horseradish sauce.

Above: Smoked haddock fillets

Above: Finnan haddock

Smoked sturgeon

This smoked fish has pale pinkish flesh with a rich flavour and a succulent texture. Like smoked salmon, it should be thinly sliced across the grain. As it is a luxury fish, it should be treated like the very best smoked salmon and served in the same way. Eat it with thinly-sliced brown bread and butter.

Below: Smoked sturgeon

Smoked haddock

There are various forms of smoked haddock, from fluorescent dyed yellow fillets to pale naturally cured fillets and finnan haddock or "haddie", which are split and look like pale golden kippers (smoked herrings). It is now known that the artificial dyes used to colour smoked haddock can be carcinogenic; dyed fillets are also often artificially flavoured with chemicals which simulate the effect of smoking, so avoid these and enjoy natural pale beige fillets.

Finnan haddock or "haddie"

These distinctively pale, whole split haddock (with the bone left in) are named after the Scottish village of Findon where the special smoking process originated. The process gives the fish a beautiful pale corn colour and a subtle smoked flavour. Finnan haddock can be used in any smoked haddock recipe, but must be boned and skinned after cooking. They are delicious served topped with a poached egg.

Glasgow pales

Similar to finnan haddock, Glasgow pales are lightly brined and smoked, resulting in a very delicate flavour.

Buying Avoid buying dyed smoked haddock whose only, dubious merit is that it adds colour to fish pies and similar dishes. Undyed smoked fillets are fine for such dishes, but for plain grilled (broiled) or poached haddock, you cannot beat finnan haddock.

Cooking Smoked haddock is succulent and delicious. It is usually eaten hot, but fillets can be thinly sliced and marinated (a splash of whisky works wonders) and eaten raw as an appetizer. Smoked haddock can be grilled (like kippers) or poached in milk or water. Serve it with butter or topped with a poached egg, or *à la florentine* on a bed of creamed spinach. A classic Scottish dish is ham 'n' haddie, in which finnan haddock is fried in ham fat and topped with fried ham.

Smoked haddock is used in another Scottish dish, cullen skink, a substantial chowder. It makes excellent mousse or pâté, and also features in kedgeree and omelette Arnold Bennett, a sumptuous omelette oozing with cheese, cream and smoked haddock.

Left: Kippers

Smoked herrings

Kippers

These are made by briefly brining split herrings, then hanging them up in pairs and smoking over oak fires for 4–18 hours. Dye is often added to the brine, resulting in deep reddish-brown kippers, but the best (notably Manx and Loch Fyne kippers) are undyed. Kippers can be unpopular because they have so many bones, but these are easy to deal with once you know how.

Buying Look for the plumpest kippers you can find; lean kippers can be dry. As a rule of thumb, the darker the fish, the poorer the quality. Always buy undyed kippers if possible. Frozen boil-in-the bag kipper fillets are convenient, boneless and odour-free, but they have a flabby texture and insipid taste, and are really hardly worth eating.

Cooking Many people are nervous about cooking kippers because of the smell. To avoid any unpleasant odour, put them head-down into a tall jug (pitcher), pour over boiling water and leave to stand for 10 minutes, by which time the kippers will be cooked. If you serve kippers often, keep a jug (pitcher) especially for cooking them. They can also be microwaved and are good grilled (broiled) or shallow fried in butter. They make a delicious breakfast dish topped with a poached egg. Poached kippers make excellent mousse and pâté. Raw kippers can be marinated and served as an appetizer.

Bloaters

Herrings that are left ungutted before being briefly salted, then smoked for 12 hours, are called bloaters. The guts impart a slightly gamey flavour and the enzymes they contain cause the herring to become bloated during smoking. Because they are not gutted, bloaters do not keep as well as other smoked herring and should be eaten within a few days. Always gut them before serving. Despite their unattractive name, they are quite pleasing to look at, with silvery skin and moist flesh.

Other varieties *Harengs saurs* are a speciality of Boulogne; they are even more bloated than English bloaters. The most bloated of all are the Swedish *surströmming*. Like *harengs saurs,* they are traditionally eaten with potatoes.

Cooking Bloaters can be eaten as they are in salads and sandwiches. They can also be mashed into a paste with lemon juice and cayenne pepper or grilled and served with butter. To skin bloaters, pour over boiling water and leave for 2 minutes, then peel off the skin.

Below: Bloaters

Boning cooked kippers

1 Lay the kipper on a plate, skin-side up. Run a knife point around the edge to lift up the skin.

2 Run the knife point down the backbone and eat the flesh that lies on top of the fine bones.

Above: Smoked eel fillets

HOT-SMOKED FISH

Fish that are cured or hot-smoked at a temperature of 80–85°C/176–185°F, which simultaneously cooks and cures them, need no further cooking. Trout, mackerel, eel and herrings can all be hot-smoked. Recently it has become fashionable to hot-smoke salmon, producing a very different flavour and texture from that of salmon that has been cold-smoked.

Arbroath smokies

These hot-smoked haddock have been beheaded and gutted but left whole. They have deep golden skin and soft pale gold flesh with a more delicate flavour than cold-smoked haddock. In their native Scotland, they are a favourite breakfast or supper dish. Smokies are sold whole, so ask the fishmonger to split them open for you. Grill (broil) gently and serve with plenty of butter. When mashed with butter and lemon juice, Arbroath smokies make a delicious pâté.

Below: Arbroath smokies are always sold in pairs, tied with string.

Below: Smoked eel

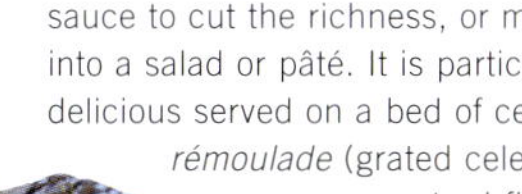

Smoked eel

This fish has a very rich, dense texture and can only be eaten in small quantities. The skin, which is easily removed, is black and shiny, and the flesh has a pinkish tinge. The eel can be served on its own as an hors d'oeuvre, with horseradish or mustard sauce to cut the richness, or made into a salad or pâté. It is particularly delicious served on a bed of celeriac *rémoulade* (grated celeriac in a mustard-flavoured mayonnaise). Smoked eel also makes a good addition to a platter of mixed smoked fish.

When buying smoked eel, check that the skin is shiny and has not dried out. For an ample serving for one, you will need about 90g/3½oz.

Brisling, Sild and Sprats

Not to everyone's taste, these small, hot-smoked herring with rich oily flesh are usually skinned and filleted and served cold as an appetizer with brown bread and butter. They can also be brushed with melted butter and lightly grilled (broiled), served hot with toast.

Below: Hot-smoked sprats

Above: Buckling

Above: Smoked trout fillets

Buckling

These are large, fat ungutted herrings with a rich flavour. They are best eaten cold with bread and butter, but can be mashed into a paste or grilled (broiled) and served with scrambled eggs.

Smoked mackerel

This has a rich flavour and a succulent velvety-smooth texture. The fillets are sold loose or pre-packed. They are sometimes coated in a thick layer of crushed peppercorns. Smoked mackerel can be eaten cold in a salad, or with horseradish sauce and lemon. It makes an excellent pâté and can be flaked and added to an omelette or quiche. Try it instead of smoked haddock in a kedgeree. Allow one fillet per person. To skin smoked mackerel, lay the fish on a board, skin side up. Starting at the tail end, peel back the skin towards the head. Pull away any fins together with their bones.

Smoked trout

Among the finest of all hot-smoked fish, trout should be plump and moist, with a beautiful golden-pink colour. The flesh has a delicate flavour and is less rich than smoked herring or mackerel. The best smoked trout is first brined, then gutted and smoked over birch with the addition of a little peat for a smokier flavour. Smoked trout is usually sold as skinned fillets, but you may occasionally find them whole, with the head on. Skin them like smoked mackerel. Smoked trout is delicious served on its own with dill or horseradish sauce. It can be made into mousses or pâté and is also good in salads, omelettes and flans. Allow one fillet per person as an appetizer; two as a main course.

Above: Smoked mackerel fillets

Below: Smoked sea trout

Below: Smoked mackerel

Fish Sauces and Pastes

For centuries, people have produced fish sauces made by fermenting whole fish or various parts, including the entrails, into a savoury, salty liquid to flavour and enhance fish dishes. The Romans' favourite condiment was *garum*, a pungent, evil-smelling sauce obtained by soaking pieces of oily fish and their guts in brine flavoured with herbs. Similar sauces exist today, notably in the Far East. The area around Nice also boasts *pissalat*, a sauce made from fermented anchovies. Don't be confused by the term "sauce"; these are flavourings or condiments, not to be served on their own.

Anchovy essence (paste)

Salted anchovies are processed into a thick, rich pinkish-brown sauce with an intensely salty flavour. A few drops will enhance the flavour of almost any savoury dish, but anchovy essence (paste) must be used sparingly, or it will overpower the other ingredients.

Thai fish sauce/Nam pla

Almost unheard of in the West a few years ago, *nam pla* is now an essential ingredient in every adventurous cook's pantry. It is a staple ingredient in all Far Eastern cooking; in Vietnam, it is called *nuoc cham*. The pungent, salty brown liquid is produced by packing small fish such as anchovies in brine in barrels and leaving them to ferment in the hot sun for several months. Curiously, the resulting sauce does not taste of fish; it is more like a very intense soy sauce. It can be added to any savoury dishes, or mixed with flavourings such as garlic, lime juice and chilli to make a dipping sauce, or can be used to add flavour to salad dressings. The colour of fish sauce should be a clear amber; if it is dark brown it will taste too fishy.

Right, from left: Thai fish sauce Worcestershire sauce and anchovy essence

Above: Shrimp paste

Shrimp paste

A speciality of Malaysia and Indonesia, shrimp paste is made from salted, fermented shrimp. This powerful smelling paste, called *blachan, terasi* or *belacan*, is sold in blocks and is mixed with other ingredients to make a flavouring for stir-fries, soups and other savoury dishes.

Worcestershire sauce

Anyone who has tasted this spicy sauce may be surprised to learn that it contains anchovies. Originally produced in India, the precise ingredients of Worcestershire sauce remain a closely-guarded secret, but they include malt and spirit vinegar, molasses, tamarind, garlic, onions and spices as well as anchovies.

Worcestershire sauce gives a lift to any savoury dish and can be used sparingly to enliven a marinade for fish or meat. It is also essential for making a Bloody Mary cocktail. The "original and genuine" Worcestershire sauce made by Lea and Perrins is superior to all its imitators.

Crustaceans

All crustaceans belong to the enormous family of decapods, ten-limbed creatures that are believed to be descendants of invertebrates that lived on the earth over 200 million and possibly up to 390 million years ago. One can only marvel at the imagination of the first person who thought of eating a crustacean. These curious-looking creatures with their hard carapaces and spidery limbs hardly look like the most attractive of foods, but the sweet flesh concealed within the shell is delicious.

Crabs and Lobsters

CRABS

There are dozens of varieties of crab, ranging from hefty common crabs that will make a meal for several people, to tiny shore crabs that are good only for making soup. They are great wanderers, travelling hundreds of miles in a year from feeding to spawning grounds. As a result, crabs are often caught in baited pots sited on the sea bed far from the shore. As their bodies grow, crabs outgrow their shells and shed them while they grow a new carapace. At first the new shells are soft. These "soft-shell" crabs are a delicacy and can be eaten shell and all. Female crabs are known as hens. They have sweeter flesh than the males, but are smaller and their claws contain less flesh.

Below: Blue crabs

Above: Common or brown crab

Right: Soft-shell crabs

Other names In French, crab is *crabe*, *tourteau* (common edible crab) or *araignée* (spider crab). In Italian, *granchio* or *granseola*; in Spanish: *cangrejo* or *centolla*.

Blue crab *(Callinectes sapidus)*

These crabs have steely-grey bodies and bright, electric blue legs and claws. They are found in American waters and are prized for their white meat.

Soft-shell crabs are blue crabs that have shed their hard carapaces, leaving them deliciously tender, with sweet creamy flesh. They are extremely delicate and do not keep or travel well, so they are generally sold frozen, although you may find fresh soft-shell crabs in the United States in the summer months.

Common edible crab/Brown crab *(Cancer pagarus)*

The bodies of these large brownish-red crabs can measure well over 20cm/8in. They have big, powerful claws that can deliver an extremely nasty nip, but they contain plenty of tasty meat. Common edible crabs are found on Atlantic coasts and parts of the Mediterranean.
Cooking These are the perfect crabs for boiling to serve cold with mayonnaise. The claws contain plenty of firm meat. After cooking, this can be removed from

Below: Spider crab

the shell in one piece, marinated in a dressing containing Worcestershire sauce and Tabasco and served as a cocktail snack. The claw meat is also delicious deep-fried. The liver and roe of these crabs are also delicious.

Dungeness/California crab *(Cancer magister)*

These trapezium-shaped crabs are found all along the Pacific coast, from Mexico to Alaska. They are very similar to common edible crabs and can be cooked in exactly the same way.

King crab *(Paralithodes camtschiatica)*

Looking like gigantic spiny spiders, king crabs are hideous to behold, but very good to eat. Their very size is awe-inspiring; a mature male king crab can weigh up to 12kg/26½lb and measure 1m/39in across. Their triangular bodies are bright red, with a pale creamy underside. Every part tastes good, from the body meat to that from the narrow claws and long, dangly legs.

Buying Only male king crabs are sold; they are much larger and meatier than the females. Cooked legs are available frozen, and king crab meat is frequently canned. Unlike most crab meat, canned king crab is of excellent quality and highly prized. The best comes from Alaska, Japan and Russia, where it is sold as Kamchatka crab.

Snow crab *(Chionoetes spp)*

Also known as queen crabs, these crabs from the north Pacific have roundish pinkish-brown bodies and exceptionally long legs. The delicious, sweet flesh is difficult to remove from the body, but the claw meat is more accessible. Snow crab meat is usually sold frozen or canned.

Spider crab *(Maia squinado)*

These alarming-looking crabs have spiny shells and long slender legs, which give them the appearance of enormous reddish-pink spiders; hence their alternative name of "sea spider". Those found along the Atlantic coasts measure about 20cm/8in across, but the giant species, found in the waters around Japan, measures up to 40cm/16in, with a claw span of almost 3m/9¾ft – a truly terrifying sight for arachnophobes.

Stone crab *(family Lithodidae)*

Similar in appearance to king crabs, stone crabs live at great depths. They have a superb flavour, but are usually sold frozen or canned rather than fresh.

Below: King crab claws

Above: Swimming crabs

Swimming crab *(family Portunidae)*

The main distinguishing feature of these crabs is their extra pair of legs, shaped rather like paddles. Among the many species of swimming crabs are mud or mangrove, shore and velvet crabs. Shore crabs are eaten in Italy in their soft-shelled state; they also make delicious soup. Mud crabs, with their excellent claw meat, are popular in Australia and South-east Asia.

Cooking Crab can be cooked in a multitude of ways. The sweet, succulent meat is rich and filling, so it needs a light touch when cooking; refreshing flavours suit it better than creamy sauces. Picking it out of the shell is hard work, but the result is well worth the effort. Recipes for crab meat include devilled crab (where the meat is removed from the shell and cooked with mustard, horseradish, spices and breadcrumbs); crab mornay, in which the meat is combined with a Gruyère cheese sauce enriched with sherry and mushrooms, and potted crab. The flesh marries well with clean Asian flavours such as lime juice, coriander (cilantro) and chilli; combined with these, it makes the perfect summer salad. Crab meat is perfect for fish cakes such as Maryland or Thai crab cakes. It also makes excellent soup; a classic Scottish dish is *partan bree*, a creamy crab soup made with fish stock, milk and rice.

In the shell, crab can be boiled and served with mayonnaise, steamed with aromatics or baked with ginger and spring onions (scallions).

Soft-shell crabs are usually lightly coated in flour and deep-fried. A Venetian speciality is *molecchie fritte;* the crabs are soaked in beaten egg before being fried. In China, soft-shell crabs are served with a garnish of chilli or ginger. They can also be sautéed in butter and sprinkled with toasted almonds, or brushed with melted butter and lemon juice, then tossed lightly in flour before grilling (broiling).

Crawfish *(Palinurus vulgaris)*

Crawfish are similar to lobsters, except that they have spiny shells and no claws. They are variously known as spiny lobsters, rock lobsters, langouste and crayfish (but must not be confused with freshwater crayfish). Crawfish are found on the rocky sea bed in many parts of the world. The colour of their shells varies according to where they come from: Atlantic crawfish are dark reddish-brown; those from the Florida coast are brown with pale spots; warm-water varieties can be pink or bluish-green. All turn pink or red when cooked. Crawfish have dense, very white flesh, similar to that of lobster, but with a milder flavour. Those from the Atlantic are the finest and sweetest. Crawfish from warmer waters can tend to be a little coarse.

Other names In France, crawfish are called *langouste*; in Italy they are *aragosta*; in Spain *langosta*.

Buying Crawfish are generally sold cooked. Females have the better flavour, so look for the egg sac underneath the thorax. Because there is no claw meat, allow one 450g/1lb crawfish per person. Florida crawfish are often sold frozen as "lobster" tails.

Cooking Cook as lobster. Crawfish benefit from spicy seasonings and are excellent in Asian recipes.

Crayfish *(Astacus astacus)* and yabby *(Cherax)*

Crayfish are miniature freshwater lobsters, which grow to a maximum length of 10cm/4in. The exception is a species found in Tasmania, which can weigh up to 6kg/13lb. Crayfish have a superb flavour and, whatever their colour when alive, turn a glorious deep scarlet when cooked. Over three hundred species are found in well-oxygenated streams throughout Europe, America and Australia, although most of the European species have been wiped out, largely through pollution and disease. Crayfish can be farmed successfully; unfortunately, the most prolific variety are the voracious American signal crayfish; these are prone to a killer disease, which they pass on to wild native crayfish, resulting in near-extinction.

Other names The most commonly available crayfish are the European, the red-claw, the American signal, the red Louisiana swamp, the greenish Turkish crayfish, the Australian yabby and the large marron, which is a deep purplish-grey colour. In France, crayfish are called *écrevisse*; in Italy, *gambero di fiume*; in Spain, *cangrejo de rio.*

Buying Fresh crayfish should be bought alive. There is a lot of wastage, so allow 8–12 crayfish per serving. Keep the shells to make stock, soup or sauces. Frozen crayfish are also available. These are fine for made-up dishes, but are not worth eating on their own.

Cooking Crayfish feature in many luxurious dishes, including bisque (a rich creamy soup), sauces and mousses. They are superb poached in a court-bouillon for about 5 minutes and served cold with mayonnaise or hot with lemony melted butter. Only the tail and claw meat is eaten; the head is often used as a garnish. The cleaned heads and shells can be used to make a shellfish stock or soup.

Below: Crayfish are tiny freshwater lobsters; there are hundreds of species.

Langoustines/Dublin Bay prawns/Scampi

(Nephrops norvegicus)

Smaller relatives of lobsters, langoustines have smooth-shelled narrow bodies with long thin, knobbly claws. They are salmon pink in colour. The largest can measure up to 23cm/9in, but the average length is about 12cm/4½in. Langoustines were originally found in Norway, hence their Latin name, and they are still sometimes known as Norway lobsters. Nowadays, they are caught all along the Atlantic coast, in the Adriatic and western Mediterranean. The colder the water in which langoustines live, the better the flavour.

Other names The French know them as *langoustine*; the Italians call them *scampo*, while in Spain they are called *cigala* or *langostina*.

Shelling cooked crayfish

1 Hold the crayfish between your finger and thumb and gently twist off the tail.

2 Hold the tail shell between your thumb and index finger, twist and pull off the flat end; the thread-like intestinal tract will come away. Peel the tail.

3 Hold the head and thorax in one hand. Use the other index finger to prise off the whole underside, including the gills and innards, and discard these.

4 Finally, gently twist off the claws from the head.

Left: These freshwater crustaceans, called cherabin in Australia and black tiger or African prawns elsewhere, are sometimes confused with crayfish and scampi, because, unlike all other prawns, they have a pair of extremely long, thin claws.

Buying Langoustines deteriorate very rapidly once caught, so are often cooked and frozen at sea. Live langoustines are therefore something of a rarity in British fish markets, although you will often find them in mainland Europe. If you are lucky enough to find live langoustines, and can be certain of cooking them soon after purchase, they will be an excellent buy. It is important to check that they are still moving; if they have died, they will have an unpleasant woolly texture. Unlike other crustaceans, langoustines do not change colour when cooked, so make sure you know what you are buying. Langoustines are graded by size; larger specimens are better value, as they contain more meat. They are also available frozen, often as scampi tails. If they have been shelled, allow about 115g/4oz per person; you will need twice this quantity if the langoustines are in the shell.

Cooking Most people must have encountered tasteless, badly cooked scampi at some time in their lives. When langoustines are properly cooked, however, their flavour is delicate and delicious. They must be cooked very briefly. Roast in oil and garlic in a hot oven for 3–5 minutes; split them and grill (broil) or cook on a barbecue for about 2 minutes on each side; or poach in a court-bouillon and serve hot with melted butter. Remember that most langoustines on sale are already cooked, so subject them to as little heat as possible. Langoustines are delicious served cold with mayonnaise. They make a wonderful addition to a *plateau de fruits de mer*. Langoustine tails can be baked *au gratin* in a creamy sauce with mushrooms and Gruyère cheese or served Scottish-style in a whisky-flavoured sauce. They can also be deep-fried and served with lemon wedges, but take care not to overcook them.

Above: Langoustines, which are also known as Dublin Bay prawns and scampi.

Left: Canadian lobsters are air-freighted live to Europe.

If you buy a live lobster, make sure that the pincers are secured with a stout elastic band.

Other names In French, lobster is called *homard*; in Italian, it is *astice* and in Spanish, *bogavante*.

Canadian/American lobster *(Homarus americanus)*

The hardiest species of lobster, these are found in large numbers in the waters around Canada and the North American Atlantic. They resemble the European lobster, but are greener in colour, and the claws are slightly rounder and fleshier. Although they make excellent eating, their flavour does not quite match up to that of the European species. The best-known American lobster is the Maine lobster. Canadian and Maine lobsters are air-freighted live to Europe to meet the demand for these crustaceans. Even taking into account the freight costs, they are considerably cheaper than their European counterparts.

Below: Maine lobster resembles the European lobster, but is less expensive.

LOBSTER

These are the ultimate luxury seafood. Their uniquely firm, sweet flesh has a delicious flavour and many people regard them as the finest crustaceans of all. The best lobsters live in cold waters, scavenging for food on the rocky sea bed. Like crabs, they "moult" every couple of years, casting off their outgrown shells. Their colour varies according to their habitat, from steely blue to greenish-brown to reddish-purple; all turn brick red when cooked. Lobsters grow very slowly, only reaching maturity at six years old, by which time they are about 18cm/7in long. If you are lucky enough to find a 1kg/2¼lb lobster, it will be about ten years old. This explains why lobsters are in such short supply.

Lobsters must be bought live or freshly boiled. The powerful pincers, which the creature uses for catching and crushing its prey, can be dangerous.

European lobster *(Homarus gammarus)*

These lobsters, which come from England, Scotland, Ireland, Norway and Brittany, are regarded as having the finest flavour of all. They have distinctive blue-black colouring, and are sometimes speckled with bright blue. European lobsters are becoming increasingly rare and expensive. If they are caught in reasonable numbers during the summer months, they are often held in vivariums, massive holding tanks built into the sea.

Unfortunately, lobsters do not eat in captivity, so although the vivariums make sure that they are available

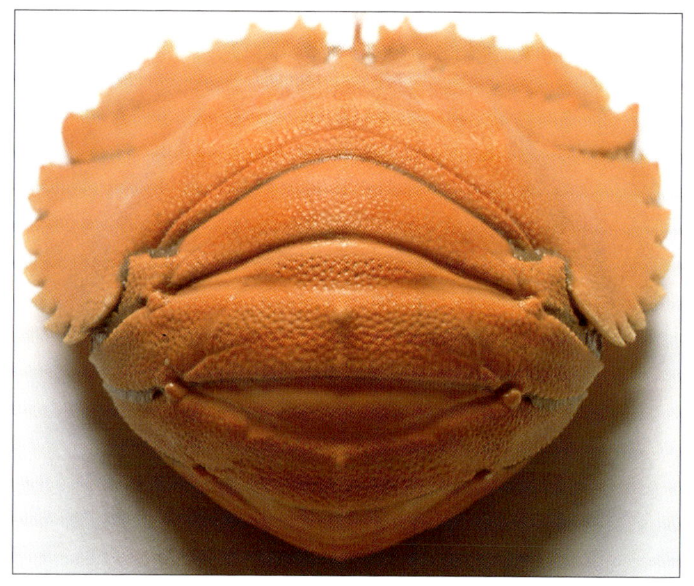

Right: The Balmain bug is a warm-water variety of squat lobster from Australia that has sweet, delicious flesh.

Below: The European lobster, which is becoming rare – and very expensive – is considered the best lobster of all.

throughout the year, the quality deteriorates as the season progresses; by early spring, they tend to be thin and undernourished.

Slipper/Squat lobster *(Scyllarus arctus)*

There are over fifty species of these warm-water lobsters. They have wide, flattened bodies and spindly clawed legs. The best known squat lobsters are the Australian "bugs", and the best known of these are the Balmain and Moreton Bay bugs. The comparatively small tails contain deliciously sweet flesh. Squat lobsters are seldom sold in Europe, but can occasionally be found in France, where they are known as *cigales* (grasshoppers). Italians call them *cicala di mare* and in Spain they are called *cigarra*.

Cooking lobster

All types of lobster are best cooked very simply to allow the delicate flavour to speak for itself. They can be boiled in salted water or court-bouillon and served hot with melted butter or cold with mayonnaise, grilled (broiled) or fried in the shell with oil and butter. A plain boiled lobster can be the crowning glory of a *plateau de fruits de mer*.

Classical French cookery has a plethora of rich lobster recipes that reflect the luxurious quality of these crustaceans. These dishes, which are usually served with rice to offset the richness, include Lobster Cardinale, with mushrooms and truffles in a velvety sauce; Lobster Newburg, with a cognac and sherry-flavoured cream sauce; Lobster Bretonne, with prawns (shrimp) and mushrooms in a white wine sauce, and the world-famous Lobster Thermidor, with its unctuous brandy and mustard-flavoured sauce. More modern recipes combine lobster with Asian flavours such as ginger and star anise, but these spices should be used in moderation.

Lobster is superb with fresh pasta. Use it as a filling for ravioli or toss it into tagliolini with lemon juice and butter. Cold boiled lobster can be diced and made into a lobster cocktail or added to a salad. When cooking lobster, keep the shells to use in a shellfish stock or soup.

Preparing a cooked lobster

You'll need a large, heavy knife or cleaver and a lobster pick to remove the meat from the legs.

1 Hold the body of the lobster firmly in one hand and twist off the claws one at a time.

2 Hold the lobster the right way up on a chopping board. Insert a large sharp knife at right angles to the seam between the body and head and press down firmly to split the body and tail lengthways.

3 Turn the lobster round to face the other way and cut firmly through the head. Separate the lobster into two halves and discard the stomach sac.

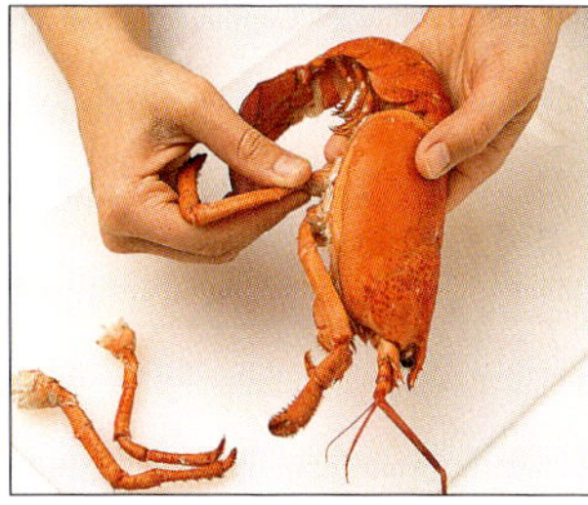

4 Twist off the legs and then flatten them lightly with the back of the knife. Use a lobster pick to remove the flesh.

5 To remove the meat from the claws, first break up the claws into sections. Hold the larger section of the claw, curved side down, in one hand and sharply pull off the smaller pincer. Twist off the lower section of the claw at the joint.

6 Gently crack the claw shell with a mallet or the end of a rolling pin and remove the flesh.

7 The lobster can be grilled (broiled) in the shell with butter, or the flesh can be diced and used in sauces.

Prawns and Shrimp

Prawns are the world's most popular crustaceans and are eaten in huge quantities around the globe. Thousands of species of prawns and shrimp are found in all of the world's oceans and also in fresh water. Technically, there is no difference between shrimp and prawns; the names merely indicate size. In the fish trade, prawns measuring less than about 5cm/2in are known as shrimp, except in America, where all prawns are known as shrimp. Most prawns have narrow, tapering bodies, curled over at the tail, and long antennae. As is the case with other crustaceans, prawns that come from colder waters have a better flavour than those from warm waters.

Above: Pink shrimp

COLD-WATER PRAWNS

Common prawn/Pink shrimp *(Palaemon serratus)*

These translucent, brownish prawns can grow up to 10cm/4in in length. They are found in deep waters in the Atlantic Ocean and Mediterranean Sea, but related species are found throughout the world. The French and Italians consider these prawns the best of all; they have an exceptionally good flavour and turn a glorious red when cooked. As a result, they command enormously high prices.

Other names Common prawns are also known as sword shrimp or Algerian shrimp. In France, they are called *crevette rose* or *bouquet*; in Italy, they are *gamberello*; in Spain, *camarón* or *quisquilla*.

Below: Mediterranean prawns

Deep-sea prawn *(Pandalus borealis)*

Sometimes sold as large shrimp, these cold-water prawns live at great depths in the North Sea. Hermaphrodite, they all begin life as males, but become female halfway through their lifespan.

Deep-sea prawns have translucent pink bodies, which turn pale salmon-pink on cooking. They have a delicate, juicy flavour and are almost always sold cooked.

Other names In France, these prawns are *crevette*; Italians know them as *gambero*; while in Spain they are *camarón*.

Peeling and deveining prawns

1 Hold the prawn in the middle and pull off the head and legs. Peel off the shell, leaving on the end of the tail if you prefer.

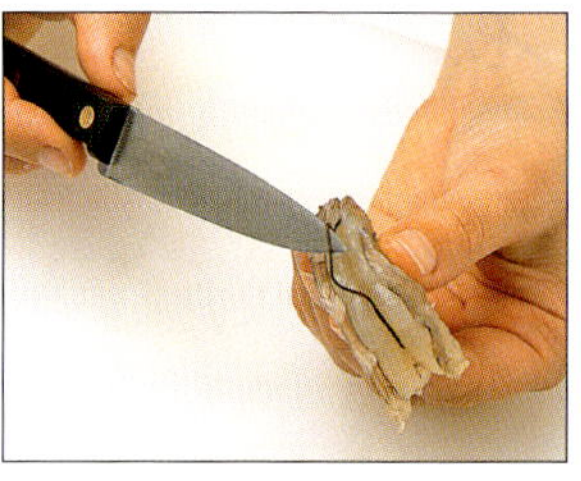

2 To devein, use a small sharp knife to make a shallow incision down the centre of the curved back of the prawn. Use the knife tip to remove the black vein (intestinal tract) and discard it.

Mediterranean prawn *(Aristeus antennatus)*

These large prawns can measure up to 10cm/4in. The colour varies – the heads can be anything from blood-red to deep coral – but once cooked, they turn a brilliant red. The flesh is delicious and very succulent. Mediterranean prawns are sold cooked and should be served simply as they are, with good-quality mayonnaise and fresh French bread. Allow 3–4 each as an appetizer.

Other names Also known as blue or red shrimp, Mediterranean prawns are called *crevette rouge* in France; they are called *gambero rosso* in Italy and *carabinero* in Spain.

Common/Brown shrimp *(Crangon crangon)*

These small shrimp have translucent grey bodies and measure only about 5cm/2in. They live in soft sand in shallow waters, emerging at night in darker camouflage to hunt for their prey. When cooked, they turn brownish-grey. Their small size makes them difficult to peel, but they can be eaten whole and their flavour is incomparable, with a wonderful tang of the sea. They are used to make potted shrimp.
Other names The French call these shrimp *crevette grise* or *boucaud*; the Italians know them as *gamberetto grigio*; the Spanish call them *quisquilla*.

Butterflied prawns
Prawns look very attractive when they are butterflied.

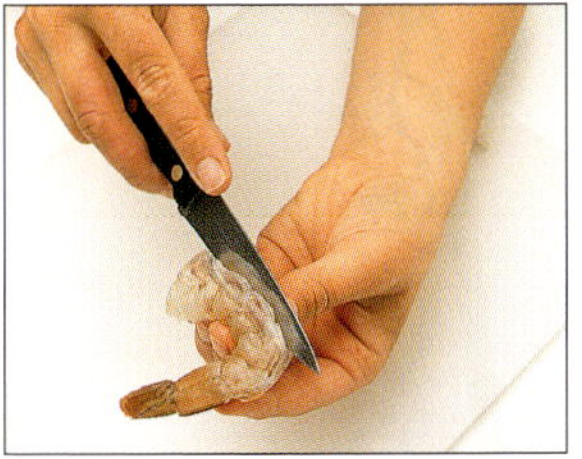

1 The easiest way of doing this is to deepen the incision made to remove the vein, cutting almost but not quite through to the belly.

2 The prawn is then opened out flat. If the prawns are large, make the incision through the belly to give a more pronounced shape.

Left: Brown shrimp

Below: Tiger prawns

WARM-WATER PRAWNS

Gulf shrimp *(Hymenopenaeus robustus)*

Warm-water prawns from the Gulf of Mexico, these are usually bright red, but may sometimes be greyish-pink. Gulf shrimp can grow up to 40g/1½oz in weight, and have succulent flesh.

Kuruma/Japanese prawn *(Penaeus japonicus)*

These large prawns can grow to a length of 23cm/9in. They have yellowish tails flecked with black. Kuruma are found throughout the Indo-Pacific region and in the Red Sea; some have migrated through the Suez Canal to the eastern Mediterranean.

Tiger/King prawn/Jumbo shrimp *(Penaeus monodon)*

These huge prawns are found throughout the Indo-Pacific. They can grow up to 33cm/13in in length and are ideal for cooking on a barbecue. When raw, they are a translucent greenish-grey. Although their flavour is not as good as that of cold-water prawns, they have succulent, firm flesh. In Europe, they are seldom sold fresh, but they freeze well and are available peeled or in the shell. Peeled tiger prawns usually have the end of the tail left on so that they can be eaten with the fingers.
Cooking The cardinal rule with any prawns or shrimp is not to overcook them. Ready-cooked prawns should preferably be eaten without further cooking. Serve them simply, with lemon and brown bread and butter, or in a prawn cocktail or salad. If you must cook them, use them in a dish such as pasta where they need only be heated through. They add extra flavour and texture to other fish dishes, such as fish pies, terrines and flans, and combine well with other shellfish. Small prawns or shrimp make an excellent filling for omelettes, vol-au-vents or tartlets.

Raw prawns can be boiled briefly in salt water or court-bouillon and are delicious grilled (broiled), cooked on a barbecue or deep-fried in batter. With squid and fish, deep-fried prawns are an essential ingredient of an Italian *fritto misto*. Warm-water prawns can be used for stir-fries, curries or kebabs.

Below: Gulf shrimp

Gastropods

Also known as univalves, gastropods are single-shelled creatures belonging to the snail family. Most marine gastropods have the familiar snail shape, with a single spiral shell, but some look more like bivalves and others have no shell at all. All gastropods have a single, large foot which they extend and contract to crawl along at a "snail's pace". Edible gastropods vary in size from tiny winkles to conches measuring up to 30cm/12in. All can be delicious if properly cooked.

Abalone/Ormer/Sea ear

You could be forgiven for thinking that abalone *(Haliotis tuberculata)* were bivalves, since their ear-shaped shells give them the appearance of large mussels. Like all gastropods, they have a large, muscled foot that they use to cling to rocks and cliffs. This immensely strong foot can withstand strains up to four thousand times the weight of the abalone, which makes it very difficult to prise them from the rocks, and helps to explain why they are so expensive. Another reason for their cost is that they feed exclusively on seaweed; as their habitat becomes polluted, they die, so they are becoming increasingly rare. In some countries abalone have become a protected species. They are highly prized not only for their flesh, but also for their beautiful shells. These are lined with iridescent mother-of-pearl. There are over a hundred species of abalone living in warm waters throughout the world. Most can grow to about 20cm/8in in length, but the shell of the red abalone *(Haliotis rufescens),* found in the American Pacific, grows up to 30cm/12in. Their firm flesh, which must be tenderized before it can be eaten, has a subtle flavour of iodine.

Other names In the Channel Islands, one of the few places in Europe where abalone are still found, they are known as ormers. In South Africa, they are known as *perlemoen* or Venus' ear. The French call them *ormeau* or *oreilles de St Pierre*; the Italians, *orecchia marina*; the Spanish, *oreja de mar.*

Buying In Europe, there is a closed season for abalone, and they are limited to only a few days in early spring. You are more likely to find fresh abalone in America, Australia and the Far East. These are often sold sliced and tenderized ready for cooking. Abalone is also available canned, frozen and dried.

Preparing and Cooking Before cooking, the intestinal sac and dark membrane and skirt must be removed. To remove the white flesh, run a sharp knife between it and the shell. Abalone flesh must be beaten vigorously with a wooden mallet to tenderize it. In Japan, it is then sliced thinly and eaten raw as sashimi. If it is cooked, the technique is the same as that for squid – it must either be cooked very briefly, or given long, slow cooking. Thin slices can be sautéed quickly in hot butter, or cut into strips and deep-fried in batter or egg and breadcrumbs. In China, abalone is braised with dried mushrooms; in France, it is stewed slowly with dry white wine and shallots. In the Channel Islands, ormers are traditionally casseroled with bacon and potatoes. Abalone makes an excellent chowder.

Below: Abalone are large shellfish, which can grow to 30cm/12in in length.

Above: Limpets

Conch *(Strombus gigas)*

Pronounced "konk", conch is a large relative of the whelk. It has a distinctive spiral shell. As with all such gastropods, the opening is protected by a hard operculum, or "trap door" which must be removed for access to the flesh inside. Conch are native to Florida, the Pacific coast and the Caribbean. The shells are sought after as ornaments and musical instruments. The pinkish flesh is tasty and chewy, and must be beaten to tenderize it before eating.

Buying In their native countries, conches are available all year round. The best are young specimens, known as "thin-lipped" conches; older conches are described as "thick-lipped". They are generally sold out of the shell.

Cooking After tenderizing, conch meat can be marinated and eaten raw, or cooked in a chowder. Some conches can cause stomach upsets; the risk of this occurring can be reduced if the conch is boiled in two changes of water.

Above: Whelks

Limpets *(Patella vulgata)*

These gastropods have conical shells. They are found throughout the world, clinging tightly to rocks. When the tide goes out, they nestle into holes in the sand, emerging at night to crawl in a 1m/39in circle around their hole in search of food. Limpets have quite a good flavour, but the small amount of flesh they contain can be very tough. It takes a great deal of effort to prise them off the rocks, so only the larger varieties, which yield more flesh, are eaten. Limpets are not available commercially so you will have to harvest them yourself.

Cooking Wash the limpets and boil them in sea water or heavily-salted water for 5–7 minutes, or cook the flesh in fish and shellfish dishes or soups.

Whelks *(Buccinum undatum)*

Smaller relatives of the conch, whelks have pretty spiral shells measuring up to 10cm/4in. They have rubbery, pinkish flesh with a good flavour, largely due to their diet. Whelks bore through the shell of other shellfish to eat their flesh.

Other names There are many varieties of whelk, including the common, the dog, the spiral and the knobbled or giant American whelk, which can grow to 20cm/8in in length. In French, they are variously known as *bulot, buccin* and *escargot de mer* (sea snail); in Italian, *buccina*; in Spanish, as *bocina* or *caracola*.

Buying Whelks should be bought alive; check that the operculum is tightly closed. They are sometimes sold ready-boiled and removed from the shell, but these can be rather dry. You will also find whelks pickled in vinegar, or ready-cooked and bottled in brine.

Cooking The best way to cook whelks is to boil them in sea water or heavily-salted water for about 5 minutes. Use a cocktail stick (toothpick) to prise the flesh out of the shell. The flesh of large whelks can be sautéed after boiling, or deep-fried in batter. It can be used instead of clams in a chowder, or added to cooked shellfish dishes or salads.

Winkles/Periwinkles *(Littorina littorea)*

These tiny marine snails have thick greenish-brown or black shells, each with a pointed end. Most grow no larger than 4cm/1½in and contain a morsel of chewy flesh.

Other names In France, they are *bigourneau* or *littorine*; in Italy, *chiocciola di mare*; in Spain, *bigaro*.

Buying Fresh winkles should be bought alive; check that the operculum is tightly closed. They are also available cooked and bottled in vinegar.

Cooking Like whelks, winkles need only brief cooking. Serve as an appetizer with vinegar or mayonnaise, or as part of a shellfish platter.

Left: Winkles

Cooking and picking winkles and whelks

1 Bring a large pan of well-salted water to the boil. Drop in the winkles or whelks and simmer for about 5 minutes for winkles; 10 minutes for whelks. Drain.

2 If the operculum is still covering the opening of the shell, remove it with a cocktail stick or pin. Insert the cocktail stick or pin into the shell and pull out the flesh.

Molluscs

The mollusc family is divided into bivalves such as mussels and oysters, which have a hinged external shell, and gastropods such as whelks and winkles, which have a single external shell. Cephalopods (squid, cuttlefish and octopus) are yet another group; unlike gastropods and bivalves, they have internal shells.

Bivalves

CLAMS

There are hundreds of species of clam, ranging from the aptly-named giant clam which can grow to a length of 1.3m/4¼ft, to tiny pebble-like Venus and littleneck clams measuring barely 5cm/2in. Americans are passionate about clams and eat them in all sizes and forms. Their enthusiasm has spread to Europe, where clams are now extensively farmed. Large species, such as the fully mature American quahog (pronounced co-hog), have very thick warty shells; small varieties have smooth shells marked with fine circular striations. Clams have a fine, sweet flavour and firm texture, and are delicious cooked or raw.

Above: Venus clams

Cherrystone/Littleneck clam *(Mercenaria mercenaria)*

These small clams have an attractive brown and white patterned shell. They are actually quahogs, the popular name deriving from their size. The smallest are the baby littlenecks, with 4–5cm/1½–2in shells. The slightly larger cherrystones (about 7.5cm/3in), named after Cherrystone Creek in Virginia, are about five years old. Both are often served raw on the half shell; cooked, they make wonderful pasta sauces. Larger quahogs, which are unsuitable for eating raw, are known as steamer clams. They have quite a strong flavour and are often used for making clam chowder or pasta sauces.

Other names The French call them *palourde*; the Italians, *vongola dura*; the Spanish, *almeja* or *clame*.

Geoduck clam *(Panopea generosa)*

These enormous clams are the largest of all American Pacific shellfish and can weigh up to 4kg/8¾lb. Half this weight is made up of two long siphons, which can be extended to more than 1.3m/4¼ft to take in and expel water. Unlike the soft-shell clam, the geoduck cannot retract these siphons into the shell, and they are often sold separately. Geoducks can bury themselves up to 1.2m/4ft deep in sand, and it takes two people to prise them out. The siphons and flesh are sliced before cooking.

Palourde/Carpetshell clam *(Venerupis decussata)*

These small (4–7.5cm/1½–3in) clams have grooved brown shells with a yellow lattice pattern. The flesh is exceptionally tender, so they can be eaten raw, but are also good grilled (broiled).

Below: Palourde or carpetshell clams have tender flesh that can be eaten raw.

Other names In French they are *palourde*; in Italian, *vongola verace*; in Spanish, *almeja fina*.

Praire/Warty Venus clam *(Venus verrucosa)*

The unattractively named warty Venus is a smallish clam measuring 2.5–7.5cm/1–3in. The thick shell has concentric stripes, some of which end in warty protuberances. These clams are widely distributed on sandy coasts, from Africa to Europe. They are often eaten raw on the half shell, but are also excellent cooked. The Italians dignify them with the name of "sea truffles".

Below: Cherrystone clams

Other names
Sometimes known as baby clams, the word *praire* comes from the French, who also call these molluscs *coque rayé*. In Italy they are *verrucosa* or *tartufo di mare*; in Spain *almeja vieja*.

Razorshell/Razor clam *(Solen marginatus)*

Resembling an old-fashioned cut-throat razor, these clams have tubular shells that are striped gold and brown. Razorshells are often served raw, but can be cooked like any other clam. Their flesh tastes delicious. They can often be found on sandy beaches at low tide, but as they can burrow into the sand at great speed to conceal themselves, you will need to act fast if you want to catch them.

Other names Razorshells are sometimes known as jack-knife clams. The French call them *couteau*; the Italians, *cannolicchio* or *cappa lunga*; their Spanish name is *navaja* or *longuerión*.

Soft-shell/Long-neck clam *(family Myidae)*

The shells of these wide oval clams gape slightly at the posterior end, giving them their nickname of "gapers". They burrow deep into sand and silt, so have a long tube that acts as a siphon for taking in and expelling water. This siphon can be eaten raw, or made into chowder or creamed dishes. Soft-shell clams are often used in clambakes.

Other names In French they are *mye*; in Italian, *vongola molle*; in Spanish, *almeja de rio*.

Cooking Small clams and razorshells can be eaten raw, steamed or cooked in soups and sauces. Larger clams can be stuffed and baked or grilled (broiled) like mussels, cut into strips and deep-fried in batter or breadcrumbs, or stewed with white wine or onions and tomatoes. Steamed clams can be added to salads or sauces or used as a garnish. Never throw away the juices which clams contain; these are extremely nutritious and delicious, and can be used for drinks such as *clamata*, shellfish stock or soup.

Below: Razor clams are often served raw.

Clambakes

A favourite American pastime is the clambake, a beach picnic in which soft-shell or hard-shell clams are steamed over seaweed laid on hot rocks. A pit is dug in the sand, rocks are placed inside and heated, then draped with wet seaweed. The clams are steamed over the seaweed, along with corn, sweet potatoes and, sometimes, lobsters or soft-shell crabs. The process of digging the pit and cooking the clams takes at least 4 hours, so a clambake can provide a whole day's entertainment.

Cockles

Although traditionally thought of as a typically British food, varieties of cockle *(Cardium edule)* are found all over the world. Their two equal heart-shaped shells are 2.5–4cm/1–1½in long and have 26 defined ribs. Inside lies a morsel of delicate flesh and its coral.

Other names In America, cockles are sometimes known as heart clams. In France, they are *coque*; in Italy, *cuore*; in Spain, *berberecho*.

Buying Fresh cockles are sold by volume; 1 pint weighs about 450g/1lb. Those with paler flesh are said to taste better than those with dark flesh.

Above: Cockles

The colour of the shell is an indication of the colour of the flesh, so choose cockles with pale shells. Shelled cockles are available frozen and bottled in brine or vinegar.

Cooking Cockles are full of sand, so must be soaked in salted cold water for several hours before eating. They can be eaten raw or boiled and served with vinegar and brown bread and butter. They are excellent steamed, stewed with tomatoes and onions or made into soup. Cockles can be added to risotto, pasta and other seafood dishes or served cold as an hors d'oeuvre or salad.

Below: Large New Zealand greenshell or green-lipped mussels.

Right: Ever-popular, black-shelled mussels

Dog cockle
(Glycymeridae)

With their large, flat striated shells, dog cockles resemble scallops. There are four known species of these tropical and warm-water bivalves – the true dog cockle, the bittersweet cockle, the violet bittersweet and the giant bittersweet. All are perfectly good to eat, but have a coarser texture and flavour than true cockles. They can be cooked in the same way as cockles and mussels.

Other names In French they are *amande*; in Italian, *pié d'asino* (ass's foot); in Spanish, *almendra de mar.*

Mussels *(Mytilus edulis)*

Once regarded as the poor relation of the shellfish family, mussels are now very popular, but still comparatively cheap. These succulent bivalves, with their elongated blue-black shells, have been eaten since earliest times. Unlike most other bivalves, they do not use a muscly foot to anchor themselves to rocks and poles, but with a byssus or "beard", a wiry substance produced by a gland at the base of the foot. Clumps of mussels grow wild on sea shores throughout the world and are great fun to harvest. It is essential that the waters they come from are unpolluted. Their sweet, tender flesh is nutritious and versatile. Nowadays, most commercial mussels are farmed.

There are many varieties of mussel. The best and most succulent are the blue or European mussels from cold British waters, which can grow to a length of 10cm/4in, although the average size is nearer 5cm/2in. They are large, with sweet-flavoured flesh which in the female is a beautiful orange; males have paler, cream-coloured flesh. The largest of all are the New Zealand greenshell or green-lipped mussels *(Perna canaliculus)*, which have a distinctive green lip around the internal border of the shell. These can grow to over 23cm/9in and are very meaty and substantial. They are ideal for stuffing, but their flavour is not so good as that of blue mussels.

Other names In French it is *moule*; in Italian, *cozza*; in Spanish, *mejillón*.

Buying Most mussels are farmed and are usually cleaned. They are available all year round and are cheap, so buy more than you think you will need to allow for wastage; 1kg/2¼lb will provide a generous meal for two people. Shelled mussels are available frozen, smoked and bottled in brine or vinegar.

Cooking Mussels are enormously versatile. They can be eaten raw or steamed very simply as in *moules marinière*. They are also good steamed with Mediterranean or Asian flavours. Large mussels can be stuffed and baked or grilled (broiled) with flavoured butter, bacon or pesto. They can be wrapped in bacon, threaded on to skewers and grilled; cooked in cream, wine or cider; deep-fried; or used in omelettes, soufflés, hot or cold soups, curries, pasta sauces, rice dishes such as paella, or shellfish salads. The national dish of Belgium is *moules frites*, crisply fried mussels with French fries, served with a glass of beer. For an unusual and piquant hors d'oeuvre, serve cold steamed mussels *à la ravigote*, with a vinaigrette flavoured with chopped hard-boiled egg, fresh herbs and gherkins.

OYSTERS

One of life's great luxuries, oysters evoke passionate feelings – people tend either to love or loathe them. Their unique, salty, iodized flavour and slippery texture may not appeal to all, but their reputation as an aphrodisiac (Casanova was said to eat at least fifty every day) has contributed to their popularity, and they are prized all over the world. It was not always so; for centuries, oysters were regarded as food for the poor. Apprentices revolted at having to eat them every day of the week. As they became scarce, however, their popularity increased.

Over 100 different varieties of oyster live in the temperate and warm waters of the world. All have thick, irregular, greyish shells, one flat, the other hollow. The highly nutritious flesh is pinkish-grey with a darker mantle and a slippery texture. Their reproductive life is highly unusual. Some are hermaphrodite; others change sex from male to female in alternate years.

Oysters have been eaten for thousands of years. They were enjoyed by the Celts and Ancient Greeks, but it was the Romans who first discovered the secret of oyster cultivation. By the 19th century, European oyster beds had been so comprehensively over-fished and stocks were so low that Napoleon III ordered that shipments of oysters be brought from abroad. It is as well that he did; in 1868, a ship carrying quantities of Portuguese oysters was forced to take shelter from a storm in the Gironde estuary. Fearing that his cargo of oysters was going bad, the captain flung them overboard. They bred prolifically, rapidly replenishing the native stocks, and managed to survive a catastrophic epidemic in 1921, which wiped out the native oysters. In 1967, however, they too were decimated by the deadly bonamia virus. Oyster cultivation on a massive scale was the only answer; nowadays, oysters are commercially produced throughout the industrialized world.

Below: Native oysters are the finest and most expensive of all oysters.

Oyster cultivation

Centuries of over-fishing and disease have decimated the world's natural stocks of oysters, a sad state of affairs which has been somewhat alleviated by oyster farming. Oysters have been farmed since Roman times, but cultivation has now become a highly lucrative business, despite being labour-intensive and very slow. Oysters need constant cosseting from the moment of hatching. A single oyster produces up to a hundred million eggs every breeding season, of which only ten oysters will survive long enough to end up on your plate. It takes at least three years to produce an oyster of marketable size; natives take up to seven years and the giant "royals" take ten years to mature. The minuscule spats must first be caught and encouraged to settle on lime-soaked tiles or slates.

After about nine months, they are transferred to oyster parks, where they are enclosed in wire grilles and carefully nurtured while they feed on plankton. After being left to grow for two or three years, they are placed in nets and fattened for about a year in shallow beds or *claires*. The final stage of the lengthy process involves placing them in clean beds for several days under stringent hygiene conditions to expel any impurities. Small wonder that they are so expensive.

Left: Gigas oysters

Eastern/Atlantic oyster *(Crassostrea virginica)*

With rounded shells like those of the native oyster, these actually belong to the Portuguese oyster family and have a similar texture and flavour. In America, they are named after their place of origin; the best known is the Blue Point.

Native oyster *(Ostrea edulis)*

Considered the finest of all oysters, Natives are slow-growers, taking three years to reach their full size of 5–12cm/ 2–4½in. Their round shells vary in colour from greyish-green to beige, depending on their habitat, and they have a wonderful flavour. Native oysters are named after their place of origin. Among the best known are the French Belon, the English Whitstable, Colchester and Helford, the Irish Galway and the Belgian Ostendes. Native oysters are the most expensive of all oysters.
Other names The French call them *huître plate* or *belon*, to the Italians they are *ostrica*, while in Spain, they are called *ostra plana*.

Pacific/Gigas oyster *(Crassostrea gigas)*

These large cupped bivalves with their craggy elongated shells are the most widely farmed oysters in the world. They are resistant to disease and can grow to 15cm/6in in the space of four years, which makes them comparatively economical to produce. Their texture is not so fine as that of native oysters, but their large size makes them more suitable for cooking than other oysters.
Other names The Pacific oyster is also known as the rock or Japanese oyster. In French, it is *creuse* (hollow); in Italian, *ostrica*; in Spanish *ostión*.

Portuguese cupped oyster *(Crassostrea angulata)*

These scaly greyish-brown oysters are considered finer than gigas, but not so good as natives. Their flesh is rather coarse and they are declining in popularity. In France, where Portuguese cupped oysters are cultivated on a large scale, they are known as *fines de claires* after the fattening beds where they are farmed. Fatter, tastier (and, of course, more expensive) specimens are called *spéciales claires*.

Sydney rock oyster *(Crassostrea commercialis)*

This sex-changing cupped oyster is extremely fertile and is farmed in huge numbers on the coast of New South Wales. It grows quickly and has a good flavour, but has the disadvantage of being difficult to open.
Buying The age-old rule that oysters should not be bought when there is no "r" in the month still holds good in the northern hemisphere, not because they are poisonous as was once supposed, but because their flesh becomes unpleasantly soft and milky during the summer breeding season from May to August. Smoked oysters are available and you may also find frozen oysters.
Cooking Oysters are best eaten raw with just a squeeze of lemon or a dash of Tabasco. If you prefer to cook them, do so very briefly. They are good poached or steamed and served with a *beurre blanc* or champagne sauce; stuffed and grilled (broiled); deep-fried in cornmeal batter; or as a luxurious addition to steak and kidney pie.

Left: Portuguese cupped oysters

SCALLOPS

Surely the most attractive of all shellfish, scallops (*Peeten maximus*) have two fan-shaped shells, one flat and the other curved, with grooves radiating out from the hinge to the outside edge. They are found on sandy seabeds in many parts of the world from Iceland to Japan. Unlike many bivalves, they do not burrow into the sand, but "swim" above the sea bed by opening and closing their shells, which gives them the appearance of leaping through the water. There are about three hundred species of scallop throughout the world, with shells ranging in colour from beige to brown, salmon pink, yellow and orange. The most common species is the common or great scallop, whose reddish-brown shell grows to a diameter of 5–6cm/2–2½in. Scallop shells contain a nugget of sweet, firm white flesh joined to the vibrant orange crescent-shaped roe or "coral", which is a delicacy in its own right.

Scallops are deeply symbolic and have long been associated with beauty. According to the legend depicted by Botticelli in one of his most famous paintings, the goddess Venus was born from a scallop shell; her Greek counterpart, Aphrodite, rode across the sea in a scallop shell pulled by six sea horses. Thanks to a miracle involving St James, scallop shells became the symbol of Christianity and the emblem of medieval pilgrims visiting the shrine at Santiago de Compostela in Spain.

Other names Sometimes known as "pilgrim shells", scallops are *coquille St Jacques* in French, *pettine* in Italian; *viera* in Spanish.

Buying Scallops are available almost all year round, but are best in winter when the roes are full and firm. The finest are individually hand-caught by divers; needless to say, they are also the most expensive. If you buy scallops in the shell, keep the shells to use as serving dishes for all sorts of fish recipes. Allow 4–5 large scallops per person as a main course, three times this number if they are small. Scallops are also available shelled, which saves the effort of cleaning them. Always try to buy scallops with their delicious coral, although this is not always possible. Avoid frozen scallops, which have little or no taste.

Above: Queen scallops

Cooking The beard and all dark coloured parts of the scallop must be removed before they are cooked and eaten. If the scallops are large, slice the white flesh in half horizontally. Scallops require very little cooking and can be thinly sliced and eaten raw with a squeeze of lemon and a drizzle of olive oil. They need only the briefest of cooking to preserve their uniquely firm yet tender texture. Scallops can be poached for a couple of minutes in court-bouillon and served warm or cold in a salad with a tomato and basil vinaigrette or mayonnaise.

Above: King scallops

Whole scallops in the shell can be baked; seal the shells with a flour and water paste to trap the juices. They are equally delicious wrapped in bacon and grilled (broiled); pan-fried for about 30 seconds on each side; coated in egg and breadcrumbs and deep-fried; stir-fried with colourful vegetables or steamed with ginger and soy sauce. They make wonderful pâtés and mousses. A classic dish is *coquilles St Jacques*, in which poached scallops and corals are sliced, returned to the half shell and coated with Mornay (cheese) sauce, then grilled (broiled) or baked until browned. A border of mashed potato is often piped around the edge of the shell.

Queen scallop *(Chlamys opercularis)*

These miniature scallops measure only about 3cm/1¼in across. Their cream-coloured shells are marked with attractive brown ridges and contain a small nugget of white flesh and a tiny pointed coral. Queen scallops are considerably cheaper than larger scallops, but have the same sweet flavour. They are often sold out of the shell; allow at least a dozen per person. "Queenies" as they are sometimes known, are commercially farmed. They are popular in Asia and are widely used in Chinese cooking.

CEPHALOPODS

Despite their appearance, cephalopods, which include cuttlefish, octopus and squid, are molluscs and are more closely related to snails than to fish. They are highly developed creatures with three-dimensional vision, memory and the ability to swim at high speeds. They can also change colour according to the environment. Their name derives from the Greek for "head with feet", which sums up their appearance very accurately. The bulbous head contains the mouth, which has two jaws, rather like a parrot's beak. This is surrounded by tentacles covered with suckers, which are used for crawling and for seizing their prey. The sack-shaped body contains a mantle cavity which houses the stomach, gills and sex organs. Although they developed from snail-like creatures, cephalopods no longer have an external shell; instead, most have an internal calcareous shell made from spongy material which they can inflate to make themselves buoyant. The most familiar of these is the cuttlebone, from the cuttlefish. Cuttlebones often wash up on beaches, and are used by bird-owners to provide calcium for budgerigars. In Roman times, ladies ground up cuttlebones and used the powder on their faces and to clean their teeth and their jewellery.

Most cephalopods also contain an ink sac which emits a blackish fluid designed to repel predators and provide a "smokescreen" for the creature when it is under attack. This fluid, or ink, is delicious and can be used for cooking.

Below: Baby cuttlefish

Right: Cuttlefish

Cephalopods are found in almost all the world's oceans. Unlike many sea creatures, they have not yet suffered from overfishing and are still a sustainable food source.

Cuttlefish

The common cuttlefish *(Sepia officinalis)* has a flattened oval head with brownish camouflage stripes on the back and light coloration on the underside. It has eight stubby tentacles and two long tentacles for catching its prey. These are kept rolled up and hidden in openings near its mouth. Cuttlefish are comparatively small, with bodies measuring 25–30cm/10–12in. When unfurled, the catching tentacles double its length. As is the case with all cephalopods, the smaller the cuttlefish, the more tender the flesh. The smallest species is the Mediterranean little or dwarf cuttlefish *(sepiola)*, which grows to only 3–6cm/1¼–2½in. They are delicious, but time-consuming to prepare, as the tiny cuttlebones must be removed before cooking.

Other names The common cuttlefish is *seiche* in French, *seppia* in Italian, *sepia* in Spanish. Dwarf cuttlefish are *supion* or *chipiron* in French, *seppiolina* in Italian, and *chipirón* in Spanish.

Cooking Tiny cuttlefish are delicious left whole and either sautéed quickly in olive oil and garlic or deep-fried. They make an excellent addition to rice dishes. Larger specimens can be cooked like squid. A classic Spanish dish is *sepia en su tinta*, cuttlefish cooked in its own ink.

Octopus *(Octopus vulgaris)*

Unlike cuttlefish and squid, the octopus has no internal shell, nor does it possess catching tentacles or fins. Octopuses spend their lives lurking in clefts in the rocks on the sea bed, blocking the entrance to their secret holes with shellfish and stones. Their eight equal-size tentacles each have two rows of suckers and can grow to a length of 5m/16¼ft. The larger an octopus grows, the tougher it becomes, so smaller specimens make the best eating. Octopus ink is contained in the liver and has a much stronger flavour than cuttlefish or squid ink.

Other names Octopus is *poulpe* or *pieuvre* in French; *polpo* in Italian; *pulpo* in Spanish.

Buying It is usually sold ready-prepared and frozen, although you may find whole fresh octopus in Mediterranean fish markets. Look for specimens with two rows of suckers on the tentacles; those with only a single row are curled octopus, which are inferior.

Right: Baby octopus

Cooking Octopus needs long, slow cooking. Before including it in a recipe, it is a good idea to blanch or marinate it. If the octopus has not been prepared already, cut off the tentacles and press out the beak from the head. Discard the head, turn the body inside out and discard the entrails. Rinse it thoroughly, then pound the body and tentacles with a mallet to tenderize them before cutting them into strips. Simmer the octopus in stock or salted water for at least 1 hour, until tender. Octopus can also be stewed with Mediterranean vegetables or robust red wine, or stuffed and baked slowly. Small specimens can be cut into rings and sautéed gently in olive oil. Octopus is best served warm as a salad, dressed with a simple olive oil and lemon vinaigrette. Whole octopus can be casseroled slowly in its own juices and ink, but be aware that the ink has a strong flavour which is not to everyone's taste. The Japanese are very fond of octopus and use the boiled tentacles for sushi.

Squid *(Loliginidae)*

These have elongated heads and slender, torpedo-shaped bodies, which end in a kite-shaped fin. Their internal shell is a transparent quill, which looks like a piece of clear acetate. They have ten tentacles, two of which are very long. Squid range from tiny creatures only 7.5cm/3in long to the giant squid which weighs several tons and can grow to a length of 17m/55¼ft. The most common squid is the calamary or long-finned squid *(Loligo vulgaris)*, which is found throughout Europe. It has smooth, sandy-red spotted skin and weighs up to 2kg/4½lb. The so-called flying squid does not actually fly, but propels itself out of the water and glides through the air like a guided missile. Squid has firm, lean, white flesh that can be tender and delicious when properly cooked.

Other names In French squid is *encornet* or *calmar*; in Italian it is *calamaro*; in Spanish *calamar* or *puntilla*.

Buying Whole squid are sold fresh or frozen and are available all year round. Make sure they contain their ink sac. Some fish-mongers and supermarkets also sell squid ink separately. Squid is also available ready-cleaned, which is very labour-saving. Whole tentacles and rings are available frozen, sometimes as part of a mixed *fruits de mer*. You can also buy ready-battered squid rings for deep-frying, but these are best avoided. Allow about 200g/7oz squid per person.

Cooking The cardinal rule with squid is to cook it either very briefly or for a long time; anything in between and it becomes tough and rubbery. The bodies can be stuffed and baked in tomato sauce, or braised with onions and tomatoes. Squid rings can be coated in batter and deep-fried, or boiled briefly and used for a salad. Tiny squid are delicious chargrilled, sautéed, or coated with egg and breadcrumbs and deep-fried. Squid can be added to pasta sauces and rice dishes such as paella. It goes well with such apparently unlikely ingredients as chorizo sausage and black pudding (blood sausage). Squid is often used in Asian recipes and lends itself to flavourings such as ginger, chilli and lime. The ink can be used to colour and flavour home-made pasta and risotto.

Above: Squid

Above: Octopus

Other Edible Sea Creatures

The sea is full of weird and wonderful creatures whose strange appearance belies their delicious taste. They may be soft and gelatinous like jellyfish, warty like sea cucumbers or menacingly spiny like sea urchins, but somewhere in the world, they will be regarded as a great delicacy.

Above: Dried jellyfish

Jellyfish *(Scyphoza)*

Jellyfish can strike terror into the hearts of those who have been stung by them. These strange, transparent creatures, with their dangling tentacles, look like open parachutes. They inhabit every ocean of the world, but are eaten almost exclusively in Asia, where they are dried and used to add texture and flavour to many seafood dishes.

Buying and using You will find dried jellyfish in any Asian food store, together with jellyfish preserved in brine. Both types must be soaked in several changes of water before use. In China, slices of dried jellyfish are scalded in boiling water until they curl up, then drained and served in a dressing of soy sauce, sesame oil and rice vinegar. They are also added to shellfish or chicken stir-fries. In Japan, crisply fried strips of jellyfish are served with vinegar, and are sometimes combined with sea urchins.

Sea cucumber *(Holothurioidea)*

These rather enigmatic, warty, cucumber-shaped creatures rejoice in the alternative name of sea slugs. Despite their strange appearance they are considered a great delicacy in Japan and China, where they are reputed to be an aphrodisiac. The plethora of prickles along one side are actually feet, which enable them to crawl along the sea bed. Sea cucumber is known in Asia as *trepang* or *balatin*. In Japan, it is sliced and eaten raw as sashimi. Sea cucumber is available dried, but requires many hours of soaking to make it palatable. It is used in soup and in several complicated recipes which take so long to prepare that one feels it must have charms that are not immediately apparent to Western perception.

Above: Sea cucumber

Sea squirt *(Ascidiacea)*

There are over a thousand species of sea squirts, small invertebrates whose bodies are enclosed in thick leathery "tunics". They have two orifices or spouts through which they siphon water in and squirt it out, and attach themselves to the sea bed or rocks and crevices. They are found in the Mediterranean, where they are a popular if esoteric food, particularly in Spain and the south of France, where the local name, violet, refers to the sea squirt's resemblance to a large purple fig. Enthusiasts eat them by splitting them in half, then scooping out the soft yellow part inside and eating it raw, despite the strong aroma of iodine. Sea squirts can accumulate

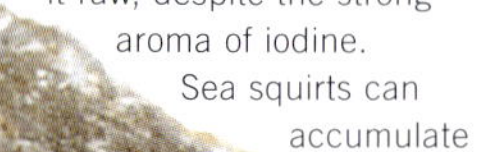

Right: Sea squirt

Opening sea urchins

1 Wearing rubber gloves, hold the sea urchin in the palm of your hand and carefully cut around the soft tissue on the underside, using a special knife or a pair of sharp, pointed scissors.

2 Lift off the top of the sea urchin and remove the mouth and innards, which are inedible. Keep the juices to flavour shellfish sauces, egg dishes or soup.

3 Use a teaspoon to scoop out the bright orange coral.

Right: Prickly sea urchins

toxins, so should never be eaten if they come from polluted waters.

Other names In French, sea squirt is *violet* or *figue de mer;* in Italian, *ovo di mare.*

Sea urchin *(Echinoidea)*

One of the most unpleasant experiences a swimmer can have is to tread on the long, poisonous spines of a sea urchin. To lovers of seafood, however, eating these marine creatures is one of life's great gastronomic pleasures. There are over eight hundred species of sea urchin, found all over the world, but only a few are edible. The most common European variety is the *Paracentrotus lividus*, a greenish or purplish-black hemispherical creature which measures about 7.5cm/3in across, and whose shell is covered with long spines, rather like those of a hedgehog. The females are slightly larger than the males and are said to taste better. Only the orange or yellow ovaries or gonads (known as the coral) are eaten; these have a pungent taste reminiscent of iodine.

Other names In French, sea urchins are variously known as *oursin*, *châtaigne de mer* (sea chestnut) and *hérisson de mer* (sea hedgehog); in Italian, they are *riccio di mare*; in Spanish *erizo de mar.*

Buying Overfishing has made sea urchins rare and expensive. The best are the purple or green urchins with long spines; short-spined, whitish species have an extremely strong flavour and are best used in cooked dishes. Look for urchins with firm spines and a tightly closed mouth (on the underside). If you find a source of fresh sea urchins, they can be kept in the refrigerator for up to three days.

Preparing The best implement for opening sea urchins is a purpose-made *coupe oursin*. Failing this, use very sharp scissors. Wearing gloves, cut into the soft tissue around the mouth and lift off the top to reveal the coral. Alternatively, slice off the top like a boiled egg.

Cooking Sea urchins can be eaten raw or used to flavour sauces, pasta, omelettes and scrambled eggs. They make wonderful soup, which can be served in small portions in the shell and eaten with a teaspoon. The shells can also be used as containers for other seafood such as langoustines in a sea urchin sauce.

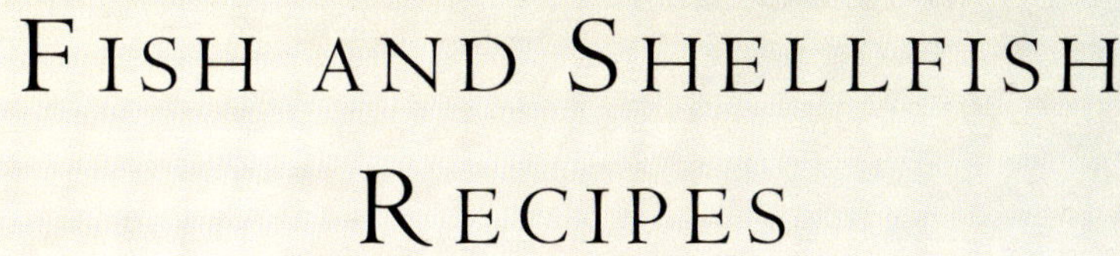

FISH AND SHELLFISH RECIPES

Fish and shellfish are both nutritious and enticing, and when properly cooked, can be among the most delicious foods imaginable. Every fish and shellfish has its own unique flavour, offering something for all tastes. In this collection of inspirational recipes there is a host of stunning contemporary creations as well as time-honoured classic dishes. With the increasingly wide range of fish and shellfish available in fishmongers and supermarkets, you can allow yourself the pleasure of experimenting and enjoying these wonderful dishes.

Soups

From light, spicy broths to hearty one-pot meals, fish and shellfish soups are a delight. Chilled Cucumber and Prawn Soup is perfect for summer eating, while Scallop and Jerusalem Artichoke Soup and substantial Bouillabaisse make wonderful winter warmers along with Clam Chowder from New England. For real luxury, treat yourself and your guests to creamy Lobster Bisque, or travel to Asia with spicy Malaysian Prawn Laksa and the wonderfully fragrant Thai Fish Broth.

CHILLED CUCUMBER AND PRAWN SOUP

If you've never served a chilled soup before, this is the one to try. Delicious, attractive and light, it's the perfect way to celebrate summer.

SERVES FOUR

INGREDIENTS
- 25g/1oz/2 tbsp butter
- 2 shallots, finely chopped
- 2 garlic cloves, crushed
- 1 cucumber, peeled, seeded and diced
- 300ml/½ pint/1¼ cups milk
- 225g/8oz/2 cups cooked peeled prawns (shrimp)
- 15ml/1 tbsp each finely chopped fresh mint, dill, chives and chervil
- 300ml/½ pint/1¼ cups whipping cream
- salt and ground white pepper

For the garnish
- 30ml/2 tbsp crème fraîche (optional)
- 4 large, cooked prawns (shrimp), peeled with tail intact
- fresh dill and chives

1 Melt the butter in a pan and cook the shallots and garlic over a low heat until soft but not coloured. Add the cucumber and cook gently, stirring frequently, until tender.

COOK'S TIP

If you prefer hot soup, reheat it gently until hot but not boiling. Do not boil, or the delicate flavour will be spoilt.

2 Stir in the milk, bring almost to boiling point, then lower the heat and simmer for 5 minutes. Tip the soup into a blender or food processor and process until very smooth. Season to taste.

3 Pour the soup into a large bowl and leave to cool. When cool, stir in the prawns, chopped herbs and cream. Cover, transfer to the refrigerator and chill for at least 2 hours.

4 To serve, ladle the soup into four individual bowls and top each portion with a spoonful of crème fraîche, if using, and place a prawn over the edge of each dish. Sprinkle a little extra chopped dill over each bowl of soup and tuck two or three chives under the prawns on the edge of the bowls to garnish. Serve immediately.

VARIATION

If you like, you can use other cooked shellfish in place of the peeled prawns (shrimp) – try fresh, frozen or canned crab meat, or cooked, flaked salmon.

Scallop and Jerusalem Artichoke Soup

The subtle sweetness of scallops combines well with the flavour of Jerusalem artichokes in this attractive golden soup. For an even more colourful version, substitute pumpkin for the artichokes and use extra stock instead of the milk.

SERVES SIX

INGREDIENTS
- 1kg/2¼lb Jerusalem artichokes
- juice of ½ lemon
- 115g/4oz/½ cup butter
- 1 onion, finely chopped
- 600ml/1 pint/2½ cups fish stock
- 300ml/½ pint/1¼ cups milk
- generous pinch of saffron threads
- 6 large or 12 small scallops, with their corals
- 150ml/¼ pint/⅔ cup whipping cream
- salt and ground white pepper
- 45ml/3 tbsp flaked (sliced) almonds and 15ml/1 tbsp finely chopped fresh chervil, to garnish

1 Working quickly, scrub and peel the Jerusalem artichokes, cut them into 2cm/¾in chunks and drop them into a bowl of cold water, which has been acidulated with the lemon juice. This will prevent the artichokes from turning brown.

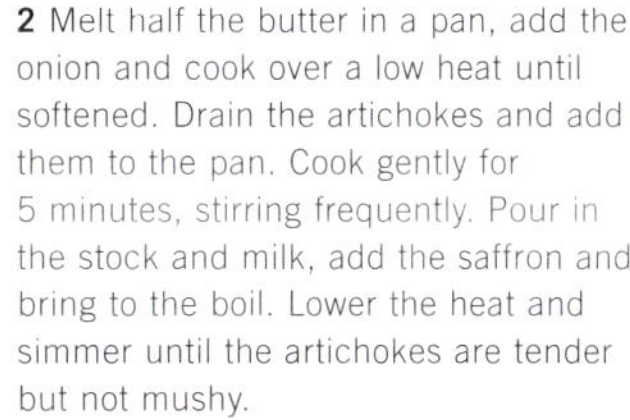

2 Melt half the butter in a pan, add the onion and cook over a low heat until softened. Drain the artichokes and add them to the pan. Cook gently for 5 minutes, stirring frequently. Pour in the stock and milk, add the saffron and bring to the boil. Lower the heat and simmer until the artichokes are tender but not mushy.

3 Meanwhile, carefully separate the scallop corals from the white flesh. Prick the corals and slice each scallop in half horizontally. Heat half the remaining butter in a frying pan, add the scallops and corals and cook very briefly (for about 1 minute) on each side. Dice the scallops and corals, keeping them separate, and set them aside until needed.

4 When the artichokes are cooked, tip the contents of the pan into a blender or food processor. Add half the white scallop meat and process until very smooth. Return the soup to the clean pan, season with salt and white pepper and keep hot over a low heat while you prepare the garnish.

5 Heat the remaining butter in a frying pan, add the almonds and toss over a medium heat until golden brown. Add the diced corals and cook for about 30 seconds. Stir the cream into the soup and add the remaining diced white scallop meat. Ladle the soup into individual bowls and garnish each serving with the almonds, scallop corals and a sprinkling of chervil.

MATELOTE

TRADITIONALLY THIS FISHERMEN'S CHUNKY SOUP INCLUDES CONGER EEL, BUT ANY FIRM FISH CAN BE USED. IF YOU CAN FIND IT, DO INCLUDE AT LEAST SOME EEL, AND USE A ROBUST DRY WHITE OR RED WINE FOR EXTRA FLAVOUR.

SERVES SIX

INGREDIENTS

- 1kg/2¼lb mixed fish, including 450g/1lb conger eel if possible
- 50g/2oz/¼ cup butter
- 1 onion, thickly sliced
- 2 celery sticks, thickly sliced
- 2 carrots, thickly sliced
- 1 bottle dry white or red wine
- 1 fresh bouquet garni containing parsley, bay leaf and chervil
- 2 cloves
- 6 black peppercorns
- *beurre manié* for thickening, see Cook's Tip
- salt and cayenne pepper

For the garnish

- 25g/1oz/2 tbsp butter
- 12 baby (pearl) onions, peeled
- 12 button (white) mushrooms
- chopped flat leaf parsley

1 Cut all the fish into thick slices, removing any obvious bones. Melt the butter in a large pan, put in the fish and sliced vegetables and stir over a medium heat until lightly browned. Pour in the wine and enough cold water to cover. Add the bouquet garni and spices and season. Bring to the boil, lower the heat and simmer gently for 20–30 minutes, until the fish is tender, skimming the surface occasionally.

2 Meanwhile, prepare the garnish. Heat the butter in a deep frying pan and sauté the baby onions until golden and tender. Add the mushrooms and cook until golden. Season and keep hot.

3 Strain the soup through a large strainer into a clean pan. Discard the herbs and spices in the strainer, then divide the fish among deep soup plates (you can skin the fish if you wish, but this is not essential) and keep hot.

4 Reheat the soup until it boils. Lower the heat and whisk in the *beurre manié*, little by little, until the soup thickens. Season it and pour over the fish. Garnish each portion with the golden baby onions and mushrooms and sprinkle with chopped parsley.

COOK'S TIP

To make the *beurre manié* for thickening, mix 15g/½oz/1 tbsp softened butter with 15ml/1 tbsp plain (all-purpose) flour. Add to the boiling soup a pinch at a time, whisking constantly.

Fish Soup with Rouille

Making this soup is simplicity itself, yet the flavour suggests it is the product of painstaking preparation and cooking.

SERVES SIX

INGREDIENTS

- 1kg/2¼lb mixed fish
- 30ml/2 tbsp olive oil
- 1 onion, chopped
- 1 carrot, chopped
- 1 leek, chopped
- 2 large ripe tomatoes, chopped
- 1 red (bell) pepper, seeded and chopped
- 2 garlic cloves, peeled
- 150g/5oz/⅔ cup tomato purée (paste)
- 1 large fresh bouquet garni, containing 3 parsley sprigs, 3 celery sticks and 3 bay leaves
- 300ml/½ pint/1¼ cups white wine
- salt and ground black pepper

For the rouille

- 2 garlic cloves, coarsely chopped
- 5ml/1 tsp coarse salt
- 1 thick slice of white bread, crust removed, soaked in water and squeezed dry
- 1 fresh red chilli, seeded and coarsely chopped
- 45ml/3 tbsp olive oil
- salt and cayenne pepper

For the garnish

- 12 slices of baguette, toasted in the oven
- 50g/2oz/½ cup finely grated Gruyère cheese

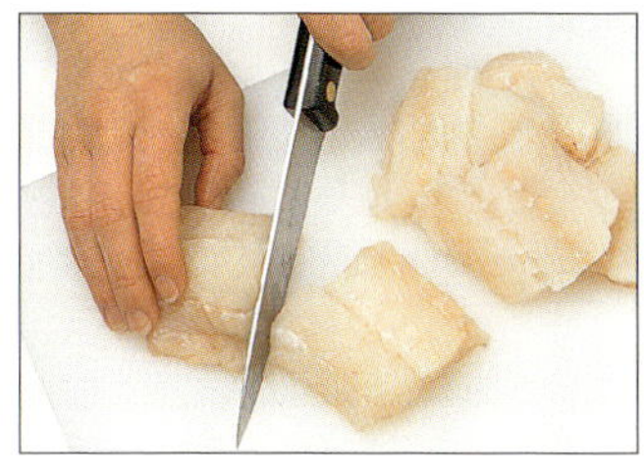

1 Cut the fish into 7.5cm/3in chunks, removing any obvious bones. Heat the oil in a large pan, then add the fish and chopped vegetables. Stir until these begin to colour.

2 Add all the other soup ingredients, then pour in just enough cold water to cover the mixture. Season well and bring to just below boiling point, then lower the heat to a bare simmer, cover and cook for 1 hour.

3 Meanwhile, make the rouille. Put the garlic and coarse salt in a mortar and crush to a paste with a pestle. Add the soaked bread and chilli and pound until smooth, or process in a food processor. Whisk in the olive oil, a drop at a time, to make a smooth, shiny sauce that resembles mayonnaise. Season with salt and add a pinch of cayenne if you like a fiery taste. Set the rouille aside.

4 Lift out and discard the bouquet garni from the soup. Process the soup in batches in a food processor, then strain through a fine strainer placed over a clean pan, pushing the solids through with the back of a ladle.

5 Reheat the soup without letting it boil. Check the seasoning and ladle into individual bowls. Top each serving with two slices of toasted baguette, a spoonful of rouille and some grated Gruyère.

COOK'S TIP

Any firm fish can be used for this recipe. If you use whole fish, include the heads, which enhance the flavour of the soup.

Lobster Bisque

Bisque is a luxurious, velvety soup, which can be made with any crustaceans.

SERVES SIX

INGREDIENTS
- 500g/1 1/4 lb fresh lobster
- 75g/3oz/6 tbsp butter
- 1 onion, chopped
- 1 carrot, diced
- 1 celery stick, diced
- 45ml/3 tbsp brandy, plus extra for serving (optional)
- 250ml/8fl oz/1 cup dry white wine
- 1 litre/1 3/4 pints/4 cups fish stock
- 15ml/1 tbsp tomato purée (paste)
- 75g/3oz/scant 1/2 cup long grain rice
- 1 fresh bouquet garni
- 150ml/1/4 pint/2/3 cup double (heavy) cream, plus extra to garnish
- salt, ground white pepper and cayenne pepper

1 Cut the lobster into pieces. Melt half the butter in a large pan, add the vegetables and cook over a low heat until soft. Add the lobster and stir until the shell on each piece turns red.

2 Pour over the brandy and set it alight. When the flames die down, add the wine and boil until reduced by half. Pour in the fish stock and simmer for 2–3 minutes. Remove the lobster.

3 Stir in the tomato purée and rice, add the bouquet garni and cook until the rice is tender. Meanwhile, remove the lobster meat from the shell and return the shells to the pan. Dice the lobster meat and set it aside.

COOK'S TIP

It is best to buy a live lobster, chilling it in the freezer until it is comatose and then killing it just before cooking. If you can't face this procedure, use a cooked lobster; take care not to over-cook the flesh. Stir for only 30–60 seconds.

4 When the rice is cooked, discard all the larger pieces of shell. Tip the mixture into a blender or food processor and process to a purée. Press the purée through a fine strainer placed over the clean pan. Stir the mixture, then heat until almost boiling. Season with salt, pepper and cayenne, then lower the heat and stir in the cream. Dice the remaining butter and whisk it into the bisque. Add the diced lobster meat and serve immediately. If you like, pour a small spoonful of brandy into each soup bowl and swirl in a little extra cream.

BOUILLABAISSE

Authentic bouillabaisse comes from the south of France and includes rascasse (scorpion fish) as an essential ingredient. It is, however, perfectly possible to make this wonderful main-course soup without it. Use as large a variety of fish as you can.

SERVES FOUR

INGREDIENTS
- 45ml/3 tbsp olive oil
- 2 onions, chopped
- 2 leeks, white parts only, chopped
- 4 garlic cloves, chopped
- 450g/1lb ripe tomatoes, peeled and chopped
- 3 litres/5 pints/12 cups boiling fish stock or water
- 15ml/1 tbsp tomato purée (paste)
- large pinch of saffron threads
- 1 fresh bouquet garni, containing 2 thyme sprigs, 2 bay leaves and 2 fennel sprigs
- 3kg/6½lb mixed fish, cleaned and cut into large chunks
- 4 potatoes, peeled and thickly sliced
- salt, pepper and cayenne pepper
- a bowl of rouille (see Fish Soup) and a bowl of aioli (see Provençal Aioli with Salt Cod), to serve

For the garnish
- 16 slices of French bread, toasted and rubbed with garlic
- 30ml/2 tbsp chopped fresh parsley

1 Heat the oil in a large pan. Add the onions, leeks, garlic and tomatoes. Cook until slightly softened. Stir in the stock or water, tomato purée and saffron. Add the bouquet garni and boil until the oil is amalgamated. Lower the heat; add the fish and potatoes.

COOK'S TIP
Suitable fish for Bouillabaisse include rascasse, conger eel, monkfish, red gurnard and John Dory.

2 Simmer the soup for 5–8 minutes, removing each type of fish as it becomes cooked. Continue to cook until the potatoes are very tender. Season well with salt, pepper and cayenne.

3 Divide the fish and potatoes among individual soup plates. Strain the soup and ladle it over the fish. Garnish with toasted French bread and parsley. Serve with rouille and aioli.

Seafood Soup with Rouille

This is a really chunky, aromatic mixed fish soup from France, flavoured with plenty of saffron and herbs. Rouille, a fiery hot paste, is served separately for everyone to swirl into their soup according to taste.

SERVES SIX

INGREDIENTS
- 3 gurnard, red mullet or snapper, scaled and gutted
- 12 large raw or cooked prawns (shrimp)
- 675g/1½lb white fish, such as cod, haddock, halibut or monkfish
- 225g/8oz fresh mussels
- 1 onion, quartered
- 1.2 litres/2 pints/5 cups water
- 5ml/1 tsp saffron threads
- 15ml/1 tbsp boiling water
- 75ml/5 tbsp olive oil
- 1 fennel bulb, coarsely chopped
- 4 garlic cloves, crushed
- 3 strips orange rind
- 4 fresh thyme sprigs
- 675g/1½lb tomatoes or 400g/14oz can chopped tomatoes
- 30ml/2 tbsp sun-dried tomato paste
- 3 bay leaves
- salt and ground black pepper

For the rouille
- 1 red (bell) pepper, seeded and coarsely chopped
- 1 fresh red chilli, seeded and sliced
- 2 garlic cloves, chopped
- 75ml/5 tbsp olive oil
- 15g/½oz/¼ cup fresh white breadcrumbs

1 To make the rouille, put the red pepper, chilli, garlic, olive oil and breadcrumbs in a blender or food processor and process until smooth. Transfer to a serving dish, cover with clear film (plastic wrap) and chill in the refrigerator.

2 Fillet the gurnard, red mullet or snapper by cutting away the flesh from either side of the backbone, reserving the heads and bones. Cut the fillets into small chunks.

3 Peel half the prawns and reserve the trimmings to make the stock. Skin the white fish, discarding any bones, and cut the flesh into large chunks with a sharp knife.

4 Scrub the mussels well, discarding any damaged ones and any that do not close immediately when tapped sharply with the back of a knife. Remove and discard the "beards".

5 Put the fish trimmings and prawn trimmings in a pan with the onion and measured cold water. Bring to the boil, then lower the heat and simmer gently for 30 minutes. Remove the pan from the heat, leave to cool slightly and strain.

6 Place the saffron in a small bowl, add the boiling water and leave to soak. Meanwhile, heat 30ml/2 tbsp of the olive oil in a large, deep sauté pan or frying pan. Add the gurnard, mullet or snapper and the white fish and cook over a high heat for 1 minute. Remove from the pan and drain on kitchen paper.

7 Heat the remaining olive oil in the pan, then add the fennel, garlic, strips of orange rind and thyme sprigs and cook over a medium heat, stirring occasionally, until beginning to colour. Measure the strained stock and make up to about 1.2 litres/2 pints/5 cups with water.

8 If using fresh tomatoes, plunge them into boiling water for about 30 seconds, then drain and refresh in cold water. Peel off the skins and chop the flesh.

9 Add the stock to the pan with the saffron, tomatoes, sun-dried tomato paste and bay leaves. Season to taste. Bring almost to the boil, lower the heat, then cover and simmer gently for 20 minutes.

10 Stir in the gurnard, mullet or snapper, white fish and both the peeled and unpeeled prawns and add the mussels. Cover the pan and cook for 3–4 minutes. Discard any mussels that do not open. Ladle the soup into warm bowls and serve immediately with the dish of rouille.

COOK'S TIP

To save time, order the fish in advance and ask the fishmonger to fillet the gurnard, mullet or snapper for you.

Prawn Bisque

The classic French recipe for bisque requires pushing the shellfish through a tamis, or drum sieve. The simpler method given here has an equally smooth, delicious result.

SERVES SIX TO EIGHT

INGREDIENTS

- 675g/1½lb cooked prawns (shrimp) in the shell
- 25ml/1½ tbsp vegetable oil
- 2 onions, halved and sliced
- 1 large carrot, sliced
- 2 celery sticks, sliced
- 2 litres/3⅓ pints/8 cups water
- a few drops of lemon juice
- 30ml/2 tbsp tomato purée (paste)
- bouquet garni
- 50g/2oz/¼ cup butter
- 50g/2oz/½ cup plain (all-purpose) flour
- 45–60ml/3–4 tbsp brandy
- 150ml/¼ pint/⅔ cup whipping cream
- salt and ground white pepper
- flat leaf parsley sprigs, to garnish

1 Remove the heads and peel off the shells from the prawns, reserving them for the stock. Chill the prawns.

2 Heat the oil in a large pan, add the prawn heads and shells and cook over a high heat, stirring frequently, until they start to brown. Reduce the heat to medium, add the onions, carrot and celery and cook gently, stirring occasionally, for about 5 minutes, until the onions are just starting to soften.

3 Add the water, lemon juice, tomato purée and bouquet garni. Bring the stock to the boil, then reduce the heat, cover and simmer gently for 25 minutes. Strain the stock through a sieve into a bowl. Discard the contents of the sieve.

4 Melt the butter in a heavy pan over a medium heat. Stir in the flour and cook until just golden in colour, stirring occasionally. Add the brandy and gradually pour in about half of the prawn stock, whisking vigorously with a balloon whisk until the mixture is smooth, then whisk in the remaining liquid. Season to taste with salt and pepper. Reduce the heat, cover the pan and simmer gently for 5 minutes, stirring frequently.

5 Strain the soup into a clean pan. Add the cream and a little extra lemon juice to taste, if you like, then stir in most of the reserved prawns and cook over a medium heat until hot. Ladle the soup into warm bowls and serve immediately, garnished with the reserved prawns and parsley.

Mussel Bisque

This delicious soup is equally good served hot or cold.

SERVES SIX

INGREDIENTS

675g/1½lb fresh mussels
150ml/¼ pint/⅔ cup dry white wine or dry (hard) cider
475ml/16fl oz/2 cups water
25g/1oz/2 tbsp butter
1 small red onion, chopped
1 small leek, thinly sliced
1 carrot, finely diced
2 tomatoes, peeled, seeded and chopped
2 garlic cloves, crushed
15ml/1 tbsp chopped fresh parsley
15ml/1 tbsp chopped fresh basil
1 celery stick, thinly sliced
½ red (bell) pepper, seeded and chopped
250ml/8fl oz/1 cup whipping cream
salt and ground black pepper

1 Scrub the mussels and pull off the beards. Discard any with broken shells or any that do not close when sharply tapped. Place them in a large pan with half the wine or cider and 150ml/¼ pint/⅔ cup of the water.

2 Cover the pan and cook the mussels over a high heat until they open up, occasionally shaking the pan vigorously. (Discard any mussels that do not open in 4–6 minutes.) Transfer the mussels with a slotted spoon to a dish and leave until they are cool enough to handle. Remove the mussels from their shells, leaving a few in their shells for the garnish if you like.

3 Strain the cooking liquid through a clean piece of muslin (cheesecloth) or other fine cloth to remove any traces of sand or grit.

4 Melt the butter in the same large pan and cook the onion, leek, carrot, tomatoes and garlic over a high heat for 2–3 minutes.

5 Reduce the heat to low and cook for a further 2–3 minutes, then add the reserved cooking liquid, the remaining water and wine or cider, the parsley and basil and simmer for a further 10 minutes. Add the mussels, celery, red pepper and cream and season to taste with salt and pepper. Serve the soup hot or cold.

Mediterranean Fish Soup

This soup is a rich and colourful mixture of fish and shellfish, flavoured with tomatoes, saffron and orange.

SERVES FOUR TO SIX

INGREDIENTS

- 1.5kg/3¼lb mixed fish and raw shellfish, such as red mullet, John Dory, monkfish, red snapper, whiting, large raw prawns (shrimp) and clams
- 225g/8oz well-flavoured tomatoes
- pinch of saffron threads
- 90ml/6 tbsp olive oil
- 1 onion, sliced
- 1 leek, sliced
- 1 celery stick, sliced
- 2 garlic cloves, crushed
- 1 bouquet garni
- 1 strip orange rind
- 2.5ml/½ tsp fennel seeds
- 15ml/1 tbsp tomato purée (paste)
- 10ml/2 tsp Pernod
- salt and ground black pepper
- 4–6 thick slices French bread, to serve
- 45ml/3 tbsp chopped fresh parsley, to garnish

1 Remove the heads, tails and fins from the fish and set the fish aside. Put the fish trimmings in a large, heavy pan and add 1.2 litres/2 pints/5 cups water. Bring to the boil, then lower the heat, cover and simmer gently for 15 minutes. Strain into a bowl and reserve the liquid. Discard the contents of the sieve.

2 Cut the fish into large chunks. Leave the shellfish in their shells. Plunge the tomatoes into boiling water for 30 seconds, then drain and refresh in cold water. Peel off the skins and coarsely chop the flesh. Soak the saffron in 15–30ml/1–2 tbsp hot water.

3 Heat the oil in a large pan, add the onion, leek and celery and cook until softened. Add the garlic, bouquet garni, orange rind, fennel seeds and tomatoes, then stir in the saffron and soaking liquid and the fish stock. Season with salt and pepper, then bring to the boil and simmer for 30 minutes.

4 Add the shellfish and continue to boil for about 6 minutes. Lower the heat, add the fish and cook for a further 6–8 minutes, until the flesh flakes easily.

5 Using a slotted spoon, transfer the fish to a warmed serving platter. Keep the liquid boiling gently to allow the oil to emulsify with the broth. Add the tomato purée and Pernod and stir well, then taste and adjust the seasoning if necessary.

6 To serve, place a slice of French bread in the base of each soup bowl, pour the broth over the top and serve the fish separately, sprinkled with the chopped parsley.

COOK'S TIP

Saffron comes from the orange and red stigmas of a type of crocus. These must be harvested by hand and it requires about 250,000 crocus flowers for a yield of 500g/1¼lb saffron. Consequently, it is extremely expensive – the highest-priced spice in the world. However, its slightly bitter flavour and pleasantly sweet aroma are unique and cannot be replaced by any other spice. It is an essential ingredient in virtually all traditional Mediterranean fish soups and stews and should not be omitted.

Classic Italian Fish Soup

In this Ligurian soup the fish are cooked in a broth with vegetables and then puréed.

SERVES SIX

INGREDIENTS

- 1kg/2¼lb mixed fish, such as coley, dogfish, whiting, red mullet, snapper, pollock or cod
- 90ml/6 tbsp olive oil, plus extra to serve
- 1 onion, finely chopped
- 1 celery stick, chopped
- 1 carrot, chopped
- 60ml/4 tbsp chopped fresh parsley
- 175ml/6fl oz/¾ cup dry white wine
- 3 medium tomatoes, peeled and chopped
- 2 garlic cloves, finely chopped
- 1.5 litres/2½ pints/6¼ cups boiling water
- salt and ground black pepper
- rounds of French bread, to serve

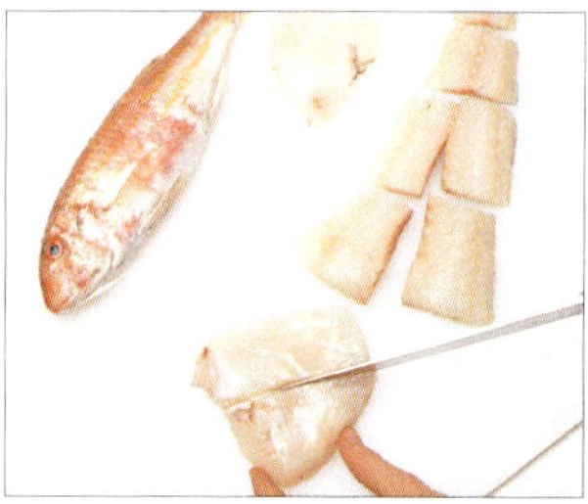

1 If necessary, scale and clean the fish, discarding all the innards, but leaving the heads on. Using a sharp knife, cut them into large pieces. Rinse well in cool water.

2 Heat the oil in a large, heavy pan and add the onion. Cook over low to medium heat, stirring occasionally, until it begins to soften. Stir in the celery and carrot and cook, stirring frequently, for a further 5 minutes. Add the parsley.

3 Pour in the wine, increase the heat to high, and cook until the liquid has reduced by about half. Stir in the chopped tomatoes and garlic. Cook, stirring occasionally, for 3–4 minutes. Pour in the boiling water and bring back to the boil. Lower the heat to medium and cook gently for a further 15 minutes.

4 Stir in the fish and simmer gently for 10–15 minutes, or until the fish pieces are tender and flake easily. Season to taste with salt and pepper.

5 Remove the fish from the soup with a slotted spoon. Discard the heads and any bones. Transfer the fish to a food processor and process to a purée. Taste and adjust the seasoning, if necessary. If the soup is too thick, add a little more water.

6 To serve, return the soup to the pan and heat just to simmering point. Meanwhile, toast the rounds of French bread and sprinkle them with a little extra olive oil. Place two or three rounds in the base of each soup plate before pouring the soup over. Serve immediately.

SHELLFISH WITH SEASONED BROTH

LEAVE ONE OR TWO MUSSELS AND PRAWNS IN THEIR SHELLS TO ADD AN EXTRA TOUCH TO THIS ELEGANT DISH.

SERVES FOUR

INGREDIENTS

- 675g/1½lb fresh mussels, scrubbed and bearded
- 1 small fennel bulb, thinly sliced
- 1 onion, thinly sliced
- 1 leek, thinly sliced
- 1 small carrot, cut into julienne strips
- 1 garlic clove
- 1 litre/1¾ pints/4 cups water
- pinch of curry powder
- pinch of saffron threads
- 1 bay leaf
- 450g/1lb raw prawns (shrimp)
- 450g/1lb small shelled scallops
- 175g/6oz cooked lobster meat, sliced (optional)
- salt and ground black pepper
- 15–30ml/1–2 tbsp chopped fresh chervil or parsley, to serve

1 Put the mussels in a large heavy pan or flameproof casserole and add just enough water to cover. Cover the pan with a tight-fitting lid and cook over a high heat for 4–6 minutes, until the shells open, occasionally shaking the pan or casserole vigorously. Remove the mussels with a slotted spoon and, when cool enough to handle, discard any mussels that did not open and remove the remainder from their shells. Strain the cooking liquid through a sieve lined with muslin (cheesecloth) and reserve.

2 Put the fennel, onion, leek, carrot and whole garlic clove in another pan and add the measured water, reserved mussel cooking liquid, spices and bay leaf. Bring to the boil, skimming any foam that rises to the surface, then reduce the heat, cover and simmer gently for 20 minutes, until the vegetables are tender. Meanwhile, peel the prawns and remove their heads.

3 Remove the garlic clove from the pan. Add the prawns, scallops and lobster meat, if using, and cook for 1 minute. Add the mussels and simmer gently for about 3 minutes, until the scallops are opaque and all the shellfish are heated through. Taste and adjust the seasoning, if necessary, then ladle the soup into a heated tureen and sprinkle with the chervil or parsley. Serve immediately.

Spiced Mussel Soup

Chunky and colourful, this Turkish fish soup is similar to a chowder in its consistency. It is flavoured with harissa sauce, more familiar in North African cooking.

SERVES SIX

INGREDIENTS

- 1.5kg/3¼lb fresh mussels
- 150ml/¼ pint/⅔ cup white wine
- 3 tomatoes
- 30ml/2 tbsp olive oil
- 1 onion, finely chopped
- 2 garlic cloves, crushed
- 2 celery sticks, thinly sliced
- bunch of spring onions (scallions), thinly sliced
- 1 potato, diced
- 7.5ml/1½ tsp harissa sauce
- 45ml/3 tbsp chopped fresh parsley
- ground black pepper
- thick yogurt, to serve

1 Scrub the mussels thoroughly under cold water and remove the beards, discarding any with damaged shells or any open ones that do not close immediately when tapped sharply with a knife.

2 Bring the wine to the boil in a large, heavy pan. Add the mussels and cover with a tight-fitting lid. Cook for 4–5 minutes, until the mussels have opened fully. Discard any mussels that remain closed.

3 Drain the mussels, reserving the cooking liquid. Strain the cooking liquid through a clean piece of muslin (cheesecloth) or fine cloth to remove any traces of grit. Reserve a few of the mussels in their shells for garnish and shell the remainder.

4 Plunge the tomatoes into boiling water for 30 seconds, then refresh in cold water. Peel off the skins and dice the flesh. Heat the oil in a heavy pan and cook the onion, garlic, celery and spring onions for 5 minutes.

5 Transfer a little of the onion mixture to a small bowl. Add the shelled mussels, reserved cooking liquid, potato, harissa sauce and tomatoes to the pan. Bring just to the boil, reduce the heat to low and cover. Simmer gently for 25 minutes, or until the potato is just beginning to break up.

COOK'S TIP

Harissa is a spicy purée made from chillies, cayenne, olive oil, garlic, coriander and cumin. It may also be flavoured with mint or verbena. It is available from Middle Eastern delicatessens and many supermarkets. Keep the surface covered with a thin layer of olive oil.

6 Stir in the parsley and season to taste with pepper. Add the reserved mussels and heat through for 1 minute. Ladle into a warm tureen or individual soup bowls, garnish with the reserved onion mixture and serve immediately with a spoonful of yogurt.

Fish and Okra Soup

The inspiration for this tasty and unusual soup came from a traditional Ghanaian recipe.

SERVES FOUR

INGREDIENTS

- 2 green bananas
- 50g/2oz/¼ cup butter or margarine
- 1 onion, finely chopped
- 2 tomatoes, peeled and chopped
- 115g/4oz okra, trimmed
- 225g/8oz smoked haddock or cod fillet, cut into bitesize pieces
- 900ml/1½ pints/3¾ cups fish stock
- 1 fresh chilli, seeded and chopped
- salt and ground black pepper
- parsley sprigs, to garnish

1 Slit the skins of the green bananas, but do not peel them. Place them in a large pan. Cover with water, bring to the boil and cook over a medium heat for about 25 minutes, or until the bananas are tender. Transfer to a plate and leave to cool.

2 Melt the butter or margarine in a large, heavy pan, add the onion and cook over a medium heat, stirring occasionally, for about 5 minutes until soft. Stir in the chopped tomatoes and okra and cook gently, stirring occasionally, for a further 10 minutes.

3 Add the pieces of fish, fish stock and chilli and season to taste with salt and pepper. Bring to the boil, then reduce the heat and simmer gently for about 20 minutes, or until the fish is cooked through and the flesh flakes easily.

4 Peel the cooked bananas and cut them into slices. Stir the slices into the soup and heat through gently for a few minutes. Ladle into warm soup bowls or a tureen. Garnish with the sprigs of parsley and serve the soup immediately.

SMOKED HADDOCK AND POTATO SOUP

THIS SCOTTISH SOUP IS TRADITIONALLY CALLED CULLEN SKINK. A CULLEN IS A PORT, WHILE "SKINK" MEANS BROTH.

SERVES SIX

INGREDIENTS

- 1 finnan haddock, about 350g/12oz
- 1 onion, chopped
- bouquet garni
- 900ml/1½ pints/3¾ cups water
- 500g/1¼ lb potatoes, quartered
- 600ml/1 pint/2½ cups milk
- 40g/1½oz/3 tbsp butter
- salt and ground black pepper
- chopped fresh chives, to garnish

1 Put the haddock, onion, bouquet garni and measured water into a large, heavy pan and bring to the boil over a medium heat. Skim the scum from the surface with a spoon, then cover the pan. Reduce the heat to low and poach gently for 10–15 minutes, until the haddock is cooked through and the flesh flakes easily.

COOK'S TIP

Finnan haddock is a small, whole fish that has been soaked in brine and then cold smoked. It has delicate, pale yellow flesh and is sold without the head. If you cannot find it, substitute plain smoked haddock fillets, but try to buy ones that have not been dyed to a bright yellow colour.

2 Lift the haddock from the pan, using a fish slice or metal spatula. Reserve the cooking liquid in the pan. Remove the skin and bones. Flake the flesh and set aside. Return the skin and bones to the pan and simmer, uncovered, for a further 30 minutes.

3 Strain the fish stock and return to the pan. Discard the contents of the strainer. Add the potatoes to the pan, bring back to the boil, then simmer for about 25 minutes, or until tender. Remove the potatoes from the pan using a slotted spoon. Add the milk to the pan and bring to the boil.

4 Meanwhile, mash the potatoes with the butter, then whisk them into the milk in the pan until thick and creamy. Add the flaked fish to the pan, then taste and adjust the seasoning if necessary. Pour the soup into a warmed tureen or individual bowls. Sprinkle with chopped chives and serve immediately with crusty bread.

CORN AND SCALLOP CHOWDER

FRESH CORN IS IDEAL FOR THIS CHOWDER, ALTHOUGH CANNED OR FROZEN CORN ALSO WORKS WELL.

SERVES FOUR TO SIX

INGREDIENTS

- 2 corn cobs or 200g/7oz frozen or canned corn
- 600ml/1 pint/2½ cups milk
- 15g/½oz/1 tbsp butter
- 1 small leek or onion, chopped
- 1 small garlic clove, crushed
- 40g/1½oz smoked lean bacon, finely chopped
- 1 small green (bell) pepper, seeded and diced
- 1 celery stick, chopped
- 1 medium potato, diced
- 15ml/1 tbsp plain (all-purpose) flour
- 300ml/½ pint/1¼ cups chicken or vegetable stock
- 4 scallops
- 115g/4oz cooked fresh mussels
- pinch of paprika
- 150ml/¼ pint/⅔ cup single (light) cream (optional)
- salt and ground black pepper

1 Using a sharp knife, slice down the fresh corn cobs to remove the kernels. If you are using canned corn, drain well and rinse. Place half of the corn kernels in a food processor or blender and process with a little of the milk.

2 Melt the butter in a large, heavy pan. Add the leek or onion, garlic and bacon and cook over a medium heat, stirring occasionally, for about 4–5 minutes, until the leek or onion is soft but not browned.

3 Add the green pepper, chopped celery and diced potato to the pan and cook over low heat, stirring frequently, for a further 3–4 minutes without browning.

4 Stir in the flour and cook, stirring constantly, for 1–2 minutes, until the mixture is golden and frothy. Gradually stir in the milk and corn mixture, chicken or vegetable stock, the remaining milk and the whole corn kernels. Season to taste with salt and pepper.

5 Bring to the boil, then reduce the heat and simmer, partially covered, for 15–20 minutes until the vegetables are tender.

6 Pull the corals away from the scallops and slice the white flesh into 5mm/¼in slices. Stir the scallops into the soup, cook for 4 minutes and then stir in the corals, mussels and paprika. Heat through for a few minutes and then stir in the cream, if using. Adjust the seasoning to taste and serve immediately.

Clam Chowder

If fresh clams are hard to find, use frozen or canned clams for this classic recipe from New England. Large clams should be cut into chunky pieces. Reserve a few clams in their shells for garnish, if you like. Traditionally, the soup is served with savoury saltine crackers. You should be able to find these in any good delicatessen.

SERVES FOUR

INGREDIENTS

- 100g/3¾oz salt pork or thinly sliced unsmoked bacon, diced
- 1 large onion, chopped
- 2 potatoes, peeled and cut into 1cm/½in cubes
- 1 bay leaf
- 1 fresh thyme sprig
- 300ml/½ pint/1¼ cups milk
- 400g/14oz cooked clams, cooking liquid reserved
- 150ml/¼ pint/⅔ cup double (heavy) cream
- salt, ground white pepper and cayenne pepper
- finely chopped fresh parsley, to garnish

1 Put the salt pork or unsmoked bacon in a pan, and heat gently, stirring frequently, until the fat runs and the meat is starting to brown. Add the chopped onion and cook over a low heat for about 5 minutes, until softened but not browned.

2 Add the cubed potatoes, the bay leaf and thyme sprig, stir well to coat with fat, then pour in the milk and reserved clam liquid and bring to the boil. Lower the heat and simmer for about 10 minutes, until the potatoes are tender but still firm. Lift out the bay leaf and thyme sprig and discard.

3 Remove the shells from most of the clams. Add all the clams to the pan and season to taste with salt, pepper and cayenne. Simmer gently for a further 5 minutes, then stir in the cream. Heat until the soup is very hot, but do not let it boil. Pour into a warm tureen, garnish with the chopped parsley and serve the soup immediately.

Chinese Crab and Corn Soup

Frozen white crab meat works as well as fresh in this delicately flavoured soup.

SERVES FOUR

INGREDIENTS

- 600ml/1 pint/2½ cups fish or chicken stock
- 2.5cm/1in piece fresh root ginger, peeled and very finely sliced
- 400g/14oz can creamed corn
- 150g/5oz cooked white crab meat
- 15ml/1 tbsp arrowroot or cornflour (cornstarch)
- 15ml/1 tbsp rice wine or dry sherry
- 15–30ml/1–2 tbsp light soy sauce
- 1 egg white
- salt and ground white pepper
- shredded spring onions (scallions), to garnish

COOK'S TIP

This soup is sometimes made with whole kernel corn, but creamed corn gives a better and more authentic texture. If you can't find it in a can, use thawed frozen creamed corn instead; the result will be just as good.

1 Put the stock and ginger in a large pan and bring to the boil over a medium heat. Stir in the creamed corn and bring back to the boil.

2 Switch off the heat and add the crab meat. Put the arrowroot or cornflour in a cup and stir in the rice wine or sherry to make a smooth paste; stir this into the soup. Cook over a low heat for about 3 minutes until the soup has thickened and is slightly glutinous in consistency. Add light soy sauce, salt and white pepper to taste.

3 In a bowl, whisk the egg white to a stiff foam. Gradually fold it into the soup. Ladle the soup into heated bowls, garnish each portion with spring onions and serve immediately.

VARIATION

To make prawn (shrimp) and corn soup, substitute 150g/5oz/1¼ cups cooked peeled prawns for the crab meat. Chop the prawns coarsely and add to the soup at the beginning of step 2.

THAI FISH BROTH

LEMON GRASS, CHILLIES AND GALANGAL ARE AMONG THE FLAVOURINGS USED IN THIS FRAGRANT SOUP.

SERVES TWO TO THREE

INGREDIENTS

- 1 litre/1¾ pints/4 cups fish stock
- 4 lemon grass stalks
- 3 limes
- 2 small fresh hot red chillies, seeded and thinly sliced
- 2cm/¾in piece fresh galangal, peeled and thinly sliced
- 6 coriander (cilantro) stalks, with leaves
- 2 kaffir lime leaves, coarsely chopped (optional)
- 350g/12oz monkfish fillet, skinned and cut into 2.5cm/1in pieces
- 15ml/1 tbsp rice vinegar
- 45ml/3 tbsp Thai fish sauce
- 30ml/2 tbsp chopped coriander (cilantro) leaves, to garnish

1 Pour the stock into a pan and bring it to the boil. Meanwhile, slice the bulb end of the lemon grass stalks diagonally into pieces about 3mm/⅛in thick. Peel off four wide strips of lime rind with a vegetable peeler, taking care to avoid the white pith underneath which would make the soup bitter. Squeeze the limes and reserve the juice.

2 Add the sliced lemon grass, lime rind, chillies, galangal and coriander stalks to the stock, with the kaffir lime leaves, if using. Simmer for 1–2 minutes.

VARIATIONS

Prawns (shrimp), scallops, squid or sole can be substituted for the monkfish. If you use kaffir lime leaves, you will need the juice of only 2 limes.

3 Add the monkfish, rice vinegar and fish sauce, with half the reserved lime juice. Simmer for about 3 minutes, until the fish is just cooked. Lift out and discard the coriander stalks, taste the broth and add more lime juice if necessary; the soup should taste quite sour. Sprinkle with the coriander leaves and serve very hot.

MALAYSIAN PRAWN LAKSA

This spicy prawn and noodle soup tastes just as good when made with fresh crab meat or any flaked cooked fish. If you are short of time or can't find all the spicy paste ingredients, buy ready-made laksa paste, which is available from Asian stores.

SERVES TWO TO THREE

INGREDIENTS

- 115g/4oz rice vermicelli or stir-fry rice noodles
- 15ml/1 tbsp vegetable or groundnut (peanut) oil
- 600ml/1 pint/2½ cups fish stock
- 400ml/14fl oz/1⅔ cups thin coconut milk
- 30ml/2 tbsp Thai fish sauce
- ½ lime
- 16–24 cooked peeled prawns (shrimp)
- salt and cayenne pepper
- 60ml/4 tbsp chopped fresh coriander (cilantro) sprigs and leaves, to garnish

For the spicy paste

- 2 lemon grass stalks, finely chopped
- 2 fresh red chillies, seeded and chopped
- 2.5cm/1in piece fresh root ginger, peeled and sliced
- 2.5ml/½ tsp dried shrimp paste
- 2 garlic cloves, chopped
- 2.5ml/½ tsp ground turmeric
- 30ml/2 tbsp tamarind paste

1 Cook the rice vermicelli or noodles in a large pan of salted, boiling water according to the instructions on the packet. Tip into a large strainer or colander, then rinse under cold water and drain. Keep warm.

2 To make the spicy paste, place all the prepared ingredients in a mortar and pound with a pestle. Alternatively, put the ingredients in a food processor and process until a smooth paste is formed.

3 Heat the vegetable or groundnut oil in a large, heavy pan, add the spicy paste and cook over a medium heat, stirring constantly, for a few moments to release all the flavours, but be careful not to let it burn.

4 Add the fish stock and coconut milk and bring to the boil. Stir in the fish sauce, then simmer for 5 minutes. Season with salt and cayenne, adding a squeeze of lime. Add the prawns and heat through for a few seconds.

5 Divide the noodles among two or three soup plates. Pour over the soup, making sure that each portion includes an equal number of prawns. Garnish with coriander and serve piping hot.

Crab and Egg Noodle Broth

This delicious broth is perfect when you are hungry and time is short.

SERVES FOUR

INGREDIENTS

- 75g/3oz fine egg noodles
- 25g/1oz/2 tbsp unsalted (sweet) butter
- 1 small bunch spring onions (scallions), chopped
- 1 celery stick, sliced
- 1 medium carrot, peeled and cut into batons
- 1.2 litres/2 pints/5 cups chicken stock
- 60ml/4 tbsp dry sherry
- 115g/4oz white crab meat
- pinch of celery salt
- pinch of cayenne pepper
- 10ml/2 tsp lemon or lime juice
- coarsely chopped coriander (cilantro) or flat leaf parsley, to garnish

1 Bring a large pan of water to the boil. Toss in the egg noodles and cook according to the instructions on the packet. Cool under cold running water and leave immersed in water until required.

2 Melt the butter in another large pan, add the spring onions, celery and carrot, cover and cook the vegetables over a gentle heat for 3–4 minutes, until softened.

3 Add the chicken stock and sherry to the pan, bring to the boil, reduce the heat and simmer gently for a further 5 minutes.

4 Flake the crab meat between your fingers on to a plate and remove any stray pieces of shell.

COOK'S TIP

You can use fresh or frozen crab meat for this soup. If using frozen, make sure that it is completely thawed.

5 Drain the egg noodles thoroughly and add them to the broth, together with the crab meat. Stir well and season to taste with celery salt and cayenne pepper and sharpen with the lemon or lime juice. Bring the soup back to a gentle simmer to heat through.

6 Ladle the broth into warm, shallow soup plates, sprinkle with coarsely chopped coriander or flat leaf parsley and serve immediately.

Corn and Crab Meat Soup

This soup originated in the United States, but it has since been introduced into China.

SERVES FOUR

INGREDIENTS
- 115g/4oz crab meat
- 10ml/2 tsp finely chopped fresh root ginger
- 2 egg whites
- 30ml/2 tbsp milk
- 15ml/1 tbsp cornflour (cornstarch) paste
- 600ml/1 pint/2½ cups vegetable or chicken stock
- 225g/8oz can creamed corn
- salt and ground black pepper
- chopped spring onions (scallions), to garnish

1 Flake the crab meat with your fingers or using chopsticks and mix it with the fresh root ginger in a small bowl.

2 Beat the egg whites until frothy in another bowl, add the milk and cornflour paste and beat again until smooth and well mixed. Blend with the crab meat.

3 Bring the stock to the boil in a wok or large, heavy pan over a medium heat, add the creamed corn and bring back to the boil.

4 Stir in the crab meat and egg-white mixture. Season to taste with salt and pepper and stir gently until well blended and heated through. Ladle the soup into warm bowls and serve immediately, garnished with chopped spring onions.

NOODLE SOUP WITH PORK AND SICHUAN PICKLE

This soup is a meal in itself and the hot pickle – available from Chinese food stores – gives it a delicious tang.

SERVES FOUR

INGREDIENTS
- 1 litre/1¾ pints/4 cups chicken stock
- 350g/12oz egg noodles
- 15ml/1 tbsp dried prawns (shrimp), soaked in water
- 30ml/2 tbsp vegetable or groundnut (peanut) oil
- 225g/8oz lean pork, finely shredded
- 15ml/1 tbsp yellow bean paste
- 15ml/1 tbsp soy sauce
- 115g/4oz Sichuan hot pickle, rinsed, drained and shredded
- pinch of sugar
- 2 spring onions (scallions), thinly sliced, to garnish

1 Bring the chicken stock to the boil in a large pan over a medium heat. Add the noodles and cook until almost tender.

2 Drain the dried prawns, rinse them under cold running water, drain again and add them to the stock. Lower the heat and simmer gently for a further 2 minutes. Keep hot.

3 Heat the oil in a frying pan or wok. Add the pork and stir-fry over a high heat for 3 minutes.

4 Add the bean paste and soy sauce to the pork and stir-fry for 1 minute more. Add the hot pickle with a pinch of sugar. Stir-fry for 1 minute more.

5 Divide the noodles and soup among individual serving bowls. Spoon the pork mixture on top, then sprinkle with the spring onions and serve immediately.

SNAPPER AND NOODLE SOUP

Tamarind gives this light, fragrant noodle soup a slightly sour taste.

SERVES FOUR

INGREDIENTS
- 1kg/2¼lb red snapper (or other red fish, such as mullet)
- 1 onion, sliced
- 50g/2oz tamarind pods
- 15ml/1 tbsp Thai fish sauce
- 15ml/1 tbsp sugar
- 30ml/2 tbsp vegetable oil
- 2 garlic cloves, finely chopped
- 2 lemon grass stalks, very finely chopped
- 4 ripe tomatoes, coarsely chopped
- 30ml/2 tbsp yellow bean paste
- 225g/8oz rice vermicelli, soaked in warm water until soft
- 115g/4oz/2 cups beansprouts
- 8–10 fresh basil or mint sprigs
- 25g/1oz/¼ cup peanuts, ground
- salt and ground black pepper

1 Bring 2 litres/3½ pints/8¾ cups water to the boil in a large pan. Lower the heat and add the fish and onion, with 2.5ml/½ tsp salt. Simmer gently until the fish is cooked through and the flesh flakes easily.

2 Remove the fish from the stock and set aside. Add the tamarind, Thai fish sauce and sugar to the stock. Cook for 5 minutes, then strain into a bowl. Carefully remove all the bones from the fish, keeping the flesh in big pieces.

3 Heat the oil in a large frying pan. Add the garlic and lemon grass and cook, stirring frequently, for a few seconds. Stir in the tomatoes and yellow bean paste. Cook gently for 5–7 minutes, until the tomatoes are soft. Add the strained stock, bring back to a simmer and season to taste with salt and pepper.

4 Drain the vermicelli. Plunge it into a pan of boiling water for a few minutes, drain and divide among individual serving bowls. Add the beansprouts, fish, basil or mint and sprinkle the ground peanuts on top. Top up each bowl with the hot soup and serve immediately.

COOK'S TIP

Tamarind is the pulp that surrounds the seeds of a tropical tree. It has a distinctive flavour for which there is no real substitute. It is usually sold in compacted or dried blocks and is available from large supermarkets.

Main Course Spicy Shrimp and Noodle Soup

This lavish dish is served as a hot coconut broth with a separate platter of tempting prawns, fish and noodles. Diners are invited to add their own choice of accompaniments to the broth.

SERVES FOUR TO SIX

INGREDIENTS

- 25g/1oz shelled, raw cashew nuts
- 3 shallots, or 1 medium onion, sliced
- 5cm/2in piece lemon grass, shredded
- 2 garlic cloves, crushed
- 150g/5oz spaghetti-size rice noodles, soaked for 10 minutes
- 30ml/2 tbsp vegetable oil
- 1cm/½in square piece shrimp paste, or 15ml/1 tbsp Thai fish sauce
- 15ml/1 tbsp mild curry paste
- 400g/14oz can coconut milk
- ½ chicken stock (bouillon) cube
- 3 curry leaves (optional)
- 450g/1lb white fish fillet, such as cod, haddock or whiting
- 225g/8oz raw or cooked prawn (shrimp) tails
- 1 small lettuce, shredded
- 115g/4oz/2 cups beansprouts
- 3 spring onions (scallions), shredded
- ½ cucumber, sliced and shredded
- prawn (shrimp) crackers, to serve

COOK'S TIP

To serve, line a large serving platter or shallow bowl with the shredded lettuce leaves. Arrange the beansprouts, spring onions (scallions) and cucumber in neat piles on top, together with the cooked fish, prawns (shrimp) and noodles. Serve the salad with a separate bowl of prawn crackers, if there isn't room on the platter, and the broth in a lidded stoneware pot. You can substitute other vegetables, such as Chinese leaves (Chinese cabbage) and grated mooli (daikon), or even serve them in addition if you like.

1 Grind the cashew nuts with the shallots or onion, lemon grass and garlic in a mortar with a pestle. Alternatively, process them in a food processor. Cook the noodles in a large pan of boiling water according to the packet instructions.

2 Heat the oil in a large wok or heavy pan, add the contents of the mortar or food processor and cook for about 1–2 minutes, or until the nuts begin to brown.

3 Add the shrimp paste or Thai fish sauce and curry paste, followed by the coconut milk, chicken stock cube and curry leaves, if using. Mix thoroughly and simmer gently over a low heat, stirring occasionally, for 10 minutes.

4 Cut the white fish into bitesize pieces. Place the fish and prawn tails in a large frying basket, immerse in the simmering coconut stock and cook for 3–4 minutes. Transfer the fish and prawn tails to a serving platter with the salad and noodles and transfer the broth to a tureen or lidded pot. Serve immediately (see Cook's Tip).

Appetizers

Fish and shellfish make the perfect light start to any meal, whatever the main course. Titillate your taste buds with refreshing Ceviche or that old favourite, Prawn Cocktail. Classic Oysters Rockefeller, and Gratin of Mussels with Pesto are as succulent as they are sophisticated, while deliciously crisp Devilled Whitebait provide piquancy and crunch. If you prefer fish to shellfish, Red Mullet Dolmades make an unusual appetizer.

Prawn Cocktail

There is no nicer appetizer than a good, fresh prawn cocktail – and nothing nastier than one in which soggy prawns swim in a thin, vinegary sauce embedded in limp lettuce. This recipe shows just how good a prawn cocktail can be.

SERVES SIX

INGREDIENTS

- 60ml/4 tbsp double (heavy) cream, lightly whipped
- 60ml/4 tbsp mayonnaise, preferably home-made
- 60ml/4 tbsp tomato ketchup
- 5–10ml/1–2 tsp Worcestershire sauce
- juice of 1 lemon
- ½ cos or romaine lettuce or other very crisp lettuce
- 450g/1lb/4 cups cooked peeled prawns (shrimp)
- salt, ground black pepper and paprika
- 6 large whole cooked prawns (shrimp) in the shell, to garnish (optional)
- thinly sliced brown bread with butter and lemon wedges, to serve

1 Place the lightly whipped cream, mayonnaise and tomato ketchup in a small bowl and whisk lightly to combine. Add Worcestershire sauce to taste, then whisk in enough of the lemon juice to make a really tangy sauce.

COOK'S TIP

Partly peeled prawns (shrimp) make a pretty garnish. To prepare, carefully peel the body shell from the prawns and leave the tail "fan" for decoration.

2 Finely shred the lettuce and fill six individual glasses one-third full.

3 Stir the prawns into the sauce, then check the seasoning and spoon the prawn mixture generously over the lettuce. If you like, drape a whole cooked prawn over the edge of each glass and sprinkle each of the cocktails with ground black pepper and/or paprika. Serve immediately, with thinly sliced brown bread with butter and lemon wedges.

Crab Salad with Rocket

If the dressed crabs are really small, pile the salad back into the shells for an attractive alternative presentation.

SERVES FOUR

INGREDIENTS

- 4 small fresh dressed crabs
- 1 small red (bell) pepper, seeded and finely chopped
- 1 small red onion, finely chopped
- 30ml/2 tbsp drained capers
- 30ml/2 tbsp chopped fresh coriander (cilantro)
- grated rind and juice of 2 lemons
- Tabasco sauce
- salt and ground black pepper
- lemon rind strips, to garnish

For the rocket (arugula) salad

- 40g/1½oz rocket (arugula) leaves
- 30ml/2 tbsp sunflower oil
- 15ml/1 tbsp fresh lime juice

1 Put the white and brown crab meat, red pepper, onion, capers and chopped coriander in a bowl. Add the lemon rind and juice and toss gently to mix together. Season with a few drops of Tabasco sauce, according to taste, and a little salt and pepper.

2 Wash the rocket leaves and pat dry on kitchen paper. Divide them among four plates. Mix together the oil and lime juice in a small bowl. Dress the rocket leaves, then pile the crab salad on top and serve garnished with lemon rind strips.

GRILLED SARDINES

FRESH SARDINES HAVE PLENTY OF FLAVOUR, SO THEY ARE REALLY AT THEIR BEST WHEN COOKED SIMPLY.

SERVES FOUR

INGREDIENTS
- 8 sardines, about 50g/2oz each
- sea salt
- 2 lemons, halved, to serve

1 Gut the sardines, but leave on the heads and tails. With a sharp knife, slash each side of all the sardines diagonally three times.

2 Place the sardines on a grill (broiler) rack and sprinkle with sea salt. Cook under a preheated high grill for 4 minutes on each side until the flesh is cooked and the skin is blistered and a little charred.

3 Transfer to a serving dish and serve immediately with the lemon halves to squeeze over.

COOK'S TIP
This is a great way to start a barbecue. To make turning the fish easier and avoid the risk of breaking them up, use a wire rack. Special sardine-size fish racks are available.

SALT-CURED SALMON

SERVES TEN

INGREDIENTS
- 50g/2oz sea salt
- 45ml/3 tbsp caster (superfine) sugar
- 5ml/1 tsp chilli powder
- 5ml/1 tsp ground black pepper
- 45ml/3 tbsp chopped fresh coriander (cilantro)
- 2 salmon fillets, about 250g/9oz each
- sprigs of fresh flat leaf parsley, to garnish
- garlic mayonnaise, to serve

1 Mix together the salt, sugar, chilli powder, pepper and coriander in a small bowl. Rub the mixture into the flesh of each fillet with your hands.

2 Place one of the fillets, skin side down, in a shallow glass dish. Place the other fillet on top, with the skin side up. Cover with foil, then place a weight on top.

3 Place the fish in the refrigerator for 48 hours, turning the fish every 8 hours or so and basting it well with the liquid that forms in the dish.

COOK'S TIP
Make the most of the leftover salmon skin by turning it into delicious crunchy strips: after slicing the salt-cured salmon, scrape any remaining fish off the skin and discard. Cut the skin into 1cm/½in wide strips. Cook for 1 minute in hot oil until crisp and browned. Drain thoroughly on kitchen paper and leave to cool. Serve the crisp strips as a garnish for the salt-cured salmon or as a tapas dish in its own right.

VARIATION
You can cure a variety of other fish in the same way as the salmon. Both rainbow trout and sea trout would work well and halibut would also be delicious. Whatever fish you use, it should be as fresh as possible.

4 Drain the salmon well and transfer to a board. Using a very sharp knife, remove the skin and slice the salmon diagonally, wafer-thin. Arrange on plates and garnish with sprigs of parsley. Serve with garlic mayonnaise.

Classic Gefilte Fish

Gefilte means stuffed and originally this mixture of chopped fish was stuffed back into the skin of the fish before cooking. Over the centuries, it has evolved into the classic balls of chopped fish that are served at the start of most Jewish festivities, including Shabbat, Pesach and Rosh Hashanah.

SERVES EIGHT

INGREDIENTS

- 1kg/2¼lb of 2–3 varieties of fish fillets, such as carp, whitefish, yellow pike, haddock and cod
- 2 eggs
- 120ml/4fl oz/½ cup cold water
- 30–45ml/2–3 tbsp medium matzo meal
- 15–45ml/1–3 tbsp sugar
- fish stock, for simmering
- 2–3 onions
- 3 carrots
- 1–2 pinches of ground cinnamon
- salt and ground black pepper
- chrain or horseradish and beetroot (beets), to serve

1 Place the fish fillets on a plate, sprinkle with salt and chill for 1 hour, or until the flesh has firmed. Rinse the fish well, then put in a food processor or blender and process until minced (ground).

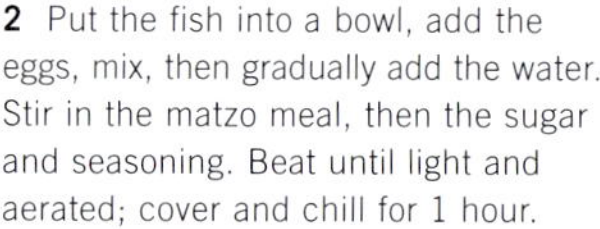

2 Put the fish into a bowl, add the eggs, mix, then gradually add the water. Stir in the matzo meal, then the sugar and seasoning. Beat until light and aerated; cover and chill for 1 hour.

3 Take 15–30ml/1–2 tbsp of the mixture and, with wet hands, roll into a ball. Continue with the remaining mixture.

4 Bring a large pan of fish stock to the boil, reduce to a simmer, then add the fishballs. Return to the boil, then simmer for 1 hour. (Add more water, if necessary, to keep the balls covered.)

5 Add the onions, carrots, cinnamon and a little extra sugar, if you like, to the pan and simmer, uncovered, for 45–60 minutes. Add more water, if necessary, to keep the balls covered.

6 Leave the fish to cool slightly, then remove from the liquid with a slotted spoon. Serve warm or cold with chrain or horseradish and beetroot.

WHITEBAIT ESCABECHE

ANY TYPE OF TINY WHITE FISH, FRIED UNTIL CRISP, THEN MARINATED WITH VEGETABLES, IS A FAVOURITE FOOD IN PERU, ESPECIALLY AMONG THE JEWS. SERVE THESE TANGY MORSELS AS AN APPETIZER WITH DRINKS OR AS A MAIN COURSE WITH CAUSA, A SALAD OF COLD MASHED POTATOES DRESSED WITH ONIONS, CHILLIES, OLIVE OIL AND LOTS OF LEMON JUICE.

SERVES FOUR

INGREDIENTS

- 800g/1¾lb whitebait or tiny white fish
- juice of 2 lemons
- 5ml/1 tsp salt
- plain (all-purpose) flour, for dusting
- vegetable oil, for frying
- 2 onions, chopped or thinly sliced
- 2.5–5ml/½–1 tsp cumin seeds
- 2 carrots, thinly sliced
- 2 jalapeño chillies, chopped
- 8 garlic cloves, coarsely chopped
- 120ml/4fl oz/½ cup white wine or cider vinegar
- 2–3 large pinches of dried oregano
- 15–30ml/1–2 tbsp chopped fresh coriander (cilantro) leaves
- slices of corn on the cob, black olives and coriander (cilantro), to garnish

1 Put the fish in a bowl, add the lemon juice and salt and leave to marinate for 30–60 minutes. Remove the fish from the bowl and dust with flour.

2 Heat the oil in a deep-frying pan until hot enough to turn a cube of bread golden brown in 30 seconds.

3 Fry the fish, in small batches, until golden brown, then put in a shallow serving dish and set aside.

4 In a separate pan, heat 30ml/2 tbsp of oil. Add the onions, cumin seeds, carrots, chillies and garlic and cook for 5 minutes, until the onions are softened. Add the vinegar, oregano and coriander, stir well and cook for 1–2 minutes.

5 Pour the onion mixture over the fried fish and leave to cool. Serve the fish at room temperature, garnished with slices of corn on the cob, black olives and coriander leaves.

COOK'S TIPS

- When selecting whitebait or any other smelt, make sure the fish are very tiny, as they are eaten whole.
- If you prefer, use chunks of any firm white fish such as cod or halibut instead of tiny whole fish. Simply flour the chunks of fish and fry as above.

Marinated Herrings

This is a classic Ashkenazi-Jewish dish, which is sweet-and-sour and lightly spiced. It is delicious for Sunday brunch and is a great choice for entertaining, as it has to be prepared in advance.

SERVES FOUR TO SIX

INGREDIENTS

- 2–3 herrings, filleted
- 1 onion, sliced
- juice of 1½ lemons
- 30ml/2 tbsp white wine vinegar
- 25ml/1½ tbsp sugar
- 10–15 black peppercorns
- 10–15 allspice berries
- 1.5ml/¼ tsp mustard seeds
- 3 bay leaves, torn
- salt

1 Soak the herrings in cold water for 5 minutes, then drain. Pour over water to cover and soak for 2–3 hours, then drain. Pour over water to cover and leave to soak overnight.

2 Hold the soaked herrings under cold running water and rinse very well, both inside and out.

3 Cut each fish into bitesize pieces, then place the pieces in a glass bowl or shallow dish.

4 Sprinkle the onion over the fish, then add the lemon juice, vinegar, sugar, peppercorns, allspice, mustard seeds, bay leaves and salt. Add enough water to just cover. Cover the bowl and chill for 2 days to allow the flavours to blend before serving.

Ceviche of Mackerel

This makes an excellent appetizer for an al fresco lunch party.

SERVES SIX

INGREDIENTS

- 450g/1lb mackerel fillets, cut into 1cm/½in pieces
- 350ml/12fl oz/1½ cups freshly squeezed lime or lemon juice
- 225g/8oz tomatoes, chopped
- 1 small onion, very finely chopped
- 2 drained canned jalapeño chillies or 4 serrano chillies, rinsed and chopped
- 60ml/4 tbsp olive oil
- 2.5ml/½ tsp dried oregano
- 30ml/2 tbsp chopped fresh coriander (cilantro)
- salt and ground black pepper
- lemon wedges and fresh coriander (cilantro), to garnish
- stuffed olives with chopped coriander (cilantro), to serve

1 Put the fish into a glass or ceramic dish and pour the lime or lemon juice over it, making sure that the fish is completely covered. Cover with clear film (plastic wrap) and chill in the refrigerator for 6 hours, turning once, by which time the fish will be opaque, "cooked" by the citrus juice.

COOK'S TIPS

- For a more delicately flavoured ceviche, you can use a white fish, such as lemon sole.
- It is important to use a glass, china or earthenware dish for marinating the fish. A metallic dish may react with the acid in the lime or lemon juice and taint the fish.

2 When the fish is opaque, lift it out of the juice and set it aside.

3 Combine the tomatoes, onion, chillies, olive oil, oregano and coriander in a bowl. Add salt and pepper to taste, then pour in the reserved juice from the mackerel. Mix well and pour over the fish.

4 Cover the dish and return the ceviche to the refrigerator for about 1 hour to allow the flavours to blend. Ceviche should not be served too cold. Leave it to stand at room temperature for 15 minutes before serving. Garnish with lemon wedges and coriander sprigs, and serve with stuffed olives sprinkled with a little chopped coriander.

CEVICHE

YOU CAN USE ALMOST ANY FIRM-FLESHED FISH FOR THIS SOUTH AMERICAN DISH, PROVIDED THAT IT IS PERFECTLY FRESH. THE FISH IS "COOKED" BY THE ACTION OF THE ACIDIC LIME JUICE. ADJUST THE AMOUNT OF CHILLI ACCORDING TO YOUR TASTE.

SERVES SIX

INGREDIENTS

- 675g/1½lb halibut, turbot, sea bass or salmon fillets, skinned
- juice of 3 limes
- 1–2 fresh red chillies, seeded and very finely chopped
- 15ml/1 tbsp olive oil
- salt

For the garnish

- 4 large firm tomatoes, peeled, seeded and diced
- 1 ripe avocado, peeled, stoned (pitted) and diced
- 15ml/1 tbsp lemon juice
- 30ml/2 tbsp olive oil
- 30ml/2 tbsp fresh coriander (cilantro) leaves

1 Cut the fish into strips measuring about 5 × 1cm/2 × ½in. Lay these in a shallow dish and pour over the lime juice, turning the strips to coat them all over in the juice. Cover with clear film (plastic wrap) and leave for 1 hour.

2 Combine all the garnish ingredients, except the coriander. Set aside.

3 Season the fish with salt and sprinkle over the chillies. Drizzle with the olive oil. Toss the fish in the mixture, then re-cover. Leave to marinate in the refrigerator for 15–30 minutes more.

4 To serve, divide the garnish among six plates. Spoon on the ceviche, sprinkle with coriander and serve.

MARINATED SMOKED HADDOCK FILLETS

THIS SIMPLE DISH COULD MAKE A LIGHT LUNCH, SERVED WITH A GREEN SALAD, AS WELL AS AN APPETIZER. EITHER WAY IT IS AN EXCELLENT SUMMER DISH AND CAN BE PREPARED IN ADVANCE.

SERVES SIX

INGREDIENTS

- 450g/1lb undyed smoked haddock fillet, skinned
- 1 onion, very thinly sliced into rings
- 5–10ml/1–2 tsp Dijon mustard
- 30ml/2 tbsp lemon juice
- 90ml/6 tbsp olive oil
- 45ml/3 tbsp dark rum
- 12 small new potatoes, scrubbed
- 30ml/2 tbsp chopped fresh dill, plus 6 dill sprigs to garnish
- ground black pepper

COOK'S TIP

Try to get a large, thick haddock fillet. If all you can find are small pieces, you can still make the dish, but serve the pieces whole instead of slicing them.

1 Cut the fish fillet in half lengthways. Arrange the pieces in a single layer in a shallow non-metallic dish. Sprinkle the onion rings evenly over the top.

2 Whisk together the mustard, lemon juice and some pepper. Gradually add the oil, whisking constantly. Pour two-thirds of the dressing over the fish. Cover the dish with clear film (plastic wrap) and leave the fish to marinate for 2 hours in a cool place. Sprinkle on the rum and leave for 1 hour more.

3 Cook the potatoes in salted, boiling water until tender. Drain, cut in half and tip into a bowl. Cool until warm, then toss in the remaining dressing. Stir in the dill, cover and set aside.

4 Slice the haddock thinly, as for smoked salmon, or leave whole. Arrange on small plates and spoon over some marinade and onion rings. Pile the potato halves on one side of each plate and garnish each portion with dill. Serve chilled or at room temperature.

Marinated Anchovies

This is one of the simplest ways to prepare these tiny fish because it requires no cooking. Marinating is particularly associated with anchovies, which tend to lose their freshness very quickly. The Spanish term for marinated anchovies is boquerones, *while* anchoas *is their word for the canned, salted variety.*

SERVES FOUR

INGREDIENTS

- 225g/8oz fresh anchovies, heads and tails removed, and split open along the belly
- juice of 3 lemons
- 30ml/2 tbsp extra virgin olive oil
- 2 garlic cloves, finely chopped
- 15ml/1 tbsp chopped fresh parsley
- flaked sea salt

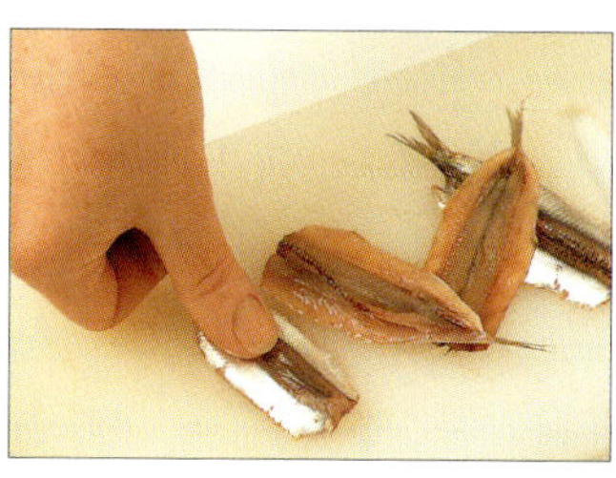

1 Turn the anchovies on to their bellies, and press down with your thumb.

2 Using the tip of a small, sharp knife, carefully remove the backbones from the flattened fish, and arrange the anchovies, skin side down, in a single layer on a large plate.

3 Squeeze two-thirds of the lemon juice over the fish and sprinkle them with the salt. Cover and leave to stand for 1–24 hours, basting occasionally with the juices, until the flesh is white and no longer translucent.

4 Transfer the anchovies to a serving plate and drizzle with the olive oil and the remaining lemon juice. Sprinkle the fish with the chopped garlic and parsley, then cover with clear film (plastic wrap) and chill until ready to serve.

FLASH-FRIED SQUID WITH PAPRIKA AND GARLIC

SQUID ARE PART OF EVERY SPANISH TAPAS BAR SELECTION, AND ARE USUALLY DEEP-FRIED. HERE IS A MODERN RECIPE, WHICH IS UNUSUAL IN THAT IT USES FRESH CHILLIES. SERVE THE DISH WITH A FINO OR MANZANILLA SHERRY AS A TAPAS DISH. ALTERNATIVELY, SERVE THE SQUID ON A BED OF SALAD LEAVES, ACCOMPANIED BY BREAD, FOR A SUBSTANTIAL FIRST COURSE TO SERVE FOUR.

SERVES SIX TO EIGHT

INGREDIENTS

- 500g/1¼lb very small squid, cleaned
- 90ml/6 tbsp olive oil, plus extra
- 1 fresh red chilli, seeded and finely chopped
- 10ml/2 tsp Spanish mild smoked paprika
- 30ml/2 tbsp plain (all-purpose) flour
- 2 garlic cloves, finely chopped
- 15ml/1 tbsp sherry vinegar
- 5ml/1 tsp grated lemon rind
- 30–45ml/2–3 tbsp finely chopped fresh parsley
- salt and ground black pepper

1 Using a sharp knife, cut the squid body sacs into rings and cut the tentacles into bitesize pieces.

2 Place the squid in a bowl and pour over 30ml/2 tbsp of the olive oil, half the chilli and the paprika. Season with a little salt and some pepper, cover with clear film (plastic wrap), place in the refrigerator and leave to marinate for 2–4 hours.

COOK'S TIPS

- Make sure the oil in the pan is very hot before adding the squid. The squid should cook for only 1–2 minutes; any longer and it will begin to toughen.
- Smoked paprika, chiefly from the Valle de Jerte, has a wonderful, subtle flavour. If you cannot find it, you can use mild paprika instead.

3 Toss the squid in the flour and divide it into two batches. Heat the remaining oil in a wok or deep frying pan over a high heat until very hot. Add the first batch of squid and quickly stir-fry for 1–2 minutes, or until it becomes opaque and the tentacles curl.

4 Add half the garlic. Stir, then turn out into a bowl. Repeat with the second batch, adding more oil if needed.

5 Sprinkle with the sherry vinegar, lemon rind, remaining chilli and parsley. Season and serve hot or cool.

SAUTÉED SCALLOPS

Scallops go well with all sorts of rich and creamy sauces, but simple cooking is probably the best way to enjoy their flavour. This dish is both simple and extremely quick.

SERVES FOUR

INGREDIENTS
- 450g/1lb shelled scallops
- 25g/1oz/2 tbsp butter
- 30ml/2 tbsp dry white vermouth
- 15ml/1 tbsp finely chopped fresh parsley
- salt and ground black pepper

1 Rinse the scallops under cold running water to remove any sand or grit and pat dry using kitchen paper. Season them lightly with salt and black pepper.

2 In a frying pan large enough to hold the scallops in one layer, heat half the butter until it begins to colour. Add the scallops and sauté over a medium heat for 3–5 minutes, turning, until golden brown on both sides and just firm to the touch. Remove to a serving platter and cover to keep warm.

3 Add the vermouth to the hot frying pan and swirl in the remaining butter. Add the chopped parsley, stir well and pour the sauce over the scallops. Serve immediately.

GARLIC SCALLOPS AND PRAWNS

Scallops and prawns are found all along the Atlantic and Mediterranean coasts of France and are enjoyed in every region. This method of cooking is a typical Provençal recipe from the south of the country.

SERVES TWO TO FOUR

INGREDIENTS
- 6 large shelled scallops
- 6–8 large raw prawns (shrimp), peeled
- plain (all-purpose) flour, for dusting
- 30–45ml/2–3 tbsp olive oil
- 1 garlic clove, finely chopped
- 15ml/1 tbsp chopped fresh basil
- 30–45ml/2–3 tbsp freshly squeezed lemon juice
- salt and ground black pepper

1 Rinse the scallops under cold running water to remove any sand or grit. Pat them dry using kitchen paper and cut in half crossways with a sharp knife.

2 Season the scallops and prawns with a little salt and pepper and dust them lightly with flour, shaking off the excess.

3 Heat the oil in a large frying pan over a high heat and add the scallops and prawns.

4 Reduce the heat to medium-high and cook for 2 minutes, then turn the scallops and prawns. Add the garlic and basil, shaking the pan to distribute them evenly. Cook for a further 2 minutes until the scallops are golden and just firm to the touch. Sprinkle over the lemon juice and toss to blend. Serve immediately.

VARIATION

To make a richer sauce, transfer the cooked scallops and prawns to a warmed serving plate and cover to keep them warm. Pour 60ml/4 tbsp dry white wine into the frying pan, bring to the boil and continue to boil until reduced by about half. Add 15g/½oz/1 tbsp unsalted (sweet) butter, whisking well until it melts and the sauce thickens slightly. Pour the sauce over the scallops and prawns and serve immediately.

SCALLOPS WRAPPED IN PROSCIUTTO

THIS IS A DELICIOUS SUMMER RECIPE FOR COOKING OVER THE BARBECUE.

SERVES FOUR

INGREDIENTS

- 24 medium-size scallops, without corals, prepared for cooking
- lemon juice
- 8–12 slices prosciutto
- olive oil, for brushing
- ground black pepper
- lemon wedges, to serve

1 Preheat the grill (broiler) or prepare a charcoal fire. Sprinkle the scallops with lemon juice. Cut the prosciutto into long strips. Wrap one strip around each scallop. Thread them on to eight skewers.

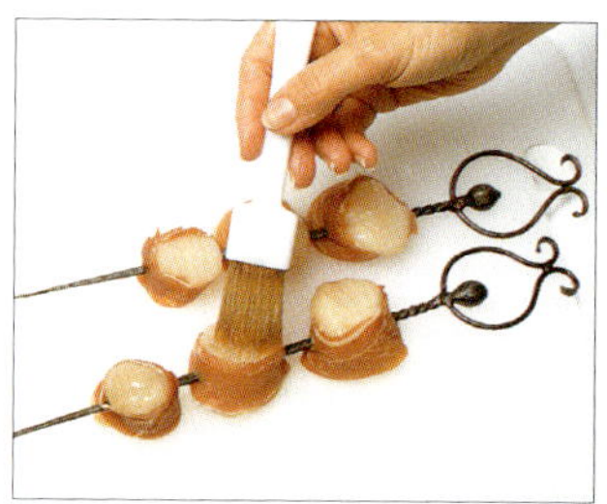

2 Brush the skewers with olive oil. Arrange them on a baking sheet if grilling (broiling). Cook about 10cm/4in from the heat under a preheated grill for 3–5 minutes on each side or until the scallops are opaque and tender. Alternatively, cook the skewers over charcoal, turning them once, until the scallops are opaque and tender.

3 Set two skewers on each plate. Sprinkle the scallops with freshly ground black pepper and serve immediately with lemon wedges.

COOK'S TIP

The edible parts of the scallop are the round white muscle and the coral or roe. When preparing fresh scallops, keep the skirt – the frilly part – for making stock.

SCALLOPS WITH SAMPHIRE AND LIME

Samphire has a wonderful taste and aroma of the sea. High-quality fishmongers sometimes stock it. It is the perfect complement to scallops and helps to create a very attractive appetizer.

SERVES FOUR

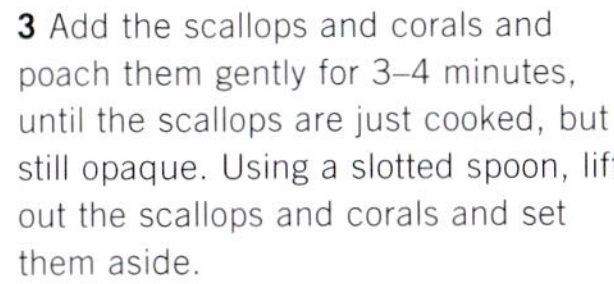

INGREDIENTS

- 225g/8oz fresh samphire
- 12 large or 24 queen scallops, out of the shell
- 300ml/½ pint/1¼ cups dry white wine
- juice of 2 limes
- 15ml/1 tbsp groundnut (peanut) or vegetable oil
- ½ cucumber, peeled, seeded and diced
- ground black pepper
- chopped fresh parsley, to garnish

1 Wash the fresh samphire in several changes of cold water. Drain, then trim off any woody ends. Bring a pan of water to the boil, then drop in the samphire and cook for 3–5 minutes, until tender but still crisp. Drain, refresh under cold water and drain again.

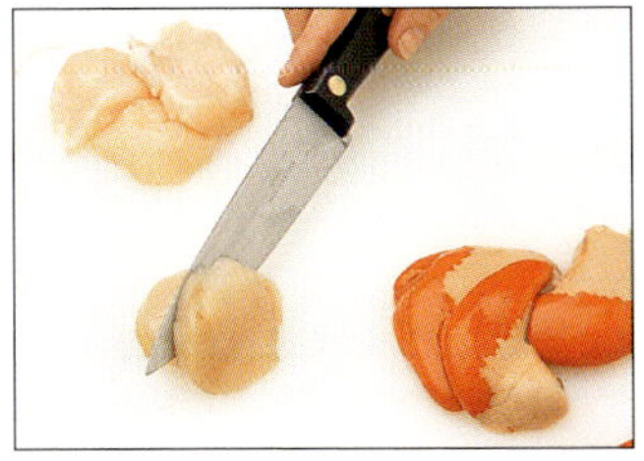

2 If the scallops are large, cut them in half horizontally. Detach the corals. In a shallow pan, bring the wine to the boil and cook until it is reduced by about one-third. Lower the heat and add the lime juice to the pan.

3 Add the scallops and corals and poach them gently for 3–4 minutes, until the scallops are just cooked, but still opaque. Using a slotted spoon, lift out the scallops and corals and set them aside.

COOK'S TIP

Samphire grows wild in estuaries and salt marshes in Europe and North America.

4 Leave the cooking liquid to cool until tepid, then whisk in the groundnut or vegetable oil. Add the samphire, cucumber, scallops and corals and toss lightly to mix. Grind over some black pepper, cover and leave at room temperature for about 1 hour to allow the flavours to develop. Divide the mixture among four individual dishes and then garnish with chopped fresh parsley. Serve the dish at room temperature.

Gratin of Mussels with Pesto

This is the perfect appetizer for serving when your time is short, since both the pesto and the mussels can be prepared in advance, and the dish assembled and cooked at the last minute.

SERVES FOUR

INGREDIENTS

- 36 large fresh mussels, scrubbed and bearded
- 105ml/7 tbsp dry white wine
- 60ml/4 tbsp finely chopped fresh flat leaf parsley
- 1 garlic clove, finely chopped
- 30ml/2 tbsp fresh white breadcrumbs
- 60ml/4 tbsp olive oil
- chopped fresh basil, to garnish
- crusty bread, to serve

For the pesto

- 2 fat garlic cloves, chopped
- 2.5ml/½ tsp coarse salt
- 100g/3¾oz/3 cups basil leaves
- 25g/1oz/¼ cup pine nuts, chopped
- 50g/2oz/⅔ cup freshly grated Parmesan cheese
- 120ml/4fl oz/½ cup extra virgin olive oil

1 Put the mussels in a pan with the wine, clamp on the lid and shake over high heat for 3–4 minutes until the mussels have opened. Discard any that remain closed.

2 As soon as the mussels are cool enough to handle, strain the cooking liquid and keep it for another recipe. Discard the empty half-shells. Arrange the mussels in their half-shells in a single layer in four individual gratin dishes. Cover and set aside.

COOK'S TIP

Home-made pesto is best, but when basil is out of season – or you are in a hurry – a jar may be used instead.

3 To make the pesto, put the chopped garlic and salt in a mortar and pound to a purée with a pestle. Then add the basil leaves and chopped pine nuts and crush to a thick paste. Work in the Parmesan cheese and, finally, gradually drip in enough olive oil to make a smooth and creamy paste. Alternatively, use a food processor.

4 Spoon pesto over the mussels placed in gratin dishes. Mix the parsley, garlic and breadcrumbs. Sprinkle over the mussels. Drizzle with the oil.

5 Preheat the grill (broiler) to high. Stand the dishes on a baking sheet and grill (broil) for 3 minutes. Garnish with basil and serve with crusty bread.

MUSSELS STEAMED IN WHITE WINE

THIS IS THE BEST AND EASIEST WAY TO SERVE THE SMALL TENDER MUSSELS, BOUCHOTS, WHICH ARE FARMED ALONG MUCH OF THE FRENCH COASTLINE.

SERVES FOUR

INGREDIENTS

- 1.8kg/4lb fresh mussels
- 300ml/½ pint/1¼ cups dry white wine
- 4–6 large shallots, finely chopped
- bouquet garni
- ground black pepper

1 Discard any broken mussels and those with open shells that do not close immediately when tapped sharply. Under cold running water, scrape the mussel shells with a knife to remove any barnacles and pull out the stringy "beards". Soak the mussels in several changes of cold water for at least 1 hour.

2 In a large, heavy, flameproof casserole combine the white wine, shallots, bouquet garni and plenty of pepper. Bring to the boil over a medium-high heat and cook for 2 minutes.

3 Add the mussels to the casserole, cover tightly with a lid and cook over a high heat, vigorously shaking and tossing the pan occasionally, for about 5 minutes, or until the mussels have opened. Discard any mussels that have not opened.

4 Using a slotted spoon, remove the mussels from the pan and divide them equally among four warmed soup plates. Keep warm. Tilt the casserole a little and hold it in that position for a few seconds to allow any sand to sink to the bottom and settle. Alternatively, strain the cooking liquid through a strainer lined with muslin (cheesecloth) into a jug (pitcher) or bowl.

5 Spoon or pour the hot cooking liquid over the mussels and serve them immediately.

VARIATION

For Mussels with Cream Sauce, cook the mussels as described here, but transfer them to a warmed bowl and cover to keep warm. Strain the cooking liquid through a sieve lined with muslin (cheesecloth) into a large pan, bring to the boil and continue to boil for about 7–10 minutes until reduced by about half. Stir in 90ml/6 tbsp whipping or double (heavy) cream and 30ml/2 tbsp chopped fresh parsley, then add the mussels. Cook for about 1 minute more to reheat the mussels. Serve immediately.

COOK'S TIP

Both the main recipe and the variation are delicious served with plenty of fresh crusty bread or warm rolls for mopping up the juices or cream sauce. No French diner would dream of doing anything else.

Moules Provençales

Eating these delectable mussels is a messy affair, which is part of their charm. Hand round plenty of crusty French bread for mopping up the juices and don't forget fingerbowls of warm water and a plate for discarded shells.

SERVES FOUR

INGREDIENTS

- 30ml/2 tbsp olive oil
- 200g/7oz rindless unsmoked streaky (fatty) bacon, cubed
- 1 onion, finely chopped
- 3 garlic cloves, finely chopped
- 1 bay leaf
- 15ml/1 tbsp chopped fresh mixed Provençal herbs, thyme, marjoram, basil, oregano and savory
- 15–30ml/1–2 tbsp sun-dried tomatoes in oil, chopped
- 4 large, very ripe tomatoes, peeled, seeded and chopped
- 50g/2oz/½ cup pitted black olives, chopped
- 105ml/7 tbsp dry white wine
- 2.25kg/5–5¼lb fresh mussels, scrubbed and bearded
- salt and ground black pepper
- 60ml/4 tbsp coarsely chopped fresh parsley, to garnish

1 Heat the oil in a large pan. Cook the bacon until golden and crisp. Remove with a slotted spoon and set aside. Add the onion and garlic to the pan and cook gently until softened. Add the herbs, with both types of tomatoes. Cook gently for 5 minutes, stirring frequently. Stir in the olives and season.

2 Put the wine and mussels in another pan. Cover and shake over a high heat for 5 minutes, until the mussels open. Discard any which remain closed.

3 Strain the cooking liquid into the pan containing the tomato sauce and boil until reduced by about one-third. Add the mussels and stir to coat them thoroughly with the sauce. Remove and discard the bay leaf.

4 Divide the mussels and sauce equally among four warm individual dishes. Sprinkle over the crispy bacon and chopped parsley and serve piping hot.

Oysters Rockefeller

This is the perfect dish for those who prefer their oysters lightly cooked. As a cheaper alternative, for those who are not "so rich as Rockefeller", give mussels or clams the same treatment; they will also taste delicious.

SERVES SIX

INGREDIENTS

- 450g/1lb/3 cups coarse salt, plus extra to serve
- 24 oysters, opened
- 115g/4oz/½ cup butter
- 2 shallots, finely chopped
- 500g/1¼lb spinach leaves, finely chopped
- 60ml/4 tbsp chopped fresh parsley
- 60ml/4 tbsp chopped celery leaves
- 90ml/6 tbsp fresh white breadcrumbs
- Tabasco sauce or cayenne pepper
- 10–20ml/2–4 tsp Pernod or Ricard
- salt and ground black pepper
- lemon wedges, to serve

COOK'S TIP

If you prefer a smoother stuffing, process to a paste in a food processor or blender.

1 Preheat the oven to 220°C/425°F/ Gas 7. Make a bed of coarse salt on two large baking sheets. Set the oysters in the half-shell in the bed of salt to keep them steady. Set aside.

2 Melt the butter in a frying pan. Add the finely chopped shallots and cook them over a low heat for 2–3 minutes, until they are softened. Stir in the spinach and let it wilt.

3 Add the parsley, celery leaves and breadcrumbs to the pan and cook gently for 5 minutes. Season with salt, pepper and Tabasco or cayenne.

4 Divide the stuffing among the oysters. Drizzle a few drops of Pernod or Ricard over each oyster, then bake for about 5 minutes, until bubbling and golden brown. Serve on a heated platter on a shallow salt bed with lemon wedges.

SOFT-SHELL CRABS WITH CHILLI AND SALT

IF FRESH SOFT-SHELL CRABS ARE UNAVAILABLE, YOU CAN BUY FROZEN ONES IN ASIAN SUPERMARKETS. ALLOW TWO SMALL CRABS PER SERVING, OR ONE IF THEY ARE QUITE LARGE. ADJUST THE QUANTITY OF CHILLI ACCORDING TO HOW HOT YOU LIKE YOUR FOOD.

SERVES FOUR

INGREDIENTS
- 8 small soft-shell crabs, thawed if frozen
- 50g/2oz/½ cup plain (all-purpose) flour
- 60ml/4 tbsp groundnut (peanut) or vegetable oil
- 2 large fresh red chillies, or 1 green and 1 red, seeded and thinly sliced
- 4 spring onions (scallions) or a small bunch of garlic chives, chopped
- sea salt and ground black pepper

To serve
- shredded lettuce, mooli (daikon) and carrot
- light soy sauce

COOK'S TIP
The vegetables make a colourful bed for the crabs. If you can't locate any mooli (daikon), use celeriac instead.

1 Pat the crabs dry with kitchen paper. Season the flour with pepper and coat the crabs lightly with the mixture.

2 Heat the oil in a shallow pan until very hot, then put in the crabs (you may need to do this in two batches). Cook for 2–3 minutes on each side, until the crabs are golden brown but still juicy in the middle. Drain the cooked crabs on kitchen paper and keep hot.

3 Add the sliced chillies and spring onions or garlic chives to the oil remaining in the pan and cook gently for about 2 minutes. Sprinkle over a generous pinch of salt, then spread the mixture on to the crabs.

4 Mix the shredded lettuce, mooli and carrot together. Arrange on plates, top each portion with two crabs and serve, with light soy sauce for dipping.

DEVILLED WHITEBAIT

SERVE THESE DELICIOUSLY CRISP LITTLE FISH WITH LEMON WEDGES AND THINLY SLICED BROWN BREAD AND BUTTER, AND EAT THEM WITH YOUR FINGERS.

SERVES FOUR

INGREDIENTS
- oil for deep-frying
- 150ml/¼ pint/⅔ cup milk
- 115g/4oz/1 cup plain (all-purpose) flour
- 450g/1lb whitebait
- salt, ground black pepper and cayenne pepper

1 Heat the oil in a large pan or deep-fryer. Put the milk in a shallow bowl and the flour into a paper bag. Season it with salt, pepper and a little cayenne.

COOK'S TIP
Most whitebait are sold frozen. Thaw them before use and dry them thoroughly on kitchen paper.

2 Dip a handful of the whitebait into the bowl of milk, drain them well, then pop them into the paper bag. Shake gently to coat them evenly in the seasoned flour. Repeat until all the fish have been coated with flour. This is the easiest method of flouring whitebait, but don't add too many at once, or they will stick together.

3 Heat the oil for deep-frying to 190°C/375°F or until a small cube of stale bread, dropped into the oil, browns in 20 seconds. Add a batch of whitebait, preferably in a frying basket, and fry for 2–3 minutes, until crisp and golden brown. Drain and keep hot while you fry the rest. Sprinkle with more cayenne and serve very hot.

Deep-Fried Whitebait

A spicy coating on these fish gives this favourite dish a crunchy bite.

SERVES SIX

INGREDIENTS

- 115g/4oz/1 cup plain (all-purpose) flour
- 2.5ml/½ tsp curry powder
- 2.5ml/½ tsp ground ginger
- 2.5ml/½ tsp cayenne pepper
- pinch of salt
- 1.1kg/2½lb fresh or frozen thawed whitebait
- vegetable oil, for deep-frying
- lemon wedges, to garnish

1 Mix together the flour, curry powder, ginger, cayenne and salt in a large bowl.

2 Coat the fish in the seasoned flour and shake off any excess.

3 Heat the oil in a large, heavy pan until it reaches a temperature of 190°C/375°F or until a small cube of stale bread, dropped into the oil, browns in 20 seconds. Fry the whitebait, in two or more batches, for about 2–3 minutes until the fish is golden and crispy. Keep warm while you cook the remaining fish.

4 Drain well on absorbent kitchen paper. Serve hot, garnished with lemon wedges.

COOK'S TIP

As whitebait are so small, they are best cooked in a frying basket; this makes them easier to remove.

Sesame Prawn Toasts

Serve four triangles each with a soy sauce dip.

SERVES SIX

INGREDIENTS

- 175g/6oz cooked prawns (shrimp)
- 2 spring onions (scallions), finely chopped
- 2.5cm/1in fresh root ginger, grated
- 2 garlic cloves, crushed
- 25g/1oz/¼ cup cornflour (cornstarch)
- 10ml/2 tsp soy sauce, plus extra for dipping
- 6 slices stale bread from a small loaf, crusts removed
- 40g/1½oz sesame seeds
- vegetable oil, for deep-frying

1 Peel the prawns, pull off their heads and devein them. Place the prawns, spring onions, grated ginger and garlic cloves into a food processor fitted with a metal blade. Add the cornflour and soy sauce and process the ingredients until they are combined into a thick paste.

COOK'S TIP

If you do not have a deep-fat thermometer, check that the oil has reached the right temperature by tossing a stale bread cube into it. If it turns golden in 30 seconds, the temperature is just right.

VARIATION

In western China, sesame prawn toasts are often served with a ham topping as well. Sprinkle 30ml/2 tbsp finely chopped, cooked ham on to the toasts with the sesame seeds before deep-frying in the same way.

2 Spread the bread slices evenly with the paste and sprinkle with the sesame seeds, making sure that they stick to the bread. Cut the slices into triangles, place them in a single layer on a large plate and chill in the refrigerator for 30 minutes.

3 Heat the oil for deep-frying in a large, heavy pan until it reaches a temperature of 190°C/375°F. Using a slotted spoon, lower half the toasts into the oil, sesame seed side down, and fry for about 2–3 minutes, turning over for the last minute. Drain on absorbent kitchen paper. Keep the cooked toasts warm while you are frying the remainder.

4 Serve the toasts immediately with extra soy sauce for dipping.

KING PRAWNS IN CRISPY BATTER

THIS IS A SPANISH, RATHER THAN CHINESE RECIPE. A HUGE RANGE OF PRAWNS IS ENJOYED IN SPAIN, EACH WITH ITS APPROPRIATE COOKING METHOD. THE BEST WAY TO ENJOY THIS EXTRA LARGE VARIETY IS DIPPED IN A SIMPLE BATTER, DEEP-FRIED AND SERVED WITH LEMON WEDGES.

SERVES FOUR

INGREDIENTS

- 120ml/4fl oz/½ cup water
- 1 large egg (US extra large)
- 115g/4oz/1 cup plain (all-purpose) flour
- 5ml/1 tsp cayenne pepper
- 12 raw king prawns (jumbo shrimp), in the shell
- vegetable oil, for deep frying
- flat leaf parsley, to garnish
- lemon wedges, to serve

COOK'S TIP

Leaving the tails on the prawns makes them easier to pick up and eat, and also look very pretty once cooked.

1 In a large bowl, whisk together the water and the egg. Whisk in the flour and cayenne pepper until smooth.

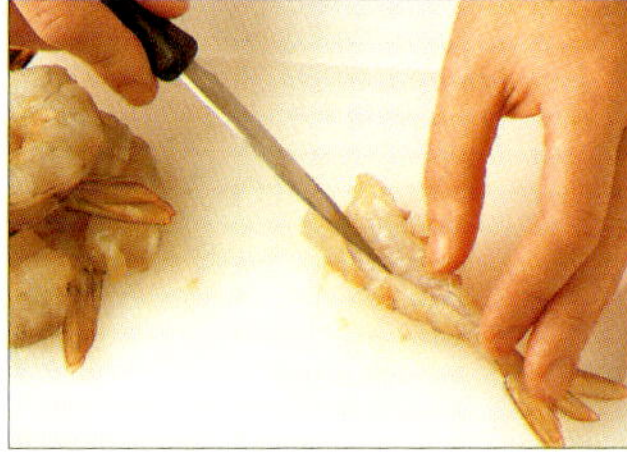

2 Peel the prawns, leaving just the tails intact. Make a shallow cut down the back of each prawn.

3 Using the tip of the knife, pull out and discard the dark intestinal tract.

4 Heat the oil in a large pan or deep-fat fryer, until a cube of bread dropped into the oil browns in 1 minute.

5 Holding the prawns by their tails, dip them into the batter, one at a time, shaking off any excess. Carefully drop each prawn into the oil and fry for 2–3 minutes until crisp and golden. Drain on kitchen paper, garnish with parsley and serve with lemon wedges.

VARIATION

If you have any batter left over, use it to coat thin strips of vegetables such as sweet potato, beetroot (beet), carrot or (bell) pepper, or use small broccoli florets or whole baby spinach leaves. Deep-fry the vegetables until golden.

Butterflied Prawns in Chocolate Sauce

There is a long tradition in Spain, which originates in Mexico, of cooking savoury food – even shellfish – with chocolate. Known as langostinos en chocolate *in Spanish, this is just the kind of culinary adventure that Basque chefs love.*

SERVES FOUR

INGREDIENTS

- 8 large raw prawns (shrimp), in the shell
- 15ml/1 tbsp seasoned plain (all-purpose) flour
- 15ml/1 tbsp pale dry sherry
- juice of 1 large orange
- 15g/½oz dark (bittersweet) chocolate, chopped
- 30ml/2 tbsp olive oil
- 2 garlic cloves, finely chopped
- 2.5cm/1in piece fresh root ginger, finely chopped
- 1 small dried chilli, seeded and chopped
- salt and ground black pepper

1 Peel the prawns, leaving just the tail sections intact. Make a shallow cut down the back of each one and carefully pull out and discard the dark intestinal tract.

2 Turn the prawns over so that the undersides are uppermost, and then carefully slit them open from tail to top, using a small sharp knife, cutting them almost, but not quite, through to the central back line.

3 Press the prawns down firmly to flatten them out. Coat with the seasoned flour and set aside.

4 Gently heat the sherry and orange juice in a small pan. When warm, remove from the heat and stir in the chopped chocolate until melted.

5 Heat the oil in a frying pan. Add the garlic, ginger and chilli and cook for 2 minutes until golden. Remove with a slotted spoon and reserve. Add the prawns, cut side down and cook for 2–3 minutes until golden brown with pink edges. Turn the prawns and cook for a further 2 minutes.

6 Return the garlic mixture to the pan and pour the chocolate sauce over. Cook for 1 minute, turning the prawns to coat them in the glossy sauce. Season to taste and serve hot.

SOLE GOUJONS WITH LIME MAYONNAISE

THIS SIMPLE DISH CAN BE RUSTLED UP VERY QUICKLY.

SERVES FOUR

INGREDIENTS

- 200ml/7fl oz/scant 1 cup mayonnaise
- 1 small garlic clove, crushed
- 10ml/2 tsp capers, rinsed and chopped
- 10ml/2 tsp chopped gherkins
- grated rind and juice of 1 lime
- 15ml/1 tbsp finely chopped fresh coriander (cilantro)
- 675g/1½lb sole fillets, skinned
- 2 eggs, beaten
- 115g/4oz/2 cups fresh white breadcrumbs
- oil, for deep-frying
- salt and ground black pepper
- lime wedges, to serve

1 To make the lime mayonnaise, mix together the mayonnaise, garlic, capers, gherkins, lime rind and juice and chopped coriander. Season with salt and pepper to taste. Transfer to a serving bowl and chill until required.

2 Cut the sole fillets into strips about the length of your finger. Dip each strip first into the beaten egg and then into the breadcrumbs.

3 Heat the oil in a deep-fat fryer to 180°C/350°F or until a cube of stale bread, dropped into it, turns golden in 45–60 seconds. Add the fish strips, in batches, and fry until they are golden brown and crisp. Drain well on kitchen paper and keep warm while you cook the remaining strips.

4 Pile the goujons on to warmed serving plates and serve immediately with the lime wedges for squeezing over. Hand the lime mayonnaise around separately.

VARIATIONS

- You can make goujons with other flat fish fillets, such as plaice, flounder, brill or dab.
- These goujons are also delicious with aioli or other flavoured, mayonnaise-based sauces.

SPICY FISH RÖSTI

THESE FISH CAKES, WITH SALAD, MAKE A GOOD MAIN COURSE FOR TWO PEOPLE.

SERVES FOUR

INGREDIENTS

- 350g/12oz large, firm waxy potatoes
- 350g/12oz salmon or cod fillet, skinned
- 3–4 spring onions (scallions), finely chopped
- 5ml/1 tsp grated fresh root ginger
- 30ml/2 tbsp chopped fresh coriander (cilantro)
- 10ml/2 tsp lemon juice
- 30–45ml/2–3 tbsp sunflower oil
- salt and cayenne pepper
- coriander (cilantro) sprigs, to garnish
- lemon wedges, to serve

1 Cook the potatoes with their skins on in a pan of salted, boiling water for 10 minutes. Drain and leave to cool for a few minutes.

2 Meanwhile, remove any pin bones from the salmon or cod fillet, finely chop the flesh and put into a bowl. Stir in the chopped spring onions, grated root ginger, chopped coriander and lemon juice. Season to taste with salt and cayenne pepper.

3 When the potatoes are cool enough to handle but still warm, peel off the skins and grate the potatoes coarsely. Gently stir the grated potato into the fish mixture.

4 Divide the fish mixture into twelve portions, then shape each into a patty with your hands, pressing the mixture together and leaving the edges slightly rough.

5 Heat the oil in a large frying pan and cook the fish rösti, a few at a time, for 3 minutes on each side, until golden brown and crisp. Remove with a fish slice or metal spatula and drain well on kitchen paper. Keep hot while you cook the remaining rösti. Serve hot, garnished with sprigs of coriander and with lemon wedges for squeezing over.

SALT COD FRITTERS WITH AIOLI

BACALAO – SALT COD – IS ONE OF THE GREAT SPANISH DELIGHTS, ADDING FLAVOUR TO BLAND INGREDIENTS SUCH AS POTATOES. IF YOU ARE UNFAMILIAR WITH IT, THEN THIS IS A DELIGHTFUL WAY TO TRY IT OUT. BITESIZE FISH CAKES, DIPPED INTO RICH, CREAMY, GARLICKY AIOLI, ARE IRRESISTIBLE AS A TAPAS DISH OR APPETIZER.

SERVES SIX

INGREDIENTS

- 450g/1lb salt cod
- 500g/1¼lb floury (mealy) potatoes
- 300ml/½ pint/1¼ cups milk
- 6 spring onions (scallions), finely chopped
- 30ml/2 tbsp extra virgin olive oil
- 30ml/2 tbsp chopped fresh parsley
- juice of ½ lemon
- 2 eggs, beaten
- plain (all-purpose) flour, for dusting
- 90g/3½oz/1¼ cups dried white breadcrumbs
- olive oil, for shallow frying
- salt and ground black pepper
- lemon wedges and salad leaves, to serve

For the aioli

- 2 large garlic cloves, finely chopped
- 2 egg yolks
- 300ml/½ pint/1¼ cups olive oil
- juice of ½ lemon, to taste

1 Soak the salt cod in cold water for at least 24 hours, changing the water two or three times. The cod should swell as it rehydrates. Sample a tiny piece. It should not taste unpleasantly salty when fully rehydrated. Drain well and pat dry with kitchen paper.

2 Cook the potatoes, unpeeled, in a pan of lightly salted, boiling water for about 20 minutes, until tender. Drain. As soon as they are cool enough to handle, peel the potatoes, then mash with a fork or use a potato masher.

3 Pour the milk into a pan, add half the spring onions and bring to a simmer. Add the soaked cod and poach very gently for 10–15 minutes, or until it flakes easily. Remove the cod and flake it with a fork into a bowl, discarding bones and skin.

4 Add 60ml/4 tbsp mashed potato to the cod and beat them together with a wooden spoon. Work in the olive oil, then gradually add the remaining mashed potato. Beat in the remaining spring onions and the parsley.

5 Season with lemon juice and pepper to taste – the mixture may also need a little salt but taste it before adding any. Add one egg to the mixture and beat in until thoroughly combined, then chill until firm.

6 Shape the chilled fish mixture into 12–18 balls, then gently flatten into small round patties. Coat each one in flour, then dip in the remaining beaten egg and coat with dried breadcrumbs. Chill until ready to fry.

7 Meanwhile, make the aioli. Place the garlic and a good pinch of salt in a mortar and pound to a paste with a pestle. Using a small whisk or a wooden spoon, gradually work in the egg yolks.

8 Beat in about half the olive oil, a drop at a time. When the sauce is as thick as soft butter, beat in 5–10ml/1–2 tsp lemon juice. Continue adding oil until the aioli is very thick. Season to taste, adding more lemon juice if you wish.

9 Heat about 2cm/¾in oil in a large, heavy frying pan. Add the fritters and cook over a medium-high heat for about 4 minutes. Turn them over and cook for a further 4 minutes on the other side, until crisp and golden. Drain on kitchen paper, then serve with the aioli, lemon wedges and salad leaves.

COOK'S TIP

Try to find a thick, creamy white piece of salt cod, preferably cut from the middle of the fish rather than the tail and fin ends. Avoid thin, yellowish salt cod, as it will be too dry and salty.

Monkfish Parcels

These little dumplings of spiced fish taste delicious with the dressing of tomato oil.

SERVES FOUR

INGREDIENTS

- 175g/6oz/1½ cups strong white bread flour, plus extra for dusting
- 2 eggs
- 115g/4oz skinless monkfish fillet, diced
- grated rind of 1 lemon
- 1 garlic clove, chopped
- 1 small fresh red chilli, seeded and sliced
- 45ml/3 tbsp chopped fresh parsley
- 30ml/2 tbsp single (light) cream
- salt and ground black pepper

For the tomato oil

- 2 tomatoes, peeled, seeded and finely diced
- 45ml/3 tbsp extra virgin olive oil
- 30ml/2 tbsp fresh lemon juice

1 Place the flour, eggs and 2.5ml/½ tsp salt in a food processor and pulse until the mixture forms a soft dough. Knead gently for 2–3 minutes until smooth, then wrap in clear film (plastic wrap). Chill for 20 minutes.

2 Place the diced monkfish, grated lemon rind, garlic, chilli and parsley in the clean food processor and process until very finely chopped. Add the cream, season with plenty of salt and pepper and process again until the mixture forms a very thick purée.

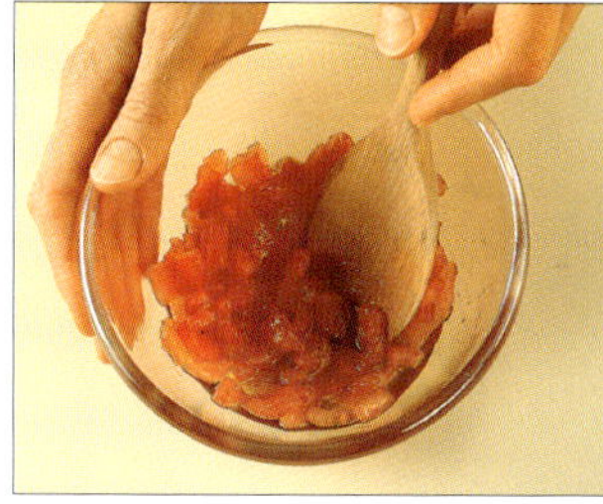

3 Make the tomato oil by stirring the diced tomato flesh with the olive oil and lemon juice in a bowl. Season with salt to taste. Cover with clear film and chill in the refrigerator until ready to serve.

4 Unwrap the dough and roll out on a lightly floured surface, then stamp out 32 rounds, using a 4cm/1½in plain cutter. Divide the filling among half the rounds, then cover with the remaining rounds. Pinch the edges tightly to seal, excluding as much air as possible.

5 Bring a large pan of water to simmering point and poach the parcels, in batches, for 2–3 minutes, or until they rise to the surface. Remove with a slotted spoon, drain well and keep warm while you cook the remaining batches. Serve the parcels immediately, drizzled with the tomato oil.

Crab and Ricotta Tartlets

Use the meat from a freshly cooked crab, weighing about 450g/1lb, if you can. Otherwise, look for frozen brown and white crab meat.

SERVES FOUR

INGREDIENTS

- 225g/8oz/2 cups plain (all-purpose) flour
- 115g/4oz/½ cup butter, diced
- about 60ml/4 tbsp iced water
- 225g/8oz/1 cup ricotta cheese
- 15ml/1 tbsp grated onion
- 30ml/2 tbsp grated Parmesan cheese
- 2.5ml/½ tsp mustard powder
- 2 eggs, plus 1 egg yolk
- 225g/8oz cooked crab meat
- 30ml/2 tbsp chopped fresh parsley
- 2.5–5ml/½–1 tsp anchovy essence (extract)
- 5–10ml/1–2 tsp lemon juice
- salt and cayenne pepper
- salad leaves, to garnish

1 Sift the flour and a good pinch of salt into a mixing bowl, add the diced butter and rub it in with your fingertips until the mixture resembles fine breadcrumbs. Gradually stir in just enough iced water to make a firm dough.

2 Turn out the dough on to a floured surface and knead lightly. Roll out the pastry and use to line four 10cm/4in tartlet tins (pans). Prick the bases with a fork, then chill in the refrigerator for 30 minutes.

3 Preheat the oven to 200°C/400°F/Gas 6. Line the pastry cases (pie shells) with greaseproof (waxed) paper or baking parchment and fill with baking beans. Bake for 10 minutes, then remove the paper and beans. Return to the oven and bake for a further 10 minutes.

4 Place the ricotta, grated onion, Parmesan and mustard in a bowl and beat until soft and thoroughly combined. Gradually beat in the eggs and egg yolk.

5 Gently stir in the crab meat and chopped parsley, then add the anchovy essence and lemon juice. Season with salt and cayenne pepper to taste.

6 Remove the tartlet cases from the oven and reduce the temperature to 180°C/350°F/Gas 4. Spoon the crab and ricotta filling evenly into the cases and bake for 20 minutes, until set and golden brown. Serve the tartlets immediately with a garnish of salad leaves.

CRAB SAVOURY

THIS SCRUMPTIOUS, BAKED SEAFOOD DISH IS RICH TASTING AND CREAMY. IT IS EXTREMELY QUICK AND EASY TO PREPARE, SO IS IDEAL FOR AN INFORMAL, MIDWEEK SUPPER PARTY.

SERVES FOUR

INGREDIENTS
- 25g/1oz/2 tbsp butter
- 1 small onion, finely chopped
- 50g/2oz/1 cup fresh brown breadcrumbs
- 225g/8oz crab meat
- 150ml/¼ pint/⅔ cup sour cream
- 10–15ml/2–3 tsp prepared mustard
- pinch of cayenne pepper
- squeeze of lemon juice
- 75ml/5 tbsp finely grated Cheddar cheese
- salt

1 Melt the butter in a large, heavy frying pan over a medium heat, then add the onion and cook gently, stirring occasionally, for 2–3 minutes, until it is soft and translucent but not brown.

2 Stir the breadcrumbs, crab meat, sour cream and prepared mustard into the onion. Add a generous sprinkling of cayenne pepper and lemon juice and season the mixture with salt to taste. Heat through gently, stirring carefully.

3 Preheat the grill (broiler). Spoon the crab mixture into a flameproof dish, sprinkle the grated cheese evenly over the top and place under the hot grill until golden and bubbling. Serve immediately.

SMOKED MACKEREL PÂTÉ

THE PÂTÉ CAN BE GIVEN EXTRA FLAVOUR BY ADDING A SPOONFUL OF CREAMED HORSERADISH, IF YOU LIKE.

SERVES FOUR

INGREDIENTS
- 275g/10oz smoked mackerel fillet, skinned
- 90ml/6 tbsp sour cream
- 75g/3oz unsalted (sweet) butter, softened
- 30ml/2 tbsp chopped fresh parsley
- 15–30ml/1–2 tbsp lemon juice
- ground black pepper
- chicory (Belgian endive) leaves and fresh parsley, to garnish
- fingers of toast, to serve

1 Remove any fine bones from the mackerel fillet, then mash it well with a fork.

2 Work the sour cream and butter into the mackerel until smooth and thoroughly combined. Stir in the chopped parsley and add lemon juice and pepper to taste.

3 Spoon the mackerel mixture evenly into a dish or bowl, packing it down well. Cover the surface tightly with clear film (plastic wrap) and chill in the refrigerator for at least 8 hours or overnight.

4 About 30 minutes before serving, remove the pâté from the refrigerator to allow it to return to room temperature.

5 To serve, spoon the pâté on to individual plates and garnish with chicory leaves and parsley. Serve with fingers of toast.

VARIATIONS

- For a less rich (and lower-calorie) version of this pâté, substitute 200g/7oz/scant 1 cup low-fat soft cheese or sieved cottage cheese for the sour cream.
- This pâté is also great made with kippers (smoked herrings). If you like, you can cook them first by placing them in a jug (pitcher), filling it with freshly boiled water and then leaving it to stand for about 10 minutes. This is not essential, as kippers may also be eaten raw.

SCRAMBLED EGGS WITH LOX AND ONIONS

SERVE THIS QUINTESSENTIAL NEW YORK SUNDAY BRUNCH DISH WITH PILES OF FRESHLY TOASTED BAGELS, MUGS OF COFFEE AND A SELECTION OF SUNDAY NEWSPAPERS. THIS DELICIOUSLY DIFFERENT VERSION OF SCRAMBLED EGGS IS CERTAIN TO APPEAL TO EVERY MEMBER OF THE FAMILY.

SERVES FOUR

INGREDIENTS

- 40g/1½oz/3 tbsp unsalted (sweet) butter
- 2 onions, chopped
- 150–200g/5–7oz smoked salmon trimmings
- 6–8 eggs, lightly beaten
- ground black pepper
- 45ml/3 tbsp chopped fresh chives, plus whole chives, to garnish
- bagels, to serve

VARIATIONS

Substitute 200–250g/7–9oz diced salami for the smoked salmon and cook in a little oil.

1 Heat half the unsalted butter in a frying pan, add the chopped onions and cook until softened and just beginning to brown. Add the smoked salmon trimmings to the onions and mix well to combine.

2 Pour the eggs into the pan and stir until soft curds form. Add the remaining butter, remove from the heat and stir until creamy. Season with pepper. Spoon on to serving plates and garnish with chives. Serve with bagels.

Glazed Garlic Prawns

This is a fairly simple and quick dish to prepare. It is best to peel the prawns, as this helps them to absorb maximum flavour. Serve with a salad as an appetizer, or as a main course for two people, with vegetables and other accompaniments.

SERVES FOUR

INGREDIENTS

- 15ml/1 tbsp vegetable oil
- 3 garlic cloves, coarsely chopped
- 3 tomatoes, chopped
- 2.5ml/½ tsp salt
- 5ml/1 tsp crushed dried red chillies
- 5ml/1 tsp lemon juice
- 15ml/1 tbsp mango chutney
- 1 fresh green chilli, chopped
- 15–20 cooked king prawns (jumbo shrimp), peeled and deveined
- fresh coriander (cilantro) sprigs, 4 unpeeled, cooked king prawns (jumbo shrimp) and 2 spring onions (scallions), chopped (optional), to garnish

1 Heat the oil in a medium pan, add the chopped garlic cloves and cook, stirring, for 1 minute. Lower the heat and add the chopped tomatoes together with the salt, crushed chillies, lemon juice, mango chutney and chopped fresh chilli. Cook, stirring frequently, for 2 minutes.

2 Finally, add the prawns, turn up the heat and stir-fry them quickly, until just heated through. Do not overcook them or they will become tough.

3 Transfer to a warmed serving dish. Serve immediately, garnished with fresh coriander, unpeeled king prawns and chopped spring onions, if you like.

COOK'S TIPS

- This is a very fiery dish – if you would prefer it less hot, carefully seed the chilli before chopping and reduce the crushed chillies to a pinch.
- You can also use raw king prawns (jumbo shrimp) for this dish. If frozen, thaw thoroughly first. Add them to the pan in step 3, but stir-fry for a little longer to make sure they are cooked through. They will be ready when they have changed colour.

AROMATIC TIGER PRAWNS

THERE IS NO ELEGANT WAY TO EAT THESE AROMATIC PRAWNS – JUST HOLD THEM BY THE TAILS, PULL THEM OFF THE STICKS WITH YOUR FINGERS AND POP THEM INTO YOUR MOUTH.

SERVES FOUR

INGREDIENTS

16 raw tiger prawns (jumbo shrimp) or scampi (extra large shrimp) tails
2.5ml/½ tsp chilli powder
5ml/1 tsp fennel seeds
5 Sichuan or black peppercorns
1 star anise, broken into segments
1 cinnamon stick, broken into pieces
30ml/2 tbsp groundnut (peanut) or sunflower oil
2 garlic cloves, chopped
2cm/¾in piece fresh root ginger, peeled and finely chopped
1 shallot, chopped
30ml/2 tbsp water
30ml/2 tbsp rice vinegar
30ml/2 tbsp soft brown or palm sugar
salt and ground black pepper
lime slices and chopped spring onion (scallion), to garnish

1 Thread the prawns or scampi tails in pairs on eight wooden cocktail sticks (toothpicks). Set aside. Heat a frying pan, put in all the chilli powder, fennel seeds, Sichuan or black peppercorns, star anise and cinnamon stick and dry-fry for 1–2 minutes to release the flavours. Leave to cool, then grind the spices coarsely in a grinder or tip into a mortar and crush with a pestle.

2 Heat the groundnut or sunflower oil in a shallow pan, add the garlic, ginger and chopped shallot and then cook gently until very lightly coloured. Add the crushed spices and seasoning and cook the mixture gently for 2 minutes. Pour in the water and simmer, stirring, for 5 minutes.

3 Add the rice vinegar and soft brown or palm sugar, stir until dissolved, then add the prawns or scampi tails. Cook for 3–5 minutes, until the shellfish has turned pink, but is still very juicy. Serve hot, garnished with lime slices and spring onion.

COOK'S TIP

If you buy whole prawns (shrimp), remove the heads before cooking them.

PRAWN AND VEGETABLE CROSTINI

USE BOTTLED CARCIOFINI (TINY ARTICHOKE HEARTS PRESERVED IN OLIVE OIL) FOR THIS SIMPLE APPETIZER, WHICH CAN BE PREPARED VERY QUICKLY.

SERVES FOUR

INGREDIENTS

450g/1lb whole cooked prawns (shrimp), in the shell
4 thick slices of ciabatta bread, cut diagonally across
3 garlic cloves, peeled and 2 halved lengthways
60ml/4 tbsp olive oil
200g/7oz/2 cups small button (white) mushrooms, trimmed
12 drained bottled *carciofini*
60ml/4 tbsp chopped flat leaf parsley
salt and ground black pepper

COOK'S TIP

Don't be tempted to use thawed frozen prawns (shrimp), especially those that have been peeled; freshly cooked prawns in their shells are infinitely nicer.

1 Peel the prawns and remove the heads. Rub the ciabatta slices on both sides with the cut sides of the halved garlic cloves, drizzle with a little of the olive oil and toast in the oven or grill (broil) until lightly browned. Keep hot.

2 Finely chop the remaining garlic. Heat the remaining oil in a pan and gently cook the garlic until golden, but do not allow it to brown.

3 Add the mushrooms and stir to coat with oil. Season and sauté for about 2–3 minutes. Gently stir in the drained *carciofini*, then add the chopped flat leaf parsley.

4 Season again, then stir in the prawns and sauté briefly to warm through. Pile the prawn mixture on to the ciabatta, pour over any remaining cooking juices and serve immediately.

Red Mullet Dolmades

If you cannot find prepared vine leaves, use blanched cabbage or large spinach leaves instead. Plaice, flounder or lemon sole can be substituted for the red mullet.

SERVES FOUR

INGREDIENTS
- 225g/8oz red mullet or red snapper fillets, scaled
- 45ml/3 tbsp dry white wine
- 115g/4oz/1 cup cooked long grain rice
- 25g/1oz/¼ cup pine nuts
- 45ml/3 tbsp chopped fresh parsley
- grated rind and juice of ½ lemon
- 8 vine (grape) leaves in brine, rinsed and dried
- salt and ground black pepper

For the orange butter sauce
- grated rind and juice of 2 oranges
- 2 shallots, very finely chopped
- 25g/1oz/2 tbsp chilled butter, diced

1 Preheat the oven to 200°C/400°F/Gas 6. Put the fish fillets in a shallow pan and season with salt and pepper. Pour over the wine, bring to the boil, then lower the heat and poach the fish gently for about 3 minutes, until it is just cooked. Strain, reserving the cooking liquid.

2 Remove the skin from the fish fillets and flake the flesh into a bowl. Gently stir in the cooked rice, pine nuts, the chopped parsley, and lemon rind and juice. Season the filling to taste with salt and ground black pepper.

3 Spoon 30–45ml/2–3 tbsp of the filling into the middle of each vine leaf. Roll up each filled leaf, tucking in the ends to make a secure package. Arrange the dolmades in an ovenproof dish, with the joins underneath. Then pour over the reserved cooking liquid and place the dolmades in the preheated oven for about 5 minutes, until they are thoroughly heated through.

4 Meanwhile, make the sauce. Mix the orange rind and juice and the shallots in a small pan and boil vigorously for a few minutes until the mixture is reduced and syrupy.

5 Strain the sauce into a clean pan, discarding the shallots. Beat in the butter, one piece at a time. Reheat gently, but do not let the sauce boil. Drizzle the sauce over the hot dolmades and serve immediately.

SALMON AND SCALLOP BROCHETTES

WITH THEIR DELICATE COLOURS AND SUPERB FLAVOUR, THESE SKEWERS MAKE THE PERFECT OPENER FOR A SOPHISTICATED MEAL AND ARE ABSOLUTELY IRRESISTIBLE.

SERVES FOUR

INGREDIENTS

- 8 lemon grass stalks
- 225g/8oz salmon fillet, skinned
- 8 queen scallops, with their corals if possible
- 8 baby (pearl) onions, peeled and blanched
- ½ yellow (bell) pepper, cut into 8 squares
- 25g/1oz/2 tbsp butter
- juice of ½ lemon
- salt, ground white pepper and paprika

For the sauce

- 30ml/2 tbsp dry vermouth
- 50g/2oz/¼ cup butter
- 5ml/1 tsp chopped fresh tarragon

1 Preheat the grill (broiler) to medium-high. Cut off the top 7.5–10cm/3–4in of each lemon grass stalk. Reserve the bulb ends for another dish. Cut the salmon fillet into twelve 2cm/¾in cubes. Thread the salmon, scallops, corals if available, onions and pepper squares on to the lemon grass and arrange the brochettes in a grill pan.

2 Melt the butter in a small pan, add the lemon juice and a pinch of paprika and then brush all over the brochettes. Grill (broil) the skewers for about 2–3 minutes on each side, turning and basting the brochettes every minute, until the fish and scallops are just cooked, but are still very juicy. Transfer to a platter and keep hot while you make the tarragon butter sauce.

3 Pour the dry vermouth and all the leftover cooking juices from the brochettes into a small pan and boil quite fiercely to reduce by half. Add the butter and melt, stirring constantly. Stir in the chopped fresh tarragon and add salt and ground white pepper to taste. Pour the tarragon butter sauce over the brochettes and serve.

CHARGRILLED SQUID

ENJOY THESE TENDER BITES OF SUCCULENT SQUID RIGHT OFF THE BARBECUE.

SERVES FOUR

INGREDIENTS

- 1kg/2¼lb prepared squid
- 90ml/6 tbsp olive oil
- juice of 1–2 lemons
- 3 garlic cloves, crushed
- 1.5ml/¼ tsp chilli flakes
- 60ml/4 tbsp chopped fresh parsley
- lemon slices, to garnish

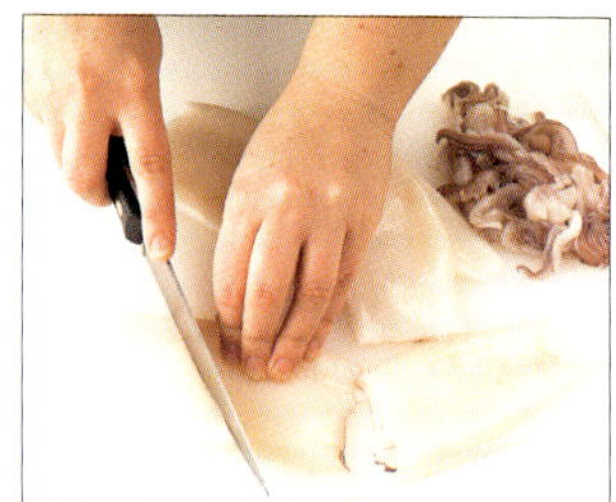

1 Cut off and reserve the squid tentacles, then, using a small, sharp knife, score the flesh of the body sacs into a diagonal pattern.

2 Place all the squid in a shallow, non-metallic dish. To make the marinade, thoroughly mix together the olive oil, lemon juice, crushed garlic and chilli flakes in a small bowl or jug (pitcher).

3 Pour the marinade over the squid, stir well to coat and set aside in a cool place for a minimum of 2 hours, stirring occasionally.

4 Prepare a barbecue or preheat the grill (broiler) to high. Lift the squid from the dish with a slotted spoon and reserve the marinade. Cook the squid for 2 minutes on each side, turning them frequently and brushing with the marinade until the outside is golden brown and crisp, with soft, moist flesh inside. On a barbecue, this is easier to do if you use a wire basket. Transfer to serving plates and keep warm.

5 Bring the remaining marinade to the boil in a small pan, stir in the chopped parsley, then pour over the squid. Garnish with lemon slices and serve immediately.

MONKFISH BROCHETTES

THESE BROCHETTES ARE COLOURFUL AS WELL AS FULL OF FLAVOUR.

SERVES FOUR

INGREDIENTS

- 675g/1½lb monkfish, skinned and boned
- 12 rashers (strips) streaky (fatty) bacon, rinded
- 2 small courgettes (zucchini)
- 1 orange (bell) pepper, seeded and cut into 2.5cm/1in cubes
- saffron rice, to serve

For the marinade

- 90ml/6 tbsp olive oil
- grated rind of ½ lime
- 45ml/3 tbsp lime juice
- 30ml/2 tbsp dry white wine
- 60ml/4 tbsp chopped fresh mixed herbs, such as dill, chives and parsley
- 5ml/1 tsp clear honey
- ground black pepper

1 To make the marinade, mix together the olive oil, lime rind and juice, wine, chopped herbs, honey and pepper in a bowl or jug (pitcher), then set aside.

2 Using a sharp knife, cut the monkfish into 24 x 2.5cm/1 in cubes. Stretch the bacon rashers with the back of a knife, then cut each one in half and wrap the halves around the monkfish cubes.

COOK'S TIPS

- If you are using wooden skewers, soak them in cold water before threading the fish and vegetables, so that they do not char when the brochettes are cooking.
- These brochettes may be cooked under a preheated grill (broiler) or on a medium barbecue.

3 Pare strips of peel from the courgettes to give a stripy effect, then cut into 2.5cm/1in chunks.

4 Thread the fish rolls on to skewers alternately with the courgettes and orange pepper. Place in a large, shallow dish. Pour over the marinade, turn the skewers to coat and leave in a cool place for 1 hour. Lift out the skewers, then grill (broil) for about 10 minutes, turning and basting occasionally with the marinade. Serve with saffron rice.

Thai Fish Cakes

These spicy fish cakes set the taste buds tingling.

SERVES FOUR

INGREDIENTS

- 450g/1lb firm white fish fillets
- 3 spring onions (scallions), sliced
- 30ml/2 tbsp chopped fresh coriander (cilantro)
- 30ml/2 tbsp Thai red curry paste
- 1 fresh green chilli, seeded and chopped
- 10ml/2 tsp grated lime rind
- 15ml/1 tbsp lime juice
- 30ml/2 tbsp sunflower oil
- salt
- crisp lettuce leaves, shredded spring onions (scallions), fresh red chilli slices, coriander (cilantro) sprigs and lime wedges, to serve

1 Skin the fish fillets, if necessary, and remove any pin bones. Using a sharp knife, cut the fish into chunks about 2.5cm/1in, then place in a blender or food processor.

2 Add the spring onions, coriander, Thai red curry paste, green chilli, lime rind and juice to the fish. Season with salt to taste. Process until finely minced (ground).

3 Using lightly floured hands, divide the fish mixture into 16 pieces and shape each one into a small, round cake about 4cm/1½in across. Place the fish cakes in a single layer on a large plate, cover with clear film (plastic wrap) and chill in the refrigerator for about 2 hours, until firm. Heat a wok or large, heavy frying pan over a high heat until hot. Add the sunflower oil and swirl it around to coat the sides.

4 Fry the fish cakes, a few at a time, for 6–8 minutes, turning them carefully, until they are evenly browned. Drain each batch on kitchen paper and keep hot while you are cooking the remainder.

5 Serve on a bed of crisp lettuce leaves with shredded spring onions, red chilli slices, coriander sprigs and lime wedges.

Seafood Wontons with Coriander Dressing

These tasty wontons resemble tortellini. Water chestnuts add a light crunch to the filling.

SERVES FOUR

INGREDIENTS

- 225g/8oz cooked prawns (shrimp), peeled and deveined
- 115g/4oz white crab meat
- 4 canned water chestnuts, finely diced
- 1 spring onion (scallion), finely chopped
- 1 small green chilli, seeded and finely chopped
- 1.5ml/¼ tsp grated fresh root ginger
- 1 egg, separated
- 20–24 wonton wrappers, thawed if frozen
- salt and ground black pepper
- fresh coriander (cilantro) leaves, to garnish

For the dressing

- 30ml/2 tbsp rice vinegar
- 15ml/1 tbsp chopped, pickled ginger
- 90ml/6 tbsp olive oil
- 15ml/1 tbsp soy sauce
- 45ml/3 tbsp chopped fresh coriander (cilantro)
- 30ml/2 tbsp finely diced red (bell) pepper

1 Finely dice the prawns and place them in a bowl. Add the crab meat, water chestnuts, spring onion, chilli, ginger and egg white. Season with salt and pepper to taste and stir well to combine.

2 Place a wonton wrapper on a board. Put about 5ml/1 tsp of the prawn filling just above the centre of the wrapper. Using a pastry brush, lightly moisten the edges of the wrapper with a little of the egg yolk. Bring the bottom of the wrapper up over the filling. Press gently to expel any air, then seal the edges of the wrapper neatly to form a triangle. Fill the remaining wonton wrappers in the same way.

3 For slightly more elaborately shaped wontons, bring the two side points up over the filling, then overlap the points and pinch the ends securely together.

4 Place the filled wontons on a large baking sheet lined with greaseproof (waxed) paper or baking parchment, spacing them well apart so that they do not stick together.

5 Half fill a large pan with water. Bring to the boil, then lower the heat to a simmer. Add the filled wontons, a few at a time, and simmer for about 2–3 minutes, or until the wontons float to the surface. When ready, the wrappers will be translucent and the filling should be cooked. Using a large slotted spoon, remove the wontons and drain them briefly, then spread them on trays. Keep warm while you cook the remaining wontons.

6 Make the coriander dressing by whisking all the ingredients together in a bowl using a balloon whisk or a fork.

7 Divide the wontons among individual serving dishes, drizzle with the coriander dressing and serve immediately, garnished with a handful of coriander leaves.

GRILLED GREEN MUSSELS WITH CUMIN

GREEN-SHELLED MUSSELS HAVE A MORE DISTINCTIVE FLAVOUR THAN THE SMALL, BLACK VARIETY.

SERVES FOUR

INGREDIENTS

- 75ml/5 tbsp fresh parsley leaves
- 45ml/3 tbsp fresh coriander (cilantro) leaves
- 1 garlic clove, crushed
- pinch of ground cumin
- 25g/1oz/2 tbsp unsalted (sweet) butter, softened
- 25g/1oz/½ cup fresh brown breadcrumbs
- 12 green mussels or 24 small mussels, on the half-shell
- ground black pepper

1 Finely chop the fresh parsley and coriander leaves. Set aside about 30ml/2 tbsp of the chopped parsley for garnish.

2 Put the remaining parsley, the coriander, garlic, ground cumin and butter in a bowl and beat together with a wooden spoon.

3 Stir in the breadcrumbs and season to taste with freshly ground black pepper.

4 Preheat the grill (broiler). Spoon a little of the mixture on to each mussel and grill (broil) for 2 minutes. Serve immediately, garnished with the reserved fresh parsley.

WELSH RAREBIT WITH ANCHOVIES

MAKE AS REQUIRED BECAUSE THE SAUCE WILL NOT KEEP FOR LONG.

SERVES FOUR

INGREDIENTS

- 40g/1½oz canned anchovies, drained
- 175g/6oz/¾ cup butter
- 6 slices of bread, crusts removed
- 4 large (US extra large) egg yolks
- 300ml/½ pint/1¼ cups double (heavy) cream
- pinch of cayenne pepper
- salt and ground black pepper
- 15ml/1 tbsp chopped fresh parsley, to garnish

1 Put the anchovy fillets and two-thirds of the butter into a food processor fitted with a metal blade and process to combine. Toast the slices of bread, spread with the anchovy butter, then set aside and keep warm.

2 Melt the remaining butter in a small, heavy pan over a low heat. Remove the pan from the heat and beat in the egg yolks.

3 Gradually add the cream. Season to taste with salt and pepper, then replace on a low heat. Stir constantly until the sauce is thick. Pour over the toast and sprinkle with the cayenne pepper. Garnish with the chopped fresh parsley.

COOK'S TIPS

- If you find canned anchovies too salty, soak them briefly in cold water before processing them with the butter.
- Anchovy butter on plain toast makes a tasty snack and it can also be used as a garnish for grilled (broiled) fish.
- If you prefer, you can use bottled salted anchovies instead of canned.
- Sardine butter can be made in the same way, using canned sardines instead of anchovies, and served with Welsh rarebit, as here.

ONION AND ANCHOVY BREAD

Not unlike Italian pizza, the less familiar Spanish cocas have a very long tradition. They are essentially fresh bread dough, baked with a variety of savoury toppings, and often include salt fish. The flavourings of this snack go back at least 1,000 years.

SERVES SIX TO EIGHT

INGREDIENTS

- 400g/14oz/3½ cups strong white bread flour
- 2.5ml/½ tsp salt
- 15g/½oz easy-blend (rapid-rise) dried yeast
- 120ml/4fl oz/½ cup olive oil
- 150ml/¼ pint/⅔ cup milk and water, in equal quantities, mixed together
- 3 large onions, thinly sliced
- 50g/2oz can anchovies, drained and coarsely chopped
- 30ml/2 tbsp pine nuts
- 30ml/2 tbsp Muscatel raisins or sultanas (golden raisins), soaked
- 5ml/1 tsp dried chilli flakes or powder
- salt and ground black pepper

VARIATION

You can eat cocas with a wide range of different toppings. Try spinach sautéed with garlic or sweet red (bell) peppers.

1 Put the flour and salt into a food processor with the yeast. Process, gradually working in 60ml/4 tbsp oil and a little of the milk and water. Gradually add the remaining milk and water, processing until well combined. Turn the dough into a bowl, cover with a dishtowel, then leave in a warm place for about 1 hour to rise.

2 Preheat the oven to 240°C/475°F/Gas 9. Heat the remaining oil in a large frying pan, add the sliced onions and cook gently until soft.

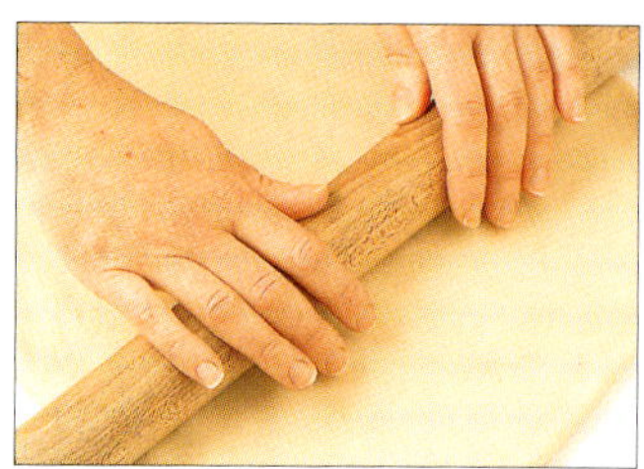

3 Return the dough to the food processor and use the pulse button to work the dough. On a lightly floured surface roll out the dough to a rectangle about 30 × 38cm/12 × 15in. Place on an oiled baking sheet.

4 Cover the dough with the onions. Sprinkle with the anchovies, pine nuts, raisins or sultanas and chilli flakes or powder and season. Bake for about 10 minutes, until puffed up and the edges are beginning to brown. Serve hot, cut into wedges.

BANDERILLAS

These miniature skewers are very popular in the north of Spain, where they are called pinchos, which literally means stuck on a thorn. Taste, colour and shape guide the choice of ingredients, which may include cold or cured meat, pickled tuna, salted fish or even hard-boiled eggs. In the South, pickled vegetables are preferred. There, the resemblance to the bullfighter's dart was noticed and so the skewers were renamed.

SERVES FOUR

INGREDIENTS

- 12 small capers
- 12 canned anchovy fillets in oil, drained
- 12 pitted black olives
- 12 cornichons or small gherkins
- 12 silverskin pickled onions

VARIATION

You can vary the ingredients if you like, using cold meats, cheeses and vegetables. Choose ingredients with different textures, tastes and colours.

1 Using your fingers, place a caper at the thicker end of each anchovy fillet and carefully roll it up, so that the caper is completely enclosed.

2 Thread one stuffed anchovy, one olive, one cornichon or gherkin and one pickled onion on to each of 12 cocktail sticks (toothpicks). Chill and serve.

OLIVE AND ANCHOVY BITES

THESE MELT-IN-THE-MOUTH MORSELS STORE WELL; FREEZE THEM FOR UP TO 3 MONTHS OR THEY CAN BE KEPT IN AN AIRTIGHT CONTAINER FOR UP TO 2 WEEKS BEFORE SERVING.

MAKES FORTY TO FORTY-FIVE

INGREDIENTS

- 115g/4oz/1 cup plain (all-purpose) flour
- 115g/4oz/½ cup chilled butter
- 115g/4oz/1 cup finely grated Cheddar cheese
- 50g/2oz can anchovy fillets in oil, drained and coarsely chopped
- 50g/2oz/½ cup pitted black olives
- 2.5ml/½ tsp cayenne pepper
- sea salt

1 Place the flour, butter, cheese, anchovies, olives and cayenne in a food processor and pulse until the mixture forms a firm dough.

2 Wrap the dough loosely in clear film (plastic wrap). Set aside in the refrigerator to chill for 20 minutes.

3 Preheat the oven to 200°C/400°F/Gas 6. Unwrap the dough and place it on a lightly floured surface. Knead it lightly and then roll it out thinly.

4 Cut the dough into 5cm/2in, wide strips, then cut across each strip diagonally, in alternate directions, to make triangles.

5 Transfer to baking sheets and bake in the oven for 8–10 minutes, until golden. Cool on a wire rack. Sprinkle the triangles generously with sea salt before serving.

SMOKED SALMON PANCAKES WITH PESTO

These pancakes are easy to prepare and are perfect for a special occasion.

MAKES TWELVE TO SIXTEEN

INGREDIENTS
- 120ml/4fl oz/½ cup milk
- 115g/4oz/1 cup self-raising (self-rising) flour
- 1 egg
- 30ml/2 tbsp pesto sauce
- vegetable oil, for frying
- 200ml/7fl oz/scant 1 cup crème fraîche
- 75g/3oz smoked salmon, cut into 1cm/½in strips
- 15g/½oz/2 tbsp pine nuts, toasted
- salt and ground black pepper
- 12–16 fresh basil sprigs, to garnish

1 Pour half of the milk into a medium mixing bowl. Sift in the flour and add the egg, pesto sauce and salt and pepper to taste. Using a wooden spoon, mix to a smooth batter.

2 Add the remainder of the milk and stir until evenly blended.

3 Heat the vegetable oil in a large, heavy frying pan. Spoon the pancake mixture into the heated oil in small heaps. Allow about 30 seconds for the pancakes to rise, then turn them over and cook briefly on the other side until just golden. Remove from the pan and keep warm. Continue cooking the pancakes in batches until all the batter has been used up.

4 Arrange the pancakes on a large serving plate and top each one with a spoonful of crème fraîche.

5 Arrange the strips of smoked salmon on top of each pancake. Sprinkle each pancake with pine nuts and garnish with a small sprig of fresh basil. Serve immediately.

Seafood Pancakes

The combination of fresh and smoked haddock imparts a wonderful flavour to the filling.

SERVES FOUR TO SIX

INGREDIENTS

For the pancakes

- 115g/4oz/1 cup plain (all-purpose) flour
- pinch of salt
- 1 egg, plus 1 egg yolk
- 300ml/½ pint/1¼ cups milk
- 15ml/1 tbsp melted butter, plus extra for cooking
- 50–75g/2–3oz/½–¾ cup grated Gruyère cheese
- curly salad leaves, to serve

For the filling

- 225g/8oz smoked haddock fillet
- 225g/8oz fresh haddock fillet
- 300ml/½ pint/1¼ cups milk
- 150ml/¼ pint/⅔ cup single (light) cream
- 40g/1½oz/3 tbsp butter
- 40g/1½oz/⅓ cup plain (all-purpose) flour
- freshly grated nutmeg
- 2 hard-boiled eggs, chopped
- salt and ground black pepper

1 To make the pancakes, sift the flour and salt into a bowl. Make a well in the centre and add the egg and yolk. Whisk the eggs, starting to incorporate some of the flour from around the edges.

2 Gradually add the milk, whisking constantly, until the batter is smooth and has the consistency of thin cream. Stir in the melted butter.

3 Heat a small crêpe pan or omelette pan until hot, then rub around the inside of the pan with a pad of kitchen paper dipped in melted butter to grease it lightly.

4 Pour about 30ml/2 tbsp of the batter into the pan, then gently tip the pan to coat the base evenly. Cook over a medium heat for about 30 seconds until the underside of the pancake is golden brown and the top of the pancake is just beginning to set.

5 Using a palette knife or metal spatula, flip the pancake over and cook the other side until lightly browned. Slide the pancake out on to a plate and keep warm. Repeat to make 12 pancakes, rubbing the pan with melted butter between cooking each one. Stack the pancakes as you make them between sheets of greaseproof (waxed) paper. Keep warm on a plate set over a pan of simmering water.

6 Put the smoked and fresh haddock fillets in a large pan. Add the milk and bring to simmering point. Poach over a low heat for 6–8 minutes, until just tender. Lift out the fish using a slotted spoon and, when cool enough to handle, remove the skin and any bones. Reserve the milk.

7 Pour the single cream into a measuring jug (cup), then strain enough of the reserved milk into the jug to make the quantity up to 450ml/¾ pint/scant 1 cup.

8 Melt the butter in a pan, stir in the flour and cook gently, stirring constantly, for 1 minute. Gradually add the cream and milk mixture, stirring constantly, to make a smooth sauce. Cook over a low heat, stirring, for 2–3 minutes, until thickened. Season with salt, pepper and nutmeg. Coarsely flake the haddock and fold the fish into the sauce with the hard-boiled eggs. Remove the pan from the heat and leave to cool.

9 Divide the filling among the pancakes. Fold the sides of each pancake into the centre, then roll them up so that the filling is completely enclosed.

10 Preheat the oven to 180°C/350°F/Gas 4. Butter four or six individual ovenproof dishes and arrange two or three filled pancakes in each. Alternatively, butter one large dish for all the pancakes. Brush the tops with melted butter and bake for 15 minutes. Sprinkle over the grated Gruyère and cook for a further 5 minutes, until warmed through and the topping is golden. Serve hot with a few curly salad leaves.

VARIATION

To ring the changes, add cooked, peeled prawns (shrimp), cooked shelled mussels or smoked mussels to the filling, instead of the chopped hard-boiled eggs.

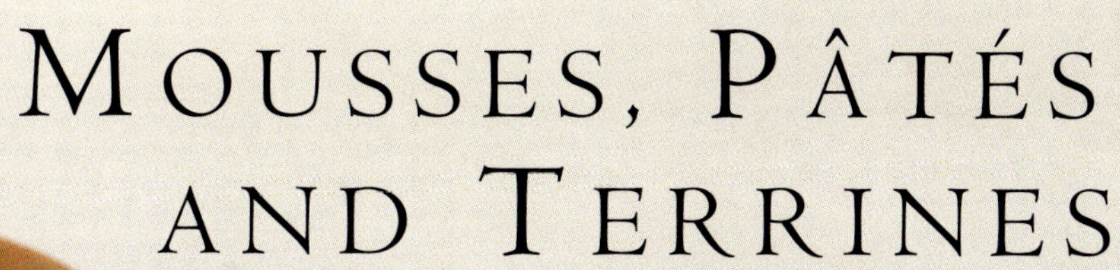

MOUSSES, PÂTÉS AND TERRINES

Soft-textured fish and shellfish can be puréed to produce attractive light-textured mousses, such as Smoked Fish and Asparagus Mousse. Hot Crab Soufflés make a substantial appetizer or light lunch or supper dish for a chilly day, and chunky Haddock and Smoked Salmon Terrine is ideal when the weather warms up. Celebrate summer with cold creamy Sea Trout Mousse. For the simplest of dishes, Fiery Mackerel Pâté takes only moments to prepare and is perennially popular.

Sea Trout Mousse

This deliciously creamy mousse makes a little sea trout go a long way. It is equally good made with salmon if sea trout is unavailable.

SERVES SIX

INGREDIENTS

- 250g/9oz sea trout fillet
- 120ml/4fl oz/½ cup fish stock
- 2 gelatine leaves, or 15ml/1 tbsp powdered gelatine
- juice of ½ lemon
- 30ml/2 tbsp dry sherry or dry vermouth
- 30ml/2 tbsp freshly grated Parmesan
- 300ml/½ pint/1¼ cups whipping cream
- 2 egg whites
- 15ml/1 tbsp sunflower oil
- salt and ground white pepper

For the garnish

- 5cm/2in piece of cucumber, with peel, thinly sliced and halved
- fresh dill or chervil

1 Put the sea trout in a shallow pan. Pour in the fish stock and heat to simmering point. Poach the fish for about 3–4 minutes, until it is lightly cooked. Strain the stock into a jug (pitcher) and leave the trout to cool.

2 Add the gelatine to the hot stock and stir until it has dissolved completely. Set aside until required.

COOK'S TIP

Serve the mousse with Melba toast, if you like. Toast thin slices of bread on both sides under the grill (broiler), then cut off the crusts and slice each piece of toast in half horizontally. Return to the grill pan, untoasted sides up, and grill (broil) again. The thin slices will swiftly brown and curl, so watch them closely.

3 When the trout is cool enough to handle, remove the skin and flake the flesh. Pour the stock into a food processor or blender. Process briefly, then gradually add the flaked trout, lemon juice, sherry or vermouth and Parmesan through the feeder tube, continuing to process the mixture until it is smooth. Scrape into a large bowl and leave to cool completely.

4 Lightly whip the cream in a bowl; fold it into the cold trout mixture. Season to taste, then cover with clear film (plastic wrap) and chill until the mousse is just beginning to set. It should have the consistency of mayonnaise.

5 In a grease-free bowl, beat the egg whites with a pinch of salt until softly peaking. Using a large metal spoon, stir one-third into the trout mixture to slacken it, then fold in the rest.

6 Lightly grease six ramekins with the sunflower oil. Divide the mousse among the ramekins and level the surface. Place in the refrigerator for 2–3 hours, until set. Just before serving, arrange a few slices of cucumber and a small herb sprig on each mousse and add a little chopped dill or chervil.

QUENELLES OF SOLE

TRADITIONALLY, THESE LIGHT FISH "DUMPLINGS" ARE MADE WITH PIKE, BUT THEY ARE EVEN BETTER MADE WITH SOLE OR OTHER WHITE FISH. IF YOU ARE FEELING EXTRAVAGANT, SERVE THEM WITH A CREAMY SHELLFISH SAUCE STUDDED WITH CRAYFISH TAILS OR PRAWNS.

SERVES SIX

INGREDIENTS

- 450g/1lb sole fillets, skinned and cut into large pieces
- 4 egg whites
- 600ml/1 pint/2½ cups double (heavy) cream
- salt, ground white pepper and grated nutmeg

For the sauce

- 1 small shallot, finely chopped
- 60ml/4 tbsp dry vermouth
- 120ml/4fl oz/½ cup fish stock
- 150ml/¼ pint/⅔ cup double (heavy) cream
- 50g/2oz/¼ cup cold butter, diced
- chopped fresh parsley, to garnish

1 Check the sole for stray bones, then put the pieces in a blender or food processor. Add a generous pinch of salt and a grinding of pepper. Switch on and, with the motor running, add the egg whites one at a time through the feeder tube to make a smooth purée. Press the purée through a metal sieve placed over a bowl. Stand the bowl of purée in a larger bowl and surround it with plenty of crushed ice or ice cubes.

2 Whip the cream until very thick and floppy, but not stiff. Gradually fold it into the fish mousse, making sure each spoonful has been absorbed completely before adding the next. Season with salt and pepper, then stir in nutmeg to taste. Cover the bowl of mousse and transfer it, still in its bowl of ice, to the refrigerator. Chill for several hours.

3 To make the sauce, combine the shallot, vermouth and fish stock in a small pan. Bring to the boil and cook until reduced by half. Add the cream and boil again until the sauce has the consistency of single (light) cream. Strain, return to the pan and whisk in the butter, one piece at a time, until the sauce is very creamy. Season and keep hot, but do not let it boil.

4 Bring a wide shallow pan of lightly salted water to the boil, then reduce the heat so that the water surface barely trembles. Using two tablespoons dipped in hot water, shape the fish mousse into ovals. As each quenelle is shaped, slip it into the simmering water.

5 Poach the quenelles, in batches, for 8–10 minutes, until they feel just firm to the touch, but are still slightly creamy inside. As each is cooked, lift it out on a slotted spoon, drain on kitchen paper and keep hot. When all the quenelles are cooked, arrange them on heated plates. Pour the sauce around. Serve garnished with parsley.

COOK'S TIP

Keep the heat low when poaching; quenelles disintegrate in boiling water.

Fiery Mackerel Pâté

Some of the most delicious dishes are also the simplest to make. Serve this popular pâté with warmed Melba toast as an appetizer, or for a light lunch with wholemeal toast.

SERVES SIX

INGREDIENTS
- 4 smoked mackerel fillets, skinned
- 225g/8oz/1 cup cream cheese
- 1–2 garlic cloves, finely chopped
- juice of 1 lemon
- 30ml/2 tbsp chopped fresh chervil, parsley or chives
- 15ml/1 tbsp Worcestershire sauce
- salt and cayenne pepper
- fresh chives, to garnish
- warmed Melba toast, to serve

VARIATION
Use peppered mackerel fillets for a more piquant flavour. This pâté can be made with smoked haddock or kipper (smoked herring) fillets.

1 Break up the mackerel and put it in a food processor. Add the cream cheese, garlic, lemon juice and herbs.

2 Process the mixture until it is fairly smooth but still has a slightly chunky texture, then add Worcestershire sauce, salt and cayenne pepper to taste. Process to mix, then spoon the pâté into a dish, cover with clear film (plastic wrap) and chill. Garnish with chives and serve with Melba toast.

Brandade of Salt Cod

There are almost as many versions of this creamy salt cod purée as there are regions of France. Some contain mashed potatoes, others truffles. This comparatively light recipe includes garlic, but you can omit it and serve the brandade on toasted slices of French bread rubbed with garlic if you like.

SERVES SIX

INGREDIENTS
- 200g/7oz salt cod
- 250ml/8fl oz/1 cup extra virgin olive oil
- 4 garlic cloves, crushed
- 250ml/8fl oz/1 cup double (heavy) or whipping cream
- ground white pepper
- shredded spring onions (scallions), to garnish
- herbed crispbread, to serve

1 Soak the fish in cold water for 24 hours, changing the water often. Drain. Cut into pieces, place in a shallow pan and pour in cold water to cover. Heat the water until simmering, then poach the fish for 8 minutes, until just cooked. Drain, then remove the skin and bones.

2 Combine the olive oil and garlic in a small pan and heat to just below boiling point. In another pan, heat the cream until it starts to simmer.

3 Put the cod into a food processor, process it briefly, then gradually add alternate amounts of the garlic-flavoured olive oil and cream, while continuing to process the mixture. The aim is to create a purée with the consistency of mashed potatoes.

4 Add pepper to taste, then scoop the brandade into a serving bowl. Garnish with shredded spring onions and serve warm with herbed crispbread.

COOK'S TIP
You can purée the fish mixture in a mortar with a pestle. This gives a better texture, but is notoriously hard work.

Hot Crab Soufflés

These delicious little soufflés must be served as soon as they are ready, so seat your guests at the table before taking the soufflés out of the oven.

Serves six

INGREDIENTS

- 50g/2oz/¼ cup butter
- 45ml/3 tbsp fine wholemeal (whole-wheat) breadcrumbs
- 4 spring onions (scallions), finely chopped
- 15ml/1 tbsp Malaysian or mild Madras curry powder
- 25g/1oz/2 tbsp plain (all-purpose) flour
- 105ml/7 tbsp coconut milk or milk
- 150ml/¼ pint/⅔ cup whipping cream
- 4 egg yolks
- 225g/8oz white crab meat
- mild green Tabasco sauce
- 6 egg whites
- salt and ground black pepper

1 Use some of the butter to grease six ramekins or a 1.75 litre/3 pint/7 cup soufflé dish. Sprinkle in the fine wholemeal breadcrumbs, roll the dishes or dish around to coat the base and sides completely, then tip out the excess breadcrumbs. Preheat the oven to 200°C/400°F/Gas 6.

2 Melt the remaining butter in a pan, add the spring onions and Malaysian or mild Madras curry powder and cook over a low heat for about 1 minute, until softened. Stir in the flour and cook for 1 minute more.

3 Gradually add the coconut milk or milk and cream, stirring constantly. Cook until smooth and thick. Remove the pan from the heat, stir in the egg yolks, then the crab. Season with salt, black pepper and Tabasco sauce.

4 In a grease-free bowl, beat the egg whites stiffly with a pinch of salt. Using a metal spoon, stir one-third into the mixture to slacken it; fold in the rest. Spoon into the dishes or dish.

5 Bake until well-risen and golden brown, and just firm to the touch. Individual soufflés will be ready in about 8 minutes; a large soufflé will take 15–20 minutes. Serve immediately.

Smoked Fish and Asparagus Mousse

This elegant mousse looks very special with its studding of asparagus and smoked salmon. Serve a mustard and dill dressing separately if you like.

SERVES EIGHT

INGREDIENTS
- 15ml/1 tbsp powdered gelatine
- juice of 1 lemon
- 105ml/7 tbsp fish stock
- 50g/2oz/¼ cup butter, plus extra for greasing
- 2 shallots, finely chopped
- 225g/8oz smoked trout fillets
- 105ml/7 tbsp sour cream
- 225g/8oz/1 cup low-fat cream cheese or cottage cheese
- 1 egg white
- 12 spinach leaves, blanched
- 12 fresh asparagus spears, lightly cooked
- 115g/4oz smoked salmon, cut into long strips
- salt
- shredded beetroot (beet) and leaves, to garnish

1 Sprinkle the gelatine over the lemon juice and leave until spongy. In a small pan, heat the fish stock, then add the soaked gelatine and stir to dissolve completely. Set aside. Melt the butter in a small pan, add the shallots and cook gently until softened but not coloured.

2 Break up the smoked trout fillets and put them in a food processor with the shallots, sour cream, stock mixture and cream or cottage cheese. Process until smooth, then spoon into a bowl.

3 In a clean bowl, beat the egg white with a pinch of salt to soft peaks. Fold into the fish. Cover the bowl; chill for 30 minutes or until starting to set.

4 Grease a 1 litre/1¾ pint/4 cup loaf tin (pan) or terrine with butter, then line it with the spinach leaves. Carefully spread half the trout mousse over the spinach-covered base, arrange the asparagus spears on top, then cover with the remaining trout mousse.

5 Arrange the smoked salmon strips lengthways on the mousse and fold over the overhanging spinach leaves. Cover with clear film (plastic wrap) and chill for 4 hours, until set. To serve, remove the clear film, turn out on to a serving dish and garnish.

STRIPED FISH TERRINE

SERVE THIS ATTRACTIVE TERRINE COLD OR JUST WARM, WITH A HOLLANDAISE SAUCE IF YOU LIKE. IT IS IDEAL AS AN APPETIZER OR LIGHT LUNCH DISH.

SERVES EIGHT

INGREDIENTS
- 15ml/1 tbsp sunflower oil
- 450g/1lb salmon fillet, skinned
- 450g/1lb sole fillets, skinned
- 3 egg whites
- 105ml/7 tbsp double (heavy) cream
- 15ml/1 tbsp finely chopped fresh chives
- juice of 1 lemon
- 115g/4oz/1 cup fresh or frozen peas, cooked
- 5ml/1 tsp chopped fresh mint leaves
- salt, ground white pepper and grated nutmeg
- thinly sliced cucumber, salad cress and chives, to garnish

1 Grease a 1 litre/1¾ pint/4 cup loaf tin (pan) or terrine with the oil. Slice the salmon thinly; cut it and the sole into long strips, 2.5cm/1in wide. Preheat the oven to 200°C/400°F/Gas 6.

2 Line the terrine neatly with alternate slices of salmon and sole, leaving the ends overhanging the edge. You should be left with about a third of the salmon and half the sole.

3 In a grease-free bowl, beat the egg whites with a pinch of salt until they form soft peaks. Purée the remaining sole in a food processor. Spoon into a mixing bowl, season, then fold in two-thirds of the egg whites, followed by two-thirds of the cream. Put half the mixture into a second bowl; stir in the chives. Add nutmeg to the first bowl.

4 Purée the remaining salmon, scrape it into a bowl; add the lemon juice. Fold in the remaining whites, then cream.

5 Purée the peas with the mint. Season the mixture and spread it over the base of the terrine, smoothing the surface with a spatula. Spoon over the sole with chives mixture and spread evenly.

6 Add the salmon mixture, then finish with the plain sole mixture. Cover with the overhanging fish fillets and make a lid of oiled foil. Stand the terrine in a roasting pan and pour in enough boiling water to come halfway up the sides.

7 Bake for 15–20 minutes, until the top fillets are just cooked and the mousse feels springy. Remove the foil, lay a wire rack over the top of the terrine and invert both rack and terrine on to a lipped baking sheet to catch the cooking juices that drain out. Keep these to make fish stock or soup.

8 Leaving the tin in place, let the terrine stand for about 15 minutes, then turn the terrine over again. Invert it on to a serving dish and lift off the tin carefully. Serve warm, or chill in the refrigerator first and serve cold. Garnish with thinly sliced cucumber, salad cress and chives before serving.

COOK'S TIPS
- Pop the salmon into the freezer about 1 hour before slicing it. If it is almost frozen, it will be much easier to slice.
- You can line the tin (pan) or terrine with oven-safe clear film (plastic wrap) after greasing and before adding the salmon and sole strips. This makes it easier to turn out the terrine.

HADDOCK AND SMOKED SALMON TERRINE

THIS SUBSTANTIAL TERRINE MAKES A SUPERB DISH FOR A SUMMER BUFFET, ACCOMPANIED BY DILL MAYONNAISE OR A FRESH MANGO SALSA.

SERVES TEN TO TWELVE AS AN APPETIZER, SIX TO EIGHT AS A MAIN COURSE

INGREDIENTS
- 15ml/1 tbsp sunflower oil, for greasing
- 350g/12oz oak-smoked salmon
- 900g/2lb haddock fillets, skinned
- 2 eggs, lightly beaten
- 105ml/7 tbsp crème fraîche
- 30ml/2 tbsp drained capers
- 30ml/2 tbsp drained soft green or pink peppercorns
- salt and ground white pepper
- crème fraîche, peppercorns and fresh dill and rocket (arugula), to garnish

1 Preheat the oven to 200°C/400°F/Gas 6. Grease a 1 litre/1¾ pint/4 cup loaf tin (pan) or terrine with the oil. Use some of the salmon to line the tin or terrine; let some of the ends overhang the mould. Reserve the remaining smoked salmon until needed.

2 Cut two long slices of haddock the length of the tin or terrine and set aside. Cut the rest of the haddock into small pieces. Season all the haddock with salt and pepper.

3 Combine the eggs, crème fraîche, capers and green or pink peppercorns in a bowl. Season with salt and pepper; stir in the small pieces of haddock. Spoon the mixture into the mould until it is one-third full. Smooth the surface with a spatula.

4 Wrap the long haddock fillets in the reserved smoked salmon. Lay them on top of the layer of the fish mixture in the tin or terrine.

5 Fill the tin or terrine with the rest of the fish mixture, smooth the surface and fold the overhanging pieces of smoked salmon over the top. Cover tightly with a double thickness of foil. Tap the terrine to settle the contents.

6 Stand the terrine in a roasting pan and pour in boiling water to come halfway up the sides. Place in the oven and cook for 45 minutes–1 hour, until the filling is just set.

7 Take the terrine out of the roasting pan, but do not remove the foil cover. Place two or three large heavy cans on the foil to weight it and leave until cold. Chill in the refrigerator for 24 hours.

8 About an hour before serving, remove the terrine from the refrigerator, lift off the weights and remove the foil. Carefully invert the terrine on to a serving plate and lift off the loaf tin.

9 Cut the terrine into thick slices using a sharp knife and serve, garnished with crème fraîche, peppercorns and fronds of dill and rocket leaves.

VARIATION

Use any thick white fish fillets for this terrine: try halibut or Arctic bass.

Smoked Salmon Terrine with Lemons

Lemons can be cut and sliced in so many ways. This melt-in-the-mouth smoked salmon terrine gives a time-honoured accompaniment an intriguing new twist.

SERVES SIX

INGREDIENTS

- 4 gelatine leaves
- 60ml/4 tbsp water
- 400g/14oz smoked salmon, sliced
- 300g/11oz/1½ cups cream cheese
- 120ml/4fl oz/½ cup crème fraîche
- 30ml/2 tbsp dill mustard
- juice of 1 lime

For the garnish

- 2 lemons
- piece of muslin (cheesecloth)
- raffia, for tying

1 Soak the gelatine in the water in a small bowl until softened. Meanwhile, line a 450g/1lb loaf tin (pan) with clear film (plastic wrap). Use some of the smoked salmon to line the tin, laying the slices widthways across the base and up the sides and leaving enough overlap to fold over the top of the filling.

2 Set aside enough of the remaining smoked salmon to make a middle layer the length of the tin. Chop the remainder finely using a sharp knife or in a food processor. Put the chopped smoked salmon, cream cheese, crème fraîche and dill mustard in a bowl and beat together well until all the ingredients are thoroughly combined.

3 Squeeze out the gelatine and melt gently in a small pan with the lime juice. Add to the smoked salmon mixture and mix thoroughly. Spoon half the mixture into the lined tin. Lay the reserved smoked salmon slices on the mixture along the length of the tin, then spoon on the rest of the filling and smooth the top.

4 Tap the tin gently on the work surface to expel any trapped air. Fold over the overhanging salmon slices to cover the top. Cover with clear film and chill in the refrigerator for at least 4 hours.

5 Meanwhile, make the garnish. Cut one lemon in half widthways. Wrap each half lemon in a small square of muslin. Gather together the muslin at the rounded end of the lemon halves and tie neatly in place with a length of raffia.

6 Cut a small "V" from the side of the other lemon. Repeat at 5mm/¼in intervals. Turn out the terrine, then slice. Garnish with muslin-wrapped lemons and lemon "leaves".

SMOKED HADDOCK AND AVOCADO MOUSSE

THE FRESH-TASTING SALSA COMPLEMENTS THE SMOOTH CREAMINESS OF THE MOUSSE.

SERVES SIX

INGREDIENTS

- 225g/8oz undyed smoked haddock fillets, skinned
- ½ onion, cut into thick rings
- 25g/1oz/2 tbsp butter
- 1 bay leaf
- 150ml/¼ pint/⅔ cup milk
- 1 ripe avocado
- 2 gelatine leaves, or 15ml/1 tbsp powdered gelatine
- 30ml/2 tbsp dry white wine
- 105ml/7 tbsp double (heavy) cream
- 1 egg white
- salt, ground white pepper and grated nutmeg

For the salsa

- 3 tomatoes, peeled, seeded and diced
- 1 avocado
- 1 small red onion, finely chopped
- 1–2 garlic cloves, finely chopped
- 1 large fresh green chilli, seeded and finely chopped
- 45ml/3 tbsp extra virgin olive oil
- juice of 1 lime
- 12 lime slices, to garnish

1 Arrange the fish in a single layer in a large shallow pan and lay the onion rings on top. Dot with butter, season with pepper, add the bay leaf and pour over the milk. Poach gently over a low heat for 5 minutes, or until the fish flakes easily when tested with the tip of a sharp knife. Remove the fish using a slotted spoon and leave to cool.

VARIATION

Undyed smoked cod can be used instead of the smoked haddock.

2 Using a slotted spoon, lift out and discard the bay leaf and onion. Set the pan over a high heat and boil the milk until it has reduced by about two-thirds. Flake the fish into a food processor and strain over the reduced milk. Process until smooth.

3 Spoon the fish mixture into a bowl. Peel the avocado and cut the flesh into 5mm/¼in dice. Fold into the fish purée.

4 In a small pan, soak the gelatine leaves in a little cold water until softened. If using powdered gelatine, sprinkle it over 30ml/2 tbsp cold water and leave until spongy. Add the wine to the softened gelatine and heat gently until completely dissolved, stirring constantly. Pour on to the fish mixture and mix well.

5 Lightly whip the cream in a bowl. In a second, grease-free bowl, beat the egg white with a pinch of salt until stiff. Fold the cream, then the egg white into the fish mixture. Season with salt and pepper and add a little nutmeg.

6 Pour the mixture into six ramekins or moulds, cover with clear film (plastic wrap) and chill for about 1 hour.

7 Meanwhile, make the salsa. Put the diced tomatoes in a bowl. Peel and dice the avocado and add it to the tomatoes with the onion, garlic and chilli. Add the olive oil and lime juice, with salt and pepper to taste. Chill until needed.

8 To release the mousse, dip the moulds into hot water for a couple of seconds, invert on to individual plates and give each mould a sharp tap. Put a spoonful of salsa on each plate and a little on the top of each mousse. Make a cut to the centre of each slice of lime and twist a couple of slices on to each plate. Serve with the remaining salsa.

SALADS

What could be nicer on a warm day than a refreshing fish or shellfish salad? Take a fresh look at fish as a salad ingredient. Meaty tuna, swordfish, skate and hake make ideal main-course medleys, while lighter offerings such as Insalata di Mare and Asparagus and Langoustine Salad are perfect for summertime al fresco *lunches. If you're looking for something out of the ordinary, Warm Monkfish Salad with pine nuts makes an unusual and delicious dish, and Red Mullet with Raspberry Dressing is an unexpected delight.*

Spinach Salad with Bacon and Prawns

Serve this hot salad with plenty of crusty bread for mopping up the delicious juices.

SERVES FOUR

INGREDIENTS

- 105ml/7 tbsp olive oil
- 30ml/2 tbsp sherry vinegar
- 2 garlic cloves, finely chopped
- 5ml/1 tsp Dijon mustard
- 12 cooked king prawns (jumbo shrimp)
- 115g/4oz streaky (fatty) bacon, rinded and cut into strips
- about 115g/4oz fresh young spinach leaves
- ½ head oak leaf lettuce, coarsely torn
- salt and ground black pepper

1 To make the dressing, whisk together 90ml/6 tbsp of the olive oil with the vinegar, garlic and mustard in a small pan, adding seasoning to taste. Heat gently until thickened slightly, then keep warm.

2 Remove and discard the heads of the prawns and carefully peel them, leaving the tails intact. Set aside.

3 Heat the remaining oil in a frying pan. Add the bacon strips and cook over a medium heat, stirring occasionally, until golden and crisp. Add the prawns and stir-fry for a few minutes until warmed through, but be careful not to overcook.

4 While the bacon and prawns are cooking, arrange the spinach and torn oak leaf lettuce leaves on four individual serving plates.

5 Spoon the bacon and prawns on to the leaves, then pour over the hot dressing. Serve immediately.

COOK'S TIP

Sherry vinegar lends its pungent flavour to this delicious salad. You can buy it from most large supermarkets and delicatessens.

PRAWN AND ARTICHOKE SALAD

ARTICHOKES ARE A VERY POPULAR VEGETABLE IN LOUISIANA, WHERE THIS RECIPE COMES FROM.

SERVES FOUR

INGREDIENTS

- 1 garlic clove
- 10ml/2 tsp Dijon mustard
- 60ml/4 tbsp red wine vinegar
- 150ml/¼ pint/⅔ cup olive oil
- 45ml/3 tbsp shredded fresh basil leaves or 30ml/2 tbsp finely chopped fresh parsley
- 1 red onion, very finely sliced
- 350g/12oz cooked peeled prawns (shrimp)
- 400g/14oz can artichoke hearts
- ½ head iceberg lettuce
- salt and ground black pepper

1 Coarsely chop the garlic, then crush it to a pulp with 5ml/1 tsp salt, using the flat of a heavy knife blade.

COOK'S TIP

Red onions have a sweet, mild flavour that makes them an ideal choice for using raw in salads. White onions are also suitable, but brown onions tend to be a little too sharp.

2 Mix the garlic and mustard to a paste in a small bowl, then beat in the vinegar and finally the olive oil, beating hard to make a thick creamy dressing. Season with freshly ground black pepper and, if necessary, a little additional salt.

3 Stir the fresh basil or parsley into the dressing, followed by the sliced onion. Leave to stand for 30 minutes at room temperature to allow the flavours to mingle, then stir in the prawns, cover with clear film (plastic wrap) and chill in the refrigerator for at least 1 hour or until you are ready to serve.

4 Drain the artichoke hearts well and halve each one. Shred the lettuce finely.

5 Make a bed of lettuce on a serving platter or four individual salad plates and spread the artichoke hearts evenly over it.

6 Immediately before serving, pour the prawns and onion and their marinade over the top of the salad.

Marinated Sardines

The Arabs invented marinades as a means of preserving poultry, meat and game. In Spain this method was enthusiastically adopted as a means of keeping fish fresh. The fish are always fried first and then stored in vinegar.

SERVES TWO TO FOUR

INGREDIENTS

- 12–16 sardines, cleaned
- seasoned plain (all-purpose) flour, for dusting
- 30ml/2 tbsp olive oil
- roasted red onion, green (bell) pepper and tomatoes, to garnish

For the marinade

- 90ml/6 tbsp olive oil
- 1 onion, sliced
- 1 garlic clove, crushed
- 3–4 bay leaves
- 2 cloves
- 1 dried red chilli, seeded and chopped
- 5ml/1 tsp paprika
- 120ml/4fl oz/½ cup wine or sherry vinegar
- 120ml/4fl oz/½ cup white wine
- salt and ground black pepper

1 Using a sharp knife, cut the heads off the sardines and split each of them along the belly. Turn the fish over so that the backbone is uppermost. Press down along the backbone to loosen it, then carefully lift out the backbone and as many of the remaining little bones as possible.

2 Close the sardines up again and dust them with seasoned flour.

3 Heat the olive oil in a frying pan and fry the sardines for 2–3 minutes on each side. With a metal spatula, remove the fish from the pan to a plate and leave to cool, then pack them in a single layer in a large shallow dish.

4 To make the marinade, add the olive oil to the oil remaining in the frying pan. Cook the onion and garlic gently for 5–10 minutes until soft and translucent, stirring occasionally. Add the bay leaves, cloves, chilli and paprika, with pepper to taste. Cook, stirring frequently, for another 1–2 minutes.

5 Stir in the vinegar, wine and a little salt. Allow to bubble up, then pour over the sardines. The marinade should cover the fish completely. When the fish is cool, cover and chill overnight or for up to 3 days. Serve the sardines and their marinade, garnished with the onion, pepper and tomatoes.

VARIATION

Other oily fish such as herrings or sprats (small whitebait) are very good prepared in this way. White fish can also be used.

PRESERVED FISH SALAD

THE SPANISH ENJOY AND MAKE THE MOST OF PRESERVED FISH. THIS IS A VERY PRETTY DISH, WHICH USES WHATEVER IS EASILY AVAILABLE, AND IT MAKES AN IDEAL LAST-MINUTE PARTY APPETIZER. IT IS ALSO EASY TO DOUBLE UP FOR A BUFFET. FOR THE BEST RESULTS TRY TO USE SPANISH CANNED FISH.

SERVES FOUR

INGREDIENTS

- 6 eggs
- cos or romaine lettuce leaves
- 75–90ml/5–6 tbsp mayonnaise
- 90g/3½oz jar Avruga herring roe, Eurocaviar grey mullet roe or undyed (or black) lumpfish roe
- 2 × 115g/4oz cans sardines in oil
- 2 × 115g/4oz cans mackerel fillets in oil
- 2 × 150g/5oz jars cockles (small clams) in brine, drained
- 2 × 115g/4oz cans mussels or scallops in tomato sauce
- fresh flat leaf parsley or dill sprigs, to garnish

COOK'S TIP

Smoked salmon, kippers (smoked herrings) and rollmops (pickled herring fillets) can also be included on the platter. Try to maintain a balance between fish or shellfish pickled in brine or vinegar, with those in oil or sauce. Huge Spanish mussels *en escabeche* (spicy sauce) are now available in large supermarkets. Also look for Spanish fish roes to top the eggs.

1 Put the eggs in a pan with enough water to cover and bring to the boil. Turn down the heat and simmer for 10 minutes. Drain immediately, then cover with cold water and set aside until completely cool. Shell the eggs and slice in half.

2 Arrange the lettuce leaves on a large serving platter, with the tips pointing outwards. (You may need to break off the bottom end of each leaf if the leaves are large).

3 Place a teaspoonful or so of mayonnaise on the flat side of each halved egg and top with a spoonful of fish caviar. Carefully arrange in the centre of the dish.

4 Arrange the sardines and mackerel fillets at four points on the plate. Spoon the pickled cockles into two of the gaps, opposite each other, and the mussels in sauce in the remaining gaps. Garnish with parsley sprigs or dill. Place in the refrigerator until needed.

Fresh Tuna Salad Niçoise

Fresh tuna transforms this classic and ever-popular colourful salad from the south of France into something really special.

SERVES FOUR

INGREDIENTS
- 4 tuna steaks, about 150g/5oz each
- 30ml/2 tbsp olive oil
- 225g/8oz fine green beans, trimmed
- 1 small cos or romaine lettuce or 2 Little Gem (Bibb) lettuces
- 4 new potatoes, boiled
- 4 ripe tomatoes, or 12 cherry tomatoes
- 2 red (bell) peppers, seeded and cut into thin strips
- 4 hard-boiled eggs
- 8 drained anchovy fillets in oil, halved lengthways
- 16 large black olives
- salt and ground black pepper
- 12 fresh basil leaves, to garnish

For the dressing
- 15ml/1 tbsp red wine vinegar
- 90ml/6 tbsp olive oil
- 1 fat garlic clove, crushed

1 Brush the tuna on both sides with a little olive oil and season with salt and pepper. Heat a ridged griddle pan or the grill (broiler) until very hot, then cook the tuna steaks for 1–2 minutes on each side; the flesh should still be pink and juicy in the middle. Set aside.

2 Cook the beans in a pan of lightly salted boiling water for 4–5 minutes or until crisp-tender. Drain, refresh under cold water and drain again.

3 Separate the lettuce leaves and wash and dry them. Arrange them on four individual serving plates. Slice the potatoes and tomatoes, if large (leave cherry tomatoes whole) and divide them among the plates. Arrange the fine green beans and red pepper strips over them.

4 Shell the hard-boiled eggs, cut them into thick slices. Place two half eggs on each plate with an anchovy fillet draped over. Sprinkle four olives on to each plate.

5 To make the dressing, whisk together the vinegar, olive oil and garlic and seasoning to taste. Drizzle over the salads, arrange the tuna steaks on top, sprinkle over the basil and serve.

COOK'S TIP

To intensify the flavour of the (bell) peppers and improve their texture, grill (broil) them until the skins are charred, then put them in a bowl and cover with several layers of kitchen paper. Leave for 10–15 minutes, then rub off the skins.

INSALATA DI MARE

YOU CAN VARY THE FISH IN THIS ITALIAN SALAD ACCORDING TO WHAT IS AVAILABLE, BUT TRY TO INCLUDE AT LEAST TWO KINDS OF SHELLFISH AND SOME SQUID. THE SALAD IS GOOD WARM OR COLD.

SERVES SIX AS AN APPETIZER, FOUR AS A MAIN COURSE

INGREDIENTS

- 450g/1lb fresh mussels, scrubbed and bearded
- 450g/1lb small clams, scrubbed
- 105ml/7 tbsp dry white wine
- 225g/8oz squid, cleaned
- 4 large scallops, with their corals
- 30ml/2 tbsp olive oil
- 2 garlic cloves, finely chopped
- 1 small dried red chilli, crumbled
- 225g/8oz whole cooked prawns (shrimp), in the shell
- 6–8 large chicory (Belgian endive) leaves
- 6–8 radicchio leaves
- 15ml/1 tbsp chopped flat leaf parsley, to garnish

For the dressing

- 5ml/1 tsp Dijon mustard
- 30ml/2 tbsp white wine vinegar
- 5ml/1 tsp lemon juice
- 120ml/4fl oz/½ cup extra virgin olive oil
- salt and ground black pepper

1 Put the mussels and clams in a large pan with the white wine. Cover and cook over a high heat, shaking the pan occasionally, for about 4 minutes, until they have opened. Discard any that remain closed. Use a slotted spoon to transfer the shellfish to a bowl, then strain and reserve the cooking liquid and set it aside.

2 Cut the squid into thin rings; chop the tentacles. Leave small squid whole. Halve the scallops horizontally.

3 Heat the oil in a frying pan, add the garlic, chilli, squid, scallops and corals, and sauté for about 2 minutes, until just cooked and tender. Lift the squid and scallops out of the pan; reserve the oil.

4 When the shellfish are cool enough to handle, shell them, keeping a dozen of each in the shell. Peel all but 6–8 of the prawns. Pour the shellfish cooking liquid into a small pan, set over a high heat and reduce by half. Mix all the shelled and unshelled mussels and clams with the squid and scallops, then add the prawns.

5 To make the dressing, whisk the mustard with the vinegar and lemon juice and season to taste. Add the olive oil, whisk vigorously, then whisk in the reserved cooking liquid and the oil from the frying pan. Pour the dressing over the shellfish mixture and toss lightly to coat well.

6 Arrange the chicory and radicchio leaves around the edge of a large serving dish and pile the mixed shellfish salad into the centre. Sprinkle with the chopped flat leaf parsley and serve immediately or chill first.

SEAFOOD SALAD

This is a very pretty and appetizing arrangement of fresh mussels, prawns and squid rings served on a colourful bed of salad vegetables. In Spain, where the dish comes from, canned albacore tuna is also often included in this type of simple salad.

SERVES SIX

INGREDIENTS

- 115g/4oz prepared squid rings
- 12 fresh mussels, scrubbed and bearded
- 1 large carrot
- 6 crisp lettuce leaves
- 10cm/4in piece cucumber, finely diced
- 115g/4oz cooked, peeled prawns (shrimp)
- 15ml/1 tbsp drained pickled capers

For the dressing

- 30ml/2 tbsp freshly squeezed lemon juice
- 45ml/3 tbsp virgin olive oil
- 15ml/1 tbsp chopped fresh parsley
- salt and ground black pepper

1 Put the squid rings into a metal sieve or vegetable steamer. Place the sieve or steamer over a pan of simmering water, cover with a lid and steam the squid for 2–3 minutes, until it just turns white. Cool under cold running water to prevent further cooking and drain thoroughly on kitchen paper.

2 Discard any open mussels that do not close when tapped. Cover the base of a large pan with water, add the mussels, then cover and steam for a few minutes until they open. Discard any that remain shut.

3 Using a swivel-style vegetable peeler, cut the carrot into wafer-thin ribbons. Tear the lettuce into pieces and arrange on a serving plate. Sprinkle the carrot ribbons on top, then sprinkle over the diced cucumber.

4 Arrange the mussels, prawns and squid rings over the salad and sprinkle the capers over the top.

5 Make the dressing. Put all the ingredients in a small bowl and whisk well to combine. Drizzle over the salad. Serve at room temperature.

POTATO, MUSSEL AND WATERCRESS SALAD

This is a speciality of Galicia in north-west Spain, where they claim that the mussels found on the Atlantic coast are the best in the world. They are also very proud of their potatoes and watercress. A creamy, well-flavoured dressing enhances all these ingredients.

SERVES FOUR

INGREDIENTS

- 675g/1½lb salad potatoes
- 1kg/2¼lb fresh mussels, scrubbed and beards removed
- 200ml/7fl oz/scant 1 cup dry white wine
- 15g/½oz fresh flat leaf parsley, chopped
- 1 bunch of watercress or rocket (arugula)
- salt and ground black pepper
- chopped fresh chives or spring onion (scallion) tops, to garnish

For the dressing

- 105ml/7 tbsp olive oil
- 15–30ml/1–2 tbsp white wine vinegar
- 5ml/1 tsp strong Dijon mustard
- 1 large shallot, very finely chopped
- 15ml/1 tbsp chopped fresh chives
- 45ml/3 tbsp double (heavy) cream
- pinch of caster (superfine) sugar (optional)

1 Cook the potatoes in salted, boiling water for 15–20 minutes, or until tender. Drain, cool, then peel. Slice the potatoes into a bowl and toss with 30ml/2 tbsp of the oil for the dressing.

2 Discard any open mussels. Bring the white wine to the boil in a large, heavy pan. Add the mussels, cover and boil vigorously, shaking the pan occasionally, for 3–4 minutes, until the mussels have opened. Discard any that do not open. Drain and shell the mussels, reserving the cooking liquid.

3 Boil the reserved mussel cooking liquid until reduced to about 45ml/3 tbsp. Strain this through a fine sieve over the potatoes and toss to mix.

4 Make the dressing. Whisk together the remaining oil, 15ml/1 tbsp of the vinegar, the mustard, shallot and chives.

5 Add the cream and whisk again to form a thick dressing. Adjust the seasoning, adding more vinegar and/or a pinch of sugar to taste.

6 Toss the mussels with the potatoes, then gently mix in the dressing and chopped parsley. Arrange the watercress or rocket on a serving platter and top with the salad. Serve sprinkled with extra chives or a little spring onion.

COOK'S TIP

Potato salads such as this one should not be chilled if at all possible because chilling alters the texture of the potatoes. For the best flavour and texture, serve this salad just cool or at room temperature.

Queen Scallop and Green Bean Salad

If you like, use lightly cooked mangetouts instead of the fine green beans.

SERVES FOUR

INGREDIENTS
- 115g/4oz fine green beans, trimmed
- 2 good handfuls of frisée or Batavia lettuce leaves, finely shredded
- 15g/½oz/1 tbsp butter
- 15ml/1 tbsp hazelnut oil
- 20 shelled queen scallops, with corals if possible
- 2 spring onions (scallions), very thinly sliced
- salt and ground black pepper
- 4 fresh chervil sprigs, to garnish

For the dressing
- 10ml/2 tsp sherry vinegar
- 30ml/2 tbsp hazelnut oil
- 15ml/1 tbsp finely chopped fresh mint leaves

1 Cook the beans in a pan of lightly salted boiling water for about 5 minutes, until crisp-tender. Drain, refresh under cold water, drain again and set aside.

2 Wash and dry the salad leaves; put in a bowl. Mix the dressing, season, pour over the salad and toss. Divide the salad among four serving plates.

3 Heat the butter and hazelnut oil in a frying pan until sizzling, then add the scallops and their corals and sauté for about 1 minute, tossing the scallops in the fat until they have just turned opaque. Stir in the green beans and spring onions. Spoon the vegetables over the salad and pile the scallops and corals into a tower. Garnish and serve.

Red Mullet with Raspberry Dressing

The combination of red mullet and raspberry vinegar is delicious in this first-course salad. Keep to the "red" theme by including salad leaves such as red oakleaf lettuce and baby red-stemmed chard. If red mullet is not available, use small red snapper fillets.

SERVES FOUR

INGREDIENTS
- 8 red mullet or red snapper fillets, scaled
- 15ml/1 tbsp olive oil
- 15ml/1 tbsp raspberry vinegar
- 175g/6oz mixed dark green and red salad leaves, such as lamb's lettuce (corn salad), radicchio, oakleaf lettuce and rocket (arugula)
- salt and ground black pepper

For the raspberry dressing
- 115g/4oz/1 cup raspberries, puréed and sieved
- 30ml/2 tbsp raspberry vinegar
- 60ml/4 tbsp extra virgin olive oil
- 2.5ml/½ tsp caster (superfine) sugar

COOK'S TIP

To make the raspberry purée, process the fruit in a blender or food processor, then press it through a strainer.

1 Lay the fish fillets in a shallow dish. Whisk together the olive oil and raspberry vinegar, add a pinch of salt and drizzle the mixture over the fish. Cover and leave to marinate for 1 hour.

2 Meanwhile, whisk together the dressing ingredients and season to taste.

3 Wash and dry the salad leaves, put them in a bowl, pour over most of the dressing and toss lightly.

4 Heat a ridged griddle pan or frying pan until very hot, put in the fish fillets and cook for 2–3 minutes on each side, until just tender. Cut the fillets diagonally in half to make rough diamond shapes.

5 Arrange a tall heap of salad in the middle of each serving plate. Prop up four fish fillet halves on the salad on each plate with the reserved dressing spooned around. Serve immediately.

Grilled Salmon and Spring Vegetable Salad

Spring is the time to enjoy sweet young vegetables. In this delicious salad they are cooked briefly, dressed and served at room temperature to bring out their flavour to the full.

SERVES FOUR

INGREDIENTS

- 350g/12oz small new potatoes, scrubbed or scraped
- 4 quail's eggs
- 115g/4oz young carrots, peeled
- 115g/4oz baby corn cobs
- 115g/4oz sugar snap peas
- 115g/4oz fine green beans
- 115g/4oz young courgettes (zucchini)
- 115g/4oz patty pan squash
- 120ml/4fl oz/½ cup French dressing
- 4 salmon fillets, each weighing 150g/5oz, skinned
- 115g/4oz sorrel or young spinach, stems removed
- salt and ground black pepper

1 Bring the potatoes to the boil in a pan of lightly salted water and cook for 15–20 minutes, until just tender. Drain, cover and keep warm.

VARIATIONS

- This salad would also be delicious with grilled (broiled) trout.
- Smoked fish fillets, such as mackerel, halibut or monkfish, also go well with these salad vegetables.

2 Cover the quail's eggs with boiling water and cook for 8 minutes. Refresh under cold water, shell and cut in half.

3 Bring a pan of lightly salted water to the boil, add the carrots, corn cobs, sugar snap peas, green beans, courgettes and patty pan squash and cook for about 3 minutes. Drain well. Place the hot vegetables and potatoes in a salad bowl, moisten with French dressing and leave to cool. Preheat the grill (broiler).

4 Brush the salmon fillets with French dressing and grill (broil) for about 6 minutes, turning once, until cooked through.

5 Place the sorrel or spinach in a stainless steel or enamel pan with 60ml/4 tbsp French dressing, cover and cook over a gentle heat for about 2 minutes, until just wilted and softened. Drain well and leave to cool to room temperature. Moisten the vegetables with the remaining French dressing.

6 Divide the potatoes and vegetables between four large plates, then position a piece of salmon to one side of each plate. Finally, place a spoonful of sorrel or spinach on each piece of salmon and top with two halves of a quail's egg. Season to taste with salt and pepper and serve at room temperature.

WARM SALMON SALAD

LIGHT AND FRESH, THIS SALAD IS PERFECT FOR AN AL FRESCO SUMMER LUNCH.

SERVES FOUR

INGREDIENTS

- 450g/1lb salmon fillet, skinned
- 30ml/2 tbsp sesame oil
- grated rind of ½ orange
- juice of 1 orange
- 5ml/1 tsp Dijon mustard
- 15ml/1 tbsp chopped fresh tarragon
- 45ml/3 tbsp groundnut (peanut) oil
- 115g/4oz fine green beans
- 175g/6oz mixed salad leaves, such as young spinach leaves, radicchio, frisée and oak leaf lettuce leaves
- 15ml/1 tbsp toasted sesame seeds
- salt and ground black pepper

1 Cut the salmon into bitesize pieces, then make the dressing. Mix together the sesame oil, orange rind and juice, mustard and chopped tarragon in a bowl and season to taste with salt and pepper. Set aside.

2 Heat the groundnut oil in a large, heavy frying pan. Add the pieces of salmon and cook for 3–4 minutes, until lightly browned on the outside but still tender inside.

3 Meanwhile, blanch the green beans in lightly salted, boiling water for about 5–6 minutes, until they are tender, but still crisp.

4 Add the dressing to the salmon, toss together gently and cook for a further 30 seconds. Remove the pan from the heat.

5 Arrange the salad leaves on four serving plates. Drain the beans and toss over the leaves. Spoon over the salmon and cooking juices and serve immediately, sprinkled with the sesame seeds.

COOK'S TIP

Serve the salad as soon as it is assembled or you'll find that the salad leaves will lose their bright colour and crisp texture.

SALMON AND TUNA PARCELS

YOU WILL NEED FAIRLY LARGE SMOKED SALMON SLICES AS THEY ARE WRAPPED AROUND A LIGHT TUNA MIXTURE BEFORE BEING SERVED ON A VIBRANT SALAD.

SERVES FOUR

INGREDIENTS
- 30ml/2 tbsp low-fat natural (plain) yogurt
- 15ml/1 tbsp sun-dried tomato paste
- 5ml/1 tsp wholegrain honey mustard
- grated rind and juice of 1 lime
- 200g/7oz can tuna in brine, drained
- 130g/4½oz smoked salmon slices
- salt and ground black pepper
- fresh mint leaves, to garnish

For the salad
- 3 tomatoes, sliced
- 2 kiwi fruit, peeled and sliced
- ¼ cucumber, cut into thin batons

For the mint vinaigrette
- 15ml/1 tbsp wine vinegar
- 45ml/3 tbsp olive oil
- 15ml/1 tbsp chopped fresh mint

1 Mix together the yogurt, sun-dried tomato paste and honey mustard in a mixing bowl. Stir in the grated lime rind and juice. Add the tuna, season with black pepper to taste and mix together well.

2 Spread out the smoked salmon slices on a board and spoon some of the tuna mixture on to each piece.

3 Roll up or fold in the sides of the smoked salmon to make neat parcels. Carefully press the edges together to seal.

4 Make the salad. Arrange the tomato and kiwi slices on four individual serving plates. Sprinkle over the cucumber batons.

5 Make the vinaigrette. Put all the ingredients in a screw-top jar, season to taste with salt and pepper and shake vigorously. Alternatively, whisk together in a bowl. Spoon a little vinaigrette over each salad.

6 Arrange three or four salmon parcels on each salad, garnish with the mint leaves and serve.

COOK'S TIP

Salads are always a popular choice for those watching their weight or following a healthy eating plan. This is an especially good option, as oily fish, including salmon and tuna, are recommended by nutritionists and kiwi fruit is a particularly rich source of vitamin C. Although healthy eating guidelines recommend reducing the amount of fat, particularly saturated fat, in the diet, salad dressings made with polyunsaturated or monounsaturated oil, such as olive oil, can and should be included, in sensible moderation. This recipe is not high in calories, but if weight control is a real issue, use an oil-free dressing instead of vinaigrette.

Warm Swordfish and Rocket Salad

Swordfish is robust enough to take the sharp flavours of rocket and Pecorino cheese. If you can't find Pecorino, use a good Parmesan instead. You could substitute marlin or shark for the swordfish, if you like.

SERVES FOUR

INGREDIENTS

- 4 swordfish steaks, about 175g/6oz each
- 75ml/5 tbsp extra virgin olive oil, plus extra for serving
- juice of 1 lemon
- 30ml/2 tbsp finely chopped fresh parsley
- 115g/4oz rocket (arugula) leaves, stalks snipped off
- 115g/4oz Pecorino cheese
- salt and ground black pepper

1 Lay the swordfish steaks in a dish. Mix 60ml/4 tbsp of the olive oil with the lemon juice. Pour over the fish. Season, sprinkle on the parsley and turn the fish to coat, cover with clear film (plastic wrap) and marinate for 10 minutes.

2 Heat a ridged griddle pan or the grill (broiler) until very hot. Take the fish out of the marinade and pat it dry with kitchen paper. Grill (broil) for 2–3 minutes on each side until the swordfish is just cooked through, but still juicy.

3 Meanwhile, put the rocket leaves in a bowl and season with a little salt and plenty of pepper. Add the remaining 15ml/1 tbsp olive oil and toss well. Shave the Pecorino over the top.

4 Place the swordfish steaks on four individual plates and arrange a little pile of salad on each steak. Serve extra olive oil separately so it may be drizzled over the swordfish.

VARIATION

Tuna or shark steaks would be equally good in this recipe.

PROVENÇAL AIOLI WITH SALT COD

This substantial salad constitutes a meal on its own and is one of the nicest dishes for summer entertaining. Vary the vegetables according to what is in season; if you like raw vegetables, include radishes, yellow pepper and celery for colour contrast.

SERVES SIX

INGREDIENTS

- 1kg/2¼lb salt cod, soaked overnight in water to cover
- 1 fresh bouquet garni
- 18 small new potatoes, scrubbed
- 1 large fresh mint sprig, torn
- 225g/8oz green beans, trimmed
- 225g/8oz broccoli florets
- 6 hard-boiled eggs
- 12 baby carrots, with leaves if possible, scrubbed
- 1 large red (bell) pepper, seeded and cut into strips
- 2 fennel bulbs, cut into strips
- 18 red or yellow cherry tomatoes
- 6 large whole cooked prawns (shrimp) or langoustines, in the shell, to garnish (optional)

For the aioli

- 600ml/1 pint/2½ cups home-made mayonnaise
- 2 fat garlic cloves (or more if you are feeling brave), crushed
- cayenne pepper

1 Drain the cod and put it into a shallow pan. Pour in barely enough water to cover the fish and add the bouquet garni. Bring to the boil, then cover and poach very gently for about 10 minutes, until the fish flakes easily when tested with the tip of a sharp knife. Drain and set aside until required.

2 Cook the potatoes with the mint in a pan of lightly salted, boiling water until just tender. Drain and set aside. Cook the beans and broccoli in separate pans of lightly salted, boiling water for about 3–5 minutes. They should still be very crisp. Refresh under cold water and drain again, then set aside.

3 Remove the skin from the cod and break the flesh into large flakes. Shell and halve the eggs lengthways.

4 Pile the cod in the middle of a large serving platter and arrange the eggs and all the vegetables around the edges or randomly. Garnish with the prawns or langoustines if you are using them.

5 To make the aioli, put the home-made mayonnaise in a bowl and stir in the crushed garlic and cayenne pepper to taste. Serve in individual bowls or one large bowl to hand around.

Whitefish Salad

Smoked whitefish is one of the glories of deli food and, made into a salad with mayonnaise and sour cream, it becomes indispensable as a brunch dish. Eat it with a stack of bagels, pumpernickel or rye bread. If you can't find smoked whitefish, use any other smoked firm white fish such as halibut or cod.

SERVES FOUR TO SIX

INGREDIENTS

- 1 smoked whitefish, skinned and boned
- 2 celery sticks, chopped
- ½ red, white or yellow onion or 3–5 spring onions (scallions), chopped
- 45ml/3 tbsp mayonnaise
- 45ml/3 tbsp sour cream or Greek (US strained plain) yogurt
- juice of ½–1 lemon
- 1 round (butterhead) lettuce
- ground black pepper
- 5–10ml/1–2 tsp chopped fresh parsley, to garnish

1 Break the smoked fish into bitesize pieces. In a bowl, combine the chopped celery, onion or spring onion, mayonnaise, and sour cream or yogurt, and add lemon juice to taste.

2 Fold the fish into the mixture and season with pepper. Arrange the lettuce leaves on serving plates, then spoon the whitefish salad on top. Serve chilled, sprinkled with parsley.

HERRING SALAD WITH BEETROOT AND SOUR CREAM

THIS SALAD, SERVED WITH BLACK PUMPERNICKEL BREAD, IS THE QUINTESSENTIAL SUMMER LUNCH DISH. SERVE IT WITH COLD BOILED POTATOES AND ALLOW YOUR GUESTS TO CUT THEM UP AND ADD TO THE SALAD AS THEY LIKE.

SERVES EIGHT

INGREDIENTS

- 1 large tangy cooking apple
- 500g/1¼lb matjes herrings (schmaltz herrings), drained and cut into slices
- 2 small pickled cucumbers, diced
- 10ml/2 tsp caster (superfine) sugar, or to taste
- 10ml/2 tsp cider vinegar or white wine vinegar
- 300ml/½ pint/1¼ cups sour cream
- 2 cooked beetroot (beets), diced
- lettuce, to serve
- fresh dill sprigs and chopped onion or onion rings, to garnish

1 Peel, core and dice the apple. Put in a bowl, add the herrings, cucumbers, sugar and cider or white wine vinegar and mix together. Add the sour cream and mix well to combine.

2 Add the beetroot to the herring mixture and chill in the refrigerator. Serve the salad on a bed of lettuce leaves, garnished with fresh dill and chopped onion or onion rings.

Smoked Eel and Chicory Salad

Smoked eel has become increasingly popular recently and is seen on some of the most sophisticated tables. It tastes marvellous in a salad with a refreshing citrus dressing.

SERVES FOUR

INGREDIENTS
- 450g/1lb smoked eel fillets, skinned
- 2 large heads of chicory (Belgian endive), separated
- 4 radicchio leaves
- flat leaf parsley leaves, to garnish

For the citrus dressing
- 1 lemon
- 1 orange
- 5ml/1 tsp sugar
- 5ml/1 tsp Dijon mustard
- 90ml/6 tbsp sunflower oil
- 15ml/1 tbsp chopped fresh parsley
- salt and ground black pepper

VARIATION

This salad can also be made with other hot-smoked fish such as trout or mackerel.

1 Cut the eel fillets diagonally into eight pieces. Make the dressing. Using a zester, carefully remove the rind in strips from the lemon and the orange. Squeeze the juice of both fruit. Set the lemon juice aside and pour the orange juice into a small pan. Stir in the rinds and sugar. Bring to the boil and reduce by half. Leave to cool.

2 Whisk the Dijon mustard, reserved lemon juice and the sunflower oil together in a bowl. Add the orange juice mixture, then stir in the chopped fresh parsley. Season to taste with salt and ground black pepper and whisk again.

3 Arrange the chicory leaves in a circle on individual plates, with the pointed ends radiating outwards like the spokes of a wheel. Take the radicchio leaves and arrange them on the plates, between the chicory leaves.

4 Drizzle a little of the dressing over the leaves and place four pieces of eel in a star-shape in the middle. Garnish with the parsley leaves and serve. Offer the remaining dressing separately.

Skate with Bitter Salad Leaves

Skate has a deliciously sweet flavour which contrasts well with the bitterness of salad leaves such as escarole, rocket, frisée and radicchio. Serve with toasted French bread.

SERVES FOUR

INGREDIENTS
- 800g/1¾lb skate wings
- 15ml/1 tbsp white wine vinegar
- 4 black peppercorns
- 1 fresh thyme sprig
- 175g/6oz bag of ready-prepared bitter salad leaves, such as frisée, rocket (arugula), radicchio, escarole and lamb's lettuce (corn salad)
- 1 orange
- 2 tomatoes, peeled, seeded and diced

For the dressing
- 15ml/1 tbsp white wine vinegar
- 45ml/3 tbsp olive oil
- 2 shallots, finely chopped
- salt and ground black pepper

1 Put the skate wings into a large shallow pan, cover with cold water and add the vinegar, peppercorns and thyme. Bring to the boil, then poach the fish gently for 8–10 minutes, until the flesh comes away easily from the bones.

2 Meanwhile, make the dressing. Whisk the vinegar, olive oil and shallots together in a bowl. Season to taste. Tip the salad leaves into a bowl, pour over the dressing and toss well.

3 Using a zester, remove the outer rind from the orange, then peel it, removing all the pith. Slice into thin rounds.

4 When the skate is cooked, flake the flesh and mix it into the salad. Add the orange rind shreds, the orange slices and tomatoes, toss gently and serve.

COOK'S TIP

When peeling the orange, take care not to include any of the bitter white pith.

Avocado and Smoked Fish Salad

Creamy avocado and smoked fish make an excellent combination, and flavoured with herbs and spices, create a delectable salad.

SERVES FOUR

INGREDIENTS
- 15g/½oz/1 tbsp butter or margarine
- ½ onion, thinly sliced
- 5ml/1 tsp mustard seeds
- 225g/8oz smoked mackerel, flaked
- 30ml/2 tbsp chopped fresh coriander (cilantro)
- 2 firm tomatoes, peeled and chopped
- 15ml/1 tbsp lemon juice
- salt and ground black pepper

For the salad
- 2 avocados
- ½ cucumber
- 15ml/1 tbsp lemon juice
- 2 firm tomatoes
- 1 fresh green chilli

1 Melt the butter or margarine in a frying pan, add the onion and mustard seeds and cook for about 5 minutes, until the onion is soft, but not coloured.

2 Add the fish, coriander, tomatoes and lemon juice and cook over a low heat for 2–3 minutes. Remove from the heat and set aside to cool while you make the salad.

3 Peel and slice the avocados and slice the cucumber. Put into a bowl and sprinkle with the lemon juice.

4 Peel the tomatoes, if you like, then slice them thinly. Seed and finely chop the chilli.

5 Place the fish mixture in the centre of a serving plate.

6 Arrange the avocados, cucumber and tomatoes around the fish. Alternatively, spoon a quarter of the fish mixture on to each of four serving plates and divide the avocados, cucumber and tomatoes equally among them. Sprinkle with the chopped chilli and a little salt and pepper and serve.

WARM FISH SALAD WITH MANGO DRESSING

THE DRESSING OF THIS LOVELY, SUMMERY SALAD COMBINES THE FLAVOUR OF RICH MANGO WITH HOT CHILLI, GINGER AND LIME.

SERVES FOUR

INGREDIENTS

- 1 French loaf
- 4 redfish, black bream or porgy, each weighing about 275g/10oz
- 15ml/1 tbsp vegetable oil
- 1 mango
- 1cm/½in fresh root ginger
- 1 fresh red chilli, seeded and finely chopped
- 30ml/2 tbsp lime juice
- 30ml/2 tbsp chopped fresh coriander (cilantro)
- 175g/6oz young spinach
- 150g/5oz pak choi (bok choy)
- 175g/6oz cherry tomatoes, halved

1 Preheat the oven to 180°C/350°F/ Gas 4 and preheat the grill (broiler). Cut the French loaf into 20cm/8in lengths. Slice lengthways, then cut into thick fingers. Place the bread on a baking sheet and dry in the oven for 15 minutes. Meanwhile, slash the fish deeply on both sides with a sharp knife and moisten with oil. Cook under the grill for 6 minutes, turning once.

2 Peel and stone (pit) the mango. Slice the flesh thinly and place about half of it in a food processor. Peel and finely grate the ginger, then add to the food processor together with the chilli, lime juice and coriander. Process until smooth. Adjust to a pouring consistency with 30–45ml/ 2–3 tbsp water.

3 Wash the salad leaves and spin dry, then divide them equally among four serving plates. Place the fish on the beds of leaves. Spoon over the mango dressing and finish with slices of mango and cherry tomato halves. Serve immediately with fingers of crispy French bread.

COOK'S TIP

You can also cook the fish on the barbecue, if you like.

VARIATION

Other fish suitable for this salad include salmon, monkfish, tuna, sea bass and halibut. Use fillets, cutlets or steaks.

MEDITERRANEAN SALAD WITH BASIL

A type of Salade Niçoise with pasta, this conjures up all the sunny flavours of the Mediterranean.

SERVES FOUR

INGREDIENTS

- 225g/8oz/2 cups chunky pasta shapes
- 175g/6oz fine green beans
- 2 large ripe tomatoes
- 50g/2oz/1 cup fresh basil leaves
- 200g/7oz can tuna fish in oil, drained and coarsely flaked
- 2 hard-boiled eggs, shelled and sliced or quartered
- 50g/2oz can anchovy fillets, drained
- salt and ground black pepper
- capers and black olives, to garnish

For the dressing

- 90ml/6 tbsp extra virgin olive oil
- 30ml/2 tbsp white wine vinegar or lemon juice
- 2 garlic cloves, crushed
- 2.5ml/½ tsp Dijon mustard
- 30ml/2 tbsp chopped fresh basil

1 Whisk all the ingredients for the dressing together, season with salt and pepper and set aside to allow the flavours to develop.

2 Cook the pasta in plenty of lightly salted, boiling water according to the manufacturer's instructions. Drain well and set aside to cool.

3 Trim the green beans and blanch them in lightly salted, boiling water for 3 minutes. Drain, then refresh in cold water.

4 Slice the tomatoes or cut them into quarters and arrange in the base of a salad bowl. Moisten with a little of the dressing and cover with a quarter of the basil leaves. Then make a layer of green beans. Moisten these with a little more of the dressing and sprinkle over about one-third of the remaining basil.

5 Cover with the pasta tossed in a little more dressing, half the remaining basil and the coarsely flaked tuna.

6 Arrange the eggs on top. Finally, sprinkle over the anchovy fillets. Pour over the remaining dressing and garnish with the capers, black olives and remaining basil. Serve immediately. Do not be tempted to chill this salad because all the flavour would be dulled.

COOK'S TIP

Olives marinated in oil flavoured with garlic, herbs and lemon peel would add an extra-special touch to this salad. Choose plump, black olives that are fully ripened. Marinated olives are available from large supermarkets and delicatessens or you could prepare them yourself.

Hake and Potato Salad

Hake is a "meaty" fish that is excellent served cold in a salad. Here the flavour is enhanced with a piquant dressing.

SERVES FOUR

INGREDIENTS

- 450g/1lb hake fillets
- 150ml/¼ pint/⅔ cup fish stock
- 1 onion, thinly sliced
- 1 bay leaf
- 450g/1lb cooked baby new potatoes, halved unless tiny
- 1 red (bell) pepper, seeded and diced
- 115g/4oz/1 cup petits pois (baby peas), cooked
- 2 spring onions (scallions), sliced
- ½ cucumber, unpeeled and diced
- 4 large red lettuce leaves
- salt and ground black pepper

For the dressing

- 150ml/¼ pint/⅔ cup Greek (US strained plain) yogurt
- 30ml/2 tbsp olive oil
- juice of ½ lemon
- 15–30ml/1–2 tbsp capers

To garnish

- 2 hard-boiled eggs, finely chopped
- 15ml/1 tbsp chopped fresh parsley
- 15ml/1 tbsp finely chopped fresh chives

1 Put the hake fillets in a large, shallow pan with the fish stock, onion slices and bay leaf. Bring to the boil over a medium heat, then lower the heat and poach the fish gently for about 10 minutes until it flakes easily when tested with the tip of a sharp knife. Leave it to cool, then remove the skin and any bones and separate the flesh into large flakes.

2 Put the baby new potatoes in a bowl with the red pepper, petits pois, spring onions and cucumber. Gently stir in the flaked hake and season with salt and pepper.

3 Make the dressing by stirring all the ingredients together in a bowl or jug (pitcher). Season and spoon or pour over the salad. Toss gently.

4 Place a lettuce leaf on each plate and spoon the salad over it. Mix the finely chopped hard-boiled eggs for the garnish with the parsley and chives. Sprinkle the mixture over each salad.

VARIATION

This is equally good made with halibut, monkfish or cod. For a change, try it with a dressing of home-made mayonnaise mixed with capers.

Piquant Prawn Salad

The Thai-inspired dressing adds a superb flavour to the noodles and prawns. This delicious salad can be served warm or cold, and will serve six as an appetizer.

SERVES FOUR

INGREDIENTS

- 200g/7oz rice vermicelli
- 8 baby corn cobs, halved
- 150g/5oz mangetouts (snow peas)
- 15ml/1 tbsp stir-fry oil
- 2 garlic cloves, finely chopped
- 2.5cm/1in piece fresh root ginger, peeled and finely chopped
- 1 fresh red or green chilli, seeded and finely chopped
- 450g/1lb raw peeled tiger prawns (jumbo shrimp)
- 4 spring onions (scallions), thinly sliced
- 15ml/1 tbsp sesame seeds, toasted
- 1 lemon grass stalk, thinly shredded, to garnish

For the dressing

- 15ml/1 tbsp chopped fresh chives
- 15ml/1 tbsp Thai fish sauce
- 5ml/1 tsp soy sauce
- 45ml/3 tbsp groundnut (peanut) oil
- 5ml/1 tsp sesame oil
- 30ml/2 tbsp rice vinegar

1 Put the rice vermicelli in a wide heatproof bowl, pour over boiling water and leave for 5 minutes. Drain, refresh under cold water and drain well again. Tip back into the bowl and set aside until required.

2 Boil or steam the corn cobs and mangetouts for about 3 minutes; they should still be crunchy. Refresh under cold water and drain. Now make the dressing. Mix all the ingredients in a screw-top jar, close tightly and shake well to combine.

3 Heat the oil in a large frying pan or wok. Add the garlic, ginger and red or green chilli and cook for 1 minute. Add the tiger prawns and stir-fry for about 3 minutes, until they have just turned pink. Stir in the spring onions, corn cobs, mangetouts and sesame seeds, and toss lightly to mix.

4 Tip the contents of the pan or wok over the rice vermicelli or noodles. Pour the dressing on top and toss well. Serve, garnished with lemon grass, or chill for an hour before serving.

Thai Seafood Salad

This unusual salad is light and refreshing.

SERVES FOUR

INGREDIENTS

- 225g/8oz ready-prepared squid
- 225g/8oz raw tiger prawns (jumbo shrimp)
- 8 scallops, shelled
- 225g/8oz firm white fish
- 30–45ml/2–3 tbsp olive oil
- mixed lettuce leaves and coriander (cilantro) sprigs, to serve

For the dressing

- 2 small fresh red chillies, seeded and finely chopped
- 5cm/2in piece lemon grass, finely chopped
- 2 fresh kaffir lime leaves, shredded
- 30ml/2 tbsp Thai fish sauce
- 2 shallots, thinly sliced
- 30ml/2 tbsp lime juice
- 30ml/2 tbsp rice vinegar
- 10ml/2 tsp caster (superfine) sugar

1 First, prepare the seafood. Using a sharp knife, slit open the squid bodies, cut them into square pieces, then score the flesh in a criss-cross pattern without cutting through. Halve the tentacles, if necessary. Remove the heads from the prawns, then peel and devein. Remove the dark beard-like fringe and tough muscle from the scallops. Skin the white fish, if necessary, and remove any pin bones, then cut the flesh into cubes.

2 Heat a wok or large, heavy frying pan until hot. Add the oil and swirl it around, then add the prawns and stir-fry for 2–3 minutes, until they turn pink. Transfer to a large bowl.

3 Stir-fry the squid and scallops for 1–2 minutes, until opaque. Remove and add to the prawns.

4 Add the white fish cubes to the wok or pan and stir-fry for 2–3 minutes. Remove and add to the cooked seafood. Reserve any juices.

5 Put all the dressing ingredients in a small bowl with the reserved juices from the wok or frying pan and whisk together well.

6 Pour the dressing over the fish and shellfish and toss gently. Arrange the salad leaves and coriander sprigs on four individual serving plates, then spoon the fish and shellfish on top, dividing it equally among them. Serve the salad immediately.

GADO GADO

GADO GADO IS A TRADITIONAL INDONESIAN SALAD AROUND WHICH FRIENDS AND FAMILY GATHER TO EAT. FILLINGS ARE CHOSEN AND WRAPPED IN A LETTUCE LEAF. THE PARCEL IS THEN DIPPED IN A SPICY PEANUT SAUCE AND EATEN.

SERVES FOUR

INGREDIENTS

- 2 medium potatoes, peeled
- 3 eggs
- 175g/6oz green beans, trimmed
- 1 cos or romaine lettuce
- 4 tomatoes, cut into wedges
- 115g/4oz/2 cups beansprouts
- ½ cucumber, peeled and cut into batons
- 150g/5oz mooli (daikon), peeled and grated
- 175g/6oz tofu, cut into large dice
- 350g/12oz large, cooked peeled prawns (shrimp)
- 1 small bunch fresh coriander (cilantro)
- salt

For the spicy peanut sauce

- 150g/5oz/⅔ cup smooth peanut butter
- juice of ½ lemon
- 2 shallots or 1 small onion, finely chopped
- 1 garlic clove, crushed
- 1–2 small fresh red chillies, seeded and finely chopped
- 30ml/2 tbsp fish sauce (optional)
- 150ml/¼ pint/⅔ cup coconut milk, canned or fresh
- 15ml/1 tbsp caster (superfine) sugar

1 To make the peanut sauce, combine all the ingredients in a food processor and process until smooth.

2 Bring the potatoes to the boil in lightly salted water and simmer for 20 minutes. Bring a second pan of salted water to the boil. To save using too many pans, cook the eggs and beans in the same pan.

3 Lower the eggs into the boiling water in the second pan; then, after 6 minutes, add the beans in a steamer for a further 6 minutes. (Hard-boiled eggs should have a total of 12 minutes.) Cool the potatoes, eggs and green beans under cold running water.

4 Wash and spin or pat dry the lettuce leaves and use the outer leaves to line a large platter. Pile the remainder to one side of the platter.

5 Thinly slice the potatoes. Shell the eggs and cut them into quarters. Arrange the potato slices, eggs, green beans and tomatoes in separate piles on the platter. Arrange the other salad ingredients and the prawns in a similar way so that the entire platter is covered. Garnish with the fresh coriander.

6 Turn the spicy peanut sauce into an attractive bowl and bring to the table with the salad.

HANDLING CHILLIES

Red chillies are generally sweeter than green ones. Smaller varieties of both red and green are likely to be more fiery than larger varieties. You can lessen the intensity of a fresh chilli by splitting it open and removing the white seed-bearing membrane. The juice that comes out when chillies are cut can cause serious irritation to the skin. You may prefer to wear rubber gloves when preparing them. Otherwise, be sure to wash your hands thoroughly after handling raw chillies and avoid touching your eyes or any sensitive skin areas.

SEAFOOD SALAD WITH FRAGRANT HERBS

This tasty seafood medley is a meal in itself.

SERVES FOUR TO SIX

INGREDIENTS

- 250ml/8fl oz/1 cup fish stock
- 350g/12oz squid, cleaned
- 12 raw king prawns (jumbo shrimp), peeled and deveined
- 12 scallops, cleaned
- 50g/2oz glass noodles, soaked in warm water for 30 minutes
- ½ cucumber, cut into thin sticks
- 1 lemon grass stalk, chopped
- 2 kaffir lime leaves, shredded
- 2 shallots, thinly sliced
- juice of 1–2 limes
- 30ml/2 tbsp fish sauce
- 30ml/2 tbsp chopped spring onion (scallion)
- 30ml/2 tbsp coriander (cilantro) leaves
- 12–15 mint leaves, coarsely torn
- 4 red chillies, seeded and sliced
- fresh coriander (cilantro) sprigs

1 Pour the fish stock into a medium pan, set over a high heat and bring to the boil. Meanwhile, cut the prepared squid into rings using a sharp knife.

2 Place each type of seafood individually in the boiling stock and cook for a few minutes, until tender. Remove from the pan with a wire basket or slotted spoon and and set aside.

3 Drain the noodles and cut them into short lengths, about 5cm/2in long. Combine the noodles with the cooked seafood.

4 Add the cucumber, lemon grass, kaffir lime leaves, shallots, lime juice, fish sauce, spring onion, coriander and mint leaves and chillies and mix together well. Serve garnished with the coriander sprigs.

COOK'S TIP

Glass noodles are also known as cellophane, transparent and bean thread noodles.

POMELO SALAD

Lots of ingredients, but this is simple to make.

SERVES FOUR TO SIX

INGREDIENTS

- 30ml/2 tbsp vegetable oil
- 4 shallots, thinly sliced
- 2 garlic cloves, thinly sliced
- 1 large pomelo
- 15ml/1 tbsp roasted peanuts
- 115g/4oz cooked peeled prawns (shrimp)
- 115g/4oz cooked crab meat
- 10–12 small mint leaves
- 2 spring onions (scallions), thinly sliced
- 2 fresh red chillies, seeded and thinly sliced
- shredded fresh coconut (optional)

For the dressing

- 30ml/2 tbsp fish sauce
- 15ml/1 tbsp palm or brown sugar
- 30ml/2 tbsp lime juice

1 Make the dressing. Whisk together the fish sauce, palm or brown sugar and lime juice in a small bowl and set aside.

2 Heat the oil in a small frying pan, add the shallots and garlic and cook for 3–4 minutes, until they are golden. Remove from the pan and set aside.

3 Peel the pomelo and break the flesh into small pieces, taking care to remove any membranes.

4 Coarsely grind the peanuts. Combine them with the pomelo flesh, prawns, crab meat, mint leaves and the cooked shallot mixture. Toss the salad in the dressing and sprinkle with the spring onions, red chillies and shredded fresh coconut, if using. Serve immediately.

COOK'S TIP

A pomelo is a large, pear-shaped fruit that resembles a grapefruit, but is slightly less juicy.

RUSSIAN SALAD

RUSSIAN SALAD BECAME FASHIONABLE IN THE HOTEL DINING ROOMS OF THE 1920S AND 1930S. THIS VERSION RECALLS THOSE DAYS AND PLAYS ON THE THEME OF THE FABERGÉ EGG.

SERVES FOUR

INGREDIENTS

- 115g/4oz/1⅔ cups large button (white) mushrooms
- 350g/12oz cooked peeled prawns (shrimp)
- 120ml/4fl oz/½ cup mayonnaise
- 15ml/1 tbsp lemon juice
- 1 large gherkin, chopped, or 30ml/2 tbsp capers
- 115g/4oz/1 cup shelled broad (fava) beans
- 115g/4oz small new potatoes, scrubbed or scraped
- 115g/4oz young carrots, trimmed and peeled
- 115g/4oz baby corn cobs
- 115g/4oz baby turnips, trimmed
- 15ml/1 tbsp olive oil, preferably French or Italian
- 4 eggs, hard-boiled and shelled
- 25g/1oz canned anchovy fillets in oil, drained and cut into fine strips
- salt and ground black pepper
- paprika, to garnish

1 Slice the mushrooms, then cut into batons. Mix with the prawns. Combine the mayonnaise and lemon juice and fold half into the mushrooms and prawns, add the gherkin or capers and season.

2 Bring a large pan of lightly salted water to the boil, add the broad beans and cook for 3 minutes. Drain and cool under cold running water, then pinch the beans between thumb and forefinger to release them from their tough skins.

3 Cook the potatoes in lightly salted, boiling water for 20 minutes and then cook the carrots, baby corn and turnips for 6 minutes. Drain and cool under running water.

4 Place all the vegetables in a bowl, mix well and moisten with olive oil, then divide them among four shallow serving bowls.

5 Spoon the dressed prawns on top of the vegetables and place a hard-boiled egg in the centre of each salad. Decorate the egg with strips of anchovy and sprinkle lightly with paprika. Serve immediately, handing the remaining mayonnaise in a separate bowl.

MELON AND CRAB SALAD

A PERFECT SUMMER SALAD FOR A RELAXED LUNCH.

SERVES SIX

INGREDIENTS

- 450g/1lb fresh cooked crab meat
- 120ml/4fl oz/½ cup mayonnaise
- 45ml/3 tbsp sour cream
- 30ml/2 tbsp olive oil
- 30ml/2 tbsp fresh lemon juice
- 2–3 spring onions (scallions), finely chopped
- 30ml/2 tbsp finely chopped fresh coriander (cilantro)
- 1.5ml/¼ tsp cayenne pepper
- 1½ canteloupe melons
- 3 medium chicory (Belgian endive) heads
- salt and ground black pepper
- fresh coriander (cilantro) sprigs, to garnish

1 Place the crab meat in a bowl and pick it over very carefully, removing any pieces of shell or cartilage. Avoid breaking up the pieces of crab meat, leaving them as large as possible.

2 Place the mayonnaise, sour cream, olive oil, lemon juice, spring onions, chopped coriander and cayenne pepper in another bowl and mix thoroughly. Season to taste with salt and pepper, then gently fold the crab meat into this dressing.

3 Halve the melons and, using a spoon, remove and discard the seeds. Cut the melons into thin slices, then remove the rind.

4 Divide the salad among six individual serving plates, making a decorative design with the melon slices and whole chicory leaves. Place a mound of dressed crab meat on each plate and garnish the salads with one or two fresh coriander sprigs. Serve immediately.

VARIATION

If you like, you can substitute natural (plain) yogurt for the sour cream, freshly squeezed lime juice for the lemon and small honeydew melons for the canteloupes.

Millionaire's Lobster Salad

When money is no object and you're in a decadent mood, this salad will satisfy your every whim. It is ideally served with a cool Chardonnay, Chablis or Pouilly-Fuissé wine.

SERVES FOUR

INGREDIENTS
- 1 medium lobster, live or cooked
- 1 bay leaf
- 1 fresh thyme sprig
- 700g/1½lb new potatoes, scrubbed
- 2 ripe tomatoes
- 4 oranges
- ½ frisée lettuce
- 175g/6oz lamb's lettuce (corn salad)
- 60ml/4 tbsp extra virgin olive oil
- 200g/7oz can young artichokes in brine, quartered
- salt
- 1 small bunch of fresh tarragon, chervil or flat leaf parsley, to garnish

For the dressing
- 30ml/2 tbsp frozen concentrated orange juice, thawed
- 75g/3oz unsalted (sweet) butter, diced
- cayenne pepper

1 If the lobster needs cooking, add to a large pan of salted cold water with the bay leaf and thyme. Cover, bring to the boil and simmer for 15 minutes. Cool under running water.

2 When the lobster is cool enough to handle, twist off the legs and claws with your fingers, and separate the tail piece from the body section. Break the claws open with a hammer and remove the meat intact. Cut the tail piece open from the underside with a pair of kitchen shears. Slice the meat and set aside.

3 Bring the potatoes to the boil in a pan of lightly salted water and simmer for 20 minutes, until tender. Drain, cover and keep warm. Place the tomatoes in a heatproof bowl, cover with boiling water and leave for 20 seconds to loosen their skins. Cool under running water and slip off the skins. Halve the tomatoes, discard the seeds, then cut the flesh into large dice.

4 To segment the oranges, remove the peel from the top, bottom and sides with a serrated knife. With a small paring knife, loosen the orange segments by cutting between the flesh and the membranes, holding the fruit over a small bowl.

5 To make the dressing, measure the thawed concentrated orange juice into a heatproof bowl and set it over a pan containing 2.5cm/1in of gently simmering water. Heat the juice for 1 minute, remove from the heat, then whisk in the butter, a little at a time, until the dressing reaches a coating consistency. Make sure each piece has been incorporated before adding the next. Season the dressing to taste with salt and a pinch of cayenne pepper, cover and keep warm over the pan with the heat turned off.

6 Wash the salad leaves and spin or pat dry. Dress them with some of the olive oil, then divide among four large serving plates.

7 Moisten the potatoes, artichokes and orange segments with the remaining olive oil and distribute them among the salad leaves.

8 Lay the sliced lobster over the salad, spoon the warm butter dressing over the salad, add the diced tomato and decorate with sprigs of fresh tarragon, chervil or flat leaf parsley. Serve the salad at room temperature.

Smoked Trout Salad

Horseradish is as good a partner to smoked trout as it is to roast beef.

SERVES FOUR

INGREDIENTS

- 1 oak leaf or other red lettuce
- 225g/8oz small tomatoes, cut into thin wedges
- ½ cucumber, peeled and thinly sliced
- 4 smoked trout fillets, about 200g/7oz each, skinned and flaked

For the dressing

- pinch of English (hot) mustard powder
- 15–20ml/3–4 tsp white wine vinegar
- 30ml/2 tbsp light olive oil
- 100ml/3½fl oz/scant ½ cup natural (plain) yogurt
- about 30ml/2 tbsp grated fresh or bottled horseradish
- pinch of caster (superfine) sugar

1 First, make the dressing. Mix together the mustard powder and vinegar in a bowl, then gradually whisk in the oil, yogurt, horseradish and sugar. Set aside for 30 minutes.

2 Tear the lettuce leaves into smaller pieces, if you like, and place them in a large bowl. Lightly whisk the dressing again, then pour half of it over the leaves and toss them lightly using two spoons.

3 Arrange the lettuce on four individual serving plates with the tomato wedges, sliced cucumber and flaked smoked trout. Spoon the remaining dressing over the salads and serve immediately.

COOK'S TIPS

- Salt should not be necessary in this recipe because of the saltiness of the smoked trout.
- Horseradish contains volatile oils that can irritate the nasal passages and eyes, so avoid bending over it if you are grating the fresh root.

TUNA AND BEAN SALAD

THIS SUBSTANTIAL SALAD MAKES A GOOD LIGHT MEAL.

SERVES FOUR TO SIX

INGREDIENTS

- 2 x 400g/14oz cans cannellini or borlotti beans
- 2 x 200g/7oz cans tuna, drained
- 60ml/4 tbsp extra virgin olive oil
- 30ml/2 tbsp fresh lemon juice
- 15ml/1 tbsp chopped fresh parsley
- 3 spring onions (scallions), thinly sliced
- salt and ground black pepper

1 Empty the cans of beans into a large strainer and rinse thoroughly under cold water. Drain well. Place in a serving dish.

2 Break the tuna into fairly large flakes and arrange over the beans in the serving dish.

COOK'S TIP

You can use tuna canned in olive or sunflower oil, or if you are watching your fat intake, in brine, but always make sure that it is well drained.

3 Make the dressing in a small bowl by combining the olive oil with the lemon juice. Season to taste with salt and pepper and stir in the chopped parsley. Mix well. Pour the dressing over the beans and tuna.

4 Sprinkle with the spring onions. Toss the salad well before serving.

Provençal Salad

There are probably as many versions of this salad as there are cooks in Provence. With chunks of good French bread, this makes a wonderful light lunch or supper.

SERVES FOUR TO SIX

INGREDIENTS

- 225g/8oz/1½ cups green beans
- 450g/1lb new potatoes, peeled and cut into 2.5cm/1in pieces
- white wine vinegar and olive oil, for sprinkling
- 1 small cos or romaine lettuce, washed, dried and torn into bitesize pieces
- 4 ripe plum tomatoes, quartered
- 1 small cucumber, peeled, seeded and diced
- 1 green or red (bell) pepper, seeded and thinly sliced
- 4 hard-boiled eggs, shelled and quartered
- 24 Niçoise or black olives
- 225g/8oz can tuna in brine, drained
- 50g/2oz can anchovy fillets in olive oil, drained
- basil leaves, to garnish
- garlic croûtons, to serve

For the anchovy vinaigrette

- 20ml/4 tsp Dijon mustard
- 50g/2oz can anchovy fillets in olive oil, drained
- 1 garlic clove, crushed
- 60ml/4 tbsp lemon juice or white wine vinegar
- 120ml/4fl oz/½ cup sunflower oil
- 120ml/4fl oz/½ cup extra virgin olive oil
- ground black pepper

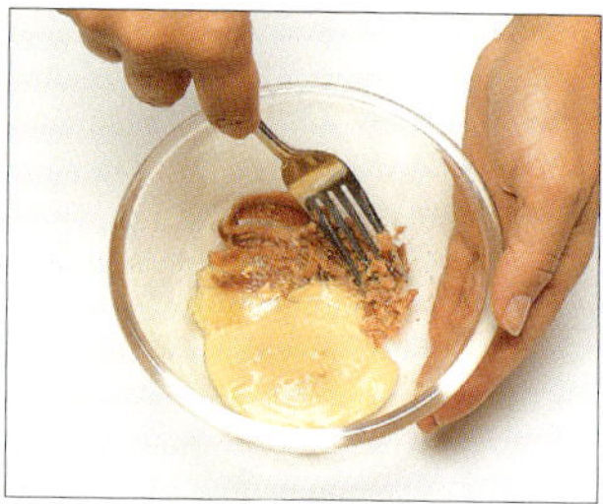

1 First, make the anchovy vinaigrette. Place the mustard, anchovies and garlic in a bowl and blend together by pressing the garlic and anchovies against the sides of the bowl with a fork. Season well with pepper.

2 Using a small whisk, blend in the lemon juice or wine vinegar. Gradually whisk in the sunflower oil in a thin stream, followed by the olive oil, whisking until the dressing is smooth and creamy.

3 Alternatively, put all the dressing ingredients except the two types of oil in a food processor fitted with the metal blade and process to combine. With the machine running, gradually add the sunflower oil and olive oil, in a thin stream through the feeder tube, until the vinaigrette is thick and creamy.

4 Drop the green beans into a large pan of boiling water and boil for 3 minutes until tender, yet crisp. Transfer the beans to a colander with a slotted spoon, then rinse under cold running water. Drain again and set aside.

5 Add the potatoes to the same pan of boiling water, return to the boil and simmer for 10–15 minutes, until just tender, then drain well. Sprinkle with a little white wine vinegar and olive oil and a tablespoonful of the anchovy vinaigrette.

6 Arrange the torn lettuce leaves on a large serving platter, top with the tomatoes, cucumber and green or red pepper, then add the green beans and potatoes.

7 Arrange the egg quarters, olives, tuna and anchovies on top and garnish with the basil leaves. Drizzle the remaining anchovy vinaigrette over the salad and serve immediately with garlic croûtons.

COOK'S TIP

To make garlic croûtons, thinly slice a French stick or cut larger loaves into 2.5cm/1in cubes. Place the bread in a single layer on a baking sheet and bake in a preheated 180°C/350°F/Gas 4 oven for 7–10 minutes, or until golden, turning once. Rub the toasted croûtons with a garlic clove and serve hot or leave to cool, then store in an airtight container to serve them at room temperature.

PRAWN SALAD WITH CURRY DRESSING

CURRY SPICES ADD AN UNEXPECTED TWIST TO THIS TASTY SALAD.

SERVES FOUR

INGREDIENTS

- 1 ripe tomato
- ½ iceberg lettuce
- 1 small onion
- 1 small bunch of fresh coriander (cilantro)
- 15ml/1 tbsp lemon juice
- 450g/1lb cooked peeled prawns (shrimp)
- 1 apple, peeled
- salt
- 8 whole cooked prawns (shrimp), 8 lemon wedges and 4 fresh coriander (cilantro) sprigs, to garnish

For the dressing

- 75ml/5 tbsp mayonnaise
- 5ml/1 tsp mild curry paste
- 15ml/1 tbsp tomato ketchup
- 30ml/2 tbsp water

1 To peel the tomato, pierce the skin with a knife and immerse in boiling water for 20 seconds. Drain and cool under cold running water. Peel off the skin.

2 Halve the tomato, push the seeds out with your thumb and discard them. Cut the flesh into large dice.

3 Finely shred the lettuce, onion and coriander and place in a bowl. Add the diced tomato, moisten with lemon juice and season to taste with salt.

4 To make the dressing, mix together the mayonnaise, curry paste and tomato ketchup in a small bowl. Add the water to thin the dressing and season to taste with salt.

5 Combine the prawns with the dressing. Quarter and core the apple and grate it into the mixture.

6 Divide the shredded lettuce and onion mixture among four serving plates or bowls. Pile the prawn mixture in the centre of each and garnish with two whole prawns, two lemon wedges and a sprig of fresh coriander. Serve immediately.

COOK'S TIP

Fresh coriander (cilantro) is inclined to wilt if it is not kept in water. Store it in a jar of water, covered with a plastic bag, in the refrigerator and it will stay fresh for several days.

AUBERGINE SALAD WITH DRIED SHRIMP

AN APPETIZING AND UNUSUAL SALAD THAT YOU WILL FIND YOURSELF MAKING OFTEN.

SERVES FOUR TO SIX

INGREDIENTS
- 2 aubergines (eggplant)
- 15ml/1 tbsp oil
- 30ml/2 tbsp dried shrimp, soaked and drained
- 15ml/1 tbsp chopped garlic
- 30ml/2 tbsp lime juice
- 5ml/1 tsp palm or brown sugar
- 30ml/2 tbsp fish sauce
- 1 hard-boiled egg, shelled and chopped
- 4 shallots, thinly sliced into rings
- fresh coriander (cilantro) leaves and 2 fresh red chillies, seeded and sliced, to garnish

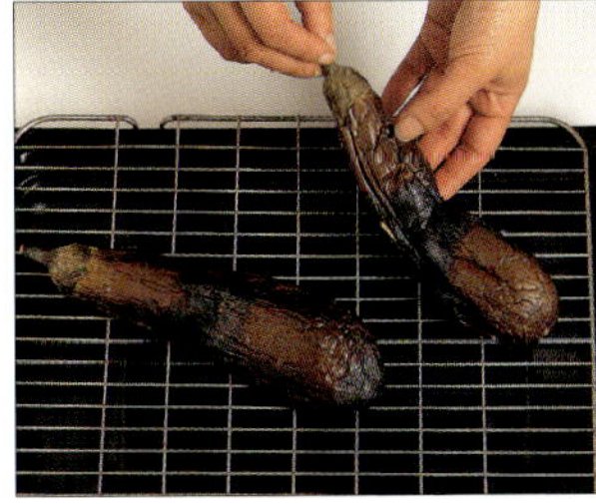

1 Grill (broil) or roast the aubergines in a preheated oven, 180°C/350°F/Gas 4, until charred and tender.

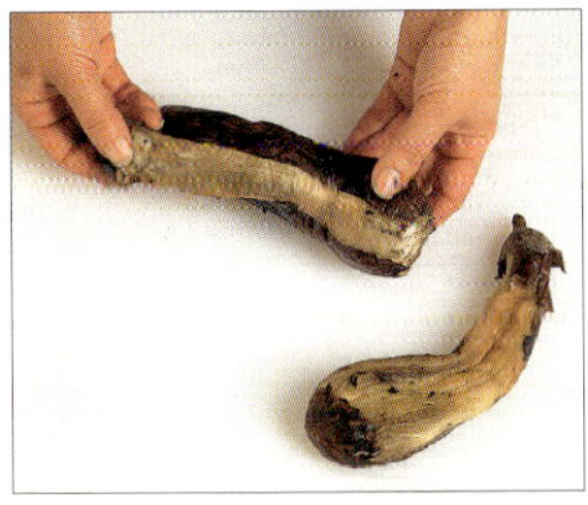

2 Leave the aubergines until they are cool enough to handle, then peel off the skins and slice the flesh.

3 Heat the oil in a small frying pan, add the drained shrimp and garlic and cook over a low heat, stirring frequently, for 3–4 minutes, until golden. Remove from the pan and set aside.

4 To make the dressing, put the lime juice, palm or brown sugar and fish sauce in a small bowl and whisk together until combined.

5 To serve, arrange the aubergines on a serving dish. Top with the egg, shallots and dried shrimp mixture. Drizzle over the dressing and garnish with coriander and chillies. Serve the salad immediately.

COOK'S TIP

Dried shrimp are lightly salted before they are dried, so you are unlikely to require any extra salt. In this recipe, they are rehydrated before being used – not always the case – and this may reduce the degree of saltiness.

VARIATION

For an interesting change, try using salted duck's or quail's eggs, cut in half, instead of the chopped eggs.

Thai Dipping Sauce

This is a traditional accompaniment to Hot Coconut, Prawn and Papaya Salad.

MAKES 120ML/4FL OZ/½ CUP

INGREDIENTS
- 15ml/1 tbsp vegetable oil
- 1cm/½in square shrimp paste, or 15ml/1 tbsp fish sauce
- 2 garlic cloves, thinly sliced
- 2cm/¾in piece fresh root ginger, peeled and finely chopped
- 3 small fresh red chillies, seeded and chopped
- 15ml/1 tbsp finely chopped coriander (cilantro) root or stem
- 20ml/4 tsp sugar
- 45ml/3 tbsp dark soy sauce
- juice of ½ lime

1 Heat the vegetable oil in a wok or heavy frying pan, add the shrimp paste or fish sauce, garlic, ginger and chillies and stir-fry over a low heat for about 1–2 minutes, until softened but not coloured.

2 Remove from the heat and add the coriander, sugar, soy sauce and lime juice. The sauce will keep in a screw-top jar for up to 10 days.

Hot Coconut Prawn and Papaya Salad

This exotic salad goes well with many Asian dishes.

SERVES FOUR TO SIX

INGREDIENTS
- 225g/8oz raw or cooked prawns (shrimp), peeled and deveined
- 2 ripe papayas
- 225g/8oz mixed lettuce leaves, Chinese leaves (Chinese cabbage) and young spinach
- 1 firm tomato, peeled, seeded and coarsely chopped
- 3 spring onions (scallions), shredded
- 1 bunch of coriander (cilantro), shredded, 1 fresh chilli, sliced, and 1 turnip, carved, to garnish
- Thai Dipping Sauce, to serve

For the dressing
- 15ml/1 tbsp creamed coconut
- 30ml/2 tbsp boiling water
- 90ml/6 tbsp vegetable oil
- juice of 1 lime
- 2.5ml/½ tsp hot chilli sauce
- 10ml/2 tsp fish sauce (optional)
- 5ml/1 tsp sugar

1 To make the dressing, place the creamed coconut in a screw-top jar and add the boiling water to soften. Add the vegetable oil, lime juice, chilli sauce, fish sauce, if using, and sugar. Shake well and set aside in a cool place, but do not chill in the refrigerator.

2 If using raw prawns, place them in a pan, add cold water to cover, bring to the boil and simmer for no longer than 2 minutes. Overcooking will make them tough. Drain well and set aside.

3 To prepare the papayas, cut each in half from top to bottom and remove the black seeds with a teaspoon. Peel off the outer skin and cut the flesh into even pieces.

4 Wash the salad leaves and toss in a bowl. Add the other ingredients. Pour on the dressing, garnish with the coriander, chilli and turnip, and serve with Thai Dipping Sauce.

COOK'S TIP

If you are unable to find creamed coconut, substitute 45ml/3 tbsp of coconut cream and omit the boiling water in the dressing.

Warm Monkfish Salad

Monkfish has a matchless flavour and benefits from being cooked simply. Teaming it with wilted baby spinach and toasted pine nuts is inspirational.

SERVES FOUR

INGREDIENTS

- 2 monkfish fillets, about 350g/12oz each
- 25g/1oz/¼ cup pine nuts
- 15ml/1 tbsp olive oil
- 15g/½oz/1 tbsp butter
- 225g/8oz baby spinach leaves, washed and stalks removed
- salt and ground black pepper

For the dressing

- 5ml/1 tsp Dijon mustard
- 5ml/1 tsp sherry vinegar
- 60ml/4 tbsp olive oil
- 1 garlic clove, crushed

VARIATION

Substitute salad leaves for the spinach.

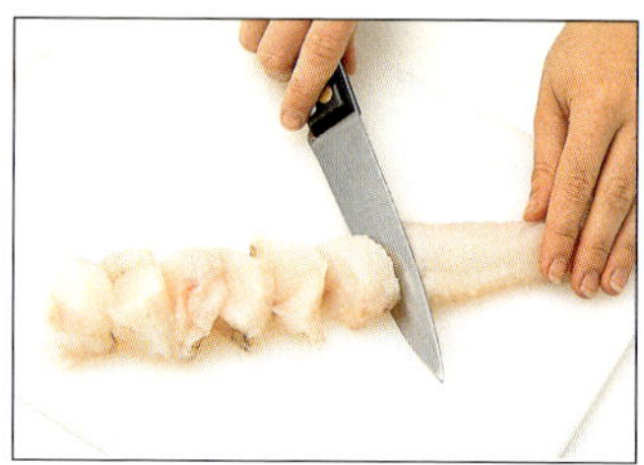

1 Holding the knife at a slight angle, cut each monkfish fillet into 12 diagonal slices. Season lightly and set aside.

2 Heat an empty frying pan, put in the pine nuts and shake them about for a while, until golden brown. Do not burn. Transfer to a plate; set aside.

3 Make the dressing by whisking all the ingredients together until smooth and creamy. Pour the dressing into a small pan, season to taste with salt and pepper and heat gently.

4 Heat the oil and butter in a ridged griddle pan or frying pan until sizzling. Add the fish; sauté for 20–30 seconds on each side.

5 Put the spinach leaves in a large bowl and pour over the warm dressing. Sprinkle on the toasted pine nuts, reserving a few, and toss together well. Divide the dressed spinach leaves among four serving plates and arrange the monkfish slices on top. Sprinkle the reserved pine nuts on top and serve.

Asparagus and Langoustine Salad

For a really extravagant treat, you could make this attractive salad with medallions of lobster. For a cheaper version, use large prawns, allowing six per serving.

SERVES FOUR

INGREDIENTS

- 16 langoustines
- 16 fresh asparagus spears, trimmed
- 2 carrots
- 30ml/2 tbsp olive oil
- 1 garlic clove, peeled
- 15ml/1 tbsp chopped fresh tarragon
- 4 fresh tarragon sprigs and some chopped, to garnish

For the dressing

- 30ml/2 tbsp tarragon vinegar
- 120ml/4fl oz/½ cup olive oil
- salt and ground black pepper

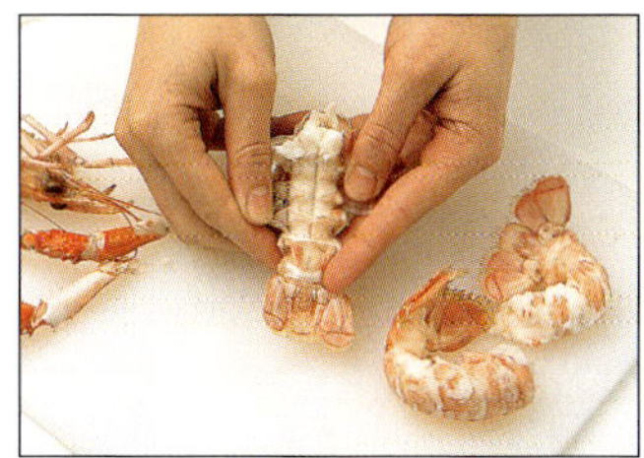

1 Shell the langoustines and keep the discarded parts for stock. Set aside.

2 Steam the asparagus over salted, boiling water until just tender, but still a little crisp. Refresh under cold water, drain and place in a shallow dish.

3 Peel the carrots and cut into fine julienne shreds. Cook in a pan of salted, boiling water for about 3 minutes, until tender but still crunchy. Drain, refresh under cold water and drain again. Place in the dish with the asparagus.

4 Make the dressing. Whisk the vinegar with the oil in a jug (pitcher). Season to taste. Pour over the asparagus and carrots and leave to marinate.

5 Heat the oil with the garlic in a frying pan until very hot. Add the langoustines and sauté quickly until just heated through. Discard the garlic.

6 Cut the asparagus spears in half and arrange on four individual plates with the carrots. Drizzle over the dressing left in the dish and top each portion with four langoustine tails. Top with the tarragon sprigs and sprinkle the chopped tarragon on top. Serve.

COOK'S TIP

Most of the langoustines we buy have been cooked at sea; this is necessary because the flesh deteriorates rapidly after death. Bear this in mind when you cook the shellfish. Because they have already been cooked, they will need only to be lightly sautéed until heated through. If you are lucky enough to buy live langoustines, kill them quickly by immersing them in boiling water, then sauté until cooked through.

EVERYDAY MAIN COURSES

Healthy everyday eating becomes a treat when you serve interesting, affordable fish dishes. Quick to prepare, low in fat and packed with nutrients, fish makes the perfect family meal. From simple-to-cook old favourites, such as Fish Pie and Haddock with Parsley Sauce, to Trout with Tamarind and Chilli Sauce, and Green Fish Curry, there's a dish to suit everyone, even those who profess not to like fish. You will be surprised how little time it takes to make these delicious everyday meals.

TROUT WITH ALMONDS

This simple and quick recipe doubles easily – you can cook the trout in batches or use two frying pans.

SERVES TWO

INGREDIENTS

- 2 trout, about 350g/12oz each, cleaned
- 40g/1½oz/⅓ cup plain (all-purpose) flour
- 50g/2oz/¼ cup butter
- 25g/1oz/¼ cup flaked (sliced) almonds
- 30ml/2 tbsp dry white wine
- salt and ground black pepper

1 Rinse the trout and pat dry with kitchen paper. Put the flour in a large plastic bag and season with salt and pepper. Place the trout, one at a time, in the bag and shake to coat with flour. Shake off the excess and discard the remaining flour.

2 Melt half the butter in a large frying pan over a medium heat. When it is foamy, add the trout and cook for 6–7 minutes on each side, until golden brown and the flesh next to the bone is opaque. Transfer the fish to warmed individual serving plates and keep warm.

3 Add the remaining butter to the pan and cook the almonds until just lightly browned. Add the wine to the pan and bring to the boil. Boil for 1 minute, stirring constantly, until slightly syrupy. Pour or spoon over the fish and serve immediately.

VARIATION

In Normandy, this traditional French dish is often prepared using hazelnuts instead of almonds.

ST RÉMY TUNA

St Rémy is a beautiful village in Provence in the South of France. Herbs, such as thyme, rosemary and oregano, grow wild on the nearby hillside.

SERVES 4

INGREDIENTS

- 4 tuna steaks, about 175–200g/6–7oz each, 2.5cm/1in thick
- 30–45ml/2–3 tbsp olive oil
- 3–4 garlic cloves, finely chopped
- 60ml/4 tbsp dry white wine
- 3 ripe plum tomatoes, peeled, seeded and chopped
- 5ml/1 tsp dried herbes de Provence
- salt and ground black pepper
- fresh basil leaves, to garnish
- fried potatoes, to serve

1 Season the tuna steaks with salt and pepper. Set a heavy frying pan over a high heat until very hot, add the oil and swirl to coat. Add the tuna steaks and press down gently, then reduce the heat to medium and cook for 6–8 minutes, turning once, until just slightly pink in the centre.

2 Using a fish slice or metal spatula, transfer the tuna steaks to a warmed serving platter and cover with foil to keep warm.

3 Add the garlic to the pan and cook for 15–20 seconds, stirring constantly, then pour in the wine, bring to the boil and continue to boil until it is reduced by half.

4 Add the tomatoes and dried herbs and cook for 2–3 minutes. Season to taste with pepper and pour the sauce over the fish steaks. Garnish with fresh basil leaves and serve with the fried potatoes.

COOK'S TIP

Tuna is often served pink in the middle, rather like beef. If you prefer it cooked through, reduce the heat and cook for an extra few minutes.

Sardine Frittata

It may seem odd to cook sardines in an omelette, but they are surprisingly delicious this way. Frozen sardines are fine for this dish. Serve the frittata with crisp sautéed potatoes and thinly sliced cucumber crescents.

SERVES FOUR

INGREDIENTS

- 4 fat sardines, cleaned, filleted and with heads removed, thawed if frozen
- juice of 1 lemon
- 45ml/3 tbsp olive oil
- 6 large (US extra large) eggs
- 30ml/2 tbsp chopped fresh parsley
- 30ml/2 tbsp chopped fresh chives
- 1 garlic clove, chopped
- salt, ground black pepper and paprika

1 Open out the sardines and sprinkle the fish with lemon juice, a little salt and paprika. Heat 15ml/1 tbsp olive oil in a frying pan and fry the sardines for about 1–2 minutes on each side to seal them. Drain on kitchen paper, trim off the tails and set aside until required.

2 Separate the eggs. In a bowl, whisk the yolks lightly with the parsley, chives and a little salt and pepper. Beat the whites in a separate bowl with a pinch of salt until fairly stiff. Preheat the grill (broiler) to medium-high.

3 Heat the remaining olive oil in a large frying pan, add the garlic and cook over a low heat until just golden. Gently mix together the egg yolks and whites and ladle half the mixture into the pan. Cook gently until just beginning to set on the base, then lay the sardines on the frittata and sprinkle lightly with paprika. Pour over the remaining egg mixture and cook gently until the frittata has browned underneath and is beginning to set on the top.

4 Put the pan under the grill and cook until the top of the frittata is golden. Cut into wedges and serve immediately.

COOK'S TIP

It is important to use a frying pan with a handle that can safely be used under the grill (broiler). If your frying pan has a wooden handle, protect it with foil.

COD CARAMBA

THIS COLOURFUL MEXICAN DISH, WITH ITS CONTRASTING CRUNCHY TOPPING AND TENDER FISH FILLING, CAN BE MADE WITH ANY ECONOMICAL WHITE FISH SUCH AS COLEY OR HADDOCK.

SERVES FOUR TO SIX

INGREDIENTS
- 450g/1lb cod fillets
- 225g/8oz smoked cod fillets
- 300ml/½ pint/1¼ cups fish stock
- 50g/2oz/¼ cup butter
- 1 onion, sliced
- 2 garlic cloves, crushed
- 1 green and 1 red (bell) pepper, seeded and diced
- 2 courgettes (zucchini), diced
- 115g/4oz/⅔ cup drained canned or thawed frozen corn kernels
- 2 tomatoes, peeled and chopped
- juice of 1 lime
- Tabasco sauce
- salt, ground black pepper and cayenne pepper

For the topping
- 75g/3oz tortilla chips
- 50g/2oz/½ cup grated Cheddar cheese
- coriander (cilantro) sprigs, to garnish
- lime wedges, to serve

1 Lay the fish in a shallow pan and pour over the fish stock. Bring to the boil, lower the heat, cover and poach for about 8 minutes, until the flesh flakes easily when tested with the tip of a sharp knife. Leave to cool slightly, then remove the skin and separate the flesh into large flakes. Keep hot.

2 Melt the butter in a pan, add the onion and garlic and cook over a low heat until soft. Add the peppers, stir and cook for 2 minutes. Stir in the courgettes and cook for 3 minutes more, until all the vegetables are tender.

3 Stir in the corn and tomatoes, then add lime juice and Tabasco to taste. Season with salt, black pepper and cayenne. Cook for a few minutes to heat the corn and tomatoes, then stir in the fish and transfer to a dish that can safely be used under the grill (broiler).

4 Preheat the grill. Make the topping by crushing the tortilla chips, then mixing in the grated cheese. Add cayenne pepper to taste and sprinkle over the fish. Place the dish under the grill until the topping is crisp and brown. Garnish with coriander sprigs and lime wedges.

KEDGEREE

This classic dish originated in India. It is best made with basmati rice, which goes well with the mild curry flavour, but other long grain rice will do. For a colourful garnish, add some finely sliced red onion and a little red onion marmalade.

SERVES FOUR

INGREDIENTS

- 450g/1lb undyed smoked haddock fillet
- 750ml/1¼ pints/3 cups milk
- 2 bay leaves
- ½ lemon, sliced
- 50g/2oz/¼ cup butter
- 1 onion, chopped
- 2.5ml/½ tsp ground turmeric
- 5ml/1 tsp mild Madras curry powder
- 2 green cardamom pods
- 350g/12oz/1¾ cups basmati or long grain rice, washed and drained
- 4 hard-boiled eggs, coarsely chopped
- 150ml/¼ pint/⅔ cup single (light) cream (optional)
- 30ml/2 tbsp chopped fresh parsley
- salt and ground black pepper

1 Put the haddock in a shallow pan and add the milk, bay leaves and lemon slices. Poach gently for 8–10 minutes, until the haddock flakes easily when tested with the tip of a sharp knife. Strain the milk into a jug (pitcher), discarding the bay leaves and lemon slices. Remove the skin from the haddock and flake the flesh into large pieces. Keep hot until required.

2 Melt the butter in the pan, add the onion and cook over a low heat for about 3 minutes, until softened. Stir in the turmeric, the curry powder and cardamom pods and cook for 1 minute.

3 Add the rice, stirring to coat it well with the butter. Pour in the reserved milk, stir and bring to the boil. Lower the heat and simmer the rice for 10–12 minutes, until all the milk has been absorbed and the rice is tender. Season to taste, going easy on the salt.

4 Gently stir in the fish and hard-boiled eggs, with the cream, if using. Sprinkle with the parsley and serve.

VARIATION

Use smoked and poached fresh salmon for a delicious change from haddock.

FRIED PLAICE WITH TOMATO SAUCE

THIS SIMPLE DISH IS PERENNIALLY POPULAR WITH CHILDREN. IT WORKS EQUALLY WELL WITH LEMON SOLE OR DABS (THESE DO NOT NEED SKINNING), OR FILLETS OF HADDOCK AND WHITING.

SERVES FOUR

INGREDIENTS

- 25g/1oz/¼ cup plain (all-purpose) flour
- 2 eggs, beaten
- 75g/3oz/¾ cup dried breadcrumbs, preferably home-made
- 4 small plaice or flounder, skinned
- 15g/½oz/1 tbsp butter
- 15ml/1 tbsp sunflower oil
- salt and ground black pepper
- 1 lemon, quartered, to serve
- fresh basil leaves, to garnish

For the tomato sauce

- 30ml/2 tbsp olive oil
- 1 red onion, finely chopped
- 1 garlic clove, finely chopped
- 400g/14oz can chopped tomatoes
- 15ml/1 tbsp tomato purée (paste)
- 15ml/1 tbsp torn fresh basil leaves

1 First make the tomato sauce. Heat the olive oil in a large pan, add the finely chopped onion and garlic and cook gently for about 5 minutes, until softened and pale golden. Stir in the chopped tomatoes and tomato purée and simmer for 20–30 minutes, stirring occasionally. Season with salt and pepper and stir in the basil.

2 Spread out the flour in a shallow dish, pour the beaten eggs into another and spread out the breadcrumbs in a third. Season the fish with salt and pepper.

3 Hold a fish in your left hand and dip it first in flour, then in egg and finally, in the breadcrumbs, patting the crumbs on with your dry right hand.

4 Heat the butter and oil in a frying pan until foaming. Fry the fish one at a time in the hot fat for about 5 minutes on each side, until golden brown and cooked through, but still juicy in the middle. Drain on kitchen paper and keep hot while you fry the rest. Serve with lemon wedges and the tomato sauce, garnished with basil leaves.

Herrings in Oatmeal with Mustard

Oatmeal makes a delicious, crunchy coating for tender herrings.

SERVES FOUR

INGREDIENTS

- 15ml/1 tbsp Dijon mustard
- 7.5ml/1½ tsp tarragon vinegar
- 175ml/6fl oz/¾ cup thick mayonnaise
- 4 herrings, about 225g/8oz each, cleaned
- 1 lemon, halved
- 115g/4oz/1 cup medium oatmeal
- salt and ground black pepper

1 Beat the mustard and vinegar into the mayonnaise in a small bowl. Cover with clear film (plastic wrap) and chill lightly.

2 Preheat the grill (broiler). Place one fish at a time on a board, cut side down and opened out. Press gently along the backbone with your thumbs. Turn over the fish and carefully lift away the backbone.

3 Squeeze lemon juice over both sides of the fish, then season with salt and pepper. Fold the fish in half, skin side outwards.

4 Place the oatmeal on a shallow plate, then coat each herring evenly in the oatmeal, pressing it in gently but firmly.

5 Place the herrings on a grill rack and cook under the grill for about 3–4 minutes on each side, until the skin is golden brown and crisp and the flesh flakes easily. Serve immediately with the lightly chilled mustard sauce, handed separately.

COOK'S TIP

You can adjust the amount of Dijon mustard and tarragon vinegar that you add to the mayonnaise to taste.

Fish and Chips

This classic British dish is quick and easy to make at home. Traditional British chips are usually chunkier and fatter than French fries.

SERVES FOUR

INGREDIENTS

- 115g/4oz self-raising (self-rising) flour
- 150ml/¼ pint/⅔ cup water
- 675g/1½lb potatoes
- vegetable oil, for deep-frying
- 675g/1½lb piece skinned cod fillet, cut into 4 pieces
- salt
- lemon wedges, to garnish

1 Sift the flour and a pinch of salt together into a bowl, then form a well in the centre. Gradually pour in the water, whisking in the flour to make a smooth batter. Cover with clear film (plastic wrap) or a dishtowel and set aside to rest for 30 minutes.

2 Peel the potatoes, then cut them into strips about 1cm/½in wide and 5cm/2in long. Place them in a colander and rinse in cold water, then drain and dry well.

3 Heat the vegetable oil in a deep-fat fryer or large heavy pan to 150°C/300°F. Using a wire basket, lower the potatoes, in batches, into the oil and cook for 5–6 minutes, shaking the basket occasionally, until the potatoes are soft but not browned.

4 Remove the chips (French fries) from the fryer or pan and drain thoroughly on plenty of kitchen paper.

5 Heat the oil in the fryer to 190°C/375°F. Season the fish with salt. Stir the batter, then dip the pieces of fish into it, one at a time, allowing the excess to drain off.

6 Working in two batches, if necessary, lower the fish into the oil and fry for 6–8 minutes, until crisp and golden brown. Drain the fish on kitchen paper and keep warm.

7 Add the chips, in batches, to the oil and cook for 2–3 minutes, until golden brown and crisp. Keep hot. Sprinkle with salt and serve with the fish, garnished with lemon wedges.

COOK'S TIP

Rinsing the potatoes under plenty of cold running water removes a lot of the starch. This, combined with frying the chips (French fries) twice, first at a lower temperature and then briefly at a higher one, is the secret of the successful British chip – crisp and crunchy on the outside, but soft and tender on the inside.

HERRINGS IN OATMEAL WITH BACON

This traditional Scottish dish is cheap and nutritious. For ease of eating, bone the herrings before coating them in the oatmeal. If you don't like herrings, use trout or mackerel instead. For extra colour and flavour, serve with grilled tomatoes.

SERVES FOUR

INGREDIENTS
- 115–150g/4–5oz/1–1¼ cups medium oatmeal
- 10ml/2 tsp mustard powder
- 4 herrings, about 225g/8oz each, cleaned, boned, heads and tails removed
- 30ml/2 tbsp sunflower oil
- 8 rindless streaky (fatty) bacon rashers (strips)
- salt and ground black pepper
- lemon wedges, to serve

COOK'S TIPS
- Use tongs to turn the herrings so as not to dislodge the oatmeal.
- Cook the herrings two at a time.
- Don't overcrowd the frying pan.

1 In a shallow dish, mix together the oatmeal and mustard powder with salt and pepper. Press the herrings into the mixture, one at a time, to coat them thickly on both sides. Shake off the excess oatmeal mixture and set the herrings aside.

2 Heat the oil in a large frying pan and fry the bacon until crisp. Drain on kitchen paper and keep hot.

3 Put the herrings into the pan and fry them for 3–4 minutes on each side, until crisp and golden brown. Serve the herrings with the streaky bacon rashers and lemon wedges.

SKATE WITH BLACK BUTTER

Skate can be quite inexpensive, and this classic dish is perfect for a family supper. Serve it with steamed leeks and plain boiled potatoes.

SERVES FOUR

INGREDIENTS
- 4 skate wings, about 225g/8oz each
- 60ml/4 tbsp red wine vinegar or malt vinegar
- 30ml/2 tbsp drained capers in vinegar, chopped if large
- 30ml/2 tbsp chopped fresh parsley
- 150g/5oz/⅔ cup butter
- salt and ground black pepper

COOK'S TIP
Despite the title of the recipe, the butter should be a rich golden brown. It should never be allowed to blacken, or it will taste unpleasantly bitter.

1 Put the skate wings in a large, shallow pan, cover with cold water and add a pinch of salt and 15ml/1 tbsp of the red wine or malt vinegar.

2 Bring to the boil, skim the surface, then lower the heat and simmer gently for about 10–12 minutes, until the skate flesh comes away from the bone easily. Carefully drain the skate and peel off the skin.

3 Transfer the skate to a warmed serving dish, season with salt and pepper and sprinkle over the capers and parsley. Keep hot.

4 In a small pan, heat the butter until it foams and turns a rich nutty brown. Pour it over the skate. Pour the remaining vinegar into the pan and boil until reduced by about two-thirds. Drizzle over the skate and serve.

GRILLED MACKEREL WITH SPICY DHAL

OILY FISH LIKE MACKEREL ARE CHEAP AND NUTRITIOUS. THEY ARE COMPLEMENTED BY A TART OR SOUR ACCOMPANIMENT, LIKE THESE TAMARIND-FLAVOURED LENTILS. SERVE WITH CHOPPED FRESH TOMATOES, ONION SALAD AND FLAT BREAD.

SERVES FOUR

INGREDIENTS

- 250g/9oz/1 cup red lentils, or yellow split peas (soaked overnight)
- 1 litre/1¾ pints/4 cups water
- 30ml/2 tbsp sunflower oil
- 2.5ml/½ tsp each mustard seeds, cumin seeds, fennel seeds, and fenugreek or cardamom seeds
- 5ml/1 tsp ground turmeric
- 3–4 dried red chillies, crumbled
- 30ml/2 tbsp tamarind paste
- 5ml/1 tsp soft brown sugar
- 30ml/2 tbsp chopped fresh coriander (cilantro)
- 4 mackerel or 8 large sardines
- salt and ground black pepper
- fresh red chilli slices and chopped coriander (cilantro), to garnish

1 Rinse the lentils or split peas, drain them thoroughly and put them in a pan. Pour in the water and bring to the boil. Lower the heat, partially cover the pan and simmer for 30–40 minutes, stirring occasionally, until the pulses are tender and soft.

2 Heat the oil in a wok or shallow pan. Add the mustard seeds, then cover and cook for a few seconds, until they pop. Remove the lid, add the rest of the seeds, with the turmeric and chillies and cook for a few more seconds.

3 Stir in the pulses, with salt to taste. Mix well; stir in the tamarind paste and sugar. Bring to the boil, then simmer for 10 minutes, until thick. Stir in the chopped fresh coriander.

4 Meanwhile, clean the fish, then heat a ridged griddle pan or the grill (broiler) until very hot. Make six diagonal slashes on either side of each fish and remove the heads if you like. Season inside and out, then grill (broil) for 5–7 minutes on each side, until the skin is crisp. Serve with the dhal, garnished with red chilli and chopped coriander.

TROUT WITH TAMARIND AND CHILLI SAUCE

TROUT IS A VERY ECONOMICAL FISH, BUT CAN TASTE RATHER BLAND. THIS SPICY, THAI-INSPIRED SAUCE REALLY GIVES IT A ZING. IF YOU LIKE YOUR FOOD VERY SPICY, ADD AN EXTRA CHILLI.

SERVES FOUR

INGREDIENTS

- 4 trout, about 350g/12oz each, cleaned
- 6 spring onions (scallions), sliced
- 60ml/4 tbsp soy sauce
- 15ml/1 tbsp stir-fry oil
- 30ml/2 tbsp chopped fresh coriander (cilantro)

For the sauce

- 50g/2oz tamarind pulp
- 105ml/7 tbsp boiling water
- 2 shallots, coarsely chopped
- 1 fresh red chilli, seeded and chopped
- 1cm/½in piece fresh root ginger, peeled and chopped
- 5ml/1 tsp soft brown sugar
- 45ml/3 tbsp Thai fish sauce

1 Slash the trout diagonally four or five times on each side with a sharp knife and place in a shallow dish.

2 Fill the cavities with spring onions and douse each fish with soy sauce. Carefully turn the fish over to coat both sides with the sauce. Sprinkle on any remaining spring onions and set aside until required.

3 Make the sauce. Put the tamarind pulp in a small bowl and pour on the boiling water. Mash well with a fork until soft. Tip the mixture into a food processor or blender, then add the shallots, fresh chilli, ginger, sugar and fish sauce and process to a fairly coarse pulp.

4 Heat the stir-fry oil in a large frying pan or wok and fry the trout, one at a time if necessary, for about 5 minutes on each side, until the skin is crisp and browned and the flesh cooked. Put on warmed plates and spoon over some sauce. Sprinkle with the coriander and serve with the remaining sauce.

MONKFISH WITH PEPPERED CITRUS MARINADE

MONKFISH IS A FIRM, MEATY FISH THAT COOKS WELL ON THE BARBECUE.

SERVES FOUR

INGREDIENTS

- 2 monkfish tails, about 350g/12oz each
- 1 lime
- 1 lemon
- 2 oranges
- handful of fresh thyme sprigs
- 30ml/2 tbsp olive oil
- 15ml/1 tbsp mixed peppercorns, coarsely crushed
- salt and ground black pepper
- lemon and lime wedges, to serve

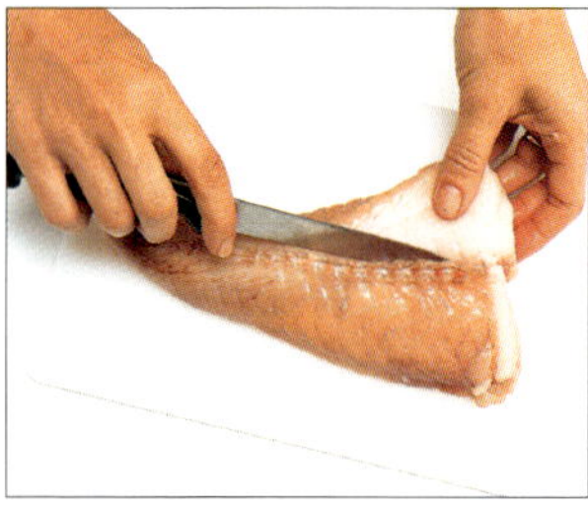

1 Remove any skin and grey membrane from the monkfish tails with a sharp knife. Cut carefully down one side of the backbone, sliding the knife between the bone and flesh, to remove the fillet on one side. (You can ask your fishmonger to do this for you.)

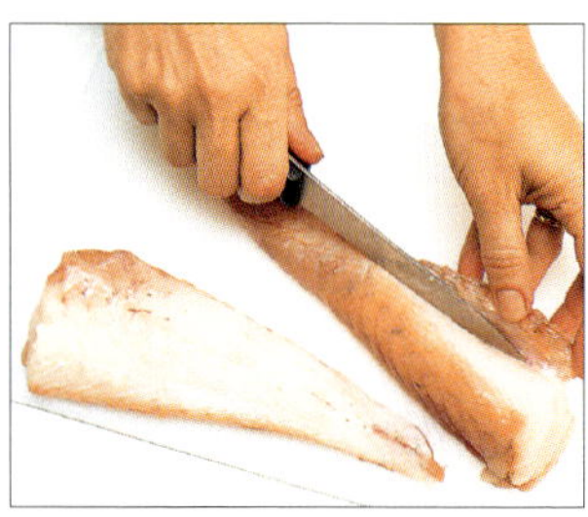

2 Turn the fish and repeat on the other side, to remove the second fillet. Repeat on the second tail.

3 Lay the four monkfish fillets out flat. Cut two slices each from the lime, lemon and one of the oranges and arrange them over two of the fish fillets. Add a few sprigs of thyme and season well with salt and pepper. Finely grate the rind from all the remaining fruit and sprinkle it evenly over the fish.

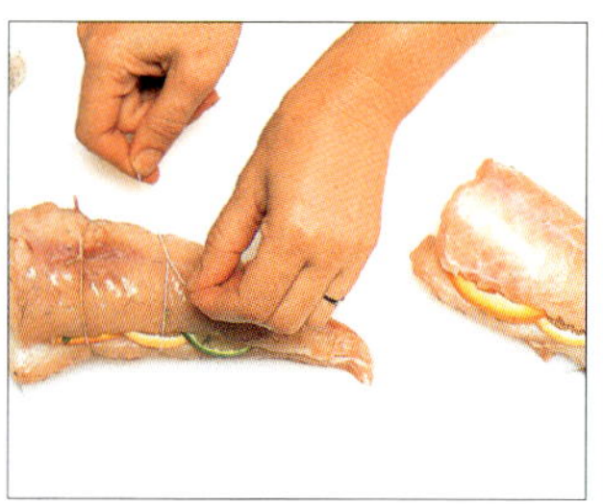

4 Lay the remaining two fish fillets on top and tie them firmly with fine cotton string to hold them in shape. Arrange them in a wide dish.

5 Squeeze the juice from the remaining lime, lemon and oranges and mix it with the oil and more salt and pepper in a bowl or jug (pitcher). Spoon or pour the mixture over the fish. Cover with clear film (plastic wrap) and leave in a cool place to marinate for about 1 hour, turning occasionally and spooning the marinade over it.

6 Drain the monkfish, reserving the marinade, and sprinkle with the crushed peppercorns. Cook on a medium-hot barbecue for about 15–20 minutes, basting it with the marinade and turning it occasionally, until it is evenly cooked through. Serve immediately with lemon and lime wedges.

COOK'S TIP

You can also cook the fish under a preheated grill (broiler). Make sure that you brush frequently with the marinade to prevent it from drying out.

VARIATION

You can also use this marinade for monkfish kebabs.

HADDOCK WITH PARSLEY SAUCE

AS THE FISH HAS TO BE KEPT WARM WHILE THE SAUCE IS BEING MADE, TAKE CARE NOT TO OVERCOOK IT.

SERVES FOUR

INGREDIENTS

- 4 haddock fillets, about 175g/6oz each
- 50g/2oz/¼ cup butter
- 150ml/¼ pint/⅔ cup milk
- 150ml/¼ pint/⅔ cup fish stock
- 1 bay leaf
- 20ml/4 tsp plain (all-purpose) flour
- 60ml/4 tbsp double (heavy) cream
- 1 egg yolk
- 45ml/3 tbsp chopped fresh parsley
- grated rind and juice of ½ lemon
- salt and ground black pepper
- boiled new potatoes and sliced carrots, to serve

1 Place the fish in a large, heavy frying pan, preferably in a single layer. Add half the butter, the milk, fish stock and bay leaf and season well with salt and pepper. Bring to simmering point over a medium heat. Lower the heat, cover the pan and gently poach the fish for about 10–15 minutes, depending on the thickness of the fillets. Cook until the fish is tender and the flesh is just beginning to flake.

2 Carefully transfer the fish to a warmed serving plate, cover with foil and keep warm while you make the sauce.

3 Return the cooking liquid to a medium heat and bring to the boil, stirring constantly. Simmer for about 4 minutes, then remove and discard the bay leaf.

4 Melt the remaining butter in another pan over a low heat, stir in the flour and cook, stirring constantly, for 1 minute. Remove the pan from the heat and gradually stir in the hot fish cooking liquid. Return the pan to the heat and bring to the boil, stirring constantly. Simmer, stirring frequently, for about 4 minutes, until the sauce is thickened and smooth.

5 Remove the pan from the heat, blend the cream into the egg yolk, then stir the mixture into the sauce with the parsley. Reheat gently, stirring, for a few minutes.

6 Remove from the heat, add the lemon juice and rind and season to taste. Pour into a sauceboat. Serve the fish with the sauce, new potatoes and carrots.

FISH WITH LEMON, RED ONION AND CORIANDER

A RICH MIXTURE OF FLAVOURS, TEXTURES AND COLOURS – AND ALL PRODUCED IN JUST ONE PAN!

SERVES FOUR

INGREDIENTS

- 4 halibut or cod steaks or cutlets, about 175g/6oz each
- juice of 1 lemon
- 5ml/1 tsp garlic granules
- 5ml/1 tsp paprika
- 5ml/1 tsp ground cumin
- 4ml/¾ tsp dried tarragon
- about 60ml/4 tbsp olive oil
- flour, for dusting
- 300ml/½ pint/1¼ cups fish stock
- 2 fresh red chillies, seeded and finely chopped
- 30ml/2 tbsp chopped fresh coriander (cilantro)
- 1 red onion, cut into rings
- salt and ground black pepper

1 Place the fish in a shallow, non-metallic dish. Mix together the lemon juice, garlic, paprika, cumin, tarragon and a little salt and pepper in a bowl. Spoon the lemon mixture over the fish, cover loosely with clear film (plastic wrap) and set aside in a cool place to marinate for 1–2 hours or overnight in the refrigerator.

2 Gently heat 45ml/3 tbsp of the olive oil in a large, non-stick frying pan. Dust the fish with flour, shaking off any excess, then add to the pan and cook over a low heat for a few minutes on each side, until golden brown all over.

3 Pour the fish stock around the fish, cover and simmer gently for about 5 minutes, until the fish is thoroughly cooked through.

4 Add the chopped red chillies and 15ml/1 tbsp of the coriander to the pan. Simmer for a further 5 minutes.

5 Transfer the fish and sauce to a serving plate and keep warm.

6 Meanwhile, heat the remaining olive oil and stir-fry the onion rings. Sprinkle over the fish with the remaining chopped coriander and serve immediately.

Marinated Fish

This dish is of Spanish origin and it is also very popular throughout the Caribbean.

SERVES FOUR TO SIX

INGREDIENTS

- 7.5ml/1½ tsp garlic granules
- 2.5ml/½ tsp coarse-grain black pepper
- 2.5ml/½ tsp paprika
- 2.5ml/½ tsp celery salt
- 2.5 ml/½ tsp curry powder
- 900g/2lb cod fillet
- ½ lemon
- 15ml/1 tbsp spice seasoning
- plain (all-purpose) flour, for dusting
- oil, for frying
- lemon wedges, to garnish

For the sauce

- 30ml/2 tbsp vegetable oil
- 1 onion, sliced
- ½ red (bell) pepper, seeded and sliced
- ½ christophene, peeled and seeded, cut into small pieces
- 2 garlic cloves, crushed
- 120ml/4fl oz/½ cup malt vinegar
- 75ml/5 tbsp water
- 2.5ml/½ tsp ground allspice
- 1 bay leaf
- 1 small hot chilli, chopped
- 15ml/1 tbsp soft dark brown sugar
- salt and ground black pepper

1 Mix together the garlic and all the spices. Place the fish in a shallow dish, squeeze over the lemon, then sprinkle with the spice seasoning and pat into the fish. Leave to marinate in a cool place for 1 hour.

2 Cut the fish into 7.5cm/3in pieces and dust with a little flour, shaking off the excess.

COOK'S TIP

A christophene is a type of gourd, sometimes known as a chayote.

3 Heat the oil in a large, heavy frying pan and cook the fish pieces over a medium heat, turning occasionally, for 2–3 minutes, until golden brown and crisp.

4 To make the sauce, heat the oil in a heavy frying pan, add the onion and cook over a low heat, stirring occasionally, for about 5 minutes, until soft. Add the pepper, christophene and garlic and stir-fry for 2 minutes. Pour in the vinegar, add all the remaining ingredients and simmer gently for 5 minutes. Leave the sauce to stand for 10 minutes, then pour it over the fish. Serve immediately, garnished with lemon wedges.

FRIED FISH WITH PIQUANT MAYONNAISE

This mayonnaise-based sauce makes fried fish just that extra bit special.

SERVES FOUR

INGREDIENTS

- 1 egg
- 45ml/3 tbsp olive oil
- squeeze of lemon juice
- 2.5ml/½ tsp finely chopped fresh dill or parsley
- 50g/2oz/½ cup plain (all-purpose) flour
- 4 whiting or haddock fillets
- 25g/1oz/2 tbsp butter or margarine
- salt and ground black pepper
- mixed salad, to serve

For the mayonnaise

- 1 egg yolk
- 30ml/2 tbsp Dijon mustard
- 30ml/2 tbsp white wine vinegar
- 10ml/2 tsp paprika
- 300ml/½ pint/1¼ cups olive or vegetable oil
- 30ml/2 tbsp creamed horseradish
- 1 garlic clove, finely chopped
- 25g/1oz/½ cup finely chopped celery
- 30ml/2 tbsp tomato ketchup

1 To make the mayonnaise, whisk together the egg yolk, mustard, vinegar and paprika in a mixing bowl. Gradually add the oil, a drop at a time to begin with, then in a thin, steady stream, beating vigorously with a wire whisk to blend it in.

2 When the mixture is smooth and thick, beat in all the remaining mayonnaise ingredients. Cover with clear film (plastic wrap) and chill until ready to serve.

3 Mix together the egg, 15ml/1 tbsp of the olive oil, the lemon juice and dill or parsley in a shallow dish and season with a little salt and pepper. Beat until thoroughly mixed.

4 Spread out the flour on a plate or in another shallow dish. Dip both sides of each fish fillet in the egg and herb mixture, then coat the fillets lightly and evenly with flour, shaking off the excess.

5 Heat the butter or margarine with the remaining olive oil in a large, heavy frying pan. Add the coated fish fillets and cook over a medium heat for 8–10 minutes, until golden brown on both sides and cooked through. If necessary, cook the fish in two batches, keeping the cooked fish warm while you are cooking the second batch.

6 Place the fish on four warmed serving plates and serve immediately, with the chilled piquant mayonnaise and accompanied by a salad of mixed leaves.

Prawns and Fish in a Herb Sauce

Bengalis are famous for their seafood dishes and always use mustard oil in recipes because it imparts a unique flavour.

SERVES FOUR TO SIX

INGREDIENTS

- 3 garlic cloves
- 5cm/2in piece fresh root ginger
- 1 large leek, coarsely chopped
- 4 green chillies
- 5ml/1 tsp vegetable oil (optional)
- 60ml/4 tbsp mustard oil
- 15ml/1 tbsp ground coriander
- 2.5ml/½ tsp fennel seeds
- 15ml/1 tbsp crushed yellow mustard seeds or 5ml/1 tsp mustard powder
- 175ml/6fl oz/¾ cup thick coconut milk
- 225g/8oz huss or monkfish, sliced
- 225g/8oz raw king prawns (jumbo shrimp), peeled and deveined with tails intact
- 115g/4oz/2 cups fresh coriander (cilantro) leaves, chopped
- salt
- green chillies, to garnish

1 Place the garlic, ginger, leek and chillies in a food processor and process to a coarse paste. Add vegetable oil if the mixture is too dry.

2 Heat the mustard oil with the paste in a heavy frying pan, stirring until it is well blended. Keep the kitchen window open and take care not to overheat the mixture, as any smoke from the mustard oil will sting the eyes and irritate the membranes of the nose.

3 Add the ground coriander, fennel seeds, mustard and coconut milk. Gently bring to the boil, then simmer, uncovered, for about 5 minutes.

4 Add the slices of huss or monkfish and simmer gently for 2 minutes, then fold in the prawns and cook until the prawns turn a bright orange-pink colour. Season to taste with salt, fold in the coriander leaves and spoon on to a warmed serving platter. Garnish with fresh green chillies and serve immediately.

FISH AND PRAWNS WITH SPINACH AND COCONUT

THIS DISH IS A TRULY DELIGHTFUL MEDLEY OF FLAVOURS THAT COMPLEMENTS THE FISH AND PRAWN MIX.

SERVES FOUR

INGREDIENTS

- 450g/1lb white fish fillets, such as cod or haddock
- 15ml/1 tbsp lemon or lime juice
- 2.5ml/½ tsp garlic granules
- 5ml/1 tsp ground cinnamon
- 2.5ml/½ tsp dried thyme
- 2.5ml/½ tsp paprika
- seasoned flour, for dusting
- vegetable oil, for shallow frying
- salt and ground black pepper

For the sauce

- 25g/1oz/2 tbsp butter or margarine
- 1 onion, finely chopped
- 1 garlic clove, crushed
- 300ml/½ pint/1¼ cups coconut milk
- 115g/4oz fresh spinach, finely sliced
- 225–275g/8–10oz cooked peeled prawns (shrimp)
- 1 fresh red chilli, seeded and finely chopped

1 Place the fish fillets in a shallow, non-metallic dish and sprinkle with the lemon or lime juice.

2 Mix together the garlic granules, cinnamon, thyme and paprika in a bowl and season with salt and pepper. Sprinkle the spice mixture over the fish, cover loosely with clear film (plastic wrap) and leave to marinate in a cool place or in the refrigerator for a few hours.

3 Meanwhile, make the sauce. Melt the butter or margarine in a large, heavy pan. Add the onion and garlic and cook over a low heat, stirring occasionally, for 5–6 minutes, until the onion is soft.

4 Pour the coconut milk into a separate pan, add the spinach and bring to the boil. Lower the heat and cook gently for a few minutes, until the spinach has just wilted and the coconut milk has reduced a little. Remove from the pan the heat and set aside to cool slightly.

5 Transfer the spinach mixture to a blender or food processor and process for 30 seconds.

6 Add the puréed spinach to the onion, together with the prawns and red chilli. Stir well and simmer gently for a few minutes, then set aside while you cook the fish.

7 Cut the fish into 5cm/2in pieces and dip in the seasoned flour to coat, shaking off any excess. Heat a little oil in a large, heavy frying pan and cook the fish pieces, in batches if necessary, for about 2–3 minutes each side, until golden brown. Drain thoroughly on kitchen paper.

8 Arrange the fish on a warmed serving plate. Gently reheat the sauce and serve separately in a sauceboat or poured over the fish.

COOK'S TIP

Coconut milk is widely available in cans from most supermarkets and Asian food stores.

SEAFOOD BALTI WITH VEGETABLES

IN THIS DISH, THE SPICY SEAFOOD IS COOKED SEPARATELY AND COMBINED WITH THE VEGETABLES ONLY WHEN IT IS EATEN, TO GIVE A TRULY DELICIOUS COMBINATION OF FLAVOURS.

SERVES FOUR

INGREDIENTS

- 225g/8oz cod
- 225g/8oz cooked peeled prawns (shrimp)
- 6 seafood sticks, halved lengthways, or 200g/7oz can crab meat, drained
- 15ml/1 tbsp lemon juice
- 5ml/1 tsp ground coriander
- 5ml/1 tsp chilli powder
- 5ml/1 tsp salt
- 5ml/1 tsp ground cumin
- 60ml/4 tbsp cornflour (cornstarch)
- 150ml/¼ pint/⅔ cup corn oil

For the vegetables

- 150ml/¼ pint/⅔ cup corn oil
- 2 medium onions, chopped
- 5ml/1 tsp onion seeds
- ½ medium cauliflower, cut into florets
- 115g/4oz green beans, cut into 2.5cm/1in lengths
- 175g/6oz/1 cup corn kernels
- 5ml/1 tsp shredded fresh root ginger
- 5ml/1 tsp chilli powder
- 5ml/1 tsp salt
- 4 fresh green chillies, seeded and sliced
- 30ml/2 tbsp chopped fresh coriander (cilantro)
- lime slices, to garnish

1 Skin the fish and cut the flesh into small cubes. Put them into a medium mixing bowl, add the prawns and seafood sticks or crab meat, mix well and set aside.

COOK'S TIP

Also known as Balti pan, a karahi is a round-based pan, usually with two handles rather like a wok. They are traditionally made of cast iron, but are now available in a range of materials.

2 Mix together the lemon juice, ground coriander, chilli powder, salt and ground cumin in a separate small bowl until well combined. Pour this mixture over the seafood and mix together gently but thoroughly, using your hands.

3 Sprinkle on the cornflour and mix again until the seafood is thoroughly coated. Cover with clear film (plastic wrap) and set aside in the refrigerator for about 1 hour to allow the flavours to develop.

4 To make the vegetable mixture, heat the oil in a preheated wok, karahi or large, heavy frying pan. Add the onions and onion seeds and stir-fry over a medium heat until softened and lightly browned.

5 Add the cauliflower florets, green beans, corn kernels, shredded ginger, chilli powder, salt, fresh green chillies and chopped fresh coriander. Stir-fry over a medium heat for about 7–10 minutes, until the vegetables are cooked through but still crisp.

6 Spoon the stir-fried vegetables around the edge of a warm, shallow serving dish, leaving a space in the middle for the seafood, cover and keep warm.

7 Wash and dry the wok, karahi or frying pan, then heat the oil to cook the pieces of seafood. Add the seafood pieces in two or three batches and stir-fry over a medium heat, until they turn a golden brown. Remove with a slotted spoon and drain on kitchen paper.

8 Arrange the batches of seafood in the middle of the dish of vegetables and keep warm while you stir-fry the remaining seafood. Garnish with lime slices and serve immediately.

Chunky Fish Balti with Peppers

Try to find differently coloured sweet peppers to make this attractive and tasty dish.

SERVES TWO TO FOUR

INGREDIENTS

- 450g/1lb cod fillet, or any other firm, white fish
- 7.5ml/1½ tsp ground cumin
- 10ml/2 tsp mango powder
- 5ml/1 tsp ground coriander
- 2.5ml/½ tsp chilli powder
- 5ml/1 tsp salt
- 5ml/1 tsp ginger pulp
- 45ml/3 tbsp cornflour (cornstarch)
- 150ml/¼ pint/⅔ cup corn oil
- 3 coloured (bell) peppers, seeded and chopped
- 8–10 cherry tomatoes

1 Skin the fish fillet, remove any pin bones and cut the flesh into small cubes. Put the fish cubes into a large mixing bowl and add the ground cumin, mango powder, ground coriander, chilli powder, salt, ginger pulp and cornflour. Mix together thoroughly, using two spoons or your hands, until the fish is thoroughly coated in the spice mixture.

2 Heat the oil in a preheated wok, karahi or large heavy frying pan. Lower the heat and add the fish pieces, three or four at a time. Cook, turning and moving them constantly, for about 3 minutes.

3 Remove the fish from the pan with a slotted spoon and drain well on kitchen paper. Transfer to a serving dish and keep warm while you cook the remaining fish pieces.

4 Add the peppers to the wok, karahi or frying pan and cook for 2 minutes. They should still be slightly crisp. Drain on kitchen paper.

5 Add the peppers to the serving dish and garnish with the cherry tomatoes. Serve immediately.

CHINESE-SPICED FISH FILLETS

SERVES FOUR

INGREDIENTS

- 65g/2½oz/generous ½ cup plain (all-purpose) flour
- 5ml/1 tsp Chinese five-spice powder
- 1 egg, lightly beaten
- 40–50g/1½–2oz/¾–1 cup fine, fresh breadcrumbs
- 8 skinned fish fillets, such as plaice, flounder or lemon sole, about 800g/1¾lb in total
- groundnut (peanut) oil, for frying
- 25g/1oz/2 tbsp butter
- 4 spring onions (scallions)
- 350g/12oz tomatoes
- 30ml/2 tbsp soy sauce
- salt and ground black pepper
- chives and strips of red (bell) pepper, to garnish

1 Sift the flour together with the Chinese five-spice powder and salt and pepper to taste on to a large plate. Place the beaten egg and breadcrumbs on separate plates. Dip the fish fillets first in the seasoned flour, then in the beaten egg, and finally in the breadcrumbs.

2 Pour the oil into a large, heavy frying pan to a depth of 1cm/½in. Heat until it is very hot and starting to sizzle. Add the coated fish fillets, a few at a time, and cook for about 2–3 minutes, according to the thickness of the fillets, until just cooked and golden brown on both sides. Do not crowd the pan or the temperature of the oil will drop and this will allow the fish to absorb too much oil.

3 Drain the fish fillets on kitchen paper, then transfer to four warm serving plates, cover and keep warm. Pour off all the oil from the frying pan and wipe it out with kitchen paper.

4 Thinly slice the spring onions diagonally, and seed and dice the tomatoes.

5 Melt the butter in the pan over a low to medium heat. Add the spring onions and tomatoes and stir-fry for 1 minute, until the spring onions are translucent. Stir in the soy sauce.

6 Spoon the tomato mixture over the fish and serve immediately, garnished with the chives and pepper strips.

Fisherman's Stew

A chunky, hearty stew that is warming in winter. The stock used here is especially aromatic, but if you do not have time to prepare it, use a basic fish stock instead.

SERVES FOUR

INGREDIENTS

- 6 streaky (fatty) bacon rashers (strips), rinded and cut into thin strips
- 15g/½oz/1 tbsp butter
- 1 large onion, chopped
- 1 garlic clove, finely chopped
- 30ml/2 tbsp chopped fresh parsley
- 5ml/1 tsp fresh thyme leaves or 2.5ml/½ tsp dried thyme
- 450g/1lb tomatoes, peeled, seeded and chopped
- 150ml/¼ pint/⅔ cup dry vermouth or white wine
- 275g/10oz potatoes, diced
- 675–900g/1½–2lb skinless white fish fillets, cut into large chunks
- salt and ground black pepper
- fresh flat leaf parsley sprig, to garnish

For the stock

- 225g/8oz white fish trimmings, including heads and bones
- 25g/1oz/2 tbsp butter
- 1 shallot, finely chopped
- 1 leek, white part only, finely chopped
- 25g/1oz/generous ⅓ cup finely chopped mushrooms
- 50ml/2fl oz/¼ cup dry white wine
- 600ml/1 pint/2½ cups water
- bouquet garni, consisting of 1 thyme sprig, 2 parsley sprigs and 1 bay leaf
- small strip of dried orange rind

1 First make the stock. Remove and discard the gills from any fish heads. Put the fish trimmings in a large bowl, cover with cold water and set aside for 1–2 hours, then drain and chop into small pieces.

2 Melt the butter in a heavy pan, add the chopped shallot, leek and mushrooms and cook gently over a low heat for 2–3 minutes, or until softened but not browned. Stir in the fish trimmings.

3 Add the wine, increase the heat to high and bring to the boil. Boil until reduced by about half, then add the water and bring back to the boil.

4 Skim off any foam from the surface, add the bouquet garni and orange rind, lower the heat and simmer gently for 25 minutes.

5 Strain the stock and set aside. Discard the vegetables, bouquet garni and orange peel.

6 Dry-fry the bacon in a large pan over a medium heat until lightly browned but not crisp, then remove the bacon and drain thoroughly on kitchen paper.

7 Add the butter to the pan and gently cook the onion over a low heat, stirring occasionally, for about 3–5 minutes, or until soft. Add the garlic, parsley and thyme and cook for 1 minute more, stirring constantly.

8 Add the tomatoes, vermouth or white wine and the strained fish stock and bring to the boil.

9 Reduce the heat to very low, cover and simmer the stew gently for about 15 minutes. Add the potatoes, cover the pan again and simmer for a further 10–12 minutes, or until they are almost tender.

10 Add the chunks of fish and the bacon to the pan. Simmer gently, uncovered, for 5 minutes, or until the fish is just cooked and the potatoes are completely tender. Taste and adjust the seasoning, if necessary. Transfer to a warmed tureen, garnish with the parsley and serve the stew immediately.

COOK'S TIP

It is worth taking the trouble to make fish stock. Fish trimmings are usually very cheap and sometimes even free, but do make sure that they are fresh. It is best to avoid oily fish, such as mackerel or sardines, but virtually all types of white fish are suitable. Remove any roe and gills before cooking, as these will make the stock bitter. Fish heads, in particular, yield the greatest flavour and nutritional content and bones are also useful. Do not overlook the value of prawn (shrimp) shells and heads, which, used on their own, make an aromatic and flavoursome stock for poaching shellfish. They add a surprising amount of strength to a basic white fish stock, too. Try experimenting with different types of fish; there is surprising variation in the flavour and body produced. The preparation and cooking take little time and it is worth bearing in mind that fish stock does not benefit from prolonged cooking, which will result in a bitter taste.

Seafood Stew

"Soups" – really stews – of mixed fish and shellfish are specialities in the cuisines of all Mediterranean countries.

SERVES SIX TO EIGHT

INGREDIENTS

- 45ml/3 tbsp olive oil
- 1 medium onion, sliced
- 1 carrot, sliced
- ½ celery stick, sliced
- 2 garlic cloves, chopped
- 400g/14oz can plum tomatoes, chopped, with their juice
- 1 litre/1¾ pints/4 cups water
- 225g/8oz raw prawns (shrimp), peeled and deveined (shells reserved)
- 450g/1lb white fish bones and heads, gills removed
- 1 bay leaf
- 1 fresh thyme sprig, or 1.5ml/¼ tsp dried thyme leaves
- 4 black peppercorns
- 675g/1½lb fresh mussels, scrubbed and bearded
- 450g/1lb fresh small clams, scrubbed
- 250ml/8fl oz/1 cup white wine
- 1kg/2¼lb mixed fish fillets, such as cod, monkfish, red mullet, red snapper or hake, cut into chunks
- 45ml/3 tbsp finely chopped fresh parsley
- salt and ground black pepper
- rounds of French bread, toasted, to serve

1 Heat the oil in a medium pan. Add the onion and cook over a low heat, stirring occasionally, for about 5 minutes, until soft but not coloured. Stir in the carrot and celery and cook for a further 5 minutes.

2 Add the garlic, tomatoes and their can juice and 250ml/8fl oz/1 cup of the measured water. Cook over a medium heat for about 15 minutes, until the vegetables are soft.

3 Process in a food processor or pass through a food mill. Set aside.

4 Place the prawn shells in a large pan with the fish bones and heads. Add the bay leaf, thyme, peppercorns and remaining measured water. Bring to the boil and simmer gently for 25 minutes, skimming off any scum that rises to the surface.

5 Strain the stock into a clean pan and add the tomato sauce. Season to taste with salt and pepper. Discard the contents of the strainer.

6 Place the mussels and clams in a large pan with the wine. Cover tightly and steam over a high heat, shaking the pan occasionally, until all the shells have opened. Discard any shellfish that have not opened after about 5 minutes.

7 Using a slotted spoon, lift the clams and mussels out of the pan and set aside. Strain the cooking liquid through a layer of kitchen paper or a sieve lined with muslin (cheesecloth) and add it to the stock and tomato sauce mixture. Taste and adjust the seasoning, if necessary.

8 Bring the sauce to the boil. Add the fish and cook for 5 minutes. Stir in the mussels and clams and cook for a further 2–3 minutes.

9 Carefully transfer the stew to a large, warmed tureen or ladle it into individual bowls. Sprinkle with the chopped parsley to garnish and serve immediately with the toasted rounds of French bread.

ITALIAN FISH STEW

ITALIANS ARE RENOWNED FOR ENJOYING GOOD FOOD, ESPECIALLY IF IT IS SHARED WITH A LARGE, EXTENDED FAMILY. THIS STEW IS A VERITABLE FEAST OF FISH AND SHELLFISH IN A DELICIOUS TOMATO BROTH, BUT THE QUANTITIES WILL SUIT A SMALLER FAMILY.

SERVES FOUR

INGREDIENTS

- 30ml/2 tbsp olive oil
- 1 onion, thinly sliced
- a few saffron threads
- 5ml/1 tsp dried thyme
- large pinch of cayenne pepper
- 2 garlic cloves, finely chopped
- 2 x 400g/14oz cans tomatoes, drained and chopped
- 175ml/6fl oz/¾ cup dry white wine
- 2 litres/3¼ pints/8 cups hot fish stock
- 350g/12oz white fish fillets, such as cod, haddock or hake, skinned and cut into pieces
- 450g/1lb monkfish, membrane removed, cut into pieces
- 450g/1lb fresh mussels, scrubbed and bearded
- 225g/8oz small squid, cleaned and cut into rings
- 30ml/2 tbsp chopped fresh basil or parsley
- salt and ground black pepper
- thickly sliced rustic bread, to serve

1 Heat the oil in a large, heavy pan or flameproof casserole. Add the onion, saffron, thyme, cayenne pepper and salt to taste. Stir well and cook over a low heat, stirring occasionally, for about 8–10 minutes, until the onion is soft. Add the garlic and cook for 1 minute more.

2 Stir in the tomatoes, white wine and hot fish stock. Bring to the boil and boil for 1 minute, then reduce the heat and simmer gently for 15 minutes.

3 Add the white fish fillet and monkfish pieces to the pan and simmer gently over a low heat for a further 3 minutes.

4 Add the mussels and squid rings and simmer for about 2 minutes, until the mussels open. Discard any that remain closed.

5 Stir in the basil or parsley and season to taste. Ladle into warmed soup bowls and serve with bread.

Crab and Corn Gumbo

Gumbos are traditional Creole dishes, which come from New Orleans.

SERVES FOUR

INGREDIENTS

- 25g/1oz/2 tbsp butter or margarine
- 25g/1oz/¼ cup plain (all-purpose) flour
- 15ml/1 tbsp vegetable oil
- 1 onion, finely chopped
- 115g/4oz okra, trimmed and chopped
- 2 garlic cloves, crushed
- 15ml/1 tbsp finely chopped celery
- 600ml/1 pint/2½ cups fish stock
- 150ml/¼ pint/⅔ cup sherry
- 15ml/1 tbsp tomato ketchup
- 2.5ml/½ tsp dried oregano
- 1.5ml/¼ tsp mixed (apple pie) spice
- 10ml/2 tsp Worcestershire sauce
- 2 corn cobs, sliced
- 450g/1lb crab claws
- cayenne pepper
- fresh coriander (cilantro), to garnish

1 Melt the butter or margarine in a large, heavy pan over a low heat. Add the flour and stir together to make a roux. Cook very gently for about 10 minutes, stirring constantly to prevent the flour from burning, while the roux turns golden brown and then darkens to a rich, nutty brown. Turn the roux on to a plate and set aside.

COOK'S TIP

If black specks appear when you are cooking the roux, you will have to discard it and start again.

2 Heat the vegetable oil in the same pan over a medium heat. Add the onion, okra, garlic and celery and stir well to mix together. Cook for a few minutes, stirring occasionally, then add the fish stock, sherry, tomato ketchup, oregano, mixed spice and Worcestershire sauce. Season with cayenne pepper to taste.

3 Bring to the boil, then lower the heat and simmer gently for about 10 minutes, until the vegetables are cooked through and tender.

4 Add the roux, stirring it well into the sauce, and cook for a few minutes, until thickened.

5 Add the corn cobs and crab claws and continue to simmer gently over a low heat for about 10 minutes, until the crab and corn are cooked.

6 Ladle the gumbo on to four warmed serving plates and garnish with sprigs of fresh coriander. Serve immediately.

VARIATION

Other fish and shellfish, as well as chicken, are traditional ingredients. Try crawfish (rock lobster) for a treat.

Tanzanian Fish Curry

A deliciously fragrant sauce full of tender fish.

SERVES TWO TO THREE

INGREDIENTS

- 1 large snapper or red bream
- 1 lemon
- 45ml/3 tbsp vegetable oil
- 1 onion, finely chopped
- 2 garlic cloves, crushed
- 45ml/3 tbsp curry powder
- 400g/14oz can chopped tomatoes
- 20ml/4 tsp smooth peanut butter
- ½ green (bell) pepper, seeded and chopped
- 2 slices fresh root ginger
- 1 fresh green chilli, seeded and finely chopped
- about 600ml/1 pint/2½ cups fish stock
- 15ml/1 tbsp finely chopped fresh coriander (cilantro)
- salt and ground black pepper

1 Season the fish inside and out with salt and pepper and place in a shallow dish. Halve the lemon and squeeze the juice all over the fish. Cover loosely with clear film (plastic wrap) and set aside in a cool place to marinate for at least 2 hours.

2 Heat the oil in a large pan. Add the onion and garlic and cook over a medium heat, stirring occasionally, for about 5–6 minutes, until soft. Reduce the heat to low, add the curry powder and cook, stirring constantly, for a further 5 minutes.

3 Stir in the tomatoes and then add the peanut butter, mixing well. Add the green pepper, ginger, chilli and stock. Stir well and simmer gently for 10 minutes.

4 Cut the fish into pieces and gently lower them into the sauce. Simmer for a further 20 minutes, or until the fish is cooked and tender. Using a slotted spoon, transfer the fish pieces to a plate.

5 Stir the chopped coriander into the sauce, then taste and adjust the seasoning, if necessary. If the sauce is very thick, add a little extra fish stock or water.

6 Return the fish pieces to the sauce and cook gently to heat through. Ladle on to warmed plates or into bowls and serve immediately.

COOK'S TIP

The fish can be fried before it is added to the sauce, if you like. Dip it in seasoned flour and fry in oil in a large frying pan or a wok for a few minutes before adding to the sauce.

Pineapple Curry with Prawns and Mussels

The delicate sweet and sour flavour of this curry comes from the pineapple and although it seems an odd combination, it is absolutely delicious. Use the freshest shellfish that you can find.

SERVES FOUR TO SIX

INGREDIENTS

- 600ml/1 pint/2½ cups coconut milk
- 30ml/2 tbsp red curry paste
- 30ml/2 tbsp fish sauce
- 15ml/1 tbsp granulated sugar
- 225g/8oz raw king prawns (jumbo shrimp), peeled and deveined
- 450g/1lb fresh mussels, scrubbed and bearded
- 175g/6oz fresh pineapple, finely crushed or chopped
- 5 kaffir lime leaves, torn
- 2 fresh red chillies, seeded and chopped, and coriander (cilantro) leaves, to garnish

1 Pour half the coconut milk into a large, heavy pan and bring to the boil. Heat, stirring constantly, until it separates.

2 Stir in the red curry paste and cook until fragrant. Add the fish sauce and sugar and continue to cook, stirring, for a few moments.

3 Stir in the remaining coconut milk and bring the mixture back to the boil over a medium heat. Add the king prawns, mussels, pineapple and kaffir lime leaves.

4 Reheat until boiling and then simmer for 3–5 minutes, until the prawns are cooked and the mussels have opened. Remove any mussels that have not opened and discard. Serve the curry immediately, garnished with chopped red chillies and coriander leaves.

COOK'S TIP

Red curry paste is so called because it is made from red chillies. It's not difficult to make, especially if you use a food processor, but is also widely available from supermarkets and Asian food stores. Commercial brands are, generally speaking, very good.

Curried Prawns in Coconut Milk

A curry-like dish where the prawns are cooked in a spicy coconut gravy.

SERVES FOUR TO SIX

INGREDIENTS

- 600ml/1 pint/2½ cups coconut milk
- 30ml/2 tbsp yellow curry paste
- 15ml/1 tbsp fish sauce
- 2.5ml/½ tsp salt
- 5ml/1 tsp granulated sugar
- 450g/1lb raw king prawns (jumbo shrimp), peeled and deveined
- 225g/8oz cherry tomatoes
- juice of ½ lime
- red chilli strips and coriander (cilantro) leaves, to garnish

1 Bring half the coconut milk to the boil in a large pan. Add the yellow curry paste, stir until it disperses, then lower the heat and simmer for about 10 minutes.

2 Add the fish sauce, salt, sugar and remaining coconut milk. Simmer for a further 5 minutes.

COOK'S TIP

To make yellow curry paste, process together 6–8 seeded yellow chillies, 1 chopped lemon grass stalk, 4 shallots, 4 garlic cloves, 15ml/1 tbsp chopped fresh root ginger, 5ml/1 tsp coriander seeds, 5ml/1 tsp mustard powder, 5ml/1 tsp salt, 2.5ml/½ tsp ground cinnamon, 15ml/1 tbsp light brown sugar and 30ml/2 tbsp groundnut (peanut) oil.

3 Add the prawns and cherry tomatoes. Simmer very gently for about 5 minutes, until the prawns are pink and tender.

4 Transfer to a warm serving dish. Sprinkle with lime juice, garnish with chillies and coriander leaves and serve immediately.

Green Curry of Prawns

A popular, fragrant, creamy curry that takes very little time to prepare and cook.

SERVES FOUR TO SIX

INGREDIENTS

- 30ml/2 tbsp vegetable oil
- 30ml/2 tbsp green curry paste
- 450g/1lb raw king prawns (jumbo shrimp), peeled and deveined
- 4 kaffir lime leaves, torn
- 1 lemon grass stalk, bruised and chopped
- 250ml/8fl oz/1 cup coconut milk
- 30ml/2 tbsp fish sauce
- ½ cucumber, seeded and cut into thin batons
- 10–15 fresh basil leaves
- 4 green chillies, sliced, to garnish

1 Heat the oil in a frying pan. Add the green curry paste and stir-fry until bubbling and fragrant.

COOK'S TIP

Leftover home-made curry paste should be spooned into a screw-top jar and stored in the refrigerator. Commercial curry paste should also be stored in the refrigerator after opening.

2 Add the prawns, kaffir lime leaves and lemon grass. Stir-fry for about 1–2 minutes, until the prawns have just turned pink.

3 Stir in the coconut milk and bring to a gentle boil. Simmer over a low heat, stirring occasionally, for about 5 minutes, or until the prawns are tender. Do not overcook them or they will become tough.

4 Stir in the fish sauce, cucumber and basil, then top with the green chillies and serve immediately.

Green Fish Curry

This is a richly aromatic dish.

SERVES FOUR

INGREDIENTS

- 1.5ml/¼ tsp ground turmeric
- 30ml/2 tbsp lime juice
- 4 cod fillets, skinned and cut into 5cm/2in chunks
- 1 onion, chopped
- 1 fresh large green chilli, seeded and coarsely chopped
- 1 garlic clove, crushed
- 25g/1oz/¼ cup cashew nuts
- 2.5ml/½ tsp fennel seeds
- 30ml/2 tbsp desiccated (dry unsweetened shredded) coconut
- 30ml/2 tbsp oil
- 1.5ml/¼ tsp cumin seeds
- 1.5ml/¼ tsp ground coriander
- 1.5ml/¼ tsp ground cumin
- 150ml/¼ pint/⅔ cup water
- 175ml/6fl oz/¾ cup single (light) cream
- 45ml/3 tbsp finely chopped fresh coriander (cilantro)
- salt
- fresh coriander (cilantro) sprig, to garnish
- vegetable pilau, to serve (optional)

1 Mix together the turmeric, lime juice and a pinch of salt and rub over the fish. Cover and leave to marinate for 15 minutes.

2 Meanwhile, process the onion, chilli, garlic, cashew nuts, fennel seeds and coconut to a paste in a food processor or pound in a mortar with a pestle. Spoon the paste into a bowl and set aside.

3 Heat the oil in a large frying pan and fry the cumin seeds over a low heat, stirring constantly, for about 2 minutes, until they begin to splutter and give off their fragrance. Add the spice paste and stir-fry for 5 minutes, then stir in the ground coriander, cumin and measured water. Cook, stirring frequently, for a further 2–3 minutes.

4 Add the cream and the chopped coriander. Simmer for 5 minutes. Add the fish and gently stir in. Cover and cook gently for 10 minutes, until the fish is tender. Garnish with coriander and serve immediately, with vegetable pilau if you like.

Hoki Curry with Herbs

Hoki is an ideal firm-fleshed fish to use for this delicious curry, which gains its rich colour from a mixture of fresh herbs; try other exotics, such as mahi mahi or swordfish, or humbler fish, such as coley. Serve it with basmati or Thai fragrant rice and lime wedges.

SERVES FOUR

INGREDIENTS

- 4 garlic cloves, coarsely chopped
- 5cm/2in piece fresh root ginger, peeled and coarsely chopped
- 2 fresh green chillies, seeded and coarsely chopped
- grated rind and juice of 1 lime
- 5–10ml/1–2 tsp shrimp paste (optional)
- 5ml/1 tsp coriander seeds
- 5ml/1 tsp Chinese five-spice powder
- 75ml/5 tbsp sesame oil
- 2 red onions, finely chopped
- 900g/2lb hoki fillets, skinned
- 400ml/14fl oz/1⅔ cups coconut milk
- 45ml/3 tbsp Thai fish sauce
- 50g/2oz/1 cup fresh coriander (cilantro) leaves
- 50g/2oz/1 cup fresh mint leaves
- 50g/2oz/1 cup fresh basil leaves
- 6 spring onions (scallions), chopped
- 150ml/¼ pint/⅔ cup sunflower or groundnut (peanut) oil
- sliced fresh green chilli and chopped fresh coriander (cilantro), to garnish
- cooked basmati or Thai fragrant rice and lime wedges, to serve

1 First make the curry paste. Combine the garlic, fresh root ginger, green chillies, the lime juice and shrimp paste, if using, in a food processor. Add the coriander seeds and five-spice powder, with half the sesame oil. Process to a fine paste, then set aside until required.

2 Heat a wok or large shallow pan and pour in the remaining sesame oil. When it is hot, stir-fry the red onions over a high heat for 2 minutes. Add the fish and stir-fry for 1–2 minutes to seal the fillets on all sides.

3 Lift out the red onions and fish and put them on a plate. Add the curry paste to the wok or pan and fry for 1 minute, stirring. Return the hoki fillets and red onions to the wok or pan, pour in the coconut milk and bring to the boil. Lower the heat, add the fish sauce and simmer for 5–7 minutes, until the fish is cooked through.

4 Meanwhile, process the herbs, spring onions, lime rind and oil in a food processor to a coarse paste. Stir into the fish curry. Garnish with chilli and coriander and serve with rice and lime wedges.

FISH PIE

FISH PIE CAN BE VARIED TO SUIT YOUR TASTE AND POCKET. THIS IS A SIMPLE VERSION, BUT YOU COULD ADD PRAWNS OR HARD-BOILED EGGS, OR MIX THE POTATO TOPPING WITH SPRING ONIONS.

SERVES FOUR

INGREDIENTS
- 450g/1lb cod or haddock fillets
- 225g/8oz smoked cod fillets
- 300ml/½ pint/1¼ cups milk
- ½ lemon, sliced
- 1 bay leaf
- 1 fresh thyme sprig
- 4–5 black peppercorns
- 50g/2oz/¼ cup butter
- 25g/1oz/¼ cup plain (all-purpose) flour
- 30ml/2 tbsp chopped fresh parsley
- 5ml/1 tsp anchovy essence (extract)
- 150g/5oz/2 cups shiitake or chestnut mushrooms, sliced
- salt, ground black pepper and cayenne pepper

For the topping
- 450g/1lb potatoes, cooked and mashed with milk
- 50g/2oz/¼ cup butter
- 2 tomatoes, sliced
- 25g/1oz/¼ cup grated Cheddar cheese (optional)

1 Put the fish, skin-side down, in a shallow pan. Add the milk, lemon slices, bay leaf, thyme and peppercorns. Bring to the boil, then lower the heat and poach gently for about 5 minutes, until just cooked. Strain off and reserve the milk. Remove the fish skin and flake the flesh, discarding any bones.

2 Melt half the butter in a small pan, stir in the flour and cook gently for 1 minute. Add the milk and boil, whisking, until smooth and creamy. Stir in the parsley and anchovy essence and season to taste.

3 Heat the remaining butter in a frying pan, add the sliced mushrooms and sauté until tender. Season and add to the flaked fish. Mix the sauce into the fish and stir gently to combine. Transfer the mixture to an ovenproof casserole.

4 Preheat the oven to 200°C/400°F/Gas 6. Beat the mashed potato with the butter until very creamy. Season, then spread the topping evenly over the fish. Fork up the surface and arrange the sliced tomatoes around the edge. Sprinkle the exposed topping with the grated cheese, if using.

5 Bake for 20–25 minutes, until the topping is lightly browned.

VARIATION

Instead of using plain mashed potatoes for the topping, try a mixture of mashed potato and mashed swede (rutabaga) or sweet potato.

Cod, Basil and Tomato with a Potato Thatch

With a green salad, this makes an ideal dish for a substantial lunch or a family supper.

SERVES EIGHT

INGREDIENTS

- 1kg/2¼lb cod fillet
- 1kg/2¼lb smoked cod fillet
- 900ml/1½ pints/3¾ cups milk
- 1.2 litres/2 pints/5 cups water
- 2 fresh basil sprigs
- 1 lemon thyme sprig
- 165g/5½oz/scant ¾ cup butter
- 1 onion, chopped
- 75g/3oz/⅔ cup plain (all-purpose) flour
- 30ml/2 tbsp tomato purée (paste)
- 30ml/2 tbsp chopped fresh basil
- 12 medium potatoes
- salt and ground black pepper
- 15ml/1 tbsp chopped parsley, to serve

1 Place the cod fillet and smoked cod fillet in a roasting pan with 600ml/1 pint/2½ cups of the milk, the water, basil sprigs and lemon thyme sprig. Bring just to the boil, then simmer over a low heat for about 3–4 minutes.

2 Remove the pan from the heat and leave to cool in the cooking liquid for about 20 minutes. Drain the fish, reserving the liquid for use in the sauce. Flake the fish, taking care to remove any skin and bones.

3 Melt 75g/3oz/6 tbsp of the butter in a large, heavy pan, add the onion and cook over a low heat, stirring occasionally, for about 5 minutes, until softened but not browned.

4 Add the flour, tomato purée and half the chopped basil and cook, stirring constantly, for 1 minute. Gradually stir in the reserved fish cooking liquid, adding a little more milk, if necessary, to make a fairly thin sauce. Bring to the boil, stirring constantly, then season to taste with salt and pepper, and add the remaining chopped basil. Add the fish carefully and stir gently. Transfer the mixture to an ovenproof dish.

5 Cook the potatoes in lightly salted, boiling water for 20–25 minutes, until tender. Meanwhile, preheat the oven to 180°C/350°F/Gas 4. Drain the potatoes, return to the pan, then add the remaining butter and milk and mash well. Season with salt and pepper to taste and spread over the fish mixture, forking to create a pattern. Bake for 30 minutes. Serve with the chopped parsley.

Creamy Fish and Mushroom Pie

Fish pie is a healthy and hearty dish for a hungry family. Mushrooms help the fish go further.

SERVES FOUR

INGREDIENTS

- 225g/8oz assorted wild and cultivated mushrooms, such as oyster, button (white), chanterelle or St George's mushrooms, trimmed and quartered
- 675g/1½lb cod or haddock fillet, skinned and diced
- 600ml/1 pint/2½ cups boiling milk

For the topping

- 900g/2lb floury (mealy) potatoes, quartered
- 25g/1oz/2 tbsp butter
- 150ml/¼ pint/⅔ cup milk
- freshly grated nutmeg
- salt and ground black pepper

For the sauce

- 50g/2oz/¼ cup unsalted (sweet) butter
- 1 medium onion, chopped
- ½ celery stick, chopped
- 50g/2oz/½ cup plain (all-purpose) flour
- 10ml/2 tsp lemon juice
- 45ml/3 tbsp chopped fresh parsley

1 Preheat the oven to 200°C/400°F/Gas 6 and butter an ovenproof dish. Spread the mushrooms over the base of the dish, add the fish and season with salt and pepper to taste. Pour on the boiling milk, cover the dish with foil and bake for 20 minutes.

2 Using a slotted spoon, transfer the fish and mushrooms to a 1.5 litre/2½ pint/6¼ cup ovenproof dish. Pour the poaching liquid into a jug (pitcher) and set aside.

3 Meanwhile, cook the potatoes in a large pan of lightly salted, boiling water for about 20 minutes, until tender. Drain well, return to the pan and mash with the butter and milk. Season to taste with salt, pepper and grated nutmeg.

4 To make the sauce, melt the butter in a pan over a low heat. Add the onion and celery and cook, stirring occasionally, until soft, but not coloured. Stir in the flour, then remove the pan from the heat.

5 Gradually add the reserved liquid, stirring until it is fully absorbed. Return to the heat and simmer, stirring constantly, until thickened. Add the lemon juice and parsley, season to taste, then pour the sauce over the fish.

6 Top with the mashed potato and return to the oven for 30–40 minutes, until the topping is golden brown. Serve immediately.

VARIATIONS

- Add 2–3 peeled garlic cloves to the pan of potatoes and mash them in when cooked.
- Stir 2–3 finely chopped spring onions (scallions) into the mashed potatoes before topping the pie.

CRUNCHY-TOPPED COD

COLOURFUL AND QUICK TO COOK, THIS IS AN IDEAL DISH FOR WEEKDAY MEALS THAT IS SURE TO PLEASE EVERYONE IN THE FAMILY.

SERVES FOUR

INGREDIENTS

- 4 pieces cod fillet, about 115g/4oz each, skinned
- 2 medium tomatoes, sliced
- 50g/2oz/1 cup fresh wholemeal (whole-wheat) breadcrumbs
- 30ml/2 tbsp chopped fresh parsley
- finely grated rind and juice of ½ lemon
- 5ml/1 tsp sunflower oil
- salt and ground black pepper
- seasonal vegetables, to serve

1 Preheat the oven to 200°C/400°F/ Gas 6. Place the cod fillets in a single layer in a wide, ovenproof dish.

2 Arrange the tomato slices on top. Mix together the breadcrumbs, fresh parsley, lemon rind and juice and the sunflower oil in a bowl. Season with salt and pepper to taste.

VARIATION

For an even easier version of this dish, substitute two 200g/7oz cans tuna for the cod fillets. Drain the fish well before spooning it into an ovenproof dish and adding the topping.

3 Spoon the breadcrumb mixture evenly over the fish, then bake for 15–20 minutes. Serve hot with a selection of seasonal vegetables.

SPECIAL FISH PIE

THIS FISH PIE IS TASTY, HEALTHY AND – BEST OF ALL – VERY EASY TO MAKE.

SERVES FOUR

INGREDIENTS

- 350g/12oz haddock fillet, skinned
- 30ml/2 tbsp cornflour (cornstarch)
- 115g/4oz cooked peeled prawns (shrimp)
- 200g/7oz can corn kernels, drained
- 75g/3oz/¾ cup frozen peas
- 150ml/¼ pint/⅔ cup milk
- 150g/5oz/⅔ cup fromage frais (farmer's cheese)
- 75g/3oz/1½ cups fresh wholemeal (whole-wheat) breadcrumbs
- 40g/1½oz/⅓ cup grated Cheddar cheese
- salt and ground black pepper
- steamed green vegetables, to serve

1 Preheat the oven to 190°C/375°F/ Gas 5. Cut the haddock into bitesize pieces. Toss the pieces of fish in the cornflour to coat evenly.

2 Arrange the fish, prawns, corn and peas in an ovenproof dish. Beat together the milk and fromage frais and season to taste with salt and pepper. Pour into the dish.

3 Mix together the breadcrumbs and grated cheese in a bowl, then spoon evenly over the top of the dish. Bake for 25–30 minutes, or until the topping is golden brown. Serve hot, with steamed green vegetables.

COOK'S TIP

For a more economical version of this pie, omit the prawns (shrimp) and use more haddock fillet.

Salmon and Prawn Tart

This tart is unusual because it is made with raw salmon, which means that the fish stays moist. Cooking it this way gives a lovely succulent result. This versatile dish may be served hot with vegetables or cool with mixed salad leaves and tomato wedges.

SERVES SIX

INGREDIENTS

- 350g/12oz shortcrust pastry, thawed if frozen
- 225g/8oz salmon fillet, skinned
- 225g/8oz/2 cups cooked peeled prawns (shrimp)
- 2 eggs, plus 2 egg yolks
- 150ml/¼ pint/⅔ cup whipping cream
- 200ml/7fl oz/scant 1 cup milk
- 15ml/1 tbsp chopped fresh dill
- salt, ground black pepper and paprika
- lime slices, tomato wedges and fresh dill sprigs, to garnish

VARIATION

For a more economical version of this flan, omit the prawns (shrimp) and use some extra salmon instead, or use a mixture of salmon and white fish.

1 Roll out the pastry on a floured work surface and use it to line a 20cm/8in quiche dish or tin (pan). Prick the base all over and mark the edges with the tines of the fork. It need not be too neat. Chill for about 30 minutes. Meanwhile, preheat the oven to 180°C/350°F/Gas 4. Bake the pastry case (pie shell) for about 30 minutes, until golden brown. Reduce the oven temperature to 160°C/325°F/Gas 3.

2 Cut the salmon into 2cm/¾in cubes. Arrange the salmon and prawns evenly in the pastry case. Dust with paprika.

3 In a bowl, beat together the eggs and yolks, cream, milk and dill and season to taste. Pour over the salmon and prawns. Bake for about 30 minutes, until the filling is just set. Serve hot or at room temperature, garnished with lime slices, tomato wedges and dill.

Coconut Baked Snapper

Adding a couple of fresh red chillies to the marinade gives this dish a really spicy flavour. Serve the baked snapper with plain boiled rice.

SERVES FOUR

INGREDIENTS

- 1 snapper, about 1kg/2¼lb, scaled and cleaned
- 400ml/14fl oz/1⅔ cups coconut milk
- 105ml/7 tbsp dry white wine
- juice of 1 lime
- 45ml/3 tbsp light soy sauce
- 1–2 fresh red chillies, seeded and thinly sliced (optional)
- 60ml/4 tbsp chopped fresh parsley
- 45ml/3 tbsp chopped fresh coriander (cilantro)
- salt and ground black pepper

COOK'S TIP

Any type of snapper or trout can be used for this recipe. If you like, use one small fish per person.

1 Lay the snapper in an ovenproof shallow dish and season with a little salt and plenty of pepper. Mix together the coconut milk, wine, lime juice, soy sauce and chillies, if using. Stir in the herbs and pour over the fish. Cover with clear film (plastic wrap) and marinate in the refrigerator for about 4 hours, turning the fish over halfway through.

2 Preheat the oven to 190°C/375°F/Gas 5. Take the fish out of the marinade and wrap loosely in foil, spooning over the marinade before sealing the parcel. Support the fish on a clean dish and bake for 30–40 minutes, until the flesh comes away easily from the bone.

GOLDEN FISH PIE

CRISP FILO PASTRY TOPS A CREAMY FISH FILLING.

SERVES FOUR TO SIX

INGREDIENTS

- 675g/1½lb white fish fillets
- 300ml/½ pint/1¼ cups milk
- 2 slices onion
- 2 bay leaves
- 6 black peppercorns
- 115g/4oz cooked peeled prawns (shrimp), thawed if frozen
- 115g/4oz/½ cup butter
- 50g/2oz/½ cup plain (all-purpose) flour
- 300ml/½ pint/1¼ cups single (light) cream
- 75g/3oz/¾ cup grated Gruyère cheese
- 1 bunch watercress, chopped
- 5ml/1 tsp Dijon mustard
- 5 sheets filo pastry
- salt and ground black pepper

1 Place the fish fillets in a large pan, pour over the milk and add the onion slices, bay leaves and peppercorns. Bring just to the boil, then lower the heat, cover and simmer gently for about 10–12 minutes, until the fish is almost tender.

2 Remove the fish from the pan with a slotted spoon. Skin and remove any bones, then coarsely flake the flesh into a shallow ovenproof dish. Sprinkle the peeled prawns over the fish. Strain the cooking liquid into a jug (pitcher) and reserve.

3 Melt 50g/2oz/¼ cup of the butter in a small pan over a low heat. Stir in the flour and cook, stirring constantly, for 1 minute. Remove the pan from the heat and gradually stir in the reserved cooking liquid and the cream. Return the pan to the heat and bring to the boil, stirring, then simmer for 2–3 minutes, until the sauce has thickened.

4 Remove the pan from the heat and stir in the grated Gruyère, watercress and mustard and season to taste with salt and pepper. Pour the sauce over the fish and set aside to cool.

5 Preheat the oven to 190°C/375°F/ Gas 5. Melt the remaining butter in a small pan over a low heat. Brush one sheet of filo pastry with a little melted butter, then crumple up loosely and place on top of the filling. Repeat with the remaining filo sheets and butter until they are all used up and the pie is completely covered.

6 Bake the pie for 25–30 minutes, until the pastry is golden and crisp. Serve immediately.

COD WITH LENTILS AND LEEKS

This unusual dish, which originated in a Parisian charcuterie, is sure to please everyone. You can cook the vegetables ahead of time, if you like.

SERVES FOUR

INGREDIENTS

- 150g/5oz/⅔ cup green lentils
- 1 bay leaf
- 1 garlic clove, finely chopped
- grated rind of 1 orange
- grated rind of 1 lemon
- pinch of ground cumin
- 15g/½oz/1 tbsp butter
- 450g/1lb leeks, thinly sliced or cut into julienne strips
- 300ml/½ pint/1¼ cups whipping cream
- 15ml/1 tbsp lemon juice
- 800g/1¾lb thick cod or haddock fillets, skinned
- salt and ground black pepper

1 Rinse the lentils and put them in a pan with the bay leaf and garlic. Add enough water to cover by 5cm/2in. Bring to the boil and boil gently for 10 minutes, then reduce the heat and simmer for a further 15–30 minutes, until the lentils are just tender.

2 Drain the lentils and discard the bay leaf, then stir in half the orange rind and all the lemon rind and season with ground cumin and salt and pepper to taste. Transfer the lentils to a shallow ovenproof dish or gratin dish.

3 Melt the butter in a pan over a medium heat, then add the leeks and cook, stirring frequently, for about 5 minutes, until just softened. Add 250ml/8fl oz/1 cup of the cream and the remaining orange rind, lower the heat and cook gently for 15–20 minutes. Stir in the lemon juice and season with salt and plenty of pepper.

4 Preheat the oven to 190°C/375°F/Gas 5. Cut the fish into four pieces and remove any small bones. Season the pieces of fish with salt and pepper, place them on top of the lentil mixture and press down slightly into the lentils.

5 Spoon a quarter of the leek mixture over each piece of fish to cover it and pour 15ml/1 tbsp of the remaining cream over each. Bake for about 30 minutes, until the fish is cooked through and the topping is a light golden brown. Serve hot.

STUFFED FISH

EVERY COMMUNITY IN INDIA PREPARES STUFFED FISH, BUT THE PARSI VERSION MUST RANK TOP OF THE LIST.

SERVES FOUR

INGREDIENTS

- 2 large pomfrets or Dover or lemon sole
- 10ml/2 tsp salt
- juice of 1 lemon
- lime slices, to serve

For the masala

- 120ml/8 tbsp desiccated (dry unsweetened shredded) coconut
- 115g/4oz/2 cups fresh coriander (cilantro)
- 8 fresh green chillies (or to taste)
- 5ml/1 tsp cumin seeds
- 6 garlic cloves
- 10ml/2 tsp caster (superfine) sugar
- 10ml/2 tsp lemon juice

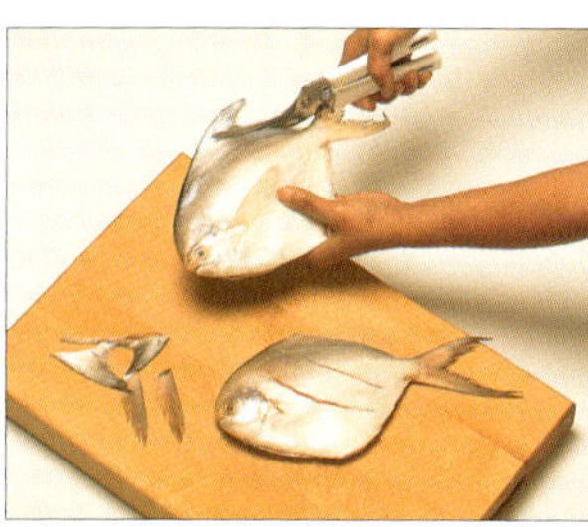

1 Scale the fish and cut off the fins. Gut the fish and remove the heads, if you like. Using a sharp knife, make two diagonal slashes on each side, then pat dry with kitchen paper.

2 Rub the fish inside and out with salt and lemon juice and leave to stand in a cool place for 1 hour. Pat dry thoroughly with kitchen paper.

3 For the masala, grind all the ingredients together using a mortar and pestle or in a food processor. Stuff both the fish with the masala mixture and rub any remaining masala into the gashes and all over the fish on both sides.

4 Place each fish on a separate piece of greased foil. Tightly wrap the foil over each fish. Place in a steamer and steam for 20 minutes or bake in a preheated oven at 200°C/400°F/ Gas 6 for 30 minutes, or until cooked through.

5 Unwrap the fish, transfer to a warm platter and serve immediately with slices of lime.

COOK'S TIP

In India, this fish dish is always steamed wrapped in banana leaves. Banana leaves are available from Indian or Chinese food stores, but vine (grape) leaves may be used instead. When you have wrapped the fish in the banana leaves, secure the parcels by pinning them together with cocktail sticks (toothpicks).

BAKED FISH CREOLE-STYLE

THERE IS NO SHORTAGE OF FISH IN LOUISIANA AND COOKS THERE HAVE A WIDE REPERTOIRE OF WAYS OF COOKING IT.

SERVES FOUR

INGREDIENTS
- 15ml/1 tbsp oil
- 25g/1oz/2 tbsp butter
- 1 onion, thinly sliced
- 1 garlic clove, chopped
- 1 red (bell) pepper, seeded and sliced
- 1 green (bell) pepper, seeded and sliced
- 400g/14oz can chopped tomatoes
- 15ml/1 tbsp tomato purée (paste)
- 30ml/2 tbsp capers, chopped
- 3–4 drops Tabasco sauce
- 4 tail end pieces cod or haddock fillets, about 175g/6oz each, skinned
- 6 basil leaves, shredded
- 45ml/3 tbsp fresh breadcrumbs
- 25g/1oz/¼ cup grated Cheddar cheese
- 10ml/2 tsp chopped fresh parsley
- salt and ground black pepper
- fresh basil sprigs, to garnish

1 Butter an ovenproof dish. Heat the oil and half the butter in a pan and add the onion. Cook over a low heat for about 6–7 minutes, until softened, then add the garlic, red and green peppers, chopped tomatoes, tomato purée, capers and Tabasco sauce and season well. Cover and cook for 15 minutes, then uncover and simmer gently for a further 5 minutes to reduce slightly.

2 Preheat the oven to 230°C/450°F/ Gas 8. Place the fish fillets in the prepared dish, dot with the remaining butter and season lightly with salt and pepper. Spoon the tomato and pepper sauce over the fish and sprinkle with the shredded basil. Bake for about 10 minutes.

3 Meanwhile, mix together the breadcrumbs, grated cheese and parsley in a bowl.

4 Remove the fish from the oven and sprinkle the breadcrumbs and cheese mixture over the top. Return to the oven and bake for a further 10 minutes, until the topping is lightly browned.

5 Let the fish stand for 1 minute, then, using a fish slice or metal spatula, carefully transfer each topped fillet to a warmed serving plate. Garnish with sprigs of fresh basil and serve immediately.

COOK'S TIP

This colourful and spicy sauce is a great way to liven up any plain white fish and it also works well with chicken portions.

Creamy Creole Crab

SERVES SIX

INGREDIENTS

- 2 x 200g/7oz cans crab meat
- 3 hard-boiled eggs, shelled
- 5ml/1 tsp Dijon mustard
- 75g/3oz/6 tbsp butter or margarine
- 1.5ml/¼ tsp cayenne pepper
- 45ml/3 tbsp sherry
- 30ml/2 tbsp chopped fresh parsley
- 120ml/4fl oz/½ cup single (light) or whipping cream
- 2–3 thinly sliced spring onions (scallions), including some of the green parts
- 50g/2oz/scant 1 cup dried white breadcrumbs
- salt and ground black pepper
- fresh chives and flat leaf parsley sprigs, to garnish

1 Preheat the oven to 180°C/350°F/ Gas 4. Drain the cans of crab meat, then, using your fingers, gently flake the crab meat into a medium bowl. Keep the pieces of crab fairly large. Pick out and discard any stray pieces of shell or cartilage.

2 Cut the eggs in half and scoop the yolks into another medium bowl, then crumble them with a fork. Add the mustard, 50g/2oz/¼ cup of the butter or margarine and the cayenne pepper, then mash well together to form a paste. Mix in the sherry and chopped parsley.

3 Chop the egg whites and add them with the cream and spring onions. Mix well. Gently fold in the crab meat and season to taste with salt and pepper.

4 Divide the crab mixture equally among six lightly greased scallop shells or individual ovenproof dishes. Sprinkle with the breadcrumbs and dot with the remaining butter or margarine.

5 Bake for about 20 minutes, until bubbling hot and golden brown. Serve immediately in the shells or dishes, garnished with fresh chives and sprigs of flat leaf parsley.

COOK'S TIP

This dish also works well with frozen crab. Make sure that it is thoroughly thawed first.

CRAB WITH SPRING ONIONS AND GINGER

THIS RECIPE IS FAR LESS COMPLICATED TO MAKE THAN IT FIRST APPEARS.

SERVES FOUR

INGREDIENTS

- 1 large or 2 medium crabs, weighing about 675g/1½lb in total
- 30ml/2 tbsp Chinese rice wine or dry sherry
- 1 egg, lightly beaten
- 15ml/1 tbsp cornflour (cornstarch) paste
- 45–60ml/3–4 tbsp vegetable oil
- 15ml/1 tbsp finely chopped fresh root ginger
- 3–4 spring onions (scallions), cut into short sections
- 30ml/2 tbsp light soy sauce
- 5ml/1 tsp soft light brown sugar
- about 75ml/5 tbsp vegetable or chicken stock
- few drops sesame oil
- shredded spring onion (scallion), to garnish

1 Using a cleaver or heavy knife, cut the crab in half from the underbelly. Break off the claws and crack them with the back of the cleaver or knife. Discard the legs and crack the shell, breaking it into several pieces. Discard the small feathery gills and the sac.

2 Put the crab pieces in a bowl. Mix together the rice wine or sherry, egg and cornflour paste in a jug (pitcher), pour the mixture over the crab and set aside in a cool place to marinate for 10–15 minutes.

3 Heat the oil in a preheated wok or large, heavy frying pan and swirl it around to coat the sides. Add the pieces of crab to the wok or pan, together with the chopped ginger and spring onions, and stir-fry over a medium heat for about 2–3 minutes.

4 Add the soy sauce, sugar and stock and blend well. Bring to the boil, then lower the heat, cover and braise gently for 3–4 minutes. Transfer to a warm platter, sprinkle with sesame oil, garnish with spring onion and serve immediately.

PRAWN SOUFFLÉ

This makes a very elegant lunch dish.

SERVES FOUR TO SIX

INGREDIENTS

- 25g/1oz/2 tbsp butter, plus extra for greasing
- 15ml/1 tbsp dried breadcrumbs
- 175g/6oz cooked peeled prawns (shrimp), deveined and chopped
- 15ml/1 tbsp finely chopped fresh tarragon or parsley
- 45ml/3 tbsp sherry or white wine
- ground black pepper
- lemon slices, whole prawn (shrimp) and flat leaf parsley sprig, to garnish

For the soufflé mixture

- 40g/1½oz/3 tbsp butter
- 37.5ml/2½ tbsp plain (all-purpose) flour
- 250ml/8fl oz/1 cup hot milk
- 4 eggs, separated
- 1 egg white
- salt

1 Preheat the oven to 190°C/375°F/ Gas 5. Butter a 1.5–1.75 litre/ 2½–3 pint/6¼–7½ cup soufflé dish. Sprinkle with the breadcrumbs, tilting the dish to coat the bottom and sides evenly. Shake out any excess.

2 Melt the butter in a small pan over a low heat. Add the chopped prawns and cook, stirring occasionally, for 2–3 minutes.

3 Stir in the chopped tarragon or parsley and sherry or white wine and season to taste with pepper. Cook for a further 1–2 minutes. Increase the heat, bring to the boil, then boil rapidly until the liquid has completely evaporated. Remove the pan from the heat and set aside.

4 To make the soufflé mixture, melt the butter in a heavy pan. Add the flour, blending well with a balloon whisk. Cook over a low heat, stirring constantly, for 2–3 minutes. Remove the pan from the heat and gradually pour in the hot milk, whisking vigorously until smooth. Return to the heat and simmer gently for 2 minutes, still whisking, then season to taste with salt.

5 Remove the pan from the heat and immediately beat in the egg yolks, one at a time, then stir in the cooled prawn mixture.

6 Whisk the egg whites in a large, grease-free bowl until they form stiff peaks. Stir about one-quarter of the egg whites into the prawn mixture to slacken it, then gently fold in the rest of the egg whites.

7 Carefully turn the mixture into the prepared dish. Bake for about 30–40 minutes, until the soufflé is puffed up and light golden brown on top. Serve immediately, with lemon slices, a whole prawn and a parsley sprig garnish.

VARIATIONS

- For lobster soufflé, substitute 1 large lobster tail for the cooked prawns. Chop it finely and add to the pan with the herbs and wine in place of the prawns.
- For crab soufflé, instead of prawns, use about 175g/6oz fresh crab meat or a 200g/7oz can, drained. Flake and pick over carefully to remove any pieces of shell or cartilage.

COOK'S TIPS

- Heating the milk before stirring it into the flour and butter mixture helps to prevent any lumps from forming.
- Resist the temptation to open the oven door before the end of the cooking time. The resulting drop in temperature, together with the current of air, will cause the soufflé to drop.
- You can prepare the soufflé up to the end of step 5 in advance, ready to whisk and add the egg whites.

BAKED MUSSELS AND POTATOES

THIS DISH ORIGINATES FROM PUGLIA IN SOUTHERN ITALY, A REGION NOTED FOR ITS IMAGINATIVE BAKED DISHES.

SERVES TWO TO THREE

INGREDIENTS

- 675g/1½lb large fresh mussels
- 250ml/8fl oz/1 cup water
- 225g/8oz potatoes, unpeeled
- 75ml/5 tbsp olive oil
- 2 garlic cloves, finely chopped
- 8 fresh basil leaves, torn
- 225g/8oz tomatoes, peeled and thinly sliced
- 45ml/3 tbsp breadcrumbs
- salt and ground black pepper

1 Pull off the "beards" and scrub the mussels under cold running water. Discard any with broken shells and ones that do not shut immediately when tapped sharply.

2 Place the mussels with the measured water in a large pan. Cover tightly and cook over high heat, shaking the pan occasionally, for 3–5 minutes, until all the mussels have opened.

3 As soon as they open, lift the mussels out. Remove and discard the empty half shells, leaving the mussels in the other half. (Discard any mussels that do not open.) Strain any liquid in the pan through a layer of kitchen paper and reserve.

4 Cook the potatoes in lightly salted, boiling water until tender but still firm. Drain, peel and slice them.

5 Preheat the oven to 180°C/350°F/ Gas 4. Pour 30ml/2 tbsp of the olive oil into the base of a shallow ovenproof dish and tilt to coat. Cover with the potato slices in a single layer. Add the mussels in their half shells in a single layer. Sprinkle with chopped garlic and pieces of basil.

6 Cover with a layer of the tomato slices. Sprinkle evenly with the breadcrumbs and season well with black pepper. Sprinkle with the reserved mussel cooking liquid and the remaining olive oil. Bake for about 20 minutes, or until the tomatoes are soft and the breadcrumb topping is golden brown. Serve immediately.

Baked Stuffed Sardines

Serve this nutritious dish with a tomato salad.

SERVES FOUR

INGREDIENTS

- 12 fresh sardines, scaled and heads removed
- 15ml/1 tbsp sunflower oil, plus extra for greasing
- 1 onion, finely chopped
- 1 garlic clove, crushed
- 75g/3oz/1½ cups fresh wholemeal (whole-wheat) breadcrumbs
- 15ml/1 tbsp wholegrain mustard
- 30ml/2 tbsp chopped fresh parsley
- 1 egg yolk
- 30ml/2 tbsp grated Parmesan cheese
- grated rind and juice of 2 lemons
- salt and ground black pepper
- lemon wedges and flat leaf parsley, to garnish

1 Preheat the oven to 190°C/375°F/ Gas 5. Using a sharp knife, slit the sardines open along their undersides. Remove and discard the innards. Then turn each fish over so that it is skin side up on a board and press it firmly along the back to loosen the backbone. Carefully remove the backbones and then rinse the inside of each sardine thoroughly under cold running water and pat dry with kitchen paper.

2 Heat the oil in a pan. Add the onion and garlic and cook over a low heat, stirring occasionally, for about 5 minutes, until softened and just beginning to brown.

3 Remove the pan from the heat and stir in the breadcrumbs, mustard, chopped parsley, egg yolk and Parmesan cheese. Stir in half the lemon rind and juice and season to taste with salt and pepper.

4 Use the stuffing to fill the cavities of the sardines.

5 Brush a shallow ovenproof dish lightly with oil and add the sardines, in a single layer. Add the remaining lemon rind and juice, cover with foil and bake for 30 minutes. Garnish with the lemon wedges and fresh parsley sprigs and serve immediately.

COOK'S TIP

Oily fish are a good source of vitamins A and D and are low in saturated fat. Larger oily fish, such as mackerel or herring, could be substituted for the sardines in this recipe. Allow one fish per person.

MEDITERRANEAN BAKED FISH

THIS DISH IS SAID TO HAVE ORIGINATED WITH FRENCH FISHERMEN, WHO WOULD COOK THE REMAINS OF THEIR CATCH FOR LUNCH IN THE STILL-WARM BAKER'S OVEN.

SERVES FOUR

INGREDIENTS

- 3 medium potatoes
- 30ml/2 tbsp olive oil, plus extra for drizzling
- 2 onions, halved and sliced
- 2 garlic cloves, very finely chopped
- 675g/1½lb thick, skinless fish fillets, such as turbot or sea bass
- 1 bay leaf
- 1 fresh thyme sprig
- 3 tomatoes, peeled and sliced
- 30ml/2 tbsp orange juice
- 60ml/4 tbsp dry white wine
- 2.5ml/½ tsp saffron threads, steeped in 60ml/4 tbsp boiling water
- salt and ground black pepper

1 Cook the potatoes in lightly salted, boiling water for 15 minutes, then drain well. Leave to cool slightly, then when the potatoes are cool enough to handle, peel off the skins and slice them thinly.

2 Preheat the oven to 190°C/375°F/ Gas 5.

COOK'S TIP

Both turbot and sea bass have a very delicate flavour, which can easily be destroyed by too rich a sauce or by overcooking.

3 Meanwhile, heat the olive oil in a large, heavy frying pan. Add the onions and cook over a medium-low heat, stirring occasionally, for about 10 minutes. Add the garlic and continue cooking for a few minutes more, until the onions are soft and golden brown.

4 Arrange half the potato slices in the base of a 2 litre/3⅓ pint/8 cup ovenproof dish. Cover with half the onions and garlic. Season with salt and pepper.

5 Place the fish fillets on top of the vegetables and tuck in the herbs between them. Top with the tomato slices and then the remaining onions and potatoes.

6 Pour over the orange juice, white wine and saffron liquid, season with salt and pepper and drizzle a little extra olive oil on top. Bake, uncovered, for about 30 minutes, until the potatoes are tender and the fish is cooked. Discard the bay leaf and thyme sprig and serve immediately.

Baked Cod with Garlic Mayonnaise

This unusual way of preparing cod is adapted from an Italian recipe that uses more typical Mediterranean fish.

SERVES FOUR

INGREDIENTS
- 4 anchovy fillets
- 45ml/3 tbsp chopped fresh parsley
- 90ml/6 tbsp olive oil
- 4 cod fillets, about 675g/1½lb total, skinned
- 40g/1½oz/¾ cup fresh breadcrumbs
- coarsely ground black pepper

For the garlic mayonnaise
- 2 garlic cloves, finely chopped
- 1 egg yolk
- 5ml/1 tsp Dijon mustard
- 175ml/6fl oz/¾ cup vegetable oil
- salt and ground black pepper

1 Preheat the oven to 200°C/400°F/ Gas 6. Make the mayonnaise. First put the garlic in a medium mixing bowl and mash it to a paste with a pestle or the end of a rolling pin. Beat in the egg yolk and mustard. Gradually add the oil, drop by drop to begin with, then in a continuous thin stream, while beating vigorously with a small wire whisk. When the mixture is thick and smooth, season to taste with salt and pepper. Transfer to a serving bowl, cover with clear film (plastic wrap) and keep cool.

2 Chop the anchovy fillets with the parsley very finely. Place in a small bowl and add pepper to taste and 45ml/3 tbsp of the olive oil. Stir well to form a paste.

3 Place the cod fillets in a single layer in an oiled ovenproof dish. Spread the anchovy paste on the top of the cod fillets. Sprinkle with the breadcrumbs and the remaining oil.

4 Bake for 20–25 minutes, or until the fish is cooked through and the breadcrumb topping is golden brown. Carefully transfer the fish to warm plates and serve immediately with the bowl of garlic mayonnaise.

Monkfish Medallions with Thyme

Monkfish has a sweet flesh that combines particularly well with Mediterranean flavours.

SERVES FOUR

INGREDIENTS
- 500g/1¼lb monkfish fillet, preferably in a single piece
- 45ml/3 tbsp extra virgin olive oil
- 75g/3oz/¾ cup small black olives, pitted
- 1 large or 2 small tomatoes, seeded and diced
- leaves from 1 fresh thyme sprig or 5ml/1 tsp dried thyme leaves, plus extra sprigs, to garnish
- salt and ground black pepper
- 15ml/1 tbsp very finely chopped fresh parsley, to garnish

1 Preheat the oven to 200°C/400°F/ Gas 6. Remove the grey membrane from the monkfish, if necessary. Using a sharp knife, cut the fish into slices 1cm/½in thick.

2 Heat a non-stick frying pan until it is quite hot, without adding any oil. Sear the fish slices quickly on both sides, in batches if necessary. Remove and set aside.

3 Pour 15ml/1 tbsp of the olive oil in the base of a shallow ovenproof dish and tilt to coat. Arrange the slices of fish in a single layer. Sprinkle the olives and diced tomato on top of the fish.

4 Sprinkle the fish with thyme, season well with salt and pepper and spoon over the remaining olive oil. Bake, uncovered, for about 10–12 minutes, until the fish is cooked through and tender.

5 Divide the medallions between four warmed plates. Spoon on the vegetables and any cooking juices. Garnish with the chopped parsley and thyme sprigs and serve immediately.

BREADED FISH WITH TARTARE SAUCE

This classic British fish dish is perfect with freshly cooked chips.

SERVES FOUR

INGREDIENTS

- 50g/2oz/scant 1 cup dried breadcrumbs
- 5ml/1 tsp dried oregano
- 2.5ml/½ tsp cayenne pepper
- 250ml/8fl oz/1 cup milk
- 10ml/2 tsp salt
- 4 pieces of cod fillet, about 675g/1½lb
- 40g/1½oz/3 tbsp butter, melted

For the tartare sauce

- 120ml/4fl oz/½ cup mayonnaise
- 2.5ml/½ tsp Dijon mustard
- 1–2 pickled gherkins, chopped
- 15ml/1 tbsp capers, drained and chopped
- 5ml/1 tsp chopped fresh parsley
- 5ml/1 tsp chopped fresh chives
- 5ml/1 tsp chopped fresh tarragon
- salt and ground black pepper

1 Preheat the oven to 230°C/450°F/Gas 8. Grease a shallow ovenproof dish. Combine the breadcrumbs, oregano and cayenne pepper on a plate and blend together. Mix the milk with the salt in a bowl, stirring well to dissolve the salt.

2 Dip the pieces of cod fillet, one at a time, in the milk, then transfer to the plate and coat both sides with the breadcrumb mixture. Pat it into place with your fingers.

3 Arrange the coated fish in the prepared ovenproof dish, in a single layer. Drizzle the melted butter over the fish.

4 Transfer to the oven and bake, uncovered, for about 10–15 minutes, until the fish fillets are cooked and the flesh flakes easily when tested with a fork.

5 Meanwhile, combine all the ingredients for the tartare sauce in a small bowl. Stir gently to mix thoroughly. Place the fish on warm plates and serve immediately, accompanied by the tartare sauce, handed separately.

SMOKED HADDOCK LYONNAISE

LYONNAISE DISHES TAKE THEIR NAME FROM THE FRENCH CITY OF LYON, KNOWN FOR ITS EXCELLENT FOOD.

SERVES FOUR

INGREDIENTS

- 450g/1lb smoked haddock
- 150ml/¼ pint/⅔ cup milk
- 15g/½oz/1 tbsp butter
- 2 onions, chopped
- 15ml/1 tbsp cornflour (cornstarch)
- 150ml/¼ pint/⅔ cup Greek (US strained plain) yogurt
- 5ml/1 tsp ground turmeric
- 5ml/1 tsp paprika
- 115g/4oz/1½ cups mushrooms, sliced
- 2 celery sticks, chopped
- 30ml/2 tbsp olive oil
- 350g/12oz firm cooked potatoes, preferably cold, diced
- 25–50g/1–2oz/½–1 cup soft white breadcrumbs
- salt and ground black pepper
- fresh flat leaf parsley, to garnish

1 Preheat the oven to 190°C/375°F/Gas 5. Put the smoked haddock into a large pan and pour in the milk. Set over a low heat and poach the fish for about 15 minutes, until just cooked. Remove the haddock, reserving the cooking liquid, then flake the fish and discard the skin and any small bones. Set aside.

VARIATION

You can also make this dish with fresh haddock or other white fish fillets, as well as with smoked cod.

2 Melt the butter in a large pan over a low heat. Add half the onions and cook, stirring occasionally, until translucent. Stir in the cornflour, then gradually blend in the fish cooking liquid and the yogurt and cook, stirring, until thickened and smooth.

3 Stir in the turmeric, paprika, mushrooms and celery. Season to taste with salt and pepper and add the flaked fish. Spoon into an ovenproof dish.

4 Heat the olive oil in a large, heavy frying pan. Add the remaining onions and cook over a low heat, stirring occasionally, for about 5 minutes, until translucent. Add the diced potatoes and stir until lightly coated all over in oil. Sprinkle on the breadcrumbs and season to taste with salt and pepper.

5 Spoon this mixture evenly over the fish and bake for 20–30 minutes, until golden. Serve.

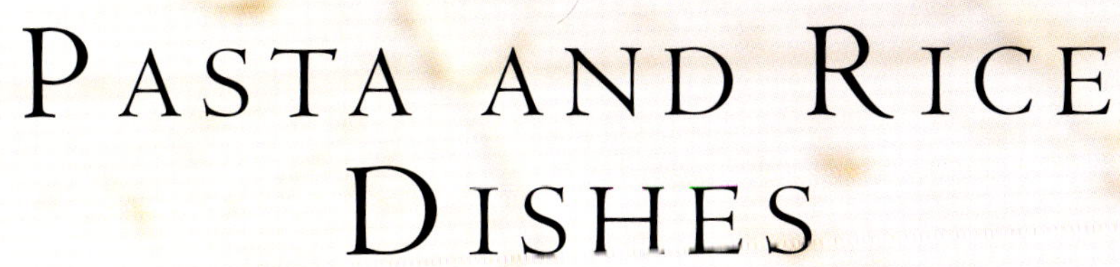

PASTA AND RICE DISHES

Fish and shellfish make perfect partners for pasta and rice, their lightness and freshness balancing the heaviness of the starch. From simple Pappardelle, Sardine and Fennel Bake to the ultra-luxurious Lobster Ravioli, there are pasta dishes to suit every occasion and palate. Risotto appears in two guises – dramatically coloured and flavoured with squid ink, and as a simple version that uses the ready-prepared shellfish that most supermarkets now stock.

PASTA WITH TUNA, CAPERS AND ANCHOVIES

This piquant sauce is also good without tomatoes – just heat the other ingredients in the oil.

SERVES FOUR

INGREDIENTS

- 2 × 200g/7oz cans tuna in oil
- 30ml/2 tbsp olive oil
- 2 garlic cloves, crushed
- 800g/1¾lb canned chopped tomatoes
- 6 canned anchovy fillets, drained
- 30ml/2 tbsp capers in vinegar, drained
- 30ml/2 tbsp chopped fresh basil
- 450g/1lb/4 cups rigatoni, penne or garganelle
- salt and ground black pepper
- fresh basil sprigs, to garnish

1 Drain the oil from the tuna into a heavy pan, add the olive oil and heat gently until it stops "spitting".

COOK'S TIP

Using the oil from the cans of tuna intensifies the flavour of the sauce. If you can only find tuna in brine, drain well and add an extra 15ml/1 tbsp olive oil in step 1. Be careful with the seasoning.

2 Add the garlic and cook over a medium heat until golden. Stir in the tomatoes, with their can juice, lower the heat and simmer for 25 minutes, until thickened.

3 Flake the tuna with a fork and cut the anchovies in half. Stir them both into the sauce with the capers and chopped basil. Season to taste with salt and pepper.

4 Cook the pasta in a large pan of lightly salted, boiling water for about 8–10 minutes, or according to the manufacturer's instructions. Drain well and put it into a warm serving dish. Add the tuna sauce and toss thoroughly, using two large forks. Garnish with fresh basil sprigs and serve immediately.

FARFALLE WITH SMOKED SALMON AND DILL

THIS LUXURIOUS SAUCE FOR PASTA HAS NOW BECOME VERY FASHIONABLE IN ITALY.

SERVES FOUR

INGREDIENTS

- 6 spring onions (scallions)
- 50g/2oz/¼ cup butter
- 90ml/6 tbsp dry white wine
- 450ml/¾ pint/1⅞ cups double (heavy) cream
- freshly grated nutmeg
- 225g/8oz smoked salmon
- 30ml/2 tbsp chopped fresh dill
- freshly squeezed lemon juice
- 450g/1lb/4 cups farfalle
- salt and ground black pepper
- fresh dill sprigs, to garnish

1 Thinly slice the spring onions. Melt the butter in a pan over a low heat. Add the spring onions and cook, stirring occasionally, for about 1 minute, until softened.

2 Add the wine, bring to the boil and boil hard to reduce to about 30ml/2 tbsp. Stir in the cream and add salt, pepper and nutmeg to taste. Bring to the boil and simmer for 2–3 minutes, until slightly thickened.

3 Cut the smoked salmon into 2.5cm/1in squares and stir into the sauce, together with the chopped dill. Stir in a little lemon juice to taste. Keep warm.

4 Cook the pasta in a large pan of lightly salted, boiling water for about 8–10 minutes, until tender. Drain and toss with the sauce. Serve garnished with sprigs of dill.

TAGLIATELLE WITH SMOKED SALMON

This is a pretty pasta sauce that tastes as good as it looks. The light texture of the cucumber perfectly complements the fish. Different effects and colour combinations can be achieved by using green or red tagliatelle – or even a mixture of colours.

SERVES FOUR

INGREDIENTS

- 350g/12oz tagliatelle
- ½ cucumber
- 75g/3oz/6 tbsp butter
- grated rind of 1 orange
- 30ml/2 tbsp chopped fresh dill
- 300ml/½ pint/1¼ cups single (light) cream
- 15ml/1 tbsp orange juice
- 115g/4oz smoked salmon
- salt and ground black pepper

1 If using dried pasta, cook in lightly salted, boiling water following the packet instructions. If using fresh pasta, cook in lightly salted, boiling water for 2–3 minutes, or until just tender but still firm to the bite.

2 Using a sharp knife, cut the cucumber in half lengthways, then using a small spoon scoop out the cucumber seeds and discard.

3 Turn the cucumber on to the flat side and slice it thinly.

4 Melt the butter in a heavy pan. Add the grated orange rind and fresh dill and stir well. Add the cucumber and cook gently over a low heat, stirring occasionally, for about 2 minutes.

5 Add the single cream and orange juice, season to taste with salt and pepper and simmer very gently for 1 minute. Do not allow the mixture to boil or the cream will probably curdle.

6 Meanwhile, cut the salmon into thin strips.

7 Stir the salmon into the sauce and heat through.

8 Drain the pasta thoroughly and put it into a warm serving dish. Add the sauce and toss. Serve immediately.

COOK'S TIPS

- A more economical way to make this special-occasion sauce is to use smoked salmon pieces, sold relatively inexpensively by most delicatessens and some supermarkets. (These are just off-cuts or trimmings and awkwardly shaped pieces that are unsuitable for recipes requiring whole slices of smoked salmon.)
- Smoked trout is a less expensive alternative, but it lacks the rich flavour and colour of smoked salmon.

PASTA WITH PRAWNS AND GREEN DRESSING

SERVES FOUR TO SIX

INGREDIENTS

- 4 anchovy fillets, drained
- 60ml/4 tbsp milk
- 225g/8oz squid
- 15ml/1 tbsp chopped capers
- 15ml/1 tbsp chopped gherkins
- 1–2 garlic cloves, crushed
- 150ml/¼ pint/⅔ cup natural (plain) yogurt
- 30–45ml/2–3 tbsp mayonnaise
- squeeze of lemon juice
- 50g/2oz watercress or arugula (rocket), finely chopped
- 30ml/2 tbsp chopped fresh parsley
- 30ml/2 tbsp chopped fresh basil
- 350g/12oz/3 cups fusilli
- 350g/12oz cooked peeled prawns (shrimp)
- salt and ground black pepper

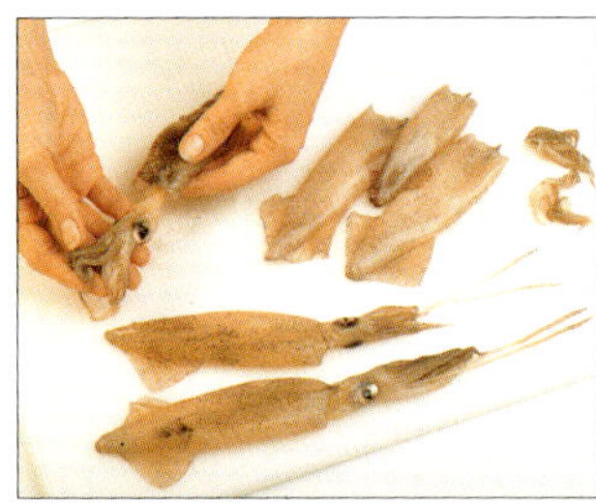

1 Put the anchovies into a small bowl and cover with the milk. Leave to soak for 10 minutes. Meanwhile, pull the heads from the squid and remove and discard the quills. Peel the outer speckled skin from the bodies and rinse well under cold running water. Cut the body sacs into 5mm/¼in rings. Cut the tentacles from the heads, rinse under cold water and cut into 5mm/¼in slices. Discard the squid heads.

2 To make the dressing, mix together the capers, gherkins, garlic, yogurt, mayonnaise, lemon juice, watercress or rocket, parsley and basil in a bowl. Drain and chop the anchovies. Add them to the dressing and season to taste with salt and pepper.

3 Drop the squid rings and tentacles into a large pan of salted, boiling water. Lower the heat and simmer for 1–2 minutes (do not overcook or the squid will become tough). Remove with a slotted spoon.

4 Bring the water back to the boil and add the pasta. Cook the pasta in the boiling water for 8–10 minutes, or according to the instructions on the packet. Drain thoroughly.

5 Mix the prawns and squid into the dressing in a large bowl. Add the pasta, toss and serve immediately. Alternatively, leave to cool and serve as a salad.

COOK'S TIP

Soaking the anchovies in milk reduces their saltiness. However, you should still be careful when seasoning the dressing in step 2.

NOODLES WITH TOMATOES AND PRAWNS

INFLUENCES FROM ITALY AND THE FAR EAST COMBINE IN A DISH WITH A LOVELY TEXTURE AND TASTE.

SERVES FOUR

INGREDIENTS
- 350g/12oz somen noodles
- 45ml/3 tbsp olive oil
- 20 raw king prawns (jumbo shrimp), peeled and deveined
- 2 garlic cloves, finely chopped
- 45–60ml/3–4 tbsp sun-dried tomato paste
- salt and ground black pepper

For the garnish
- handful of basil leaves
- 30ml/2 tbsp sun-dried tomatoes in oil, drained and cut into strips

1 Cook the noodles in a large pan of salted boiling water until tender, following the directions on the packet. Drain well and set aside.

2 Heat half the oil in a wok or large, heavy frying pan. Add the prawns and garlic and cook over a medium heat, stirring frequently, for 3–5 minutes, until the prawns turn pink and are firm to the touch.

3 Stir in 15ml/1 tbsp of the sun-dried tomato paste and mix well. Using a slotted spoon, transfer the prawns to a bowl and keep hot.

4 Reheat the oil remaining in the wok or frying pan. Stir in the rest of the oil with the remaining sun-dried tomato paste. You may need to add a spoonful of water if the mixture is very thick.

5 When the mixture starts to sizzle, toss in the well-drained noodles. Season with salt and pepper to taste and mix well.

6 Return the prawns to the pan and toss to combine. Transfer to warm plates and serve immediately, garnished with the basil and strips of sun-dried tomatoes.

COOK'S TIP

Ready-made sun-dried tomato paste is widely available from supermarkets. However, you can make your own simply by processing bottled sun-dried tomatoes with their oil in a food processor or blender. You could also add a couple of canned or bottled anchovy fillets and a few capers for extra flavour, if you like.

LINGUINE WITH CLAMS

CANNED CLAMS MAKE THIS A SPEEDY SAUCE FOR THOSE IN A REAL HURRY.

SERVES FOUR

INGREDIENTS
- 350g/12oz linguine
- 25g/1oz/2 tbsp butter
- 2 leeks, thinly sliced
- 150ml/¼ pint/⅔ cup dry white wine
- 4 tomatoes, peeled, seeded and chopped
- pinch of ground turmeric (optional)
- 250g/9oz can clams, drained
- 30ml/2 tbsp chopped fresh basil
- 60ml/4 tbsp crème fraîche
- salt and ground black pepper

1 Cook the pasta in a large pan of lightly salted, boiling water for 8–10 minutes, or according to the instructions on the packet.

2 Meanwhile, melt the butter in a small pan. Add the leeks and cook over a low heat, stirring occasionally, for about 5 minutes, until softened, but not coloured.

3 Add the white wine, tomatoes and turmeric, if using. Increase the heat to medium, bring to the boil and continue to boil until the liquid has reduced by about half.

4 Lower the heat, stir in the clams, basil and crème fraîche and season to taste with salt and pepper. Heat through gently, stirring occasionally, without allowing the sauce to come to the boil again.

5 Drain the pasta thoroughly and put it into a warm serving bowl. Add the clam sauce and toss well with two forks until coated. Serve immediately.

MACARONI WITH KING PRAWNS AND HAM

THIS QUICK-AND-EASY RECIPE IS AN IDEAL LUNCH OR SUPPER DISH.

SERVES FOUR

INGREDIENTS
- 350g/12oz/3 cups short macaroni
- 45ml/3 tbsp olive oil
- 12 raw king prawns (jumbo shrimp), peeled and deveined
- 1 garlic clove, chopped
- 175g/6oz smoked ham, diced
- 150ml/¼ pint/⅔ cup red wine
- ½ small head radicchio, shredded
- 2 egg yolks, beaten
- 30ml/2 tbsp chopped fresh flat leaf parsley
- 150ml/¼ pint/⅔ cup double (heavy) cream
- salt and ground black pepper
- shredded fresh basil, to garnish

1 Cook the pasta following the instructions on the packet.

2 Meanwhile, heat the oil in a frying pan. Add the prawns, garlic and ham and cook over a medium heat for about 5 minutes, stirring occasionally, until the prawns are tender and have turned pink.

3 Add the wine and radicchio, bring to the boil and boil rapidly until the liquid has reduced by about half.

4 Stir in the egg yolks, parsley and cream and bring almost to the boil, stirring constantly, then simmer until the sauce thickens slightly. Season to taste with salt and pepper.

5 Drain the pasta thoroughly and put it into a warm serving bowl. Add the prawn and ham sauce and toss thoroughly with two forks to coat. Serve immediately, garnished with shredded fresh basil.

COOK'S TIPS

- Widely thought of as a salad leaf, radicchio features in many cooked Italian dishes, especially in the north. Although it retains its characteristic bitter flavour, unfortunately it loses its lovely red colour.
- Flat leaf parsley has more flavour than the curly variety. Finely chop any leftover parsley and freeze it in a small plastic bag. It is then ready to use for cooking, but not garnishing.

Seafood Spaghetti Parcels

In this recipe, the cooking is finished in a paper parcel. When the parcel is opened, the most wonderful aroma wafts out. To serve as an appetizer, bake in two larger parcels.

SERVES FOUR AS A MAIN COURSE, SIX AS AN APPETIZER

INGREDIENTS

- 500g/1¼lb fresh mussels, scrubbed and bearded
- 500g/1¼lb small clams, scrubbed
- 105ml/7 tbsp dry white wine
- 60ml/4 tbsp olive oil
- 2 fat garlic cloves, chopped
- 2 dried red chillies, crumbled
- 200g/7oz squid, cut into rings
- 200g/7oz raw peeled prawns (shrimp)
- 400g/14oz dried spaghetti
- 30ml/2 tbsp chopped fresh parsley
- 5ml/1 tsp chopped fresh oregano or 2.5ml/½ tsp dried
- salt and ground black pepper

For the tomato sauce

- 30ml/2 tbsp olive oil
- 1 red onion, finely chopped
- 1 garlic clove, finely chopped
- 400g/14oz can chopped tomatoes
- 15ml/1 tbsp tomato purée (paste)
- 15ml/1 tbsp torn fresh basil leaves

1 Make the tomato sauce. Heat the oil in a pan and cook the onion and garlic over a low heat for 5 minutes. Stir in the tomatoes and tomato purée and simmer for 20–30 minutes, stirring occasionally. Season and add the basil.

2 Put the mussels, clams and wine in a large pan and bring to the boil. Put on the lid and shake the pan until all the shells have opened. Discard any that remain closed. Remove most of the mussels and clams from the shells, leaving about a dozen of each in the shell. Strain the juices and set aside.

3 Heat the olive oil in a frying pan, add the garlic and cook until lightly coloured. Add the chillies, then add the squid and prawns and sauté for 2–3 minutes, until the squid is opaque and the prawns have turned pink. Add the shellfish and their reserved juices, then stir in the tomato sauce. Set aside.

4 Preheat the oven to 240°C/475°F/Gas 9 or the grill (broiler) to hot. Cook the spaghetti in a pan of lightly salted, boiling water for about 12 minutes, or until it is just tender. Drain very thoroughly, then return to the clean pan and stir in the shellfish sauce, tossing to coat all the strands of spaghetti. Stir in the parsley and oregano, with some seasoning.

5 Cut out four 25cm/10in square pieces of greaseproof (waxed) paper. Put a quarter of the spaghetti mixture into the middle of one piece and fold up the edges, pleating them to make a secure bag. Seal the sides first, then blow gently into the top to fill the bag with air. Fold over the top to seal. Make another three parcels with the rest of the spaghetti mixture.

6 Place the parcels on a baking sheet and cook in the hot oven or under the grill until the paper is browned and slightly charred at the edges. Transfer the parcels to serving plates and open them at the table so that you can enjoy the wonderful aromas.

PAPPARDELLE, SARDINE AND FENNEL BAKE

PAPPARDELLE ARE WIDE, FLAT NOODLES. THEY ARE PERFECT FOR THIS SICILIAN RECIPE. IF YOU CAN'T FIND THEM, ANY WIDE PASTA, SUCH AS MACCHERONCINI OR BUCATINI, WILL DO INSTEAD. THE DISH IS ALSO DELICIOUS MADE WITH FRESH ANCHOVIES.

SERVES SIX

INGREDIENTS

- 2 fennel bulbs, trimmed
- large pinch of saffron threads
- 12 sardines, backbones and heads removed
- 60ml/4 tbsp olive oil
- 2 shallots, finely chopped
- 2 garlic cloves, finely chopped
- 2 fresh red chillies, seeded and finely chopped
- 4 drained canned anchovy fillets, or 8–12 pitted black olives, chopped
- 30ml/2 tbsp capers
- 75g/3oz/¾ cup pine nuts
- 450g/1lb pappardelle
- butter, for greasing
- 30ml/2 tbsp grated Pecorino cheese
- salt and ground black pepper

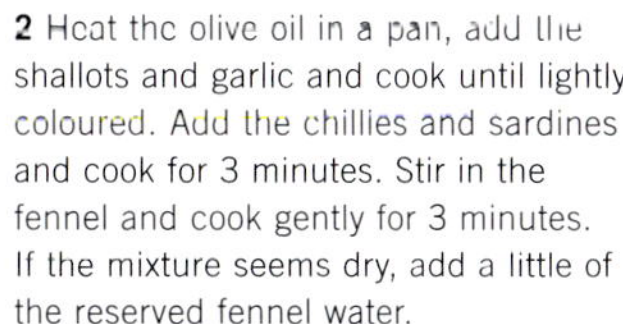

1 Preheat the oven to 200°C/400°F/Gas 6. Cut the fennel bulbs in half and cook them in a pan of lightly salted boiling water with the saffron threads for about 10 minutes, until tender. Drain, reserving the cooking liquid, and cut into small dice. Then finely chop the sardines, season with salt and ground black pepper and set aside until required.

2 Heat the olive oil in a pan, add the shallots and garlic and cook until lightly coloured. Add the chillies and sardines and cook for 3 minutes. Stir in the fennel and cook gently for 3 minutes. If the mixture seems dry, add a little of the reserved fennel water.

3 Add the anchovies or olives and cook for 1 minute; stir in the capers and pine nuts, and season. Simmer for 3 minutes more, then turn off the heat.

4 Meanwhile, pour the reserved fennel liquid into a pan and top it up with enough water to cook the pasta. Stir in a little salt, bring to the boil and add the pappardelle. Cook dried pasta for about 12 minutes; fresh pasta until it rises to the surface of the water. When the pasta is just tender, drain it.

5 Grease a shallow ovenproof dish and put in a layer of pasta, then make a layer of the sardine mixture. Continue until all the pasta and sardine mixture have been used, finishing with the fish. Sprinkle over the Pecorino; bake for 15 minutes, until bubbling and golden.

PASTA WITH SCALLOPS IN GREEN SAUCE

THE STRIKING DISH IS COMPLETELY IRRESISTIBLE.

SERVES FOUR

INGREDIENTS

- 120ml/4fl oz/½ cup crème fraîche
- 10ml/2 tsp wholegrain mustard
- 2 garlic cloves, crushed
- 30–45ml/2–3 tbsp fresh lime juice
- 60ml/4 tbsp chopped fresh parsley
- 30ml/2 tbsp chopped fresh chives
- 350g/12oz black tagliatelle
- 12 large, prepared scallops
- 60ml/4 tbsp white wine
- 150ml/¼ pint/⅔ cup fish stock
- salt and ground black pepper
- lime wedges and fresh parsley sprigs, to garnish

1 To make the green sauce, mix together the crème fraîche, wholegrain mustard, garlic, lime juice to taste, parsley and chives in a bowl. Season to taste with salt and pepper. Cover with clear film (plastic wrap) and set aside in a cool place or in the refrigerator until required.

2 Cook the pasta in a large pan of lightly salted, boiling water for 10–12 minutes, or according to the packet instructions. Drain well.

3 Using a sharp knife, slice the scallops in half horizontally. Keep any corals whole. Put the wine and fish stock into a pan and heat just to simmering point. Add the scallops and cook very gently for 3–4 minutes, until just tender.

4 Remove the scallops with a slotted spoon. Boil the wine and stock vigorously to reduce by half and add the green sauce to the pan. Heat gently to warm through, replace the scallops and cook for 1 minute. Spoon over the pasta and garnish with lime wedges and parsley.

PASTA WITH SCALLOPS IN TOMATO SAUCE

DELICATE AND SIMPLE, THIS PASTA DISH MAKES A GOOD APPETIZER OR MAIN COURSE. USE GOOD QUALITY CANNED PLUM TOMATOES FOR THE MAXIMUM FLAVOUR.

SERVES FOUR

INGREDIENTS
- 450g/1lb long, thin pasta, such as fettucine or linguine
- 30ml/2 tbsp olive oil
- 2 garlic cloves, finely chopped
- 450g/1lb prepared scallops, sliced in half horizontally
- 30ml/2 tbsp chopped fresh basil
- salt and ground black pepper
- fresh basil sprigs, to garnish

For the sauce
- 30ml/2 tbsp olive oil
- ½ onion, finely chopped
- 1 garlic clove, finely chopped
- 2 x 400g/14oz cans tomatoes

1 To make the sauce, heat the oil in a non-stick frying pan. Add the onion, garlic and a pinch of salt, and cook over a low heat, stirring occasionally, for about 5 minutes, until just softened, but not coloured.

2 Add the tomatoes, with their can juice, and crush with a fork. Bring to the boil, then lower the heat and simmer gently for 15 minutes. Remove the pan from the heat and set aside.

3 Bring a large pan of lightly salted water to the boil. Add the pasta and cook for 8–10 minutes, or according to the instructions on the packet.

4 Meanwhile, combine the oil and garlic in another non-stick frying pan and cook for about 30 seconds, until just sizzling. Add the scallops and 2.5ml/½ tsp salt and cook over a high heat for about 3 minutes, tossing, until the scallops are cooked through.

COOK'S TIP

Pasta should always be cooked in boiling, rather than merely simmering water. Bring the water back to the boil after adding the pasta to the pan and start timing its cooking from that moment. Test whether it is cooked by removing a small piece and biting it between your front teeth.

5 Add the scallops to the tomato sauce. Season with salt and pepper to taste, then stir gently, cover and keep warm.

6 Drain the pasta, rinse under hot water and drain again. Add the scallop sauce and the basil and toss thoroughly. Serve immediately, garnished with fresh basil sprigs.

SPAGHETTINI WITH VODKA AND CAVIAR

This is an elegant, yet easy, way to serve spaghettini. In Rome it is a late evening, after-theatre favourite.

SERVES FOUR

INGREDIENTS
- 60ml/4 tbsp olive oil
- 3 spring onions (scallions), thinly sliced
- 1 garlic clove, finely chopped
- 120ml/4fl oz/½ cup vodka
- 150ml/¼ pint/⅔ cup double (heavy) cream
- 150ml/¼ pint/⅔ cup black or red caviar
- 400g/14oz spaghettini
- salt and ground black pepper

COOK'S TIP

The finest caviar is salted sturgeon roe and it is notoriously expensive. Beluga is the most popular variety in Britain while both the Americans and French prefer Oscietra. Red "caviar" comes from salmon or sea trout or may be dyed lumpfish roe. It is much cheaper.

1 Heat the oil in a small frying pan. Add the spring onions and garlic and cook over a low heat, stirring occasionally, for 4–5 minutes, until softened but not coloured.

2 Add the vodka and cream, and cook over a low heat for about 5–8 minutes more.

3 Remove the pan from the heat and stir in the caviar. Season with salt and pepper to taste.

4 Meanwhile, bring a large pan of lightly salted water to the boil. Add the pasta and cook until just tender, according to the instructions on the packet.

5 Drain the pasta and put it into a warm serving dish. Add the sauce and toss well with two forks to coat. Serve immediately.

VARIATION

For a special occasion, serve the pasta on individual plates, garnished with an extra spoonful of caviar.

PENNE WITH TUNA AND MOZZARELLA

This tasty sauce is quickly made from store-cupboard ingredients, with the simple addition of mozzarella and parsley.

SERVES FOUR

INGREDIENTS
- 400g/14oz/3½ cups penne or other short pasta
- 15ml/1 tbsp capers, in brine or salt
- 2 garlic cloves
- 45g/3 tbsp chopped fresh parsley
- 200g/7oz can tuna, drained
- 75ml/5 tbsp olive oil
- 115g/4oz mozzarella cheese, cut into small dice
- salt and ground black pepper

1 Bring a large pan of lightly salted water to the boil. Add the pasta and cook for 8–10 minutes, or according to the packet instructions.

2 Rinse the capers well. Chop them finely with the garlic. Combine with the parsley and the tuna. Stir in the oil and season to taste with salt and pepper.

3 Drain the pasta when it is just tender, but still firm to the bite. Transfer it to a large, heavy frying pan. Add the tuna sauce and the diced mozzarella. Cook over a medium heat, stirring constantly, until the cheese is just beginning to melt. Spoon on to four warm plates and serve immediately.

Lobster Ravioli

It is essential to use home-made pasta to obtain the delicacy and thinness that this superb filling deserves. Before you start the recipe, make a well-flavoured fish stock, including the lobster shell and head.

SERVES SIX AS AN APPETIZER, FOUR AS A MAIN COURSE

INGREDIENTS

- 1 lobster, about 450g/1lb, cooked and taken out of the shell
- 2 soft white bread slices, about 50g/2oz, crusts removed
- 200ml/7fl oz/scant 1 cup fish stock, made with the lobster shell
- 1 egg
- 250ml/8fl oz/1 cup double (heavy) cream
- 15ml/1 tbsp chopped fresh chives, plus extra to garnish
- 15ml/1 tbsp finely chopped fresh chervil
- salt and ground white pepper
- fresh chives, to garnish

For the pasta dough

- 225g/8oz/2 cups strong plain (all-purpose) flour
- 2 eggs, plus 2 egg yolks

For the mushroom sauce

- a large pinch of saffron threads
- 25g/1oz/2 tbsp butter
- 2 shallots, finely chopped
- 200g/7oz/3 cups button (white) mushrooms, finely chopped
- juice of ½ lemon
- 200ml/7fl oz/scant 1 cup double (heavy) cream

1 Make the pasta dough. Sift the flour with a pinch of salt. Put into a food processor with the eggs and extra yolks; process until the mixture resembles coarse breadcrumbs. Turn out on to a floured surface; knead to a smooth dough. Wrap in clear film (plastic wrap) and rest in the refrigerator for 1 hour.

2 Meanwhile, make the lobster filling. Cut the lobster meat into large chunks and place in a bowl. Tear the white bread into small pieces and soak them in 45ml/3 tbsp of the fish stock. Place in a food processor with half the egg and 30–45ml/2–3 tbsp of the double cream and process until smooth. Stir the mixture into the lobster meat, then add the chives and chervil and season to taste with salt and white pepper.

3 Roll the ravioli dough to a thickness of 3mm/⅛in, preferably using a pasta machine. The process can be done by hand with a rolling pin but is quite hard work. Divide the dough into four rectangles and dust each rectangle lightly with flour.

4 Spoon six equal heaps of filling on to one sheet of pasta, leaving about 3cm/1¼in between each pile of filling. Lightly beat the remaining egg with a tablespoon of water and brush it over the pasta between the piles of filling. Cover with a second sheet of pasta. Repeat with the other two sheets of pasta and remaining filling.

5 Using your fingertips, press the top layer of dough down well between the piles of filling, making sure each is well sealed. Cut between the heaps with a 7.5cm/3in fluted pastry cutter or a pasta wheel to make twelve ravioli.

6 Place the ravioli in a single layer on a baking sheet, cover with clear film or a damp cloth, and put in the refrigerator while you make the sauces.

7 Make the mushroom sauce. Soak the saffron in 15ml/1 tbsp warm water. Melt the butter in a pan and cook the shallots over a low heat until they are soft but not coloured.

8 Add the chopped mushrooms and lemon juice and continue to cook over a low heat until almost all the liquid has evaporated. Stir in the saffron, with its soaking water, and the cream, then cook gently, stirring occasionally, until the sauce has thickened. Keep warm while you cook the ravioli.

9 In another pan, bring the remaining fish stock to the boil, stir in the rest of the cream and bubble to make a slightly thickened sauce. Season to taste and keep warm. Bring a large pan of lightly salted water to a rolling boil. Gently drop in the ravioli (left) and cook for 3–4 minutes, until the pasta is just tender.

10 Place two ravioli (three for a main course) on to the centre of individual warmed plates, spoon over a little of the mushroom sauce and pour a ribbon of fish sauce around the edge. Serve immediately, garnished with chopped and whole fresh chives.

LINGUINE ALLE VONGOLE

USE THE SMALLEST CLAMS YOU CAN FIND FOR THIS RECIPE. YOU WILL HAVE GREAT FUN SUCKING THEM OUT OF THEIR SHELLS. IF YOU CAN'T FIND LINGUINE, USE THIN SPAGHETTI.

SERVES FOUR AS A MAIN COURSE, SIX AS AN APPETIZER

INGREDIENTS

- 675g/1½lb small clams
- 45ml/3 tbsp olive oil
- 2 fat garlic cloves, finely chopped
- 15ml/1 tbsp anchovy paste, or 4 drained canned anchovy fillets, finely chopped
- 400g/14oz can chopped tomatoes
- 30ml/2 tbsp finely chopped fresh flat leaf parsley
- 450g/1lb linguine
- salt and ground black pepper

1 Wash and scrub the clams, then put them in a large pan. Cover the pan and place it over a high heat for 3–4 minutes, shaking the pan occasionally, until all the clams have opened. Discard any that remain closed. Strain the clams, reserving the juices. Shell the clams, if you like.

2 Heat the oil in a pan, add the garlic and cook gently for 2 minutes, until lightly coloured. Stir in the anchovy paste or chopped fillets, then the tomatoes and the reserved clam juices. Add the parsley, bring to the boil, then lower the heat and simmer, uncovered, for 20 minutes, until the sauce is well reduced and full of flavour. Season to taste.

3 Cook the linguine in plenty of lightly salted, boiling water until just tender. Drain the pasta, then tip it back into the pan. Add the clams to the tomato and anchovy sauce, mix together well, then pour the sauce over the linguine and toss until the pasta is well coated. Serve immediately.

BLACK FETTUCINE WITH SEAFOOD

THE DRAMATIC BLACK PASTA MAKES A WONDERFUL CONTRASTING BACKGROUND FOR THE PINK, WHITE AND GOLDEN SHELLFISH. USE WHATEVER SHELLFISH ARE AVAILABLE; TINY CUTTLEFISH, SMALL SQUID, CLAMS OR RAZORSHELL CLAMS ARE DELICIOUS IN THIS DISH.

SERVES FOUR AS A MAIN COURSE, SIX AS AN APPETIZER

INGREDIENTS

- 800g/1¾lb fresh mussels, scrubbed and bearded
- 45ml/3 tbsp olive oil
- 105ml/7 tbsp dry white wine
- 2 fat garlic cloves, chopped
- 150g/5oz queen scallops
- 200g/7oz raw prawns (shrimp), partially shelled
- 400g/14oz black fettucine, preferably fresh
- salt and ground black pepper
- 30ml/2 tbsp chopped fresh flat leaf parsley, to garnish

COOK'S TIP

If you can't find black pasta, use green spinach tagliatelle or fettucine instead.

1 Put the mussels in a pan with 15ml/1 tbsp of the oil. Add the wine, set over a high heat, cover and steam for about 3 minutes, shaking the pan occasionally, until all the mussels have opened. Discard any shellfish that remain closed. Leave to cool in the pan, then lift out and shell some of the mussels. Strain the cooking liquid and set it aside until required.

2 Heat the remaining oil in a large, deep frying pan. Add the chopped garlic and cook for 1 minute, without letting it brown. Add the queen scallops and cook for about 1–2 minutes, tossing them about until they turn opaque. Add the prawns and cook for 1 minute more, then remove the shellfish with a slotted spoon to a bowl and set it aside. Keep the frying pan handy; it will be needed for the sauce.

3 Meanwhile, cook the pasta in a large pan of lightly salted, boiling water according to the packet instructions until just tender; fresh pasta will take only about 2 minutes. Drain.

4 Pour the reserved mussel liquid into the frying pan and bring it to the boil. Lower the heat and season. Return the shellfish to the pan, heat for a few seconds, then stir in the pasta. Toss well, sprinkle the parsley on top and serve.

BLACK PASTA WITH SQUID SAUCE

TAGLIATELLE FLAVOURED WITH SQUID INK LOOKS AMAZING AND TASTES DELICIOUSLY OF THE SEA.

SERVES FOUR

INGREDIENTS

- 105ml/7 tbsp olive oil
- 2 shallots, chopped
- 2 garlic cloves, crushed
- 45ml/3 tbsp chopped fresh parsley
- 675g/1½lb cleaned squid, cut into rings and rinsed
- 150ml/¼ pint/⅔ cup dry white wine
- 400g/14oz can chopped tomatoes
- 2.5ml/½ tsp dried chilli flakes
- 450g/1lb black tagliatelle
- salt and ground black pepper

1 Heat the oil in a pan and add the shallots. Cook over a low heat, stirring occasionally, for 3–5 minutes, until pale golden in colour, then add the garlic. When the garlic colours a little, add 30ml/2 tbsp of the parsley, stir, then add the squid and stir again. Cook for 3–4 minutes, then add the wine.

2 Simmer for a few seconds, then add the tomatoes and chilli flakes and season with salt and pepper to taste. Cover and simmer gently for about 1 hour, until the squid is tender. Add more water if necessary.

3 Bring a large pan of lightly salted water to the boil. Add the pasta and cook for 8–10 minutes, or according to the instructions on the packet. It should be just tender, but still firm to the bite.

4 Drain the pasta and return it to the pan. Add the squid sauce and toss to mix well. Divide among four warm serving plates. Sprinkle each serving with the remaining chopped parsley and serve immediately.

COOK'S TIP

The labelling of olive oil can be confusing. The oil is basically divided into two types – pure and virgin. The latter comes from the first pressing, but virgin olive oil is further sub-divided, according to its level of acidity. The least acid and so the best oil is extra virgin. Use this quality for special dishes and salad dressings, but the next best oil – virgin – may be used for general cooking. Pure olive oil, although not in any way adulterated, lacks the unique flavour of virgin oil.

TAGLIATELLE WITH SAFFRON MUSSELS

MUSSELS IN A SAFFRON AND CREAM SAUCE ARE SERVED WITH TAGLIATELLE IN THIS RECIPE, BUT YOU CAN USE ANY OTHER PASTA YOU LIKE.

SERVES FOUR

INGREDIENTS

- 1.75kg/4–4½lb mussels
- 150ml/¼ pint/⅔ cup dry white wine
- 2 shallots, chopped
- 350g/12oz dried tagliatelle
- 25g/1oz/2 tbsp butter
- 2 garlic cloves, crushed
- 250ml/8fl oz/1 cup double (heavy) cream
- generous pinch of saffron threads, soaked in 30ml/2 tbsp hot water
- 1 egg yolk
- salt and ground black pepper
- 30ml/2 tbsp chopped fresh parsley, to garnish

1 Scrub the mussels under cold running water. Remove the beards. Discard any mussels with damaged shells or that do not shut immediately when sharply tapped.

2 Place the mussels in a large pan with the wine and shallots. Cover with a tight-fitting lid and cook over a high heat, shaking the pan occasionally, for 5–8 minutes, until the mussels have opened. Drain the mussels, reserving the liquid. Discard any that remain closed. Shell all but a few of the mussels and keep warm.

3 Bring the reserved cooking liquid to the boil over a high heat, then continue to boil vigorously until it is reduced by about half. Strain the liquid through a very fine sieve or through a sieve lined with muslin (cheesecloth) into a jug (pitcher) to remove any grit.

4 Bring a large pan of lightly salted water to the boil. Add the pasta and cook for 8–10 minutes, or according to the packet instructions. It should be tender, but still firm to the bite.

5 Melt the butter in a pan and cook the garlic for 1 minute. Add the mussel cooking liquid, cream and saffron. Heat gently until the sauce thickens slightly. Remove from the heat and stir in the egg yolk and shelled mussels. Season to taste with salt and pepper.

6 Drain the pasta and transfer to serving bowls. Spoon over the sauce and sprinkle with chopped parsley. Garnish with the mussels in shells and serve immediately.

SICILIAN SPAGHETTI WITH SARDINES

A traditional dish from the island of Sicily.

SERVES FOUR

INGREDIENTS

- 12 fresh sardines, cleaned and boned
- 250ml/8fl oz/1 cup olive oil
- 1 onion, chopped
- 25g/1oz/½ cup fresh dill, chopped
- 50g/2oz/½ cup pine nuts
- 25g/1oz/3 tbsp raisins, soaked in water
- 50g/2oz/1 cup fresh breadcrumbs
- 450g/1lb spaghetti
- flour, for dusting
- salt

1 Rinse the sardines under cold running water and pat them thoroughly dry on kitchen paper. Open them out flat, then, using a sharp knife, cut in half lengthways.

2 Heat 30ml/2 tbsp of the oil in a heavy pan, add the onion and cook over a medium heat, stirring occasionally, for 5–8 minutes, until golden. Lower the heat, add the dill and cook gently for 1–2 minutes. Add the pine nuts and raisins and season with salt to taste. Set aside and keep warm.

3 Dry-fry the breadcrumbs in a frying pan until golden. Set aside.

4 Bring a large pan of lightly salted water to the boil. Add the spaghetti and cook for 8–10 minutes, or according to the instructions on the packet. It should be tender, but still firm to the bite.

5 Meanwhile, heat the remaining oil in a frying pan. Lightly dust the sardines with flour, shaking off any excess, and fry in the hot oil for 2–3 minutes. Drain on kitchen paper.

6 Drain the spaghetti and return to the pan. Add the onion mixture and toss well to coat. Transfer the spaghetti mixture to a warmed platter and arrange the fried sardines on top. Sprinkle with the toasted breadcrumbs and serve immediately.

COOK'S TIP

Sardines are actually baby pilchards and weigh about 115g/4oz. They are covered in very fine scales and these are most easily removed with your hand, rather than with a scaling knife. Hold the fish by the tail under cold running water and rub your thumb and fingers gently along the body down to the head.

Smoked Haddock and Pasta in Parsley Sauce

Pasta shells with a deliciously creamy sauce.

SERVES FOUR

INGREDIENTS

- 450g/1lb smoked haddock fillet
- 1 small leek or onion, thickly sliced
- 300ml/½ pint/1¼ cups milk
- 1 bouquet garni (bay leaf, thyme and parsley stalks)
- 25g/1oz/2 tbsp margarine
- 25g/1oz/¼ cup plain (all-purpose) flour
- 225g/8oz/2 cups pasta shells
- 30ml/2 tbsp chopped fresh parsley
- salt and ground black pepper
- 15g/½oz/2 tbsp toasted flaked (sliced) almonds, to garnish

1 Remove all the skin and any bones from the haddock. Put into a pan with the leek or onion, milk and bouquet garni. Bring to the boil, lower the heat, cover and simmer gently for about 8–10 minutes, until the fish flakes easily.

2 Strain, reserving the milk for making the sauce, and discard the bouquet garni. Flake the fish.

3 Put the margarine, flour and reserved milk into a pan. Bring to the boil over a low heat and whisk constantly until the sauce is smooth and thickened. Season to taste with salt and pepper, then add the fish and leek or onion.

4 Cook the pasta in a large pan of lightly salted, boiling water for 8–10 minutes, or according to the packet instructions. It should be tender, but still firm to the bite. Drain and stir into the sauce with the parsley. Serve, garnished with almonds.

Baked Seafood Spaghetti

In this dish, each portion is baked and served in an individual parcel, which diners can then open at the table.

SERVES FOUR

INGREDIENTS

- 450g/1lb fresh mussels
- 120ml/4fl oz/½ cup dry white wine
- 60ml/4 tbsp olive oil
- 2 garlic cloves, finely chopped
- 450g/1lb tomatoes, fresh or canned, peeled and finely chopped
- 400g/14oz spaghetti
- 225g/8oz raw prawns (shrimp), peeled and deveined
- 30ml/2 tbsp chopped fresh parsley
- salt and ground black pepper

1 Scrub the mussels well under cold running water and pull off the beards using a small sharp knife. Discard any with broken shells or which do not close immediately when sharply tapped. Place the mussels and the wine in a large, heavy pan. Cover with a tight-fitting lid and cook over a high heat, shaking the pan occasionally, for about 5 minutes, until they open.

2 Lift out the mussels with a slotted spoon and set aside. Discard any that do not open. Strain the cooking liquid through a sieve lined with muslin (cheesecloth) to remove any grit and reserve until needed.

3 Put the olive oil and garlic in a medium pan and set over a medium heat for 1–2 minutes. Add the tomatoes, increase the heat to high and cook, stirring occasionally, until soft (or just heat through, if canned). Stir in 175ml/6fl oz/¾ cup of the reserved mussel cooking liquid and heat through.

4 Meanwhile, bring a large pan of lightly salted water to the boil. Add the spaghetti and cook for 8–10 minutes, or according to the packet instructions. It should be tender, but still firm to the bite.

5 Just before draining the pasta, add the prawns and chopped parsley to the tomato sauce. Simmer gently for a further 2 minutes, or until the prawns are cooked through. Taste and adjust the seasoning, if necessary. Remove from the heat and set aside. Drain the pasta.

6 Preheat the oven to 150°C/300°F/Gas 2. Prepare four pieces of baking parchment, greaseproof (waxed) paper or foil about 30 x 45cm/12 x 18in. Place each sheet in the centre of a shallow bowl. Turn the drained pasta into a mixing bowl. Add the tomato sauce and mix well. Stir in the mussels.

7 Divide the pasta and seafood between the four pieces of parchment, paper or foil, placing a mound in the centre of each, and twisting the paper ends together to make a closed packet. (The bowl under the paper will stop the sauce from spilling while the paper parcels are being closed.)

8 Place the parcels on a large baking sheet and bake for 8–10 minutes. Place an unopened parcel on each of four warm individual plates and serve immediately.

COOK'S TIP

Don't forget to provide a bowl for the shells. If you prefer, you can remove and discard the empty mussel shells, leaving the mussels on the half shell, or shell them completely.

FUSILLI WITH SMOKED TROUT

THE TROUT AND CREAMY SAUCE BLEND SUPERBLY WITH THE CRUNCHY VEGETABLES.

SERVES FOUR TO SIX

INGREDIENTS

- 2 carrots, cut into batons
- 1 leek, cut into batons
- 2 celery sticks, cut into batons
- 150ml/¼ pint/⅔ cup vegetable stock
- 225g/8oz smoked trout fillets, skinned and cut into strips
- 200g/7oz/scant 1 cup cream cheese
- 150ml/¼ pint/⅔ cup medium sweet white wine or fish stock
- 15ml/1 tbsp chopped fresh dill
- 225g/8oz long fusilli
- salt and ground black pepper
- dill sprigs, to garnish

1 Put the carrots, leek and celery into a large pan with the vegetable stock. Bring to the boil over a medium heat and cook quickly, uncovered, for 4–5 minutes, until tender and most of the stock has evaporated.

2 Remove the pan from the heat and fold in the strips of smoked trout. Set aside and keep warm.

3 To make the sauce, put the cream cheese and white wine or fish stock into a heavy pan and beat with a whisk over a low heat until smooth and thoroughly combined. Season to taste with salt and pepper. Stir in the chopped dill.

4 Bring a large pan of lightly salted water to the boil. Add the pasta and cook for 8–10 minutes, or according to the packet instructions. It should be tender, but still firm to the bite. Drain thoroughly.

5 Add the fusilli with the sauce, toss lightly and transfer to a warm serving bowl. Top with the cooked vegetables and trout. Serve immediately, garnished with fresh dill sprigs.

SPAGHETTI WITH HOT-AND-SOUR FISH

A truly Chinese spicy taste is what makes this sauce so different.

SERVES FOUR

INGREDIENTS

- 350g/12oz spaghetti tricolore
- 450g/1lb monkfish, skinned
- 225g/8oz courgettes (zucchini)
- 1 fresh green chilli, seeded
- 15ml/1 tbsp olive oil
- 1 large onion, chopped
- 5ml/1 tsp ground turmeric
- 115g/4oz/1 cup shelled peas, thawed if frozen
- 10ml/2 tsp lemon juice
- 75ml/5 tbsp hoisin sauce
- 150ml/¼ pint/⅔ cup water
- salt and ground black pepper
- fresh dill sprig, to garnish

1 Cook the pasta in a large pan of lightly salted, boiling water for 8–10 minutes, or according to the instructions on the packet.

2 Meanwhile, remove the grey membrane from the monkfish, if this hasn't already been done. Using a sharp knife, cut along either side of the central bone, then remove and discard it. Cut the monkfish flesh into bitesize pieces.

COOK'S TIPS

- This dish is quite low in calories, so it is ideal for slimmers.
- Hoisin sauce is widely available from most supermarkets and also from Chinese food stores.

3 Thinly slice the courgettes, then finely chop the fresh green chilli.

4 Heat the oil in a large, heavy frying pan. Add the onion and cook over a low heat, stirring occasionally, for 5 minutes, until softened, but not coloured. Add the turmeric.

5 Add the chilli, courgettes and peas, increase the heat to medium and cook for about 5 minutes, until the vegetables have softened.

6 Stir in the pieces of monkfish, lemon juice, hoisin sauce and measured water. Bring to the boil, then lower the heat and simmer for about 5 minutes, or until the fish is cooked through and tender. Season to taste with salt and pepper.

7 Drain the pasta thoroughly and turn it into a warm serving bowl. Add the monkfish sauce and toss well to coat. Serve immediately, garnished with fresh dill.

Seafood Laksa

For a special occasion serve creamy rice noodles in a spicy, coconut-flavoured broth, topped with a selection of seafood. There is a fair amount of work involved in the preparation, but you can make the soup base ahead.

SERVES FOUR

INGREDIENTS

- 4 fresh red chillies, seeded and coarsely chopped
- 1 onion, coarsely chopped
- 1 piece shrimp paste, the size of a stock (bouillon) cube
- 1 lemon grass stalk, chopped
- 1 small piece fresh root ginger, coarsely chopped
- 6 macadamia nuts or almonds
- 60ml/4 tbsp vegetable oil
- 5ml/1 tsp paprika
- 5ml/1 tsp ground turmeric
- 475ml/16fl oz/2 cups fish stock or water
- 600ml/1 pint/2½ cups coconut milk
- Thai fish sauce, to taste
- 12 raw king prawns (jumbo shrimp), peeled and deveined
- 8 scallops, shelled
- 225g/8oz prepared squid, cut into rings
- 350g/12oz rice vermicelli or rice noodles, soaked in warm water until soft
- salt and ground black pepper
- lime halves, to serve

For the garnish

- ¼ cucumber, cut into small batons
- 2 fresh red chillies, seeded and thinly sliced
- 30ml/2 tbsp fresh mint leaves
- 30ml/2 tbsp fried shallots

COOK'S TIP

Shrimp paste is also known as blachan and terasi and is made from dried shrimp. It is sold in small blocks and you will find it in Asian supermarkets.

1 Put the red chillies, onion, shrimp paste, lemon grass, ginger and macadamias or almonds into a food processor or blender and process until smooth and combined.

2 Heat 45ml/3 tbsp of the oil in a large, heavy pan. Add the chilli paste and stir-fry over a medium heat for 6 minutes. Stir in the paprika and turmeric and stir-fry for a further 2 minutes.

3 Add the fish stock or water and the coconut milk to the pan. Bring to the boil, reduce the heat to low and simmer gently, stirring occasionally, for 15–20 minutes. Season to taste with the Thai fish sauce.

4 Season the prawns, scallops and squid with salt and pepper. Heat the remaining oil in a wok or large, heavy frying pan. Add all the seafood and stir-fry over a medium-high heat for 2–3 minutes, until cooked.

5 Add the rice vermicelli or rice noodles to the broth and heat through. Divide the broth among four warm individual serving bowls.

6 Place the fried seafood on top of the broth, then garnish with the cucumber, chillies, mint and fried shallots. Serve immediately with the lime halves.

SWEET AND SOUR PRAWNS WITH EGG NOODLES

A QUICK AND EASY DISH FULL OF FLAVOUR.

SERVES FOUR TO SIX

INGREDIENTS

- 15g/½oz dried porcini mushrooms
- 300ml/½ pint/1¼ cups hot water
- bunch of spring onions (scallions)
- 1 red (bell) pepper, seeded
- 2.5cm/1in piece fresh root ginger, peeled and grated
- 225g/8oz can water chestnuts
- 45ml/3 tbsp light soy sauce
- 30ml/2 tbsp sherry
- 350g/12oz large cooked prawns (shrimp), peeled
- 225g/8oz Chinese egg noodles

1 Put the dried mushrooms into a bowl with the hot water and leave to soak for 15 minutes. Thickly slice the spring onions, dice the pepper and slice the water chestnuts.

2 Put the spring onions, grated ginger and red pepper into a pan with the mushrooms and their soaking liquid. Bring to the boil, lower the heat, cover and simmer gently for about 5 minutes, until the vegetables are tender.

3 Add the water chestnuts, soy sauce, sherry and prawns. Re-cover the pan and cook gently over a low heat for 2 minutes.

4 Cook the egg noodles in a pan of lightly salted boiling water according to the instructions on the packet. Drain thoroughly and transfer to a warmed serving dish. Spoon the hot prawn mixture on top. Toss lightly and serve immediately.

FARFALLE WITH PRAWNS

CREAMY SAUCES ARE NOT INVARIABLY THE BEST WAY TO SERVE SEAFOOD WITH PASTA. THIS SIMPLE, FRESH PRAWN SAUCE IS QUITE DELICIOUS.

SERVES FOUR

INGREDIENTS
- 225g/8oz/2 cups farfalle
- 350g/12oz raw or cooked prawns (shrimp)
- 115g/4oz/½ cup unsalted (sweet) butter
- 2 garlic cloves, crushed
- 45ml/3 tbsp chopped fresh parsley
- salt and ground black pepper

1 If using fresh pasta, cook in a large pan of lightly salted, boiling water for 2–3 minutes, or until tender but still firm to the bite. Cook dried pasta for 8–10 minutes, or according to the packet instructions. Peel and devein the prawns.

2 Melt the butter in a large, heavy pan with the garlic and parsley. Toss in the prawns and cook over a medium heat for 8 minutes, until the prawns are tender and have turned pink. If you are using cooked prawns, 4 minutes will be sufficient.

3 Drain the pasta thoroughly and rinse with boiling water to remove any starch.

4 Stir the pasta into the prawn mixture. Season with salt and pepper to taste and serve immediately.

BAMIE GORENG

THIS FABULOUS FRIED NOODLE DISH FROM INDONESIA IS WONDERFULLY VERSATILE. TO THE BASIC RECIPE YOU CAN ADD OTHER VEGETABLES, SUCH AS MUSHROOMS, BROCCOLI, LEEKS OR BEANSPROUTS, IF YOU LIKE.

SERVES SIX TO EIGHT

INGREDIENTS

- 450g/1lb dried egg noodles
- 1 boneless, skinless chicken breast portion
- 115g/4oz pork fillet (tenderloin)
- 115g/4oz calf's liver (optional)
- 2 eggs, beaten
- 90ml/6 tbsp oil
- 25g/1oz/2 tbsp butter or margarine
- 2 garlic cloves, crushed
- 115g/4oz cooked peeled prawns (shrimp)
- 115g/4oz spinach or Chinese leaves (Chinese cabbage)
- 2 celery sticks, thinly sliced
- 4 spring onions (scallions), shredded
- about 60ml/4 tbsp chicken stock
- dark soy sauce and light soy sauce
- salt and ground black pepper
- deep-fried onions and celery leaves, to garnish
- mixed fruit and vegetable salad, to serve (optional)

1 Cook the noodles in a pan of lightly salted, boiling water for 3–4 minutes, or according to the packet instructions. Drain, rinse with cold water and drain well again. Set aside until required.

2 Using a sharp knife, thinly slice the chicken breast portion, pork fillet and calf's liver, if using.

3 Season the eggs with salt and pepper. Heat 5ml/1 tsp of the oil with the butter or margarine in a small pan until the butter has melted. Stir in the eggs and continue stirring until scrambled. Remove from the heat and set aside.

4 Heat the remaining oil in a preheated wok. Add the garlic, chicken, pork and liver, if using, and stir-fry for 2–3 minutes, until they have changed colour. Stir in the prawns, spinach or Chinese leaves, celery and spring onions.

5 Add the drained noodles and toss the mixture well so that all the ingredients are thoroughly combined. Add just enough chicken stock to moisten and stir in dark and light soy sauce to taste. Finally, stir in the scrambled eggs.

6 Garnish the dish with deep-fried onions and celery leaves. Serve with a mixed fruit and vegetable salad, if you like.

COOK'S TIP

Light and dark soy sauce differ in flavour, as well as colour. Light soy sauce has a stronger, more pungent taste, while dark soy sauce is usually quite sweet.

Buckwheat Noodles with Smoked Trout

The light, crisp texture of the pak choi balances the earthy flavour of the mushrooms, the buckwheat noodles and the smokiness of the trout.

SERVES FOUR

INGREDIENTS

- 350g/12oz buckwheat noodles
- 30ml/2 tbsp vegetable oil
- 115g/4oz fresh shiitake mushrooms, quartered
- 2 garlic cloves, finely chopped
- 15ml/1 tbsp grated fresh root ginger
- 225g/8oz pak choi (bok choy)
- 1 spring onion (scallion), thinly sliced diagonally
- 15ml/1 tbsp dark sesame oil
- 30ml/2 tbsp mirin
- 30ml/2 tbsp soy sauce
- 2 smoked trout, skinned and boned
- salt and ground black pepper
- 30ml/2 tbsp coriander (cilantro) leaves and 10ml/2 tsp sesame seeds, toasted, to garnish

1 Cook the buckwheat noodles in boiling water for 7–10 minutes, or according to the packet instructions.

2 Meanwhile, heat the oil in a large, heavy frying pan. Add the shiitake mushrooms and cook over a medium heat, stirring occasionally, for about 3 minutes. Add the garlic, ginger and pak choi and continue to cook, stirring frequently, for a further 2 minutes.

3 Drain the buckwheat noodles thoroughly and add them to the mushroom mixture, together with the spring onion, sesame oil, mirin and soy sauce. Toss well over the heat and then season to taste with salt and pepper.

4 Break up the trout into bitesize pieces. Arrange the noodle mixture on four warm individual serving plates and top with trout.

5 Garnish the noodles with fresh coriander leaves and sesame seeds and serve immediately.

COOK'S TIP

Mirin is sweet, cooking sake, available from Japanese stores. If you can't find it, you can substitute sweet sherry.

STIR-FRIED NOODLES WITH SWEET SALMON

A DELICIOUS SAUCE FORMS THE MARINADE FOR THE SALMON IN THIS RECIPE.

SERVES FOUR

INGREDIENTS
- 350g/12oz salmon fillet
- 30ml/2 tbsp Japanese soy sauce (shoyu)
- 30ml/2 tbsp sake
- 60ml/4 tbsp mirin or sweet sherry
- 5ml/1 tsp soft light brown sugar
- 10ml/2 tsp grated fresh root ginger
- 3 garlic cloves, 1 crushed, and 2 sliced into rounds
- 30ml/2 tbsp groundnut (peanut) oil
- 225g/8oz dried egg noodles, cooked and drained
- 50g/2oz/1 cup alfalfa sprouts
- 30ml/2 tbsp sesame seeds, lightly toasted

1 Using a sharp knife, slice the salmon very thinly, then place in a shallow dish.

2 Mix together the soy sauce, sake, mirin or sherry, sugar, grated ginger and crushed garlic in a jug (pitcher). Pour the mixture over the salmon, turning to coat. Cover with clear film (plastic wrap) and leave in a cool place to marinate for 30 minutes.

3 Preheat the grill (broiler). Drain the salmon, scraping off and reserving the marinade. Place the salmon in a single layer on a baking sheet. Cook under the hot grill for 2–3 minutes, without turning the fish.

4 Meanwhile, heat a wok or large, heavy frying pan until hot, add the oil and gently swirl it around to coat the sides. Add the garlic rounds and cook until golden brown, but do not allow them to burn.

5 Add the cooked noodles and reserved marinade to the wok. Cook, stirring constantly, for 3–4 minutes, until the marinade has reduced slightly to make a syrupy glaze that coats the egg noodles.

6 Toss in the alfalfa sprouts, then remove immediately from the heat. Transfer to four warmed serving plates and top with the salmon. Sprinkle over the toasted sesame seeds. Serve immediately.

COOK'S TIPS
- It is important to scrape all the marinade off the fish as any remaining pieces of ginger or garlic would burn during grilling (broiling) and spoil the finished dish.
- Keep a sharp eye on the salmon while it is cooking, as it can burn very easily.

VARIATION
This is a good way to cook other oily fish. Try it with thinly sliced tuna.

SMOKED TROUT CANNELLONI

SMOKED TROUT CAN BE BOUGHT ALREADY FILLETED OR AS WHOLE FISH. THEY MAKE A DELICIOUS CHANGE FROM THE TOMATO-BASED FILLINGS USUALLY FOUND IN CANNELLONI DISHES.

SERVES FOUR TO SIX

INGREDIENTS
- 1 large onion, finely chopped
- 1 garlic clove, crushed
- 60ml/4 tbsp vegetable stock
- 2 x 400g/14oz cans chopped tomatoes
- 2.5ml/½ tsp dried mixed herbs
- 1 smoked trout, weighing about 400g/14oz, or 225g/8oz smoked trout fillets
- 75g/3oz/¾ cup frozen peas, thawed
- 75g/3oz/1½ cups fresh breadcrumbs
- 16 cannelloni tubes, cooked
- salt and ground black pepper
- mixed salad, to serve

For the cheese sauce
- 25g/1oz/2 tbsp butter or margarine
- 25g/1oz/¼ cup plain (all-purpose) flour
- 350ml/12fl oz/1½ cups skimmed milk
- freshly grated nutmeg
- 25ml/1½ tbsp freshly grated Parmesan cheese

1 Preheat the oven to 190°C/375°F/Gas 5. Put the onion, garlic and stock in a large pan. Bring to the boil, then lower the heat, cover and simmer for 3 minutes. Uncover and continue to cook, stirring occasionally, until the stock has reduced entirely.

2 Stir in the tomatoes and dried herbs. Simmer gently, uncovered, for a further 10 minutes, or until the mixture is very thick.

VARIATION

You can use a 200g/7oz can of tuna in brine in place of the trout, if you like.

3 Meanwhile, skin the smoked trout with a sharp knife. Carefully flake the flesh and discard all the bones.

4 Stir the fish into the tomato mixture, then add the peas and breadcrumbs. Season to taste with salt and pepper and remove the pan from the heat.

5 Carefully spoon the filling into the cannelloni tubes and arrange them in a single layer in a large ovenproof dish.

6 For the sauce, put the butter or margarine, flour and milk into a pan and cook over a medium heat, beating constantly with a whisk, until the sauce thickens. Simmer gently for 2–3 minutes, stirring constantly. Season to taste with salt, ground black pepper and grated nutmeg.

7 Pour the sauce over the filled cannelloni and sprinkle evenly with the grated Parmesan cheese. Bake for about 30–45 minutes, or until the top is golden and bubbling. Serve immediately with a mixed salad.

Tuna Lasagne

SERVES SIX

INGREDIENTS

- 350g/12oz no pre-cook lasagne
- 15g/½oz/1 tbsp butter
- 1 small onion, finely chopped
- 1 garlic clove, finely chopped
- 115g/4oz/1⅔ cups mushrooms, thinly sliced
- 60ml/4 tbsp dry white wine
- 600ml/1 pint/2½ cups white sauce
- 150ml/¼ pint/⅔ cup whipping cream
- 45ml/3 tbsp chopped fresh parsley
- 2 x 200g/7oz cans tuna, drained
- 2 canned pimientos, cut into strips
- 75g/3oz/¾ cup frozen peas, thawed
- 115g/4oz/1 cup grated mozzarella cheese
- 25g/1oz/⅓ cup freshly grated Parmesan cheese
- salt and ground black pepper

1 Preheat the oven to 180°C/350°F/ Gas 4. Soak the sheets of lasagne in a bowl of hot water for 3–5 minutes, or according to the packet instructions. Drain and rinse with cold water. Lay them on a dishtowel, in a single layer, to drain.

2 Melt the butter in a pan. Add the onion and cook over a medium heat, stirring occasionally, for 2–3 minutes, until soft but not coloured. Add the garlic and mushrooms and cook, stirring occasionally, for a further 5 minutes.

3 Pour in the wine. Bring to the boil and boil for 1 minute. Stir in the white sauce, cream and chopped parsley and season to taste with salt and pepper.

4 Spoon a thin layer of sauce over the base of a 30 x 23cm/12 x 9in ovenproof dish. Cover with a layer of lasagne sheets.

5 Flake the tuna. Sprinkle half of the tuna, pimiento strips, peas and grated mozzarella over the pasta. Spoon one-third of the remaining sauce evenly over the top and cover with another layer of lasagne sheets.

6 Repeat the layers, ending with lasagne and sauce. Sprinkle evenly with the grated Parmesan.

7 Bake for 30–40 minutes, or until bubbling hot and the top is lightly browned. Leave to stand for about 120 minutes, then cut into squares and serve.

Seafood Lasagne

This dish can be as simple or as elegant as you like. For a dinner party, dress it up with scallops, mussels or prawns and a really generous pinch of saffron in the sauce; for a family supper, use simple fish, such as cod and smoked haddock. The lasagne can be prepared in advance and baked at the last moment.

SERVES EIGHT

INGREDIENTS

- 350g/12oz monkfish
- 350g/12oz salmon fillet
- 350g/12oz undyed smoked haddock
- 1 litre/1¾ pints/4 cups milk
- 500ml/17fl oz/generous 2 cups fish stock
- 2 bay leaves or a good pinch of saffron threads
- 1 small onion, peeled and halved
- 75g/3oz/6 tbsp butter, plus extra for greasing
- 45ml/3 tbsp plain (all-purpose) flour
- 150g/5oz/2 cups mushrooms, sliced
- 225–300g/8–11oz no-precook or fresh lasagne
- 60ml/4 tbsp freshly grated Parmesan cheese
- salt, ground black pepper, grated nutmeg and paprika
- rocket (arugula) leaves, to garnish

For the tomato sauce

- 30ml/2 tbsp olive oil
- 1 red onion, finely chopped
- 1 garlic clove, finely chopped
- 400g/14oz can chopped tomatoes
- 15ml/1 tbsp tomato purée (paste)
- 15ml/1 tbsp torn fresh basil leaves

1 Make the tomato sauce. Heat the oil in a pan and cook the onion and garlic over a low heat for 5 minutes, until softened and golden. Stir in the tomatoes and tomato purée and simmer for 20–30 minutes, stirring occasionally. Season and stir in the basil.

COOK'S TIP

It is preferable to use fresh lasagne, if available. Cook the sheets in a large pan of lightly salted boiling water for 3 minutes. Do not overcrowd the pan, or the sheets will stick together.

2 Put all the fish in a shallow flameproof dish or pan with the milk, stock, bay leaves or saffron and onion. Bring to the boil over a medium heat; poach for 5 minutes, until almost cooked. Leave to cool.

3 When the fish is almost cold, strain it, reserving the liquid. Remove the skin and any bones and flake the flesh.

4 Preheat the oven to 180°C/350°F/Gas 4. Melt the butter in a pan, stir in the flour; cook for 2 minutes, stirring. Gradually add the poaching liquid and bring to the boil, stirring. Add the mushrooms, cook for 2–3 minutes; season with salt, pepper and nutmeg.

5 Lightly grease a shallow ovenproof dish. Spoon a thin layer of the mushroom sauce over the base of the dish and spread it with a spatula. Stir the fish into the remaining mushroom sauce in the pan.

6 Make a layer of lasagne, then a layer of fish and sauce. Add another layer of lasagne, then spread over all the tomato sauce. Continue to layer the lasagne and fish, finishing with a layer of fish.

7 Sprinkle over the grated Parmesan cheese. Bake for 30–45 minutes, until bubbling and golden. Before serving, sprinkle with paprika and garnish with rocket leaves.

Seafood Chow Mein

This basic recipe can be adapted using different items for the "dressing".

SERVES FOUR

INGREDIENTS

- 75g/3oz squid, cleaned
- 75g/3oz raw prawns (shrimp)
- 3–4 fresh scallops, shelled
- ½ egg white
- 15ml/1 tbsp cornflour (cornstarch) paste
- 250g/9oz egg noodles
- 90ml/6 tbsp vegetable oil
- 50g/2oz/¾ cup mangetouts (snow peas)
- 2.5ml/½ tsp salt
- 2.5ml/½ tsp light brown sugar
- 15ml/1 tbsp Chinese rice wine or dry sherry
- 30ml/2 tbsp light soy sauce
- 2 spring onions (scallions), finely shredded
- vegetable or chicken stock, if necessary
- few drops sesame oil

1 Open up the squid and, using a sharp knife, score the inside in a criss-cross pattern. Cut the squid into pieces, each about the size of a postage stamp. Soak the squid in a bowl of boiling water until all the pieces curl up. Rinse in cold water and drain.

2 Peel and devein the prawns, then cut each of them in half lengthways.

3 Using a sharp knife, cut each scallop into three or four slices. Mix the scallops and prawns with the egg white and cornflour paste in a bowl and set aside.

4 Cook the noodles in boiling water according to the packet instructions, then drain, rinse under cold water and drain well again. Mix with 15ml/1 tbsp of the oil.

COOK'S TIPS

- To make cornflour (cornstarch) paste, mix four parts dry cornflour with about five parts cold water until smooth.
- Although normally served hot, chow mein is also delicious served at room temperature. However, do not chill it in the refrigerator, as this tends to make the noodles brittle.

5 Heat 45ml/3 tbsp of the oil in a preheated wok until hot. Add the mangetouts and seafood mixture and stir-fry for 2 minutes, then add the salt, brown sugar, rice wine or sherry, half of the soy sauce and the shredded spring onions. Toss over the heat to mix well and add a little stock, if necessary. Transfer the mixture to a large bowl, cover and keep warm.

6 Heat the remaining oil in the wok. Add the noodles and stir-fry for 2–3 minutes with the remaining soy sauce until heated through.

7 Place the noodles in a large, warm serving dish, pour the seafood "dressing" on top and sprinkle with sesame oil. Serve immediately.

STIR-FRIED NOODLES IN SHELLFISH SAUCE

THE CHINESE WOULD HAVE US BELIEVE THAT IT WAS THEY WHO INVENTED PASTA, SO IT SEEMS APPROPRIATE TO INCLUDE A CHINESE-STYLE PASTA DISH.

SERVES SIX TO EIGHT AS AN APPETIZER
FOUR AS A MAIN COURSE

INGREDIENTS

- 225g/8oz Chinese egg noodles
- 8 spring onions (scallions), trimmed
- 8 asparagus spears, plus extra steamed asparagus spears, to serve (optional)
- 30ml/2 tbsp stir-fry oil
- 5cm/2in piece fresh root ginger, peeled and cut into very fine batons
- 3 garlic cloves, chopped
- 60ml/4 tbsp oyster sauce
- 450g/1lb cooked crab meat (all white, or two-thirds white and one-third brown)
- 30ml/2 tbsp rice wine vinegar
- 15–30ml/1–2 tbsp light soy sauce

1 Put the noodles in a large pan or wok, cover with lightly salted, boiling water, place a lid on top and leave for 3–4 minutes, or for the time suggested on the packet. Drain and set aside.

2 Cut off the green spring onion tops and slice them thinly. Set aside. Cut the white parts into 2cm/¾in lengths and quarter them lengthways. Cut the asparagus spears on the diagonal into 2cm/¾in pieces.

3 Heat the stir-fry oil in a pan or wok until very hot, then add the ginger, garlic and white spring onion batons. Stir-fry over a high heat for 1 minute. Add the oyster sauce, crab meat, rice wine vinegar and soy sauce to taste. Stir-fry for about 2 minutes, until the crab and sauce are hot. Add the noodles and toss until heated through. At the last moment, toss in the spring onion tops and serve with a few extra asparagus spears, if you like.

Shellfish Paella

There are as many versions of paella as there are regions of Spain. Those from near the coast contain a lot of shellfish, while inland versions add chicken or pork. Here the only meat is the chorizo, essential for an authentic flavour.

SERVES FOUR

INGREDIENTS

- 45ml/3 tbsp olive oil
- 1 Spanish onion, chopped
- 2 fat garlic cloves, chopped
- 150g/5oz chorizo sausage, sliced
- 300g/11oz small squid, cleaned
- 1 red (bell) pepper, cut into strips
- 4 tomatoes, peeled, seeded and diced, or 200g/7oz can tomatoes
- 500ml/17fl oz/generous 2 cups chicken stock
- 105ml/7 tbsp dry white wine
- 200g/7oz/1 cup short grain Spanish rice or risotto rice
- a large pinch of saffron threads
- 150g/5oz/1 cup fresh or frozen peas
- 12 large cooked prawns (shrimp), in the shell, or 8 langoustines
- 450g/1lb fresh mussels, scrubbed
- 450g/1lb medium clams, scrubbed
- salt and ground black pepper

1 Heat the olive oil in a paella pan or wok, add the onion and garlic and cook until translucent. Add the chorizo and cook until lightly golden.

2 If the squid are very small, leave them whole, otherwise cut the bodies into rings and the tentacles into pieces. Add the squid to the pan and sauté over a high heat for 2 minutes.

3 Stir in the pepper strips and tomatoes and simmer gently for 5 minutes, until the pepper strips are tender. Pour in the stock and wine, stir well and bring to the boil.

4 Stir in the rice and saffron threads and season well with salt and pepper. Spread the contents of the pan evenly. Bring the liquid back to the boil, then lower the heat and simmer gently for about 10 minutes.

5 Add the peas, prawns or langoustines, mussels and clams, stirring them gently into the rice.

6 Cook the paella gently for a further 15–20 minutes, until the rice is tender and all the mussels and clams have opened. If any remain closed, discard them. If the paella seems dry, add a little more hot chicken stock. Gently stir everything together and serve piping hot.

Seafood Rice

This tasty dish uses a frozen fish mixture that saves lots of time.

SERVES FOUR

INGREDIENTS

- 30ml/2 tbsp oil
- 1 onion, sliced
- 1 red (bell) pepper, seeded and chopped
- 115g/4oz/1⅔ cups mushrooms, chopped
- 10ml/2 tsp ground turmeric
- 225g/8oz rice and grain mix
- 750ml/1¼ pints/3 cups stock, made with a pilau-rice stock (bouillon) cube
- 400g/14oz bag frozen cooked seafood selection, thawed
- 115g/4oz large, cooked prawns (shrimp), peeled and deveined
- salt and ground black pepper

1 Heat the oil in a deep frying pan. Add the onion and cook over a low heat, stirring occasionally, until it is starting to soften. Add the chopped pepper and mushrooms and cook for 1 minute more.

2 Stir in the turmeric and then the rice and grain mix. Stir until thoroughly mixed, then carefully pour on the stock. Season with salt and pepper, cover with a lid or foil and simmer gently over a low heat for 15 minutes.

VARIATION

You can also make this dish with risotto rice, such as arborio or Carnaroli, or with a mixture of long grain and wild rice.

3 Add the seafood selection and the prawns, stir well and turn up the heat slightly to bring the liquid back to the boil. Cover again and simmer for 15–20 minutes more, until the grains are cooked and the seafood is hot. Serve immediately.

COOK'S TIP

If you don't like this fish mixture, choose your own – use more prawns (shrimp) and seafood sticks or crab meat, if you prefer, but cut down on the cooking time for the fish.

FISH WITH RICE

THIS ARABIC FISH DISH, SAYADIEH, IS VERY POPULAR IN THE LEBANON.

SERVES FOUR TO SIX

INGREDIENTS
- juice of 1 lemon
- 45ml/3 tbsp oil
- 900g/2lb cod steaks
- 4 large onions, chopped
- 5ml/1 tsp ground cumin
- 2–3 saffron threads, soaked in 30ml/2 tbsp hot water
- 1 litre/1¾ pints/4 cups fish stock
- 500g/1¼lb basmati or other long grain rice
- 115g/4oz/1 cup pine nuts, lightly toasted
- salt and ground black pepper
- fresh parsley, to garnish

1 Mix together the lemon juice and 15ml/1 tbsp of the oil in a shallow dish. Add the fish steaks, turning to coat, then cover and set aside to marinate for 30 minutes.

2 Heat the remaining oil in a large pan or flameproof casserole and cook the onions over a low heat, stirring occasionally, for 5–6 minutes, until softened and golden.

3 Drain the cod steaks, reserving the marinade, and add them to the pan. Cook for 1–2 minutes on each side until lightly golden, then add the cumin and saffron threads and season with a little salt and pepper.

4 Pour the fish stock into the pan or casserole, together with the reserved marinade. Bring to the boil and then simmer very gently over a low heat for 5–10 minutes, until the fish is nearly done.

5 Using a slotted spoon, transfer the fish to a plate, cover and set aside. Add the rice to the pan or casserole. Bring the stock to the boil, then reduce the heat and simmer very gently over a low heat for about 15 minutes, until nearly all the stock has been absorbed.

6 Arrange the fish on the rice and cover. Steam over a low heat for a further 15–20 minutes.

7 Transfer the fish to a plate, then spoon the rice on to a large, flat serving dish and arrange the fish on top. Sprinkle with lightly toasted pine nuts and garnish with fresh parsley. Serve immediately.

COOK'S TIP

Take care when cooking the rice that the pan does not boil dry. Check it occasionally and add more stock or water, if it becomes necessary.

VARIATION

This method of cooking also works well with other white fish, especially Mediterranean varieties such as hake.

Salmon Risotto

Fresh tarragon and cucumber combine superbly with salmon.

SERVES FOUR

INGREDIENTS

- 25g/1oz/2 tbsp butter
- 1 small bunch spring onions (scallions), white part only, chopped
- ½ cucumber, peeled, seeded and chopped
- 400g/14oz/2 cups risotto rice
- 900ml/1½ pints/3¾ cups chicken or fish stock
- 150ml/¼ pint/⅔ cup dry white wine
- 450g/1lb salmon fillet, skinned and diced
- 45ml/3 tbsp chopped fresh tarragon
- salt and ground black pepper

1 Melt the butter in a large pan and add the spring onions and cucumber. Cook over a low heat for 2–3 minutes without colouring.

2 Add the rice, chicken or fish stock and wine and bring to the boil. Lower the heat and simmer, uncovered, for 10 minutes, stirring occasionally.

3 Stir in the diced salmon and chopped tarragon, and season to taste. Continue cooking for a further 5 minutes, then switch off the heat. Cover the pan and leave to stand for 5 minutes before serving.

VARIATION

Risotto rice, which has a round, medium-size grain, cooks to a unique creamy consistency because it can absorb plenty of liquid. Long grain rice can be used, but will not produce the same texture. Choose non-pre-cooked rice and reduce the quantity of stock to 750ml/1¼ pints/3 cups.

TRUFFLE AND LOBSTER RISOTTO

This elegant dish is the ultimate in luxury.

SERVES FOUR

INGREDIENTS

- 50g/2oz/¼ cup unsalted (sweet) butter
- 1 onion, chopped
- 400g/14oz/2 cups risotto rice
- 1 fresh thyme sprig
- 1.2 litres/2 pints/5 cups chicken stock
- 150ml/¼ pint/⅔ cup dry white wine
- 1 freshly cooked lobster
- 45ml/3 tbsp chopped fresh parsley and chervil
- 3–4 drops truffle oil
- 2 hard-boiled eggs, shelled and sliced
- 1 fresh black or white truffle, shaved
- salt and ground black pepper

1 Melt the butter in a large shallow pan. Add the onion and cook over a low heat, stirring occasionally, for about 5 minutes, until soft but not coloured. Add the rice and thyme and stir well to coat the grains evenly with butter. Pour in the chicken stock and wine, stir once and cook gently, uncovered, for 15 minutes, until the rice is tender and almost all the stock has been absorbed.

2 Meanwhile, twist off the lobster tail, cut open the underside with scissors and remove the white tail meat. Slice half of the meat, then coarsely chop the remainder. Break open the claws with a small hammer and remove the flesh, in one piece if possible.

3 Remove the rice from the heat, and stir in the chopped lobster meat, herbs, truffle oil, and salt and pepper to taste. Cover and leave to stand for 5 minutes.

4 Divide the risotto among four warmed plates and arrange the slices of lobster and hard-boiled egg on top. Sprinkle evenly with the truffle shavings and serve immediately.

Risotto Nero

If you happen to have some squid or cuttlefish complete with ink sacs, retrieve the ink yourself to make this black risotto. Otherwise, you can buy sachets of squid or cuttlefish ink at fishmongers and some delicatessens.

SERVES FOUR

INGREDIENTS

- 450g/1lb small cuttlefish or squid, with their ink, or 350g/12oz cuttlefish and 4 sachets cuttlefish or squid ink
- 1.2 litres/2 pints/5 cups light fish stock
- 50g/2oz/¼ cup butter
- 30ml/2 tbsp olive oil
- 3 shallots, finely chopped
- 350g/12oz/1¾ cups risotto rice
- 105ml/7 tbsp dry white wine
- 30ml/2 tbsp chopped fresh flat leaf parsley
- salt and ground black pepper

1 If the cuttlefish or squid contain ink, squeeze it out into a small bowl and set it aside. Cut the bodies into thin rings and chop the tentacles. Set aside.

2 Add the ink to the fish stock. Bring to the boil and lower the heat so that the liquid is at a gentle simmer. Heat half the butter and all the olive oil in a large pan. Add the chopped shallots and cook for about 3 minutes, until they are soft and translucent.

COOK'S TIP

If you prefer, make the risotto without the cuttlefish or squid and serve it with other fish or shellfish.

3 Add the cuttlefish or squid and cook very gently for 5–7 minutes, until tender. Add the rice and stir well to coat all the grains with fat. Pour in the wine and simmer until most of it has been absorbed by the rice. Add a ladleful of the hot stock and cook, stirring constantly, until it has been absorbed.

4 Continue cooking and stirring for 20–25 minutes, adding the remaining stock a ladleful at a time after the previous quantity has been absorbed.

5 Season to taste, then stir in the parsley. Beat in the remaining butter to make the risotto shiny. Spoon the risotto into four warmed dishes and serve.

Shellfish Risotto

Most supermarkets now stock packs of ready-prepared mixed shellfish, such as prawns, squid and mussels, which are ideal for making this quick and easy risotto.

SERVES FOUR

INGREDIENTS

- 1 litre/1¾ pints/4 cups fish or shellfish stock
- 50g/2oz/¼ cup butter
- 2 shallots, chopped
- 2 garlic cloves, chopped
- 350g/12oz/1¾ cups risotto rice
- 150ml/¼ pint/⅔ cup dry white wine
- 2.5ml/½ tsp powdered saffron, or a pinch of saffron threads
- 400g/14oz mixed prepared shellfish
- 30ml/2 tbsp freshly grated Parmesan cheese
- 30ml/2 tbsp chopped fresh flat leaf parsley, to garnish
- salt and ground black pepper

1 Pour the fish or shellfish stock into a large pan. Bring it to the boil, then reduce the heat and keep it at a gentle simmer. The water needs to be hot when it is added to the rice.

2 Melt the butter in a heavy pan, add the shallots and garlic and cook over a low heat until soft but not coloured. Add the rice, stir well to coat the grains with butter, then pour in the wine. Cook over a medium heat, stirring occasionally, until all the wine has been absorbed by the rice.

3 Add a ladleful of hot stock and the saffron and cook, stirring constantly, until the liquid has been absorbed. Add the shellfish and stir well. Continue to add stock a ladleful at a time, waiting until each quantity has been absorbed before adding more. Stir the mixture for about 20 minutes, until the rice is swollen and creamy, but still with a little bite in the middle.

4 Vigorously mix in the freshly grated Parmesan cheese and season to taste, then sprinkle over the chopped parsley and serve immediately.

COOK'S TIP

It is essential to use risotto rice for this dish. You can buy arborio or carnaroli risotto rice in an Italian delicatessen or a large supermarket.

VARIATION

Use peeled prawns (shrimp), or cubes of fish, such as cod or salmon, in place of the mixed prepared shellfish.

BAKED TROUT WITH RICE, TOMATOES AND NUTS

Trout is very popular in Spain, particularly in the North, where it is fished in many rivers. Here is a modern version of a traditional dish, trout baked in foil with a rice stuffing in which sun-dried tomatoes have been used in place of the more usual chillies.

SERVES FOUR

INGREDIENTS

- 2 fresh trout, about 500g/1¼lb each
- 75g/3oz/¾ cup mixed unsalted almonds, pine nuts or hazelnuts
- 25ml/1½ tbsp olive oil, plus extra for drizzling
- 1 small onion, finely chopped
- 10ml/2 tsp grated fresh root ginger
- 175g/6oz/1½ cups cooked white long grain rice
- 4 tomatoes, peeled and very finely chopped
- 4 sun-dried tomatoes in oil, drained and chopped
- 30ml/2 tbsp chopped fresh tarragon
- 2 fresh tarragon sprigs
- salt and ground black pepper
- dressed green salad leaves, to serve

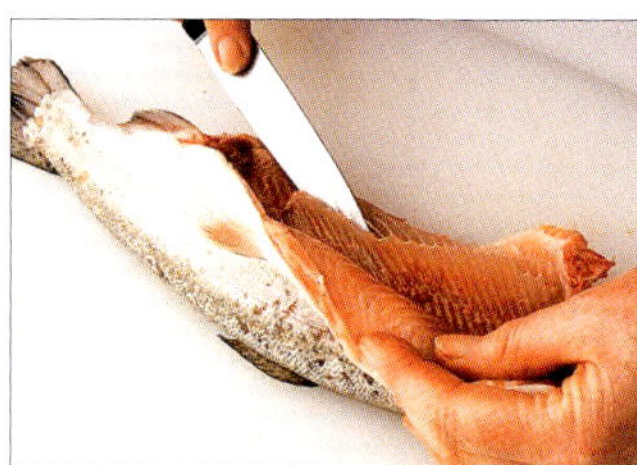

1 Preheat the oven to 190°C/375°F/ Gas 5. If the trout is unfilleted, use a sharp knife to fillet it. Remove any tiny bones remaining in the cavity using a pair of tweezers.

2 Spread out the nuts in a shallow tin (pan) and bake for 3–4 minutes until golden brown, shaking the tin occasionally. Chop the nuts coarsely.

3 Heat the olive oil in a small frying pan and cook the onion for 3–4 minutes, until soft and translucent. Stir in the grated ginger, cook for 1 minute more, then spoon into a mixing bowl.

4 Stir the rice, chopped tomatoes, sun-dried tomatoes, toasted nuts and tarragon into the onion mixture. Season the stuffing well.

5 Place the trout on individual large pieces of oiled foil and spoon the stuffing into the cavities. Add a sprig of tarragon and a drizzle of olive oil or oil from the sun-dried tomatoes.

6 Fold the foil over to enclose each trout completely, and put the parcels in a large roasting pan. Bake for about 20 minutes, or until the fish is just tender. Cut the fish into thick slices. Serve with the salad leaves.

COOK'S TIP

You will need about 75g/3oz/¾ cup of uncooked rice to produce 175g/6oz/ 1½ cups cooked rice.

CALAMARES RELLENOS

SQUID ARE OFTEN JUST STUFFED WITH THEIR OWN TENTACLES BUT, IN THIS RECIPE, HAM AND RAISINS, WHICH CONTRAST WONDERFULLY WITH THE SUBTLE FLAVOUR OF THE SQUID, ARE ALSO INCLUDED. THE STUFFED SQUID ARE COOKED IN A RICHLY FLAVOURED TOMATO SAUCE AND MAKE A PERFECT APPETIZER. TO SERVE AS A MAIN COURSE, SIMPLY ACCOMPANY WITH PLAIN BOILED RICE.

SERVES FOUR

INGREDIENTS

- 2 squid, about 275g/10oz each
- 60ml/4 tbsp olive oil
- 1 small onion, finely chopped
- 2 garlic cloves, finely chopped
- 50g/2oz Serrano ham or gammon steak, diced small
- 75g/3oz/scant ½ cup long grain rice
- 30ml/2 tbsp raisins, chopped
- 30ml/2 tbsp finely chopped fresh parsley
- ½ small (US medium) egg, beaten
- plain (all-purpose) flour, for dusting
- 250ml/8fl oz/1 cup white wine
- 1 bay leaf
- 30ml/2 tbsp chopped fresh parsley
- salt, paprika and black pepper

For the tomato sauce

- 30ml/2 tbsp olive oil
- 1 onion, finely chopped
- 2 garlic cloves, finely chopped
- 200g/7oz can tomatoes
- salt and cayenne pepper

1 Make the tomato sauce. Heat the oil in a flameproof casserole large enough to hold the squid. Cook the onion and garlic over a gentle heat. Add the tomatoes and cook for 10–15 minutes. Season with salt and cayenne pepper.

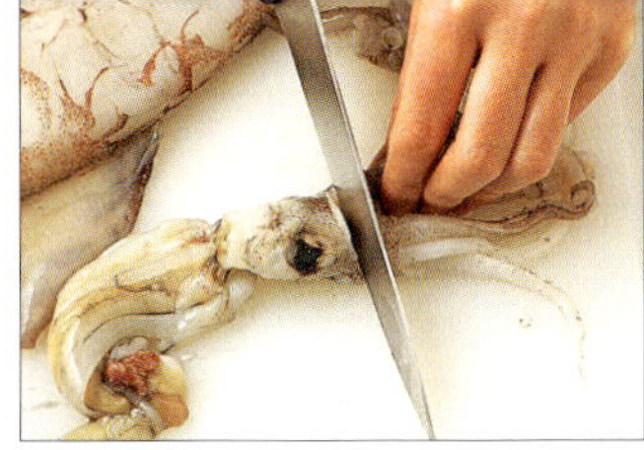

2 To prepare the squid, use the tentacles to pull out the body. Cut off the tentacles, discarding the eyes and everything below. Flex the bodies to pop out the quill. Chop the fin flaps and rinse the bodies well.

3 Heat half the oil in a pan and gently cook the onion and garlic together. Add the ham and squid tentacles and stir-fry. Remove from the heat stir in the rice, raisins and parsley. Season well and add the egg to bind the ingredients.

4 Spoon the mixture into the squid bodies, then stitch each of them shut using a small poultry skewer. Blot the bodies with kitchen paper, then flour them very lightly. Heat the remaining oil in a frying pan and fry the squid, turning until coloured on all sides.

5 Move the squid with two spoons and arrange them in the tomato sauce. Add the wine and bay leaf. Cover the casserole tightly and simmer for about 30 minutes, turning the squid over halfway through cooking if the sauce does not cover them completely. Serve sliced into rings, surrounded by the sauce and garnished with parsley.

Rice Layered with Prawns

SERVES FOUR TO SIX

INGREDIENTS

- 2 large onions, thinly sliced and deep-fried
- 300ml/½ pint/1¼ cups natural (plain) yogurt
- 25ml/1½ tbsp tomato purée (paste)
- 60ml/4 tbsp green masala paste
- 25ml/1½ tbsp lemon juice
- 5ml/1 tsp black cumin seeds
- 5cm/2in piece cinnamon stick or 1.5ml/¼ tsp ground cinnamon
- 4 green cardamoms
- 450g/1lb cooked king prawns (jumbo shrimp), peeled and deveined
- 225g/8oz/3¼ cups small button (white) mushrooms
- 225g/8oz/2 cups frozen peas, thawed and drained
- 450g/1lb/2¼ cups basmati rice, soaked for 5 minutes in boiled water and drained
- 300ml/½ pint/1¼ cups water
- 1 sachet saffron powder mixed in 90ml/6 tbsp milk
- 30ml/2 tbsp ghee or unsalted (sweet) butter
- salt

1 Mix together the onions, yogurt, tomato purée, masala paste, lemon juice, cumin seeds, cinnamon and cardamoms in a large bowl. Fold in the prawns, mushrooms and peas. Cover with clear film (plastic wrap) and leave to marinate for 2 hours.

2 Grease the base of a heavy pan and add the prawns, vegetables and any marinade juices. Cover with the drained rice and smooth the surface gently until you have an even layer.

3 Pour the water all over the surface of the rice. Make random holes through the rice with the handle of a spoon and pour a little saffron milk into each.

4 Place a few knobs (pats) of ghee or butter on the surface and place a circular piece of foil directly on top of the rice. Cover and cook over a low heat for 45–50 minutes, until the rice is tender. Gently toss the rice, prawns and vegetables together and serve immediately.

Seafood Paella

Paella is also the name of the heavy pan traditionally used for this dish.

SERVES FOUR

INGREDIENTS

- 60ml/4 tbsp olive oil
- 225g/8oz monkfish or cod fillet, skinned and cut into chunks
- 3 prepared baby squid, body cut into rings and tentacles chopped
- 1 red mullet, filleted, skinned and cut into chunks (optional)
- 1 onion, chopped
- 3 garlic cloves, finely chopped
- 1 red (bell) pepper, seeded and sliced
- 4 tomatoes, peeled and chopped
- 225g/8oz/generous 1 cup risotto rice
- 450ml/¾ pint/scant 2 cups fish stock
- 150ml/¼ pint/⅔ cup white wine
- 75g/3oz/¾ cup frozen peas
- 4–5 saffron threads soaked in 30ml/2 tbsp hot water
- 115g/4oz cooked peeled prawns (shrimp)
- 8 fresh mussels, scrubbed
- salt and ground black pepper
- 15ml/1 tbsp chopped fresh parsley, to garnish
- lemon wedges, to serve

1 Heat 30ml/2 tbsp of the olive oil in a paella pan or large, heavy frying pan and add the chunks of monkfish or cod, the squid and chunks of red mullet, if using. Stir-fry over a medium heat for 2 minutes, then transfer the fish to a bowl with all the pan juices and set aside.

2 Heat the remaining 30ml/2 tbsp of oil in the pan and add the onion, garlic and red pepper. Cook over a low heat, stirring occasionally, for about 6–7 minutes, until the onion and pepper have softened.

3 Stir in the tomatoes and cook for 2 minutes, then add the rice, stirring well to coat all the grains with oil, and cook for 2–3 minutes.

4 Pour on the fish stock and wine and add the peas and saffron together with its soaking water. Season well with salt and pepper and mix thoroughly.

5 Gently stir in the fish with all the juices, followed by the prawns, and then push the mussels down into the rice. Cover and cook over a gentle heat for about 30 minutes, or until the stock has been absorbed but the mixture is still moist.

6 Remove the pan from the heat, keep covered and leave to stand for 5 minutes. Transfer to a warm serving dish, or serve in the paella pan, if you like. Discard any mussels that have not opened. Sprinkle the paella with chopped parsley and serve immediately with lemon wedges.

Smoked Trout Pilaff

This aromatic rice dish works surprisingly well with the smoked trout.

SERVES FOUR

INGREDIENTS

- 225g/8oz/generous 1 cup basmati rice
- 40g/1½oz/3 tbsp butter
- 2 onions, sliced into rings
- 1 garlic clove, crushed
- 2 bay leaves
- 2 cloves
- 2 green cardamom pods
- 2 cinnamon sticks
- 5ml/1 tsp cumin seeds
- 600ml/1 pint/2½ cups boiling water
- 4 smoked trout fillets, skinned
- 50g/2oz/½ cup flaked (sliced) almonds, toasted
- 50g/2oz/scant ½ cup raisins
- 30ml/2 tbsp chopped fresh parsley

1 Wash the rice thoroughly in several changes of cold water and drain well. If you have time, leave to soak for 30 minutes. Set aside. Melt the butter in a large frying pan and cook the onions, stirring frequently, for about 10 minutes, until browned.

2 Add the crushed garlic, bay leaves, cloves, cardamom pods, cinnamon sticks and cumin seeds to the pan and stir-fry over a medium heat for 1 minute.

3 Stir in the drained rice, then add the boiling water and bring back to the boil. Stir the rice once. Cover with a tight-fitting lid, reduce the heat to low and cook very gently for 20–25 minutes, until the water has been completely absorbed and the rice is tender.

4 Flake the smoked trout and add to the pan with the almonds and raisins. Fork through gently. Cover the pan and leave the smoked trout to warm in the rice for a few minutes. Transfer to a warm serving dish, sprinkle over the parsley and serve immediately.

COOK'S TIP

Mango chutney and poppadoms would be the perfect accompaniments.

MIXED FISH JAMBALAYA

JAMBALAYA IS NOT UNLIKE A PAELLA, BUT MUCH SPICIER. THE NAME COMES FROM THE FRENCH "JAMBON", AS THE DISH WAS ORIGINALLY BASED ON HAM, BUT YOU CAN ADD MANY OTHER INGREDIENTS.

SERVES FOUR

INGREDIENTS

- 30ml/2 tbsp oil
- 115g/4oz smoked bacon, rinded and diced
- 1 onion, chopped
- 2 celery sticks, chopped
- 2 large garlic cloves, chopped
- 5ml/1 tsp cayenne pepper
- 2 bay leaves
- 5ml/1 tsp dried oregano
- 2.5ml/½ tsp dried thyme
- 4 tomatoes, peeled and chopped
- 150ml/¼ pint/⅔ cup ready-made tomato sauce
- 350g/12oz/1¾ cups long grain rice
- 475ml/16fl oz/2 cups fish stock
- 175g/6oz firm white fish fillets, skinned and cubed
- 115g/4oz cooked peeled prawns (shrimp)
- salt and ground black pepper
- 2 chopped spring onions (scallions), to garnish

1 Preheat the oven to 180°C/350°F/Gas 4. Heat the oil in a large, heavy pan or flameproof casserole. Add the smoked bacon and cook until crisp. Add the onion and celery and cook over a low heat, stirring frequently, until they are just beginning to stick to the base of the pan.

2 Add the garlic, cayenne pepper, bay leaves, oregano, thyme and chopped tomatoes. Season to taste with salt and pepper and stir well to combine. Stir in the tomato sauce, rice and fish stock and bring the mixture to the boil.

3 Gently stir in the cubes of fish. Transfer to an ovenproof dish and cover tightly with foil, or cover the casserole with a lid. Bake for 20–30 minutes, until the rice is just tender and the liquid has been absorbed. Stir in the prawns and heat through gently. Serve immediately, sprinkled with the spring onions.

Indonesian Pork and Prawn Rice

Nasi Goreng is an attractive way of using up leftovers and appears in many different variations throughout Indonesia. Rice is the main ingredient, although almost anything can be added to provide colour and flavour.

SERVES FOUR TO SIX

INGREDIENTS

- 3 eggs
- 60ml/4 tbsp vegetable oil
- 6 shallots, or 1 large onion, chopped
- 2 garlic cloves, crushed
- 2.5cm/1in piece fresh root ginger, chopped
- 2–3 small fresh red chillies, seeded and finely chopped
- 15ml/1 tbsp tamarind sauce
- 1cm/½in square piece shrimp paste or 15ml/1 tbsp fish sauce
- 2.5ml/½ tsp ground turmeric
- 30ml/2 tbsp coconut cream
- juice of 2 limes
- 10ml/2 tsp sugar
- 350g/12oz lean pork or chicken breast portions, skinned and sliced
- 350g/12oz raw or cooked prawn (shrimp) tails, peeled
- 175g/6oz/3 cups beansprouts
- 175g/6oz Chinese leaves (Chinese cabbage), shredded
- 175g/6oz/1½ cups frozen peas, thawed
- 250g/9oz/1¼ cups long grain rice, cooked
- salt
- 1 small bunch coriander (cilantro) or basil, coarsely chopped, to garnish

1 Beat the eggs with a pinch of salt in a bowl. Heat a non-stick frying pan over a medium heat. Pour in the eggs and move the pan around until they are beginning to set. Cook until set, then roll up, slice thinly, cover and set aside.

2 Heat 15ml/1 tbsp of the oil in a preheated wok or large, heavy frying pan. Add the shallots or onion and cook over a medium heat, stirring occasionally, for 8–10 minutes, until evenly browned. Remove from the wok, set aside and keep warm.

3 Heat the remaining 45ml/3 tbsp of oil in the wok or frying pan. Add the garlic, ginger and chillies and cook over a low heat, stirring frequently, for a few minutes until softened but not coloured.

4 Stir in the tamarind and shrimp paste or fish sauce, turmeric, coconut cream, lime juice, sugar and salt to taste. Cook briefly over a medium heat, stirring constantly. Add the pork or chicken and prawns and stir-fry for 3–4 minutes.

5 Toss the beansprouts, Chinese leaves and peas in the spice mixture and cook briefly. Add the cooked rice and stir-fry for 6–8 minutes, keeping it moving constantly to prevent it from burning. Transfer to a large, warm serving plate and garnish with the shredded egg pancake, the fried shallots or onion and the chopped fresh coriander or basil.

Mixed Smoked Fish Kedgeree

An ideal brunch dish on a cold weekend. Garnish with hard-boiled eggs and season well.

SERVES SIX

INGREDIENTS

- 450g/1lb mixed smoked fish such as smoked cod, smoked haddock, smoked mussels or oysters
- 300ml/½ pint/1¼ cups milk
- 175g/6oz long grain rice
- 1 slice lemon
- 50g/2oz butter
- 5ml/1 tsp medium curry powder
- 2.5ml/½ tsp freshly grated nutmeg
- 15ml/1 tbsp chopped fresh parsley
- salt and ground black pepper
- 3 eggs, hard-boiled, shelled and quartered, to serve

1 Put the smoked fish and milk in a pan, cover and poach for 10 minutes, or until it flakes. Drain off the milk and flake the fish. Mix with the smoked shellfish.

2 Cook the rice in lightly salted, boiling water, together with a slice of lemon, for 10–15 minutes, until just cooked and tender. Drain well.

3 Melt the butter in a large heavy pan over a low heat. Add the rice and fish and shellfish mixture, then shake the pan gently to mix all the ingredients together.

4 Stir in the curry powder, nutmeg and parsley and season with salt and pepper to taste. Divide the kedgeree among six warm plates and serve immediately, each garnished with two quarters of the hard-boiled eggs.

VARIATION

Substitute fresh salmon fillet for the smoked fish and poach it in water rather than milk.

LIGHT AND HEALTHY DISHES

What could be healthier than a meal based on simply cooked fish and shellfish? We should all include fish in our diet at least twice a week, particularly the oily fish that are so beneficial to health. Here are vibrant, attractive dishes certain to inspire, such as Roast Cod with Pancetta and Beans, Moroccan Spiced Mackerel, and Hoki Stir-Fry. All are quick to prepare and so full of fresh, natural flavours that healthy eating becomes pure pleasure.

Steamed Lettuce-Wrapped Sole

If you can afford it, use Dover sole fillets for this recipe; if not, lemon sole, trout, plaice, flounder and brill are all excellent cooked this way.

SERVES FOUR

INGREDIENTS

- 2 large sole fillets, skinned
- 15ml/1 tbsp sesame seeds
- 15ml/1 tbsp sunflower or groundnut (peanut) oil
- 10ml/2 tsp sesame oil
- 2.5cm/1in piece fresh root ginger, peeled and grated
- 3 garlic cloves, finely chopped
- 15ml/1 tbsp soy sauce or Thai fish sauce
- juice of 1 lemon
- 2 spring onions (scallions), thinly sliced
- 8 large soft lettuce leaves
- 12 large fresh mussels, scrubbed and bearded

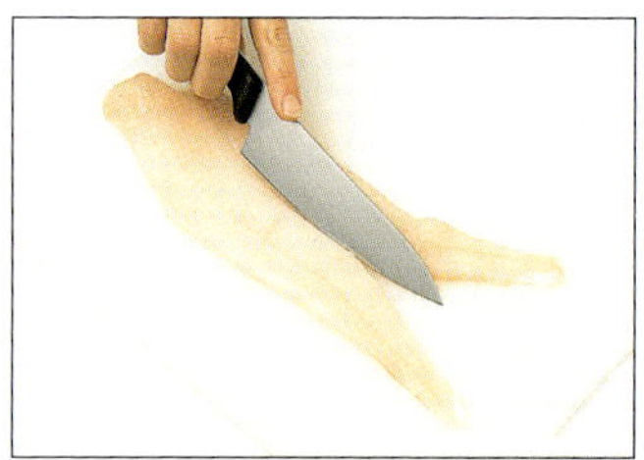

1 Cut the sole fillets in half lengthways. Season; set aside. Prepare a steamer.

2 Heat a heavy frying pan until hot. Toast the sesame seeds lightly but do not allow them to burn. Set aside in a bowl until required.

3 Heat the oils in the frying pan over a medium heat. Add the ginger and garlic and cook until lightly coloured; stir in the soy sauce or fish sauce, lemon juice and spring onions. Remove from the heat; stir in the toasted sesame seeds.

4 Lay the pieces of fish on baking parchment, skinned-side up; spread each evenly with the ginger mixture. Roll up each piece, starting at the tail end. Place on a baking sheet.

5 Plunge the lettuce leaves into the boiling water you have prepared for the steamer and immediately lift them out with tongs or a slotted spoon. Lay them out flat on kitchen paper and gently pat them dry. Wrap each sole parcel in two lettuce leaves, making sure that the filling is well covered to keep it in place.

6 Arrange the fish parcels in a steamer basket, cover and steam over simmering water for 8 minutes. Add the mussels and steam for 2–4 minutes, until opened. Discard any that remain closed. Put the parcels on individual warmed plates, halve and garnish with mussels. Serve immediately.

Smoked Haddock with Mustard Cabbage

This simple dish takes less than twenty minutes to make and is quite delicious. Serve it with new potatoes.

SERVES FOUR

INGREDIENTS

- 1 Savoy or pointu cabbage
- 675g/1½lb undyed smoked haddock fillet
- 300ml/½ pint/1¼ cups milk
- ½ onion, sliced into rings
- 2 bay leaves
- ½ lemon, sliced
- 4 white peppercorns
- 4 ripe tomatoes
- 50g/2oz/¼ cup butter
- 30ml/2 tbsp wholegrain mustard
- juice of 1 lemon
- salt and ground black pepper
- 30ml/2 tbsp chopped fresh parsley, to garnish

1 Cut the cabbage in half, remove the central core and thick ribs, then shred the cabbage. Cook in a pan of lightly salted, boiling water, or steam over boiling water for about 10 minutes, until just tender. Leave in the pan or steamer until required.

2 Meanwhile put the haddock in a large shallow pan with the milk, onion and bay leaves. Add the lemon slices and peppercorns. Bring to simmering point, cover and poach until the fish flakes easily when tested with the tip of a sharp knife. Depending on the thickness of the fish, this takes 8–10 minutes. Remove the pan from the heat. Preheat the grill (broiler).

3 Cut the tomatoes in half horizontally, season them with salt and pepper and grill (broil) until lightly browned. Drain the cabbage, refresh under cold water and drain again.

4 Melt the butter in a shallow pan or wok, add the cabbage and toss over the heat for 2 minutes. Mix in the mustard and season to taste, then tip the cabbage into a warmed serving dish.

5 Drain the haddock. Skin and cut the fish into four pieces. Place on top of the cabbage with some onion rings and grilled tomato halves. Pour on the lemon juice, then sprinkle with chopped parsley and serve.

FISH STEAKS WITH MUSTARD SAUCE

THE SIMPLEST OF DISHES, THIS MUSTARD SAUCE TURNS A PLAINLY COOKED FISH INTO SOMETHING SPECIAL. AS IT'S QUICK AND EASY, THIS IS A GREAT DISH FOR A MIDWEEK DINNER PARTY.

SERVES FOUR TO SIX

INGREDIENTS

- 4–6 halibut or turbot steaks, 2.5cm/1in thick
- 50g/2oz/¼ cup butter, melted
- salt and ground black pepper
- frisée lettuce and lemon wedges, to garnish

For the mustard sauce

- 60ml/4 tbsp Dijon mustard
- 300ml/½ pint/1¼ cups double (heavy) or whipping cream
- 2.5ml/½ tsp caster (superfine) sugar
- 15ml/1 tbsp white wine vinegar or lemon juice

1 Preheat the grill (broiler). Season the fish steaks well with salt and pepper. Arrange them on an oiled rack in the grill pan and brush the tops of the steaks generously with melted butter.

2 Cook under the grill, about 10cm/4in from the heat, for 4–5 minutes on each side, or until cooked through and the flesh flakes easily. Brush the second side of the fish generously with more melted butter, when you turn the steaks.

3 Meanwhile, make the sauce. Combine all the ingredients in a pan and bring to the boil over a low heat, stirring constantly with a wooden spoon. Simmer, whisking constantly, until the sauce thickens. Remove from the heat, set aside and keep warm.

4 Transfer the fish to warmed serving plates. Spoon the sauce evenly over the fish and serve immediately, garnished with frisée lettuce and lemon wedges.

SPICED FISH BAKED THAI-STYLE

BANANA LEAVES MAKE A PERFECT, NATURAL WRAPPING FOR FOOD, BUT YOU CAN USE FOIL INSTEAD.

SERVES FOUR

INGREDIENTS

- 4 red snapper or mullet, about 350g/12oz each
- banana leaves (optional)
- 1 lime, plus extra slices to garnish
- 1 garlic clove, thinly sliced
- 2 spring onions (scallions), thinly sliced
- 30ml/2 tbsp Thai red curry paste
- 60ml/4 tbsp coconut milk

1 Clean the fish, removing the scales, and then cut several deep, diagonal slashes in the sides of each one with a sharp knife. Place each fish on a layer of banana leaves or on a double thickness of foil.

2 Thinly slice half the lime and tuck the slices into the slashes in the fish, together with slivers of garlic. Sprinkle the spring onions evenly over the fish.

3 Finely grate the rind and squeeze the juice from the remaining half of the lime and mix both with the red curry paste and coconut milk in a small bowl until thoroughly combined. Spoon the mixture evenly over the fish.

4 Wrap the banana leaves or foil over the fish to enclose them completely. Tie the banana leaves securely with string or fold over the edges of the foil to secure. Cook the fish on a medium-hot barbecue or under a preheated grill (broiler) for about 15–20 minutes, turning occasionally until cooked through. Alternatively, you can bake the fish in a preheated oven, 200°C/400°F/Gas 6, for 20–25 minutes. Serve immediately, garnished with extra lime slices.

COOK'S TIP

A large, whole fish, such as sea bass or sea bream, can also be cooked this way. Allow about 10 minutes per 2.5cm/1in thickness.

Mackerel with Mustard and Lemon Butter

Look for bright, firm-looking fresh mackerel for the best flavour.

SERVES FOUR

INGREDIENTS

- 4 fresh mackerel, about 275g/10oz each, cleaned
- 175–225g/6–8oz young spinach leaves
- salt and ground black pepper

For the mustard and lemon butter

- 115g/4oz/½ cup butter, melted
- 30ml/2 tbsp wholegrain mustard
- grated rind of 1 lemon
- 30ml/2 tbsp lemon juice
- 45ml/3 tbsp chopped fresh parsley

1 Preheat the grill (broiler). To prepare each mackerel, using a sharp knife, cut off the heads just behind the gills, if this has not already been done, then cut along the line of the belly so that the fish can be opened out flat.

2 Place each fish, in turn, on a board, skin side up. Then, with the heel of your hand, press firmly along the length of the backbone to loosen it.

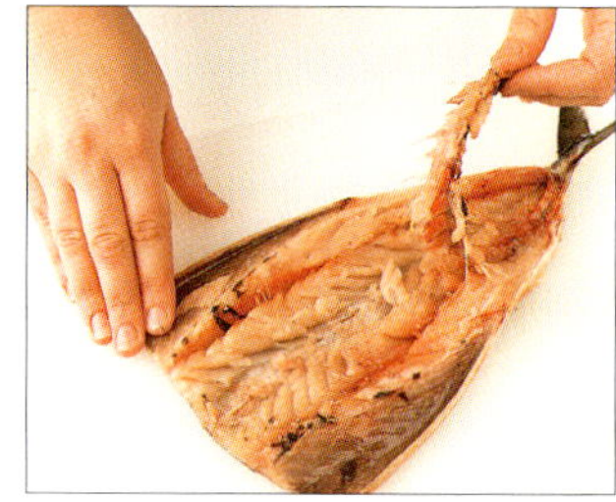

3 Turn the fish the other way up and carefully pull the bone away from the flesh. Remove the tail and cut each fish in half lengthways. Rinse under cold running water and pat dry with kitchen paper.

4 Score the skin three or four times, then season the fish well with salt and pepper.

5 To make the mustard and lemon butter, mix the melted butter, mustard, lemon rind and juice, parsley and seasoning.

6 Place the mackerel on a grill rack. Brush a little of the butter over the mackerel and grill (broil) for about 5 minutes each side, basting occasionally, until cooked through.

7 Arrange the spinach leaves in the centre of four large plates. Place the mackerel on top. Heat the remaining butter in a small pan until sizzling, pour over the mackerel and serve.

TURKISH COLD FISH

COLD FISH DISHES ARE APPRECIATED IN THE MIDDLE EAST AND FOR GOOD REASON – THEY ARE DELICIOUS! THIS VERSION CAN ALSO BE MADE WITH MACKEREL.

SERVES FOUR

INGREDIENTS
- 60ml/4 tbsp olive oil
- 900g/2lb porgy or snapper
- 2 onions, sliced
- 1 green (bell) pepper, seeded and sliced
- 1 red (bell) pepper, seeded and sliced
- 3 garlic cloves, crushed
- 15ml/1 tbsp tomato purée (paste)
- 50ml/2fl oz/¼ cup fish stock, bottled clam juice or water
- 5–6 tomatoes, peeled and sliced, or 400g/14oz can tomatoes
- 30ml/2 tbsp chopped fresh parsley
- 30ml/2 tbsp lemon juice
- 5ml/1 tsp paprika
- 20 green and black olives
- salt and ground black pepper
- bread and salad, to serve

1 Heat 30ml/2 tbsp of the oil in a large roasting pan or frying pan. Add the fish and cook on both sides until golden brown. Remove from the pan with a fish slice or metal spatula, cover and keep warm.

2 Heat the remaining oil in the pan and cook the onions over a medium heat for 2–3 minutes, until softened. Add the peppers and continue cooking for 3–4 minutes, stirring occasionally, then add the garlic and stir-fry for 1 more minute.

3 Mix together the tomato purée and the fish stock, clam juice or water in a small bowl and stir into the pan with the tomatoes, parsley, lemon juice and paprika. Season to taste with salt and pepper. Lower the heat and simmer very gently, stirring occasionally, for 15 minutes.

4 Return the fish to the pan and spoon the sauce over them to cover. Cook gently for 10 minutes, then add the olives and cook for a further 5 minutes or until just cooked through and the fish flakes easily.

5 Transfer the fish to a large serving dish and pour the sauce over the top. Leave to cool, then cover with clear film (plastic wrap) and chill in the refrigerator until completely cold. Serve cold with fresh bread and plenty of crisp salad.

VARIATION

One large fish looks spectacular and would make a good centrepiece for a dinner party. However, it can be tricky both to cook and to serve. If you want to prepare this dish for a family meal, buy four smaller fish and cook for a shorter time, until just tender and cooked through.

SALMON FISH CAKES

THE SECRET OF A GOOD FISH CAKE IS TO MAKE IT WITH FRESHLY PREPARED FISH AND POTATOES, HOME-MADE BREADCRUMBS AND PLENTY OF INTERESTING SEASONING.

SERVES FOUR

INGREDIENTS

- 450g/1lb cooked salmon fillet
- 450g/1lb freshly cooked potatoes, mashed
- 25g/1oz/2 tbsp butter, melted
- 10ml/2 tsp wholegrain mustard
- 15ml/1 tbsp each chopped fresh dill and chopped fresh parsley
- grated rind and juice of ½ lemon
- 15ml/1 tbsp plain (all-purpose) flour
- 1 egg, lightly beaten
- 150g/5oz/1¼ cups dried breadcrumbs
- 60ml/4 tbsp sunflower oil
- salt and ground black pepper
- rocket (arugula) and chives, to garnish
- lemon wedges, to serve

1 Flake the cooked salmon, discarding any skin and bones. Put it in a bowl with the mashed potato, melted butter and wholegrain mustard and mix well. Stir in the dill and parsley and lemon rind and juice. Season to taste with salt and pepper.

2 Divide the mixture into eight portions and shape each into a ball, then flatten into a round. Dip the fish cakes in flour, then in egg and finally in breadcrumbs, making sure that they are evenly coated.

3 Heat the oil in a frying pan until it is very hot. Fry the fish cakes, in batches, until golden brown and crisp all over. As each batch is ready, drain on kitchen paper and keep hot. Garnish with rocket leaves and chives and serve with lemon wedges.

COOK'S TIP

Almost any fresh white or hot-smoked fish is suitable; smoked cod and haddock are particularly good.

CRAB CAKES

UNLIKE FISH CAKES, CRAB CAKES ARE BOUND WITH EGG AND MAYONNAISE OR TARTARE SAUCE INSTEAD OF POTATOES, WHICH MAKES THEM LIGHT IN TEXTURE. IF YOU LIKE, THEY CAN BE GRILLED INSTEAD OF FRIED; BRUSH WITH A LITTLE OIL FIRST.

SERVES FOUR

INGREDIENTS

- 450g/1lb mixed brown and white crab meat
- 30ml/2 tbsp mayonnaise or tartare sauce
- 2.5–5ml/½–1 tsp mustard powder
- 1 egg, lightly beaten
- Tabasco sauce
- 45ml/3 tbsp chopped fresh parsley
- 4 spring onions (scallions), finely chopped (optional)
- 50–75g/2–3oz/½–¾ cup dried breadcrumbs, preferably home-made
- sunflower oil, for frying
- salt, ground black pepper and cayenne pepper
- chopped spring onions (scallions), to garnish
- red onion marmalade, to serve

1 Put the crab meat in a bowl and stir in the mayonnaise or tartare sauce, with the mustard and egg. Season with Tabasco, salt, pepper and cayenne.

2 Stir in the parsley, spring onions, if using, and 50g/2oz/½ cup of the breadcrumbs. The mixture should be just firm enough to hold together; depending on how much brown crab meat there is, you may need to add some more breadcrumbs.

3 Divide the mixture into eight portions, roll each into a ball and flatten slightly to make a thick flat disc. Spread out the crab cakes on a platter and put in the refrigerator for 30 minutes before frying.

4 Pour the oil into a shallow pan to a depth of about 5mm/¼in. Fry the crab cakes in two batches until golden brown all over. Drain on kitchen paper and keep hot. Serve with a spring onion garnish and red onion marmalade.

SALMON CAKES WITH SPICY MAYONNAISE

TASTE THE DIFFERENCE BETWEEN HOME-MADE FISH CAKES AND THE INFERIOR STORE-BOUGHT VARIETY WITH THIS DELICIOUS RECIPE.

SERVES FOUR

INGREDIENTS

- 2 large potatoes, about 350g/12oz
- 350g/12oz salmon fillet, skinned and finely chopped
- 45ml/3 tbsp chopped fresh dill
- 15ml/1 tbsp lemon juice
- plain (all-purpose) flour, for coating
- 45ml/3 tbsp vegetable oil
- salt and ground black pepper
- spicy mayonnaise (see Cook's Tip) and salad leaves, to serve

1 Put the potatoes in a pan of lightly salted, boiling water and parboil them for 15 minutes.

2 Meanwhile, mix together the salmon, dill and lemon juice in a large bowl and season well with salt and pepper. Cover with clear film (plastic wrap) and set aside.

3 Drain the potatoes well and leave them to cool. When they are cool enough to handle, peel off the skins.

4 Shred the potatoes into large strips on a coarse flat grater or the coarse side of a box grater.

5 Add the potato strips to the salmon mixture. Very gently mix together with your fingers, breaking up the strips of potato as little as possible.

6 Divide the salmon and potato mixture into eight portions. Gently roll each portion into a round, then shape into a compact cake, pressing well together. Finally, flatten the cakes to a thickness of about 1cm/½in.

7 Coat the salmon cakes lightly with flour, shaking off excess.

8 Heat the oil in a large, heavy frying pan. Add the salmon cakes and cook for about 5 minutes or until crisp and golden brown on both sides.

9 Drain the salmon cakes well on kitchen paper and serve with the spicy mayonnaise and salad.

COOK'S TIP

To make spicy mayonnaise, mix together 350ml/12fl oz/1½ cups mayonnaise, 10ml/2 tsp Dijon mustard, 2.5–5ml/½–1 tsp Worcestershire sauce and a dash of Tabasco sauce. You can use home-made mayonnaise or a good-quality commercial variety.

TUNA AND CORN FISH CAKES

THESE ECONOMICAL LITTLE TUNA FISH CAKES ARE QUICK TO MAKE.

SERVES FOUR

INGREDIENTS

- 300g/11oz cooked mashed potatoes
- 200g/7oz can tuna in soya oil, drained and flaked
- 115g/4oz canned or frozen corn
- 30ml/2 tbsp chopped fresh parsley
- 50g/2oz/1 cup fresh white or brown breadcrumbs
- salt and ground black pepper
- lemon wedges, to garnish
- fresh vegetables or salad, to serve

1 Place the mashed potato in a large bowl and stir in the drained tuna, corn and chopped parsley until thoroughly combined.

2 Season to taste with salt and pepper, then divide the mixture into eight portions. Shape each portion into a patty shape with your hands.

3 Spread out the breadcrumbs on a plate and gently press the fish cakes into the breadcrumbs to coat them lightly, then transfer to a baking sheet. If you have time, cover the fish cakes with clear film (plastic wrap) and chill in the refrigerator for 30 minutes to firm up.

4 Preheat the grill (broiler). Cook the fish cakes under a medium-hot grill until crisp and golden brown, turning once. Garnish with the lemon wedges and serve immediately with the fresh vegetables or salad.

COOK'S TIPS

- For simple variations, which are just as tasty and nutritious, try using canned sardines, red or pink salmon, or smoked mackerel in place of the tuna.
- If you are in a hurry, you can use instant mash, made up following the instructions on the packet.
- If you are using frozen corn, leave it to thaw first. If using canned, drain thoroughly in a sieve.

FRESH TUNA SHIITAKE TERIYAKI

TERIYAKI, A SWEET SOY MARINADE GIVES A RICH FLAVOUR TO FRESH TUNA STEAKS.

SERVES FOUR

INGREDIENTS
- 4 x 175g/6oz fresh tuna steaks
- 175g/6oz shiitake mushrooms, sliced
- 150ml/¼ pint/⅔ cup teriyaki sauce
- 225g/8oz white radish, peeled
- 2 large carrots, peeled
- salt
- boled rice, to serve

1 Season the tuna steaks with a sprinkling of salt, then set aside for 20 minutes to allow it to penetrate. Mix together the fish and sliced mushrooms, pour the teriyaki sauce over them and set aside to marinate for a further 20–30 minutes, or longer if you have the time. Preheat the grill (broiler), or light the barbecue coals.

COOK'S TIP

You can make your own teriyaki sauce by mixing together 90ml/6 tbsp shoyu (Japanese soy sauce), 15ml/1 tbsp caster (superfine) sugar, 15ml/1 tbsp dry white wine and 15ml/1 tbsp rice wine or dry sherry.

2 Drain the tuna, reserving the marinade and mushrooms. Cook the tuna under a medium grill or on the barbecue for about 4 minutes on each side, until done.

3 Transfer the mushrooms and marinade to a stainless steel pan and simmer gently over a medium heat for 3–4 minutes.

4 Slice the radish and carrots thinly, then shred finely with a chopping knife. Arrange in heaps on four serving plates and add the fish, with the mushrooms and sauce poured over. Serve with boiled rice.

VARIATION

You can substitute salmon for the tuna, but it may need less cooking.

Whiting Fillets in a Polenta Crust

Use quick and easy polenta if you can, as it will give a better and crunchier coating.

SERVES FOUR

INGREDIENTS

- 8 small whiting fillets
- finely grated rind of 1 lemon
- 225g/8oz/1⅔ cups polenta
- 30ml/2 tbsp olive oil
- 15g/½ oz/1 tbsp butter
- 30ml/2 tbsp mixed fresh herbs, such as parsley, chervil and chives
- salt and ground black pepper
- toasted pine nuts and sliced red onion, to garnish
- steamed spinach, to serve

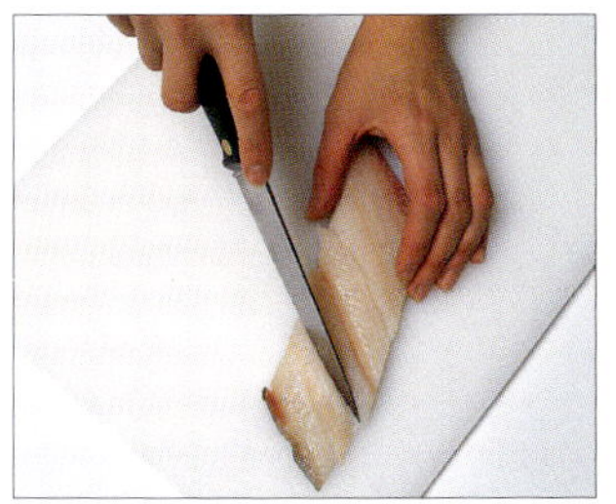

1 With a sharp knife, make four small cuts in each whiting fillet to prevent the fish from curling up when it is being cooked.

2 Season the fish generously with salt and pepper and sprinkle the lemon rind over it.

3 Press the polenta evenly on to the fillets. Cover with clear film (plastic wrap) and chill in the refrigerator for 30 minutes.

COOK'S TIP

Whiting is very delicate in texture, so handle with care. Buy really fresh fish, as the longer it has been out of the sea, the more easily it breaks up.

4 Heat the oil and butter in a large, heavy frying pan. Add the fish fillets and cook gently for 3–4 minutes on each side, until cooked through.

5 Transfer the fish to four warm serving plates. Sprinkle over the fresh herbs and garnish with toasted pine nuts and red onion slices. Serve immediately with steamed spinach.

Fish Fillets with Orange and Tomato Sauce

SERVES FOUR

INGREDIENTS

- 45ml/3 tbsp plain (all-purpose) flour
- 4 fillets of firm white fish, such as cod, sea bass or sole, about 675g/1½lb
- 15g/½oz/1 tbsp butter
- 30ml/2 tbsp olive oil
- 1 onion, sliced
- 2 garlic cloves, chopped
- 1.5ml/¼ tsp ground cumin
- 500g/1¼lb tomatoes, peeled, seeded and chopped
- 120ml/4fl oz/½ cup fresh orange juice
- salt and ground black pepper
- orange wedges, to garnish
- steamed vegetables, such as mangtetouts or green beans, to serve

1 Put the flour on a plate and season well with salt and pepper. Coat the fish fillets lightly with the seasoned flour, shaking off any excess.

2 Heat the butter and half the oil in a large, heavy frying pan. Add the fish fillets to the pan and cook for about 3 minutes on each side, until golden brown and the flesh flakes easily when tested with a fork.

COOK'S TIP

If possible, use sun-ripened plum tomatoes for the best flavour. Alternatively, substitute 400g/14oz canned chopped tomatoes for the fresh. (Chopped tomatoes tend to be less watery than whole.) You may need to cook the sauce for a little longer in step 5 to be sure that it is thickened.

3 When the fish is cooked, transfer to a warmed serving platter. Cover with foil and keep warm while you make the sauce.

4 Heat the remaining oil in the pan. Add the onion and garlic and cook for about 5 minutes, until softened but not coloured.

5 Stir in the ground cumin, chopped tomatoes and orange juice. Bring to the boil over a medium heat and cook, stirring frequently, for about 10 minutes, until thickened. Garnish the fish with orange wedges and serve immediately with steamed vegetables, handing the sauce separately.

CAJUN-STYLE COD

THIS RECIPE WORKS EQUALLY WELL WITH ANY FIRM-FLESHED FISH, SUCH AS SWORDFISH, SHARK, TUNA, MONKFISH OR HALIBUT.

SERVES FOUR

INGREDIENTS

- 4 cod steaks, each weighing about 175g/6oz
- 30ml/2 tbsp natural (plain) yogurt
- 15ml/1 tbsp lime or lemon juice
- 1 garlic clove, crushed
- 5ml/1 tsp ground cumin
- 5ml/1 tsp paprika
- 5ml/1 tsp mustard powder
- 2.5ml/½ tsp cayenne pepper
- 2.5ml/½ tsp dried thyme
- 2.5ml/½ tsp dried oregano
- vegetable oil, for brushing
- lemon wedges, baby potatoes and mixed salad, to serve

1 Pat the fish dry on kitchen paper. Mix together the yogurt and lime or lemon juice and brush lightly over both sides of the fish.

2 Mix together the garlic, cumin, paprika, mustard powder, cayenne, thyme and oregano. Coat both sides of the fish with the seasoning mix, rubbing in well.

COOK'S TIP

The technique of coating fish – or even meat – in dry spices and then cooking until almost black is, to many people's surprise, quite a modern innovation in Cajun cooking and not a long-standing tradition. However, it soon achieved great popularity.

3 Brush a ridged grill pan or heavy frying pan with a little oil. Heat until very hot. Add the fish and cook over a high heat for 4 minutes, or until the underside is well browned. Brush the fish with a little more oil, if necessary, turn it over and cook for a further 4 minutes, or until the steaks have cooked through.

4 Transfer the fish to four warmed serving plates and serve with boiled baby potatoes, mixed salad and lemon wedges.

MONKFISH WITH MEXICAN SALSA

THIS IS A GREAT DISH FOR A SUMMER MEAL.

SERVES FOUR

INGREDIENTS

- 675g/1½lb monkfish tail
- 45ml/3 tbsp olive oil
- 30ml/2 tbsp lime juice
- 1 garlic clove, crushed
- 15ml/1 tbsp chopped fresh coriander (cilantro)
- salt and ground black pepper
- fresh coriander (cilantro) sprigs and lime slices, to garnish

For the salsa

- 4 tomatoes
- 1 avocado
- ½ red onion, chopped
- 1 green chilli, seeded and chopped
- 30ml/2 tbsp chopped fresh coriander (cilantro)
- 30ml/2 tbsp olive oil
- 15ml/1 tbsp lime juice

1 Make the salsa. Cut a cross in the base of the tomatoes and plunge into boiling water for 30 seconds. Drain, refresh under cold water, then peel off the skins. Halve, seed and dice, then place in a bowl. Peel, stone (pit) and dice the avocado, then add to the bowl. Add all the remaining salsa ingredients, mix well, cover and set aside at room temperature for about 40 minutes.

COOK'S TIP

It is important to remove the tough, pinkish-grey membrane covering the monkfish tail before cooking, otherwise it will shrink and toughen the monkfish.

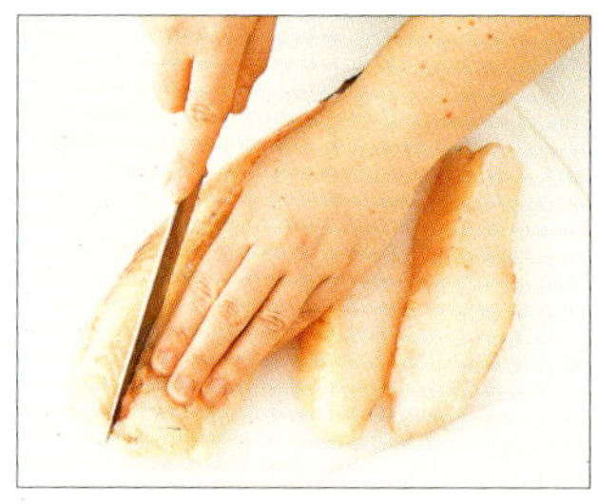

2 Prepare the monkfish. Using a sharp knife, remove the pinkish-grey membrane that may still cover the fish. Cut the fillets from either side of the backbone, then cut each fillet in half lengthways.

3 Mix together the olive oil, lime juice, garlic and chopped coriander in a non-metallic dish and season with salt and pepper.

4 Add the monkfish to the dish. Turn the fillets several times to coat evenly with the marinade, then cover the dish with clear film (plastic wrap) and leave to marinate at cool room temperature for about 30 minutes or in the refrigerator for about 1 hour.

5 Preheat the grill (broiler). Remove the monkfish from the dish, drain well and reserve the marinade. Cook the fish fillet under the grill for 10–12 minutes, turning once and brushing frequently with the marinade, until cooked through and the flesh flakes easily.

6 Serve the monkfish immediately, garnished with fresh coriander sprigs and lime slices and accompanied by the Mexican salsa.

RED SNAPPER WITH CORIANDER SALSA

SNAPPER IS A FIRM FISH WITH LITTLE FAT AND BENEFITS FROM A SAUCE WITH LOTS OF TEXTURE AND FLAVOUR.

SERVES FOUR

INGREDIENTS

- 4 red snapper fillets, about 175g/6oz each
- 25ml/1½ tbsp vegetable oil
- 15g/½oz/1 tbsp butter
- salt and ground black pepper
- coriander (cilantro) sprigs and orange rind, to garnish
- salad, to serve (optional)

For the salsa

- 1 bunch fresh coriander (cilantro), stalks removed
- 250ml/8fl oz/1 cup olive oil
- 2 garlic cloves, chopped
- 2 tomatoes, seeded and chopped
- 30ml/2 tbsp fresh orange juice
- 15ml/1 tbsp sherry vinegar

1 To make the salsa, place the coriander, oil and garlic in a food processor or blender. Process until almost smooth. Add the tomatoes and pulse on and off several times; the mixture should be well mixed but slightly chunky.

2 Transfer the mixture to a bowl. Stir in the orange juice and vinegar and season with salt to taste. Cover with clear film (plastic wrap) and set the salsa aside until ready to serve.

3 Rinse the red snapper fillets under cold running water and pat dry with kitchen paper, then season well with salt and pepper on both sides. Heat the oil and butter in a large, heavy frying pan. When hot, add the fish fillets and cook over a medium heat for about 2–3 minutes on each side, or until opaque and the flesh flakes easily. Cook the fish in two batches, if necessary.

4 Transfer the snapper fillets to four warmed serving plates. Top with a spoonful of salsa. Serve immediately, garnished with coriander and orange rind and accompanied with a salad, if you like.

COOK'S TIP

If you order the snapper, ask your supplier for the bones, as they make a rich, gelatinous stock.

SIZZLING PRAWNS

Garlic prawns are hugely popular in Spain, both with and without the addition of chilli. They are normally cooked in small, individual earthenware casseroles, which stand on an iron baking sheet. A frying pan will produce an authentic Spanish result.

SERVES FOUR

INGREDIENTS

- 1–2 dried chillies (to taste)
- 60ml/4 tbsp olive oil
- 3 garlic cloves, finely chopped
- 16 large raw prawns (shrimp), unpeeled
- salt and ground black pepper
- French bread, to serve

VARIATION

To make classic *gambas al ajillo* – garlic prawns (shrimp) – simply omit the chilli. The word *ajillo* tells you how the garlic is prepared. The diminutive means finely chopped, like the garlic in the final dish. The alternative is *gambas con ajo*, which means with garlic. For this dish, slices of garlic are fried until brown, to flavour the oil, then discarded.

1 Split the chillies lengthways and discard the seeds. It is best to do this with a knife and fork, because the membranes, in particular, contain hot capsicum, which can be very irritating to the eyes, nose and mouth.

2 Heat the oil in a large frying pan and stir-fry the garlic and chilli for 1 minute, until the garlic begins to turn brown.

3 Add the whole prawns and stir-fry for 3–4 minutes, coating them well with the flavoured oil.

4 Remove from the heat and divide the prawns among four dishes. Spoon over the flavoured oil and serve immediately. (Remember to provide a plate for the heads and shells, plus plenty of napkins for messy fingers.)

SPICED CLAMS

SPANISH CLAMS, ESPECIALLY IN THE NORTH, ARE MUCH LARGER THAN CLAMS FOUND ELSEWHERE, AND HAVE MORE SUCCULENT BODIES. THIS MODERN RECIPE USES ARAB SPICING TO MAKE A HOT DIP OR SAUCE. SERVE WITH PLENTY OF FRESH BREAD TO MOP UP THE DELICIOUS JUICES.

SERVES THREE TO FOUR

INGREDIENTS

- 1 small onion, finely chopped
- 1 celery stick, sliced
- 2 garlic cloves, finely chopped
- 2.5cm/1in piece fresh root ginger, grated
- 30ml/2 tbsp olive oil
- 1.5ml/¼ tsp chilli powder
- 5ml/1 tsp ground turmeric
- 30ml/2 tbsp chopped fresh parsley
- 500g/1¼ lb small, fresh clams, scrubbed
- 30ml/2 tbsp dry white wine
- salt and ground black pepper
- celery leaves, to garnish
- fresh bread, to serve

COOK'S TIPS

- There are many different varieties of clam fished off the coast of Spain. One of the best is the *almeja fina* (the carpet shell clam), which is perfect used in this dish. They have grooved brown shells with a yellow lattice pattern.
- Before cooking the clams, check that all the shells are closed. Any clams that do not open after cooking should be discarded.

1 Place the onion, celery, garlic and ginger in a large pan, add the olive oil, spices and chopped parsley and stir-fry for about 5 minutes. Add the clams to the pan and cook for 2 minutes.

2 Add the wine, then cover and cook gently for 2–3 minutes, shaking the pan occasionally. Season. Discard any clams whose shells remain closed, then serve, garnished with the celery leaves.

CRUMB-COATED PRAWNS

THESE PRAWNS ARE DELICIOUSLY SPICY.

SERVES FOUR

INGREDIENTS

- 90g/3½oz/¾ cup polenta
- about 5–10ml/1–2 tsp cayenne pepper, to taste
- 2.5ml/½ tsp ground cumin
- 5ml/1 tsp salt
- 30ml/2 tbsp chopped fresh coriander (cilantro) or parsley
- 1kg/2¼lb large raw prawns (shrimp), peeled and deveined
- plain (all-purpose) flour, for dredging
- 50ml/2fl oz/¼ cup vegetable oil
- 115g/4oz/1 cup coarsely grated Cheddar cheese
- lime wedges and tomato salsa, to serve

1 Put the polenta, cayenne pepper, cumin, salt and chopped coriander or parsley in a bowl and mix well until thoroughly combined.

2 Coat the prawns lightly in a little flour, then dip them in cold water and roll in the polenta mixture until they are evenly coated.

3 Heat the oil in a large, heavy frying pan. When hot, add the prawns, in batches if necessary. Cook over a medium heat, stirring and tossing well, for 2–3 minutes on each side, until they are cooked through. Drain on kitchen paper.

4 Preheat the grill (broiler). Place the prawns in a flameproof dish, or in four individual ones. Sprinkle over the grated cheese. Grill (broil) for 2–3 minutes until the cheese is bubbling. Serve immediately with lime wedges and tomato salsa.

Sweet and Sour Prawns

It is best to use raw prawns. If you are using cooked ones, add them to the sauce without the initial deep-frying.

SERVES FOUR TO SIX

INGREDIENTS

- 450g/1lb raw king prawns (jumbo shrimp), unpeeled
- vegetable oil, for deep-frying
- lettuce leaves, to serve

For the sauce

- 15ml/1 tbsp vegetable oil
- 15ml/1 tbsp finely chopped spring onions (scallions)
- 10ml/2 tsp finely chopped fresh root ginger
- 30ml/2 tbsp light soy sauce
- 30ml/2 tbsp soft light brown sugar
- 45ml/3 tbsp rice vinegar
- 15ml/1 tbsp Chinese rice wine
- 120ml/4fl oz/½ cup chicken or vegetable stock
- 15ml/1 tbsp cornflour (cornstarch) paste
- few drops sesame oil

1 Remove the prawn heads if necessary. Pull the soft legs off the prawns without removing the tail shells. Dry well with kitchen paper.

2 Heat the vegetable oil in a large pan or deep-fryer to 180–190°C/350–375°F or until a cube of stale bread browns in 30 seconds. Add the prawns, preferably in a deep-frying basket, and fry for 35–40 seconds, or until their colour changes from grey to bright orange. Remove and drain on kitchen paper.

3 To make the sauce, heat the oil in a preheated wok or frying pan. Add the spring onions and ginger, followed by the soy sauce, sugar, vinegar, rice wine and stock, and bring to the boil.

4 Add the prawns, mix well, then thicken the sauce with the cornflour paste, stirring constantly. Sprinkle with the sesame oil. Arrange a bed of lettuce on a large serving dish, top with the prawns and sauce and serve immediately.

MUSSELS WITH A PARSLEY CRUST

The stormy Atlantic coast of Spain produces the best mussels in the world. Known as mejillones *in Spain, they grow to enormous size in a very short time, without becoming tough. Here they are grilled with a deliciously fragrant topping of Parmesan cheese, garlic and parsley, which helps to prevent the mussels from becoming overcooked.*

SERVES FOUR

INGREDIENTS

- 450g/1lb fresh mussels
- 45ml/3 tbsp water
- 15ml/1 tbsp melted butter
- 15ml/1 tbsp olive oil
- 45ml/3 tbsp freshly grated Parmesan cheese
- 30ml/2 tbsp chopped fresh parsley
- 2 garlic cloves, finely chopped
- 2.5ml/½ tsp coarsely ground black pepper
- crusty bread, to serve

COOK'S TIP

Steaming the mussels produces about 250ml/8fl oz/1 cup wonderful shellfish stock that can be used in other fish and shellfish recipes. Once the mussels have been steamed, remove them from the pan and leave the broth liquor to cool, then store it in a sealed container in the refrigerator or freezer.

Combining fish and shellfish stock is the backbone of many Spanish fish dishes such as *merluza con salsa verde* (hake with green sauce). It is said that the stock from one shellfish makes the best sauce for another.

1 Scrub the mussels thoroughly, scraping off any barnacles with a round-bladed knife and pulling out the gritty beards. Sharply tap any open mussels and discard any that fail to close or whose shells are broken.

2 Place the mussels in a large pan and add the water. Cover the pan with a lid and steam for about 5 minutes, or until the mussel shells have opened.

3 Drain the mussels well and discard any that remain closed. Carefully snap off the top shell from each mussel, leaving the actual flesh still attached to the bottom shell.

4 Balance the shells in a flameproof dish, packing them closely together to make sure that they stay level.

5 Preheat the grill (broiler) to high. Put the melted butter, olive oil, grated Parmesan cheese, parsley, garlic and black pepper in a small bowl and mix well to combine.

6 Spoon a small amount of the cheese and garlic mixture on top of each mussel and gently press down with the back of the spoon.

7 Grill (broil) the mussels for about 2 minutes, or until they are sizzling and golden. Serve the mussels in their shells, with plenty of bread to mop up the delicious juices.

COOK'S TIP

Give each guest one of the discarded top shells of the mussels. They can be used as a little spoon to free the body from the shell of the next. Scoop up the mussel in the empty shell and tip the shellfish and topping into your mouth.

Spanish-style Hake

Cod and haddock cutlets will also work well.

SERVES FOUR

INGREDIENTS
- 30ml/2 tbsp olive oil
- 25g/1oz/2 tbsp butter
- 1 onion, chopped
- 3 garlic cloves, crushed
- 15ml/1 tbsp plain (all-purpose) flour
- 2.5ml/½ tsp paprika
- 4 hake cutlets, about 175g/6oz each
- 225g/8oz fine green beans, cut into 2.5cm/1in lengths
- 350ml/12fl oz/1½ cups fish stock
- 150ml/¼ pint/⅔ cup dry white wine
- 30ml/2 tbsp dry sherry
- 16–20 fresh mussels, scrubbed
- 45ml/3 tbsp chopped fresh parsley
- salt and ground black pepper

1 Heat the oil and butter in a sauté pan or large, heavy frying pan. Add the chopped onion and cook over a low heat, stirring occasionally, for about 5 minutes, until softened and translucent, but not browned. Add the crushed garlic cloves and cook for 1 minute more.

VARIATION
You can substitute fresh clams for the mussels or even a mixture of mussels and clams, if you like.

2 Mix together the flour and paprika in a small bowl, then lightly dust the mixture over the hake cutlets. Push the onion and garlic to one side of the frying pan. Increase the heat to medium, add the hake cutlets to the pan and cook until they are golden on both sides.

3 Stir in the green beans, fish stock, wine and sherry and season with salt and pepper to taste. Bring to the boil and cook for 2 minutes.

4 Add the mussels and parsley, cover and cook for about 5–8 minutes, until all the mussels open. Discard any closed ones.

5 Divide among warmed, shallow bowls and serve immediately.

HALIBUT WITH TOMATO VINAIGRETTE

SAUCE VIERGE, AN UNCOOKED MIXTURE OF TOMATOES, AROMATIC FRESH HERBS AND OLIVE OIL, CAN BE SERVED AT ROOM TEMPERATURE OR, AS IN THIS DISH, SLIGHTLY WARM.

SERVES FOUR

INGREDIENTS

- 3 large, ripe beefsteak tomatoes, peeled, seeded and chopped
- 2 shallots or 1 small red onion, finely chopped
- 1 garlic clove, crushed
- 90ml/6 tbsp chopped mixed fresh herbs, such as parsley, basil, tarragon, chervil or chives
- 120ml/4fl oz/½ cup extra virgin olive oil
- 4 halibut fillets or steaks, 175–200g/6–7oz each
- salt and ground black pepper
- green salad, to serve

1 Mix together the tomatoes, shallots or onion, garlic and mixed herbs in a medium bowl. Stir in the olive oil and season to taste with salt and freshly ground black pepper. Cover the bowl with clear film (plastic wrap) and set aside at room temperature for about 1 hour to allow the flavours to blend.

2 Preheat the grill (broiler). Line a grill pan with foil and brush the foil lightly with oil.

COOK'S TIP

Some manufacturers specifically advise against lining the grill (broiler) pan with foil. In that case, simply brush the base of the clean grill pan with oil.

3 Season the halibut fillets or steaks well on both sides with salt and pepper. Place the fish on the foil and brush with a little extra oil. Grill (broil) for 5–6 minutes, turning once, until the fish is a light golden brown and cooked through.

4 Pour the sauce into a small pan and heat gently for a few minutes, until warm.

5 Place the fish on four warm plates and spoon over the sauce, then serve immediately with a green salad.

Mackerel California-style

Fish, well coated with spices, are often fried until "blackened" in California, but this does make a lot of smoke and smell in the kitchen. This recipe doesn't go quite that far.

SERVES 2–4

INGREDIENTS

- 10ml/2 tsp paprika
- 7.5ml/1½ tsp salt
- 2.5ml/½ tsp onion powder
- 2.5ml/½ tsp garlic powder
- 2.5ml/½ tsp white pepper
- 2.5ml/½ tsp black pepper
- 2.5ml/½ tsp dried dill
- 2.5ml/½ tsp dried oregano
- 2 large, thick mackerel, cleaned and filleted
- 115g/4oz/½ cup butter
- fresh oregano sprigs, to garnish
- lemon slices, to serve

1 Mix together the paprika, salt, onion powder, garlic powder, white and black pepper, dill and dried oregano in a small bowl. Sprinkle the spice mixture over each fillet of mackerel until well coated.

2 Heat half the butter in a large, heavy frying pan until really hot. Add two fish fillets and cook over a medium heat for about 2 minutes on each side. Remove immediately, cover and keep warm, then add the remaining butter and, when it has melted, cook the rest of the mackerel fillets in the same way.

3 Transfer the fish to warm serving plates and garnish with oregano sprigs. Serve piping hot with a little of the butter from the pan poured over and with slices of lemon.

COOK'S TIP

Other fish, such as salmon, red snapper and tuna, are also suitable, but thick cuts are best.

Trout with Curried Orange Butter

Small trout are delicious served with this tangy butter. Children love the buttery curry flavour, but for them it is best to fillet the cooked trout and remove the bones.

SERVES FOUR

INGREDIENTS

- 25g/1oz/2 tbsp butter, softened
- 5ml/1 tsp curry powder
- 5ml/1 tsp grated orange rind
- 4 small trout, gutted and heads removed
- vegetable oil, for brushing
- salt and ground black pepper
- 4 orange wedges, to garnish
- boiled new potatoes, to serve

1 Mix together the butter, curry powder and orange rind in a bowl. Season with salt and pepper. Wrap in foil and freeze for 10 minutes.

2 Brush the fish all over with oil and sprinkle well with salt and pepper. Make three diagonal slashes through the skin and flesh, on each side of the fish.

3 Preheat the grill (broiler). Cut the flavoured butter into small pieces and insert them into the slashes. Place the fish on the grill tray and cook under a high heat for 3–4 minutes on each side, until cooked through.

4 Serve the fish immediately, with new potatoes, garnished with wedges of orange.

BAKED SEA BASS WITH FENNEL

SEA BASS HAS A WONDERFUL FLAVOUR, BUT CHEAPER ALTERNATIVES, SUCH AS SNAPPER, BREAM OR PORGY, CAN BE USED. SERVE WITH CRISPLY COOKED GREEN BEANS TOSSED IN OLIVE OIL AND GARLIC.

SERVES FOUR

INGREDIENTS

- 4 fennel bulbs, trimmed
- 4 tomatoes, peeled and diced
- 8 drained canned anchovy fillets, halved lengthways
- a large pinch of saffron threads, soaked in 30ml/2 tbsp hot water
- 150ml/¼ pint/⅔ cup chicken or fish stock
- 2 red or yellow (bell) peppers, seeded and each cut into 12 strips
- 4 garlic cloves, chopped
- 15ml/1 tbsp chopped fresh marjoram
- 45ml/3 tbsp olive oil
- 1 sea bass, about 1.75kg/4–4½lb, scaled and cleaned
- salt and ground black pepper
- chopped parsley, to garnish

1 Preheat the oven to 200°C/400°F/Gas 6. Quarter the fennel bulbs lengthways. Cook in lightly salted boiling water for 5 minutes, until barely tender. Drain and arrange in a shallow ovenproof dish. Season with pepper; set aside.

2 Spoon the diced tomatoes and anchovy strips on top of the fennel. Stir the saffron and its soaking water into the stock and pour the mixture over the tomatoes. Lay the strips of pepper alongside the fennel and sprinkle with the garlic and marjoram. Drizzle 30ml/2 tbsp of the olive oil over the peppers and season with salt and pepper.

VARIATION

If you like, use large pieces of thick-cut halibut or turbot for this dish.

3 Bake the vegetables for 15 minutes. Season the prepared sea bass inside and out and lay it on top of the fennel and pepper mixture. Drizzle the remaining olive oil over the fish and bake for 30–40 minutes more, until the sea bass flesh comes away easily from the bone when tested with the point of a sharp knife. Serve, garnished with parsley.

MOROCCAN SPICED MACKEREL

MACKEREL IS EXTREMELY GOOD FOR YOU, BUT SOME PEOPLE FIND ITS HEALTHY OILINESS TOO MUCH TO TAKE. THE MOROCCAN SPICES IN THIS RECIPE COUNTERACT THE RICHNESS OF THE FISH.

SERVES FOUR

INGREDIENTS

- 150ml/¼ pint/⅔ cup sunflower oil
- 15ml/1 tbsp paprika
- 5–10ml/1–2 tsp harissa (chilli sauce) or chilli powder
- 10ml/2 tsp ground cumin
- 10ml/2 tsp ground coriander
- 2 garlic cloves, crushed
- juice of 2 lemons
- 30ml/2 tbsp chopped fresh mint leaves
- 30ml/2 tbsp chopped fresh coriander (cilantro)
- 4 mackerel, cleaned
- salt and ground black pepper
- mint sprigs, to garnish
- lemon wedges, to serve

1 In a bowl, whisk together the oil, spices, garlic and lemon juice. Season, then stir in the mint and coriander.

2 Make two or three diagonal slashes on either side of each mackerel so that they will absorb the marinade. Pour the marinade into a shallow non-metallic dish that is large enough to hold the fish in a single layer.

3 Put in the mackerel and turn them over in the marinade, spooning it into the slashes. Cover the dish with clear film (plastic wrap) and place in the refrigerator for at least 3 hours.

4 When you are ready to cook the mackerel, preheat the grill (broiler) to medium-high. Transfer the fish to the grill rack and grill (broil) for 5–7 minutes on each side, until just cooked, turning the fish once and basting them several times with the marinade. Serve hot or cold with lemon wedges, garnished with mint. Herb-flavoured couscous or rice make good accompaniments.

COOK'S TIP

These spicy mackerel can be cooked on a barbecue. Make sure the coals are very hot before you begin cooking. Arrange the fish on a large hinged rack to make turning easier and barbecue (grill) for 5–7 minutes, turning once.

VARIATION

Trout, bonito, trevally or bluefish are also good cooked this way.

Stuffed Plaice Rolls

Plaice fillets are an excellent choice for family meals because they are economical, easy to cook and free of bones.

SERVES FOUR

INGREDIENTS

- 2 carrots, grated
- 1 courgette (zucchini), grated
- 60ml/4 tbsp fresh wholemeal (whole-wheat) breadcrumbs
- 15ml/1 tbsp lime or lemon juice
- 4 plaice or flounder fillets
- salt and ground black pepper
- boiled new potatoes, to serve

1 Preheat the oven to 200°C/400°F/ Gas 6. Mix together the grated carrots and courgette in a large bowl. Add the wholemeal breadcrumbs and lime or lemon juice and season with salt and pepper. Stir well.

2 Lay the fish fillets skin side up and divide the stuffing among them, spreading it evenly.

3 Roll up to enclose the stuffing and place the fish in a single layer in an ovenproof dish. Cover and bake for about 30 minutes, or until the fish flakes easily. Serve immediately with boiled new potatoes.

COOK'S TIP

If you like, you can remove the skin from the fish fillets before cooking. As a general rule, most cooks prefer to remove the dark, spotty skin, but often leave the white skin.

VARIATION

This recipe creates its own delicious juices, but for an extra sauce, stir chopped fresh parsley into a little fromage frais, or ricotta cheese mixed with yogurt or sour cream, and serve with the fish.

Fillets of Hake Baked with Thyme

Quick cooking is the essence of this dish – it's amazingly simple and easy to make, yet tastes really special. Use the freshest garlic available.

SERVES FOUR

INGREDIENTS
- 4 x 175g/6oz hake fillets
- 1 shallot, finely chopped
- 2 garlic cloves, thinly sliced
- 4 fresh thyme sprigs
- grated rind and juice of 1 lemon
- 30ml/2 tbsp extra virgin olive oil
- salt and ground black pepper
- coarsely grated lemon rind and fresh thyme sprigs, to garnish

1 Preheat the oven to 180°C/350°F/Gas 4. Arrange the hake fillets on the base of a large roasting pan. Sprinkle the shallot, garlic cloves, thyme and lemon rind on top.

2 Season the fish well with salt and freshly ground pepper. Whisk the lemon juice and olive oil together in a jug (pitcher) and drizzle the mixture evenly over the fish.

3 Bake in the preheated oven for about 15 minutes, or until the fish flakes easily. Transfer the fish to four warmed plates or a serving platter and serve immediately, garnished with coarsely grated lemon rind and fresh thyme sprigs.

VARIATIONS
- If hake is not available, you can use cod or haddock fillets for this recipe.
- You can substitute a mixture of fresh herbs, such as tarragon, parsley and chervil, for the thyme.
- To add colour to the dish, use half a small red onion instead of the shallot or look for pink shallots.

COOK'S TIPS
- Hake is a round fish extensively found in the North and South Atlantic and is extremely popular in Spain and Portugal. Its milky white flesh is delicate in flavour and quite fragile, so fillets need very careful handling, as they break up easily.
- Fresh thyme is best for this recipe, but if you can't find it, you can use 10ml/2 tsp of dried thyme – it will still give a good flavour.

Tahini Baked Fish

This dish is a favourite in many Middle Eastern countries, especially Egypt, Lebanon and Syria.

SERVES SIX

INGREDIENTS

- 6 × 175g/6oz cod or haddock fillets
- juice of 2 lemons
- 60ml/4 tbsp olive oil
- 2 large onions, chopped
- 250ml/8fl oz/1 cup tahini
- 1 garlic clove, crushed
- 45–60ml/3–4 tbsp water
- salt and ground black pepper
- rice and salad, to serve

1 Preheat the oven to 180°C/350°F/ Gas 4. Arrange the cod or haddock fillets in a large shallow casserole or ovenproof dish. Mix together 15ml/ 1 tbsp of the lemon juice and 15ml/1 tbsp of the olive oil in a jug (pitcher) and pour the mixture evenly over the fish. Bake for about 20 minutes.

2 Meanwhile, heat the remaining oil in a large frying pan and cook the onions over a medium heat for about 6–8 minutes, until well browned and almost crisp.

3 Put the tahini and garlic in a small bowl. Mix together the remaining lemon juice and measured water in another bowl and gradually beat into the tahini mixture, a little at a time, until the sauce is light and creamy. Season to taste with salt and pepper.

4 Remove the fish from the oven. Sprinkle the onions over it and pour over the tahini sauce. Bake the fish for a further 15 minutes, until the flesh is cooked through and the sauce is bubbling. Serve the fish immediately with rice and a salad.

ROAST MONKFISH WITH GARLIC AND FENNEL

MONKFISH WAS ONCE USED AS A SUBSTITUTE FOR LOBSTER BECAUSE IT IS SIMILAR IN TEXTURE. IT IS NOW MORE FULLY APPRECIATED AND IS DELICIOUS QUICKLY ROASTED.

SERVES FOUR

INGREDIENTS
- 1.1kg/2½lb monkfish tail
- 8 garlic cloves
- 15ml/1 tbsp olive oil
- 2 fennel bulbs, sliced
- juice of 1 lemon
- 1 bay leaf
- salt and ground black pepper
- fresh bay leaves and coarsely grated lemon rind, to garnish

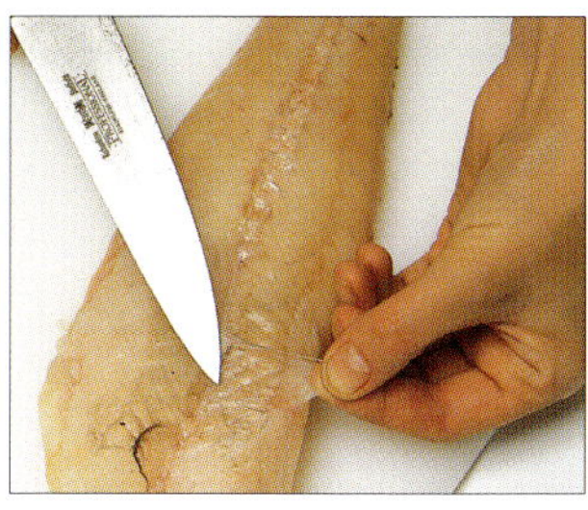

1 With a filleting knife or other pointed knife, cut away the thin, transparent membrane covering the outside of the fish to avoid its shrinking during cooking.

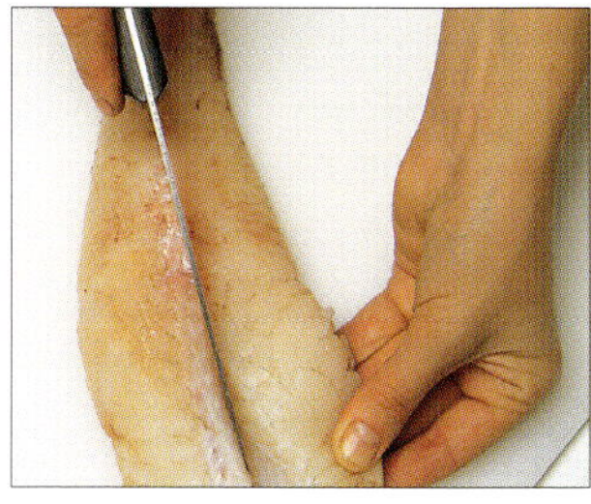

2 Cut along one side of the central bone to remove the fillet. Repeat on the other side. Tie the two fillets together with string. Preheat the oven to 220°C/425°F/Gas 7.

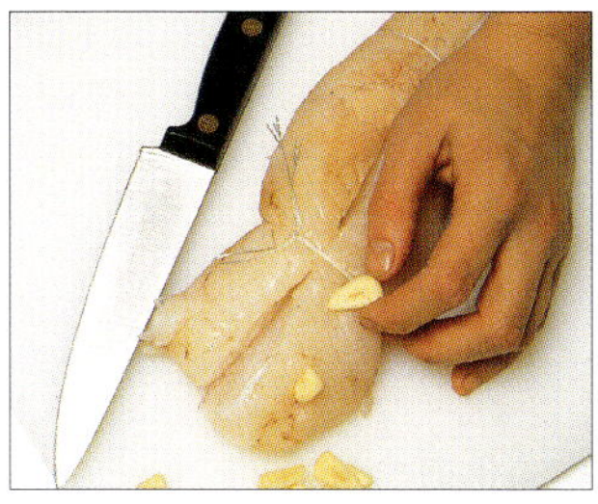

3 Peel the garlic cloves and cut them into small slivers. Make small incisions into the flesh of the fish and insert the slivers of garlic into these "pockets".

4 Heat the oil in a large, heavy pan. Add the fish and cook, turning frequently, until sealed on all sides.

5 Place the fish in a roasting pan, together with the fennel, lemon juice and bay leaf. Season with salt and pepper. Roast the monkfish for about 20 minutes, until cooked through and the flesh flakes easily. Untie the fillets and cut into slices. Garnish with bay leaves and lemon rind and serve immediately.

ASIAN FISH EN PAPILLOTE

The aromatic smell that wafts out of these fish parcels as you open them is deliciously tempting. If you don't like Asian flavours, use white wine, herbs and thinly sliced vegetables, or Mediterranean ingredients, such as tomatoes, basil and olives.

SERVES FOUR

INGREDIENTS

- 2 carrots
- 2 courgettes (zucchini)
- 6 spring onions (scallions)
- 2.5cm/1in piece fresh root ginger, peeled
- 1 lime
- 2 garlic cloves, thinly sliced
- 30ml/2 tbsp teriyaki marinade or Thai fish sauce
- 5–10ml/1–2 tsp clear sesame oil
- 4 salmon fillets, about 200g/7oz each
- ground black pepper
- rice, to serve

VARIATION

Thick fillets of hake, halibut, hoki and fresh or undyed smoked haddock and cod can all be used for this dish.

1 Cut the carrots, courgettes and spring onions into thin sticks and set them aside. Cut the ginger into thin sticks and put these in a small bowl. Using a zester, pare the lime thinly. Add the pared rind to the ginger, with the garlic. Squeeze the lime juice.

2 Place the teriyaki marinade or fish sauce in a bowl and stir in the lime juice and sesame oil.

3 Preheat the oven to 220°C/425°F/Gas 7. Cut out four rounds of baking parchment, each with a diameter of 40cm/16in. Season the salmon with pepper. Lay a fillet on one side of each paper round, about 3cm/1¼in off centre. Sprinkle a quarter of the ginger mixture over each and pile a quarter of the vegetable sticks on top. Spoon a quarter of the teriyaki or fish sauce mixture over the top.

4 Fold the bare side of the baking parchment over the salmon and roll the edges of the parchment over to seal each parcel very tightly.

5 Place the salmon parcels on a baking sheet and cook in the oven for about 10–12 minutes, depending on the thickness of the fillets. Put the parcels on plates and serve with rice.

ROAST COD WITH PANCETTA AND BEANS

THICK COD STEAKS WRAPPED IN PANCETTA AND ROASTED MAKE A SUPERB SUPPER DISH WHEN SERVED ON A BED OF BUTTER BEANS, WITH SWEET AND JUICY CHERRY TOMATOES ON THE SIDE.

SERVES FOUR

INGREDIENTS

- 200g/7oz/1 cup butter (lima) beans, soaked overnight in cold water
- 2 leeks, thinly sliced
- 2 garlic cloves, chopped
- 8 fresh sage leaves
- 90ml/6 tbsp fruity olive oil
- 8 thin slices of pancetta
- 4 thick cod steaks, skinned
- 12 cherry tomatoes
- salt and ground black pepper

1 Drain the beans, tip into a pan and cover with cold water. Bring to the boil and skim off the foam on the surface. Lower the heat, then stir in the leeks, garlic, four sage leaves and 30ml/2 tbsp of the olive oil. Simmer for 1–1½ hours until the beans are tender, adding more water if necessary. Drain, return to the pan, season, stir in 30ml/2 tbsp olive oil and keep warm.

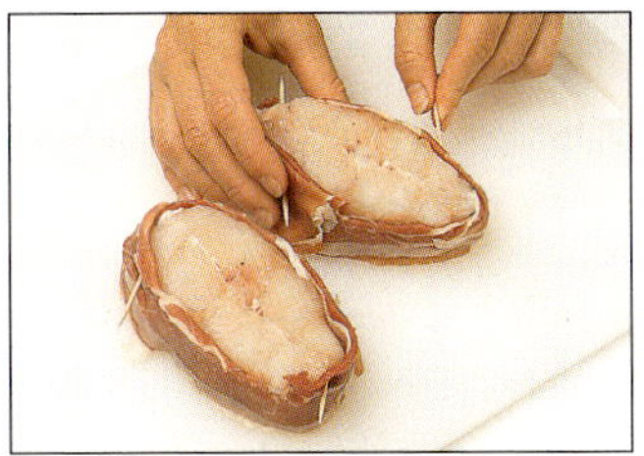

2 Preheat the oven to 200°C/400°F/Gas 6. Wrap two slices of pancetta around the edge of each cod steak, tying it on with kitchen string or securing it with a wooden cocktail stick or toothpick. Insert a sage leaf between the pancetta and the cod. Season the fish.

VARIATION

You can use cannellini beans for this recipe, and streaky (fatty) bacon instead of pancetta. It is also good made with halibut, hake, haddock or salmon.

3 Heat a heavy frying pan, add 15ml/1 tbsp of the remaining oil and seal the cod steaks, two at a time, for 1 minute on each side. Transfer them to an ovenproof dish and roast in the oven for 5 minutes.

4 Add the tomatoes to the dish and drizzle over the remaining olive oil. Roast for 5 minutes more, until the cod steaks are cooked but still juicy. Serve them on a bed of butter beans with the roasted tomatoes. Garnish with parsley.

COD WITH CAPER SAUCE

THIS QUICK AND EASY SAUCE, WITH A SLIGHTLY SHARP AND NUTTY FLAVOUR, IS A VERY EFFECTIVE WAY OF LIVENING UP RATHER BLAND FISH.

SERVES FOUR

INGREDIENTS

- 4 cod steaks, about 175g/6oz each
- 115g/4oz/½ cup butter
- 15ml/1 tbsp white wine vinegar
- 15ml/1 tbsp capers
- 15ml/1 tbsp chopped fresh parsley
- salt and ground black pepper
- fresh tarragon sprigs, to garnish

1 Preheat the grill (broiler). Season the cod with salt and pepper to taste. Melt 25g/1oz/2 tbsp of the butter, then brush some over one side of each piece of cod.

2 Cook the cod under a medium grill for about 6 minutes, turn it over, brush the second side with the remaining melted butter and grill (broil) for a further 5–6 minutes, or until lightly golden, when the fish flakes easily.

3 Meanwhile, heat the remaining butter until it turns golden brown, but do not allow it to burn. Add the white wine vinegar, followed by the capers, and stir well.

4 Transfer the fish to four warm serving plates. Pour the vinegar, butter and capers over it, sprinkle with the chopped parsley and garnish with the tarragon sprigs. Serve immediately.

COOK'S TIP

This also makes a quick and easy dish for the barbecue. Make the caper sauce first, then stand the pan on the side of the barbecue to keep warm while you cook the fish. Put the fish steaks in a hinged wire basket to make them easier to turn.

VARIATION

Thick tail fillets of cod or haddock could be used in place of the cod steaks, if you like.

COD WITH SPICED RED LENTILS

THIS DELICIOUS DISH MARRIES THE SPICES OF INDIA WITH THE DELICATE FLAVOUR OF COD.

SERVES FOUR

INGREDIENTS
- 175g/6oz/¾ cup red lentils
- 1.5ml/¼ tsp ground turmeric
- 600ml/1 pint/2½ cups fish stock
- 30ml/2 tbsp vegetable oil
- 7.5ml/1½ tsp cumin seeds
- 15ml/1 tbsp grated fresh root ginger
- 2.5ml/½ tsp cayenne pepper
- 15ml/1 tbsp lemon juice
- 30ml/2 tbsp chopped fresh coriander (cilantro)
- 450g/1lb cod fillets, skinned and cut into large chunks
- salt
- coriander (cilantro) leaves and 4–8 lemon wedges, to garnish

1 Put the lentils in a pan with the turmeric and stock. Bring to the boil, lower the heat, cover and simmer gently for 20–25 minutes, until the lentils are just tender. Remove the pan from the heat and season the lentils with salt to taste.

2 Heat the oil in a small frying pan. Add the cumin seeds and, when they begin to pop and give off their aroma, add the ginger and cayenne pepper. Stir-fry the spices over a low heat for a few seconds, then pour on to the lentils. Add the lemon juice and the chopped coriander and stir in gently.

COOK'S TIP
Do not add salt to the lentils during cooking, as this makes them tough.

3 Lay the pieces of cod on top of the lentils, re-cover the pan and then cook very gently over a low heat for about 10–15 minutes, until the fish is tender and the flesh flakes easily.

4 Using a metal spatula, divide the lentils and pieces of cod among four warmed serving plates. Sprinkle over the whole coriander leaves and garnish each serving with one or two lemon wedges. Serve the fish and lentils immediately.

SAND DAB PROVENÇAL

RE-CREATE THE TASTE OF THE MEDITERRANEAN.

SERVES FOUR

INGREDIENTS

- 4 large sand dab fillets
- 2 small red onions
- 120ml/4fl oz/½ cup vegetable stock
- 60ml/4 tbsp dry red wine
- 1 garlic clove, crushed
- 2 courgettes (zucchini), sliced
- 1 yellow (bell) pepper, seeded and sliced
- 400g/14oz can chopped tomatoes
- 15ml/1 tbsp chopped fresh thyme
- salt and ground black pepper
- potato gratin, to serve (optional)

1 Preheat the oven to 180°C/350°F/Gas 4. Skin the sand dab fillets with a sharp knife by laying them skin-side down. Holding the tail end, push the knife between the skin and flesh in a sawing movement. Hold the knife at an angle, with the blade angled towards the skin.

2 Cut each onion into eight wedges. Place them in a heavy pan, together with the stock. Cover and simmer over a low heat for 5 minutes.

3 Uncover the pan and continue to cook, stirring occasionally, until the stock has reduced entirely.

4 Add the red wine and crushed garlic to the pan and continue to cook until the onions are softened.

5 Add the courgettes, yellow pepper, chopped tomatoes, together with their can juice, and thyme and season with salt and pepper to taste. Simmer for 3 minutes. Spoon the sauce into a large casserole or ovenproof dish.

6 Fold each fish fillet in half and place on top of the sauce. Cover with a lid or sheet of foil and bake for 15–20 minutes, until the fish is opaque and cooked through. Serve the fish immediately with potato gratin, if you like.

STUFFED SWORDFISH ROLLS

SWORDFISH IS ABUNDANT AROUND SICILY, AND IT FEATURES IN MANY OF THE LOCAL DISHES.

SERVES FOUR

INGREDIENTS

- 4 slices fresh swordfish about 1cm/½in thick
- 90ml/6 tbsp olive oil
- 1 garlic clove, finely chopped (optional)
- 50g/2oz/1 cup fresh white breadcrumbs
- 30ml/2 tbsp capers, rinsed, drained and chopped
- 10 fresh basil leaves, chopped
- 60ml/4 tbsp fresh lemon juice
- salt and ground black pepper

For the tomato sauce

- 30ml/2 tbsp olive oil
- 1 garlic clove, crushed
- 1 small onion, finely chopped
- 450g/1lb tomatoes, peeled
- 120ml/4fl oz/½ cup dry white wine

1 Cut the swordfish slices in half, removing any bones. Brush with 30ml/2 tbsp of the olive oil, place on a plate and leave in the refrigerator until needed.

2 Make the tomato sauce. Heat the oil in a medium, heavy pan. Add the garlic and cook until golden. Remove and discard the garlic.

3 Add the onion, and cook over a low heat until soft. Stir in the tomatoes and wine. Season with salt and pepper. Cover the pan, and cook over medium heat for 15 minutes.

4 Pass the sauce through a food mill or process in a food processor or blender to a purée. Keep the sauce warm while you are preparing the fish.

5 Preheat the oven to 200°C/400°F/Gas 6. Mix together 30ml/2 tbsp of the olive oil with the garlic, if using, the breadcrumbs, capers, basil and lemon juice in a bowl. Season with salt and pepper and stir well to make a paste.

6 Remove the swordfish slices from the refrigerator and lay them flat on a chopping board. Divide the stuffing mixture equally among the slices and spread it evenly over the centre of each. Roll up the swordfish slices and secure with wooden cocktail sticks or toothpicks.

7 Heat the remaining oil in a flameproof dish. Add the swordfish rolls and brown them for 3–4 minutes over a high heat, turning them once or twice.

8 Pour in the tomato sauce and transfer the dish to the oven. Bake for 15 minutes, basting occasionally with the sauce. Serve warm.

Salmon with a Tarragon Mushroom Sauce

Tarragon has a distinctive flavour that is good with fish, cream and mushrooms. This recipe uses oyster mushrooms to provide both texture and flavour.

SERVES FOUR

INGREDIENTS

- 50g/2oz/¼ cup unsalted (sweet) butter
- 4 x 175g/6oz salmon steaks
- 1 shallot, finely chopped
- 175g/6oz assorted wild and cultivated mushrooms, including oyster mushrooms, sliced
- 200ml/7fl oz/scant 1 cup chicken or vegetable stock
- 10ml/2 tsp cornflour (cornstarch)
- 2.5ml/½ tsp mustard
- 50ml/2fl oz/¼ cup crème fraîche
- 45ml/3 tbsp chopped fresh tarragon
- 5ml/1 tsp white wine vinegar
- salt and cayenne pepper
- boiled new potatoes and green salad, to serve

1 Melt half the butter in a large, heavy frying pan. Season the salmon with salt and pepper and cook over a medium heat for 8 minutes, turning once. Transfer to a plate, cover and keep warm.

2 Heat the remaining butter in the pan. Add the shallot and cook over a low heat to soften. Add the mushrooms and cook until the juices begin to flow. Add the stock and simmer for 2–3 minutes.

3 Mix together the cornflour and mustard and blend with 15ml/1 tbsp of water. Stir into the mushroom mixture and bring to a simmer, stirring, to thicken. Add the crème fraîche, tarragon, vinegar and salt and pepper to taste.

4 Place the salmon steaks on four warm serving plates. Spoon the mushrooms and sauce evenly over each salmon steak and serve immediately with new potatoes and a green salad.

COOK'S TIPS

- Fresh tarragon will bruise and darken quickly after chopping, so prepare the herb as and when you need it.
- If you are watching your intake of saturated fats, cook the salmon in a ridged griddle pan rather than a frying pan. It will need only a light brushing of oil, so you can halve the quantity of butter used in the recipe. Similarly, you could substitute low-fat yogurt for the crème fraîche.

Grilled Butterflied Salmon

Ask your fishmonger to bone the salmon for butterflying.

SERVES SIX TO EIGHT

INGREDIENTS

- 25ml/1½ tbsp dried juniper berries
- 10ml/2 tsp dried green peppercorns
- 5ml/1 tsp caster (superfine) sugar
- 45ml/3 tbsp vegetable oil
- 30ml/2 tbsp lemon juice
- 2.25kg/5–5¼lb salmon, scaled, gutted and boned for butterflying
- salt
- lemon wedges and fresh parsley sprigs, to garnish

1 Coarsely grind the juniper berries and peppercorns in a spice mill or in a mortar with a pestle. Tip into a small bowl and stir in the sugar, oil, lemon juice and salt to taste.

2 Open out the salmon like a book, skin-side down. Spread the juniper mixture evenly over the flesh. Fold the salmon closed again and place on a large plate. Cover with clear film (plastic wrap) and marinate in the refrigerator for at least 1 hour.

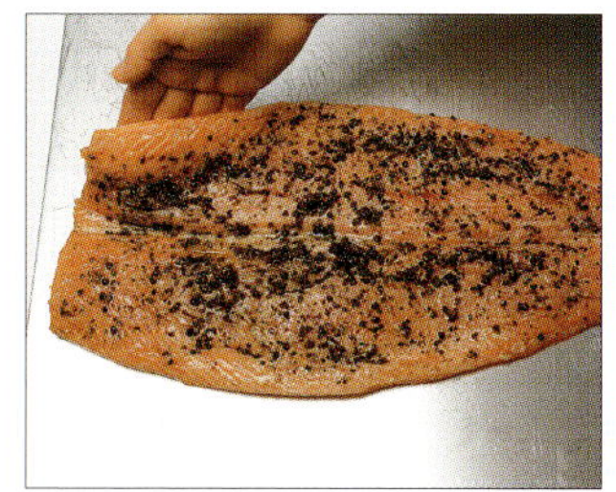

3 Preheat the grill (broiler). Remove the salmon from the refrigerator and open it out again. Place the salmon, skin-side down, on a lightly oiled baking sheet. Spoon any juniper mixture that has been left on the plate over the fish.

4 Cook under the grill, about 10cm/4in from the heat, for 8–10 minutes or until the fish is cooked through and the flesh flakes easily.

5 Carefully transfer the salmon to a large, warm platter. Garnish with the lemon wedges and parsley and serve immediately.

COOK'S TIP

To prepare the salmon for butterflying yourself, follow the instructions for boning a round fish through the stomach. Remove both the head and tail but do not separate the fillets. Unfortunately, because salmon is an oily fish, the trimmings are not suitable for making fish stock.

Halibut with Fennel and Orange

Sweet halibut is enhanced by strong flavourings.

SERVES FOUR

INGREDIENTS

- 50g/2oz/¼ cup butter, plus extra for greasing
- 1 fennel bulb, thinly sliced
- grated rind and juice of 1 orange
- 150ml/¼ pint/⅔ cup white wine
- 4 halibut steaks, 200g/7oz each
- salt and ground black pepper
- fresh fennel fronds, to garnish

1 Preheat the oven to 180°C/350°F/ Gas 4. Butter a shallow ovenproof dish and set aside. Add the fennel to a pan of boiling water, return to the boil and cook for about 4–6 minutes, until just tender.

2 Meanwhile, put the grated orange rind, orange juice and white wine in a small pan, bring to the boil over a medium heat and boil until reduced by about half. Remove the pan from the heat.

3 Drain the fennel, then place the slices in the prepared dish and season to taste with salt and pepper. Arrange the halibut on top of the fennel, season, dot with butter, then pour over the reduced orange and wine mixture.

4 Cover the dish with a lid or foil and bake for about 20 minutes, until the fish is cooked through and the flesh flakes easily. Serve immediately, garnished with fennel fronds.

Salmon with Cucumber Sauce

Cucumber and fresh dill are a perfect combination in this unusual hot sauce, which really complements the baked salmon.

SERVES SIX TO EIGHT

INGREDIENTS

- 1.8kg/4lb salmon, cleaned and scaled
- melted butter, for brushing
- 3 fresh parsley or thyme sprigs
- ½ lemon, halved
- fresh dill sprigs, to garnish
- orange slices and salad leaves, to serve

For the cucumber sauce

- 1 large cucumber, peeled
- 25g/1oz/2 tbsp butter
- 120ml/4fl oz/½ cup dry white wine
- 45ml/3 tbsp chopped fresh dill
- 60ml/4 tbsp sour cream
- salt and ground black pepper

1 Preheat the oven to 220°C/425°F/ Gas 7. Season the salmon with salt and pepper and brush inside and out with melted butter. Place the parsley or thyme sprigs and lemon half in the cavity of the fish.

2 Wrap the salmon in foil, folding the edges together securely, then place on a baking sheet and bake for 15 minutes. Remove the fish from the oven and leave to stand in the foil for 1 hour, then unwrap and remove the skin from the salmon.

3 Meanwhile, make the cucumber sauce. Cut the cucumber in half lengthways, scoop out the seeds with a spoon, then dice the flesh.

4 Place the cucumber in a colander, toss lightly with salt and leave for about 30 minutes to drain. Rinse well and pat dry.

5 Melt the butter in a small pan, add the cucumber and cook over a low heat, stirring frequently, for about 2 minutes, until translucent but not soft. Add the wine to the pan, increase the heat to medium and boil briskly until the cucumber is dry.

6 Stir the dill and sour cream into the cucumber and season to taste with salt and pepper. Fillet the salmon and transfer to serving plates. Garnish with the fresh dill and serve immediately with the cucumber sauce, orange slices and salad.

TUNA WITH PEAS AND TOMATOES

THIS JEWISH ITALIAN DISH OF FRESH TUNA AND PEAS IS ESPECIALLY ENJOYED AT PESACH, WHICH FALLS IN SPRING. BEFORE THE DAYS OF THE FREEZER, SPRING WAS THE TIME FOR LITTLE SEASONAL PEAS. AT OTHER TIMES OF THE YEAR CHICKPEAS WERE USED INSTEAD.

SERVES FOUR

INGREDIENTS

- 60ml/4 tbsp olive oil
- 1 onion, chopped
- 4–5 garlic cloves, chopped
- 45ml/3 tbsp chopped fresh flat leaf parsley
- 1–2 pinches of fennel seeds
- 350g/12oz tuna steaks
- 400g/14oz can chopped tomatoes
- 120ml/4fl oz/½ cup dry white wine or fish stock
- 30–45ml/2–3 tbsp tomato purée (paste)
- pinch of sugar, if needed
- 350g/12oz/3 cups fresh shelled or frozen peas
- salt and ground black pepper

1 Preheat the oven to 190°C/375°F/Gas 5. Heat the olive oil in a large frying pan, then add the chopped onion, garlic, flat leaf parsley and fennel seeds, and cook over a low heat for about 5 minutes, or until the onion is softened but not browned.

2 Sprinkle the tuna steaks on each side with salt and pepper. Add to the pan and cook for 2–3 minutes on each side until lightly browned. Transfer the tuna steaks to a shallow ovenproof dish, in a single layer.

3 Add the canned tomatoes along with their juice and the wine or fish stock to the onions and cook over a medium heat for 5–10 minutes, stirring, until the flavours blend together and the mixture thickens slightly.

4 Stir the tomato purée, sugar, if needed, and salt and pepper into the tomato sauce, then add the fresh or frozen peas. Pour the mixture over the fish steaks and bake, uncovered, for about 10 minutes, or until tender.

VARIATIONS

This recipe works well with other fish. Use tuna fillets in place of the steaks or try different fish steaks, such as salmon or swordfish.

POACHED FISH IN SPICY TOMATO HERB SAUCE

THIS TRADITIONAL JEWISH DISH IS KNOWN AS SAMAK. YEMENITE SPICING IS REFRESHING IN THE SULTRY HEAT OF THE MIDDLE EAST AND IS VERY POPULAR WITH ISRAELIS. SERVE THIS DISH WITH FLAT BREADS SUCH AS PITTA OR MATZOS, AND HILBEH, A TOMATO AND FENUGREEK RELISH.

SERVES EIGHT

INGREDIENTS

- 300ml/½ pint/1¼ cups passata (bottled strained tomatoes)
- 150ml/¼ pint/⅔ cup fish stock
- 1 large onion, chopped
- 60ml/4 tbsp chopped fresh coriander (cilantro) leaves
- 60ml/4 tbsp chopped fresh parsley
- 5–8 garlic cloves, crushed
- chopped fresh chilli or chilli paste, to taste
- large pinch of ground ginger
- large pinch of curry powder
- 1.5ml/¼ tsp ground cumin
- 1.5ml/¼ tsp ground turmeric
- seeds from 2–3 cardamom pods
- juice of 2 lemons, plus extra if needed
- 30ml/2 tbsp vegetable or olive oil
- 1.5kg/3¼lb mixed white fish fillets
- salt and ground black pepper

1 Put the passata, stock, onion, herbs, garlic, chilli, ginger, curry powder, cumin, turmeric, cardamom, lemon juice and oil in a pan and bring to the boil.

VARIATIONS

- This dish is just as good using only one type of fish, such as cod or flounder.
- Instead of poaching the fish, wrap each piece in puff pastry and bake at 190°C/375°F/Gas 5 for 20 minutes, then serve with the tomato sauce.

2 Remove the pan from the heat and add the fish fillets to the hot sauce. Return to the heat and allow the sauce to boil briefly again. Reduce the heat and simmer very gently for about 5 minutes, or until the fish is tender. (Test the fish with a fork. If the flesh flakes easily, then it is cooked.)

3 Taste the sauce and adjust the seasoning, adding more lemon juice if necessary. Serve hot or warm.

HADDOCK AND BROCCOLI STEW

THIS EASY ONE POT MEAL IS FULL OF FLAVOUR

SERVES FOUR

INGREDIENTS

- 4 spring onions (scallions), sliced
- 450g/1lb new potatoes, diced
- 300ml/½ pint/1¼ cups fish stock
- 300ml/½ pint/1¼ cups milk
- 1 bay leaf
- 225g/8oz broccoli florets, sliced
- 450g/1lb smoked haddock fillets
- 200g/7oz can corn, drained
- ground black pepper
- chopped spring onions (scallions), to garnish

1 Place the sliced spring onions and diced potatoes in a large, heavy pan and add the fish stock, milk and bay leaf. Bring the mixture to the boil, then lower the heat, cover the pan and simmer gently for about 10 minutes.

2 Add the broccoli to the pan. Using a sharp knife, skin the haddock fillets, cut them into bitesize chunks and add them to the pan with the drained corn.

3 Season the stew well with black pepper, then cover the pan and simmer for a further 5 minutes, or until the fish is cooked through and the flesh flakes easily.

4 Remove and discard the bay leaf and transfer the stew to a warm serving dish. Sprinkle over the chopped spring onion and serve hot.

COOK'S TIP

When new potatoes are not available, old ones can be used, but choose a waxy variety which will not disintegrate during cooking.

VARIATION

Substitute cauliflower florets for the broccoli. Choose a variety that is an attractive colour, such as Romanesco or purple.

HOKI BALLS IN TOMATO SAUCE

THIS QUICK MEAL IS A GOOD CHOICE FOR CHILDREN, AS YOU CAN GUARANTEE NO BONES. ITS LOW FAT CONTENT ALSO MAKES IT AN IDEAL DISH FOR ANYONE ON A LOW-FAT DIET.

SERVES FOUR

INGREDIENTS
- 450g/1lb hoki or other white fish fillets
- 60ml/4 tbsp fresh wholemeal breadcrumbs
- 30ml/2 tbsp chopped fresh chives or spring onion (scallion)
- 400g/14oz can chopped tomatoes
- 50g/2oz button (white) mushrooms, sliced
- salt and ground black pepper
- fresh chives, to garnish

1 Using a sharp knife, skin the fish fillets, cut them into large chunks and place in a food processor. Add the wholemeal breadcrumbs, chives or spring onion. Season to taste with salt and pepper and process until the fish is finely chopped, but still has some texture left.

2 Scrape out the fish mixture on to a board and divide it into about 16 even-size pieces, then mould them into balls with your hands. (You may find this easier and less sticky if you dampen your hands with cold water first.)

3 Place the tomatoes and mushrooms in a large pan and cook over a medium heat until boiling. Carefully add the fish balls, cover and simmer for about 10 minutes, until cooked. Serve hot, garnished with chives.

COOK'S TIP

Hoki is a good choice for this dish, but if it is not available, use cod, haddock or whiting instead.

VARIATION

For a spicier version, add a dash of Tabasco or other chilli sauce to the pan in step 3 before adding the fish balls.

Spanish Trout with Serrano Ham

Traditionally, the trout would have come from mountain streams and been stuffed and wrapped in locally cured ham. One of the beauties of this method is that the skins come off in one piece, leaving the succulent, moist flesh to be eaten with the crisped, salt ham.

SERVES FOUR

INGREDIENTS

- 4 brown or rainbow trout, about 250g/9oz each, cleaned
- 16 thin slices Serrano ham, about 200g/7oz
- 50g/2oz/¼ cup melted butter, plus extra for greasing
- salt and ground black pepper
- buttered potatoes, to serve (optional)

1 Extend the belly cavity of each trout, cutting up one side of the backbone. Slip a knife behind the rib bones to loosen them (sometimes just flexing the fish makes them pop up). Snip these off from both sides with scissors, and season the fish well inside.

2 Preheat the grill (broiler) to high, with a shelf in the top position. Line a baking tray with foil and butter it.

3 Working with the fish on the foil, fold a piece of ham into each belly. Use smaller or broken bits of ham for this, and reserve the eight best slices.

4 Brush each trout with a little butter, seasoning the outside lightly with salt and pepper. Wrap two ham slices round each one, crossways, tucking the ends into the belly. Grill (broil) the trout for 4 minutes, then carefully turn them over with a metal spatula, rolling them across on the belly, so the ham doesn't come loose, and grill for a further 4 minutes.

5 Serve the trout very hot, with any spare butter spooned over the top. Diners should open the trout on their plates, and eat them from the inside, pushing the flesh off the skin.

GRILLED RED MULLET WITH BAY LEAVES

Red mullet are called SALMONETES *– little salmon – in Spain because of their delicate, pale pink colour. They are simple to cook on a barbecue, with bay leaves for flavour and a drizzle of tangy dressing instead of a marinade.*

SERVES FOUR

INGREDIENTS

- 4 red mullet, about 225–275g/8–10oz each, cleaned and descaled if cooking under a grill (broiler)
- olive oil, for brushing
- fresh herb sprigs, such as fennel, dill, parsley, or thyme
- 2–3 dozen fresh or dried bay leaves

For the dressing

- 90ml/6 tbsp olive oil
- 6 garlic cloves, finely chopped
- ½ dried chilli, seeded and chopped
- juice of ½ lemon
- 15ml/1 tbsp parsley

COOK'S TIP

If you are cooking on the barbecue, the fish do not need to be scaled.

1 Prepare the barbecue or preheat the grill (broiler) with the shelf 15cm/6in from the heat source.

2 Brush each fish with oil and stuff the cavities with the herb sprigs. Brush the grill pan with oil and lay bay leaves across the cooking rack. Place the fish on top and cook for 15–20 minutes until cooked through, turning once.

3 To make the dressing, heat the olive oil in a small pan and cook the chopped garlic with the dried chilli. Add the lemon juice and strain the dressing into a small jug (pitcher). Add the chopped parsley and stir to combine.

4 Serve the mullet on warmed plates, drizzled with the dressing.

COOK'S TIPS

- Nicknamed the woodcock of the sea, red mullet are one of the fish that are classically cooked uncleaned to give them extra flavour. In this recipe however, the fish are cleaned and herbs are used to add extra flavour to the fish.
- If cooking on a barbecue, light the barbecue well in advance. Before cooking, the charcoal or wood should be grey, with no flames.

Herbed Chargrilled Shark Steaks

Shark is very low in fat, with dense, well-flavoured flesh. Other close-textured fish like tuna, bonito and marlin work equally well in this recipe, which is ideal for a barbecue. Serve the fish with a tangy tomato salad.

SERVES FOUR

INGREDIENTS

- 45ml/3 tbsp olive oil
- 2 fresh bay leaves, chopped
- 15ml/1 tbsp chopped fresh basil
- 15ml/1 tbsp chopped fresh oregano
- 30ml/2 tbsp chopped fresh parsley
- 5ml/1 tsp finely chopped fresh rosemary
- 5ml/1 tsp fresh thyme leaves
- 2 garlic cloves, crushed
- 4 pieces drained sun-dried tomatoes in oil, chopped
- 4 shark steaks, about 200g/7oz each
- juice of 1 lemon
- 15ml/1 tbsp drained small capers in vinegar (optional)
- salt and ground black pepper

1 Whisk the oil, herbs, garlic and sun-dried tomatoes in a bowl, then pour the mixture into a shallow dish that is large enough to hold the shark steaks in a single layer. Season the shark steaks with salt and pepper and brush the lemon juice over both sides. Lay the fish in the dish, turning the steaks to coat them all over. Cover and marinate in the refrigerator for 1–2 hours.

2 Heat a ridged griddle pan or barbecue until it is very hot. Lift the shark steaks out of the marinade, pat dry with kitchen paper and grill (broil) or cook on the barbecue for about 5 minutes on each side, until they are cooked through. Pour the marinade into a small pan and bring to the boil. Stir in the capers, if using. Spoon over the shark steaks and serve immediately.

Chinese-style Scallops and Prawns

Serve this light, delicate dish for lunch or supper accompanied by aromatic steamed rice or fine rice noodles and stir-fried pak choi.

SERVES FOUR

INGREDIENTS

- 15ml/1 tbsp stir-fry or sunflower oil
- 500g/1¼lb raw tiger prawns (jumbo shrimp), peeled
- 1 star anise
- 225g/8oz scallops, halved if large
- 2.5cm/1in piece fresh root ginger, peeled and grated
- 2 garlic cloves, thinly sliced
- 1 red (bell) pepper, seeded and cut into thin strips
- 115g/4oz/1¾ cups shiitake or button (white) mushrooms, thinly sliced
- juice of 1 lemon
- 5ml/1 tsp cornflour (cornstarch), mixed with 30ml/2 tbsp cold water
- 30ml/2 tbsp light soy sauce
- chopped fresh chives, to garnish
- salt and ground black pepper

1 Heat the oil in a wok until very hot. Put in the prawns and star anise and stir-fry over a high heat for 2 minutes. Add the scallops, ginger and garlic and stir-fry for 1 minute more, by which time the prawns should have turned pink· and the scallops opaque. Season with a little salt and plenty of pepper and then remove from the wok using a slotted spoon. Discard the star anise.

2 Add the red pepper and mushrooms to the wok and stir-fry for 1–2 minutes. Pour in the lemon juice, cornflour paste and soy sauce, bring to the boil and bubble for 1–2 minutes, stirring constantly, until the sauce is smooth and slightly thickened.

3 Stir the prawns and scallops into the sauce, cook for a few seconds until heated through, then season with salt and ground black pepper and serve garnished with chopped chives.

VARIATIONS

Use other prepared shellfish in this dish; try thinly sliced rings of squid, or mussels or clams, or substitute chunks of firm white fish, such as monkfish fillet, for the scallops.

SEA BASS WITH CITRUS FRUIT

THE SEA BASS FAMILY IS FOUND THROUGHOUT MOST OF THE WORLD'S SEAS AND IS ESPECIALLY POPULAR IN COUNTRIES ALONG THE MEDITERRANEAN COAST. ITS DELICATE FLAVOUR IS COMPLEMENTED BY CITRUS FRUITS AND FRUITY FRENCH OLIVE OIL.

SERVES SIX

INGREDIENTS

- 1 small grapefruit
- 1 orange
- 1 lemon
- 1 sea bass, about 1.35kg/3lb, cleaned and scaled
- 6 fresh basil sprigs
- 6 fresh dill sprigs
- plain (all-purpose) flour, for dusting
- 45ml/3 tbsp olive oil
- 4–6 shallots, halved
- 60ml/4 tbsp dry white wine
- 15g/½oz/1 tbsp butter
- salt and ground black pepper

1 Preheat the oven to 190°C/375°F/ Gas 5. Using a vegetable peeler, remove the rind from the grapefruit, orange and lemon. Cut into thin julienne strips, cover and set aside.

2 Peel off and discard all the white pith from the fruits and, working over a bowl to catch the juices, cut out the segments from the grapefruit and orange with a sharp knife. Set them aside for the garnish. Slice the lemon thickly.

3 Wipe the fish dry inside and out with kitchen paper and season the cavity with salt and pepper. With a sharp knife, make three diagonal slashes on each side.

4 Reserve a few basil and dill sprigs for the garnish and fill the cavity of the fish with the remaining basil, dill, the lemon slices and half the julienne strips of citrus rind.

5 Dust the fish lightly with flour. In a roasting pan or flameproof casserole large enough to hold the fish, heat 30ml/2 tbsp of the olive oil over a medium-high heat. Add the fish and cook for about 1 minute, until the skin just crisps and browns on one side. Add the halved shallots.

COOK'S TIP

For extra colour, use a ruby or pink grapefruit, which have the extra advantage of being slightly less sharp than yellow varieties. You could also use a blood orange.

6 Transfer the roasting pan or casserole to the oven and bake for about 15 minutes.

7 Remove the pan or casserole from the oven and carefully turn the fish over and stir the shallots. Drizzle the fish with the remaining oil. Return to the oven and bake for a further 10–15 minutes, until the flesh is opaque throughout.

8 Carefully transfer the fish to a warm serving dish and remove and discard the cavity stuffing. Keep warm.

9 Pour off any excess oil and add the wine and 30–45ml/ 2–3 tbsp of the fruit juices to the pan. Bring to the boil over a high heat, stirring constantly. Stir in the remaining julienne strips of citrus rind and boil for 2–3 minutes, then whisk in the butter. Spoon the shallots and sauce around the fish and garnish with dill and the reserved basil and grapefruit and orange segments.

SESAME BAKED FISH

TROPICAL FISH ARE OFTEN AVAILABLE IN SUPERMARKETS, BUT ASIAN MARKETS USUALLY HAVE A WIDER SELECTION.

SERVES FOUR TO SIX

INGREDIENTS
- 2 red snapper, parrot fish, or monkfish tails, weighing about 350g/12oz each
- 30ml/2 tbsp vegetable oil
- 10ml/2 tsp sesame oil
- 30ml/2 tbsp sesame seeds
- 2.5cm/1 in piece fresh root ginger, thinly sliced
- 2 garlic cloves, crushed
- 2 small fresh red chillies, seeded and finely chopped
- 4 shallots or 1 medium onion, halved and sliced
- 30ml/2 tbsp water
- 1cm/½in square piece shrimp paste or 15ml/1 tbsp fish sauce
- 10ml/2 tsp caster (superfine) sugar
- 2.5ml/½ tsp cracked black pepper
- juice of 2 limes
- 3–4 banana leaves or foil
- lime wedges, to garnish (optional)

1 Rinse the fish inside and out under cold running water. Pat thoroughly dry with kitchen paper. Using a sharp knife, make three deep diagonal slashes on both sides of each fish to enable the marinade to penetrate effectively. If using parrot fish, rub them all over with fine salt and leave to stand for about 15 minutes. Then rinse well and pat dry. (This will remove the chalky coral flavour often associated with the parrot fish.)

2 To make the marinade, heat the vegetable and sesame oils in a preheated wok, add the sesame seeds and fry until golden.

3 Add the ginger, garlic, chillies and shallots or onion and cook over a low heat without burning. Add the water, shrimp paste or fish sauce, sugar, pepper, and lime juice. Simmer for 2–3 minutes, then remove from the heat and set aside to cool.

4 If using banana leaves, remove and discard the central stem. Soften the leaves by dipping them in boiling water. To keep them supple, rub all over with vegetable oil.

5 Spread the marinade over the fish, then wrap them in the banana leaves and fasten with bamboo skewers, weaving the skewers in and out like a pin. Alternatively, wrap the fish in aluminium foil, folding the edges to seal. Set aside in a cool place for up to 3 hours to allow the flavours to mingle.

6 Preheat the oven to 180°C/350°F/Gas 4. Place the wrapped fish on a baking sheet and bake for about 35–40 minutes. Alternatively, place on a wire rack and cook over a barbecue for 35–40 minutes.

7 Carefully transfer the fish, still wrapped, to a warm serving platter. Garnish with lime wedges, if you like, and serve immediately.

COOK'S TIP

Banana leaves make attractive wrappers that also add flavour to the fish, but do not eat them.

FILO-WRAPPED FISH

This delicious dish comes from Jerusalem, where whole fish are wrapped in filo pastry and served with a zesty tomato sauce. The choice of fish can be varied according to what is in season and what is freshest on the day of purchase.

SERVES THREE TO FOUR

INGREDIENTS

- 450g/1lb salmon or cod steaks or fillets
- 1 lemon
- 30ml/2 tbsp olive oil, plus extra for brushing
- 1 onion, chopped
- 2 celery sticks, chopped
- 1 green (bell) pepper, diced
- 5 garlic cloves, chopped
- 400g/14oz fresh or canned tomatoes, chopped
- 120ml/4fl oz/½ cup passata (bottled strained tomatoes)
- 30ml/2 tbsp chopped fresh flat leaf parsley
- 2–3 pinches of ground allspice or ground cloves
- cayenne pepper, to taste
- pinch of sugar
- about 130g/4½oz filo pastry (6–8 large sheets)
- salt and ground black pepper

1 Sprinkle the salmon or cod steaks or fillets with salt and black pepper and a squeeze of lemon juice. Set aside while you prepare the sauce.

2 Heat the olive oil in a pan, add the chopped onion, celery and pepper and cook for about 5 minutes, until the vegetables are softened. Add the garlic and cook for a further 1 minute, then add the tomatoes and passata and cook until the tomatoes are of a sauce consistency.

3 Stir the parsley into the sauce, then season with allspice or cloves, cayenne pepper, sugar and salt and pepper.

4 Preheat the oven to 200°C/400°F/Gas 6. Take a sheet of filo pastry, brush with a little olive oil and cover with a second sheet. Place a piece of fish on top of the pastry, towards the bottom edge, then top with 1–2 spoonfuls of the sauce, spreading it evenly.

5 Roll the fish in the pastry, taking care to enclose the filling completely. Arrange on a baking sheet and repeat with the remaining fish and pastry. You should have about half the sauce remaining, to serve with the fish.

6 Bake for 10–15 minutes, or until golden. Meanwhile, reheat the remaining sauce, if necessary. Serve immediately with the remaining sauce.

Moroccan Grilled Fish Brochettes

Serve these delicious skewers with potatoes, aubergine slices and strips of red peppers, which can be cooked on the barbecue alongside the fish brochettes. Accompany with a stack of warm, soft pitta breads or flour tortillas.

SERVES FOUR TO SIX

INGREDIENTS

- 5 garlic cloves, chopped
- 2.5ml/½ tsp paprika
- 2.5ml/½ tsp ground cumin
- 2.5–5ml/½–1 tsp salt
- 2–3 pinches of cayenne pepper
- 60ml/4 tbsp olive oil
- 30ml/2 tbsp lemon juice
- 30ml/2 tbsp chopped fresh coriander (cilantro) or parsley
- 675g/1½ lb firm-fleshed white fish, such as haddock, halibut, sea bass, snapper or turbot, cut into 2.5–5cm/1–2in cubes
- 3–4 green (bell) peppers, cut into 2.5–5cm/1–2in pieces
- 2 lemon wedges, to serve

1 Put the garlic, paprika, cumin, salt, cayenne pepper, oil, lemon juice and coriander or parsley in a large bowl and mix together. Add the fish and toss to coat. Leave to marinate for at least 30 minutes, and preferably 2 hours, at room temperature, or chill overnight.

2 About 40 minutes before you are going to cook the brochettes, light the barbecue. The barbecue is ready when the coals have turned white and grey.

3 Meanwhile, thread the fish cubes and pepper pieces alternately on to wooden or metal skewers.

4 Grill the brochettes on the barbecue for 2–3 minutes on each side, or until the fish is tender and lightly browned. Serve with lemon wedges.

COOK'S TIP

If you are using wooden skewers for the brochettes, soak them in cold water for 30 minutes before using to prevent them from burning.

FILO FISH PIES

THESE LIGHT FILO-WRAPPED FISH PIES CAN BE MADE WITH ANY FIRM WHITE FISH FILLETS, SUCH AS ORANGE ROUGHY, COD, HALIBUT OR HOKI. SERVE WITH SALAD LEAVES AND MAYONNAISE ON THE SIDE.

SERVES SIX

INGREDIENTS

- 400g/14oz spinach, trimmed
- 1 egg, lightly beaten
- 2 garlic cloves, crushed
- 450g/1lb orange roughy or other white fish fillet
- juice of 1 lemon
- 50g/2oz/¼ cup butter, melted
- 8–12 filo pastry sheets, thawed if frozen, quartered
- 15ml/1 tbsp finely chopped fresh chives
- 200ml/7fl oz/scant 1 cup half-fat crème fraîche
- 15ml/1 tbsp chopped fresh dill
- salt and ground black pepper

VARIATION

To make one large pie, use a 20cm/8in tin (pan) and cook for 45 minutes.

1 Preheat the oven to 190°C/375°F/Gas 5. Wash the spinach, then cook it in a lidded heavy pan with just the water that clings to the leaves. As soon as the leaves are tender, drain, squeeze as dry as possible and chop. Put the spinach in a bowl, add the egg and garlic, season with salt and pepper and set aside. Dice the fish and place it in a bowl. Stir in the lemon juice. Season with salt and pepper and toss lightly.

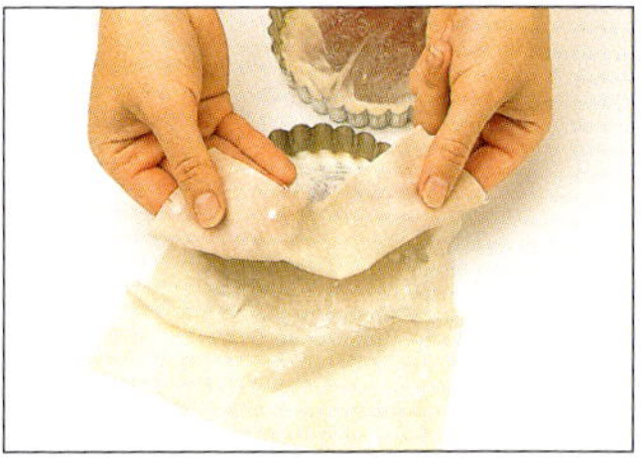

2 Brush the inside of six 13cm/5in tartlet tins (muffin pans) with a little of the melted butter. Fit a piece of filo pastry into the tins, draping it so that it hangs over the sides. Brush with butter, then add another sheet at right-angles to the first. Brush with butter. Continue to line the tins in this way.

3 Spread the spinach evenly over the pastry. Add the diced fish and season well. Stir the chives into the crème fraîche and spread the mixture over the top of the fish. Sprinkle the dill over.

4 Draw the overhanging pieces of pastry together and scrunch lightly to make a lid. Brush with butter. Bake for about 15–20 minutes, until golden brown.

Hoki Stir-fry

Any firm white fish, such as monkfish, hake or cod, can be used for this attractive stir-fry. Vary the vegetables according to what is available, but try to include at least three different colours. Shrimp-fried rice would be the perfect accompaniment.

SERVES FOUR TO SIX

INGREDIENTS

- 675g/1½lb hoki fillet, skinned
- pinch of five-spice powder
- 2 carrots
- 115g/4oz/1 cup mangetouts (snow peas)
- 115g/4oz asparagus spears
- 4 spring onions (scallions)
- 45ml/3 tbsp groundnut (peanut) oil
- 2.5cm/1in piece fresh root ginger, peeled and cut into thin slivers
- 2 garlic cloves, finely chopped
- 300g/11oz beansprouts
- 8–12 small baby corn cobs
- 15–30ml/1–2 tbsp light soy sauce
- salt and ground black pepper

1 Cut the hoki into finger-size strips and season with salt, pepper and five-spice powder. Cut the carrots diagonally into slices as thin as the mangetouts.

2 Trim the mangetouts. Trim the asparagus spears and cut in half crossways. Trim the spring onions and cut them diagonally into 2cm/¾in pieces, keeping the white and green parts separate. Set aside.

3 Heat a wok, then pour in the oil. As soon as it is hot, add the ginger and garlic. Stir-fry for 1 minute, then add the white parts of the spring onions and cook for 1 minute more.

COOK'S TIP

When adding the oil to the hot wok, drizzle it around the inner rim like a necklace. The oil will run down to coat the entire surface of the wok. Swirl the wok to make sure the coating is even.

4 Add the hoki strips and stir-fry for 2–3 minutes, until all the pieces of fish are opaque. Add the beansprouts. Toss them around to coat them in the oil, then put in the carrots, mangetouts, asparagus and corn. Continue to stir-fry for 3–4 minutes, by which time the fish should be cooked, but all the vegetables will still be crunchy. Add soy sauce to taste, toss everything quickly together, then stir in the green parts of the spring onions. Serve immediately.

BRAISED BREAM WITH SHELLFISH

This versatile dish is extremely low in calories, but full of flavour. Use any mixture of fresh or frozen shellfish you like (a few mussels or clams in the shell are particularly attractive). Serve with noodles or pasta shells.

SERVES FOUR

INGREDIENTS
- 30ml/2 tbsp olive oil
- 1 onion, thinly sliced
- 1 yellow or orange (bell) pepper, seeded and cut into strips
- 400ml/14fl oz/1⅔ cups well-reduced tomato sauce
- 45ml/3 tbsp dry white wine or fish stock
- 2 courgettes (zucchini), sliced
- 350g/12oz bream or porgy fillets, skinned and cut into 5cm/2in chunks
- 450g/1lb ready-prepared mixed shellfish, thawed if frozen
- juice of ½ lemon
- 15ml/1 tbsp shredded fresh marjoram or basil leaves
- salt and ground black pepper
- basil leaves, to garnish
- cooked pasta or noodles, to serve

1 Heat the olive oil in a large frying pan. Add the onion slices and yellow or orange pepper strips and stir-fry the vegetables for about 2 minutes, until the onion is translucent.

2 Stir in the tomato sauce, with the white wine or fish stock and bring to the boil. Lower the heat, then simmer for about 2 minutes.

3 Add the courgettes and the chunks of fish; cover and cook gently for about 5 minutes, stirring once or twice during this time. Add the shellfish and stir well to coat it with the sauce.

4 Season to taste with salt, pepper and lemon juice, cover the pan and simmer for 2–3 minutes, until heated through. Stir in the shredded marjoram or basil, and garnish with basil leaves. Serve with noodles or pasta.

COOK'S TIP
If you are short of time, use a 400ml/14fl oz jar of good quality ready-prepared tomato sauce.

VARIATIONS
Fillets of snapper, bass or red mullet could be used in place of the bream in this recipe.

MALAYSIAN STEAMED TROUT FILLETS

This simple dish can be prepared extremely quickly, and is suitable for any fish fillets. Serve it on a bed of noodles accompanied by ribbons of colourful vegetables.

SERVES FOUR

INGREDIENTS
- 8 pink trout fillets of even thickness, about 115g/4oz each, skinned
- 45ml/3 tbsp grated creamed coconut (coconut cream)
- grated rind and juice of 2 limes
- 45ml/3 tbsp chopped fresh coriander (cilantro)
- 15ml/1 tbsp sunflower oil
- 2.5–5ml/½–1 tsp chilli oil
- salt and ground black pepper
- lime slices and coriander (cilantro) sprigs, to garnish

1 Cut four rectangles of baking parchment, twice the size of the trout. Place a fillet on each piece and season.

2 Mix together the coconut, lime rind and chopped coriander and spread a quarter of the mixture over each trout fillet. Sandwich another trout fillet on top. Mix the lime juice with the oils, adjusting the quantity of chilli oil to your own taste, and drizzle the mixture over the trout "sandwiches".

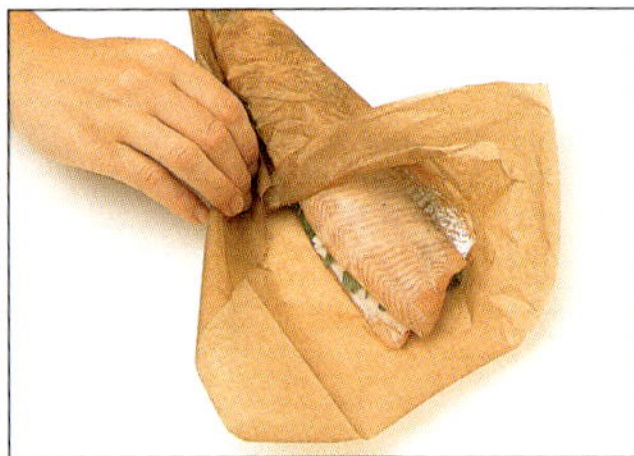

3 Prepare a steamer. Fold up the edges of the parchment and pleat them over the trout to make parcels, making sure they are well sealed. Place in the steamer insert and steam over the simmering water for about 10–15 minutes, depending on the thickness of the fish. Serve immediately.

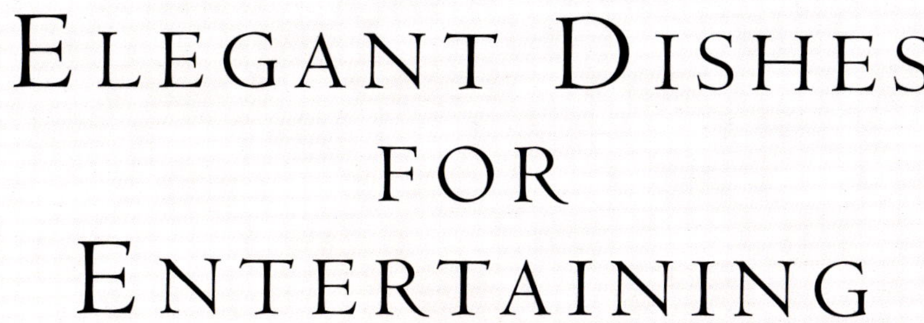

Elegant Dishes for Entertaining

For sheer elegance, fish and shellfish are hard to beat and so quick to prepare that they make light work of entertaining. A whole fish baked in a salt crust looks intriguing and tastes superb. For breathtaking elegance and taste, treat your guests to Lobster Thermidor, Vegetable-stuffed Squid or Fillets of Turbot with Oysters. Whatever the occasion, delight your guests with these superb party dishes.

Hake au Poivre with Red Pepper Relish

This piscine version of the classic steak au poivre can be made with monkfish or cod instead of hake. Vary the quantity of peppercorns according to your personal taste.

SERVES FOUR

INGREDIENTS

- 30–45ml/2–3 tbsp mixed peppercorns (black, white, pink and green)
- 4 hake steaks, about 175g/6oz each
- 30ml/2 tbsp olive oil

For the red (bell) pepper relish

- 2 red (bell) peppers
- 15ml/1 tbsp olive oil
- 2 garlic cloves, chopped
- 4 ripe tomatoes, peeled, seeded and quartered
- 4 drained canned anchovy fillets, chopped
- 5ml/1 tsp capers
- 15ml/1 tbsp balsamic vinegar
- 12 fresh basil leaves, shredded, plus a few extra to garnish
- salt and ground black pepper

1 Put the peppercorns in a mortar and crush them coarsely with a pestle. Alternatively, put them in a plastic bag and crush them with a rolling pin. Season the hake fillets lightly with salt, then coat them evenly on both sides with the crushed peppercorns. Set the coated fish steaks aside while you make the red pepper relish.

2 Make the relish. Cut the red peppers in half lengthways, remove the core and seeds from each and cut the flesh into 1cm/½in wide strips. Heat the olive oil in a wok or a shallow pan that has a lid. Add the peppers and stir them for about 5 minutes, until they are slightly softened. Stir in the chopped garlic, tomatoes and the anchovies, then cover the pan and simmer the mixture very gently for about 20 minutes, until the peppers are very soft.

3 Tip the contents of the pan into a food processor and process to a coarse purée. Transfer to a bowl and season to taste. Stir in the capers, balsamic vinegar and basil. Keep the relish hot.

4 Heat the olive oil in a shallow pan, add the hake steaks and cook them, in batches if necessary, for 5 minutes on each side, turning them once or twice, until they are just cooked through.

5 Place the fish on individual plates and spoon a little red pepper relish on to each plate. Garnish with basil leaves and a little extra balsamic vinegar. Serve the rest of the relish separately.

MOROCCAN FISH TAGINE

THIS SPICY, AROMATIC DISH PROVES JUST HOW EXCITING AN INGREDIENT FISH CAN BE. SERVE IT WITH COUSCOUS FLAVOURED WITH CHOPPED MINT, AND GARNISH WITH EXTRA CORIANDER SPRIGS.

SERVES EIGHT

INGREDIENTS

- 1.4kg/3lb firm fish fillets, skinned
- 3 large fresh red chillies, seeded and chopped
- 3 garlic cloves, peeled
- 15ml/1 tbsp ground coriander
- 30ml/2 tbsp ground cumin
- 5ml/1 tsp ground cinnamon
- grated rind of 1 lemon
- 30ml/2 tbsp sunflower oil
- 60ml/4 tbsp olive oil
- 4 onions, chopped
- 1 large aubergine (eggplant), cut into 1cm/½in cubes
- 2 courgettes (zucchini), cut into 1cm/½in cubes
- 400g/14oz can chopped tomatoes
- 400ml/14fl oz/1⅔ cups passata (bottled strained tomatoes)
- 200ml/7fl oz/scant 1 cup fish stock
- 1 preserved lemon, chopped
- 90g/3½oz/scant 1 cup olives
- 60ml/4 tbsp chopped fresh coriander (cilantro)
- salt and ground black pepper

1 Cut the fish into 5cm/2in chunks. Make a chilli sauce by processing the next seven ingredients in a blender to a smooth paste. Place the fish chunks in a wide bowl and add 30ml/2 tbsp of the sauce. Toss to coat, cover and chill for at least 1 hour, or overnight.

2 Heat half the olive oil in a shallow, heavy pan. Cook the onions over a low heat for 10 minutes, until golden brown. Stir in the remaining chilli sauce and cook for 5 minutes, stirring occasionally.

3 Heat the remaining olive oil in a separate shallow pan. Add the aubergine cubes and cook for about 10 minutes, until they are golden brown. Add the cubed courgettes and cook for a further 2 minutes.

4 Tip the mixture into the shallow pan and combine with the onions, then stir in the chopped tomatoes, the passata and fish stock. Bring to the boil, then lower the heat and simmer the mixture for about 20 minutes.

5 Stir the fish chunks and preserved lemon into the pan. Add the olives and stir gently. Cover and simmer over a low heat for about 15–20 minutes, until the fish is just cooked through. Season to taste. Stir in the chopped coriander. Serve with couscous and garnish with coriander sprigs, if you like.

COOK'S TIP

If you want to make the fish go further, you could add 225g/8oz/1¼ cups cooked chickpeas to the tagine.

PAN-FRIED GARLIC SARDINES

LIGHTLY FRY A SLICED CLOVE OF GARLIC IN OLIVE OIL TO GARNISH THE FISH. THIS DISH COULD ALSO BE MADE WITH SPRATS OR FRESH ANCHOVIES, IF AVAILABLE.

SERVES FOUR

INGREDIENTS

- 1.1kg/2½lb fresh sardines
- 30ml/2 tbsp olive oil
- 4 garlic cloves
- finely grated rind of 2 lemons
- 30ml/2 tbsp chopped fresh parsley
- salt and ground black pepper

For the tomato bread

- 2 large ripe beefsteak tomatoes
- 8 slices crusty bread, toasted

1 Clean the sardines thoroughly and scale them.

2 Heat the oil in a frying pan and add the garlic cloves. Cook until soft.

3 Add the sardines and cook over a medium heat for 4–5 minutes, until they are cooked through and the flesh flakes easily. Sprinkle over the lemon rind and parsley and season to taste with salt and pepper.

4 Cut the tomatoes in half and rub the cut sides on to the toasted bread, discarding the skins. Divide the sardines among serving plates and serve with the tomato bread.

Sea Bream with Orange Sauce

Sea bream is a taste revelation to anyone not yet familiar with its creamy rich flavour. The fish has a firm white flesh that scrumptiously partners a rich butter sauce, sharpened here with a dash of orange.

SERVES TWO

INGREDIENTS

- 2 x 350g/12oz sea bream, cleaned and scaled
- 10ml/2 tsp Dijon mustard
- 5ml/1 tsp fennel seeds
- 30ml/2 tbsp olive oil
- 50g/2oz/1 cup watercress
- 175g/6oz mixed salad leaves
- baked potatoes and orange slices, to serve

For the sauce

- 30ml/2 tbsp frozen orange juice concentrate
- 175g/6oz unsalted (sweet) butter, diced
- salt and cayenne pepper

1 Preheat the grill (broiler). Slash the bream diagonally four times on either side with a sharp knife. Mix together the mustard and fennel seeds in a small bowl, then spread over both sides of the fish. Moisten with some of the oil and cook under the grill for 12 minutes, turning once.

VARIATION

For a sharper sauce, substitute frozen grapefruit juice concentrate for the orange. Stir in a pinch of caster (superfine) sugar if you like.

2 To make the sauce, place the orange juice concentrate in a heatproof bowl and set over a pan containing about 2.5cm/1in of boiling water. When it is hot, remove the pan from the heat and gradually whisk the butter, one piece at a time, into the juice until creamy. Season to taste with salt and cayenne, cover and set aside.

3 Lightly toss the watercress and salad leaves with the remaining olive oil in a bowl. Arrange the fish on two large, warm plates, spoon over the sauce and serve with the salad leaves, baked potatoes and slices of orange.

COOK'S TIPS

- For speedy baked potatoes, microwave small potatoes on 100% high power for 8 minutes, then crisp in a hot oven preheated to 200°C/400°F/ Gas 6 for a further 10 minutes. Cut a cross in the tops, split them open, insert a knob (pat) of butter and serve.
- For the best presentation, choose a selection of colourful and curly salad leaves, such as frisée, oak leaf and lollo biondo. You could also substitute rocket (arugula) for the watercress.

GRILLED SQUID WITH CHORIZO

THE BEST WAY TO COOK THIS DISH IS ON A GRIDDLE OR IN A RIDGED GRIDDLE PAN. IF YOU HAVE NEITHER, USE AN OVERHEAD GRILL, MAKING SURE IT IS VERY HOT. IF YOU CAN ONLY FIND MEDIUM-SIZE SQUID, ALLOW TWO PER SERVING AND HALVE THEM LENGTHWAYS FROM THE TAIL END TO THE CAVITY.

SERVES SIX

INGREDIENTS
- 24 small squid, cleaned
- 150ml/¼ pint/⅔ cup extra virgin olive oil
- 300g/11oz cooking chorizo, cut into 12 slices
- 3 tomatoes, halved and seasoned with salt and pepper
- juice of 1 lemon
- 24 cooked new potatoes, halved
- fresh rocket (arugula) leaves
- salt and ground black pepper
- lemon slices, to garnish

1 Separate the body and tentacles of the squid and cut the bodies in half lengthways if they are large.

2 Pour half the oil into a bowl, season with salt and pepper, then toss all the squid in the oil. Heat a ridged griddle pan or grill (broiler) to very hot.

3 Grill (broil) the prepared squid bodies for about 45 seconds on each side until the flesh is opaque and tender. Then transfer to a plate and keep hot. Grill the tentacles for about 1 minute on each side, then place them on the plate. Grill the chorizo slices for about 30 seconds on each side, until golden brown, then set them aside with the squid. Grill the tomato halves for 1–2 minutes on each side, until they are softened and browned.

4 Place the potatoes and a handful of rocket in a large bowl.

5 Pour the lemon juice into a bowl and whisk in the remaining oil. Season. Reserve 30ml/2 tbsp of this dressing. Pour the dressing over the potatoes and rocket, toss lightly and divide among six plates. Pile a portion of the squid, tomatoes and chorizo on each salad, and drizzle over the reserved dressing. Garnish with lemon slices and serve immediately.

SOLE WITH WILD MUSHROOMS

IF POSSIBLE, USE CHANTERELLES FOR THIS DISH; THEIR GLOWING ORANGE COLOUR COMBINES REALLY WONDERFULLY WITH THE INTENSELY GOLDEN SAUCE. OTHERWISE, USE ANY PALE-COLOURED OR OYSTER MUSHROOMS THAT YOU CAN FIND INSTEAD.

SERVES FOUR

INGREDIENTS
- 4 Dover sole fillets, about 115g/4oz each, skinned
- 50g/2oz/4 tbsp butter
- 500ml/17fl oz/generous 2 cups fish stock
- 150g/5oz/2 cups chanterelles
- a large pinch of saffron threads
- 150ml/¼ pint/⅔ cup double (heavy) cream
- 1 egg yolk
- salt and ground white pepper
- finely chopped fresh parsley, and parsley sprigs to garnish
- boiled new potatoes, to serve

1 Preheat the oven to 200°C/400°F/Gas 6. Cut the sole fillets in half lengthways and place them on a board with the skinned side uppermost. Season them with salt and white pepper, then roll them up. Use a little of the butter to grease an ovenproof dish just large enough to hold all the sole fillets in a single layer. Arrange the sole rolls in the dish, then pour over the fish stock. Cover tightly with foil and bake for 12–15 minutes, until cooked through.

2 Meanwhile, pick off any bits of fern or twig from the chanterelles and wipe the mushrooms with a damp cloth. Halve or quarter any large ones. Heat the remaining butter in a frying pan until foaming and sauté the mushrooms for 3–4 minutes, until just tender. Season with salt and pepper and keep hot.

3 Lift the cooked sole fillets out of the cooking liquid and place them on a heated serving dish. Keep hot. Strain the liquid into a small pan, add the saffron threads, set over a very high heat and boil until reduced to about 250ml/8fl oz/1 cup. Stir in the cream and then let the sauce bubble gently once or twice.

4 Lightly beat the egg yolk in a small bowl, pour on a little of the hot sauce and stir well. Stir the mixture into the remaining sauce in the pan and cook over a very low heat for 1–2 minutes, until slightly thickened. Season to taste. Stir the chanterelles into the sauce and pour it over the sole fillets. Garnish with fresh parsley sprigs and serve immediately. Boiled new potatoes make the perfect accompaniment.

SPICY SQUID

This aromatically spiced squid dish, Cumi Cumi Smoor, is a favourite in Madura, Indonesia and is simple yet utterly delicious. You can use ready prepared squid or clean the squid yourself.

SERVES THREE TO FOUR

INGREDIENTS

- 675g/1½lb prepared squid
- 45ml/3 tbsp groundnut (peanut) oil
- 1 onion, finely chopped
- 2 garlic cloves, crushed
- 1 beefsteak tomato, peeled and chopped
- 15ml/1 tbsp dark soy sauce
- 2.5ml/½ tsp freshly grated nutmeg
- 6 cloves
- 150ml/¼ pint/⅔ cup water
- juice of ½ lemon or lime
- salt and ground black pepper
- boiled rice, to serve

1 Using a sharp knife, cut the squid bodies into thin ribbons and chop the tentacles. Rinse in a colander under cold running water and drain well.

2 Heat a wok or large heavy frying pan. Toss in the squid and stir constantly over a medium heat for 2–3 minutes, by which time the squid will have curled into attractive shapes or firm rings. Lift out to a plate, cover and set aside in a warm place.

3 Heat the oil in a clean pan. Add the onion and garlic, and cook over a medium heat, stirring occasionally, for about 5 minutes, until softened and beginning to brown. Add the tomato, soy sauce, nutmeg, cloves, measured water and lemon or lime juice and stir well. Bring to the boil, then reduce the heat and add the squid. Season to taste with salt and pepper.

4 Simmer gently over a low heat for a further 3–5 minutes, stirring occasionally. Take care not to overcook the squid. Serve either hot or warm, with boiled rice.

VARIATION

Try using 450g/1lb cooked, peeled tiger prawns (jumbo shrimp) in this recipe. Add them for the final 1–2 minutes of the cooking time.

Donu's Lobster Piri Piri

Lobster in its shell, in true Nigerian style.

SERVES TWO TO FOUR

INGREDIENTS

- 2 cooked lobsters, halved
- fresh coriander (cilantro) sprigs, to garnish
- boiled white rice, to serve

For the piri piri sauce

- 60ml/4 tbsp vegetable oil
- 2 onions, chopped
- 5ml/1 tsp chopped fresh root ginger
- 450g/1lb fresh or canned tomatoes, chopped
- 15ml/1 tbsp tomato purée (paste)
- 225g/8oz cooked peeled prawns (shrimp)
- 10ml/2 tsp ground coriander
- 1 green chilli, seeded and chopped
- 15ml/1 tbsp ground, dried prawns (shrimp) or crayfish
- 600ml/1 pint/2½ cups water
- 1 green (bell) pepper, seeded and sliced
- salt and ground black pepper

1 To make the piri piri sauce, heat the oil in a large, flameproof casserole. Add the onions, ginger, tomatoes and tomato purée and cook over a low heat, stirring occasionally, for about 5 minutes, or until the onions are soft.

2 Add the prawns, ground coriander, chilli and ground, dried prawns or crayfish and stir well to mix.

COOK'S TIP

Piri piri is said to be the sound the sauce makes as it bubbles.

3 Stir in the measured water and green pepper strips and season with salt and pepper to taste. Bring to the boil over a high heat, then lower the heat to medium and simmer gently, uncovered, for about 20–30 minutes, until the sauce is well reduced and has thickened.

4 Add the lobster halves to the sauce and cook for a few minutes just to heat through. Arrange the lobster halves on warmed serving plates and pour the sauce over each one. Garnish with fresh coriander sprigs and serve immediately with fluffy white rice.

Lobster Thermidor

One of the classic French dishes, Lobster Thermidor makes a little lobster go a long way. It is best to use one big rather than two small lobsters, as a larger lobster will contain a higher proportion of flesh and the meat will be sweeter. Ideally, use a live crustacean and cook it yourself, but a boiled lobster from the fishmonger will do.

SERVES TWO

INGREDIENTS

- 1 large lobster, about 800g–1kg/1¾–2¼lb, boiled
- 45ml/3 tbsp brandy
- 25g/1oz/2 tbsp butter
- 2 shallots, finely chopped
- 115g/4oz/1½ cups button (white) mushrooms, thinly sliced
- 15ml/1 tbsp plain (all-purpose) flour
- 105ml/7 tbsp fish or shellfish stock
- 120ml/4fl oz/½ cup double (heavy) cream
- 5ml/1 tsp Dijon mustard
- 2 egg yolks, beaten
- 45ml/3 tbsp dry white wine
- 45ml/3 tbsp freshly grated Parmesan
- salt, ground black pepper and cayenne pepper

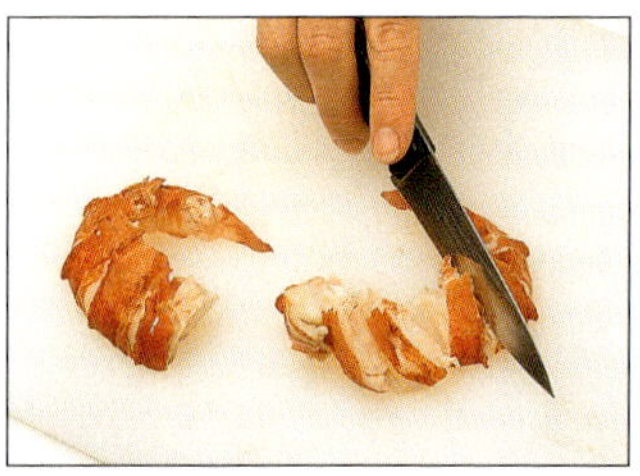

1 Split the lobster in half lengthways; crack the claws. Discard the stomach sac; keep the coral for another dish. Keeping each half-shell intact, extract the meat from the tail and claws, then cut into large dice. Place in a shallow dish; sprinkle over the brandy. Cover and set aside. Wipe and dry the half-shells and set them aside.

2 Melt the butter in a pan and cook the shallots over a low heat until soft. Add the mushrooms and cook until just tender, stirring constantly. Stir in the flour and a pinch of cayenne; cook, stirring, for 2 minutes. Gradually add the stock, stirring until the sauce boils and thickens.

3 Stir in the cream and mustard and continue to cook until the sauce is smooth and thick. Season to taste with salt, black pepper and cayenne. Pour half the sauce on to the egg yolks, stir well and return the mixture to the pan. Stir in the wine; adjust the seasoning, being generous with the cayenne.

4 Preheat the grill (broiler) to medium-high. Stir the diced lobster and the brandy into the sauce. Arrange the lobster half-shells in a grill pan and divide the mixture among them. Sprinkle with Parmesan and place under the grill until browned. Serve with steamed rice and mixed salad leaves.

RED MULLET SALTIMBOCCA

THE RICH RED COLOUR OF THE MULLET IS INTENSIFIED BY RUBBING SAFFRON INTO THE SKIN, COMPLEMENTING THE PROSCIUTTO BEAUTIFULLY. SERVE WITH BRIGHTLY COLOURED ROASTED MEDITERRANEAN VEGETABLES AND CRISPLY COOKED GREEN BEANS, IF YOU LIKE.

SERVES FOUR

INGREDIENTS

- 8 red mullet or red snapper fillets, scaled but not skinned
- a pinch of saffron threads or powdered saffron
- 15ml/1 tbsp olive oil
- 8 fresh sage leaves
- 8 thin slices of prosciutto
- 25g/1oz/2 tbsp butter
- 115g/4oz/1 cup mixed olives
- salt and ground black pepper

For the dressing

- 15ml/1 tbsp caster (superfine) sugar
- 105ml/7 tbsp balsamic vinegar
- 300ml/½ pint/1¼ cups extra virgin olive oil
- 5cm/2in slice red (bell) pepper, diced
- 1 small courgette (zucchini), diced
- 1 ripe tomato, peeled, seeded and very finely diced

1 Score the fish skin lightly in three or four places. Season both sides of each fillet with salt and ground black pepper. If you are using saffron threads, crumble them over the skin side of each fish fillet, or sprinkle the powdered saffron over the skin. Drizzle on a little olive oil and then rub the saffron in well with your fingertips. This will dramatically enhance the colour of the fish skin.

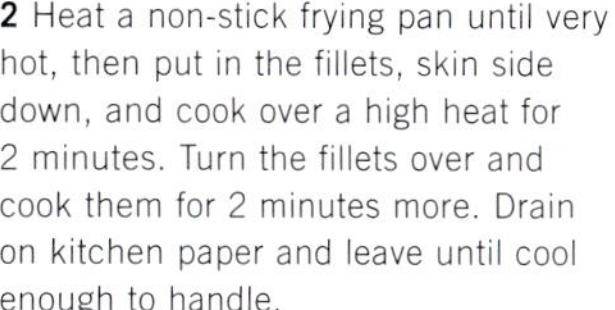

2 Heat a non-stick frying pan until very hot, then put in the fillets, skin side down, and cook over a high heat for 2 minutes. Turn the fillets over and cook them for 2 minutes more. Drain on kitchen paper and leave until cool enough to handle.

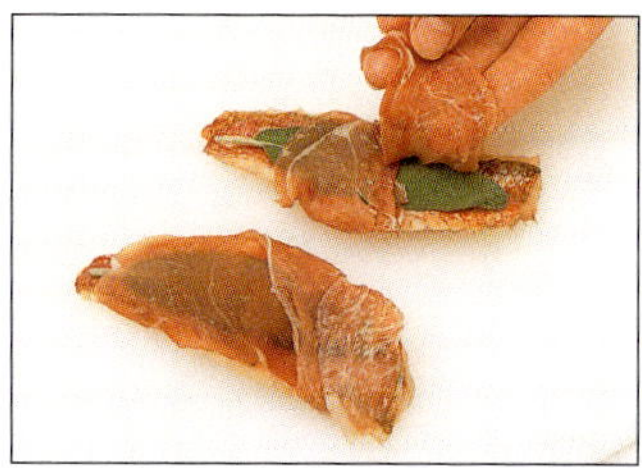

3 Place a sage leaf on each cooked fillet, then wrap the fillets in a slice of prosciutto to cover them completely. Melt the butter in the frying pan and continue to heat until it foams. Fry the ham and red mullet parcels over a high heat for 1–2 minutes on each side, until the ham is pale golden. Transfer to warmed serving plates and keep hot while you make the dressing.

4 Mix the sugar and balsamic vinegar in a small pan, set over a high heat and boil until syrupy.

5 Meanwhile, pour the olive oil into a bowl, stir in the diced vegetables and season. Stir the vinegar syrup into the dressing. Drizzle it over and around the ham-wrapped fish. Place the olives on the plates and serve immediately.

Roast Monkfish with Garlic

Monkfish tied up and cooked in this way is known in French as a "gigot", because it resembles a leg of lamb. The combination of monkfish and garlic is superb. For a contrast in colour, serve it with vibrant green beans.

SERVES FOUR TO SIX

INGREDIENTS

- 1kg/2¼lb monkfish tail, skinned
- 14 fat garlic cloves
- 5ml/1 tsp fresh thyme leaves
- 30ml/2 tbsp olive oil
- juice of 1 lemon
- 2 bay leaves
- salt and ground black pepper

1 Preheat the oven to 220°C/425°F/Gas 7. Remove any membrane from the monkfish tail and cut out the central bone. Peel two garlic cloves and cut them into thin slivers. Sprinkle a quarter of these and half the thyme leaves over the cut side of the fish, then close it up and use fine kitchen string to tie it into a neat shape, like a boned piece of meat. Pat dry with kitchen paper.

2 Make incisions on either side of the fish and push in the remaining garlic slivers. Heat half the olive oil in a frying pan which can safely be used in the oven. When the oil is hot, put in the monkfish and brown it all over for about 5 minutes, until evenly coloured. Season with salt and pepper, sprinkle with lemon juice and sprinkle over the remaining thyme.

3 Tuck the bay leaves under the monkfish, arrange the remaining (unpeeled) garlic cloves around it and drizzle the remaining olive oil over the fish and the garlic. Transfer the frying pan to the oven and roast the monkfish for 20–25 minutes, until the flesh is cooked through.

4 Place on a warmed serving dish with the garlic and some green beans. To serve, remove the string and cut the monkfish into 2cm/¾in thick slices.

COOK'S TIPS

- The garlic heads can be used whole.
- When serving the monkfish, invite each guest to pop out the soft garlic pulp with a fork and spread it over the monkfish.
- Use two smaller monkfish tails.

SEA BASS WITH GINGER AND LEEKS

YOU CAN USE WHOLE FISH OR THICK FILLETS FOR THIS RECIPE, WHICH IS ALSO EXCELLENT MADE WITH BREAM, PORGY, SNAPPER, POMFRET AND TREVALLY. SERVE THE FISH WITH FRIED RICE AND STIR-FRIED CHINESE GREEN VEGETABLES, SUCH AS PAK CHOI, IF YOU LIKE.

SERVES FOUR

INGREDIENTS

- 1 sea bass, about 1.4–1.5kg/3–3½lb, scaled and cleaned
- 8 spring onions (scallions)
- 60ml/4 tbsp teriyaki marinade or dark soy sauce
- 30ml/2 tbsp cornflour (cornstarch)
- juice of 1 lemon
- 30ml/2 tbsp rice wine vinegar
- 5ml/1 tsp ground ginger
- 60ml/4 tbsp groundnut (peanut) oil
- 2 leeks, shredded
- 2.5cm/1in piece fresh root ginger, peeled and grated
- 105ml/7 tbsp chicken or fish stock
- 30ml/2 tbsp rice wine or dry sherry
- 5ml/1 tsp caster (superfine) sugar
- salt and ground black pepper

1 Make several diagonal slashes on either side of the sea bass so it can absorb the flavours, then season the fish inside and out with salt and ground black pepper. Trim the spring onions, cut them in half lengthways, then slice them diagonally into 2cm/¾in lengths. Put half of the spring onions in the cavity of the fish and reserve the rest for later use.

2 In a shallow dish, mix together the teriyaki marinade or dark soy sauce, the cornflour, lemon juice, rice wine vinegar and ground ginger to make a smooth, runny paste. Turn the fish in the marinade to coat it thoroughly, working it into the slashes, then leave it to marinate for 20–30 minutes, turning it several times.

3 Heat a wok or frying pan that is large enough to hold the sea bass comfortably. Add the oil, then the leeks and grated ginger. Cook gently for about 5 minutes, until the leeks are tender. Remove the leeks and ginger with a slotted spoon and drain on kitchen paper. leaving the oil in the wok or pan.

4 Lift the sea bass out of the marinade and lower it carefully into the hot oil. Cook over a medium heat for 2–3 minutes on each side. Stir the stock, rice wine or sherry and sugar into the marinade, with salt and pepper to taste. Pour the mixture over the fish. Return the leeks and ginger to the wok, together with the reserved spring onions. Cover and simmer for about 15 minutes, until the fish is cooked through. Serve.

GRILLED LANGOUSTINES WITH HERBS

THIS SIMPLE COOKING METHOD ENHANCES BOTH THE DELICATE COLOUR AND FLAVOUR OF THE LANGOUSTINES. TRY TO FIND LIVE LANGOUSTINES FOR THIS RECIPE. CHOOSE THE LARGEST YOU CAN FIND (OR AFFORD) FOR THIS DISH, AND ALLOW FIVE OR SIX PER SERVING. LOBSTER AND CRAYFISH ARE ALSO DELICIOUS COOKED THIS WAY.

SERVES FOUR AS A MAIN COURSE, SIX AS AN APPETIZER

INGREDIENTS

- 60ml/4 tbsp extra virgin olive oil
- 60ml/4 tbsp hazelnut oil
- 15ml/1 tbsp each finely chopped fresh basil, chives, chervil, parsley and tarragon
- pinch of ground ginger
- 20–24 large langoustines, preferably live
- lemon wedges and rocket (arugula) leaves, to garnish
- salt and ground black pepper

COOK'S TIPS

- Don't forget to provide your guests with fingerbowls of warm water and plenty of paper napkins.
- If you use cooked langoustines, then grill (broil) them for just 2–3 minutes to warm them through.

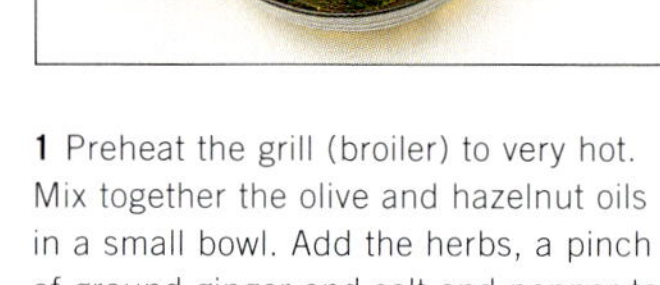

1 Preheat the grill (broiler) to very hot. Mix together the olive and hazelnut oils in a small bowl. Add the herbs, a pinch of ground ginger and salt and pepper to taste. Whisk thoroughly until slightly thickened and emulsified.

2 If you are using live langoustines, immerse them in a pan of boiling water for 1–2 minutes, then drain and leave them to cool.

3 Split the langoustines lengthways using a large sharp knife and arrange them on a foil-lined grill pan. Spoon over the herb-flavoured oil.

4 Grill (broil) for 8–10 minutes, basting the langoustines two or three times until they are cooked and lightly browned.

5 Arrange the langoustines on a warmed serving dish, pour the juices from the grill pan over and serve immediately garnished with lemon wedges and rocket leaves.

SEA BASS IN A SALT CRUST

BAKING FISH IN A CRUST OF SEA SALT ENHANCES THE FLAVOUR AND BRINGS OUT THE TASTE OF THE SEA. ANY FIRM FISH CAN BE COOKED IN THIS WAY. BREAK OPEN THE CRUST AT THE TABLE TO RELEASE THE GLORIOUS AROMA.

SERVES FOUR

INGREDIENTS

- 1 sea bass, about 1kg/2¼lb, cleaned and scaled
- 1 sprig each of fresh fennel, rosemary and thyme
- 2kg/4½lb/13½ cups coarse sea salt
- mixed peppercorns
- seaweed or samphire, blanched, and lemon slices, to garnish

1 Preheat the oven to 240°C/475°F/Gas 9. Fill the cavity of the sea bass with all the herbs and grind over some of the mixed peppercorns.

2 Spread half the salt on a shallow baking tray (ideally oval) and lay the sea bass on it. Cover the fish all over with a 1cm/½in layer of salt, pressing it down firmly. Moisten the salt lightly by spraying with water from an atomizer. Bake the fish in the hot oven for 30–40 minutes, until the salt crust is just beginning to colour.

3 Garnish the baking tray with seaweed or samphire and bring the fish to the table in its salt crust. Use a sharp knife to break open the crust. Serve the fish, adding lemon slices to each plate.

SALMON WITH WATERCRESS SAUCE

THIS IS A PARTNERSHIP MADE IN HEAVEN.

SERVES FOUR

INGREDIENTS

- 300ml/½ pint/1¼ cups crème fraîche
- 30ml/2 tbsp chopped fresh tarragon
- 25g/1oz/2 tbsp butter
- 15ml/1 tbsp sunflower oil
- 4 salmon fillets, skinned
- 1 garlic clove, crushed
- 100ml/3½fl oz/scant ½ cup dry white wine
- 1 bunch watercress
- salt and ground black pepper
- salad leaves, to serve

1 Gently heat the crème fraîche in a small pan until just beginning to boil. Remove the pan from the heat and stir in half the tarragon. Leave the herb cream to infuse (steep) while you cook the fish.

2 Heat the butter and oil in a frying pan, add the salmon and cook for 3–5 minutes on each side. Remove from the pan and keep warm.

3 Add the garlic to the pan and cook over a low heat, stirring frequently, for 1 minute, then pour in the wine and let it bubble until reduced to about 15ml/1 tbsp.

4 Meanwhile, strip the leaves off the watercress stalks and chop them very finely. Discard any damaged or discoloured leaves. (You can save the watercress stalks for making soup, if you like.)

5 Strain the herb cream into the pan and cook for a few minutes, stirring until the sauce has thickened. Stir in the remaining chopped tarragon and the watercress, then cook for a few minutes, until wilted but still bright green. Season to taste with salt and black pepper.

6 Place the salmon on warm plates, spoon over the sauce and serve immediately with salad leaves.

SALMON WITH GREEN PEPPERCORNS

A FASHIONABLE DISCOVERY OF NOUVELLE CUISINE, GREEN PEPPERCORNS ADD PIQUANCY TO ALL KINDS OF SAUCES. AVAILABLE PICKLED IN JARS OR CANS, THEY ARE GREAT TO KEEP ON HAND.

SERVES FOUR

INGREDIENTS

- 15g/½oz/1 tbsp butter
- 2–3 shallots, finely chopped
- 15ml/1 tbsp brandy (optional)
- 60ml/4 tbsp white wine
- 90ml/6 tbsp fish or chicken stock
- 120ml/4fl oz/½ cup whipping cream
- 30–45ml/2–3 tbsp green peppercorns in brine, rinsed
- 15–30ml/1–2 tbsp vegetable oil
- 4 salmon fillets, 175–200g/6–7oz each
- salt and ground black pepper
- fresh parsley, to garnish

1 Melt the butter in a heavy pan over a medium heat. Add the shallots and cook, stirring occasionally, for about 1–2 minutes, until just softened but not coloured.

2 Add the brandy, if using, and the white wine, then stir in the stock. Increase the heat to high and bring to the boil. Boil vigorously, stirring occasionally, until reduced by about three-quarters.

COOK'S TIP

Use a heat diffuser when you are keeping the sauce warm, so that it doesn't come to the boil.

3 Reduce the heat, then add the cream and half the peppercorns, crushing them slightly with the back of a spoon. Cook very gently for about 4–5 minutes, until the sauce is slightly thickened, then strain, return to the pan and stir in the remaining peppercorns. Keep the sauce warm over a very low heat, stirring occasionally, while you cook the salmon fillets.

4 In a large, heavy frying pan, heat the oil over a medium-high heat until very hot. Lightly season the salmon with salt and pepper and cook for 3–4 minutes, until the flesh is opaque throughout. To check, pierce the fish with the tip of a sharp knife; the juices should run clear. Transfer the fish to warmed plates and pour over the sauce. Garnish with parsley and serve immediately.

Braised Fish in Chilli and Garlic Sauce

This recipe reflects its Chinese origins. When served in a restaurant, the head and tail are usually discarded before cooking. A whole fish may be used, however, and always looks impressive.

SERVES FOUR TO SIX

INGREDIENTS

- 1 carp, bream, sea bass, trout, grouper or striped mullet, weighing about 675g/1½lb, cleaned
- 15ml/1 tbsp light soy sauce
- 15ml/1 tbsp Chinese rice wine or dry sherry
- vegetable oil, for deep-frying

For the sauce

- 2 garlic cloves, finely chopped
- 2–3 spring onions (scallions), finely chopped, with the white and green parts separated
- 5ml/1 tsp finely chopped fresh root ginger
- 30ml/2 tbsp hot bean sauce
- 15ml/1 tbsp tomato purée (paste)
- 10ml/2 tsp soft light brown sugar
- 15ml/1 tbsp rice vinegar
- about 120ml/4fl oz/½ cup stock
- 15ml/1 tbsp cornflour (cornstarch) paste
- few drops sesame oil

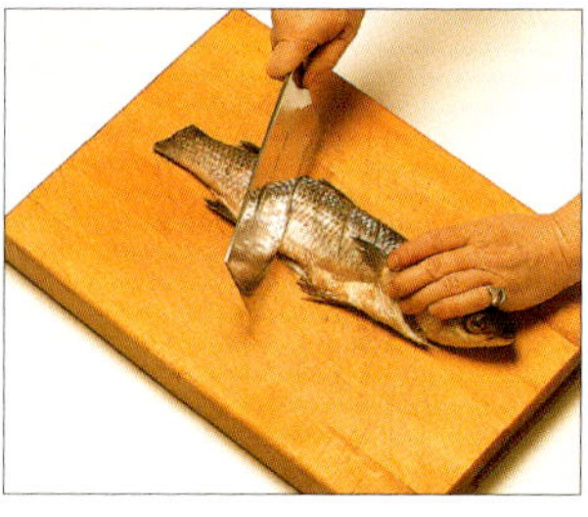

1 Rinse and dry the fish. Score both sides of the fish, as deep as the bone, with diagonal cuts about 2.5cm/1in apart. Rub the fish with soy sauce and rice wine or sherry on both sides, then leave to marinate for 10–15 minutes.

2 Heat the oil in a preheated wok or large, heavy frying pan and deep-fry the fish for about 3–4 minutes on both sides, or until golden brown. Pour off the excess oil, leaving about 15ml/1 tbsp in the wok.

COOK'S TIP

Chinese rice wine can be found in Asian food stores and is available from some supermarkets. It is not necessary to use the best quality and most expensive wine for cooking.

3 Push the fish to one side of the wok and add the garlic, the white part of the spring onions, ginger, hot bean sauce, tomato purée, sugar, vinegar and stock. Bring to the boil and braise the fish in the sauce for 4–5 minutes, turning it over once. Add the green part of the spring onions. Thicken the sauce with the cornflour paste and sprinkle with the sesame oil. Transfer to a warm platter and serve immediately.

Tilapia in Fruit Sauce

Tilapia is widely used in African cooking, but can now be found in most fishmongers and markets.

SERVES FOUR

INGREDIENTS
- 4 tilapia, cleaned
- ½ lemon
- 2 garlic cloves, crushed
- 2.5ml/½ tsp dried thyme
- 30ml/2 tbsp chopped spring onions (scallions)
- vegetable oil, for shallow frying
- plain (all-purpose) flour, for dusting
- 30ml/2 tbsp groundnut (peanut) oil
- 15g/½oz/1 tbsp butter
- 1 onion, finely chopped
- 3 tomatoes, peeled and finely chopped
- 5ml/1 tsp ground turmeric
- 60ml/4 tbsp white wine
- 1 fresh green chilli, seeded and finely chopped
- 600ml/1 pint/2½ cups fish stock
- 5ml/1 tsp sugar
- 1 medium underripe mango, peeled, stoned (pitted) and diced
- 15ml/1 tbsp chopped fresh parsley
- salt and ground black pepper

1 Place the fish in a shallow bowl, squeeze the lemon juice all over it and gently rub in the garlic, thyme and some salt and pepper. Place some of the spring onion in the cavity of each fish, cover loosely with clear film (plastic wrap) and leave to marinate for a few hours or overnight in the refrigerator.

2 Heat a little vegetable oil in a large, heavy frying pan. Coat the fish with flour, shaking off any excess, then cook the fish on both sides over a medium heat for a few minutes, until golden brown. Remove from the pan to a plate, using a slotted spoon, and set aside.

3 Heat the groundnut oil and butter in a pan. Add the onion and cook over a low heat, stirring occasionally, for 4–5 minutes, until softened. Stir in the tomatoes, increase the heat to medium and cook briskly for a few minutes more.

4 Add the turmeric, white wine, chilli, fish stock and sugar, stir well and bring to the boil, then lower the heat, cover and simmer gently for 10 minutes.

5 Add the fish and cook over a gentle heat for 15–20 minutes, until the fish is cooked through. Add the mango, arranging it around the fish, and cook briefly for 1–2 minutes to heat through.

6 Arrange the fish on a warmed serving platter with the mango and tomato sauce poured over. Garnish with the chopped fresh parsley and serve immediately.

FISH IN TAHINI SAUCE

IN THIS RECIPE, WHOLE FISH ARE WRAPPED IN VINE LEAVES, THEN SPREAD WITH TAHINI SAUCE AND BAKED. A FINAL SPRINKLING OF POMEGRANATE SEEDS ADDS A FRESH, INVIGORATING FLAVOUR. YOU COULD USE FISH FILLETS OR STEAKS, IF YOU PREFER.

SERVES FOUR

INGREDIENTS

- 4 small fish, such as trout, sea bream or red mullet, each weighing about 300g/11oz, cleaned
- at least 5 garlic cloves, chopped
- juice of 2 lemons
- 75ml/5 tbsp olive oil
- about 20 brined vine leaves
- tahini, for drizzling
- 1–2 pomegranates
- fresh mint and coriander (cilantro) sprigs, to garnish

VARIATION

Instead of whole fish, use fish fillets or steaks such as fresh tuna. Make a bed of vine leaves and top with the fish and marinade. Bake for 5–10 minutes until the fish is half cooked, then top with the tahini as above and grill (broil) until golden brown and lightly crusted on top.

1 Preheat the oven to 180°C/350°F/ Gas 4. Put the fish in a shallow, ovenproof dish, large enough to fit the whole fish without touching each other. In a bowl, combine the garlic, lemon juice and oil; spoon over the fish. Turn the fish to coat.

2 Rinse the vine leaves well under cold water, then wrap the fish in the leaves. Arrange the fish in the same dish and spoon any marinade in the dish over the top of each. Bake for 30 minutes.

3 Drizzle the tahini over the top of each wrapped fish, making a ribbon so that the tops and tails of the fish and some of the vine leaf wrapping still show. Return to the oven and bake for a further 5–10 minutes until the top is golden and slightly crusted.

4 Meanwhile, cut the pomegranates in half and scoop out the seeds. Sprinkle the seeds over the fish, garnish with mint and coriander, and serve.

SPICY BAKED FISH WITH PINE NUTS

A whole fish, cooked in spices, is a festival treat in the Jewish calendar. It is especially popular at Rosh Hashanah. The wholeness symbolizes the full year to come and the head symbolizes the wisdom that we ask to be endowed with.

SERVES SIX TO EIGHT

INGREDIENTS

- 1–1.5kg/2¼–3¼lb fish, such as snapper, cleaned, with head and tail left on (optional)
- 2.5ml/½ tsp salt
- juice of 2 lemons
- 45–60ml/3–4 tbsp extra virgin olive oil
- 2 onions, sliced
- 5 garlic cloves, chopped
- 1 green (bell) pepper, seeded and chopped
- 1–2 fresh green chillies, seeded and finely chopped
- 2.5ml/½ tsp ground turmeric
- 2.5ml/½ tsp curry powder
- 2.5 ml/½ tsp ground cumin
- 120ml/4fl oz/½ cup passata (bottled strained tomatoes)
- 5–6 fresh or canned tomatoes, chopped
- 45–60ml/3–4 tbsp chopped fresh coriander (cilantro) leaves and/or parsley
- 65g/2½oz pine nuts, toasted
- fresh parsley, to garnish

1 Prick the fish all over with a fork and rub with the salt. Put the fish in a roasting pan or dish and pour over the lemon juice. Leave to stand for 2 hours.

VARIATION

The spicy tomato sauce is very good served with fish patties. Omit step 1 and simply warm fried patties through in the spicy sauce.

2 Preheat the oven to 180°C/350°F/Gas 4. Heat the oil in a pan, add the onions and half the garlic and cook for about 5 minutes, or until softened.

3 Add the pepper, chillies, turmeric, curry powder and cumin to the pan and cook gently for 2–3 minutes. Stir in the passata, tomatoes and herbs.

4 Sprinkle half of the pine nuts over the base of an ovenproof dish, top with half of the sauce, then add the fish and its marinade. Sprinkle the remaining garlic over the fish, then add the remaining sauce and the remaining pine nuts. Cover tightly with a lid or foil and bake for 30 minutes, or until the fish is tender. Garnish with parsley.

Fish Steaks with Coriander-Lime Butter

Cook this dish under the grill or on the barbecue.

SERVES FOUR

INGREDIENTS

- 675g/1½lb swordfish or tuna steak, 2.5cm/1in thick
- 60ml/4 tbsp vegetable oil
- 30ml/2 tbsp lemon juice
- 15ml/1 tbsp lime juice
- salt and ground black pepper
- coriander-lime (cilantro-lime) butter (see Cook's Tip)
- asparagus and lime slices, to serve

1 Cut the fish steaks into four pieces and place them in a shallow dish. Mix together the oil, lemon juice and lime juice, season with salt and pepper and pour over the fish. Cover and chill for 1–2 hours, turning the fish once or twice.

2 Drain the fish steaks and arrange them on the rack in the grill (broiler) pan or set over the hot charcoal about 13cm/5in from the coals. Cook, turning the steaks once, for about 3–4 minutes, or until the fish is just firm to the touch but still succulent in the centre.

3 Transfer to four warmed plates and top each fish steak with a pat of coriander-lime butter. Serve the fish immediately with steamed asparagus and slices of lime.

COOK'S TIPS

- For the butter, finely chop 25g/1oz/½ cup fresh coriander (cilantro). Mix into 115g/4oz/½ cup softened, unsalted (sweet) butter, together with the grated rind and juice of 1 lime. Roll the butter neatly in greaseproof (waxed) paper and chill in the refrigerator until firm.
- Other flavoured butters can be made in the same way. Try parsley-lemon butter, made from 30ml/2 tbsp chopped fresh parsley, 115g/4oz/½ cup unsalted butter and 15ml/1 tbsp lemon juice.
- For anchovy butter, drain 50g/2oz canned anchovy fillets and soak in milk for 10 minutes to reduce the saltiness. Pat dry, chop finely and beat into 115g/4oz/½ cup unsalted butter.

Trout in Wine Sauce with Plantain

Tropical fish would add a distinctive flavour to this Caribbean dish.

SERVES FOUR

INGREDIENTS

- 15ml/1 tbsp garlic granules
- 7.5ml/1½ tsp coarse black pepper
- 7.5ml/1½ tsp paprika
- 7.5ml/1½ tsp celery salt
- 7.5ml/1½ tsp curry powder
- 5ml/1 tsp caster (superfine) sugar
- 4 trout fillets
- 25g/1oz/2 tbsp butter
- 150ml/¼ pint/⅔ cup white wine
- 150ml/¼ pint/⅔ cup fish stock
- 10ml/2 tsp clear honey
- 15–30ml/1–2 tbsp chopped fresh parsley
- 1 yellow plantain
- oil, for frying

1 Mix together the spices and the caster sugar, sprinkle over the trout and leave to marinate for 1 hour.

2 Melt the butter in a frying pan. Add the trout fillets and cook over a low heat for about 5 minutes, until cooked through, turning once. Transfer to a plate and keep warm.

3 Add the white wine, fish stock and honey to the pan and bring to the boil, stirring well to mix. Lower the heat and simmer to reduce slightly. Return the fish fillets to the pan and spoon the sauce over them. Sprinkle with parsley and simmer gently for a few minutes.

4 Meanwhile, peel the plantain and slice it into rounds. Heat a little oil in another frying pan. Add the plantain slices and cook over a medium heat until golden, turning once. Transfer the fish to warmed serving plates, stir the sauce and pour over the fish. Garnish with the fried plantain.

Turbot in Parchment

Cooking in parcels is not new, but it is an ideal way to cook fish. Serve this dish plain or with a little hollandaise sauce.

SERVES FOUR

INGREDIENTS

- 2 carrots, cut into julienne strips
- 2 courgettes (zucchini), cut into julienne strips
- 2 leeks, cut into julienne strips
- 1 fennel bulb, cut into julienne strips
- 2 tomatoes, peeled, seeded and diced
- 30ml/2 tbsp chopped fresh dill
- 4 turbot or Dover sole fillets, about 200g/7oz each, cut in half
- 20ml/4 tsp olive oil
- 60ml/4 tbsp white wine
- salt and ground black pepper

1 Preheat the oven to 190°C/375°F Gas 5. Cut four pieces of non-stick baking parchment, about 45cm/ 18in long. Fold each piece in half and cut into a heart shape.

VARIATION

If you prefer, you can substitute fresh tarragon or chervil for the dill and use fish stock instead of white wine. Other flat fish, such as brill – also known as poor man's turbot – work well.

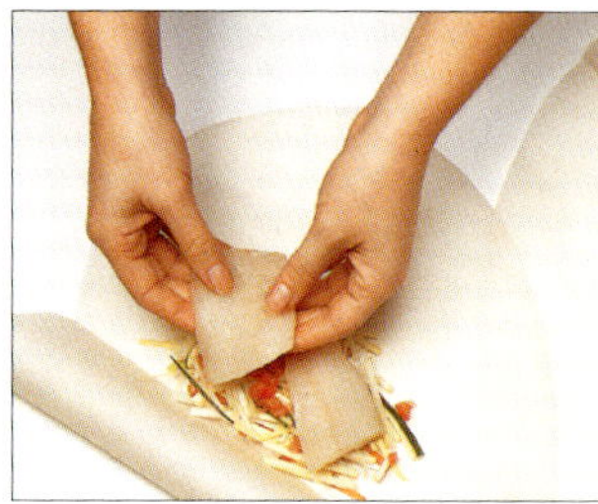

2 Open the paper hearts. Arrange one quarter of each of the carrots, courgettes, leeks, fennel and tomatoes next to the fold of each heart. Sprinkle with salt and pepper and half the chopped dill. Arrange two pieces of fish fillet over each bed of vegetables, overlapping the thin end of one piece and the thicker end of the other.

3 Sprinkle the remaining herbs, the olive oil and white wine evenly over the fish.

4 Fold the top half of one of the paper hearts over the fish and vegetables and, beginning at the rounded end, fold the edges of the paper over, twisting and folding to form an airtight parcel. Repeat with the remaining three.

5 Slide the parcels on to one or two baking sheets and bake for about 10 minutes, or until the parchment is lightly browned and well puffed up.

6 Slide each parcel on to a warmed serving plate and serve immediately. Each diner can then open their own parcel and savour the aroma.

Fish Soufflé with Cheese Topping

This is an easy-going soufflé, which will not drop too much if kept waiting. On the other hand, it might be best to get the family seated before you take it out of the oven!

SERVES FOUR

INGREDIENTS

- 350g/12oz white fish fillet, skinned
- 150ml/¼ pint/⅔ cup milk
- 225g/8oz cooked potatoes, still warm
- 1 garlic clove, crushed
- 2 eggs, separated
- grated rind and juice of ½ small lemon
- 115g/4oz cooked peeled prawns (shrimp)
- 50g/2oz/½ cup grated Cheddar cheese
- salt and ground black pepper

1 Place the fish in a large pan and add the milk. Bring just to the boil, lower the heat and simmer gently for 12 minutes, or until it flakes easily.

2 Drain the fish, reserving the milk, and place it in a bowl. Mash the potatoes with a potato masher or fork until they are really creamy, using as much of the reserved fish milk as necessary. Mash the garlic, egg yolks, lemon rind and juice into the potatoes and season to taste with salt and pepper. Preheat the oven to 220°C/425°F/Gas 7.

3 Flake the fish and gently stir into the potato mixture with the prawns. Adjust the seasoning if necessary.

4 Whisk the egg whites until stiff, but not dry, and gently fold them into the fish mixture. When smoothly blended, spoon into a greased gratin dish.

5 Sprinkle with the cheese and bake for about 25–30 minutes, until the top is golden brown and just about firm to the touch. (If the soufflé browns too quickly, reduce the oven temperature to 200°C/400°F/Gas 6.) Serve immediately.

COOK'S TIP

Instead of poaching the fish in a pan on the hob (stovetop) in step 1, you can cook it in the microwave. Place the fish fillet and milk in a microwave-safe bowl and cook for 3–4 minutes on high, 100% power.

VARIATION

This soufflé is also delicious made with smoked haddock or cod.

Baked Red Snapper

The flesh of the red snapper is made flavourful by rubbing in spices.

SERVES THREE TO FOUR

INGREDIENTS

- 1 large red snapper, cleaned
- juice of 1 lemon
- 2.5ml/½ tsp paprika
- 2.5ml/½ tsp garlic granules
- 2.5ml/½ tsp dried thyme
- 2.5ml/½ tsp ground black pepper
- boiled rice and lemon wedges, to serve

For the sauce

- 30ml/2 tbsp palm or vegetable oil
- 1 onion, chopped
- 400g/14oz can chopped tomatoes
- 2 garlic cloves, crushed
- 1 thyme sprig or 2.5ml/½ tsp dried thyme
- 1 fresh green chilli, seeded and finely chopped
- ½ green (bell) pepper, seeded and chopped
- 300ml/½ pint/1¼ cups fish stock or water

1 Preheat the oven to 200°C/400°F/Gas 6. Prepare the sauce. Heat the palm or vegetable oil in a pan. Add the onion and cook over a low heat, stirring occasionally, for 5 minutes, until softened, then add the tomatoes, garlic, thyme and chilli.

2 Add the pepper and stock or water. Bring to the boil, stirring, then reduce the heat, cover and simmer for about 10 minutes, until the vegetables are soft. Leave to cool a little and then place in a blender or food processor and process to a purée.

3 Rinse the fish under cold running water and pat dry with kitchen paper. Score the skin with a sharp knife in a criss-cross pattern. Mix together the lemon juice, paprika, garlic, thyme and black pepper in a small bowl. Spoon the mixture over the fish and rub in well.

4 Place the fish in a greased ovenproof dish and pour the sauce over the top. Cover with foil and bake for about 30–40 minutes, or until the fish is cooked and flakes easily when tested with a knife. Serve with boiled rice and lemon wedges.

COOK'S TIP

If you prefer less sauce, remove the foil after 20 minutes and bake, uncovered, until the fish is cooked through and the flesh flakes easily.

VARIATION

Other whole fish are also very tasty cooked in this spice mixture. Try some more unusual varieties, such as gurnard or parrot fish.

TROUT WRAPPED IN A BLANKET

THE "BLANKET" OF BACON BASTES THE FISH DURING COOKING, KEEPING IT MOIST AND ADDING FLAVOUR.

SERVES FOUR

INGREDIENTS

- juice of ½ lemon
- 4 trout, about 275g/10oz each
- 4 fresh thyme sprigs
- 8 thin slices streaky (fatty) bacon, rinds removed
- salt and ground black pepper
- chopped fresh parsley, and thyme sprigs, to garnish
- lemon wedges, to serve

1 Squeeze lemon juice over the skin and inside the cavity of each trout. Season the fish all over with salt and pepper, then put one thyme sprig in each cavity.

2 Stretch each bacon slice using the back of a knife, then wind two slices around each fish. Preheat the oven to 200°C/400°F/Gas 6.

3 Place the fish in a single layer in a lightly greased, shallow ovenproof dish with the loose ends of bacon tucked underneath to prevent them from unwinding during cooking.

4 Bake in the preheated oven for about 15–20 minutes, until the trout flesh flakes easily when tested with the point of a sharp knife and the bacon is quite crisp and is just beginning to brown.

5 To serve, transfer the trout to four warm plates and sprinkle with chopped parsley, then garnish with sprigs of thyme and accompany with lemon wedges.

COOK'S TIPS

- You can partially prepare this dish in advance.The trout can be wrapped in bacon and kept, covered, in the refrigerator until you are ready to cook. Return them to room temperature about 20 minutes before baking.
- This is also an excellent way to cook trout on the barbecue, as it prevents it from drying out.Use 12 slices of bacon instead of 8 to wrap the trout more closely and brush all over with a little olive oil. Place the fish in a hinged wire rack. Grill on a medium-hot barbecue for about 10–15 minutes, turning the fish once.

FILLETS OF BRILL IN RED WINE SAUCE

FORGET THE OLD MAXIM THAT RED WINE AND FISH DO NOT GO WELL TOGETHER. THE ROBUST SAUCE ADDS COLOUR AND RICHNESS TO THIS EXCELLENT DISH. TURBOT, HALIBUT AND JOHN DORY ARE ALSO GOOD COOKED THIS WAY.

SERVES FOUR

INGREDIENTS

- 4 brill fillets, about 175–200g/6–7oz each, skinned
- 150g/5oz/⅔ cup chilled butter, diced, plus extra for greasing
- 115g/4oz shallots, thinly sliced
- 200ml/7fl oz/scant 1 cup robust red wine
- 200ml/7fl oz/scant 1 cup fish stock
- salt and ground white pepper
- fresh chervil or flat leaf parsley leaves, to garnish

1 Preheat the oven to 180°C/350°F/Gas 4. Season the fish on both sides with salt and pepper. Generously butter a flameproof dish, which is large enough to take all the brill fillets in a single layer without overlapping. Spread the shallots over the base and lay the fish fillets on top. Season.

2 Pour in the red wine and fish stock, cover the dish and bring the liquid to just below boiling point. Transfer to the oven and bake for 6–8 minutes, until the brill is just cooked.

3 Using a fish slice (spatula), carefully lift the fish and shallots on to a serving dish, cover with foil and keep hot.

4 Transfer the casserole to the hob (stovetop) and bring the cooking liquid to the boil over a high heat. Cook it until it has reduced by half. Lower the heat and whisk in the chilled butter, one piece at a time, to make a smooth, shiny sauce. Season with salt and white pepper, set aside and keep hot.

5 Divide the shallots among four warmed plates and lay the brill fillets on top. Pour the sauce over and around the fish and garnish with the chervil or flat leaf parsley.

BAKED SEA BREAM WITH TOMATOES

JOHN DORY, TURBOT OR SEA BASS CAN ALL BE COOKED THIS WAY. IF YOU PREFER TO USE FILLETED FISH, CHOOSE A CHUNKY FILLET, LIKE COD, AND ROAST IT SKIN-SIDE UP. ROASTING THE TOMATOES BRINGS OUT THEIR SWEETNESS, WHICH CONTRASTS BEAUTIFULLY WITH THE FLAVOUR OF THE FISH.

SERVES FOUR TO SIX

INGREDIENTS

- 8 ripe tomatoes
- 10ml/2 tsp caster (superfine) sugar
- 200ml/7fl oz/scant 1 cup olive oil
- 450g/1lb new potatoes
- 1 lemon, sliced
- 1 bay leaf
- 1 fresh thyme sprig
- 8 fresh basil leaves
- 1 sea bream or porgy, about 900g–1kg/2–2¼lb, cleaned and scaled
- 150ml/¼ pint/⅔ cup dry white wine
- 30ml/2 tbsp fresh white breadcrumbs
- 2 garlic cloves, crushed
- 15ml/1 tbsp finely chopped fresh parsley
- salt and ground black pepper
- fresh flat parsley or basil leaves, chopped, to garnish

1 Preheat the oven to 240°C/475°F/Gas 9. Cut the tomatoes in half lengthways and arrange them in a single layer in an ovenproof dish, cut side up. Sprinkle with sugar, salt and pepper and drizzle over a little of the olive oil. Roast for 30–40 minutes, until soft and lightly browned.

2 Meanwhile, cut the potatoes into 1cm/½in slices. Par-boil for 5 minutes. Drain and set aside.

3 Grease an ovenproof dish with oil. Arrange the potatoes in a single layer with the lemon slices over them; sprinkle on the bay leaf, thyme and basil. Season and drizzle with half the remaining olive oil. Lay the fish on top, season; pour over the wine and the rest of the oil. Arrange the tomatoes around the fish.

4 Mix together the breadcrumbs, garlic and parsley; sprinkle over the fish. Bake for 30 minutes, until the flesh comes away easily from the bone. Garnish with chopped parsley or basil.

Fillets of Sea Bream in Filo Pastry

Any firm fish fillets can be used for this dish – bass, grouper, red mullet and snapper are particularly good. Each little parcel is a meal in itself and can be prepared several hours in advance, which makes this an ideal recipe for entertaining. If you like, serve the pastries with fennel braised with orange juice or a mixed leaf salad.

SERVES FOUR

INGREDIENTS

- 8 small waxy salad potatoes, preferably red-skinned
- 200g/7oz sorrel or spinach, stalks removed
- 30ml/2 tbsp olive oil
- 16 filo pastry sheets, thawed if frozen
- 4 sea bream or porgy fillets, about 175g/6oz each, scaled but not skinned
- 50g/2oz/¼ cup butter, melted
- 120ml/4fl oz/½ cup fish stock
- 250ml/8fl oz/1 cup whipping cream
- salt and ground black pepper
- finely diced red (bell) pepper, to garnish

1 Preheat the oven to 200°C/400°F/Gas 6. Cook the potatoes in a pan of lightly salted boiling water for about 15–20 minutes, until just tender. Drain and leave to cool. Set about half the sorrel or spinach leaves aside. Shred the remaining leaves by piling up six at a time, rolling them up like a fat cigar and slicing them with a sharp knife.

2 Thinly slice the potatoes lengthways. Brush a baking sheet with a little of the oil. Lay a sheet of filo pastry on the sheet, brush it with oil, then lay a second sheet crossways over the first. Repeat with two more sheets. Arrange a quarter of the sliced potatoes in the centre, season and add a quarter of the shredded sorrel or spinach. Lay a fish fillet on top, skin-side up. Season.

3 Loosely fold the filo pastry up and over to make a neat parcel. Make three more parcels; place on the baking sheet. Brush with half the butter. Bake for about 20 minutes, until the filo is puffed up and golden brown.

4 Meanwhile, make the sorrel sauce. Heat the remaining butter in a pan, add the reserved sorrel and cook gently for 3 minutes, stirring, until it wilts. Stir in the stock and cream. Heat almost to boiling point, stirring so that the sorrel breaks down. Season to taste and keep hot until the fish parcels are ready. Serve garnished with red pepper. Hand around the sauce separately.

OCTOPUS STEW

THIS RUSTIC STEW IS A PERFECT DISH FOR ENTERTAINING, AS IT TASTES EVEN BETTER IF MADE A DAY IN ADVANCE. SERVE WITH A COLOURFUL SALAD OF BABY CHARD, ROCKET AND RADICCHIO.

SERVES FOUR TO SIX

INGREDIENTS

- 1kg/2¼lb octopus, cleaned
- 45ml/3 tbsp olive oil
- 1 large red onion, chopped
- 3 garlic cloves, finely chopped
- 30ml/2 tbsp brandy
- 300ml/½ pint/1¼ cups dry white wine
- 800g/1¾lb ripe plum tomatoes, peeled and chopped, or two 400g/14oz cans chopped tomatoes
- 1 fresh red chilli, seeded and chopped (optional)
- 450g/1lb small new potatoes
- 15ml/1 tbsp chopped fresh rosemary
- 15ml/1 tbsp fresh thyme leaves
- 1.2 litres/2 pints/5 cups fish stock
- 30ml/2 tbsp fresh flat leaf parsley leaves
- salt and ground black pepper
- rosemary sprigs, to garnish

For the garlic croûtes

- 1 fat garlic clove, peeled
- 8 thick slices of baguette or ciabatta
- 30ml/2 tbsp olive oil

1 Cut the octopus into large pieces, put these in a pan and pour in cold water to cover. Season with salt, bring to the boil, then lower the heat and simmer for 30 minutes to tenderize. Drain and cut into bitesize pieces.

2 Heat the oil in a large shallow pan. Cook the onion for 2–3 minutes, until lightly coloured, then add the garlic and cook for 1 minute more. Add the octopus and cook for 2–3 minutes, stirring and tossing to colour it lightly.

3 Pour the brandy over the octopus and ignite it. When the flames have died down, add the wine, bring to the boil and bubble gently for about 5 minutes. Stir in the tomatoes, with the chilli, if using, then add the potatoes, rosemary and thyme. Simmer for 5 minutes.

4 Pour in the fish stock and season well. Cover the pan and simmer for 20–30 minutes, stirring occasionally. The octopus and potatoes should be very tender, and the sauce should have thickened slightly. At this stage, you can leave the stew to cool, then put it in the refrigerator overnight.

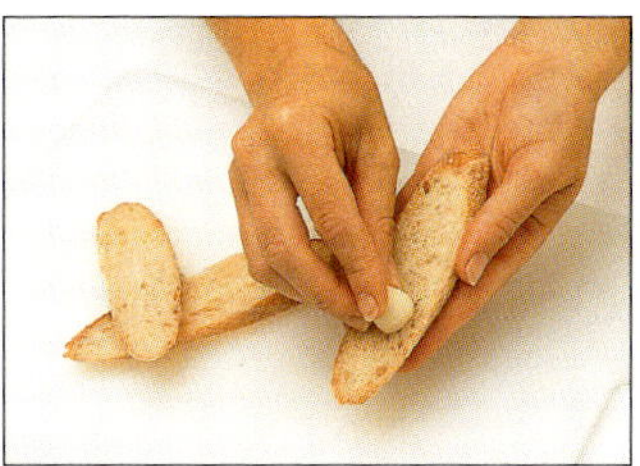

5 Preheat a medium-hot grill (broiler). To make the croûtes, cut the garlic clove in half and rub both sides of the bread slices with the cut side. Crush the garlic, stir it into the oil and brush the mixture over both sides of the bread. Grill (broil) on both sides until the croûtes are golden brown and crisp.

6 To serve the stew, reheat it gently if it has been in the refrigerator overnight, check the seasoning and stir in the parsley leaves. Serve piping hot in individual warmed bowls, garnished with rosemary sprigs and accompanied by the warm garlic croûtes.

Fish Plaki

Every Mediterranean country has a slightly different version of this simple but very delicious dish, which makes the most of the local fresh fish. A whole fish can be used instead of a large fillet, if you prefer. This dish also works well with sea bass or bream, John Dory, turbot, halibut or brill.

SERVES FOUR

INGREDIENTS

- 150ml/¼ pint/⅔ cup olive oil
- 2 large Spanish onions, chopped
- 2 celery sticks, chopped
- 4 fat garlic cloves, chopped
- 4 potatoes, peeled and diced
- 4 carrots, cut into small dice
- 15ml/1 tbsp caster (superfine) sugar
- 2 bay leaves
- 1 thick middle-cut fillet of grouper or cod, about 1kg/2¼lb
- 16–20 large black olives (optional)
- 4 large ripe tomatoes, peeled, seeded and chopped
- 150ml/¼ pint/⅔ cup dry white wine or vermouth
- salt and ground black pepper
- fresh herb leaves, to garnish
- saffron rice, to serve

1 Preheat the oven to 190°C/375°F/ Gas 5. Heat the olive oil in a large frying pan, add the chopped onions and celery and sauté until they are transparent. Add the garlic and cook for 2 minutes more. Stir in the potatoes and carrots and cook for about 5 minutes, stirring occasionally. Sprinkle with the sugar and season to taste with salt and ground black pepper.

2 Spoon the vegetable mixture into an oval or rectangular ovenproof dish slightly larger than the fish and tuck in the bay leaves. Season the fish and lay it on the bed of vegetables, skin side up. Sprinkle the olives around the edge, if using. Spread the chopped tomatoes over the fish, pour over the wine or vermouth and season.

3 Bake for 30–40 minutes, until the fish is cooked through. Serve straight from the dish. Garnish with herb leaves. Saffron rice would be the ideal accompaniment.

COOK'S TIP

If you use a whole fish, be sure to season it inside as well as outside.

Salmon Escalopes with Whisky and Cream

This dish combines two of the finest flavours of Scotland – salmon and whisky. It takes very little time to make, so cook it at the last moment when you are ready to serve. Your guests will deem it worth the wait. Serve with new potatoes and green beans.

SERVES FOUR

INGREDIENTS

- 4 salmon escalopes (scallops), about 175g/6oz each
- 5ml/1 tsp chopped fresh thyme leaves
- 50g/2oz/¼ cup butter
- 75ml/5 tbsp whisky
- 150ml/¼ pint/⅔ cup double (heavy) cream
- juice of ½ lemon (optional)
- salt and ground black pepper
- fresh dill sprigs, to garnish

1 Season the salmon with salt, pepper and thyme. Melt half the butter in a frying pan large enough to hold two escalopes side by side. When the butter is foaming, cook the first two escalopes for about 1 minute on each side, until they are golden on the outside and just cooked through.

2 Pour in 30ml/2 tbsp of the whisky and ignite it. When the flames have died down, carefully transfer the salmon escalopes to a plate and keep them hot. Heat the remaining butter and cook the second two escalopes in the same way. Keep them hot.

3 Pour the cream into the pan and bring to the boil, stirring constantly and scraping up the cooking juices from the base of the pan. Allow to bubble until reduced and slightly thickened, then season and add the last of the whisky and a squeeze of lemon if you like.

4 Place the salmon escalopes on individual warmed plates, pour the sauce over and serve garnished with dill.

FILLETS OF TURBOT WITH OYSTERS

This luxurious dish is perfect for special occasions. It is worth buying a whole turbot and asking the fishmonger to fillet and skin it for you. Keep the head, bones and trimmings for stock. Sole, brill and halibut can all be substituted for the turbot.

SERVES FOUR

INGREDIENTS

- 12 Pacific (rock) oysters
- 115g/4oz/½ cup butter
- 2 carrots, cut into julienne strips
- 200g/7oz celeriac, cut into julienne strips
- the white parts of 2 leeks, cut into julienne strips
- 375ml/13fl oz/generous 1½ cups champagne or dry white sparkling wine (about ½ bottle)
- 105ml/7 tbsp whipping cream
- 1 turbot, about 1.75kg/4–4½lb, filleted and skinned
- salt and ground white pepper

1 Using an oyster knife, open the oysters over a bowl to catch the juices, then carefully remove them from their shells, discarding the shells, and place them in a separate bowl. Set aside until required.

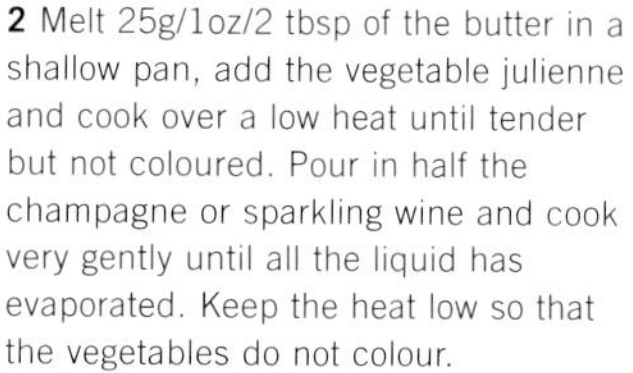

2 Melt 25g/1oz/2 tbsp of the butter in a shallow pan, add the vegetable julienne and cook over a low heat until tender but not coloured. Pour in half the champagne or sparkling wine and cook very gently until all the liquid has evaporated. Keep the heat low so that the vegetables do not colour.

3 Strain the oyster juices into a small pan and add the cream and the remaining champagne or sparkling wine. Place over a medium heat until the mixture has reduced to the consistency of thin cream. Dice half the remaining butter and whisk it into the sauce, one piece at a time, until smooth. Season to taste, then pour the sauce into a blender and process until velvety smooth.

4 Return the sauce to the pan, bring it to just below boiling point, then drop in the oysters. Poach for about 1 minute, to warm but barely cook. Keep warm, but do not let the sauce boil.

5 Season the turbot fillets with salt and pepper. Heat the remaining butter in a large frying pan until foaming, then cook the fillets over a medium heat for about 2–3 minutes on each side until cooked through and golden.

6 Cut each turbot fillet into three pieces and arrange on individual warmed plates. Pile the vegetable julienne on top, place three oysters around the turbot fillets on each plate and pour the sauce around the edge.

JOHN DORY WITH LIGHT CURRY SAUCE

THIS EXCELLENT COMBINATION OF FLAVOURS ALSO WORKS WELL WITH OTHER FLAT FISH LIKE TURBOT, HALIBUT AND BRILL, OR MORE EXOTIC SPECIES LIKE MAHI-MAHI OR ORANGE ROUGHY. THE CURRY TASTE SHOULD BE VERY SUBTLE, SO USE A MILD CURRY POWDER. SERVE THE FISH WITH PILAU RICE AND MANGO CHUTNEY. IT LOOKS WONDERFUL ARRANGED ON BANANA LEAVES, IF YOU CAN FIND SOME.

SERVES FOUR

INGREDIENTS

- 4 John Dory fillets, each about 175g/6oz, skinned
- 15ml/1 tbsp sunflower oil
- 25g/1oz/2 tbsp butter
- salt and ground black pepper
- 15ml/1 tbsp fresh coriander (cilantro) leaves and 1 small mango, peeled and diced, to garnish

For the curry sauce

- 30ml/2 tbsp sunflower oil
- 1 carrot, chopped
- 1 onion, chopped
- 1 celery stick, chopped
- white of 1 leek, chopped
- 2 garlic cloves, crushed
- 50g/2oz creamed coconut (coconut cream), crumbled
- 2 tomatoes, peeled, seeded and diced
- 2.5cm/1in piece fresh root ginger, grated
- 15ml/1 tbsp tomato purée (paste)
- 5–10ml/1–2 tsp mild curry powder
- 500ml/17fl oz/generous 2 cups chicken or fish stock

1 Make the sauce. Heat the oil in a pan; add the vegetables and garlic. Cook gently until soft but not brown.

2 Add the coconut, tomatoes and ginger. Cook for 1–2 minutes; stir in the tomato purée and curry powder to taste. Add the stock, stir and season.

3 Bring to the boil, then lower the heat, cover the pan and cook the sauce over the lowest heat for about 50 minutes. Stir once or twice to prevent burning. Leave the sauce to cool; pour into a food processor or blender and process until smooth. Return to a clean pan and reheat very gently, adding a little water if too thick.

4 Season the fish fillets with salt and pepper. Heat the oil in a large frying pan, add the butter and heat until sizzling. Put in the fish and cook for about 2–3 minutes on each side, until pale golden and cooked through. Drain on kitchen paper.

5 Arrange the fillets on individual warmed plates, pour the sauce around the fish and sprinkle on the finely diced mango. Decorate with coriander leaves and serve immediately.

COOK'S TIP

The coconut sauce must be cooked over a very low heat, so use a heat diffuser if you have one.

Grilled Halibut with Sauce Vierge

Any thick white fish fillets can be cooked in this versatile dish; turbot, brill and John Dory are especially delicious, but the flavoursome sauce also gives humbler fish like cod, haddock or hake a real lift.

SERVES FOUR

INGREDIENTS
- 105ml/7 tbsp olive oil
- 2.5ml/½ tsp fennel seeds
- 2.5ml/½ tsp celery seeds
- 5ml/1 tsp mixed peppercorns
- 675–800g/1½–1¾lb middle cut of halibut, about 3cm/1¼in thick, cut into 4 pieces
- coarse sea salt
- 5ml/1 tsp fresh thyme leaves, chopped
- 5ml/1 tsp fresh rosemary leaves, chopped
- 5ml/1 tsp fresh oregano or marjoram leaves, chopped

For the sauce
- 105ml/7 tbsp extra virgin olive oil
- juice of 1 lemon
- 1 garlic clove, finely chopped
- 2 tomatoes, peeled, seeded and diced
- 5ml/1 tsp small capers
- 2 drained canned anchovy fillets, chopped
- 5ml/1 tsp chopped fresh chives
- 15ml/1 tbsp shredded fresh basil leaves
- 15ml/1 tbsp chopped fresh chervil

1 Heat a ridged griddle pan or preheat the grill (broiler) to high. Brush the griddle pan or grill pan with a little of the olive oil. Mix the fennel and celery seeds with the peppercorns in a mortar. Crush with a pestle, and then stir in the coarse sea salt to taste. Spoon the mixture into a shallow dish and stir in the herbs and the remaining olive oil.

2 Add the halibut pieces to the olive oil mixture, turning them to coat them thoroughly, then arrange them with the dark skin uppermost in the oiled griddle pan or grill pan. Cook or grill (broil) for about 6–8 minutes, until the fish is cooked all the way through and the skin has browned.

3 Combine all the sauce ingredients except the fresh herbs in a pan and heat gently until warm but not hot. Stir in the chives, basil and chervil.

4 Place the halibut on four warmed plates. Spoon the sauce around and over the fish and serve immediately, with lightly-cooked green cabbage.

VEGETABLE-STUFFED SQUID

Shirley Conran famously said that life is too short to stuff a mushroom. The same might be said of squid, except that the result is so delicious that it makes the effort seem worthwhile. Small cuttlefish can be prepared in the same way. Serve with saffron rice.

SERVES FOUR

INGREDIENTS

- 4 medium squid, or 12 small squid, skinned and cleaned
- 75g/3oz/6 tbsp butter
- 50g/2oz/1 cup fresh white breadcrumbs
- 2 shallots, chopped
- 4 garlic cloves, chopped
- 1 leek, finely diced
- 2 carrots, finely diced
- 150ml/¼ pint/⅔ cup fish stock
- 30ml/2 tbsp olive oil
- 30ml/2 tbsp chopped fresh parsley
- salt and ground black pepper
- rosemary sprigs, to garnish
- saffron rice, to serve

1 Preheat the oven to 220°C/425°F/Gas 7. Cut off the tentacles and side flaps from the squid and chop these finely. Set the squid aside. Melt half the butter in a large frying pan that can safely be used in the oven. Add the fresh white breadcrumbs and cook until they are golden brown, stirring to prevent them from burning. Using a slotted spoon, transfer the breadcrumbs to a bowl and set aside until required.

2 Heat the remaining butter in the frying pan and add the chopped and diced vegetables. Cook until softened but not browned, then stir in the fish stock and cook until it has reduced and the vegetables are very soft. Season to taste with salt and ground black pepper and transfer to the bowl with the breadcrumbs. Mix lightly together.

3 Heat half the olive oil in the frying pan, add the chopped squid and cook over a high heat for 1 minute. Remove the squid with a slotted spoon; stir into the vegetable mixture. Stir in the parsley.

4 Put the stuffing mixture into a piping (pastry) bag, or use a teaspoon to stuff the squid tubes with the mixture. Do not overfill them, as the stuffing will swell slightly during cooking. Secure the openings with cocktail sticks or toothpicks, or sew up with fine kitchen thread.

5 Heat the remaining olive oil in the frying pan, place the stuffed squid in the pan and cook until they are sealed on all sides and golden brown. Transfer the frying pan to the oven and roast the squid for 20 minutes.

6 Unless the squid are very small, carefully cut them into three or four slices and arrange on a bed of saffron rice. Spoon the cooking juices over and around the squid and serve immediately, garnished with rosemary.

Salmon Coulibiac

This is a complicated Russian dish that takes a lot of preparation, but is worth it. Traditionally sturgeon is used, but since this is difficult to obtain, salmon may be substituted. Serve with shots of chilled vodka for a truly authentic Russian flavour.

SERVES EIGHT

INGREDIENTS

- butter, for greasing
- plain (all-purpose) flour, for dusting
- 450g/1lb puff pastry
- 1 egg, beaten
- salt and ground black pepper
- lemon wedges and fresh dill sprigs, to garnish

For the pancakes

- 2 eggs, separated
- 750ml/1¼ pints/3 cups milk
- 225g/8oz/2 cups plain (all-purpose) flour
- 350g/12oz/1½ cups butter, melted
- 2.5ml/½ tsp salt
- 2.5ml/½ tsp caster (superfine) sugar

For the filling

- 50g/2oz/¼ cup butter
- 350g/12oz/4¾ cups chestnut mushrooms, sliced
- 100ml/3½fl oz/scant ½ cup white wine
- juice of ½ lemon
- 675g/1½lb salmon fillet, skinned
- 115g/4oz/generous ½ cup long grain rice
- 30ml/2 tbsp chopped fresh dill
- 1 large onion, chopped
- 4 hard-boiled eggs, shelled and sliced

1 First make the pancakes. Whisk the egg yolks together and add the milk. Gradually beat in the flour, almost all the melted butter, the salt and sugar until smooth. Leave to stand for about 30 minutes.

2 Whisk the egg whites in a clean, grease-free bowl until they just form stiff peaks, then fold into the batter.

3 Heat a little of the remaining butter in a heavy frying pan over a medium heat and add about 45ml/3 tbsp of the batter. Turn and cook until golden. Repeat until all the mixture has been used up, brushing on a little melted butter when stacking the pancakes. When they are cool, cut them into long rectangles, cover and set aside.

4 For the filling, melt most of the butter in a large, heavy frying pan, add the mushrooms and cook for 3 minutes. Add 60ml/4 tbsp of the wine, bring to the boil and boil for 2 minutes, then lower the heat and simmer for a further 5 minutes. Add almost all the remaining wine and the lemon juice.

5 Place the salmon fillet on top of the cooked mushrooms, cover with foil, and gently steam over a low heat for about 8–10 minutes, until just cooked. Using a fish slice or metal spatula, remove the salmon from the pan and set aside.

6 Set aside the mushrooms and pour the cooking liquid into a large clean pan. Add the rice and cook for 10–15 minutes, until tender, adding more wine if necessary. Remove from the heat, stir in the dill and season to taste with salt and pepper. Melt the remaining butter and cook the onion until brown. Set aside.

7 Grease a large baking sheet. Flour a clean dishtowel, place the pastry on it and roll into a rectangle 30 x 55cm/12 x 20in. Leaving a 3cm/1¼in margin at the top and bottom ends of the pastry, place half the pancakes in a strip up the middle of the dough. Top with half the rice, half the onion, half the eggs and half the mushrooms. Place the salmon on top of the mushrooms and press down gently. Continue the layering process in reverse.

8 Take the 3cm/1¼in ends and wrap over the filling, then fold over the long edges. Brush with beaten egg and transfer to the baking sheet, rolling it so that it ends up seam side down. Chill for 1 hour.

9 Preheat the oven to 220°C/425°F/Gas 7. Cut four small slits in the top, brush with beaten egg and bake for 10 minutes. Reduce the oven temperature to 190°C/375°F/Gas 5 and cook for a further 30 minutes, until golden brown. Serve sliced, garnished with lemon and dill.

COOK'S TIP

Puff pastry has a high proportion of fat to flour, so handle it as little as possible and chill well before baking.

SEAFOOD IN PUFF PASTRY

This classic combination is found as an hors d'oeuvre on the menus of many elegant restaurants in France.

SERVES SIX

INGREDIENTS
- butter, for greasing
- plain (all-purpose) flour, for dusting
- 350g/12oz rough puff or puff pastry
- 1 egg beaten with 15ml/1 tbsp water, to glaze
- 60ml/4 tbsp dry white wine
- 2 shallots, finely chopped
- 450g/1lb fresh mussels, scrubbed and bearded
- 15g/½oz/1 tbsp butter
- 450g/1lb shelled scallops, cut in half crossways
- 450g/1lb raw prawns (shrimp), peeled and deveined
- 175g/6oz cooked lobster meat, sliced

For the sauce
- 225g/8oz/1 cup unsalted (sweet) butter, diced
- 2 shallots, finely chopped
- 250ml/8fl oz/1 cup fish stock
- 90ml/6 tbsp dry white wine
- 15–30ml/1–2 tbsp double (heavy) cream
- lemon juice
- salt and ground white pepper
- fresh dill sprigs, to garnish

1 Lightly grease a large baking sheet and sprinkle with a little water. On a lightly floured surface, roll out the pastry into a rectangle slightly less than 5mm/¼in thick. Using a sharp knife, cut into six diamond shapes about 13cm/5in long.

2 Transfer to the baking sheet. Brush the pastry with the egg glaze. Using the tip of a knife, score a line 1cm/½in from the edge without cutting all the way through, then lightly mark the centre in a criss-cross pattern.

3 Chill the pastry cases in the refrigerator for 30 minutes. Preheat the oven to 220°C/425°F/ Gas 7, then bake the pastry cases for about 20 minutes, until well puffed up and golden brown.

4 Transfer to a wire rack and, while they are still hot, remove each lid, cutting along the scored line to free it. Scoop out any uncooked dough from the bases and discard, then leave the cases to cool completely.

5 Put the wine and shallots in a large pan and bring to the boil over a high heat. Add the mussels to the pan, cover tightly and cook, shaking the pan occasionally, for 4–6 minutes, until the shells open. Remove and discard any mussels that have failed to open.

6 Reserve six mussels for the garnish, then remove the rest from their shells and set aside in a bowl, covered. Strain the cooking liquid through a sieve lined with muslin (cheesecloth) and reserve.

7 Melt the butter in a heavy frying pan over a medium heat. Add the scallops and prawns, cover tightly and cook for 3–4 minutes, shaking and stirring occasionally, until they feel just firm to the touch and the prawns have turned pink; do not overcook or they will become tough.

8 Using a slotted spoon, transfer the scallops and prawns to the bowl with the mussels and add any cooking juices from the frying pan to the reserved mussel cooking liquid.

9 To make the sauce, melt 25g/1oz/ 2 tbsp of the butter in a heavy pan. Add the shallots and cook over a low heat for 2 minutes. Pour in the fish stock, bring to the boil and cook over a high heat for about 15 minutes, until reduced by three-quarters. Add the white wine and reserved cooking liquid and boil for 5–7 minutes, until reduced by half.

10 Lower the heat to medium and whisk in the remaining butter, a little at a time, to make a smooth thick sauce (lift the pan from the heat if the sauce begins to boil). Whisk in the cream and season with salt, if necessary, pepper and lemon juice. Keep the sauce warm over a very low heat, stirring frequently.

11 Warm the pastry cases in a low oven for about 10 minutes. Put the mussels, scallops and prawns in a large pan. Stir in a quarter of the sauce and reheat gently over a low heat. Gently stir in the lobster meat and cook for 1 further minute.

12 Arrange the pastry case bases on individual plates. Divide the seafood mixture equally among them and top with the lids. Garnish each with a mussel in its half-shell and a dill sprig and spoon the remaining sauce around the edges or serve separately.

COOK'S TIP

Although not difficult, making puff or rough puff pastry is a time-consuming activity. Fortunately, the quality of ready-made pastry is very good, and it is available chilled or frozen. Thaw frozen dough completely before use.

PUFF PASTRY SALMON WITH CHANTERELLE CREAM

THE SLIGHTLY BLAND FLAVOUR OF FARMED SALMON IS GIVEN A DELICIOUS LIFT BY A CREAMY LAYER OF CHANTERELLE MUSHROOMS.

SERVES SIX

INGREDIENTS

- 675g/1½lb puff pastry, thawed if frozen
- 1 egg, beaten, to glaze
- 2 large salmon fillets, about 900g/2lb total weight, skinned
- 375ml/13fl oz/1⅝ cups dry white wine
- 1 small carrot
- 1 small onion, halved
- ½ celery stick, chopped
- 1 fresh thyme sprig
- curly kale, to garnish

For the chanterelle cream

- 25g/1oz/2 tbsp unsalted (sweet) butter
- 2 shallots, chopped
- 225g/8oz chanterelle mushrooms, trimmed and sliced
- 75ml/5 tbsp white wine
- 150ml/¼ pint/⅔ cup double (heavy) cream
- 45ml/3 tbsp chopped fresh chervil
- 30ml/2 tbsp chopped fresh chives

For the hollandaise sauce

- 175g/6oz/¾ cup unsalted butter
- 2 egg yolks
- 10ml/2 tsp lemon juice
- salt and ground black pepper

1 Roll out the pastry on a lightly floured surface to form a rectangle 10cm/4in longer and 5cm/2in wider than the salmon fillets. Trim into a fish shape, decorate with a pastry cutter to represent scales and glaze with beaten egg. Place on a baking sheet and chill for 1 hour.

2 Preheat the oven to 200°C/400°F/Gas 6. Bake the pastry "fish" for about 30–35 minutes, until well risen and golden. Remove from the oven and split open horizontally. Reduce the oven temperature to 170°C/325°F/Gas 3.

3 To make the chanterelle cream, melt the butter in a pan over a low heat. Add the shallots and cook gently, stirring occasionally, for about 3 minutes, until soft but not coloured. Add the mushrooms and cook until their juices begin to run.

4 Pour in the white wine, increase the heat and bring to the boil. Continue to boil until the liquid has evaporated. When dry, add the cream, chervil and chives and bring to a simmer. Season to taste with salt and pepper, transfer to a bowl, cover and keep warm.

5 Place the salmon in a fish kettle or roasting pan. Add the wine, carrot, onion, celery, thyme and enough water to cover. Gradually bring just to boiling point, remove from the heat, cover and leave the fish to cook in this gentle heat for 30 minutes.

6 To make the sauce, melt the butter in a small pan, skim the surface and pour into a jug (pitcher), leaving behind the milky residue.

7 Place the egg yolks and 15ml/1 tbsp of water in a glass bowl and place over a pan of simmering water. Whisk the yolks until thick and foamy. Remove from the heat and very slowly pour in the butter, whisking constantly. Add the lemon juice and season with salt and pepper to taste.

8 Place one salmon fillet on the base of the pastry, spread with the chanterelle cream and cover with the second fillet. Cover with the top of the pastry "fish" and warm through in the oven for about 10–15 minutes. Transfer to a warm platter, garnish with curly kale and serve immediately with the sauce.

WHOLE COOKED SALMON

FARMED SALMON HAS MADE THIS FISH MORE AFFORDABLE AND LESS OF A TREAT, BUT A WHOLE SALMON STILL FEATURES AS A CENTREPIECE AT PARTIES AND ON BUFFET TABLES. AS WITH ALL FISH, THE TASTE DEPENDS ON FRESHNESS AND ON NOT OVERCOOKING IT.

SERVES ABOUT TEN AS PART OF A BUFFET

INGREDIENTS

- 2–3kg/5–6lb fresh whole salmon
- 30ml/2 tbsp oil
- 1 lemon
- salt and ground black pepper
- lemon wedges, cucumber and fresh dill sprigs, to garnish

1 Preheat the oven to 200°C/400°F/Gas 6. Rinse the salmon and dry it well, inside and out. Pour half the oil on to a large piece of strong foil, or a double thickness, and place the fish in the centre.

2 Put a few slices of lemon inside the cavity of the salmon and arrange some more slices on the top. Season well with salt and pepper and sprinkle over the remaining oil. Wrap up the foil to make a loose parcel. Put the parcel on another sheet of foil or on a large baking sheet.

3 Cook the salmon in the oven for 10 minutes. Turn off the oven, do not open the door, and leave the fish for several hours.

4 To serve the same day, remove the foil and peel off the skin. If you are keeping it for the following day, leave the skin on and chill the fish overnight. Arrange the fish on a large platter and garnish with lemon wedges, cucumber cut into thin ribbons and sprigs of dill.

COOK'S TIP

Although it is traditional to leave the head and tail intact, you can remove these if you like.

PRAWN CURRY WITH QUAIL'S EGGS

QUAIL'S EGGS ARE AVAILABLE FROM MANY SUPERMARKETS NOW. HEN'S EGGS MAY BE SUBSTITUTED IF QUAIL'S EGGS ARE HARD TO FIND. USE ONE HEN'S EGG TO EVERY FOUR QUAIL'S EGGS.

SERVES FOUR

INGREDIENTS

- 12 quail's eggs
- 30ml/2 tbsp vegetable oil
- 4 shallots or 1 medium onion, finely chopped
- 2.5cm/1in piece galangal or fresh root ginger, chopped
- 2 garlic cloves, crushed
- 5cm/2in piece lemon grass, finely shredded
- 1–2 small, fresh red chillies, seeded and finely chopped
- 2.5ml/½ tsp ground turmeric
- 1cm/½ in square piece shrimp paste or 15ml/1 tbsp fish sauce
- 900g/2lb raw prawns (shrimp), peeled and deveined
- 400ml/14fl oz/1⅔ cups canned coconut milk
- 300ml/½ pint/1¼ cups chicken stock
- 115g/4oz Chinese leaves (Chinese cabbage), coarsely shredded
- 10ml/2 tsp sugar
- 2.5ml/½ tsp salt
- 2 spring onions (scallions), green part only, shredded, and 30ml/2 tbsp shredded coconut, to garnish

1 Cook the quail's eggs in boiling water for 8 minutes. Refresh in cold water, shell and then set aside.

2 Heat the vegetable oil in a large wok or frying pan, add the shallots or onion, galangal or ginger and garlic and cook over a low heat until soft but not coloured. Add the lemon grass, chillies, turmeric and shrimp paste or fish sauce and cook briefly to bring out their flavours.

3 Add the prawns and cook briefly. Pour the coconut milk through a strainer over a bowl, then add the thin part of the milk to the wok or pan with the chicken stock. Add the Chinese leaves, sugar and salt and bring to the boil. Simmer gently for 6–8 minutes.

4 Turn out on to a warm serving dish, halve the quail's eggs and toss them in the sauce. Sprinkle with the spring onions and the shredded coconut and serve.

COOK'S TIP

It is important to shell the quail's eggs immediately after refreshing them in cold water. If you leave them to stand, they become very difficult to shell.

Parsi Prawn Curry

This dish comes from the west coast of India, where fresh seafood is eaten in abundance.

SERVES FOUR TO SIX

INGREDIENTS

- 60ml/4 tbsp vegetable oil
- 3 medium onions, 1 thinly sliced and 2 finely chopped
- 6 garlic cloves, finely crushed
- 5ml/1 tsp chilli powder
- 7.5ml/1½ tsp ground turmeric
- 50ml/2fl oz/¼ cup tamarind juice
- 5ml/1 tsp mint sauce
- 15ml/1 tbsp demerara (raw) sugar
- 450g/1lb raw king prawns (jumbo shrimp), peeled and deveined
- 75g/3oz/1½ cups fresh coriander (cilantro) leaves, chopped
- salt
- fresh coriander (cilantro) sprig, to garnish

1 Heat the oil in a frying pan and cook the sliced onion until golden brown. In a bowl, mix the garlic, chilli powder and turmeric with a little water to form a paste. Add to the browned onion and simmer gently for 3 minutes.

2 Add the chopped onions to the pan and cook until they become soft and translucent, then fold in the tamarind juice, mint sauce and sugar. Season to taste with salt. Simmer for a further 3 minutes.

3 Pat the prawns dry with kitchen paper. Add them to the spice mixture with a small amount of water and cook over a medium heat, stirring constantly, until the prawns turn a bright orange-pink colour.

COOK'S TIP

If you can't find tamarind juice, you can substitute the same quantity of lemon or lime juice.

4 When the prawns are cooked, add the chopped coriander leaves and stir-fry over a high heat for a few minutes to thicken the sauce. Garnish with the coriander sprig and serve immediately.

Creole Fish Stew

A simple dish – good for an informal dinner party.

SERVES FOUR TO SIX

INGREDIENTS

- 2 whole red bream, porgy or large snapper, cleaned and cut into 2.5cm/1in pieces
- 30ml/2 tbsp spice seasoning
- 30ml/2 tbsp malt vinegar
- plain (all-purpose) flour, for dusting
- oil, for frying

For the sauce

- 30ml/2 tbsp vegetable oil
- 15g/½oz/1 tbsp butter or margarine
- 1 onion, finely chopped
- 275g/10oz fresh tomatoes, peeled and finely chopped
- 2 garlic cloves, crushed
- 2 fresh thyme sprigs
- 600ml/1 pint/2½ cups fish stock
- 2.5ml/½ tsp ground cinnamon
- 1 hot fresh chilli, chopped
- 115g/4oz red (bell) pepper, finely chopped
- 115g/4oz green (bell) pepper, finely chopped
- salt
- fresh oregano sprigs, to garnish

1 Place the fish in a large, shallow dish and sprinkle it with the spice seasoning and vinegar, turning to coat. Cover and set aside in the refrigerator to marinate for a minimum of 2 hours or overnight.

2 When ready to cook, place a little flour on a large plate and coat the fish pieces all over, shaking off any excess flour.

3 Heat a little oil in a large frying pan and cook the fish pieces over a medium heat for about 5 minutes, until golden brown, then remove from the pan and set aside. Do not worry if the fish is not cooked through, it will finish cooking in the sauce.

4 To make the sauce, heat the oil and butter or margarine in a large frying pan or wok and stir-fry the onion over a low heat for 5 minutes.

5 Add the tomatoes, garlic and thyme, stir well and simmer gently for a further 5 minutes. Stir in the fish stock, ground cinnamon and chopped chilli.

6 Return the fish pieces to the pan and add the chopped red and green peppers. Simmer until the fish is cooked through and the stock has reduced to a thick sauce. Adjust the seasoning with salt. Serve hot, garnished with oregano.

INDIAN FISH STEW

A colourful fish stew made with potatoes, peppers and traditional Indian spices.

SERVES FOUR

INGREDIENTS

- 30ml/2 tbsp oil
- 5ml/1 tsp cumin seeds
- 1 onion, chopped
- 1 red (bell) pepper, seeded and thinly sliced
- 1 garlic clove, crushed
- 2 fresh red chillies, finely chopped
- 2 bay leaves
- 2.5ml/½ tsp salt
- 5ml/1 tsp ground cumin
- 5ml/1 tsp ground coriander
- 5ml/1 tsp chilli powder
- 400g/14oz can chopped tomatoes
- 2 large potatoes, cut into 2.5cm/1in chunks
- 300ml/½ pint/1¼ cups fish stock
- 4 cod fillets
- chappatis, to serve

1 Heat the oil in a large, deep-sided frying pan and fry the cumin seeds for 2 minutes until they begin to splutter and give off their aroma. Add the onion, red pepper, garlic, chillies and bay leaves and cook over a low heat, stirring occasionally, for about 5–7 minutes, until the onions have softened and browned.

2 Add the salt, ground cumin, ground coriander and chilli powder and cook, stirring constantly, for a further 3–4 minutes.

3 Increase the heat to medium and stir in the chopped tomatoes, potatoes and fish stock. Bring to the boil, then lower the heat and simmer for a further 10 minutes.

4 Add the fish to the pan, then cover and simmer for about 10 minutes, or until the fish is tender and the flesh flakes easily. Serve immediately with freshly cooked chappatis.

Ragoût of Shellfish with Sweet Scented Basil

Green curry paste will keep for up to 3 weeks stored in a jar in the refrigerator.

SERVES FOUR TO SIX

INGREDIENTS

- 450g/1lb fresh mussels, scrubbed and bearded
- 60ml/4 tbsp water
- 225g/8oz medium squid
- 400ml/14fl oz/1⅔ cups canned coconut milk
- 300ml/½ pint/1¼ cups chicken or vegetable stock
- 350g/12oz monkfish, hoki or red snapper fillet, skinned
- 150g/5oz raw or cooked prawns (shrimp), peeled and deveined
- 4 scallops, sliced (optional)
- 75g/3oz green beans, trimmed and cooked
- 50g/2oz canned bamboo shoots, drained and rinsed
- 1 ripe tomato, peeled, seeded, and coarsely chopped
- 4 large-leaf basil sprigs, torn, and strips of fresh red chilli, to garnish
- rice, to serve (optional)

For the green curry paste

- 10ml/2 tsp coriander seeds
- 2.5ml/½ tsp caraway or cumin seeds
- 3–4 fresh green chillies, finely chopped
- 20ml/4 tsp caster (superfine) sugar
- 10ml/2 tsp salt
- 7.5cm/3in piece lemon grass
- 2cm/¾in piece galangal or fresh root ginger, finely chopped
- 3 garlic cloves, crushed
- 4 shallots or 1 medium onion, finely chopped
- 2cm/¾in square piece shrimp paste
- 50g/2oz/1 cup fresh coriander (cilantro) leaves, finely chopped
- 45ml/3 tbsp fresh mint or basil, finely chopped
- 2.5ml/½ tsp ground nutmeg
- 30ml/2 tbsp vegetable oil

1 Place the mussels in a large pan, add the measured water, cover with a tight-fitting lid and cook over a high heat, shaking the pan occasionally, for about 6–8 minutes, until the shells open. Take three-quarters of them out of their shells and set aside. (Discard any which have not opened.) Strain the cooking liquid.

2 To prepare the squid, trim off the tentacles beneath the eye. Rinse under cold running water, discarding the gut. Remove the "quill" from inside the body and rub off the paper-thin skin. Cut the body open and score, criss-cross, with a sharp knife. Cut into strips and set aside.

3 To make the green curry paste, dry fry the coriander and caraway or cumin seeds in a wok to release their flavour. Grind the chillies with the sugar and salt in a mortar with a pestle or in a food processor to make a smooth paste. Combine the seeds from the wok with the chillies, add the lemon grass, galangal or ginger, garlic and shallots or onion, then grind or process until smooth.

4 Add the shrimp paste, coriander, mint or basil, nutmeg and vegetable oil. Mix thoroughly to combine, then transfer to a bowl.

5 Pour the coconut milk into a strainer set over a bowl or jug (pitcher). Pour the thin part of the milk, together with the chicken or vegetable stock and the reserved mussel cooking liquid, into a wok. Reserve the coconut milk solids.

6 Add 60–75ml/4–5 tbsp of the green curry paste, according to taste. You can add more paste later, if you need to. Boil rapidly until the liquid has reduced completely.

7 Add the coconut milk solids, then add the squid and monkfish, hoki or red snapper. Simmer gently for 15–20 minutes.

8 Add the prawns, scallops, if using, and cooked mussels with the beans, bamboo shoots and tomato. Simmer for 2–3 minutes, until heated through. Transfer to a warm serving bowl and garnish with the basil and chillies. Serve immediately with rice, if you like.

Fish Stew with Calvados and Herbs

This rustic stew harbours all sorts of interesting and pleasing flavours.

SERVES FOUR

INGREDIENTS

- 1kg/2¼lb assorted white fish fillets
- 15ml/1 tbsp chopped fresh parsley, plus leaves to garnish
- 225g/8oz/3¼ cups mushrooms
- 200g/7oz can tomatoes
- 1 large bunch fresh dill sprigs
- 10ml/2 tsp plain (all-purpose) flour
- 15g/½oz/1 tbsp butter
- 450ml/¾ pint/scant 2 cups (hard) cider
- 45ml/3 tbsp Calvados
- salt and ground black pepper

1 Preheat the oven to 180°C/350°F/Gas 4. Skin the fish fillets, if you like, then chop them coarsely and place in a flameproof casserole or stewing pot with the parsley, mushrooms and tomatoes. Season with salt and pepper to taste. Reserve four dill sprigs for the garnish and chop the remainder. Add the chopped dill to the casserole.

2 Work the flour into the butter with a fork in a small bowl. Heat the cider in a pan over a low heat and stir in the flour and butter mixture, a little at a time. Cook, stirring constantly, until it has thickened slightly.

3 Add the cider mixture and the Calvados to the casserole and mix gently. Cover and bake for about 30 minutes, or until cooked through, when the fish flakes easily. Serve immediately, garnished with reserved sprigs of dill and the parsley leaves.

COOK'S TIP

Calvados is an apple brandy from the Normandy region of France. Its production and export are strictly controlled. Although not the same as American applejack, this spirit may be used instead.

Coconut Salmon

This is an ideal dish to serve at dinner parties.

SERVES FOUR

INGREDIENTS

- 10ml/2 tsp ground cumin
- 10ml/2 tsp chilli powder
- 2.5ml/½ tsp ground turmeric
- 30ml/2 tbsp white wine vinegar
- 1.5ml/¼ tsp salt
- 4 x 175g/6oz salmon steaks
- 45ml/3 tbsp oil
- 1 onion, chopped
- 2 fresh green chillies, seeded and chopped
- 2 garlic cloves, crushed
- 10ml/2 tsp grated fresh root ginger
- 5ml/1 tsp ground coriander
- 175ml/6fl oz/¾ cup coconut milk
- fresh coriander (cilantro) sprigs
- spring onion (scallion) rice, to serve

1 Mix 5ml/1 tsp of the ground cumin together with the chilli powder, turmeric, vinegar and salt in a small bowl. Place the salmon steaks in a large, shallow dish. Rub the paste all over them, then cover with clear film (plastic wrap) and leave to marinate in a cool place for about 15 minutes.

COOK'S TIP

For an alternative accompaniment, put 350g/12oz/scant 1½ cups Thai jasmine rice, 400ml/14fl oz/1⅔ cups canned coconut milk, 300ml/½ pint/1¼ cups water, 2.5ml/½ tsp ground coriander and a cinnamon stick in a pan. Bring to the boil, stir, cover and simmer for 10–12 minutes. Fork through, remove the cinnamon, cover and cook for 3–5 minutes more.

2 Heat the oil in a large, deep-sided frying pan or wok. Add the onion, green chillies, garlic and grated ginger and cook over a low heat, stirring occasionally for about 5–6 minutes, until the onion is softened but not browned. Remove the pan from the heat and leave to cool slightly, then transfer the mixture to a food processor or blender and process to a paste.

3 Return the paste to the pan or wok. Add the remaining cumin, the ground coriander and coconut milk. Bring to the boil, lower the heat and simmer gently for 5 minutes.

4 Add the salmon. Cover and cook for 15 minutes, until the fish is tender. Transfer to a warm serving dish and garnish with coriander. Serve with spring onion rice.

Moroccan Baked Fish Tagine

Tagine is the name of the large Moroccan cooking pot used for this type of cooking, but you can use an ordinary casserole.

SERVES FOUR

INGREDIENTS
- 2 garlic cloves, crushed
- 30ml/2 tbsp ground cumin
- 30ml/2 tbsp paprika
- 1 fresh red chilli, chopped
- 30ml/2 tbsp tomato purée (paste)
- 60ml/4 tbsp lemon juice
- 4 whiting or cod cutlets, about 175g/6oz each
- 350g/12oz tomatoes, sliced
- 2 green (bell) peppers, seeded and thinly sliced
- salt and ground black pepper
- chopped fresh coriander (cilantro), to garnish

1 Mix together the garlic, cumin, paprika, chilli, tomato purée and lemon juice in a small bowl. Place the fish cutlets on a plate and spread this mixture evenly over them, then cover with clear film (plastic wrap) and chill in the refrigerator for about 30 minutes to let the flavours mingle and penetrate.

2 Preheat the oven to 200°C/400°F/Gas 6. Arrange half the tomato slices and half the green pepper slices in an ovenproof dish. Season to taste with salt and black pepper.

3 Cover with the fish, placing the cutlets in a single layer, then arrange the remaining tomato slices and green pepper slices on top. Cover the dish with foil and bake for about 45 minutes. Garnish with chopped coriander and serve immediately. Lightly steamed broccoli would be a suitable accompaniment.

COOK'S TIPS
- If you are preparing this dish for a dinner party, it can be assembled completely and stored in the refrigerator, ready to bake when your guests have arrived.
- For a milder flavour, seed the chilli before chopping it. If you don't like hot food, you can omit it, as the remaining spices still have plenty of flavour.

OCTOPUS AND RED WINE STEW

UNLESS YOU ARE HAPPY TO CLEAN OCTOPUS FOR THIS GREEK DISH, BUY ONE THAT IS READY FOR COOKING.

SERVES FOUR

INGREDIENTS

- 900g/2lb prepared octopus
- 450g/1lb onions, sliced
- 2 bay leaves
- 450g/1lb ripe tomatoes
- 60ml/4 tbsp olive oil
- 4 garlic cloves, crushed
- 5ml/1 tsp caster (superfine) sugar
- 15ml/1 tbsp chopped fresh oregano or rosemary
- 30ml/2 tbsp chopped fresh parsley
- 150ml/¼ pint/⅔ cup red wine
- 30ml/2 tbsp red wine vinegar
- chopped fresh herbs, to garnish
- warm bread and pine nuts, to serve

1 Put the octopus in a large pan of gently simmering water with one-quarter of the sliced onions and the bay leaves. Cook gently for 1 hour.

2 While the octopus is cooking, cut a cross in the base of the tomatoes, plunge them into boiling water for 30 seconds, then refresh in cold water. Peel off the skins and coarsely chop the flesh.

COOK'S TIP

It is a complete myth that octopus is tough. However, it must be thoroughly beaten to tenderize it after cleaning and skinning. If you are not sure whether this has been done, place it in a plastic bag and beat well with a meat mallet or rolling pin.

3 Drain the octopus thoroughly and, using a sharp knife, cut it into bitesize pieces. Discard the onions and bay leaves.

4 Heat the oil in a heavy pan. Add the octopus, the remaining chopped onions and the crushed garlic and cook over a low heat, stirring occasionally for 3 minutes.

5 Add the tomatoes, sugar, oregano or rosemary, parsley, red wine and vinegar and cook, stirring constantly, for about 5 minutes until the mixture is thickened and pulpy.

6 Cover the pan and cook over the lowest possible heat for about 1½ hours, until the sauce is thickened and the octopus is tender.

7 Garnish with fresh herbs and serve immediately with plenty of warm bread and pine nuts to sprinkle over the top.

INDEX

P

Q

R

T